Science and Technology of Terrorism and Counterterrorism

Second Edition

PUBLIC ADMINISTRATION AND PUBLIC POLICY

A Comprehensive Publication Program

EDITOR-IN-CHIEF

EVAN M. BERMAN

Distinguished University Professor
J. William Fulbright Distinguished Scholar
National Chengchi University
Taipei, Taiwan

Founding Editor

JACK RABIN

1. *Public Administration as a Developing Discipline,* Robert T. Golembiewski
2. *Comparative National Policies on Health Care,* Milton I. Roemer, M.D.
3. *Exclusionary Injustice: The Problem of Illegally Obtained Evidence,* Steven R. Schlesinger
5. *Organization Development in Public Administration,* edited by Robert T. Golembiewski and William B. Eddy
7. *Approaches to Planned Change,* Robert T. Golembiewski
8. *Program Evaluation at HEW,* edited by James G. Abert
9. *The States and the Metropolis,* Patricia S. Florestano and Vincent L. Marando
11. *Changing Bureaucracies: Understanding the Organization before Selecting the Approach,* William A. Medina
12. *Handbook on Public Budgeting and Financial Management,* edited by Jack Rabin and Thomas D. Lynch
15. *Handbook on Public Personnel Administration and Labor Relations,* edited by Jack Rabin, Thomas Vocino, W. Bartley Hildreth, and Gerald J. Miller
19. *Handbook of Organization Management,* edited by William B. Eddy
22. *Politics and Administration: Woodrow Wilson and American Public Administration,* edited by Jack Rabin and James S. Bowman
23. *Making and Managing Policy: Formulation, Analysis, Evaluation,* edited by G. Ronald Gilbert
25. *Decision Making in the Public Sector,* edited by Lloyd G. Nigro
26. *Managing Administration,* edited by Jack Rabin, Samuel Humes, and Brian S. Morgan
27. *Public Personnel Update,* edited by Michael Cohen and Robert T. Golembiewski
28. *State and Local Government Administration,* edited by Jack Rabin and Don Dodd
29. *Public Administration: A Bibliographic Guide to the Literature,* Howard E. McCurdy
31. *Handbook of Information Resource Management,* edited by Jack Rabin and Edward M. Jackowski
32. *Public Administration in Developed Democracies: A Comparative Study,* edited by Donald C. Rowat
33. *The Politics of Terrorism: Third Edition,* edited by Michael Stohl
34. *Handbook on Human Services Administration,* edited by Jack Rabin and Marcia B. Steinhauer
36. *Ethics for Bureaucrats: An Essay on Law and Values, Second Edition,* John A. Rohr
37. *The Guide to the Foundations of Public Administration,* Daniel W. Martin
39. *Terrorism and Emergency Management: Policy and Administration,* William L. Waugh, Jr.

40. *Organizational Behavior and Public Management: Second Edition,* Michael L. Vasu, Debra W. Stewart, and G. David Garson
43. *Government Financial Management Theory,* Gerald J. Miller
46. *Handbook of Public Budgeting,* edited by Jack Rabin
49. *Handbook of Court Administration and Management,* edited by Steven W. Hays and Cole Blease Graham, Jr.
50. *Handbook of Comparative Public Budgeting and Financial Management,* edited by Thomas D. Lynch and Lawrence L. Martin
53. *Encyclopedia of Policy Studies: Second Edition,* edited by Stuart S. Nagel
54. *Handbook of Regulation and Administrative Law,* edited by David H. Rosenbloom and Richard D. Schwartz
55. *Handbook of Bureaucracy,* edited by Ali Farazmand
56. *Handbook of Public Sector Labor Relations,* edited by Jack Rabin, Thomas Vocino, W. Bartley Hildreth, and Gerald J. Miller
57. *Practical Public Management,* Robert T. Golembiewski
58. *Handbook of Public Personnel Administration,* edited by Jack Rabin, Thomas Vocino, W. Bartley Hildreth, and Gerald J. Miller
60. *Handbook of Debt Management,* edited by Gerald J. Miller
61. *Public Administration and Law: Second Edition,* David H. Rosenbloom and Rosemary O'Leary
62. *Handbook of Local Government Administration,* edited by John J. Gargan
63. *Handbook of Administrative Communication,* edited by James L. Garnett and Alexander Kouzmin
64. *Public Budgeting and Finance: Fourth Edition,* edited by Robert T. Golembiewski and Jack Rabin
67. *Handbook of Public Finance,* edited by Fred Thompson and Mark T. Green
68. *Organizational Behavior and Public Management: Third Edition,* Michael L. Vasu, Debra W. Stewart, and G. David Garson
69. *Handbook of Economic Development,* edited by Kuotsai Tom Liou
70. *Handbook of Health Administration and Policy,* edited by Anne Osborne Kilpatrick and James A. Johnson
72. *Handbook on Taxation,* edited by W. Bartley Hildreth and James A. Richardson
73. *Handbook of Comparative Public Administration in the Asia-Pacific Basin,* edited by Hoi-kwok Wong and Hon S. Chan
74. *Handbook of Global Environmental Policy and Administration,* edited by Dennis L. Soden and Brent S. Steel
75. *Handbook of State Government Administration,* edited by John J. Gargan
76. *Handbook of Global Legal Policy,* edited by Stuart S. Nagel
78. *Handbook of Global Economic Policy,* edited by Stuart S. Nagel
79. *Handbook of Strategic Management: Second Edition,* edited by Jack Rabin, Gerald J. Miller, and W. Bartley Hildreth
80. *Handbook of Global International Policy,* edited by Stuart S. Nagel
81. *Handbook of Organizational Consultation: Second Edition,* edited by Robert T. Golembiewski
82. *Handbook of Global Political Policy,* edited by Stuart S. Nagel
83. *Handbook of Global Technology Policy,* edited by Stuart S. Nagel
84. *Handbook of Criminal Justice Administration,* edited by M. A. DuPont-Morales, Michael K. Hooper, and Judy H. Schmidt
85. *Labor Relations in the Public Sector: Third Edition,* edited by Richard C. Kearney
86. *Handbook of Administrative Ethics: Second Edition,* edited by Terry L. Cooper
87. *Handbook of Organizational Behavior: Second Edition,* edited by Robert T. Golembiewski
88. *Handbook of Global Social Policy,* edited by Stuart S. Nagel and Amy Robb
89. *Public Administration: A Comparative Perspective, Sixth Edition,* Ferrel Heady

90. *Handbook of Public Quality Management*, edited by Ronald J. Stupak and Peter M. Leitner
91. *Handbook of Public Management Practice and Reform*, edited by Kuotsai Tom Liou
93. *Handbook of Crisis and Emergency Management*, edited by Ali Farazmand
94. *Handbook of Comparative and Development Public Administration: Second Edition*, edited by Ali Farazmand
95. *Financial Planning and Management in Public Organizations*, Alan Walter Steiss and Emeka O. Cyprian Nwagwu
96. *Handbook of International Health Care Systems*, edited by Khi V. Thai, Edward T. Wimberley, and Sharon M. McManus
97. *Handbook of Monetary Policy*, edited by Jack Rabin and Glenn L. Stevens
98. *Handbook of Fiscal Policy*, edited by Jack Rabin and Glenn L. Stevens
99. *Public Administration: An Interdisciplinary Critical Analysis*, edited by Eran Vigoda
100. *Ironies in Organizational Development: Second Edition, Revised and Expanded*, edited by Robert T. Golembiewski
101. *Science and Technology of Terrorism and Counterterrorism*, edited by Tushar K. Ghosh, Mark A. Prelas, Dabir S. Viswanath, and Sudarshan K. Loyalka
102. *Strategic Management for Public and Nonprofit Organizations*, Alan Walter Steiss
103. *Case Studies in Public Budgeting and Financial Management: Second Edition*, edited by Aman Khan and W. Bartley Hildreth
104. *Handbook of Conflict Management*, edited by William J. Pammer, Jr. and Jerri Killian
105. *Chaos Organization and Disaster Management*, Alan Kirschenbaum
106. *Handbook of Gay, Lesbian, Bisexual, and Transgender Administration and Policy*, edited by Wallace Swan
107. *Public Productivity Handbook: Second Edition*, edited by Marc Holzer
108. *Handbook of Developmental Policy Studies*, edited by Gedeon M. Mudacumura, Desta Mebratu and M. Shamsul Haque
109. *Bioterrorism in Medical and Healthcare Administration*, Laure Paquette
110. *International Public Policy and Management: Policy Learning Beyond Regional, Cultural, and Political Boundaries*, edited by David Levi-Faur and Eran Vigoda-Gadot
111. *Handbook of Public Information Systems, Second Edition*, edited by G. David Garson
112. *Handbook of Public Sector Economics*, edited by Donijo Robbins
113. *Handbook of Public Administration and Policy in the European Union*, edited by M. Peter van der Hoek
114. *Nonproliferation Issues for Weapons of Mass Destruction*, Mark A. Prelas and Michael S. Peck
115. *Common Ground, Common Future: Moral Agency in Public Administration, Professions, and Citizenship*, Charles Garofalo and Dean Geuras
116. *Handbook of Organization Theory and Management: The Philosophical Approach, Second Edition*, edited by Thomas D. Lynch and Peter L. Cruise
117. *International Development Governance*, edited by Ahmed Shafiqul Huque and Habib Zafarullah
118. *Sustainable Development Policy and Administration*, edited by Gedeon M. Mudacumura, Desta Mebratu, and M. Shamsul Haque
119. *Public Financial Management*, edited by Howard A. Frank
120. *Handbook of Juvenile Justice: Theory and Practice*, edited by Barbara Sims and Pamela Preston
121. *Emerging Infectious Diseases and the Threat to Occupational Health in the U.S. and Canada*, edited by William Charney
122. *Handbook of Technology Management in Public Administration*, edited by David Greisler and Ronald J. Stupak
123. *Handbook of Decision Making*, edited by Göktuğ Morçöl
124. *Handbook of Public Administration, Third Edition*, edited by Jack Rabin, W. Bartley Hildreth, and Gerald J. Miller
125. *Handbook of Public Policy Analysis*, edited by Frank Fischer, Gerald J. Miller, and Mara S. Sidney

126. *Elements of Effective Governance: Measurement, Accountability and Participation,* edited by Kathe Callahan
127. *American Public Service: Radical Reform and the Merit System,* edited by James S. Bowman and Jonathan P. West
128. *Handbook of Transportation Policy and Administration,* edited by Jeremy Plant
129. *The Art and Practice of Court Administration,* Alexander B. Aikman
130. *Handbook of Globalization, Governance, and Public Administration,* edited by Ali Farazmand and Jack Pinkowski
131. *Handbook of Globalization and the Environment,* edited by Khi V. Thai, Dianne Rahm, and Jerrell D. Coggburn
132. *Personnel Management in Government: Politics and Process, Sixth Edition,* Norma M. Riccucci and Katherine C. Naff
133. *Handbook of Police Administration,* edited by Jim Ruiz and Don Hummer
134. *Handbook of Research Methods in Public Administration, Second Edition,* edited by Kaifeng Yang and Gerald J. Miller
135. *Social and Economic Control of Alcohol: The 21st Amendment in the 21st Century,* edited by Carole L. Jurkiewicz and Murphy J. Painter
136. *Government Public Relations: A Reader,* edited by Mordecai Lee
137. *Handbook of Military Administration,* edited by Jeffrey A. Weber and Johan Eliasson
138. *Disaster Management Handbook,* edited by Jack Pinkowski
139. *Homeland Security Handbook,* edited by Jack Pinkowski
140. *Health Capital and Sustainable Socioeconomic Development,* edited by Patricia A. Cholewka and Mitra M. Motlagh
141. *Handbook of Administrative Reform: An International Perspective,* edited by Jerri Killian and Niklas Eklund
142. *Government Budget Forecasting: Theory and Practice,* edited by Jinping Sun and Thomas D. Lynch
143. *Handbook of Long-Term Care Administration and Policy,* edited by Cynthia Massie Mara and Laura Katz Olson
144. *Handbook of Employee Benefits and Administration,* edited by Christopher G. Reddick and Jerrell D. Coggburn
145. *Business Improvement Districts: Research, Theories, and Controversies,* edited by Göktuğ Morçöl, Lorlene Hoyt, Jack W. Meek, and Ulf Zimmermann
146. *International Handbook of Public Procurement,* edited by Khi V. Thai
147. *State and Local Pension Fund Management,* Jun Peng
148. *Contracting for Services in State and Local Government Agencies,* William Sims Curry
149. *Understanding Research Methods: A Guide for the Public and Nonprofit Manager,* Donijo Robbins
150. *Labor Relations in the Public Sector, Fourth Edition,* Richard Kearney
151. *Performance-Based Management Systems: Effective Implementation and Maintenance,* Patria de Lancer Julnes
152. *Handbook of Governmental Accounting,* edited by Frederic B. Bogui
153. *Bureaucracy and Administration,* edited by Ali Farazmand
154. *Science and Technology of Terrorism and Counterterrorism, Second Edition,* edited by Tushar K. Ghosh, Mark A. Prelas, Dabir S. Viswanath, and Sudarshan K. Loyalka

Available Electronically

Principles and Practices of Public Administration, edited by Jack Rabin, Robert F. Munzenrider, and Sherrie M. Bartell

PublicADMINISTRATION*netBASE*

Science and Technology of Terrorism and Counterterrorism

Second Edition

Edited by

Tushar K. Ghosh
University of Missouri
Columbia, Missouri, U.S.A.

Mark A. Prelas
University of Missouri
Columbia, Missouri, U.S.A.

Dabir S. Viswanath
University of Missouri
Columbia, Missouri, U.S.A.

Sudarshan K. Loyalka
University of Missouri
Columbia, Missouri, U.S.A.

CRC Press
Taylor & Francis Group
Boca Raton London New York

CRC Press is an imprint of the
Taylor & Francis Group, an **informa** business

CRC Press
Taylor & Francis Group
6000 Broken Sound Parkway NW, Suite 300
Boca Raton, FL 33487-2742

Printed in the United States of America on acid-free paper
10 9 8 7 6 5 4 3 2 1

International Standard Book Number: 978-1-4200-7181-8 (Hardback)

Library of Congress Cataloging-in-Publication Data

Science and technology of terrorism and counterterrorism / editors: Tushar K. Ghosh ... [et al.]. -- 2nd ed.
p. cm. -- (Public administration and public policy ; 156)
Includes bibliographical references and index.
ISBN 978-1-4200-7181-8 (alk. paper)
1. Terrorism--Technological innovations. 2. Bioterrorism. 3. Chemical terrorism. 4. Nuclear terrorism. I. Ghosh, Tushar K., Dr. II. Title. III. Series.

HV6431.S3786 2010
363.325--dc22 2009017578

Visit the Taylor & Francis Web site at
http://www.taylorandfrancis.com

and the CRC Press Web site at
http://www.crcpress.com

Contents

Preface xiii

Authors xvii

1 Introduction 1
DABIR S. VISWANATH

2 A Brief Theory of Terrorism and Technology 15
HERBERT K. TILLEMA

3 Group Psychology of Terrorism 31
MICHAEL A. DIAMOND

4 Aerosols: Fundamentals 41
SUDARSHAN K. LOYALKA AND ROBERT V. TOMPSON, JR.

5 Biological Terrorism: Effects, Toxicity, and Effectiveness 51
GORDON D. CHRISTENSEN

6 Biological Terrorism: Classification and Manufacture 79
MARK A. PRELAS

7 Biological Terrorism: Weaponization and Delivery Systems 89
MARK A. PRELAS

8 Biological Terrorism: Sensors and Detection Systems 99
TUSHAR K. GHOSH AND MARK A. PRELAS

9 Biological Terrorism: Consequences and Medical Preparedness 153
L. DAVID ORMEROD

10 Biological Terrorism: Preparation for Response—What the Government Can Do in Defending the Homeland 185
MARION C. WARWICK

11 Agroterrorism: Agroeconomic Bioterrorism 233
KEITH A. HICKEY

12 Agroterrorism: Attributes and Implications of High-Impact Targets in U.S. Agriculture 251
KATIE THOMPSON

13 Nuclear Terrorism: Nature of Radiation 267
WILLIAM H. MILLER

14 Nuclear Terrorism: Radiation Detection 273
WILLIAM H. MILLER

15 Nuclear Terrorism: Radiation Detectors—Applications in Homeland Security 277
TUSHAR K. GHOSH, MARK A. PRELAS, AND ROBERT V. TOMPSON, JR.

16 Nuclear Terrorism: Dose and Biological Effects 307
WILLIAM H. MILLER AND ROBERT LINDSAY

17 Nuclear Terrorism: Nuclear Weapons 313
SUDARSHAN K. LOYALKA

18 Nuclear Terrorism: Threats and Countermeasures 321
SUDARSHAN K. LOYALKA AND MARK A. PRELAS

19 Chemical Terrorism: Classification, Synthesis, and Properties 329
DABIR S. VISWANATH AND TUSHAR K. GHOSH

20 Chemical Terrorism: Toxicity, Medical Management, and Mitigation 355
L. DAVID ORMEROD

21 Chemical Terrorism: Destruction and Decontamination 379
DABIR S. VISWANATH AND TUSHAR K. GHOSH

22 Chemical Terrorism: Sensors and Detection Systems 409
MARK A. PRELAS AND TUSHAR K. GHOSH

23 Chemical Terrorism: Weaponization and Delivery System 447
MARK A. PRELAS AND TUSHAR K. GHOSH

24 Chemical Terrorisms: Threats and Countermeasures 457
L. DAVID ORMEROD, TUSHAR K. GHOSH, AND DABIR S. VISWANATH

25 Cyber-Terrorism 469
HARRY W. TYRER

26 Personal Protective Equipment 493
GLENN P. JIRKA AND WADE THOMPSON

27 National Response Plan and Preparedness 509
TUSHAR K. GHOSH

28 Government and Voluntary Agencies 529
JULIE A. BENTZ AND THERESA M. CROCKER

29 The National Infrastructure Protection Plan 557
ALLEN KROTMAN, JANICE R. BALLO, AND MARION C. WARWICK

Index 571

Preface

Since the first edition of this book was published in 2002, many changes have taken place with respect to the issues concerning homeland security. Scientists, engineers, political scientists, politicians, and any other professional who have anything to do with this subject should ask themselves the following questions:

Is the fear of terrorism greater today than it was in 2002?
Is the situation better or worse today than it was in 2002?

When we look at things impassionedly, the answers to both these questions appear to be that we are more fearful and the situation is worsening. Why is this so when we live in a world that has better communications, better science and technology, and more financial power than was the case in 2002? After the events of 9/11 (September 11, 2001), we have witnessed bombs being detonated in Madrid (Madrid train bombing in March 2004) that killed 191 and wounded over 600; the bus hijacking in Ulghur, Krygyzstan (March 2003) that resulted in 20 deaths; suicide attacks in 2004 at the Port of Ashdod, Israel, that resulted in 10 deaths; the London subway attacks (July 7, 2005) that killed 52 and injured nearly 800; four attempted bomb attacks on July 21 again in London that were disrupted; failed attempts on August 9, 2006, to detonate liquid explosives aboard flights from London to the United States; the ongoing suicide bombings in Iraq; and many more incidents that attest to the increase in terroristic acts across the world.

Terroristic activities are on the rise on the global scene, and it is generally believed that such activities can be contained or eliminated by controlling the proliferation of nuclear, biological, and chemical (NBC) weapons; by building a strong defense system; by having in place different types of treaties; and by punishing countries that fail to follow such agreements. One may ask why these procedures, which are in place at the present time, failed to stop activities such as the Tokyo subway gassing, the Oklahoma City bombing, the World Trade Center bombing and attack, the bombing at the Atlanta Olympic games, and many more similar incidents. This book is a direct outcome of several recent group discussions by the editors. These discussions were motivated by the fact that some of us were involved in research in the area of sensors, and that one of us, Mark A. Prelas, spent a year at the U.S. State Department as a Foster fellow. Another motivating factor was that the Nuclear Engineering Program organized a series of seminars on the nonproliferation of nuclear materials and weapons in 1998. This series included presentations by Dr. Sudarshan Loyalka, Dr. Mark Prelas, Dr. Dale Klein (formerly Assistant Secretary of Defense for NBC Defense and the former chairman of the Nuclear Regulatory Commission), LTC Charles Kelsey, and Dr. Herb Tillema. A third major motivation was to introduce undergraduate and graduate students from several disciplines to this important area with an emphasis on the scientific and technological aspects. All of these factors led us to organize and offer courses in the area of terrorism and counterterrorism. One of us, Dabir S. Viswanath, did a survey on the courses offered in this area in other engineering departments and found that most courses were confined to social, behavioral, and law departments. We found that none of the courses addressed the scientific and technological aspects of this subject. Therefore, during the fall 2000 semester we organized this course and sought the help of other faculty members. Dabir S. Viswanath took on the responsibility of drawing up the syllabus and arranging the lectures, and two other editors, Mark A. Prelas and Tushar K. Ghosh, took on the responsibility of taping the lectures, putting the material onto CDs, and putting the lectures onto the Web (http://prelas.nuclear.missouri.edu/NE401/NE401.htm).

The first defense with regard to several areas such as pollution control, waste management, terrorism, and a host of other issues is education. It is essential to educate a core group—the students who can spread the word. We received a good response from the student community. Our initial idea that students from various departments should take this course was amply rewarded. The class had students from political science, journalism, microbiology, nuclear engineering, mechanical engineering, computer science and computer engineering, and electrical engineering, as well as some with undeclared majors. The class was a 50–50 mix of graduate and undergraduate students. This mix allowed room for extensive discussions, and the faculty and students felt that this was one of the strengths of this course. The course received substantial press, radio, and TV coverage both on a local and on a national scale. We are glad to see that our efforts have culminated in the form of this book. The enthusiasm of the faculty, the students, and the press was overwhelming. We express our sincere gratitude to all these groups.

We hope that this book will help students who will be our future policy makers and diplomats to understand some basic information on the nature of terrorism, the materials used by terrorists, how to detect them, and how to destroy such materials, while at the same time showing how to deal with terrorist groups. We also anticipate that this book will help our current politicians and policy makers. We hope that it will be a catalyst for several engineering departments to offer innovative courses in this area, and enhance our capabilities in counterterrorism.

The current revision has been expanded from 26 to 29 chapters. The bulk of the material is directed toward understanding the why, how, and what of each type of terrorism. It is possible to expand and combine each of the nuclear, biological, chemical, and agro- and cyber-terrorism chapters and develop the material into a 3 h course. To appeal to a wider audience, an attempt has been made to streamline both the political and technological parts of terrorism and counterterrorism. We hope this book will inspire faculties to innovate courses encompassing several disciplines and to provide students with a wide perspective. The future in this area is unknown, as we cannot predict where, when, and how terrorists will strike, but we hope we can take all possible preventive measures to minimize the disaster.

Chapter 1 introduces the broad thinking on terrorist attacks after September 11, 2001, and summarizes selected case studies. Chapters 2 and 3 lay the foundation for this book by discussing the origin and nature of terrorism and the factors involved in diplomacy. Chapter 4 deals with the fundamentals of aerosol dispersion as many of the toxic materials are released as aerosol particles. Chapters 5 through 10 deal with the fundamentals of bioterrorism, the manufacture of certain biological agents, and their delivery. In addition, these chapters deal with the detection of biological agents and countermeasures that need to be taken. Chapters 11 and 12 deal with agricultural terrorism. This section has been expanded to include a second chapter on the attributes and implications of agroterrorism. Nuclear terrorism is dealt with in Chapters 13 through 18. Besides discussing the fundamentals, these chapters also discuss nuclear weapons systems, threats, and safeguards. Chemical terrorism is described in Chapters 19 through 24. These chapters discuss various chemicals used and their manufacture, detection, delivery, and decontamination. Chapter 25 deals with cyber-terrorism, its nature and scope, how it takes place, its consequences, and what we can do to protect against such attacks. When a disaster occurs, one simple but very effective measure is to protect ourselves with proper clothing. This is discussed in Chapter 26. The role of the government at the federal and state levels and the role of international agencies, along with their respective resources, capabilities, and responsibilities, are discussed in Chapters 27 through 29. This section has been extended to include the current national infrastructure to protect citizens from terrorist attacks.

Today we know that citizens have to be very vigilant and should learn as much as possible about terrorism. The September 11, 2001, World Trade Center attack has awakened the country like no other single event in the history of the United States, presumably not even the Pearl Harbor attack. The public needs to know the profile of a terrorist, the threat of NBC weapons, what measures to take in case of an attack, how to respond in case of an emergency, and a host of other things. We have tried to present as comprehensive a report as possible. We recognize that we have not covered all the materials that should be included in a text of this nature. Sections of this book can be expanded to cover more comprehensive courses.

In closing, it is a pleasure to thank the faculty and the guest lecturers who willingly participated in this course; contributors to this book who, in spite of their busy schedules, cooperated in getting the manuscript completed in a short period; students who participated in the course and whose enthusiasm encouraged the faculty to do their best; the local and national media who interviewed us about this course; the reviewers for their comments that significantly improved the presentation; and Taylor & Francis for their help and cooperation. Additionally, this text is the first manuscript from the newly formed Nuclear Science and Engineering Institute at the University of Missouri-Columbia. We wish to express our gratitude to the University of Missouri.

Tushar K. Ghosh
Mark A. Prelas
Dabir S. Viswanath
Sudarshan K. Loyalka

Authors

Janice R. Ballo is a lead information analyst in the Knowledge Management Services Department at the MITRE Corporation in McLean, Virginia. She has a BA in history and an MA in library and information science from the University of South Florida, as well as an MA in history from Florida State University.

Julie A. Bentz is the principal deputy for nuclear defense within the Office of the Deputy Assistant to the Secretary of Defense for Nuclear Matters. In this role, Colonel Bentz provides oversight, coordination, review, and advocacy within the Department of Defense (DoD) for counterproliferation and counterterrorism initiatives such as nuclear/radiological detection, interdiction, collection, render safe procedure, forensics, and attribution. She currently provides subject-matter expertise in defining and implementing the nuclear defense mission for the DoD, including the development of acquisition, research, and development strategies. She advises the assistant to the Secretary of Defense for Nuclear and Chemical and Biological Defense Programs on the oversight responsibilities for all DoD programs within this mission space.

Colonel Bentz's previous assignment was on the Homeland Security Council (HSC) as the director for Nuclear Defense Policy. She was instrumental in writing presidential policy for nuclear detection, technical nuclear forensics, and other nuclear defense issues. Prior to her HSC experience, Colonel Bentz served as the science advisor for National Guard Bureau on homeland defense, where she aided in the development and procurement of the Civil Support Team Analytical Laboratory System.

Colonel Bentz is a recent graduate of the National War College and holds a PhD in nuclear engineering from the University of Missouri-Columbia.

Gordon D. Christensen is the associate chief of staff for research and development at the Harry S Truman Memorial Veterans Hospital in Columbia, Missouri, and a professor of internal medicine at the University of Missouri-Columbia. He is a fellow of the Infectious Diseases Society of America, the American Academy of Microbiology, and the American College of Physicians. He is the author or coauthor of over 120 professional papers and abstracts. Dr. Christensen received his MD from Creighton University in Omaha, Nebraska, in 1974 and completed his postgraduate training in infectious diseases and internal medicine at the University of Texas Medical Branch in Galveston, Texas, in 1979.

Theresa M. Crocker has more than 25 years of experience in planning and training for disaster preparedness, emergency medicine, and public health. She has the required experience to develop and conduct Chemical, Biological, Radiological, Nuclear, and Explosive (CBRNE) exercises and training courses and has conducted training for the National Incident Management System (NIMS), HSEEP, National Response Plan (NRP), Incident Command System (ICS), and weapons of mass destruction (WMD). She planned and coordinated interdepartmental/interagency/intergovernmental emergency response operations for all levels of government, nongovernmental organizations, volunteer agencies, and private businesses. Crocker represented the National Association of City and County Health Officials (NACCHO) for the Department of Homeland Security, State/Local/Tribal Work Group (SLTWG). This group was involved in authoring the National Preparedness Goal and its component parts, including the Universal Task List and the Targeted Capabilities List. The group was historically an integral participant in authoring both the NRP and the NIMS. Crocker has an MS in science of disaster response from Indiana University of Pennsylvania, which consisted of intensive training in the principles involved in detecting, identifying, and safe handling of chemical, biological, radiological, and nuclear agents and their precursors as they are related to WMDs. She also has a BS in nursing from the University of Steubenville, Ohio.

Michael A. Diamond is a professor of public affairs and the director of the Center for the Study of Organizational Change at the Truman School of Public Affairs at the University of Missouri. He teaches and writes on organizational analysis, group dynamics and conflict resolution, and the group psychology of terrorism. Diamond was awarded the 1994 Harry Levinson Award for Excellence in Consulting Psychology from the American Psychological Association, the 1999 William T. Kemper Fellow for Excellence in Teaching, and the 2005 Faculty-Alumni Award from the University of Missouri-Columbia. He is the founder and past president of the International Society for the Psychoanalytic Study of Organizations and has published over 50 journal articles and several books. He is a practicing psychoanalytic organizational consultant with over 25 years of experience. He is also former coeditor in chief of the *American Review of Public Administration*, and is currently coeditor in chief of the forthcoming e-journal, the *Journal of Organizational Psychodynamics* (*JOP*).

Tushar K. Ghosh is a professor of nuclear engineering at the University of Missouri-Columbia (MU). After receiving his PhD in chemical engineering in July 1989 from Oklahoma State University in Stillwater, Dr. Ghosh worked at MU as a research assistant professor in conjunction with the chemical and nuclear engineering departments and the Particulate Systems Research Center. His research interests include the development of ultrasensitive sensors for chemical and biological agents. He is the author or coauthor of more than 100 journal articles and several books. He has also played an instrumental role in developing several courses on homeland security and counterterrorism at MU.

Keith A. Hickey is a medical physicist and a radiation safety officer at Missouri Cancer Associates, and an adjunct assistant professor at the University of Missouri. He is a member of the American Association of Physicists in Medicine, the Health Physics Society, and the Institute of Electrical and Electronics Engineers; he is also a certified health physicist and is board certified by the American Board of Radiology in Therapeutic Radiological Physics. Dr. Hickey is a former U.S. Army reserve nuclear medical science officer with several years of experience in defense related advanced technology and systems engineering. He received his PhD in nuclear engineering from the University of Missouri-Columbia in 1989.

Glenn P. Jirka was the environmental emergency response program manager for the University of Missouri-Columbia Extension Division's Fire and Rescue Training Institute and an adjunct assistant professor in the College of Engineering at the University of Missouri-Columbia. Jirka is a member of the National Fire Protection Association Technical Committee on Hazardous Materials Protective Clothing and Equipment, the Department of Justice–Department of Defense Joint Interagency Board for Equipment Standardization and Interoperability, and the Federal Emergency Management Agency's First Responder Technology Transfer Committee on Weapons of Mass Destruction and Hazardous Materials, among others. He is also the author or coauthor of numerous professional papers and curricula. Jirka received his MS in chemistry from Southern Illinois University-Carbondale in 1990 and completed his postgraduate work from the School of Chemical Sciences at the University of Illinois Urbana-Champaign.

Allen Krotman is a senior project leader in the Healthcare Mission Area in MITRE Corporation's Center for Enterprise Modernization. He has over 25 years of experience in the practice of forming and leading technical and nontechnical teams, designing and implementing new and improved systems and processes, and managing large programs. Since joining MITRE in 2005, Krotman has contributed technically to and managed large programs for the Department of Health and Human Services (HHS). Currently, he is the MITRE project lead for the Healthcare & Public Health Sector Critical Infrastructure Protection (CIP) Program. In this role, Krotman supports the Office of the Assistant Secretary for Preparedness and Response within HHS. The Healthcare and Public Health CIP Program supports Homeland Security Presidential Directive-7 and the implementation of the National Infrastructure Protection Plan of 2006. Krotman graduated with distinction from Purdue University with a bachelor's degree in computer science.

Robert Lindsay is a professor in the physics department at the University of the Western Cape in South Africa. He was awarded a Rhodes scholarship in 1978 to study at Oxford in England after obtaining his BSc in physics at Stellenbosch University in South Africa. He obtained a DPhil in theoretical physics at Oxford in 1982. He spent two years as a postdoc at Daresbury Laboratory in the United Kingdom and then joined the University of the Western Cape. His present research interests are in applied nuclear physics, specifically radon measurements and the use of natural radioactivity.

Sudarshan K. Loyalka is a curators' professor of nuclear engineering and chemical engineering and the director of the Particulate Systems Research Center at the University of Missouri-Columbia. His research interests are in transport theory, aerosol mechanics, the kinetic theory of gases, and neutron reactor physics and safety. Dr. Loyalka is a fellow of both the American Physical Society (since 1982) and the American Nuclear Society (since 1985). He has published more than 170 papers and provided guidance to approximately 70 graduate students. He has received numerous awards for his research and teaching, including the David Sinclair Award (1995) of the American Association for Aerosol Research and the Glenn Murphy Award (1998) of the American Association for Education.

William H. Miller is the James C. Dowell research professor of nuclear engineering and the director of the Energy Systems and Resources Program at the University of Missouri-Columbia, where he has taught graduate nuclear engineering for 28 years. He is the author of approximately 100 papers and has made over 1000 presentations to the public on issues concerning energy, the environment, radiation, and nuclear power. Dr. Miller received his PhD in nuclear engineering from the University of Missouri-Columbia.

L. David Ormerod is currently with Genentech Inc., San Francisco, California. He was the chief of vitreoretinal surgery and an associate professor of ophthalmology at the University of Missouri-Columbia School of Medicine. He is a fellow of the Royal College of Surgeons, a fellow of the Royal College of Ophthalmologists, and a member of the Royal College of Physicians, and has been educated in St. Bartholomew's Medical College at the University of London. He is a diplomate in tropical medicine and hygiene (London School of Hygiene and Tropical Medicine) and has an MS in immunology from the University of Birmingham, United Kingdom. He has served in a professional capacity at the Hospital for Tropical Diseases, London, and at Ahmadu Bellow University, Zaria, Nigeria. Ormerod received a fellowship from the U.S. government for training in cornea and external diseases (Harvard University) and in the retina (Wayne State University) and has received the Honor Award of the American Academy of Ophthalmology. He is the author of 85 publications in ophthalmology, internal and tropical medicine, immunology, visual rehabilitation, and the medical aspects of terrorism.

Mark A. Prelas is H. O. Croft professor of nuclear engineering at the University of Missouri-Columbia. Prelas received his PhD from the University of Illinois in 1979. Dr. Prelas received the Presidential Young Investigator Award in 1984, was a Gas Research Institute fellow in 1981, was a Fulbright fellow at the University of New South Wales in 1992, was named a fellow of the American Nuclear Society in 1999, and was a William C. Foster fellow with the U.S. Department of State in 1999–2000. In addition to being a professor at the University of Missouri, he worked at the U.S. Department of State in the Bureau of AM1S Control in 1999–2000 and with the Idaho National Engineering Laboratory of the U.S. Department of Energy in 1987. He has worked in the areas of arms control for weapons of mass destruction; in the development of nuclear, chemical, and biological sensors; in the synthesis and application of wide band-gap materials; in directed energy weapons; in direct energy conversion; and in gaseous electronics. He has published over 200 papers and 5 books and holds 12 national and international patents.

Katie Thompson writes about agriculture and biotechnology for *Farming Magazine*, *Agriculture Online*, and other publications. She has a master's degree in molecular pathology from the University of California.

Wade Thompson is an adjunct associate instructor at the University of Missouri-Columbia Extension Division's Fire and Rescue Training Institute. He is also a lieutenant with the Columbia, MO Fire Department; a member of the weapons of mass destruction response unit housed at the Boone County (MO) Fire Protection District; and a former member of the United States Marine Corps, Second Recon Battalion. Thompson has over 10 years of experience in hazardous materials and emergency response.

Herbert K. Tillema is a professor of political science at the University of Missouri-Columbia. His received his BA from Hope College in 1964 and his PhD from Harvard University in 1969. Dr. Tillema served as commissioner, State of Missouri Peace Officer Standards and Training Commission from 1992 to 1994. He has written several books and articles on the use of force in international relations, including *Appeal to Force—American Military Intervention in the Era of Containment* and *International Armed Conflict Since 1945*.

Robert V. Tompson, Jr. is an associate professor of nuclear engineering in the Nuclear Science and Engineering Institute at the University of Missouri-Columbia (MU). He received his BS in physics in 1980, his MS in nuclear engineering in 1984, and his PhD in nuclear engineering in 1988, all from MU. Dr. Tompson subsequently worked for three years as a postdoctoral research associate, first at the University of Kentucky for one year and then back at MU for two more years. Dr. Tompson was the recipient of a NASA Summer 1991 Faculty Fellowship at the Langley Research Center, following which he became a tenure-track assistant professor at MU. He is deeply involved in the activities of the Particulate Systems Research Center at MU, where he is the associate director. His research interests are in the experimental and theoretical aspects of nuclear reactor safety, aerosol mechanics, rarefied gas dynamics, indoor air quality, particulate-based and particle-related materials, and particle manufacturing and applications. He is a member of the American Nuclear Society, the American Physical Society, the American Vacuum Society, the American Association for Aerosol Research, the Society for Industrial and Applied Mathematics, and Sigma Xi. Dr. Tompson has about 70 publications including almost 40 refereed journal articles as well as a number of transactions and proceedings.

Harry W. Tyrer is a professor in and chairman of computer engineering and computer science at the University of Missouri-Columbia. He holds several degrees in electrical engineering and received his PhD from Duke University in 1972. Dr. Tyrer has edited three volumes and several special issues, and has contributed to over 60 publications. He has developed biomedical instrumentation, object-oriented applications, and wireless communication systems. Additionally, he has written on real-time operating systems, digital systems, computer networks, and computer network performance.

Dabir S. Viswanath is an emeritus professor and Dowell chair of chemical engineering at the University of Missouri-Columbia. Since his retirement in 2000, Dr. Viswanath has been associated with the Nuclear Science and Engineering Institute at the university. He is a fellow of both the American Institute of Chemical Engineers and the American Institute of Chemists. He has provided guidance to over 50 graduate students and has published over 130 peer-reviewed papers and 4 American Petroleum Institute monographs. He has coauthored two books: *Data Book on the Viscosity of Liquids*, published by Hemisphere in 1989, and *Liquid Viscosity*, published by Springer in 2006. His research interests are in thermodynamic properties and transport of liquids and gases, process development, wastewater treatment, and thermal degradation of polymers in ceramics. He has taught at Bucknell University, the Indian Institute of Science, and Texas A&M.

Marion C. Warwick was a medical epidemiologist and the bioterrorism coordinator for the Missouri Department of Health and Senior Services. Dr. Warwick currently practices medicine, is the author of several papers on subjects related to both medicine and public health, and is a member of the American Society of Tropical Medicine and Hygiene; she is also board certified in both family practice and preventive medicine. She received her MD from the University of Minnesota in 1985 and her MPH from the University of Massachusetts, Worcester, in 1996. She has also been associated with the MITRE Corporation in McLean, Virginia.

Chapter 1

Introduction

Dabir S. Viswanath

CONTENTS

World Trade Center Bombing 8
Tokyo Subway Attack 8
Oklahoma City Bombing 9
Internal Terrorism: Republic of Texas (Terrorist Activities of Wise, Grebe, and Emigh) 10
Second World Trade Center Attack 11
Anthrax Threat 12
References 14

We started teaching a course entitled "Science and Technology of Terrorism and Counterterrorism" in 2000, before the USS *Cole* incident in October 2000. The manuscript for the first edition of this text was completed after the September 11, 2001, World Trade Center (WTC) disaster, and the book was published in August 2002. The Iraq war started on March 20, 2003, to eliminate weapons of mass destruction (WMDs), but it has now become a war against terrorism and terrorists. Today, in 2009, we are living in a world fearful of terrorism. We may not be able to completely eliminate terrorism, but we can work toward reducing terrorism. Education is one of the avenues to reduce terrorism, and we hope this book will contribute toward this goal.

The Rand report [1] under the chairmanship of Governor Gilmore of Virginia stated that

> The United States needs a functional, coherent national strategy for domestic preparedness against terrorism. Administrative measurements of program implementation are not meaningful for the purposes of strategic management and obscure the more fundamental and important question: To what end are these programs being implemented? The Advisory Panel therefore recommends that the next President develops and

> presents to the Congress a national strategy for combating terrorism within one year of assuming office. As the Advisory Panel recognized in its first report, our nation's highest goal must be the deterrence and prevention of terrorism. The United States cannot, however, prevent all terrorist attacks.

The programs recommended by the panel are

> Domestic Preparedness Programs: We recommend an Assistant Director for Domestic Preparedness Programs in the National Office to direct the coordination of Federal programs designed to assist response entities at the local and State levels, especially in the areas of "crisis" and "consequence" planning, training, exercises, and equipment programs for combating terrorism. The national strategy that the National Office should develop—in coordination with State and local stakeholders—must provide strategic direction and priorities for programs and activities in each of these areas.
>
> Health and Medical Programs: Much remains to be done in the coordination and enhancement of Federal health and medical programs for combating terrorism and for coordination among public health officials, public and private hospitals, prehospital emergency medical service (EMS) entities, and the emergency management communities. We recommend that the responsibility for coordinating programs to address health and medical issues be vested in an Assistant Director for Health and Medical Programs in the National Office for Combating Terrorism. The national strategy should provide direction for the establishment of national education programs for the health and medical disciplines, for the development of national standards for health and medical response to terrorism, and for clarifying various legal and regulatory authorities for health and medical response.
>
> Research, Development, Test, and Evaluation (RDT&E), and National Standards: We recommend that the responsibility for coordinating programs in these two areas be assigned to an Assistant Director for Research, Development, Test, and Evaluation, and National Standards in the National Office for Combating Terrorism. The national strategy should provide direction and priorities for RDT&E for combating terrorism. We believe that the Federal government has primary responsibility for combating terrorism RDT&E. Local jurisdictions and most states will not have the resources to engage in the research and development required in the sophisticated environment that may be a part of the nation's response to terrorism. Moreover, we have essentially no nationally recognized standards in such areas as personal protective equipment, detection equipment, and laboratory protocols and techniques.

Thus the report clearly points to the fact that counterterrorism measures must be developed and should be in place, and that research, development, testing, and evaluation must be supported. To carry out significant research in any area, students must be educated and future research needs to be explored. It was with this objective in mind that we developed a curriculum in the area of the scientific and technological aspects of terrorism and counterterrorism. Our search for courses that dealt with the scientific and technological aspects of terrorism and counterterrorism revealed that the engineering and science departments did not teach any course of this nature, but a large number of such courses were taught by faculty in political science, public policy, and related areas.

The motivation to start a program of this type was enhanced when we found that there are hundreds of books and a host of journals dealing with this subject; however, the scientific and technological aspects of terrorism and counterterrorism are loosely and thinly spread in some journal articles, for example, in the August 1997 (Volume 278, No. 5) issue of the *Journal of American Medical Association* on biological warfare.

Just when the first edition of this book was published, President George W. Bush had formed the Department of Homeland Security under the leadership of Governor Tom Ridge. Now Secretary Janet Napolitano heads the department. The organization and other details are discussed in later chapters.

The events that have taken place after September 11, 2001, particularly the ongoing wars in Afghanistan and Iraq, have not only changed the thinking of world leaders but even that of every citizen. What are some of the things we learned after September 11, 2001? The following are some of them:

1. That terrorism is part of our daily lives, and that no country, irrespective of its strong and technical advancement, is immune from terrorism. Before September 11, 2001, not many individuals paid much attention to terrorism, but now it is in the minds of all individuals. Terrorism has been there and will be there, but we need to take steps to reduce terrorist acts. Figure 1.1 shows that terrorist acts, based on the type of tactics used, have stayed fairly the same from 1980 to 2004. However, recent events (in 2005 and 2006), such as the London bus and underground train bombings, suicide bombings in Iraq, India, Bangladesh, commuter train bomb explosion in India which killed 209 and injured 720, unexploded suitcase bombs found in Dortmund and Koblenz in Germany,

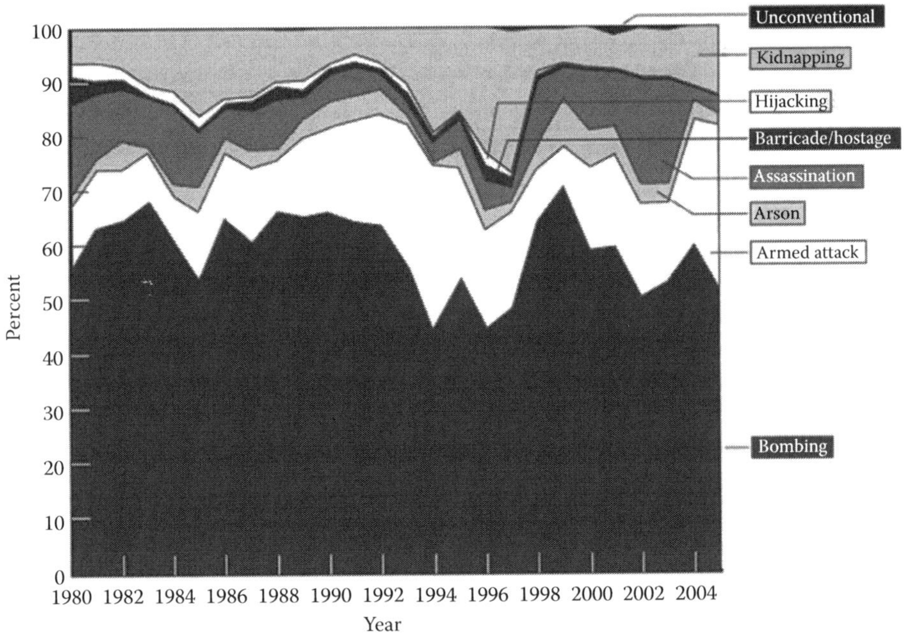

Figure 1.1 Terrorist acts based on type. (From Lal, R. and Jackson, B.A., MIPT Annual Report, 2006, pp. 3–18.)

John F. Kennedy International Airport terror plot, and many more, point to the fact that we need better methods of deterring terrorist acts.
2. That there is a sustained fear of Al-Qaeda, and that homegrown terrorists are on the increase.
3. That we have to sacrifice some amount of freedom, and freedom and security go hand in hand. This is evident from the security at the airports, the restrictions we face in traveling, the price we have to pay to protect our freedom, restrictions to our freedom of expression, restrictions on civil liberties, economic sacrifices to build a secure nation, and many more. We have also come to realize that the relationship among security, democracy, and terrorism is extremely complex.
4. That there is a feeling that we are winning the war on terrorism. It is not clear whether we are winning the battle and losing the war. In democratic nations, as we are witnessing today, the minds of the politicians/governments change but an organization such as Al-Qaeda may not change. We noticed this change when the Clinton administration changed to the Bush administration. However, Al-Qaeda has not changed but has grown stronger.
5. That strength and might are not the only ways of dealing with terrorists. International opinion is important and should not be ignored. Diplomacy is a very important and integral part of the equation in fighting terrorism.
6. That a complex but necessary infrastructure has to be built to take care of the aftermath of a terrorist attack or a major disaster.
7. That history cannot be ignored and historical perspective should be a part in fighting terrorism. For example, Afghanistan has never been subjugated to a foreign rule.
8. That terrorism is a threat to democracy and market economy. However, democracy cannot be forced on the people.
9. That the human mind can be directed to cause evil, hatred, pain, and suffering. Even civil and democratic governments do not disclose all the information they have and do not always base their actions on credible information.

Hundreds of such thoughts based on what has or has not been learnt after September 11, 2001, can be enumerated, but it is left to the readers to use their imagination and knowledge.

The Five-Year Interagency Counterterrorism and Technology Crime Plan [3] lists specific goals that are to be addressed. They are to

1. Identify critical technologies for targeted research and development efforts
2. Outline strategies for preventing, deterring, and reducing vulnerabilities to terrorism and improving law enforcement agency capabilities to respond to terrorist acts while ensuring interagency cooperation
3. Outline strategies for integrating crisis and consequence management
4. Outline strategies to protect our national information infrastructure
5. Outline strategies to improve state and local capabilities for responding to terrorist acts involving bombs, improvised explosive devices, chemical and biological agents, and cyber attacks

Education and research are key components in combating terrorism. To have a better understanding of terrorism and then to counter it, one should understand

1. The psychology of the terrorist or terrorist groups, the prevailing atmosphere in some countries which encourage and promote terrorist activities, and their religious, cultural, and economic background.
2. How to manage terrorist events, and the short- and long-term effects of terrorist acts.

3. What measures have to be taken to prevent terrorist acts? This involves educating both the terrorist (which is not easy) and the victim.
4. The underlying details of the weapons used in B-NCCE (biological, nuclear, chemical, cyber, and explosives) acts so that countermeasures can be devised.

Terrorism, by nature, is difficult to define. Even the U.S. government cannot agree on one single definition. The old adage, "One man's terrorist is another man's freedom fighter" is still alive and well. Listed below are several definitions of terrorism.

Terrorism is the use or threatened use of force designed to bring about political change. Laqueur [4] defines terrorism as an act that constitutes the illegitimate use of force to achieve a political objective when innocent people are targeted.

According to Poland [4], terrorism is the premeditated, deliberate, systematic murder, mayhem, and threatening of the innocent to create fear and intimidation to gain a political or tactical advantage, usually to influence an audience.

The Vice President's Task Force in 1986 defined terrorism as the unlawful use or threat of violence against persons or property to further political or social objectives [5]. It is usually intended to intimidate or coerce a government, individuals or groups, or to modify their behavior or politics.

According to the Federal Bureau of Investigation (FBI), terrorism is the unlawful use of force or violence against persons or property to intimidate or coerce a government, the civilian population, or any segment thereof, in furtherance of political or social objectives.

All these definitions have some connotation to political activity. However, certain acts such as the poisoning of Tylenol tablets, the bombing of Centennial Olympic Games in Atlanta, and a score of others, do not lend themselves to any political motives. Therefore, a much more general definition seems in order, which should include nonpolitical aspects of a terrorist act. We would like to define terrorism as "an organized act committed, with or without a political motive, to create fear resulting in death and destruction." The analysis carried out by Schmidt and Jongman [6] shows that our definition takes into account several views expressed by various authors. They found that among the various terms used in defining terrorism, violence and force appeared in 83.5 percent of the definitions, political 65 percent, fear 51 percent, threat 47 percent, and so on. However, it can be concluded that defining terrorism is not easy; changes have to be made from time to time, and have to be dynamic.

Some of the terrorist acts that have taken place during the past few years can help in understanding the complexity of this subject. A collection of case studies can help identify the following:

- The type of people involved in terrorist attacks. Can we profile them?
- The types of weapons used in these attacks.
- Possible motives behind such attacks.
- Whether any information was available before such attacks and what action, if any, was taken?
- What measures have been taken to prevent such attacks in the future?
- Where the resources should be spent to maximize the benefit?
- Are the terrorists homegrown? If so what made them terrorists? Can this be reversed?

During 1997 and 1998, the number of cases or threats investigated on weapons of mass destruction (WMD) is as follows: nuclear 25 and 20; chemical 20 and 23; biological 22 and 112; and others 7 and 17, respectively. Although the nuclear threat has come from the breakup of the Soviet Union and the clandestine removal of nuclear materials, the number of chemical and biological threats has also increased several fold. We will outline some of the chemical and biological threats, and try to raise questions. We will not discuss the details of the attacks, as the primary focus is to generate questions resulting from these incidents.

On the basis of data given above, from the free flow of information, religious fundamentalism, increasing lethality of current biological and chemical weapons, the ease with which terrorist groups can acquire or develop weapons, and other factors, it can only be surmised that the number of terrorist activities will increase and cause more damage. In spite of the availability of technology in the open literature, it is not easy for the terrorists to manufacture biological and chemical weapons. However, timely action might prevent terrorist activities and could be a lesson for others. At the same time, it is important to understand that the current political unrest in various parts of the world and the economic disparity between the haves and the have-nots are drawing more and more educated people into different terrorist camps, and this is a cause for alarm. This may lead to a faster implementation of the technology available in the open literature. It is a fairly complex issue, and an increased vigilance on the part of all citizens is important to reduce terrorist activities. This increased vigilance can come by educating the public and through their efforts.

Table 1.1 shows a list of terrorist events from 1990 to 1999 in the United States. However, it was not until September 11, 2001, that most paid any attention to terrorist attacks either in this country or in any other county in the world.

Although the number of terrorist incidents has reduced in the United States, except for the major incident on September 11, 2001, the number of terrorist attacks in other parts of the world has increased. The number of U.S. noncombatant citizens killed worldwide as a result of terrorist incidents was 56 in 2005 and 28 in 2006. Also, 17 and 27 people were injured in 2005 and 2006, respectively. The number of people kidnapped were 11 and 12 in 2005 and 2006, respectively. (U.S. Department of State, Country Reports on Terrorism 2006, http://www.terrorisminfo.mipt.org/pdf/Country-Reports-Terrorism-2006.pdf). Table 1.2 shows the incidents worldwide for 2005 and 2006, and the damage resulting out of these incidents.

Table 1.1 Listing of Terrorist Events in the United States from 1990 to 1999

Year	*Incidents*	*Suspected Incidents*	*Prevention*
1990	7	1	5
1991	5	1	5
1992	4	0	0
1993	12	1	7
1994	0	1	0
1995	1	1	2
1996	3	0	5
1997	2	2	20
1998	5	0	12
1999	10	2	7

Source: Federal Bureau of Investigation, National Security Division, Terrorism in the United States, Report 1998, 1999.

Table 1.2 Incidents Worldwide during 2005 and 2006

	2005	*2006*
Incidents of terrorism worldwide	11,153	14,338
Number of individuals killed	14,618	20,498
Number of individuals injured	24,761	38,191
Number of individuals kidnapped	34,838	15,854

Source: U.S. Department of State Country Reports on Terrorism 2006, http://www.terrorisminfo.mipt.org/pdf/Country-Reports-Terrorism-2006.pdf.

It is evident from Table 1.2 that the number of terrorist activities is on the rise, and creative ways have to be found to contain terrorism. To bring things up to date, we have mentioned other major terrorist attacks since September 11, 2001. The total number of significant incidents as reported by the State Department is shown in Table 1.3. The data shown in Table 1.3 was compiled from the

Table 1.3 Significant Terrorist Incidents as Reported by the U.S. State Department

Year	*No. of Incidents*	*Year*	*No. of Incidents*	*Year*	*No. of Incidents*
1961	1	1983	6	1996	22
1968	1	1984	4	1997	12
1969	2	1985	8	1998	8
1970	2	1986	3	1999	12
1973	3	1987	3	2000	9
1974	1	1988	4	2001	19
1975	1	1989	3	2002	38
1976	3	1990	1	2003	45
1978	1	1991	3	2004	25
1979	3	1992	2	2005	39
1980	1	1993	3	2006	43
1981	3	1994	3	2007 (as of September)	82
1982	1	1995	8		

Source: U.S. Department of State, Country Reports on Terrorism 2006, http://www.terrorisminfo.mipt.org/pdf/Country-Reports-Terrorism-2006.pdf.

information provided by the U.S. Department of State as reported by the Office of the Historian, Bureau of Public Affairs. It is likely that many incidents that are not considered significant by the State Department are not included in this compilation. However, it will suffice to say that there is an increase in the number of such incidents particularly after September 11, 2001 terrorist attack on the U.S. soil. The major point to note is that although several governments claim that terrorism is under control and terrorists have been killed, the rise in the number of terrorist incidents does not justify such a conclusion.

We would like to present a brief study of six terrorist acts that have occurred in recent years. We hope an in-depth study of these case studies will reveal the inherent problems in the design of the security management, weaknesses in the design of such security management systems, adequacy or inadequacy of response, interface requirements such as sharing intelligence among various groups/agencies or even countries in combating terrorism, deep understanding of religious and cultural aspects, profiling of terrorists and terrorist organizations, and a host of other questions.

World Trade Center Bombing

On February 26, 1993, a car bomb exploded at the B2 level of the World Trade Center (WTC) killing six persons and injuring hundreds. The blast created a 6 m diameter hole. The event posed a number of questions:

1. What kind of intelligence did the government had about this attack? Was the attack instrumental in getting through a quick passage of the 1995 Counter Terrorism Bill?
2. Was this stateless warfare? If so, how can a government protect its citizens?
3. How many states or countries can the United States punish to contain such attacks? Would this work?
4. Is this a deep psychological problem?
5. Is this a religious problem? Do we know the basic tenets of different religions, and which ones can we trust?
6. Why do terrorists target the United States and citizens of the United States? Can we draw broad-based conclusions or correlations of the different terrorist attacks based on the policies of the United States at different times and support given to different types of governments and people?

Tokyo Subway Attack

The Tokyo subway attack by the Aum Shinrikyo, or Supreme Truth, cult occurred on March 20, 1995, and killed over a dozen people and injured more than 5000. The chemical used in this attack was sarin gas (GB), although there were indications that the group was experimenting with biological agents such as anthrax, botulism toxin, and the Ebola virus. There were widespread reports that this was a trial attack by the Aum group before a larger attack, and that the Aum group experimented with sheep in the Banjawarn area in Australia. The latter news was based on an Australian Broadcasting Company report and was thought to be incorrect for various reasons, and the European experts in chemical and nerve gas detection laughed at the suggestion that experiments on sheep were carried out with sarin. Aum members in this Australian ranch were apparently warned of a police attack. There are hundreds of reports and writings on this incident just like the Oklahoma Federal Building attack or the WTC attack. What important lessons can we learn from this Tokyo subway incident? Besides the points mentioned in the attack of WTC, some other points are:

1. Sarin was the chemical used, and like sarin there are many other nerve gases and toxic chemicals. Have we reached a time when some of the chemicals should be restricted, even if they are of commercial importance?
2. Should we pay more attention to the reports, such as that of the Australian Broadcasting Company, and investigate more thoroughly?
3. Should there be more financial commitment for research and development in areas such as sensor technology?
4. In the event of an attack, what is the minimum amount of information the public should know to defend or help themselves?
5. What was the motive of Aum Shinrikyo?
6. Will chemicals like sarin create allergy problems? How will one answer this question? Should there be research in this area?
7. Are the components of chemical and biological weapons available too easily?
8. How far can we go in preventing the proliferation of biological and chemical weapons?

Oklahoma City Bombing

On April 19, 1995, a bomb destroyed the Alfred Murrah Federal Building in Oklahoma City, and killed 168 people and injured hundreds more. Several agencies and teams were involved in the investigation. These agencies were Bureau of Alcohol, Tobacco, Firearms, and Explosives (ATF), the FBI, local police and fire departments, Secret Service, many voluntary groups, and many other independent agencies. The investigation was intense, but from the point of view of terrorism and counterterrorism, what are the important factors and what lessons have we learned?

The bomb was made with approximately 2 tons of ammonium nitrate fertilizer mixed with combustible fuel oil, and it was taken in a Ryder truck, and parked in front of the north side of the building before it was detonated. Some questions are:

1. Was the building designed to withstand such blasts?
2. Should a chemical like ammonium nitrate be restricted? If so, what about ammonia and nitric acid? Can terrorists get hold of chemicals sold normally in the open market and make destructive chemicals?
3. How did the morale of the people in the country and around the world suffer? What was the impact on the people in the city, and what type of psychological counseling should be provided? What are the political implications? At first it was thought that a Middle-Eastern group had carried out this attack, particularly in view of the WTC bombing on February 26, 1993. What would have happened if McVeigh was not arrested quickly?
4. What type of response was available immediately after the bombing—emergency, medical, etc.? Was it satisfactory? In public buildings where a large number of people work, should there be a common area where all personnel are required to go to report to get further instruction before leaving the building? Should most of the people in that building receive Emergency Medical Technician (EMT) training? How about communications?

5. In the Oklahoma City, WTC, and USS *Cole* bombings, vehicles were involved. Should there be restrictions regarding the vehicular traffic (to keep them at a distance from the buildings), plans to transport materials that arrive at the building (unload from the carrying vehicle to a vehicle owned by the Security at the building), etc.?
6. In these situations, the FBI and the Federal Emergency Management Agency (FEMA) had control. Would this hinder the assistance efforts of other organizations, such as the Red Cross, church organizations, etc.? How should the relief efforts be coordinated? What type of measures should be in place for issuing identifications, etc.? The president signed an emergency declaration within 8 h of the occurrence—section 501(b) of the Stafford Act—granting FEMA the primary federal responsibility for responding to a domestic consequence management incident. The president subsequently declared a major disaster on April 26, 1995.

Internal Terrorism: Republic of Texas (Terrorist Activities of Wise, Grebe, and Emigh)

Political objectives and motives appear to be the major reasons for some terrorist activities. Almost all national or international terrorist attacks can be traced to political ends. In some of the cases, it is not clear how far the authorities follow tips or information to crack down on terrorist groups. This particular incident reveals how one attack was prevented.

Three men belonging to the Republic of Texas group, Johnny Wise, Jack Abbott Grebe, Jr., and Oliver Dean Emigh, plotted to kill several members of the government including President Clinton. They were to obtain anthrax from sources outside the country, and were trying to make devices to target a federal judge in Texas. Fortunately, FBI agents arrested these suspects on July 1, 1998. The FBI acted quickly in this case and thus prevented what could have been a major catastrophe. The trial of this case began on October 19, 1998, and concluded on October 29, 1998, when two of the three were convicted. What can we learn from this episode?

1. Did the FBI act timely to arrest the perpetrators?
2. Under what circumstances would the FBI think that a report is credible or not? In this case, it is reported that an FBI agent thought that the "alleged plot to assassinate government officials with poisoned cactus needles shot out of BIC lighters was far-fetched."
3. What type of devices did this group put together? The lighters were to be rigged to shoot cactus needles dipped in substances such as anthrax, AIDS-tainted blood, and rabies, according to an account by federal officers.
4. Where did they get information to make the devices that they were trying to assemble?
5. Are the regulations for importing materials adequate?
6. If they succeeded in getting anthrax from a foreign source, what could have been the consequences?
7. Are they part of a larger group, and if so, what measures have been taken to keep a watch on this group?
8. Did the investigation end with their conviction or did it continue? If it continued, was the public informed?
9. What is the profile of these people? Can the citizens be familiarized with these profiles, and be guarded?

10. Were there any psychological tests carried out to profile the type of individuals who could carry out such threats?
11. What is their educational background, and did they understand what they were doing?
12. What measures are in place to disseminate information? Should this information be disseminated at all?
13. How far can the government go before constitutional rights are violated?

Second World Trade Center Attack

On September 11, 2001, two jets from Boston, one bound to Los Angeles and the other one to San Francisco, crashed into Towers 1 and 2 of the WTC. In all, four passenger jets were involved in different attacks on that day, killing over 3000 persons. In addition, the immediate economic losses to the City of New York could be as high as 30 billion dollars, and the long-term economic losses to the United States could amount to hundreds of billions of dollars.

The loss of life in this attack was heavy, and mostly unaccounted. Simple calculations show temperatures in excess of several thousand degrees could have resulted inside the tower building. The towers, 415.5 m (1,363.25 ft) and 417 m (1,368.2 ft) tall, housed 418,600 m^2 (4,504,136 ft^2) of office space. The airplanes that hit the WTC were Boeing 767 and 757. Taking aviation fuel as a saturated hydrocarbon, and assuming that less than 5 percent of the total fuel (approximately 63,210 L or 16,700 gal) burned in an area of 3,011 m^2 (32,400 ft^2) (approximate area/floor), the amount of heat generated will be, approximately, 7.6×10^{10} J (72×10^6 Btu). The air inside a volume of 11,011 m^3 (388,800 ft^3) (assuming a height of 3.65 m (12 ft)) gets heated to more than thousands of degree centigrade.

This attack raises several questions besides those raised in the previous cases. We will raise these questions in two sets; one similar to those raised in the examples cited above, and the other set pertaining to long-range policy. The first set of questions is

1. Is there anything close to foolproof airport security? What steps should be taken to enhance airport security?
2. It was reported that some of the persons involved in this attack took part in other attacks such as the bombing of USS *Cole*. These persons were residing in the United States without proper documents. Is this a failure on the part of the FBI or failure of the Immigration and Naturalization Service (INS)? Do these agencies work separately? Is there a need for these two agencies to work closely at least in certain cases? Should several departments such as law enforcement, the Central Intelligence Agency (CIA), the FBI, and, the INS work together? In that case, who should be in charge of these departments? Should the federal government create a separate umbrella to oversee the work of these departments?
3. The New York City Fire Department, hospitals, volunteers, police, and other agencies did a heroic job. Was the emergency preparedness adequate? Do we have the same type of preparedness in other parts of the country as in New York?
4. Do we need new codes for buildings of the type of WTC?
5. We seem to be dealing with a particular set of people in this world who are identified with terrorist acts. Do we have the psychological profiles of the people who commit such terrible terrorist acts? Do we have a deep understanding of their religion and beliefs? Why do these countries hate the United States?
6. What type of terrorism is this? Is this chemical terrorism?
7. How can the injured and dead bodies be recovered in an organized and respectful way?

The second set of questions is

1. Why is the United States the main target of terrorist attack?
2. What is the origin of the persons who carried out this attack?
3. Being the most powerful nation in the world, what should be the U.S. policy toward other countries?
4. President Bush very correctly said "Terrorism in any form is bad." Would this be the cornerstone of the U.S. policy? Can the United States boldly follow this principle? Would this jeopardize the U.S. interests in trade and commerce? How far can the United States go in sacrificing its standard of living?
5. Has the Iraq war produced more terrorists? Was the war worth the effort?
6. What would have been the result if the United States had concentrated in Afghanistan instead of going to Iraq? Did Al-Qaeda exist in Iraq before the war?
7. And many more.

Anthrax Threat

Bioterrorism threats have emerged since October 2001, and the anthrax scare came to Capitol Hill. The spores of the bacterium were discovered in several places including Senator Daschle's office at the Hart Senate Office building in Washington, DC; mail-sorting equipment in Brentwood road, NBC anchor Tom Brokaw's office in New York; the office of a photo editor of the *Sun* tabloid in Boca Raton, Florida; Kansas City, Missouri, and other places. Two postal workers in the Washington, DC area, Thomas Morris, Jr. and Ottilie Lundgren, of Oxford, Connecticut, died due to anthrax inhalation. September 18 to the middle of December 2001 was a very anxious period for all, not knowing how this scare came about and who was responsible. Although the case remained unsolved till August 2008, Bruce Lvins, an army microbiologist, was suspected to be responsible for anthrax attack by mail. However, he committed suicide on August 21, 2008 bringing the case to a possible closure.

This threat appeared to be more at home than a threat due to a chemical weapon, and a host of questions can be asked:

1. How can one find out if the threat is anthrax?
2. If exposed to anthrax spores, where should one go?
3. How does one know whether she or he is in a high-or low-risk category?
4. What precautions should be taken before handling mail?
5. How can the public get information on postoffices closed due to anthrax contamination?
6. How can one tell if one is exposed to cutaneous anthrax?
7. How can one be sure that the mail is not contaminated by anthrax?
8. People who got infected were in different places such as mailrooms, hospitals, and other areas. Did they get infected by mail or by some other method?
9. Are there enough medical facilities to cope with a major threat? How should the healthcare personnel respond in case of an emergency?
10. What should a person do to get prepared to deal with an anthrax scare?
11. How resistant are the spores?

In 1979, the city of Sverdlovsk in the former Soviet Union experienced an anthrax outbreak. There was a difference of opinion regarding the source of anthrax. While the Soviet Union believed it was from contaminated meat, the U.S. sources maintained that it was due to a leak from an anthrax-manufacturing facility. This epidemic claimed 68 lives and 17 suffered skin infections. In all likelihood, the spores of anthrax spread as an aerosol, and affected people close to the manufacturing facility. It is reported that there has been only 18 cases of anthrax between 1900 and 1976 (cnn.com/health, October 5, 2001).

As we see from these six examples, the motivation in all cases appears to be political, one way or the other, either internal or external to the state. The profile of the individual or individuals involved has not been analyzed to draw conclusions to help identify future terrorists. Except in the case of the Tokyo subway incident, the individuals involved were not highly educated and technically skilled persons, but had some practical experience. All cases are of chemical terrorism in nature, and the chemicals used could be purchased or synthesized. It is evident that the chemicals used have a dual purpose as industrial chemicals and chemicals that can be used for terrorist activities.

These examples were cited in the first edition of this book, and we have left them as presented earlier. After the publication of this book came the Iraq war. On March 19, 2003, the Iraq war started, Saddam Hussein fell on April 9, 2003, and was captured on December 13, 2003, executed on December 30, 2006, close to 2 million Iraqis have become refugees, 3564 American and 281 allied troops have lost their lives, 111 troops have died of self-inflicted wounds, and close to 35,000 troops have been wounded as reported by the U.S. Department of Defense (USDOD) the data and is shown in Table 1.4.

Although the Iraq war was started on the premise that Saddam Hussein possessed WMDs, and we wanted to destroy these WMDs, it has now turned out to be a war on terrorism. But it is not clear whether this war has

1. Reduced/increased the global threat of terrorism
2. Been useful in identifying the character and boundaries of the threat
3. Nurtured homegrown terrorists
4. Shown that there are better methods of reducing global terrorism

Table 1.4 Wounded and Medical Evacuations

Nonmortal Casualties	*Army*	*Navy*	*Marines*	*Air Force*	*Total*
Wounded—no medical air transport required	11,197	411	6,083	230	17,921
Wounded—medical air transport required	5,514	149	1,904	61	7,628
Nonhostile-related medical air transports	22,792	833	2,214	1,183	27,022
Nonhostile injuries—medical air transport required	5,705	236	942	293	7,176
Diseases/other medical—medical air transport required	17,087	597	1,272	890	19,846
Medical air transport (hostile and nonhostile)	28,306	982	4,118	1,244	34,650

Note: As reported by the DOD as of May 19, 2007.

5. Revealed the magnitude of human and economic losses
6. Managed to show people beyond the Western Hemisphere that democracy and market economy is the answer for all evils
7. Justified that diplomacy is better than armed conflict (President John Kennedy used diplomacy instead of armed conflict during the Cuban Missile Crisis against the advice of the military)
8. Impacted the coalition of other countries with the United States on policies affecting the world events in future
9. Helped to design counterterrorism strategies and methods
10. And many more

One thing is certain that we can only hope to contain terrorism but not eliminate it completely. We need to be extremely cautious in our approach, and devise methods to counter terrorism through education, economic uplift, a sense of participation but not dictation in the affairs of other countries, democratization through the will of the people and not by stick and carrot approach, selflessness and not selfishness (this is what may happen in Pakistan with the recent elections), humility and not arrogance, and so on.

References

1. Second Annual Report of the Advisory Panel to Assess Domestic Response Capabilities for Terrorism Involving Weapons of Mass Destruction, James S. Gillmore, Chairman, December 15, 2000.
2. R Lal and BA Jackson, The MIPT Terrorism Annual Report, 2006, National Memorial Institute for the Prevention of Terrorism, Oklahoma City, OK, pp. 3–18.
3. The Five-Year Interagency Counterterrorism and Technology Crime Plan, Attorney General, 1999 Report, February 1, 1999.
4. Terrorism Research Center, Definition Page, 1996–2000. http//www:terrorism.com/ terrorism.def.shtml
5. Vice President of the United States. Public Report of the Vice President's Task Force on Combating Terrorism, February, 1986.
6. AP Schmidt and AI Jongman. *Political Terrorism*, Transaction Books, Amsterdam, 1988.
7. Federal Bureau of Investigation, National Security Division, Terrorism in the United States, Report 1998, 1999.

Chapter 2

A Brief Theory of Terrorism and Technology

Herbert K. Tillema

CONTENTS

Introduction 15
What Is Terrorism 16
Why Terrorism 18
Who Are Terrorists 19
Counterterrorism 20
Technology and Terrorism 22
Counterterrorism and Technology 27
Summary 28
References 29

Introduction

What and why is terrorism? What can be done about it? Terrorism is undeniably horrific. It kills, maims, and destroys property for political purposes. Few praise terrorism in itself, not now and not in the past. Nevertheless, the practice has persisted for literally thousands of years. In some ways, terrorism is more horrifying than other awful forms of violence, including war, criminal brutality, and psychopathic mayhem, each of which also has a long history. Soldiers in war at least expect violence. Victims of crime at least comprehend violence inflicted for material gain. Those who suffer at the hands of the psychopath may at least attribute loss to fate. Victims and witnesses of terrorist acts, on the other hand, seldom expect the event, cannot easily understand why violence strikes when and where it does, but know that damage is inflicted for a purpose. They are made fearful. That is the immediate purpose.

Contemporary possibilities of terrorism are especially frightening due to new technologies. Potentially, weapons of mass destruction might be involved. Terror is not simply a function of technology, however. The means are often simple. Motives are usually indirect. Effects are invariably complex.

The terrorist wreaks havoc to terrorize those who see or hear about it. He expects to gain more from the symbolic consequences of violence than from its destructive physical effects. The terrorist intends to alter states of mind as well as to change things physically. At the same time, terror is seldom an end in itself. Ultimately, the terrorist aims to influence the prospective behavior of others by affecting their will to act. For this reason, terrorism necessarily represents a political act. Political effects are almost always complex. Effective counterterrorism must usually address the politics involved as well as apply physical defense.

Terrorism is neither rare nor new. Thousands of terrorist incidents occur around the world in any given year. It is more frequent than major wars, less frequent than other efforts to bring change by peaceful means. There is probably no more of it now than in the past, controlling for growth of societies, but the general public is assuredly more aware of it due in part to advances in international communications. Five hundred years ago, North Americans did not know that there was a Europe, much less that terrorist events occurred within it. Forty years ago, the Viceque Rebellion was almost entirely unknown outside East Timor at the time that it occurred. Today, many terrorist events in far-flung corners of the world are instantly recognized around the globe.

What Is Terrorism?

Modern usage of the word "terrorism" owes much to the Jacobins during the French Revolution. The Jacobin movement advocated democracy in the form of universal suffrage and also proclaimed very high standards of probity for personal and public conduct. In September 1793, the radical Committee of Public Safety in France under the leadership of Robespierre and the Jacobins publicly decreed "terror," called by that name, against enemies of the Revolution to assure the "reign of virtue." Agents of the Committee murdered, maimed, and also seized and destroyed property of alleged enemies for nine months until Robespierre's arrest and execution. Foreign and domestic critics of Jacobin political objectives and methods, including Britain's Edmund Burke and conservative continental European governments, fulminated against the French "Reign of Terror." Critics spoke louder to later generations than did the Jacobins. That period of French history is still commonly identified as "The Reign of Terror." Perhaps this helps to explain the persistently perjorative connotations associated with the word "terrorism."

Terrorism is the subject of much recent study and comment. Many book-length treatises and collected works have general import, including Clutterbuck [1], Crenshaw [2], Ford [3], Hoffman [4], Laqueur [5,6], Long [7], Kegley [8], Rubenstein [9], Schlagheck [10], and Wieviorka [11]. Contemporary theory is also represented within several important essays, including Adkinson et al. [12], Enders and Sandler [13], Hamilton and Hamilton [14], and Merari [15]. A few recent studies systematically examine connections between terrorism and other manifestations of political conflict, including O'Brien [16]. Many additional scholarly monographs, collections, and articles speak to specific forms of terrorism or specific instances of it. A few journals devote themselves particularly to the subject, notably including *Terrorism and Political Violence*. Several compendia document recent terrorist events, including several iterations of the dataset *International Terrorism: Attributes of Terrorist Events*, which contributes to numerous systematic studies [17]. The *Rand-St. Andrews Chronology of Terrorism*, also iterated, is another frequently employed compendium [18]. Government reports and individual political commentaries are too numerous to mention.

The term "terrorism" is generally employed today to denote fearful violence inflicted for explicit political purpose. There is disagreement about what else, if anything, to include under the label. Consensus upon a strict definition exists among most scholars who study terrorism consistently over time and space [19]. Governments and public commentators, most of whom attend primarily to a few attention-getting events of the moment, do not necessarily agree. Some seek to excuse some actions that they prefer not to call "terrorism." Others conflate terrorism done for political purpose with other forms of reprehensible violence without regard to motive or long-term effect. Broad and behaviorally inconsistent definitions are potentially misleading.

It may not be surprising that interested parties in government and the public frequently confound terminology in discussion of terrorism. The label "terrorism" itself has practical consequences. To call another a "terrorist" is to name one an outcast, given traditional prejudice against the word. To call a terrorist by another name—perhaps "freedom fighter"—grants superficially greater political and moral legitimacy. Whether or not to attribute an event to terrorism may even affect whether or not insurance policies that exclude acts of terrorism will compensate for losses [20].

It is also not surprising that some interested parties conflate terrorism with other acts of violence. Terrorism is merely one of several forms of violence that threaten ordered societies. Others of these, including simple criminality, may be even more widespread. The physical effects of violence are damaging no matter the cause. It is tempting to clump all bad things together in hope of addressing them all at once.

Conflating terrorism for political purpose with other forms of violence may be seriously misleading. The motives of terrorism, guerrilla warfare, simple criminal violence, and psychopathology are presumably different. The terrorist seeks primarily symbolic political effect. The guerrilla warrior seeks, along with other things, to sap the strength of established security forces by unconventional means. The simple criminal presumably inflicts violence incidentally in pursuit of personal material gain. The psychopath may have no comprehensible reason at all.

In addition, the more broadly is terrorism defined, the less clear it is how to counter it [19]. Counterinsurgency warfare against guerrillas has well-developed doctrine and training. So does criminal justice and peace officer training. Psychiatrists possess their own theory and methods for dealing with irrationally destructive personal behavior, if given the chance. These are different from each other, however and none is sufficient to the special requirements of curbing politically motivated terrorism. The methods that one can and ought to use in response to each are not identical. Martial law and other suspensions of political liberties may be tolerable in the face of guerrilla warfare but are seldom politically or morally acceptable in response to mere terrorism. Counterthreats directed primarily to personal material interest are largely wasted upon the terrorist; he seeks more than just tribute. On the other hand, appeals to political interest and principle are largely wasted upon both the criminal and the psychopath.

The purpose of this chapter is to briefly elaborate and extend contemporary theory of terrorism to facilitate comprehensive discussion of technology within terrorism and counterterrorism. Technical literature abounds, especially relating to particular technologies, and especially relating to especial needs of law enforcement and military defense. Very little has been done since Wilkinson [21] comprehensively and explicitly related technology to terrorism, strictly defined.

For present purposes, the term "terrorism" is defined strictly and in accordance with present scholarly convention. "Terrorism represents a publicized program of episodic violence targeted upon noncombatant persons and property for purpose of affecting political attitudes and behavior." Publicity is essential to terrorism's purposes, even if limited to word of mouth, to communicate demands, and to signal accomplishments. Terrorism normally involves a succession of destructive events. It is difficult to change attitudes and behavior by means of a single isolated act. At the same time, it is customary to distinguish episodic terrorism from continuous military campaigns, including strategic bombing of civilian targets during World War II and other major wars. Terrorism is further distinguished from guerrilla warfare and conventional military operations that target soldiers and other recognized combatants. Terrorist violence aims ultimately to affect public policy and governance and not necessarily other matters. It aims to do so by changing attitudes and behavior among immediate and secondary witnesses, primarily through intimidation.

Why Terrorism?

Terrorism is by definition a tactic undertaken for strategic political effect. It helps to think like a terrorist to comprehend the political context within which the terrorist operates. Politics generally resembles a strategic game whose outcome rests upon interdependent choices among two or more parties. Parties to politics may include individuals, governments, or other organizations, depending upon circumstances. Politics further involves a bargaining process, not necessarily peaceful, in which parties attempt to influence one another's choices [22]. One may seek to induce another to act in ways one did not originally intend. Alternatively, one may seek to deter another from doing what one planned. Various general strategies are available for this purpose, including argumentation (both affirmative and negative), reward, promise, punishment, and threat. Several instruments are available to suit each of these strategies.

Terrorism is one of many instruments that may be employed in an attempt to change political behavior by the application of punishment and threat. It is an intermediate technique in the spectrum of violence. It is more destructive than most strikes and other demonstrations, and less damaging than most conventional military campaigns. The deadly logic of terrorism relies upon the insight that death and damage inflicted upon noncombatants may demoralize observant citizens and government officials, undermine support of established leaders, and eventually lead to change of policies or governments. He who resorts to terrorism may also employ other instruments at other times, including conventional military force if he is able. The terrorist presumably employs terrorism because it suits his purpose and is consistent with his abilities.

A terrorist attack constitutes a nonverbal signal intended primarily to convey an intimidating message to particular audiences. Any such act demonstrates ability and willingness to behave destructively. The magnitude of an attack further signals terrorist strength [23]. Apparent strength implies ability to conduct more attacks in future.

A terrorist attack may intend to send a signal to any of several audiences for any of several instrumental purposes. It may be employed in an attempt to demoralize agents of an established government, including the wave of assassinations inflicted upon village leaders within South Vietnam during the late 1950s by opposition groups associated with the Viet Cong. It may be employed in an effort to undermine public support of a government by demonstrating that government's inability to protect its citizens. This is a frequent aim among insurrectionist movements now and in the past. It may be employed abroad to discourage foreign support for domestic policies and governments, including Palestinian attacks within Europe from the 1960s onward aimed to coerce change in foreign support of Israel. It may be employed to attract new adherents to one's own cause by demonstrating will and capacity for action. This presumably was an important purpose of the Boston Tea Party of 1773. It may be employed to reinforce commitment among one's own followers and to forestall decay of organization due to inaction. One suspects that was one reason why the Provisional Irish Republican Army broke so many truce agreements in Northern Ireland during the 1980s. In practice, the signal represented by a terrorist attack may reach several audiences at once and may serve more than one political objective.

Terrorism is not necessarily best for all purposes, however, and some terrorists may wish to employ more powerful instruments instead. Guerilla warfare targeted upon security forces is sometimes an alternative to terrorism targeted upon noncombatants, if one is able to do it [24–26]. Guerrilla warfare impacts governments directly and may precipitate swift change of policy. The devastating attack upon U.S. Marine barracks in Beirut in 1982 by Islamic militants led to U.S. withdrawal a few months later. The problem with guerilla warfare is that it usually requires more resources, more skill, and more organization than does a mere terrorist campaign. The targets of the guerrilla are at least supposed to be prepared to fight back.

Conventional military force is even more effective for some purposes [27,28]. Terrorism does not work well to gain and retain control of territory. It may help to undermine existing authority but does not immediately establish new authority, any more than does guerrilla warfare. To control territory, the terrorist and the guerrilla are both advised to turn to conventional military force, if they are able to do so [29]. Terrorism is not even the best means for inflicting maximum physical damage. The physical consequences of a terrorist attack are frequently small, temporary, and uncertain compared to what may be achieved by a conventional military operation. Conventional military force, of course, requires even more resources than does guerrilla warfare; many terrorists refrain from it more from weakness than preference.

The terrorist may also wish that he could rely upon less destructive instruments, including peaceful methods of coercion. Terrorism, to the extent that it is physically successful, damages persons and property that the terrorist might prefer to remain intact if he becomes politically successful. Moreover, practice of terrorism frequently prejudices claims of moral legitimacy on behalf of the terrorist's demands for change. Some terrorists resort to terror in sadness as well as anger, convinced that less violent means alone will not produce desired political effects.

Who Are Terrorists?

Individual agents execute most terrorist operations. The individual who pulls the trigger or plants a bomb is not necessarily fully aware of the strategic purpose that directs his actions. The primary terrorist, often behind the scene, is he who purposefully employs and directs individual agents and operations.

Serious terrorists are generally well known. Terrorism is a public activity. It is not and cannot be entirely clandestine. The terrorist may seek to hide the time and place of planned attacks and may also try to obscure the names of his individual agents. The event itself cannot be secret because terrorism must be visible to terrorize. The authority and purpose behind terrorist attacks must also be apparent to influence attitudes and behavior in desired directions.

Political conditions that give rise to terrorism are also usually obvious and typically involve conspicuous, although controversial, claims of injustice. Most who embrace terrorism do so on the basis of dire expectations. They do not like the way things are and despair of other means to affect the future. Those who see themselves as revolutionaries, leaders of resistance, or guardians of declining order are especially likely to resort to terror. It is a conscionable instrument among some who are dispossessed, disadvantaged, or downtrodden [30]. It is also occasionally appealing as a last resort to beleaguered authorities who are desperate to extend or hold onto power.

Terrorists are comparatively weak in most cases and often embrace terrorism because they are not strong enough to do things differently. They are able to inflict episodic damage but are usually deficient in constructive power and compelling authority [31]. Dominant parties associated with the established order may rest upon their laurels. The wealthy may buy change. Powerful authorities may be able to sustain conventional military campaigns. Those known to be strong may get their way merely by threatening military action. The terrorist often resorts to terror because he is unable to employ effective alternatives. Terrorist tactics are comparatively easy to execute and involve comparatively small risks if one has little to lose from retaliation.

Terrorists are not new. Nor do they always serve unworthy purposes. Jewish Zealots employed terror in an effort to resist Roman policies within Jerusalem and other parts of Palestine 2000 years ago. Terrorism erupted after Roman edict of direct taxation at the beginning of the present era and persisted at least until the fall of Masada decades later. The American Revolution began with terrorism, including the destructive but not lethal Boston Tea Party of 1773. Ethan Allen and the fabled "Green Mountain Boys" behaved as little more than terrorists during their 1775 rampage across New York and southern Canada although they occasionally also attacked lightly defended British military installations. The modern state of Israel grew out of terrorism. The Irgun and other Jewish groups violently resisted British administration of Palestine before and after World War II, including attacks upon property and persons that served or supported British authority. Some Arab Palestinian groups did similarly at the same time. Growing strength allowed Jewish nationalists to develop also conventional military units by 1948; these were subsequently incorporated within the Israeli Defense Force after independence.

Many well-known parties employ terrorism today and did so in the recent past. Notable recent terrorists include agents for numerous nongovernmental organizations. Among these are various Palestinian entities such as the Popular Front for the Liberation of Palestine and Al Fatah; the Kurdish Workers' Party within Turkey and Iraq; Sikh nationalist organizations within Punjab and other parts of India; and the Provisional Irish Republican Army acting within Northern Ireland and England. No short list can do justice to the whole. Various "watch lists" distributed by the Federal Bureau of Investigation and other U.S. intelligence agencies identify thousands of political organizations connected to terrorism today and denote hundreds that deserve constant attention.

Some terrorism is popularly attributed to particular individuals. Osama bin Laden, an exiled Saudi who took refuge in Afghanistan, is frequently mentioned in this regard. Strictly personal terrorism is uncommon, however. It is difficult to sustain a program without durable organization. It is difficult to effect important political change if others interpret violence merely as personal vendetta. Effective terrorist leaders typically portray themselves as representatives of conspicuous groups and movements. Usually they are.

Some governments also contribute to terrorism, although more sponsor it indirectly than employ it directly. Most refrain from conspicuous involvement in terrorism, either because they have no need for it, do not approve of its methods, or fear retaliation. Governments that employ terrorism directly and conspicuously are often comparatively weak and insecure. A few employ terror against their own peoples in an effort to consolidate power, as did France's Committee of Public Safety in the 1790s. Others terrorize their own in an effort to forestall collapse, as did the government of Mohammed Reza Shah Pahlavi in Iran prior to its downfall in 1979. Some employ terror against hostile neighbors or other foes for ostensibly defensive purposes. Modern Israel, since 1948, has periodically attacked noncombatants within Jordan, Lebanon, and elsewhere. A few others occasionally employ terrorism for blatantly coercive purposes, including Libya within Chad during the 1970s and 1980s.

Counterterrorism

Counterterrorism attempts to negate terrorism. Of necessity, it is as old as terrorism itself. Governments and other established authorities threatened by terrorism have each relied upon it for thousands of years. Many have cooperated with one another for this purpose. The international community as a whole took notice at least, as early as 1934, when the League of Nations established the Committee for the International Repression of Terrorism.

Counterterrorism resembles terrorism in a few respects. Both involve programs of action and not merely singular acts. Both counterterrorism and terrorism depend upon political influence, not merely physical prowess. To fully prevent terrorism one usually has to influence the terrorist to choose to stop. Both usually require institutional organization, perhaps counterterrorism even more than terrorism. Effective counterterrorism typically requires large social investments and political programs beyond the reach of most small groups. In many cases, only strong governments are empowered to do counterterrorism well.

In some other respects, counterterrorism represents the opposite of terrorism, including who is most likely to undertake a serious counterterrorist program. While anyone who fears to be a target may worry about, those with most to lose are most likely to do something about it. Thus counterterrorism is usually associated with those privileged to take comfort in the present social and political order. The counterterrorist typically represents the established order of monetary wealth, property, political power, and policy within and among societies. This is opposite to the typical terrorist distressed and dissatisfied by the present state of order.

The tactical and political objectives of counterterrorism are also opposite to that of terrorism. The tasks of counterterrorism typically emphasize defense, not attack, and deterrence, not inducement. Defense in this context involves protection of specific persons and property to defeat a terrorist operation underway. This usually includes physical security, either passive or active, connected to specific sites. The focus of concern is the terrorist and the weapons in his hands. Physical security alone is usually insufficient unless protective devices that provide broad shields are omnipresent and perfect. The terrorist has many potential weapons to choose from, many potential targets to select from, and many ways to get around incomplete defenses.

Deterrence aims to dissuade the terrorist from commencing an attack [32]. Assuming that a terrorist resorts to violence deliberately as a means to a political end, and assuming that defense is uncertain, it makes sense to try to influence the terrorist either to abandon his political objectives or choose less destructive methods. Deterrence does not necessarily require physical action by the counterterrorist although it often includes such. The primary focus of concern for deterrence is the primary terrorist who directs agents for a purpose.

Counterterrorism occasionally includes preemptive attacks upon known terrorist bases, usually for purpose of deterrence. Such operations rarely expect to eradicate terrorist capabilities, something virtually impossible to accomplish against dispersed and easy-to-replace agents and weaponry. Attacks upon terrorists usually aim merely to punish and be punishment to deter future terrorist operations.

An important question to answer before devising any counterterrorist strategy is whether one objects more to terrorists' methods or to terrorists' political objectives. If one particularly deplores violence, one way to limit it is to accommodate all or part of terrorists' demands. Appeasement works, up to a point, despite a bad name earned following the Munich Conference of 1938, provided that one is willing to accept the ultimate political results. If, on the other hand, one objects most to the substance of terrorist demands, some terrorism may be an acceptable price to pay for standing up for one's own political principles.

Another question is to what extent to rely upon defense and to what extent upon deterrence. A strong defense against terrorism does not necessarily imply effective deterrence, nor vice versa. The defense against terrorism is almost invariably probabilistic. Some defenses may protect some sites some of the time. Few known defenses are sufficient to protect all potential targets against all potential weapons. Further, most terrorists know that it is not necessary to succeed in every instance to inflict terror overall. Terrorists, therefore, are generally motivated to keep trying if at first they do not succeed, they probably will succeed eventually. At the same time, deterrence is seldom perfect either, and leaves no immediate protection when it fails.

Counterterrorist defense is complicated by problems related to the offensive–defensive balance. The marginal social cost of deploying and maintaining counterterrorist devices and procedures often exceeds the cost to terrorists to overcome those same defenses. The price of full spectrum defense may exceed the expected value of objective losses likely to be halted. Partly for this reason, counterterrorist defense is customarily selective. Wise effort assesses the likelihood of various terrorist possibilities before committing large sums to uncertain defense.

Deterrence of terrorism is also complicated. The object of deterrence is to dissuade another party from doing what he intends. This requires a clear and consistent signal regarding what another ought not to do. Generally, the more broadly deterrence is aimed, the more diffuse is the signal. Diffuse signals are usually less effective. Unfortunately, assuming that another party has many alternatives from which to choose, selective deterrence may prevent one bad outcome but fail to prevent other undesirable results. Reliance upon deterrence is thus doubly risky: deterrence may fail outright; or deterrence may succeed narrowly but undeterred alternatives prove unfortunate, too [33].

Selective deterrence involves difficult choices regarding what to deter and what to tolerate. Some sorts of violence may be judged most needful to prevent, including certain targets using certain awful weapons. Assuming that the terrorist's will to do violence may find an outlet somewhere, it may be necessary to leave some targets at risk to more effectively deter attacks upon targets that one worries most about. Worse yet, as Enders and Sandler [34] report upon the basis of systematic study of terrorist events, a terrorist's alternatives are demonstrably substitutable: improvement in deterring one type of terrorist attack is associated with increased likelihood of other forms of attack.

Another issue in deterrent strategy concerns where to concentrate influence within the terror process. One may try to persuade a potential terrorist that his political aims are unworthy or lie beyond reach by any means. One may try to undermine confidence in the ability to do damage. One may attempt to convince a potential terrorist that he cannot gain any specific benefit from damage as he admittedly can inflict. Or one may seek to assure a potential terrorist that his destructive acts will result in unacceptable retaliation [35]. The ultimate objective remains the same at each step of the process: to influence would-be terrorists to refrain from terrorism. Methods of imparting influence differ, however.

In sum, counterterrorism is generally more difficult to accomplish than to arrest mere criminal violence. For one thing, the criminal seldom chooses targets indiscriminately. He usually attacks where money is. Sadly, even sophisticated counterterrorist strategy may not suffice to prevent destruction owed to seemingly irrational personal impulses, including bombing of the U.S. Federal Building in Oklahoma City in 1995 by Timothy McVeigh, and violence inflicted by the "Unabomber," Theodore Kaczynski.

Technology and Terrorism

Technology shapes terrorist events. Terrorism is initiated for political reasons and political consequences are ultimately paramount. Nevertheless, the political path from start to finish is restricted by available technologies. Many recent and sophisticated technical advances enhance horrible possibilities of terrorism, including advanced munitions, energy devices, chemical, biological, radiological, or cyber-weapons. Some of these potentially could do extraordinary harm whether employed as weapons of mass destruction or as weapons of mass disruption to disarray the infrastructure of a society [36]. The danger of immediate super-terrorism based upon such new technologies is real but improbable compared to the virtual certainty that ordinary terrorism will persist [37]. The substratum of widely installed technologies guides ordinary terrorism most of the time. The terrorist, by and large, is more imitative and habitual than technically imaginative [38,39]. To this day, most death and destruction due to terrorism results from knives, guns, and simple bombs. The savvy terrorist and the prudent counterterrorist both recognize ordinary technologies that determine what is practical for each. Readily available technologies have improved with time although they usually lag behind the latest laboratory developments. A contemporary terrorist is able to do things that his predecessors found impractical or did not imagine.

Technology ordinarily relates to terrorism in at least three ways, all of which have changed over time: (1) weapons technology produces implements that terrorists may use; (2) transportation technology limits the speed, distance, and magnitude of terrorist operations; and (3) communications technology also governs the speed and distance of political effects.

1. The terrorist usually employs readily available and easily controlled weapons. By and large, he adopts new weapons technologies belatedly, after military, commercial, and sometimes even criminal uses are established. The terrorist prefers simple and familiar weapons for several reasons. They are often readily available. Most are comparatively inexpensive. Less complexity predicts greater reliability. Often used weapons are frequently small, portable, easy to hide before the event, disposable, do not require great skill among agents to prepare or use, and have long records of accomplishment.

   For centuries, most terrorists relied primarily upon the knife. Zealots used knives to kill prominent citizens at public gatherings in Jerusalem and other cities. The knife remained the preferred implement of terrorism until the nineteenth century. Guns existed long before most terrorists began to use them. Guns appeared occasionally during the American Revolution and the 1790s Reign of Terror in postrevolutionary France but were not commonly found in terrorists' hands until a half-century later. Rapid-fire hand weapons date from the late nineteenth century but were not commonly employed for terrorism until well into the twentieth century. Indeed, some devices such as the submachine were used for criminal purposes even before many terrorists adopted them. Fully automatic weapons did not become frequent tools of terror until the 1960s or later, depending upon locality. Now, of course, fully automatic rifles and handguns are widely employed.

   The story of explosives follows a similar course. The gunpowder bomb, as old or older than the gun itself, was used for military purposes from the beginning, but did not find much employment among terrorists until the eighteenth century. Most subsequent developments in explosives were also long known before finding use in terrorism. Nitroglycerin, picric acid, and combustible derivatives of petroleum were commonly available before Anarchists employed them across Europe in the late nineteenth century. Dynamite, invented by Alfred Nobel in 1866, quickly found both military and commercial applications, and eventually appeared as a frequent terrorist weapon at the beginning of the twentieth century. Other high explosives, including trinitrotoluene (TNT) followed with similar delays. Most recently, plastic explosives have belatedly appeared in terrorist use. To this day, however, many important terrorist bombings rely upon old-fashioned technologies, including the so-called fertilizer bomb.

Poisonous and infectious chemical–biological–radiological (CBR) agents developed as military weapons during the twentieth century also have terrorist potential but are seldom used for this purpose. Some chemical weapons have been employed on battlefields from World War I to the Persian Gulf War of the 1980s. A few chemical agents are widely available. None is ordinarily used in deliberate attacks upon civilian targets for purpose of inflicting terror. Attacks such as that undertaken by Aum Shinrikyo (Sacred Truth) using sarin nerve gas within a Tokyo subway in 1995 are very rare. Most CBR agents have technical disadvantages as weapons for any use, including terrorism: most are difficult to transport; many have uncertain reliability; and nearly all are difficult to control in use.

Some governments also routinely equip military forces with deadly and far-reaching weapon systems capable of instilling terror by bombing or bombarding civilian targets. So far, most governments refrain from using such weapons except in conjunction with major military campaigns. Threats of nuclear attack upon cities, the basis for contemporary nuclear deterrence, are especially horrifying. Nuclear weapons, although now available in several forms to several governments, have not ever been employed since Hiroshima and Nagasaki at the end of World War II. Conventional munitions delivered by tanks, long-range artillery, bomber and fighter-bomber aircraft, and subsonic and ballistic missiles are also frightening. Civilians sometimes suffer incidental damage from such military weapons aimed primarily at combatants. Sometimes civilian damage appears to be more than incidental. Nonetheless, governments seldom admit to deliberate invocation of terror except in wartime, and not always even then. Most have too much to lose from retaliation in kind.

2. Technology of transport also makes a difference. Historically, terrorism is mostly local. Terrorist agents traditionally strike close to home, although, increasingly, some also undertake operations far away. Advances in the speed of personal transportation facilitate extended reach of terrorism. In principle, a contemporary terrorist agent could travel to a target thousands of miles away in less than a day, complete his mission, and return at similar speed. Some do. This has become possible only recently. From earliest civilization until little more than 200 years ago the speed of long distance transport was generally limited to no more than 4 mi/hour. Men on foot or horses normally go no faster than this, nor did most sailing ships until the late eighteenth century. The pace of transport in some parts of the world increased by an order of magnitude during the nineteenth century with the introduction of railroads and fast steamships. Automobiles and trucks built upon the internal combustion engine, introduced in the twentieth century, helped to reach places not served by railroads. The airplane, also introduced in the twentieth century, increased maximum speed of personal transport by another order of magnitude. At the beginning of the twenty-first century a terrorist agent relying upon commercial or general jet aviation can travel between major cities around the world hundreds of times faster than his eighteenth century predecessors. One cannot reach all points of the globe so rapidly. Some locations, including many rural areas of the world, remain beyond the immediate reach of recent technologies.

Ease of moving weapons has not necessarily kept pace with improvement of personal transport. Terrorists traveling by commercial air must usually rely upon weapons cached or found at or near the scene. Personal weapons and other light arms are otherwise mobile but usually move at land- or sea-speed when carried over appreciable distances. Long-range transport of heavy weapons is and always has been difficult except for the military forces of a few countries. These technological limitations restrict terrorists' choice of weapons and reinforce tendency to rely upon small arms and locally available explosives.

3. Communications technology is also significant to both tactical and strategic aspects of terrorism. Tactical communications between the terrorist and his agents, as well as communications among agents if there is more than one, are necessary to execute most effective attacks. Strategic communications, both verbal and nonverbal, are essential to the political purposes of terrorism. The terrorist must signal responsible parties what he demands as condition for ending terrorism. Violent actions must be reported beyond the immediate scene if terror is to spread. The terrorist needs also to signal his accomplishments to present and prospective supporters to maintain and build his organization. Verbal communication is not necessarily required in every instance and at every step of the way provided that sufficient ground is previously established to be confident that nonverbal signals will be interpreted as one desires. For example, the terrorist does not necessarily announce a public claim of responsibility for each and every atrocity he commits [40]. Some form of communication, verbal or nonverbal, is always essential, nonetheless.

Advances in communications technology have enabled more complex and more far-reaching terrorist campaigns than previously practical. In some instances, technology now permits orchestrated terrorism where previously it was impossible.

In 1840–1841, small units under U.S. Navy Lt. Charles Wilkes, commander of the United States Exploring Expedition repeatedly attacked and destroyed villages in the Pacific, including Fiji, Samoa, and Drummond Island in the Gilberts. Superficially and in hindsight, this might appear to constitute a conscious campaign of political terror directed by the U.S. government. It was not and could not be. Communications technology of that day permitted no quick means to communicate with ships at sea and Wilkes remained entirely out of touch with Washington most of this time. The U.S. Exploring Expedition set out in 1838 to investigate the rumored existence of Antarctica and returned in 1842 after also surveying the North American coast and visiting various unfamiliar places in the Pacific. The Secretary of the Navy initially directed the expedition, when in contact with native populations, "to appeal to their good will rather than to their fears." Ensuing violence reflected mostly personal motives, including efforts to bring alleged cannibals to justice and reprisal for theft and injury inflicted upon members of the expedition who, among other things, seized artifacts that later became the foundation of the Smithsonian Institution collection. Wilkes was belatedly brought to court-martial for exceeding instructions after return of the expedition in 1842 and after men under his command reported what had been done. He was eventually acquitted of all charges relating to mistreatment of civilians and retained his commission.

Critical dimensions of communications technology affecting terrorism include the range, speed, and carrying capacity of signals transmitted via particular media. Dramatic advances in communications technology over the past century and a half permit the terrorist to convey messages further, faster, and with more content than before. As is true of weapons and transportation, installed technologies matter most. The terrorist usually relies upon widely available communications media.

Until the 1840s, with few exceptions, no message traveled faster or further than the pace and range of human transport. In effect, nearly all communications, including tactical communications, signals of terrorist demands, and news of terrorist attacks, used to be limited to word of mouth and hand-carried paper. Exceptions generally had limited applications. The "ancient telegraph"—smoke-signals relayed from hilltop to hilltop—known at least as long ago as fifth century B.C. Greece, conveyed little information, worked only in presence of appropriate hilltops, and only for those who controlled the hilltops, which terrorists seldom did. Pigeons and other trained birds occasionally were employed for centuries to carry bits of information, including first news to London of Wellington's victory at the Battle of Waterloo in 1815, but also saw limited use for obvious reasons relating to reliable range and carrying capacity.

The bulk of information still travels at human pace, although that pace is faster now than it once was. Some new technologies have increased carrying capacity of long-distance communications without breaking the human speed barrier. Printed media, including books, magazines, and newspapers, as well as ephemeral publications such as newsletters, are more numerous due in part to computer-assisted design and production. As a result, more is put to print than previously and the terrorist has more opportunities to make known his demands and accomplishments, provided that his intended audience identifies his signal within the burgeoning noise of numerous other messages.

Other technologies newly available in the late twentieth century provide additional channels to transmit large amounts of information, including audio, video, and data tape, plus parallel disk media. The Iranian revolutionary movement inspired by the Ayatollah Khomeini that toppled the Shah in 1979 relied in part upon audio cassette tapes dispatched from Paris to direct agents and other followers within Iran.

The velocity of some communications increased significantly in the later half of the nineteenth century. Invention of the telegraph in 1844 provided the first reliable means to send signals more rapidly than human transport over long distances. Bandwidth was limited. Messages could travel fast only where wires existed and these initially followed railroad lines. Telegraphy across large bodies of water was enabled only decades later. The telephone, introduced in the late 1870s, improved upon the telegraph in some respects, including ability to carry more information, but was also limited at first to land-wires. The radiotelegraph, invented in 1895, reduced dependence upon installed wiring but was initially limited to use between designated facilities, including, for the first time, instantaneous communication with some ships at sea. These technologies at first conferred more tactical benefit upon governmental counterterrorism than upon insurgent terrorism. Nineteenth century terrorists, by and large, did not control these media. Terrorists gained some benefit in spreading terror from early use of telegraphy and telephony among some urban newspapers that used these new devices to acquire information more rapidly than before. Once in print, however, newspapers reached the public little more rapidly than before.

Broadcast technology introduced in the twentieth century expanded the scope of rapid communications but initially remained outside direct control of most terrorists. Commercial radio and, more recently, television permit the terrorist to convey political messages rapidly to distant audiences, provided that he can cause the broadcaster to transmit his message. The graphic content of television is particularly helpful to spread terror if one can exploit it.

Today's Internet connections among computers and telephonic facsimile transmission provide additional high-speed channels to transmit both words and images. The rapidly growing Internet facilitates several forms of instantaneous and far-reaching communication, including point-to-point transmission via electronic mail and largely self-regulated global broadcasting via the World Wide Web. Some contemporary terrorists employ the Internet for these reasons. "Fax" transmission is not necessarily so versatile but also finds use for some point-to-point terrorist communications.

Terrorists generally rely upon publicly available technology for communication just as they do with regard to weapons and transport. In principle, public access to fast moving and content-rich communication is now available through several channels throughout most of the world. In practice, the effective speed, range, and carrying capacity of public communications vary greatly for different purposes and from place to place. Telephone and e-mail are more or less instantaneous and are widely available but do not provide satisfactorily secure media for tactical messages to and among terrorist agents. For political purposes, including dissemination of reports of terrorist attacks, most terrorist signals still follow circuitous paths through multiple media before reaching all of their intended audiences, including transmission and retransmission via radio, television, and newspapers. Nor do advanced communications presently extend to all localities, especially not to rural areas within developing societies. It is not accidental that terrorist attacks appear to congregate within and near major cities today. Not merely do cities include many inviting targets; reports of violence spread further and faster out of major cities that are directly connected to global communications networks.

Interconnected urban mass media are especially important to the contemporary terrorist. For political purposes, the terrorist now depends greatly upon the journalist to help convey his signals. This does not imply that journalists necessarily subscribe to terrorists' purposes. It is, and generally recognized as a symbiotic relationship [41]. Journalists report "news." "News," according to a widespread bias within modern journalism, necessarily includes threats of political violence and, especially, violent political events themselves. The terrorist makes "news," partly but not merely to stimulate journalistic reports of what he wants and what he has done. Images and words emanating from an observant reporter may reverberate widely once transmitted and retransmitted among radio stations, television stations, newspapers, and other mass media, many of which pluck "news" from one another as well as from their own proprietary reporters. The Web work of modern journalism penetrates more corners of the globe today than in the past. It now extends among most major cities of the world although it does not necessarily extend everywhere into the countryside. It is now practical in some cases for a terrorist to attack close to home, confident that word will get out, to terrorize far away; or vice versa. This is the most important meaning of the current catch phrase "global terrorism."

Counterterrorism and Technology

Counterterrorism depends upon technology to deter as well as to defend against terrorism. The counterterrorist benefits from many advances in technology, sometimes more quickly than the terrorist. Some governments may be able to mobilize new devices and procedures not yet generally available for public use. Generally speaking, however, most successful counterterrorist strategies rely primarily upon widely disseminated technologies. This applies similarly to weapons, transport, and communications.

Effective counterterrorism faces a broader challenge than does terrorism. The terrorist may choose where, when, and how to attack. The counterterrorist must prepare to defend any likely target at times and by means of the terrorist's choosing without knowing in advance what the terrorist will choose. He must try to deter many possible actions, not merely one. Ideally, counterterrorism is omnipresent because there are many potential terrorists to deter and many potential targets to defend. This is practically impossible, if only because it is too costly to achieve. Focused effort and widely available methods are at least as valuable to the counterterrorist as the terrorist.

Technical requirements of defense and deterrence are not necessarily identical. For purpose of defense, the counterterrorist wants to stop the terrorist from completing destructive operations. The first line of defense is to eradicate or incarcerate all prospective terrorists. This is more easily said than done in any morally or socially acceptable way. The second line of defense is to deny terrorist agents access to things that they need to do their deeds, including weapons, transport, and tactical communications. It is sometimes possible, within limits, for governments to deny access to some advanced technologies that are not yet available for public use. Secrecy and physical security are the primary instruments for this purpose. The U.S. government and most other nuclear powers treat information relating to nuclear weapons technology as restricted data and prohibit dissemination. Advanced military weaponry, transport, and communications devices are usually stored under heavy guard. It is more difficult to deny access to publicly available weapons or other technologies although magnetic security gates and other familiar second line defenses are deployed for precisely this purpose. The third line of defense is to arrest a terrorist operation at the scene, hopefully before destruction is fully unleashed. This necessarily involves physical security. Many devices, new and old, are potentially helpful. The challenge of physical security includes more than merely to invent appropriate techniques. It is also to deploy the right devices at the right place at the right time, along with personnel to employ them, properly trained in their use. Advanced defense technologies that are not ordinarily widely distributed are especially difficult to deploy in timely fashion.

The technical requirements of deterrence depend in part upon what strategy of counterterrorism one pursues. Many deterrent strategies require more than mere technical proficiency and depend also upon propaganda, diplomatic skill, and expenditures for other than defense. To convince terrorists to abandon their objectives as hopeless or to persuade them that they cannot gain specific benefit from terrorism, one must usually invest in nation-building to reinforce the solidity of established order. Extended deterrence of terrorism aimed at change abroad may require foreign aid to assist nation-building within vulnerable societies. Technical requirements for undermining terrorists' confidence in ability to inflict damage are similar to those required for effective defense. The additional requirement for this purpose is to publicize the efficacy of those defenses. Unfortunately, publicity may assist the terrorist to identify ways to avoid existing defenses. As a result, the counterterrorist sometimes knowingly weakens defense in effort to strengthen deterrence. Technical requirements for a strategy of retaliation against terrorists and terrorist agents are at least as onerous as those required in counterinsurgency warfare against guerrillas. This includes capability to inflict terror upon terrorists. This is sometimes technically more difficult than to terrorize guerrilla warriors whose more elaborate infrastructure may be easier to locate and to damage.

An important challenge in devising any counterterrorist strategy is to anticipate probable events. It helps to identify who are likely terrorists. This is an intelligence task. Most good estimates depend as much or more upon open sources of information available to the public as they do upon advanced intelligence technologies. It also helps to anticipate likely targets and likely techniques of terrorism. This is also in part an intelligence task. Success depends, in part, upon adequate specification of intelligence requirements in advance. Unguided, even the best intelligence sources and the most sophisticated intelligence methods presently available, including signals intelligence, are unlikely to provide timely warning of all impending terrorist attacks. As noted previously, contemporary terrorists usually select conspicuous targets whose damage or destruction is likely to attract journalistic attention. In addition, terrorists generally rely upon widely available weaponry, transport, and communications. While it may be prudent to investigate techniques for dealing with possible but improbable super-terrorism based upon new technologies, this is not enough [42]. One wants also to find better ways to deal with ordinary terrorism, remembering that even ordinary terrorism is usually more difficult to control than simple criminality.

Summary

Terrorism represents a program of political action by violent means. It deliberately inflicts damage upon noncombatant persons and property. Its immediate purpose is to induce fear among those who witness the events. It ultimately aims to alter prospective political behavior among immediate witnesses and other parties. Terrorism differs from superficially similar damages inflicted for other reasons, including criminal violence in pursuit of material gain.

Terrorism is an ancient political instrument used mainly by parties who are aggrieved by the present political and social order. The issues are usually obvious and customarily include claims of injustice. The terrorist's methods may always be unworthy. His ultimate objectives are sometimes admirable. Terrorism is especially appealing to those who think that they have much to gain and little to lose. Terrorists customarily represent political organizations that are more capable than most individuals to sustain a campaign of terror. At the same time, terrorist organizations ordinarily lack sufficient power to succeed without violence and are also usually too weak to employ conventional military force.

Terrorism involves nonverbal as well as verbal signaling. The bomb blast, the bullet, and worse are recognizable symbols of punishment and threat if conspicuously coupled to demands for political change. The terrorist depends as much upon his ability to communicate demands and spread report of his deeds as he does upon his ability to inflict physical harm. Recent advances in international communications help to spread the terrorist's messages widely and quickly. This may lend the appearance that terrorism is more common today than in the past but that appearance may be deceiving. The world as a whole is certainly more aware of terrorism now.

The terrorist's political objectives, as well his immediate tactics, depend upon installed technologies, including weapons, transport, and communications. Generally speaking, the terrorist relies mostly upon simple and widely available methods.

Counterterrorism seeks to negate terrorism. It, too, requires political strategy. It is usually desirable to deter as well as to defend against terrorist attacks. To do both these things well one must anticipate likely terrorism because it is practically impossible to deter all potential terrorists and to defend all possible targets against all possible forms of attack. Effective counterterrorism, therefore, distinguishes that which is likely from that which is merely possible. A savvy estimation along this line combines both political and technical analyses. Wise technical investments in counterterrorism also address likely sources, forms, and targets of attack as well as help to prepare against the newest but improbable dangers.

References

1. R Clutterbuck. *Terrorism in an Unstable World*. London: Routledge, 1994.
2. M Crenshaw, ed. *Terrorism in Context*. University Park, PA: The Pennsylvania State University Press, 1995.
3. FL Ford. *Political Murder: From Tyrannicide to Terrorism*. Cambridge, MA: Harvard University Press, 1985.
4. B Hoffman. *Inside Terrorism*. New York: Columbia University Press, 1998.
5. W Laqueur. *The Age of Terrorism*. Boston, MA: Little, Brown, 1987.
6. W Laqueur. *The New Terrorism: Fanaticism and the Arms of Mass Destruction*. New York: Oxford University Press, 1999.
7. DE Long. *The Anatomy of Terror*. New York: Free Press, 1990.
8. CW Kegley, ed. *International Terrorism*. New York: St. Martin's, 1990.
9. RE Rubenstein. *Alchemists of Revolution: Terrorism in the Modern World*. New York: Basic Books, 1987.
10. DM Schlagheck. *International Terrorism: An Introduction to the Concepts and Actors*. Lexington, MA: Lexington Books, 1988.
11. M Wieviorka. *The Making of Terrorism* (Translated by DG White). Chicago, IL: The University of Chicago Press, 1993.
12. SE Adkinson, T Sandler, and J Tschirhart. Terrorism in a bargaining framework. *Journal of Law and Economics* 30: 1–21, 1987.

13. W Enders and T Sandler. Terrorism: Theory and application. In: K Hartley and T Sandler, eds., *Handbook of Defense Economics*, vol.1. Amsterdam The Netherlands: Elsevier, 1995, pp. 213–249.
14. LC Hamilton and JD Hamilton. The dynamics of terrorism. *International Studies Quarterly* 27: 39–54, 1983.
15. A Merari. Terrorism as a strategy of insurgency. *Terrorism and Political Violence* 5 (4, Winter): 213–251, 1993.
16. SP O'Brien. Foreign policy crises and the resort to terrorism. *Journal of Conflict Resolution* 40: 320–335, 1996.
17. W Enders and T Sandler. Transnational terrorism in the post-Cold War era. *International Studies Quarterly* 43: 145–167, 1999.
18. B Hoffman and DK Hoffman. The Rand-St. Andrews chronology of international terrorist incidents, 1995. *Terrorism and Political Violence* 8 (3, Autumn): 87–127, 1996.
19. AP Schmid. The response problem as a definition problem. *Terrorism and Political Violence* 4 (4, Winter): 7–13, 1992.
20. VT LeVine. The logomachy of terrorism: On the political uses and abuses of definition. *Terrorism and Political Violence* 7 (4, Winter): 45–59, 1995.
21. P Wilkinson, ed. Technology and terrorism. *Special Issue of Terrorism and Political Violence* 5 (2, Summer): 1–150, 1993.
22. TC Schelling. *The Strategy of Conflict*. Cambridge, MA: Harvard University Press, 1960.
23. PB Overgaard. The scale of terrorist attacks as a signal of resources. *Journal of Conflict Resolution* 38: 452–478, 1994.
24. R Clutterbuck. *Terrorism and Guerrilla Warfare: Forecasts and Remedies*. London, U.K.: Routledge, 1990.
25. E Guevara. *Guerrilla Warfare* (Translated by BA Loveman and TM Davis). Lincoln, NE: University of Nebraska Press, 1985.
26. VN Giap. *The Military Art of People's War*, R Stetler, ed. New York: Monthly Review Press, 1970.
27. HK Tillema. *International Armed Conflict Since 1945*. Boulder, CO: Westview Press, 1991.
28. HK Tillema. *Appeal to Force*. New York: T. Y. Crowell, 1973.
29. T-T Mao. *Selected Military Writings*. Peking, China: Foreign Languages Press, 1966.
30. G Sorell. *Reflections on Violence* (Translated by TE Hulme and J Roth). Glencoe, IL: Free Press, 1950.
31. KE Boulding. *Three Faces of Power*. Beverly Hills, CA: Sage, 1989.
32. PM Morgan. *Deterrence*, 2nd edn. Beverly Hills, CA: Sage, 1983.
33. T Sandler and HE Lapan. The calculus of dissent: An analysis of terrorists' choice of targets. *Synthese* 76: 245–261, 1988.
34. W Enders and T Sandler. The effectiveness of antiterrorism policies: A vector-autoregression-intervention analysis. *American Political Science Review* 87: 829–844, 1993.
35. B Brophy-Baermann and JAC Conybeare. Retaliating against terrorism: Rational expectations and the optimality of rules versus discretion. *American Journal of Political Science* 38: 196–210, 1994.
36. RJ Bunker. Weapons of disruption and terrorism. *Terrorism and Political Violence* 12 (1, Spring): 37–46, 2000.
37. M Taylor and J Horgan, eds. The future of terrorism. *Special Issue of Terrorism and Political Violence* 11 (4, Winter): 1–230, 1999.
38. B Hoffman. Terrorist targeting: Tactics, trends and potentialities. *Terrorism and Political Violence* 5 (2, Summer): 12–29, 1993.
39. MA Wilson. Toward a model of terrorist behavior in hostage-taking incidents. *Journal of Conflict Resolution* 44: 403–424, 2000.
40. DC Rapoport. To claim or not to claim: That is the question—Always! *Terrorism and Political Violence* 9 (1, Spring): 11–17, 1997.
41. P Wilkinson. The media and terrorism: A reassessment. *Terrorism and Political Violence* 9 (2, Summer): 51–64, 1997.
42. B Hoffman. Responding to terrorism across the technological spectrum. *Terrorism and Political Violence* 6 (3, Autumn): 366–390, 1994.

Chapter 3

Group Psychology of Terrorism

Michael A. Diamond

CONTENTS

Introduction 31
Changing Face of Terrorism 32
Internal Psychologic of Terrorist Acts 33
Dynamics of Large-Group Identity 34
Terrorism as a Group Activity: Large-Group Identity 36
Large Groups and Totalistic Belief Systems 37
Conclusion 39
References 39

Introduction

Today fewer acts of terrorism are state sponsored. Increasingly, acts of terrorism are rooted in ethnic, religious, cultural, and nationalistic, large-group identities. Given the combined ambiguity and vulnerability of nation-state boundaries and affiliations in a global economy, understanding individual motives behind violent, large-group memberships, is crucial. The psychology of large-group defense of borders and boundaries must be understood and appreciated if one wants to increase tolerance and decrease intergroup conflicts and ethnic and religious tensions worldwide. Effective counterterrorism requires our contemplation of the group psychology of terrorism. It demands an answer to the twenty-first-century riddle: why are so many people affiliating with extremist and fundamentalist groups that condone terrorism?

In 2005, according to the Stockholm International Peace Research Institute (SIPRI), intrastate conflicts were on the increase [1]. There were 19 internationalized major armed intrastate conflicts in 2004. Only three of these—the conflict against Al-Qaeda, the conflict in Iraq, and the conflict in Darfur, Sudan—were less than ten years old.* International in nature and in effects, these intrastate conflicts are complex and diverse, rendering the distinction between the "internal" and the "external" nation-state borders and boundaries particularly complicated and ambiguous, and calling into question the basis on which conflicts are classified and addressed [1].

According to SIPRI (2005), global patterns from 1990 to 2004 observed 19 armed conflicts in 17 locations throughout the world. There were no interstate conflicts recorded for 2004. In the 15-year period from 1990 to 2004 only 4 of the 57 active conflicts were fought between states. The remaining 53 were fought within states and concerned with either control over government (29 conflicts) or control of territory (24 conflicts).

Conflicts in Afghanistan, Algeria, Angola, Azerbaijan, Bangladesh, Burundi, Cambodia, Colombia, Georgia, Guatemala, India, Indonesia, Iran, Iraq, Israel, Liberia, Myanmar (Burma), Peru, Philippines, Rwanda, Somalia, Sri Lanka, Sudan, Tajikistan, Turkey, N. Ireland, and Zaire have claimed hundreds of thousands more lives. For example, in Burundi a conflict that began in 1991 has claimed approximately 200,000 lives. Conflicts in Colombia, since 1970, have claimed 70,000 lives; in Sudan 70,000 have been killed and 2 million displaced; 11,000 have been killed in Nepal (some 2,700 since 2003); 70,000–80,000 have been killed and hundreds of thousands made refugees in Russia (Chechnya); 15,000 lives lost in Indonesia; and over 98,000 dead in Iraq [1]. For the most part, these conflicts have taken place within the boundaries of a single country. They were ethnic, racial, religious, and cultural large-group identity-based conflicts rather than national conflicts between sovereign countries.

Changing Face of Terrorism

The face of terrorism has changed. Today, terrorism is associated with public acts of violence and mass destruction, dramatic public feats intended to shock bystanders and symbolize a war between good and evil. According to Crenshaw [2], the "new" terrorists

> seek nothing less than to transform the world. Motivated by religious imperatives, they are feared by many observers and bystanders to lack an earthly constituency and thus feel accountable only to a deity or some transcendental or mystical idea.

Many terrorists are more "inclined to use highly lethal methods to destroy (as they perceive) an impure world and bring about the apocalypse—unlimited ends lead to unlimited means" [2]. These "new" terrorists seek to cause high numbers of casualties and are willing to commit suicide or use weapons of mass destruction to do so [2].

Terrorism is a group activity where members share a common ideology, group solidarity, and persecutory group identity. Typically, the group ideology is fundamentalist and homogeneous, a totalistic system of beliefs that governs a way of life, which promotes group cohesion. Members merge via group solidarity behind the idealized godlike image and grandiosity of their charismatic leaders and the perpetuation of absolutist ideas.

The terrorist group identity stems from a shared subjective experience of persecution among members of a common ethnic, religious, nationalistic, or cultural group. This shared experience

---

* According to the 2005 statistics of the Stockholm International Peace Research Institute (SIPRI) in Sweden.

and collective tragic and traumatic memory (what Volkan [3] calls chosen trauma) consists of shame, anger, and a lethal perception of outsiders. These toxic sentiments are then fueled and solidified at historically urgent and opportune moments of intergroup tension and vulnerability.

The essence of this bond of persecution symbolizes a shared experience of unjust treatment by others, specifically those outside of their ethnic, religious, nationalistic, or racial group. This fear of and hostility toward outsiders may simply derive from the others' rejection of the group's ideas and belief system, or it may emerge from the possible threat alleged of outsiders infiltrating and destroying the large-group identity (as is often the case in ethnic tensions). Inevitably, a vulnerable sense of "we-ness," low group self-image, resentment for persecution, and/or opposition (whether real or imagined) fosters a social structure of "us against them." The polarization of group insiders and outsiders is driven by the psychologic of large-group identity and requires further elaboration.

Internal Psychologic of Terrorist Acts

Juergensmeyer [4] observes that "acts of terrorism are usually products of an internal logic and not of random crazy thinking: These acts of terrorism are done not to achieve a strategic goal but to make a symbolic statement." For Juergensmeyer what matters to terrorists is the symbolism, the theatrical nature of an act that draws attention worldwide, rather than a well-planned maneuver intended to defeat the evil enemy. Some experts such as Pape [5] argue that suicide terrorism, in particular, is strategic and represents a logical choice on the part of otherwise disenfranchised and relatively powerless extremists. And, although there may be a rationale for these acts of desperation as Pape suggests, it would also seem that the symbolism of particular acts of terror are assumed to reinforce the strategic goals of terrorists. Nevertheless, this does not explain why some individuals become suicide terrorists, and what motivates them and not others to engage in mass killings.

Ethnic, religious, cultural, and nationalistic large-group affiliations are vulnerable to provocation of regressive, primitive, and fanatical thinking and extreme emotions, particularly when these groups espouse fundamentalist ideologies and simultaneously feel defenseless and in danger of losing their identity or "we-ness." In the minds of extremists, holding onto that identity and protecting the integrity and preservation of the group are acts worthy of self-sacrifice, and thereby in the group mind, a threat, real or imagined, justifies violence and mayhem.

In Lifton's [6] study of Aum Shinrikyo, the Japanese cult that released sarin nerve gas in the Tokyo subways, he writes

> Any imagined Armageddon is violent, but the violence tends to be distant and mythic, to be brought about by evil forces that leave God with no other choice, but a total cleansing of this world. With Aum's Armageddon the violence was close at hand and palpable.

Lifton continues

> Aum was always an actor in its own Armageddon drama, whether as a target of world-destroying enemies or as a fighting force in a great battle soon to begin or already under way. As time went on, however, Aum increasingly saw itself as the initiator, the trigger of the final event.

Similar to rightist American militia groups, these groups perceive themselves as destined to "save the world" and, as Lifton points out, they are driven to do so even if the means necessary to meet their ultimate goal necessitate "destroying the world to save it." Moreover, as is often the case, the vulnerable cult (or large-group identity) comes to believe in the evil of the *other* by demonizing and dehumanizing the other and thereby rationalizing the destruction of the other as an act of God's will rather than a mass killing. Psychologically, group members perpetrate murderous acts on outsiders when they come to view the *other* as a nonhuman object of evil (such as vermin, pests, and insects).

Staub [7], among others, has noted that underlying the hostility and violence is a collective self-image of vulnerability. His research indicates that the presence of "difficult life conditions" and "certain cultural and personal characteristics" contribute to violent group activities such as genocide, terrorism, and ethnic cleansing. Difficult life conditions include economic and political problems, crime, widespread violence, rapid changes in technology, social institutions, values, ways of life, and social disorganization. These conditions promote feelings of powerlessness and confusion. In addition, cultural and personal characteristics provide further context for group violence and encompass low self-concept among group members. The group's low self-image and shared vulnerability foster in-group–out-group differentiation ("us and them" mentality), exaggerated obedience to authority (as in authoritarianism), monolithic (versus pluralistic) culture, emerging totalitarian or fascistic ideology, and cultural aggressiveness. Staub also suggests that societal and political organizations with authoritarian and totalitarian characteristics are factors contributing to group violence.

Violent group members come to view themselves as potentially innocent victims of the other group's (societal and political institutions) inherently evil nature—the psychologic of what psychoanalysts call "projective identification." Projective identification is a mode of projection in which the subject locates part of himself or herself (psychologically speaking) inside someone else, which permits knowing this person to have the projected attributes [8]. At the same time, the other takes in and identifies with the projected image. Controlling others (into which parts of the self are projected) is central to projective identification. Thus, group members are driven to act out in some fashion as a reaction to their imagined demise. In the case of projective identification, group members externalize and project all bad and evil attributes onto the image of the outsider's group and its leadership. Eventually, the outsiders are depersonalized and dehumanized in the minds of the insiders. In some instances, the outsiders react with aggression and violence, which reinforces one group's image of the other and ties the volatile emotional knot between them—the essence of projective identification. Moreover, as is the case with ethnic tensions, a vicious cycle of conflict is then set in motion with seemingly little hope of finding a peaceful exit. These are the dynamics of large-group identity and what Volkan [9] calls "the need to have enemies and allies"—a proclivity shared by all human beings.

Dynamics of Large-Group Identity

Although some prefer to avoid calling these violent acts (such as projective identification) "mad" or psychotic, these are in fact psychotic processes acted out on the social and political stage of international human relations. Thus, exploring the underlying, primitive, motivating psychological dynamics of large-group identities can illuminate our understanding of group violence and terrorism. These large-group characteristics do in fact resemble psychotic thinking and acting-out. For example, group members' devotion to totalistic ideologies and grand conspiracies are typical of paranoid–schizoid processes of splitting objects (the world of "others") into good and bad camps—viewing the world as black or white. Totalistic, absolutist, and fundamentalist belief systems require compartmentalization and the psychology of splitting.

Group vulnerability and the impulse to act out is then triggered by anxieties further provoked by difficult life conditions that often reflect poverty and disenfranchisement; societal–cultural characteristics that foster and reinforce extremist and conspiratorial belief systems; and relatively recent political changes within the larger economic and social systems.

Beck [10] argues for distinguishing between the paranoid perspective of militia groups in the United States and mental illness:

> The militants confine their conspiratorial beliefs to a relatively circumscribed domain: their relation with the government and their group. They have normal relations with members of their families and friends, carry on normal business transactions, and appear rational when testifying in court.

Nevertheless, Beck submits that "although there are decided differences between people who are members of an extremist group and those who are psychologically disturbed, it is illuminating to examine the similarities in their beliefs and thinking. The comparison between militant group think and paranoid delusions is useful for the light it shines on the nature of the human mind and its tendency to create fantastic explanations for distressing circumstances"—what Freud observed as the human proclivity toward "magical thinking"—a tendency more commonplace in human groups. My approach to group violence and the development of a deeper understanding of the group mind or "group-in-the-mind" of terrorists shares Beck's assumption of a parallel with cognitive, psychotic processes.

Following this line of psychologic, Lifton [11] describes the phenomena of "doubling" and "numbing" in his extensive study of the Nazi doctors and their culpability for mass killings and genocide. Lifton reports that despite their horrific and murderous daily chores and the concomitant decision-making responsibilities, sentencing millions to death in gas chambers and many other millions to die in labor camps, he found that these same Nazi physicians were capable of carrying on relatively normal relations with their families—seemingly evil by day and apparently loving by night—a mental feat he assumed was made possible by a combination of "doubling" and "numbing."

Doubling encompasses processes of (what psychologists call) psychological "splitting." Splitting describes a process in which the self-in-mind cognitively and emotionally splits apart good and bad images of the other based upon one's memories and subjective experiences of the other. It is a form of internal compartmentalization and fragmentation of self and other. When internalized splits cannot be contained, the individual self projects, typically, bad images onto the other. This is what is meant by the psychological concept of projection. Fear, pain, and anguish often provoke these projections, leaving the self, if only momentarily, with the internalized good images. In large groups with common ideologies and emotional cohesion, these projections are commonplace under stressful and vulnerable circumstances. Numbing indicates a psychological distancing and desensitization of one's actions, despite their horrific nature. Hence, it is common for a perpetrator (such as a terrorist) to convey that he felt nothing or has no remorse for his actions. His or her commitment to the grand idea, the ideology, provides a cognitive focal point that takes the self beyond the present experience of destruction and violence.

Under certain circumstances, joining a group may require relinquishing one's true self for the group's required ideological cloak, resulting in the performance of a false self among large-group members, something akin to Lifton's "doubling." For example, in *The Roots of Evil*, Ervin Staub [7] writes

> The greater the demands a group makes on its members and the more it guides their lives, the more completely the members can relinquish their burdensome identity and

> assume a group identity. However, submerging oneself in a group makes it difficult to maintain independent judgment of the group's conduct and more problematic to exert a contrary influence.

A loss of individuality or individuation and a lack of inhibition of the usual moral constraint on individual action are likely consequences: Experiments show that aggressiveness is increased by conditions that weaken a sense of identity or increase anonymity, such as wearing masks. Stripping individuals of their distinct individuality and self-identity is correlated with increased aggression and violence. Group membership is acquired at a rather high cost of individual integrity and identity to self and a much greater price to society in the members' ability to commit acts of murder and destruction without guilt or remorse.

The notion of "deindividuation" here has significance in human development. Cognitive and emotional growth and maturity occur along a developmental path from infantile attachment (deindividuation) to childhood (early individuation) toward (eventual separation) relative adult autonomy. Hence, deindividuation signifies a psychologically regressive and backward process taking hold of the individual in his or her experience of group membership. Members of a group, when they regress in the face of stressful conditions, come close to experiencing their enemy as the original container of unintegrated bad parts (punishers) of their childhood selves. Further, as Volkan [3] points out, such reservoirs typically contain nonhuman objects, such as a pig for a Muslim child or the turban for a Christian child. Similarly, adults, when regressed, reactivate a sense of experiencing the enemy as nonhuman.

Surrendering individuation and the capacity for critical judgment may promote group solidarity and identity while, at the same time, fostering a deeper underlying sense of powerlessness and dissociation. While the group identity offers the illusion of compensatory power for its members, it is an illusion that does not solve the problem of members' deeper feelings of helplessness. Ultimately, this form of suppression is unsuccessful because powerlessness persists in the group's unconsciousness. Inevitably, group violence is a likely outcome.

Weston's [12] far-reaching study of Yugoslavia as it was breaking up provides a disturbing illustration of psychological splitting and regression within large (Serbian and Croatian) groups and their leaders' abilities to manipulate and provoke conflict between ethnic groups:

> In Yugoslavia we found a strong tendency toward splitting. Images were split into good/bad and into we/them categories. Almost everyone idealized their own ethnic group and demonized others.... The black and white thinking was further encouraged by nationalistic leaders who actively played on group antipathy, using propaganda aimed at creating fear, rage and insecurity about people's safety.

Slobodan Milosevic was successful at stirring up the hostilities of Serbs in Kosovo and promoting ethnic cleansing in just this manner. By evoking the collective memory of the 1539 Battle of Kosovo and insisting to his fellow Serbs that they will never be forced to leave Kosovo, Milosevic solidified the large group against its neighboring enemy, the Ethnic Albanians in Kosovo.

Terrorism as a Group Activity: Large-Group Identity

Ethnic, religious, cultural, and nationalistic groups are characterized by homogeneous subcultures in which psychological and physical boundaries between and among individual members seem to disintegrate and vanish from consciousness. The terrorist group identity and its concomitant belief system transcend the individual identities of members themselves. The group and its leadership come to replace the ideals, fantasies, and ambitions of individual members. Thus, psychological processes of deindividuation abdicate power to the group and its leadership through emotional bonds that require intense loyalties and social cohesion.

In his article "The Origins of Ethnic Strife" Firestone [13] writes

> Identification with a particular ethnic or religious group is at once a powerful defense against death anxiety and a system of thought and belief that can set the stage for hatred and bloodshed. Conformity to the belief system of the group, that is, to its collective symbols of immortality, protects one against the horror of feeling the objective loss of self. In merging his or her identity with that of a group, each person feels that although he or she may not survive as an individual entity, he or she will live on as part of something larger which will continue to exist after he or she is gone.

Joining the group and identifying with its leadership and ideology is a defense against death anxiety—the ultimate experience of individual vulnerability that leads to a merger (deindividuation) with the leadership and its associated large-group identity. Firestone's application of the "defense against death anxiety" is synonymous with the notion of group vulnerability (discussed earlier) and the perceived threat of outsider groups.

For example, Volkan [3,14,15] warns

> When anxiety about identity occurs, members of a large group may consider killing a threatening neighbor rather than endure the anxiety caused by losing their psychological borders: In such a climate, chosen traumas and chosen glories, mourning difficulties, and feelings of entitlement to revenge, are reactivated.

These psychological processes underlie ethnic, racial, and religious acts of terrorism. A group's core identity is derived from the "pride" of attachment between members/followers and their leader(s). Members merge with like-minded blood brothers, all of whom come to idealize their charismatic leader and his governing ideology. Yet, as is the case with individual pride, group pride is often a mask for group self-hatred and low self-concept.

Large Groups and Totalistic Belief Systems

These psychological processes of merger, deindividuation, and attachment then contribute to the leader's ideological influence over the actions of members. Individual morality and conscience are replaced by group ideology and worldview. Members forfeit their individual liberties for affiliation and identification with an omnipotent, godlike leader or guru who gives them hope of a better world.

Typically, group members come to adopt a totalistic and conspiratorial belief system that embodies the struggles of a cosmic war of good against evil. Once the merging of individual and group leadership is complete, the psychology of splitting and paranoia—"us against them"—takes over. A persecutory group identity shapes and cements the members together through a common subjective experience and shared perception of evil and threatening outsiders. Primitive thinking and fanatic belief systems then promote group members, unwitting resignation to simplistic solutions to otherwise complex societal problems. Enemies and scapegoats are identified, solidifying the group and targeting the aim of its aggression.

As Staub [7] notes

> History shows that people will sacrifice themselves to promote ideologies. Followers of ideologies identify some people as a hindrance and commit horrifying acts in the name of creating a better world and fulfilling higher ideals. This scapegoating occurs partly because the new social or spiritual order is defined in contrast to an existing order and partly because the ideal way of life is difficult to bring about or the new social system does not fulfill its promise.

Disappointment stirs resentment and anger: "Examples include the great blood bath after the French Revolution, the Inquisition and other religious persecutions, as well as genocides and mass killings [3]."

Whether it refers to religious affiliation, nationality, or ethnicity, large-group identity is defined as the subjective experience of hundreds of thousands or even millions of people who are linked by a persistent sense of sameness while also sharing numerous characteristics with others in foreign groups [3]. Our understanding of the concept of large-group identity begins with the work of Freud and, in particular, his view of group psychology and institutions.

In Freud's *Group Psychology and the Analysis of the Ego* [16], he suggests that individual psychology and group psychology are not mutually exclusive. In particular, he argues in this and in later works that our understanding of the intrapersonal world is derived from our knowledge of the psychodynamics of self and other from infancy through adolescence and adulthood—the internalization of interpersonal (self and other) experience over time. Thus, one can come to learn that the emergence of one's sense of self, and thereby one's sense of his or her core identity, evolves from the mental internalization of self and other relations in dyads, groups, and institutions. In other words, our internalized subjective experiences, particularly those early on in life and through adolescence, then help to shape our mental images of ourself, others, and the world.

Leadership and authority are key components in our developing identity, as they are central to our understanding of the nature of individual attachments and affiliations with large groups (religious, ethnic, and other primary associations) and nation-states. Furthermore, as Naimark [17] points out in *Fires of Hatred: Ethnic Cleansing in the Twentieth Century,*

> Although the modern state and integral nationalism have been critical to ethnic cleansing in this century, political elites nevertheless bear the major responsibility for its manifestations. In competing for political power, they have exploited the appeal of nationalism to large groups of resentful citizens in the dominant ethnic population. Using the power of the state, the media, and their political parties, national leaders have manipulated distrust of the "other" and purposely revived and distorted ethnic tensions, sometimes long-buried, sometimes closer to the surface.

Naimark stresses the assumption of personal responsibility ultimately coming to rest on the shoulders of political elites, leaders. Yet, leadership does not exist without followership. It is a dyadic relationship, a merger of like-mindedness and shared responsibility. Naimark, however, is correct in pointing out the manipulative and influential power of leaders in large groups, which is critical and ought to be viewed as an appropriate starting point if one is moved to understand more deeply the phenomenon of group violence and hold accountable those most responsible. Consider the earlier example of Milosevic and his provocation of the Serbs against ethnic Albanians.

In Freud's original essay, he explains the dynamics of group psychology via the individual's emotional attachment to the group. He argues that the individual surrenders his or her autonomy and independence to the group leadership by unconsciously replacing his or her own ego ideal with that of the leadership. In other words, group affiliation that may be characterized as hypnotic and suggestive takes place by a process in which the individual relinquishes to the leadership his or her own conscience, values, liberties, and integrity. In joining the group, the self is forced into a psychologically regressive flight from individuality and autonomy to a more infantile state of deindividuation, merger, and social cohesion, which explains why one observes primitive thinking such as splitting and compartmentalization, as well as shared fantasies and delusions, among vulnerable large groups.

The group image of collective utopia is then represented for the membership by their loyalty and admiration of the group leader. So, although Naimark [17] is correct in highlighting the responsibilities of political elites in fostering ethnic cleansing and other forms of violence, his analysis marginalizes the role of followers in endorsing and empowering their leaders. As I have already stated, it is a dyadic phenomenon and thereby ought to be examined and understood as such.

Conclusion

When large groups, whether ethnic, racial, religious, nationalistic, or cultural, feel vulnerable, that is, when they feel the potential loss of their attachment and emotional investment in the group's belief system and leadership, they fear the annihilation of the group-self or (what has been called) the large-group identity. Psychological regression is a common yet primitive defense mechanism used by groups under these stressful circumstances, whether the fear is legitimate or not, real or fantasized. Psychological regression and the associated cognitive and emotional splitting are typical responses to the experience of such profound anxiety (what Firestone calls death anxiety).

Under these conditions of psychological regression, members assume a collective, psychological flight behind their leaders and toward more primitive and infantile feelings. Charismatic spiritual leaders and gurus reflecting and articulating expansive visions and absolute ideologies offer the illusion of a safe haven for the seemingly fearful, disenfranchised, and powerless members of society who are searching for simple, black and white solutions to complex social and political problems.

Group solidarity emerges from a foundation of ethnic, religious, cultural, and nationalistic similarity and like-mindedness. There is safety in the comfort of the large-group identity and its godlike leader. The combination of homogeneity and group cohesion fosters a loss of individuality and separateness (self and other boundaries) among members. This loss of independence and critical thinking then reinforces polarized, compartmentalized thinking, which produces psychological splitting and regression among group members. It is this black and white, absolutist thinking rooted in infantile anxieties that fosters dehumanization of and violence against the *other*.

In the presence of social disorganization and economic and political problems, charismatic leaders can manipulate and provoke group violence by exploiting the "us and them" mentality of the large (ethnic, religious, cultural, or nationalistic) group. By identifying the enemy and then leading the group in attack against a popular scapegoat, terrorist leaders diminish followers' anxieties while proffering them a target for their long-held resentment and hostility.

References

1. Stockholm International Peace Research Institute. *SIPRI Yearbook 2005: Armaments, Disarmament and International Security*. Oxford and New York: Oxford University Press, 2005.
2. M Crenshaw. The psychology of terrorism: An agenda for the 21st century. *Political Psychology* 21 (2): 405–420, 2000.

3. V Volkan. *Blood Lines: From Ethnic Pride to Ethnic Terrorism*. New York: Farrar, Straus and Giroux, 1997.
4. M Juergensmeyer. *Terror in the Mind of God: The Global Rise of Religious Violence*. Berkeley: University of California Press, 2000.
5. RA Pape. *Dying to Win: The Strategic Logic of Suicide Terrorism*. New York: Random House, 2005.
6. RJ Lifton. *Destroying the World to Save It: Aum Shinrikyo, Apocalyptic Violence and the New Global Terrorism*. New York: Metropolitan Books, 1999.
7. E Staub. *The Roots of Evil: The Origins of Genocide and Other Group Violence*. New York: Cambridge University Press, 1992.
8. M Klein. Notes on some schizoid mechanisms. *International Journal of Psychoanalysis* 27: 99–110, 1946.
9. V Volkan. *The Need to Have Enemies & Allies: From Clinical Practice to International Relationships*. New Jersey: Jason Aronson Inc., 1988.
10. AT Beck. *Prisoners of Hate: The Cognitive Basis of Anger, Hostility, and Violence*. New York: HarperCollins Publishers, 1999.
11. RJ Lifton. *The Nazi Doctors: Medical Killing and the Psychology of Genocide*. New York: Basic Books, 1986.
12. MC Weston. When words lose their meaning: From societal crisis to ethnic cleansing. *Mind and Human Interaction* 8 (1): 20–32, 1997.
13. RW Firestone. The origins of ethnic strife. *Mind and Human Interaction* 7 (4): 167–191, 1996.
14. V Volkan. Psychoanalysis and diplomacy: Part 1. Individual and large group identity. *Journal of Applied Psychoanalysis* 1 (1): 29–55, 1999.
15. V Volkan. *Killing in the Name of Identity: A Study of Bloody Conflicts*. Charlottesville, VA: Pitchstone Publishing, 2006.
16. S Freud. *Group Psychology and the Analysis of the Ego*. New York: Norton & Company, 1921.
17. NM Naimark. *Fires of Hatred: Ethnic Cleansing in Twentieth Century Europe*. Cambridge, MA: Harvard University Press, 2001.

Chapter 4

Aerosols: Fundamentals

Sudarshan K. Loyalka and Robert V. Tompson, Jr.

CONTENTS

Introduction 41
Generation 47
Dispersion 47
Sampling and Characterization 49
References 50
Bibliography 50

Introduction

One cubic centimeter of atmospheric air contains approximately 2.5×10^{19} molecules. About 1000 of these molecules may be charged (ions). The molecules of N_2, O_2, and the various trace gases have sizes (diameters) of about 3×10^{-8} cm. The average distance between the molecules is about ten times the molecular size. In addition to the molecules and the ions, 1 cm^3 of air also contains a substantial number of particles varying in size from a few times the molecular size to several microns (μm, 1 μm = 10^{-4} cm). In relatively clean air, there are about 1000 particles with diameters 0.001–50.0 μm while in polluted air there can be 100,000 or more, including pollen, bacteria, dust, and industrial emissions. These particles, which can be both beneficial and detrimental, arise from a number of natural sources as well as from the activities of the earth's inhabitants. The particles can have complex chemical compositions and morphologies, and may even be radioactive or toxic. A suspension of particles in a gas is known as an aerosol. Atmospheric aerosol is of global interest and has an important impact on our lives.

Aerosols are characterized by a few fundamental properties. Most importantly, aerosol particles have large residence times (settling speeds on the order of a fraction of a centimeter per second) and, because of their small size and large number, present a large surface area for interactions with

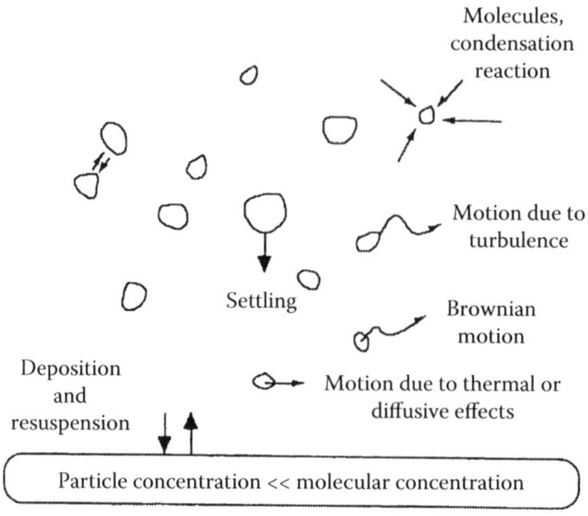

Figure 4.1 Aerosol interactions and motion.

the host medium. In addition, they can have a substantial effect on the transmission of light as they tend to occur in a size range that leads to substantial interaction (scattering and absorption) with light (see Figure 4.1).

For particles of a given composition, size and shape determine residence time as well as other dynamical properties that bear on particle removal by filtration or collection devices. Liquid particles are almost always spherical, but solid particles can occur in many different shapes varying from spherical to fibrous (needlelike forms). They can be chain-like agglomerates, or can be amorphous clumps. Typical size ranges of particles are shown in Figure 4.2.

Usually, aerosol particles contain numerous species with varying physicochemical properties. The processes that lead to their initial creation and their subsequent interactions with the host medium and electromagnetic radiation determine the compositions of the particles. Coarse particles ($\geq 2\,\mu m$) are generally created by mechanical processes such as fragmentation and hence are rich in Ca, Fe, SiO_2, and other constituents of the earth. Fine particles ($<2\,\mu m$) are generally derived from processes such as combustion or gas to particle conversion and are rich in C, Pb, sulfates, and ammonium and nitrate ions. The trace and often toxic species such as As, Cd, Cs, Sr, Zn, and Se are also mostly concentrated in the fine particles. Nuclear explosions produce large numbers of radioactive particles that can disperse globally. Volcanic eruptions lead to the production of particles, some of which reside in the atmosphere for years.

Since the number of particles in an aerosol is large, and since each particle can have a multitude of physical and chemical characteristics, a description that accounts for individual particles is not sought. Rather, one focuses on the important attributes of the aerosol and considers a distribution function based on particle properties and size. It has been observed in many applications that the aerosol distributions are close to some simple forms.

The distribution of chemicals with respect to particle sizes is, indeed, quite complex. One also observes complex surface distributions of different species on particle surfaces. Chemicals are transported to different locations in human respiratory tracts as dictated by different particle sizes, and these specifications play a major role in the delivery of toxic dosages to specific cells in human

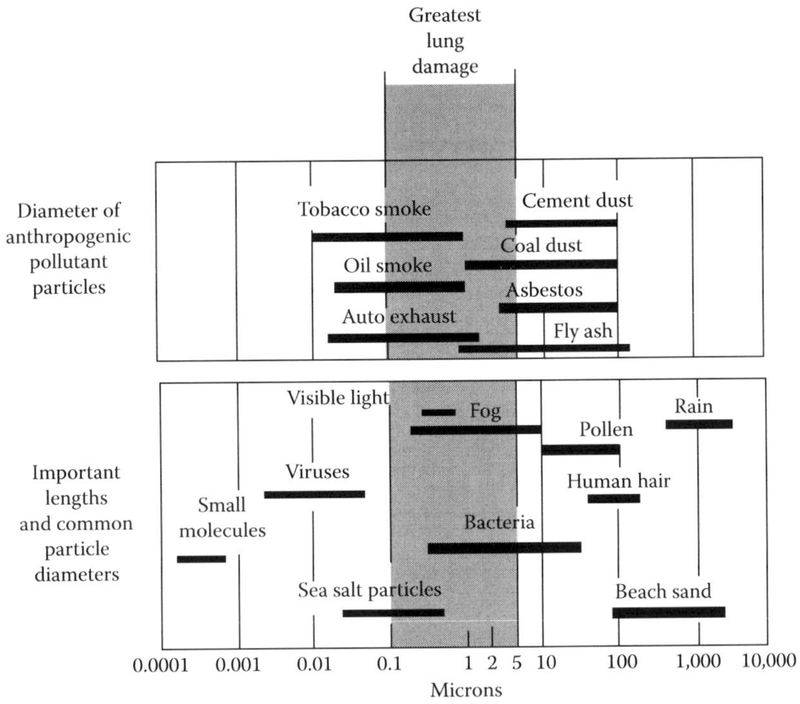

Figure 4.2 Typical size range of aerosols. (Data from Hines, A.L. et al., *Indoor Air: Quality and Control*, Prentice Hall, Englewood Cliffs, NJ, 1993.)

lungs. The atmospheric environment can be viewed as a giant and complex chemical reactor. Control strategies require sound scientific understandings at both microscopic and macroscales in time and space, and interplay of theory, modeling, and experiments.

To consider a simple example, a person breathes about 20 m^3 of air per day. Even if there were 1 particle/cm^3 of air, a person would breathe about 20 million particles in a day, or about a million in an hour. Particle concentration in a polluted city may be about 100 μg/m^3. Suppose these particles have a diameter of 0.1 μm, and density of 1 gm/cm^3, then there would be about 2×10^5 particles/cm^3 of air. Hence, a person would be breathing about 4000 billion particles per day. Of course the particles are distributed over a size range, and a large number deposits in the upper respiratory tract [1]. Still a sufficiently large number reaches the lower respiratory tract, and interacts with the large surface there (see Figure 4.3). Thus, aerosols, with chemical, radioactive, or biological implications for lungs, are particularly attractive to terrorists. The aerosols also deposit externally on the human body, and can cause reactions there also.

In this chapter, some fundamental properties of aerosols are described, followed by a discussion on how they are generated and dispersed in the atmosphere and in confined spaces. There is also a discussion on how particles are sampled and characterized. These understandings lead to means by which one can guard against terrorist actions that seek to disperse aerosols.

The most important aspect of aerosol particles is, perhaps, their interaction with gas molecules. Under standard conditions, a current of 10^{23} gas molecules/cm^2 s impinges on a particle and, in equilibrium, a current of the same magnitude is returned from the particle's surface to the surrounding gas.

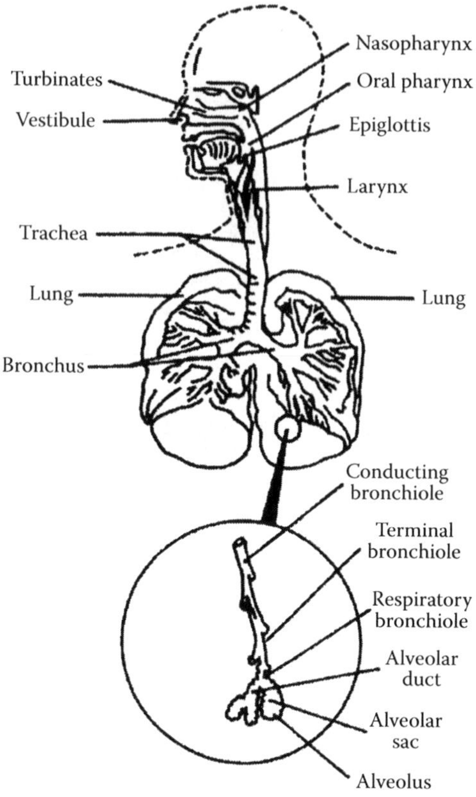

Figure 4.3 The human respiratory tract.

Generally, the molecules incident on a particle's surface can react with the particle constituents, they can be absorbed or adsorbed, or they can be scattered back into the gas (see Figure 4.4). For an isolated single particle in an infinite expanse of a stationary gas and in absence of gravity and other forces, one would assume that the particle would not move.

However, this is not true, as the molecules incident on the surface of a particle impart impulse to the particle, and while on the average there is no net force on the particle, there is a fluctuating force. The particle moves randomly ("diffuses") under this force, with a velocity determined by this force and an opposing force due to friction exerted by the gas (or the molecules through which the particle moves). This motion is known as the Brownian motion, and its quantitative aspects were first clarified by Einstein and Smoluchowski. Using the nomenclature,

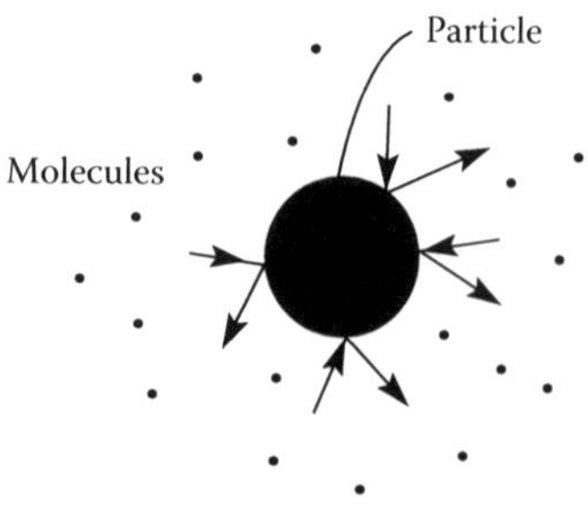

Figure 4.4 Molecular interactions with a particle.

T	Temperature of the environment (K)
B	Particle mobility ($\mathrm{T\,M^{-1}}$)
D	Diffusion coefficient ($\mathrm{L^2\,T^{-1}}$)
d_p	Particle diameter (L)
g	Acceleration due to gravity ($\mathrm{L\,T^{-2}}$)
L	Characteristic dimension of a body or flow (L)

m	Particle mass (M)
U	Characteristic flow speed (L T^{-1})
V_S	Sedimentation velocity (L T^{-1})
x	Some arbitrary distance (L)
λ_c	Molecular mean free path (L)
μ	Fluid dynamic viscosity (M L^{-1} T^{-1})
ρ	Fluid mass density (M L^{-3})
$\tau = mB$	Relaxation time (T)
Kn	Knudsen number, $Kn = \lambda_c/d_p$
C_c	Cunningham correction factor, depends on Kn
n	Particle concentration (L^{-3})
J	Particle current (L^{-2} T^{-1})
S	Particle source (L^{-3} T^{-1})
Units	K—temperature, L—length, M—mass, T—time

The frictional force, F_D, is given as

$$F_D = 3\pi\mu d_p v/C_e$$

where v is the instantaneous velocity of the particle. The diffusive motion of the particle (see Figure 4.5) is determined through a "diffusion" coefficient,

$$D = BkT$$

where

k is the Boltzmann constant

B is the "mobility" (defined as velocity/force) of the particle given as

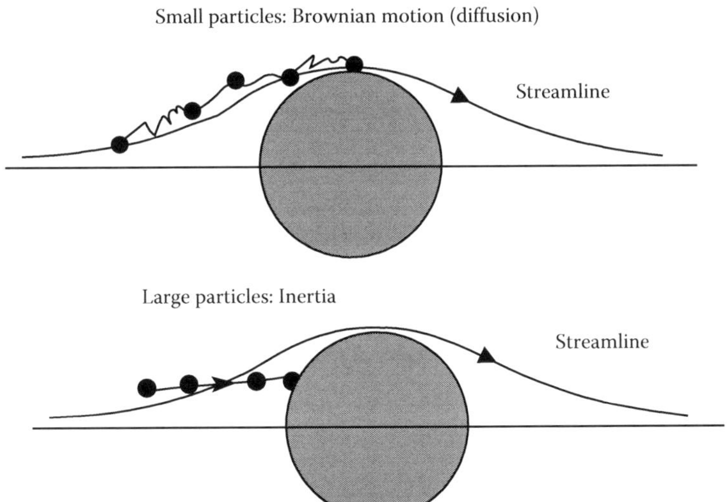

Figure 4.5 Aerosol diffusive and inertial motions.

$$B = v/F_D = \frac{C_e}{3\pi\mu d_p}$$

The root mean square distance traveled in time, t, by a particle undergoing linear (one-dimensional) diffusion is expressed as

$$x = \sqrt{2Dt}$$

Particles also move under external forces, and in particular all particles settle under gravity (see Figure 4.6). The particle motion under an external force can be described by the equation:

$$m\frac{dv}{dt} = F - \frac{v}{B}$$

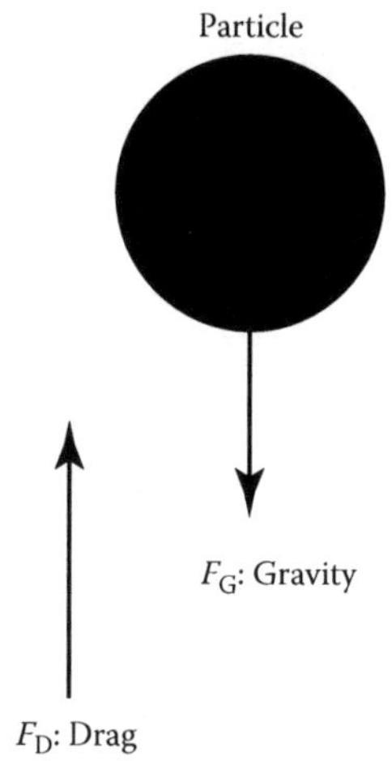

Figure 4.6 Aerosol motion: gravity and drag.

or

$$\frac{dv}{dt} = -\frac{v}{\tau} + \frac{F}{m}; \quad \tau = Bm$$

where τ is known as the relaxation time, and it is a measure of how quickly the particle adapts to a flow. The settling velocity, V_S, is thus simply given as

$$V_S = Bmg = \frac{mgC_e}{3\pi\mu d_p}$$

Table 4.1 shows typical values of the quantities discussed here. It should be noted that the smaller the particles, the more rapidly they diffuse and the more slowly they settle. Thus, particles of intermediate size are likely to remain suspended for the longest time, as the larger particles settle out, and the smaller particles attach to other larger particles or deposit on surfaces. It should be emphasized that particles do move with air (gas) flow—the convective motion (or the mean speed of flow), and the diffusive and gravitational motions are superimposed on this convective motion. In fact, this convective motion (e.g., plumes) is the principal means of aerosol dispersion in most cases. In addition, the convective motion (e.g., breathing, spraying) is the principal means of deposition, as it brings particles near surfaces where particles deposit because of diffusion and settling, and other forces.

As has been noted, particles grow because of condensation of water vapor; they can also diminish in size because of evaporation. They can react with gases and vapors, and they can coagulate (adhere) when they collide with other particles. The particles can fragment, and react with sunlight and other radiation. Bioaerosols may not survive because of atmospheric conditions, or internal causes. Radioactive particles can decay, and charged particles can have a host of other reactions. Particles stick to or repel from surfaces because of short-range molecular forces. They can be charged, and they can accumulate ions. They can mediate transport of many molecular species. All these processes are complex, and in addition to deposition, these affect aerosol evolution and dispersion, and the aerosol uptake by humans and animals.

Table 4.1 Aerosol Properties as a Function of Size of a Unit Density Sphere in Air at Standard Temperature and Pressure (STP)

Particle Diameter *(μm)* d_p	*Sedimentation Velocity (cm/s)* $V_s = \frac{mgC_c}{3\pi\mu d_p}$	*Diffusion Coefficient (cm²/s)* $D = Bk_BT$	*Mobility (s/g)* $B = \frac{V_s}{mg}$	*Particle Relaxation Time (s)* $\tau = mB$
0.001	6.5530E−07	5.1084E−02	1.2719E+12	6.6595E−10
0.01	6.6901E−06	5.2312E−04	1.3025E+10	6.8197E−09
0.1	8.6316E−05	6.7494E−06	1.6804E+08	8.7988E−08
1.0	3.5054E−03	2.7410E−07	6.8245E+06	3.5733E−06
10.0	3.0605E−01	2.3931E−08	5.9583E+05	3.1198E−04
100.0	2.4844E+01	2.3583E−09	5.8717E+04	3.0744E−02

These fundamental properties play the most important role in particle filtration and removal. Fine particles are preferentially removed by fabric filters and electrostatic devices, while large particles are removed through use of cyclones and impactors. Intermediate size particles (~0.3 μm) are harder to remove as they neither diffuse nor settle as much. Generally, for all efficient filtration one needs high volume flows. Particles can also be scavenged by use of sprays and mists. It is also known that heat and sunlight can dissipate fogs.

Generation

Fogs, mists, power plant plumes, automobile exhaust, cigarette smoke, fire and combustion, pollen, dust, bacteria, and viruses are part of our common experiences. Fine aerosols generally form through nucleation and condensation/reaction processes in the environment as well as combustion. Coarse particles arise from many mechanical processes and human activities.

A fire will invariably lead to large aerosol production. It is known that explosions lead to dense aerosol (large concentrations) release. Burning some oils is an effective way of producing large quantities of aerosols. Crop dusters release large amounts of pesticides in an aerosol form. Sprayers or blowers can also generate large amounts of aerosols. Volcanic eruptions and nuclear explosions release huge amounts of aerosols. Violent destruction of buildings releases copious amounts of aerosols through combustion as well as fragmentation.

Bioaerosols (viruses, bacteria, pollen, etc.) can be generated in laboratories, stored, and then released into the environment through use of sprayers, dusters, blowers, balloons, or explosives.

Dispersion

Aerosols disperse more rapidly with wind, but they disperse even in the absence of the wind. It is recognized that in open environments, release at a greater height, as well as wind, lead to greater dispersion of aerosols. One can determine the direction of wind, as well as estimate its turbulence, by watching the movement of the plume (fine particles are used in wind tunnels, etc. to visualize flow). It is known that rain washes out aerosols from the atmosphere. It is also common knowledge that air currents or human activities can cause resuspension of dust from surfaces, and then disperse it in the environment. Quite clearly in confined environments (homes, offices, factories, shopping malls, airports, automobiles, and train stations) aerosol dispersion is strongly influenced by the ventilation (air exchange, flow, and filtration) and heating/air-conditioning systems, and a release of aerosols into a ventilation system could be a very effective means of dispersing them. In open environments, wind patterns, height of release, humidity and rain, sunlight, and the like play important roles. It should be noted, though, that fine particles are generally likely to disperse very widely in the open if released at multiple points (to avoid coagulation inherent in a dense aerosol, which leads to larger particles and greater settling near the source), a good height, and in low humidity (to avoid growth and coagulation or reactions) and in the absence of rain (to avoid washout).

Sophisticated physicochemical and mathematical descriptions of aerosol dispersion have been studied. Computer programs are being developed that would make possible semirealistic and real-time computations of aerosol dispersion. Neglecting aerosol coagulation and growth processes, an equation that can provide simple and suitable description of aerosol dispersion and deposition can be written as

$$\frac{\partial n}{\partial t} = -\nabla \cdot \mathbf{J} - \Re n + S$$

where S is the particle source, and the particle current, $\mathbf{J}$, can be written as

$$\mathbf{J} = \mathbf{U}n - D\nabla n + \mathbf{V}_s n$$

Here n is the particle concentration, and it could be a function of position and time, as well as particle size. U is the convective velocity, and the flow could be turbulent or laminar, depending upon the conditions. The flowfield can be estimated or calculated from the flow conditions and appropriate fluid dynamic equations. A removal rate constant, $\Re$, is included in the equation to indicate additional removal (death, for example, of a bioaerosol or washout) of particles. This equation will be subject to appropriate initial and boundary conditions. Solutions of this and/or a spatially homogenized equation provide considerable insights into aerosol concentration over the space of interest. The major points of departure from the dispersion of a gaseous contaminant are the presence of settling and comparatively low values of diffusion coefficient. There exist many popular descriptions of gas dispersions, and for short times, these also provide useful descriptions of aerosol dispersion.

Consider, for example, dispersion of aerosols resulting from a nuclear weapon explosion. The explosion leads to vaporization of the weapon material within fractions of a second. If it is a near surface explosion then the surface material (soil, water, and structures) in the vicinity is also immediately vaporized and suspended. This material is cooled as the fireball expands. It condenses, and forms into fine particles, which will contain radioactive species such as cesium, iodine, strontium, uranium, molybdenum, plutonium, and the like. These fine particles disperse, and eventually settle out depending upon the heights at which these are formed, and the wind patterns involved. Particles formed high in the atmosphere could travel around the world. Since the explosion will set structures/wood on fire within a few miles, these fires would contribute additional smoke aerosols, upon which radioactive species would condense or attach. These smoke aerosols would also undergo further dispersion and settling/diffusion. Thus, a nuclear explosion would result in some immediate and some long-term "fallout" of particles, both near the explosion and far away from it. It can be known from weapons tests that wind directions and weather conditions can change the course of fallout immensely.

Sampling and Characterization

The fundamental dynamic properties of aerosols dictate their sampling. For the same speed of flow, coarse (heavier) particles have greater inertia than fine (lighter) particles, and hence any change in flow direction can cause coarse particles to deposit on a collection surface preferentially (i.e., fine particles have a low relaxation time, and they adjust to change in flow more rapidly, and do not depart from streamlines that easily). However, particles of almost all sizes can be collected in samplers that employ high speeds. A continual variation in flow speeds can be employed for size-specific deposition of aerosols on collection plates [2]. A device based on this principle is known as an aerosol impactor, and a schematic is shown in Figure 4.7. Generally, one employs one or several (two, six, or more) stages, and collects particles on filters or growth media for bioaerosols

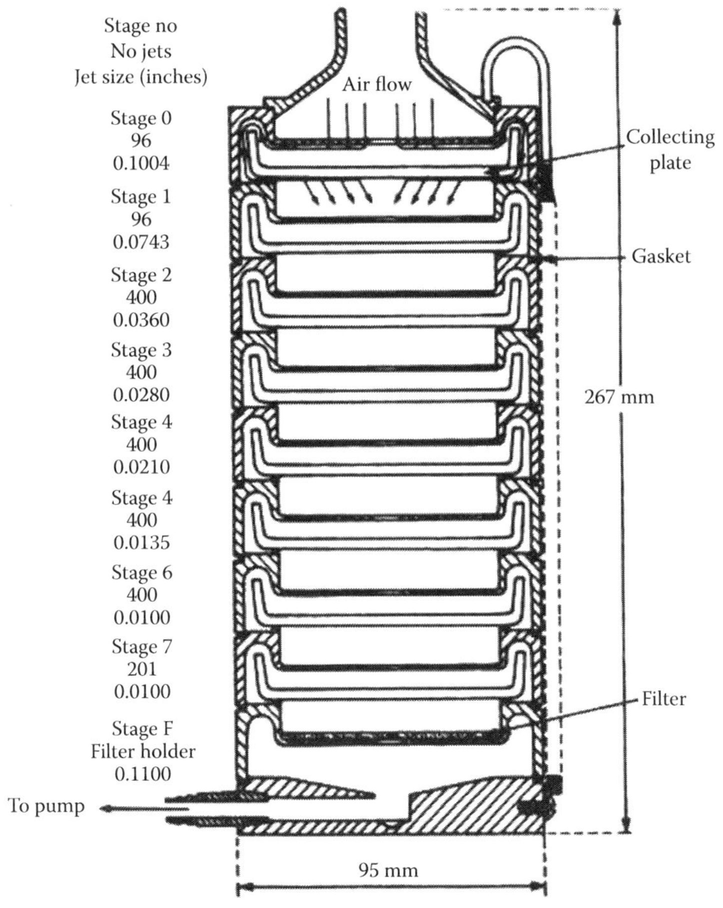

Figure 4.7 Schematic diagram of a Andersen Mark II ambient impactor. (Data from Cox, C.S., Wathes, C.M., *Bioaerosis Handbook,* CRC Press Inc., 1995.)

(e.g., agar) [3]. The physical, chemical, and biological properties of the collected particles can be obtained in laboratories from a number of analytical methods such as gravimetry, optical and electron microscopy, neutron activation analysis, spectroscopy, and DNA sequencing.

Quite often, for bioaerosol sampling, one also employs liquid impingers. Here the aerosol is flowed at sonic speed through a liquid medium, thus resulting in high collection rates. The liquid is the collection medium, and the particles collected in it can then be conveniently analyzed in laboratories.

For collection of fine and ultrafine particles, with low particle concentration, impaction may not be very effective. Here one can employ fabric bags (narrow passages lead to high deposition because of diffusion) or electrostatic devices (that charge and then collect particles).

The sampling and characterization are always of limited value if the sample size is small, and if characterization is affected, for example, by the viability of a sample (for bioaerosols). Improved methods of nondestructive and rapid testing are areas of current research interest. An important challenge is identification of the source of aerosols, as the collected aerosol particles could be substantially different from the particles that are generated (the primary aerosol).

References

1. AL Hines, TK Ghosh, SK Loyalka, and RC Warder. *Indoor Air: Quality and Control.* Englewood Cliffs, NJ: Prentice Hall, 1993.
2. AA Andersen. New sampler for the collection, sizing, and enumeration of viable airborne particles. *J. Bacteriol.* 76: 471–484, 1958.
3. CS Cox, CM Wathes, *Bioaerosis Handbook*, CRC Press Inc., 1995.

Bibliography

CN Davies, Ed. *Aerosol Science.* London, U.K.: Academic Press, 1966.
R Dennis. *Handbook on Aerosols.* Washington, DC: U.S. Department of Energy, 1976.
SK Friedlander. *Smoke, Dust and Haze.* New York: Wiley, 1977.
NA Fuchs. *The Mechanics of Aerosols.* New York: Pergamon, 1964.
GM Hidy. *Aerosols, An Industrial and Environmental Science.* New York: Academic Press, 1984.
GM Hidy, JR Brock, Eds. *Topics in Aerosol Research.* Vols. 1–3. Oxford, U.K.: Pergamon, 1972.
WC Hinds, *Aerosol Technology.* New York: Wiley, 1982.
WH Marlow, Ed. *Aerosol Microphysics.* Vols. I&II, New York: Springer-Verlag, 1982.
J Seinfeld. *Atmospheric Chemistry and Physics of Air Pollution.* New York: Wiley, 1986.
S Twomey. *Atmospheric Aerosols.* New York: Elsevier, 1977.
MMR Williams and SK Loyalka. *Aerosol Science: Theory and Practice, with Special Applications to the Nuclear Industry.* New York: Elsevier, New York, 1991. (A part of the introduction follows from this text).

Chapter 5

Biological Terrorism: Effects, Toxicity, and Effectiveness

Gordon D. Christensen

CONTENTS

Background 52
Focus on Anthrax Hoaxes 53
Historical Use of Biological Weapons 55
Focus on Fort Detrick 57
Focus on Biopreparat 57
Anthrax 58
Focus on Sverdlovsk 59
Focus on Anthrax in the U.S. Postal Service, 2001 (Known to the FBI as "Amerithrax") 61
Smallpox 62
Focus on Smallpox in New York City, 1947 63
Tularemia 64
Plague 65
Viral Hemorrhagic Fevers 67
Botulism 69
Future Perspectives and Countermeasures 72
Appendix A Electronic Resources for Bioterrorism 74
References 75

Throughout the history of mankind, military organizations have occasionally used biological agents as weapons. With the advent of the field of microbiology in the twentieth century, multiple national research and development programs have applied microbes to the creation of weapons of mass destruction. In recent years, terrorist organizations—particularly organizations with strong religious affiliations—have also begun deploying biological weapons. Fortunately, the capacity to create sophisticated biological weapons and carry out a massive biological attack appears to be beyond the resources of most terrorist organizations. Unfortunately, these organizations seem unrestrained by the humanitarian concerns that normally limit biological warfare. In the last three decades, we have witnessed an increase in the number and lethality of bioterrorist attacks, raising the specter of a successful large-scale attack in the future. To prepare for the worst, we must anticipate the agent the bioterrorist will use in an attack. Although "germ" warfare and "bioterrorism" have different goals and different limitations, they often use the same biological agents for weapons. Six organisms appear to be the weapons of choice: anthrax, smallpox, plague, tularemia, hemorrhagic fever, and the toxin from *Clostridium botulinum*. The following pages examine in greater detail the background and limitations of bioterrorism, the variety of weapons in the biological armory, and the specific bacteriologic and clinical features of these six potential terrorist weapons.

Background

To defend ourselves from bioterrorism, we must anticipate which biological weapon the bioterrorist will use and how the bioterrorist will deploy the weapon.

Biological weapons use microorganisms or toxins derived from microorganisms to produce death or disease in humans, animals, or plants.* Over the years, humans have used a large number of biological agents as weapons, but the arsenal for bioterrorism is not the same as the arsenal for biological warfare. The difference lies in the difference between the goal of bioterrorism and the goal of biological warfare.

The goal of biological warfare is to eliminate or incapacitate the enemy. The goal of bioterrorism is to instill fear in the enemy to achieve a political goal or promote an ideology [1].† Illness, death, and destruction may result from the bioterrorists' activities, but these casualties are only a secondary concern. For this reason, the bioterrorist has a wider selection of biological weapons than does the combatant preparing for biological warfare [2].

Biological warfare uses either weapons of mass destruction or small-scale weapons. Weapons of mass destruction are targeted against an armed force, civilian population, or the national economy. Small-scale weapons are targeted against an individual, a unit, or a facility. Either way, the military use of biological weapons has tactical, strategic, financial, and political considerations that determine the selection and deployment of the biologic agent. For tactical reasons, the weapon must be of military grade, meaning the munitions have known performance characteristics such as lethality, range, and shelf life. This requires a large research and development program. For strategic reasons, weapons of mass destruction must be safely produced in large quantities. This requires a major manufacturing plant capable of handling large volumes of biohazardous materials. Both large- and small-scale weapons require safe storage in secure locations; this requires guarded armories designed to store biological weapons. Because civilization universally condemns biological weapons

* The focus of this chapter is on antipersonnel weapons. Bioterrorism, however, also includes the use of biologic agents to destroy livestock, crops, and machinery.

† In addition to warfare and terrorism, biological weapons can be used to commit criminal acts or "biocrimes." Biocrimes include crimes against individuals for personal gain or revenge [1] as well as mischievous acts by disturbed individuals.

as immoral and cruel, the entire weapons program must be kept secret. Only a few nations have the financial resources and political structure to fund and hide the research and development programs, manufacturing plants, and armories required for biological warfare.

To use military-grade munitions, bioterrorists must have either stolen the weapon or had it supplied to them. Because the existence and location of the weapons are both secret and secure, these armaments are rarely stolen. Stolen weapons suggest an "inside job" with only a small amount of material available to the thief.*

The terrorist may receive a military grade weapon as a gift because the provider shares goals with the bioterrorist. An outright gift of a weapon of mass destruction is probably rare, because the gift would jeopardize the provider's biological weapons program to public exposure and condemnation. Although gifts of small-scale weapons pose less danger of public censure, such gifts would also have a diminished capacity to cause terror.

For these reasons, bioterrorists will often use weapons fabricated by themselves with or without the assistance of national agencies. This can be accomplished at a low cost, but the product will most likely be unsophisticated [2,4], available in limited quantities, with unknown and variable properties such as lethality, range, and shelf life. Moreover, like building a bomb in one's basement, the homebuilt biological weapon could "blow-up" during assembly, meaning the bioterrorists themselves have a substantial risk of succumbing to their "weaponized" infectious disease [4]. For suicidal terrorists this may not pose a threat or may even be the objective, but for all others, the potential for accidental "occupational" illness will place limitations on the choice, manufacture, and deployment of the weapon.

Strategic, tactical, and financial constraints on bioterrorism can be simply avoided by using the ruse of a biological weapon to create terror. Because of the ease and low cost involved in its manufacture, this is the weapon of choice for many bioterrorists. While such a weapon has no capacity to produce illness and death, it can cause tremendous fear and publicity because the victim does not know the weapon is a hoax. The bioterrorist seeks fear and publicity, but repeated use of such a fraudulent weapon can rapidly extinguish the fear and even lead to ridicule or scorn.

Focus on Anthrax Hoaxes

Many bioterrorists have threatened an attack with anthrax with bogus weapons [1]. Perhaps the best example of such a hoax was the April 24, 1997 attack on the Washington Offices of B'nai B'rith, an international Jewish service organization. As described by Leonard Cole ([5], see also [6]), the attack began when a mail room employee discovered a package leaking foul smelling, red, gelatinous material. Security called police, who opened the package, finding a "Petri dish"† with a microbial growth labeled "Anthracis Yersinia." This nonsensical label suggested that the plate contained one or more strains of deadly bacteria, prompting a series of well-intended, but inappropriate actions, which in turn led to widespread terror and chaos. Problems began when the local fire department HAZMAT unit isolated a dozen people who were near the package;

* For example, the Associated Press reported that, in 1992, an internal audit of stocks found missing specimens of anthrax, Ebola virus, and other pathogens at the Army's biological warfare research center [3].

† A Petri dish is a flat-rimmed plate, usually made of clear plastic, with matching cover. These plates are filled, like jelly in a mold, with agar; agar is a gelatin-like material, sometimes mixed with blood, which supports the growth of bacteria spread on the surface of the agar. These inexpensive Petri plates are universally used in bacteriology laboratories to support the growth and storage of a wide variety of bacteria and fungi.

eventually the HAZMAT sealed off a one-block square of downtown Washington—severely disrupting rush-hour traffic—and quarantined 109 people in the B'nai B'rith office building as well as many additional people in a neighboring hotel. A decision was made to decontaminate 30 of these "exposed" people by having them completely disrobe on the street outside the building and then be hosed down with a 1 percent bleach solution. The disrobing was videotaped by local news organizations causing severe mortification to the "victims." Some "exposed" police officers resisted the command to disrobe, causing at least one physical altercation. The terror was so severe that one of the police officers had to be taken to an emergency room for chest pain. Cole quoted another "exposed" police officer as saying he feared for his life. After nine hours of terror in downtown Washington, the incident was found to be a complete hoax; the microbial growth was incapable of causing disease. Although no one was sickened by the incident, from the viewpoint of the bioterrorist, the incident was a complete success. With a cheap prop, the terrorist caused severe emotional distress to dozens of people, frightened hundreds of people, and disrupted the lives of many more, and all of this took place in the United States (US) capital.

Another well-known example occurred in February, 1998, when Larry Wayne Harris boasted to an informant that he had enough military grade anthrax to "wipe out" Las Vegas [4,7]. A member of the white supremacist group "Aryan Nation," Harris was a registered microbiologist and the author of a self-published Internet book *Bacteriological Warfare—Major Threat to North America* [7]. He had previously been convicted in 1995 for fraudulently obtaining three vials of freezedried *Yersinia pestis* for $240 from the American Type Culture Collection [7]. For these reasons, the Federal Bureau of Investigation (FBI) took the boast seriously. But the FBI found that Harris had only an avirulent vaccine strain of anthrax in his possession, a strain incapable of producing illness [4]. Nevertheless, this incident provoked considerable public angst and publicity; it also provoked a proliferation of "copycat" anthrax hoaxes through the rest of 1998 and 1999 [4]. For example, on reviewing public domain reports of anthrax incidents, Jessica Stern found just two such incidents for the period 1992–1997. After the 1998 Harris incident, however, she counted 37 anthrax incidents in 1998 affecting some 5500 people [4]. These hoaxes included anonymous letters purporting to contain anthrax sent to medical clinics in Indiana, Kentucky, and Tennessee and anonymous threats of using anthrax to contaminate the air-handling systems for various public buildings in California [8].

Likewise, after the attack on the World Trade Center and the subsequent mailing of military grade anthrax to political and media targets, the general public had a heightened awareness of bioterrorism. In this setting, numerous "copycat terrorists" found ample opportunity to instigate additional terror and mischief simply by labeling innocent powders as "anthrax" and then sending the material with threatening letters to their victims. Based on a telephone survey of health departments over the period September 11 to October, the Centers for Disease Control and Prevention (CDC) estimated that U.S. health departments had received an estimated 7000 reports of potential bioterrorist threats [9]. In comparison, the number of anthrax threats reported to federal authorities during 1996–2000 did not exceed 180 [9].

Hoaxes continue. As recently as the Fall of 2008, the FBI indicted a man from Sacramento, California for mailing packets of sugar labeled "anthrax" to more than a 100 newspapers, public officials, and businesses in 2007 and 2008 [10].

The community of nations regards biological weapons as inhumane, unnecessarily cruel, and fabulously dangerous. Nations that openly manufacture such weapons—such as Iraq—expose themselves to public censure and preemptive strikes by other nations to eliminate the terrifying program [11]. These political considerations might not restrain militaristic religious and extremist groups from considering bioterrorism [4]. Such terrorist organizations do not respect governmental authority because they view secular rulers and the law they uphold as illegitimate [4]. The terrorists' objective is to destroy the legitimacy of the government by creating as much fear and chaos as possible [4]. The terrorists do not fear public censure for their misdeeds because the terrorists believe their actions please God, and they consider their victims to be subhuman because the victims do not subscribe to the terrorists' religious beliefs [4]. Stern noted that in the last decade, the number of terrorist acts committed by religiously motivated groups has increased and the acts have become more violent [4]. From this perspective, it is easy to understand why authorities view with such alarm the credible threats of bioterrorism made by militaristic religious orders like the white supremacist groups, Aum Shinrikyo, and Al Qaeda.

So what weapons does the bioterrorist include in the biological arsenal? Our examination of this armory begins with the history of biological weapons and concludes with a review of prospective agents.

Historical Use of Biological Weapons

Probably because of a poor understanding of biology, prior to World War I, combatants infrequently used biologic agents with uncertain results [12]. Characteristically, these attempts used simple devices to spread contaminated material or expose individuals to hazardous materials. For example, ancient history records that the Carthaginian leader, Hannibal, hurled clay pots filled with venomous snakes onto the decks of an opposing naval force, the resulting chaos allowed Hannibal to rout the enemy [13]. Medieval history includes multiple attempts to use plague as a weapon; during the siege of Caffa, the Tartars threw the carcasses of plague victims into the fortified town expecting to cause an outbreak of the plague [11,13]. The history of the New World includes several attacks on the Native American population with smallpox [13]. During the French Indian War, the British distributed contaminated blankets to French loyalist Native Americans; the blankets had been previously inoculated with the crusts from smallpox lesions with the expectation of causing an epidemic of smallpox [11,13]. Throughout human history combatants have used animal carcasses, cadavers, and sewage to practice a simple form of biological warfare. By dumping the putrid material into an enemy's drinking water supplies, the attackers expected to incapacitate their adversaries with fouled water [11–13]. During the Vietnam War, the Viet Cong practiced another elemental form of biological warfare using a strategy also employed by many other peoples in many other situations. The Viet Cong dug pits and lined the bottoms with bamboo and wood spikes ("pungi sticks") soiled with human feces, expecting unwary passersby to fall into the pits, impale themselves on the sticks, and develop severe wound infections [11,14].

The advent of microbiology provided specific agents for conducting biological warfare. During World War I, the Germans reputedly tried to sabotage cavalry horses in Baltimore with glanders and military pack mules in Rumania with both glanders and anthrax [13]. During World War II, the Japanese conducted an extensive program for the development of biological weapons, reputedly resulting in the death of some 10,000 prisoners [11]. The Japanese reportedly used a variety of agents to attack China, including contaminated foodstuffs, drinking water, and air, as well as plague-infected fleas [11,15]. Some of these attacks backfired; in an attack on Changteh in 1941, the Japanese forces reportedly suffered 10,000 casualties and 1700 deaths due to their own biological weapons [11]. In 1984, members of the Bhagwan Shree Rajneesh commune attempted to incapacitate voters in a local election with food poisoning by contaminating salad bars in Dalles, Oregon, with homegrown *Salmonella typhimurium* [12].

Even though the Geneva Protocol of 1925 and the 1972 Biological Weapons Convention specifically banned biological warfare, after World War I, a number of nations—including treaty signatories—used the new science of microbiology to establish large programs for the discovery, development, and production of biological weapons [13]. Propelling this development was the promise of developing indefensible weapons with the capacity to cause massive destruction, primarily through the dissemination of infectious aerosols. As a result, national research programs explored the military utility of numerous agents, but only a small number appear to have become serious candidates for conversion into weapons, i.e., "weaponized" (Table 5.1) and even fewer have been actually deployed (Table 5.2) [12,14].

Table 5.1 Prospective Agents of Biological Warfare in the Modern Era

Disease (Agent) {National Arsenal} |CDC Risk Category|
Viral encephalitis (particularly Venezuelan equine encephalitis) {US and USSR} |B|
Agents of viral hemorrhagic fevers (including Marburg and Ebola) {USSR} |A|
Smallpox (variola major) {USSR} |A|
Typhus (*Rickettsia prowazekii*) {USSR} |unranked|
Q fever (*Coxiella burnetti*) {US and USSR} |B|
Brucellosis (*Brucella suis*) {US} |B|
Tularemia (*Francisella tularensis*) {US and USSR} |A|
Glanders (*Burkholderia mallei*) {USSR} |B|
Melioidosis (*Pseudomonas pseudomallei*) {USSR} |B|
Plague (*Yersinia pestis*) {Japan and USSR} |A|
Cholera (*Vibrio cholerae*) |B|
Food poisoning (*Clostridium perfringens*) |unranked|
Enterotoxin B (from *Staphylococcus aureus*) {US} |B|

Sources: Adapted from Rotz, L.D. et al., *Emerg. Infect. Dis.*, 8(2), 225, 2002; Christopher, G.W. et al., *J. Am. Med. Assoc.*, 278(5), 412, 1997; Kleitmann, W.F. and Ruoff, K.L., *Clin. Microbiol. Rev.*, 14, 364, 2001; Kortepeter, M.G. and Parker, G.W., *Emerg. Infect. Dis.*, 5(4), 523, 1999; Davis, C.J., *Emerg. Infect. Dis.*, 5(4), 509, 1999.

Table 5.2 Deployed Agents of Biological Warfare in the Modern Era

Disease (Agent) |CDC Risk Category|	*Deploying Nations (Conflict)*
Anthrax (*Bacillus anthracis*) |A|	Multiple nations and conflicts {US and USSR}
Assassination (ricin toxin) |B|	USSR (Cold War)
Botulism (*Clostridium botulinum* toxin) |A|	Iraq (Persian Gulf War); {US}

Sources: Adapted from Kortepeter, M.G. and Parker, G.W., *Emerg. Infect. Dis.*, 5(4), 523, 1999; Davis, C.J., *Emerg. Infect. Dis.*, 5(4), 509, 1999; Olson, K.B., *Emerg. Infect. Dis.*, 5(4), 513, 1999.

Tables 5.1 and 5.2 include a bracketed abbreviation for the United States {US}, indicating the United States reportedly included this agent in our biological arsenal before President Nixon unilaterally banned the use of offensive biological weapons in 1969 and had all stocks destroyed by 1973 [11,18].

Focus on Fort Detrick

In 1942, the U.S. Army Chemical Warfare Service began an offensive and defensive biological weapons research program headquartered at a small National Guard airfield named Camp Detrick (later renamed Fort Detrick), Maryland [18]. The field became the location for extensive laboratories and testing facilities, including a 1-million-L, 40-ft-high steel sphere known as the "Eight Ball." Between 1954 and 1973, Fort Detrick enrolled some 2300 volunteers—primarily Seventh-day Adventists—into a human research program known as "Operation Whitecoat" [19]. In some experiments, investigators detonated biological weapons in the Eight Ball and then exposed the volunteers to the aerosols [11,19]; other experiments tested new vaccines and therapeutic agents [19]. The sphere remains today as a historical monument to the program [18]. Ultimately, the Fort Detrick investigators determined that with great effort biological weapons could be safely produced and effectively deployed [18], in the process they developed modern principles of biosafety and containment [18]. Between 1943 and 1969, Fort Detrick workers acquired 456 cases of illnesses from their work; three patients died, two with anthrax and one with encephalitis [11]. Currently, the Fort Detrick facilities include a large-scale maximum containment laboratory and a small-scale maximum containment medical evacuation and hospitalization unit [18]. With the change to a pure defensive mission in 1969, the facility was renamed the U.S. Army Medical Research Institute of Infectious Diseases (USAMRIID) [18]. The USAMRIID has led the continued development of medical and public health countermeasures to biologic agents; all USAMRIID research is unclassified [11]. The USAMRIID has published online detailed manuals on defense against biological and chemical warfare: (http://www.usamriid.army.mil/education/instruct.htm).

Also included in Tables 5.1 and 5.2 is a bracketed abbreviation for the former Soviet Union (Union of Soviet Socialist Republics) {USSR} which was dissolved in 1991. The USSR reportedly included these agents in their arsenal of biological weapons [14,16]. The Soviet Union selected agents and toxins for possible weaponization by scoring each candidate for infectivity, toxicity, environmental stability, ease of large-scale manufacture, disease severity, and stability in the atmosphere [14].

Focus on Biopreparat

After signing the 1972 Biological and Toxic Weapons Convention, the Soviet Union secretly continued their biological weapons research and development program under the aegis of a civilian biotechnology research program known as "Biopreparat" [11,12]. During the 1970s and the 1980s, the program operated a string of research laboratories and production facilities employing 55,000 people [11]. After Russia inherited the program from the Soviet Union in 1992, President Yeltsin announced that he would discontinue the program [11]. Despite this declaration, high-level defectors revealed that the program continued. One of these defectors, the deputy director of Biopreparat, Ken Alibek, described an extensive secret biological weapons program in his popular book: *Biohazard: The Chilling True Story of the Largest Covert Biological Weapons Program, Told from the Inside by the Man Who Ran It*. According to Alibek, Biopreparat activities included [20]

- Multiple "on demand" biological warfare production facilities for the wartime annual production of 300–1000 tons of anthrax and up to 100 annual tons of plague, tularemia, glanders, and brucellosis.

- "On demand" biological warfare production facilities for the wartime production of smallpox, and Marburg virus.
- Research into creating a weapon out of HIV.
- Research into creating new vaccine and drug-resistant varieties of conventional biological weapons.
- Research into creating new viruses with secret virulence properties and unknown countermeasures by fusing different viruses.

The preceding discussion does not mean that only the United States and the USSR produced and stockpiled biological weapons. Various authorities have claimed that as many as 5–12 nations currently have biological weapons in their national armories [12,14,21].

In 1999, the CDC embarked on a congressionally mandated program to improve the national response to bioterrorism. To guide this effort, the CDC convened a panel of experts to categorize biological agents, for the potential of the agent, to be used as weapons for biological terrorism [2]. To make this assignment the panel used the following four criteria [2]:

- Potential for causing massive illness and death
- Potential for delivery to large populations
- Potential for causing fear and civil disruption
- Public health preparedness needs for surveillance, diagnosis, and stockpiling countermeasures (i.e., vaccine and antimicrobial agents)

With these criteria in mind, the panel assigned the agents to three risk categories (A–C) [2]:

- Category A: greatest threat
- Category B: moderate threat
- Category C: potential to become a major threat in the future

To signify their relative value for bioterrorism, Tables 5.1 and 5.2 also include a bracketed |A, B, or "unranked"| designation for the CDC risk category. The tables do not include new diseases that have the potential to become threats in the future (Category C) like the Nipah virus and Hantavirus.

The following sections discuss in detail the six Category A agents that the CDC considers the greatest threat for bioterrorism.

Anthrax

When authorities list infectious diseases as potential biological weapons, anthrax always seems to be at the top of the list [2,12,14,21]. Indeed, there are probably more examples of the use of this agent as a biological weapon than for any other agent.

Anthrax is a large, encapsulated, Gram positive, spore-forming, bacillus, bacterium [22,23]. Normally the microbe causes a disease of herbivores resulting in occasional epidemics in livestock [22,23] and sporadic occupational infections of farmers, sheepherders, butchers, taxidermists, weavers, and wool handlers [24], from which the organism gets the name "woolsorter's disease." Anthrax is also known as "charcoal," "blackbane," and "malignant pustule" in recognition of the pitch black "scab" (or more formally the "eschar") that characteristically, covers the painless ulcer at the site of the skin ("cutaneous") infection [22]. Moreover, characteristically, the rim of the ulcer develops an unusual amount of swelling ("edema") [22]. Anthrax-contaminated foodstuffs can also cause a gastrointestinal form of the disease with a high fatality rate (25–60 percent). The disease is not transmissible from person to person.

While cutaneous disease can be lethal (20 percent lethality in untreated patients, <1 percent in treated patients) [24], the fearsome reputation of the disease comes from the high fatality (80 percent lethality) rate that follows inhalational anthrax [24] and the low, lethal inhalational dose (one millionth of a gram of spores) required to produce disease.

When spores come into contact with the host, either by direct contact, inhalation, or ingestion, the spores transform ("germinate") into a rapidly growing ("vegetative") form [22]. It is believed that germination can take place as long as 60 days after inhalation [23,24]. The number of spores required to kill 50 percent of exposed individuals has been estimated to be 2,000–55,000 spores [24,25]. Vegetative cells produce two toxins, edema toxin and lethal toxin, killing the local tissues ("necrosis") and causing local swelling and bleeding ("hemorrhage") [22,24,25]. While the incubation period for the gastrointestinal and cutaneous diseases is relatively short (0.5–12 days), the incubation period for inhalational anthrax can be long. As noted in the following discussion of the Sverdlovsk incident (see the following text), cases occurred as late as 43 days after exposure [26]. For this reason, authorities fear that inhaled spores will survive and germinate if the antimicrobial therapy is not continued for at least 60 days [23,24].

Inhalational anthrax begins as a nonspecific illness with fever, malaise, muscle aches and pains, and a dry cough for one to three days [22–24]. The first phase is followed by a precipitous decline with high fever, acute shortness of breath, sweating, and a blue discoloration of the skin due to lack of oxygen ("cyanosis") [22–24]. At this time, the patient may wheeze and develop swelling of the chest and neck [22,23]. Ultimately, the patient loses consciousness, develops shock, and dies within in one to two days [23]. Characteristically, x-ray examination of the chest shows widening of the central structures ("mediastinum") that include the major blood vessels, airways, and lymph nodes; swelling and localized bleeding causes the widening of the mediastinum [22–24]. For the physician, this mediastinal widening in a previously healthy patient with a flu-like illness signals the diagnosis of inhalational anthrax [22,24]. In a quarter of cases the patient also has a bloody localized pneumonia believed to mark the site of the original inhalation and implantation of the anthrax spores [23,24].

Anthrax is diagnosed by recovering the causative organism from normally sterile body fluids and tissues [12,23]. For epidemiological purposes of mapping exposure, microbiologists will obtain swab cultures of the nasal passages for anthrax. When positive, these cultures indicate exposure, but not necessarily infection [23]. The microbiologist may also call upon a variety of molecular and antibody techniques to confirm infection investigate outbreaks [23], and expose hoaxes [24].

With early diagnosis, the illness can be cured by antimicrobial therapy. The drugs penicillin, tetracycline, and ciprofloxacin are all effective [24]. There is concern, however, that any group that would weaponize anthrax would take the additional step to make the organism resistant to multiple antibiotics (particularly penicillin and tetracycline) [23,24]—a maneuver that can be accomplished fairly readily in the research laboratory. For this reason, authorities recommend the drug ciprofloxacin as the first choice of defense against anthrax in the setting of a terrorist attack [23,24,26].

Focus on Sverdlovsk

The 1979 accidental release of anthrax in Sverdlovsk illustrates what could happen in an anthrax attack. Figure 5.1 is based on the report by Meselson et al. [26] who described this outbreak. The larger drawing shows the city limits of Sverdlovsk, a city of 1.2 million located in the former USSR (now Ekaterinburg, Russia). In 1980, reports began appearing of anthrax in residents of Sverdlovsk as well as in animals to the south of the city; the triangles on the larger map mark the locations of villages that reported livestock anthrax. The investigative team examined old records and interviewed survivors and the families of victims. They counted 77 victims, 66 of whom died from their infection

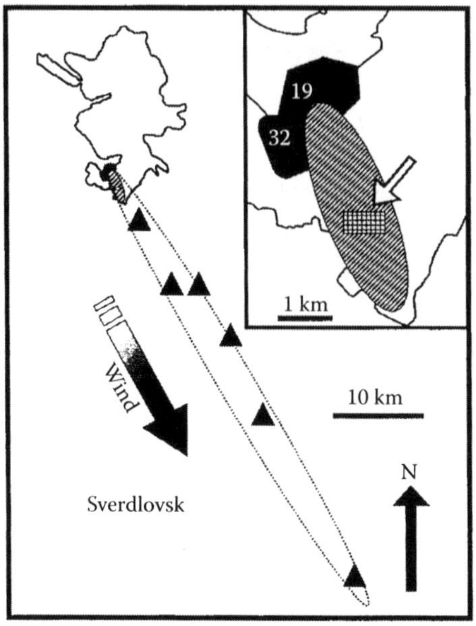

Figure 5.1 Geographic epidemiology of the 1979 anthrax outbreak in Sverdlovsk as described by Meselson et al. (Modified from Meselson, M. et al., *Science*, 266, 1202, 1994.)

[26]. The outbreak began suddenly with 28 victims identified in the first week, and then tapered off with the last victims occurring in the sixth week [26]. This "epidemic curve" characterizes a "point source" outbreak. The team's information allowed them to map the location of 66 of the victims on April 2, 1979, the day they believed the accidental release took place. Meselson found that 57 of these 66 victims lived or worked within a narrow zone approximately 4 km long that stretched from a military facility (Compound 19) to the Sverdlovsk city limits [26]; the slashed ellipse in the inset maps this exposure zone. This zone paralleled the direction of the prevailing winds (large broken arrow) on April 2. Eighteen victims worked in a ceramics factory located in the middle of the exposure zone (the hatched box designated by the open arrow in the inset) [26]. The inset also shows the location of two military facilities, Compounds 19 and 32 (gray polygons); Compound 19 produced anthrax and is believed to be the source of the outbreak. To account for the geographic clustering, Meselson et al. postulated that an anthrax plume (dotted ellipse on the larger map) originated from Compound 19 and followed the prevailing winds. The plume stretched some 50 km downwind of Sverdlovsk and contaminated the environment, resulting in human and animal anthrax [26]. Government officials responded to the outbreak by vaccinating animals and nearly 50,000 humans [26]. Apparently, since the outbreak there have been no further cases of anthrax [26].

A crude anthrax vaccine, Anthrax Vaccine Adsorbed (AVA), exists that provides protective immunity against cutaneous anthrax [23,24,28]. The material is made from a culture filtrate harvested from a noninfectious, avirulent strain of anthrax [23,24]. Vaccination can be performed to prevent illness (prophylaxis) as well as to prevent the activation of illness after exposure (postexposure prophylaxis) [23]. There is concern, however, that weaponized anthrax may also have been manipulated so that the vaccine would also be ineffective [24].

Controversy surrounds AVA concerning an unconfirmed reputation for causing troublesome side effects [23] and because vaccine efficacy to prevent inhalational anthrax has not been—for understandable reasons—rigorously tested [29]. The Institute of Medicine reviewed the controversy concerning the anthrax vaccine, and reported in 2002 that AVA was both effective and safe [30].

Because AVA has not been produced since 1998 [27], supplies are limited [23,24]. Generally speaking, the vaccine is not available to civilians [27,28]. After the 2001 attack through mails in the United States (see the following text), the Department of Health and Human Services agreed to make the vaccine available as an investigational drug to civilians exposed to inhalational anthrax [29]. Subsequently, the federal government has established and funded a program to provide a sufficient stock of AVA to meet both military needs and a national emergency as well as to develop new vaccines to replace AVA (see the discussion at the end).

Weaponization requires fabricating the anthrax spores into particles, 5–17 μm, in size by drying the material, mixing it with a powdery substance like silica, grinding the preparation into a fine powder, and treating the powder to diminish the static charge [25]. Particulate matter prepared in this manner can be easily dispersed as an aerosol that remains aloft for a prolonged period and can be inhaled deeply into the lungs [14]. The resulting weapon has the advantage of broad dispersal from a single delivery point, but the disadvantage of easy dispersability makes it difficult for the aggressor to limit the attack to the target population. After the material has settled, further disturbance can resuspend the dust leading to further infections ("secondary dispersal") [24].

Focus on Anthrax in the U.S. Postal Service, 2001 (Known to the FBI as "Amerithrax")

Just 11 days after the terrorist attack on the New York World Trade Center, cases of anthrax began appearing in the United States. Initially considered coincidental, it soon became evident that someone had used the mail system to attack politicians and members of the print and broadcast media with anthrax. In addition to the targeted individuals, mail workers and uninvolved citizens also developed anthrax. Altogether anthrax struck some 22 individuals, 11 had inhalational anthrax of which 5 died [31,32]. Even though the investigation is still incomplete, the bioterrorist apparently packaged in mailing envelopes a dry powder preparation of an antibiotic susceptible, but highly virulent, "Ames" strain of anthrax [31]. The anthrax powder had high dispersability; as a consequence the spores penetrated the mailing envelopes, cross-contaminated mail and mailing machinery, and contaminated office buildings [31]. The dispersal characteristics of the powder suggested to some authorities that the powder had been "weaponized" [33,34]. Although the number of casualties was relatively small, the terrorist* succeeded in causing tremendous national fear and disruption of government facilities (i.e., terror) resulting in considerable cost [25].

* This incident may actually represent a crime committed with a biological weapon or "biocrime" rather than "bioterrorism" *per se*. From the beginning, authorities speculated that the perpetrator was an American microbiologist connected to the American biological weapons program, who had inadvertently caused casualties in a misplaced attempt to draw attention to either a secret and illegal offensive weapons program (which is not known to exist) or dramatize the lack of funding for a defensive program to combat bioterrorism [35]. Authorities suspected the casualties were accidental because the perpetrator had used tape to seal the mailing envelopes containing the anthrax powder and the perpetrator had urged the mail recipients to take antibiotics for anthrax exposure [35]. These precautions suggested that the perpetrator did not realize that the envelopes were not impervious to anthrax but actually had pores large enough to allow the anthrax spores to penetrate the paper and disperse throughout the surroundings [35]. In July 2008, a Fort Detrick microbiologist apparently committed suicide after learning that the Justice Department was preparing to charge him with this crime. Whether or not this scientist committed these crimes is unknown [34]; on the other hand, the federal government has made a persuasive argument that the source of the anthrax used in this attack came from a culture flask stored in this scientist's laboratory refrigerator at USAMRIID [34].

Reportedly the Soviet Union produced 30 metric tons of anthrax and the United Nations Special Commission (UNSCOM) claims that Iraq manufactured 84,250 L of anthrax spores [16]. In comparison, different authorities have reported that the release of 50 kg of anthrax over an urban population of 5 million would cause 100,000 deaths and 250,000 casualties [24] and the release of 100 kg over Washington, DC would cause 130,000–3,000,000 deaths [24].

The high fatality rate, rapid clinical pace, and limited countermeasures make this a fearsome illness, and therefore a great weapon from the viewpoint of the terrorist. The capacity to spread the material by aerosols enables the terrorists to attack large numbers of people providing the terrorist has access to military grade material. Because of the infrastructure required to produce weapons grade material, it is unlikely that weaponized anthrax can be obtained from any source other than a nation-state [24]. The terrorists contemplating an attack with anthrax will either have to steal the material, solicit a gift, or prepare it themselves. Terrorist-manufactured anthrax will probably not have the dispersability and infectivity of weapons grade material, although it could still represent a potent weapon [4].

Smallpox

The last reported case of wild smallpox occurred in Somalia in 1977 [36]. In 1980, the General Assembly of the World Health Organization declared smallpox extinct [36] and recommended that all remaining stocks of the virus be transferred to secure laboratories in either the United States or the USSR [37]. Despite calls for the destruction of these residual stocks, the organism remains in the United States and Russia [37]. Reportedly, the USSR biological weapons program produced 20 metric tons of this material [12].

The organism is a DNA virus of the Orthopoxvirus family that includes monkeypox, vaccinia, and cowpox [37]. Two types of smallpox exist: the virulent variola major (with a case fatality rate of 30 percent) and the less virulent variola minor (or alastrim) (with a case fatality rate of 1 percent or less) [37]. The infectious dose is unknown but believed to be only a few viral particles ("virions") [37]. Infection begins with implantation of the virus on the oropharyngeal and respiratory mucosa, from there it migrates to regional lymph nodes where it multiplies [37]. Three to four days after exposure, smallpox enters the bloodstream ("viremia") and spreads to the spleen, bone marrow, and lymph nodes [36]. A secondary cycle of viremia occurs on day eight, resulting in fever and toxemia. The incubation period is 12–14 days; the illness begins with a two-to-four day prodrome of high fever, malaise, prostration, headache, and backache [36]. In some 30 percent of patients, the natural immune response leads to a severe toxic reaction that ends in death [36].

The characteristic feature of the illness is a skin rash ("exanthem") that begins as small red bumps ("papules") that over time fill with clear fluid to become "vesicles" [36]. The vesicles then fill with pus ("pustules") and break open leaving a crusted ulcer, known as the "pox," that heals with a deep pit [37]. The onset of the exanthem heralds greatest communicability [37], but communicability at this time is through the saliva [37]. Prior to onset of the exanthem and during the first week of illness, a similar rash—known as an "enanthem"—develops on the inner lining ("mucosa") of the mouth and throat. As mucosal lesions form they quickly ulcerate releasing infective virus [25]. At first, when the saliva contains relatively small numbers of virions, communicability is limited to contaminated eating and drinking utensils [25]. As the number of oral lesions increases, the number of virions in the saliva increases, increasing communicability and reaching a maximum just prior to the onset of the exanthem [25]. At this time smallpox can be transmitted through close contact by aerosolized saliva [25]. When the exanthem appears, the vesicles rupture and release fluid containing infective virions. The virion-laden vesicular fluid soils clothing and bedding, which can in turn transmit the illness [25]. The virus is also present in large numbers in the blood clot or scab covering the pox, but the encasing fibrin network of the clot makes the scabs noninfective [37].

The illness is diagnosed by the characteristic rash, confirmed by electron microscopic examination of the vesicular fluid, and reconfirmed by propagating the organism on tissue culture and verifying the genetic identity by molecular techniques [37]. Needless to say, such an analysis must be conducted in high-containment laboratories [37].

Aside from supportive nursing care, there is no therapy for smallpox [27,37]. In an unimmunized population, 10–20 secondary cases occur for every primary case [37]. The public health response depends entirely on identification and isolation of the infected patients followed by contacting and immunizing all those who are exposed to the patient.

Smallpox can be prevented by vaccination; the worldwide vaccination program led to the illness becoming extinct. With eradication of smallpox from the United States, the medical necessity for immunization ceased, as a result routine vaccination stopped after 1972 [37].

Smallpox vaccination does not lead to lifelong immunity, so with the cessation of vaccination, public health authorities began to worry that the overall immunity to smallpox had begun to wane [38]. At the same time, vaccine manufacturing had ended, so over the next three decades the remaining stocks of vaccine were both gradually depleted and aged. As the twenty-first century approached and concerns about biological weapons emerged, public health officials began to worry that the American population was both susceptible to smallpox and guarded by inadequate stocks of vaccine [37,38]. These concerns prompted public health officials to create new stocks of smallpox and stage a vaccination campaign for the armed forces and emergency workers. Although the initial plan called for the vaccination of some 500,000 civilian emergency workers [39], the program vaccinated only 39,000 people [40]. In this group there were 100 serious adverse events with 3 deaths [40]. The serious adverse events included 21 cases of cardiac inflammation (myocarditis and pericarditis), 10 excess cases of ischemic heart disease, 2 cases of generalized vaccinia (infection with the vaccine strain), and 1 case of postvaccinal encephalitis [40]. In light of the significant morbidity and mortality of the vaccine and the failure to find stocks of smallpox weapons in Iraq, the Institute of Medicine called for an end to the vaccination program [39]. Although the vaccination program has ended, in 2007 the FDA licensed a new, "second generation" smallpox vaccine [41]; this vaccine is being stockpiled by the CDC for emergency use in the event of an attack.

Focus on Smallpox in New York City, 1947

The 1947 New York outbreak of smallpox serves as an encouraging example of an effective public health response to an unrecognized outbreak of smallpox in an unvaccinated U.S. population [25]. In 1947, a 47 year old man, the "index" case, who was a U.S. citizen, journeyed to Mexico where he acquired smallpox [42]. Shortly after returning to New York City, he developed a severe but atypical form of smallpox that resulted in hospitalization and later his death, the first death in New York City due to smallpox since 1939 [42]. Because of the atypical presentation and the presence of a well-formed childhood smallpox scar, the index patient's physicians failed to make the diagnosis until two typical secondary cases of smallpox appeared [42]. Both of these secondary cases were initially thought to have chickenpox, but it became evident that the true diagnosis was smallpox [42]. Ultimately, the index case generated 11 additional cases [42] and 2 patients died, the index patient and a secondary case [42]. Public health officials responded to the outbreak by isolating the "index" patient and the secondarily infected patients, and then vaccinating a potentially exposed population of 6.3 million [42]. By these measures, public health officials limited the outbreak to 3 deaths and 12 cases [42]. The vaccination campaign had an associated mortality due to the capacity of the live vaccine to cause overwhelming illness in compromised patients: a 66-year-old man and two infants died as a result of infection with the vaccine strain [42]. It is possible that there was additional morbidity and mortality due to the vaccination; however, the technology and public health resources available at that time would not have detected such events if they occurred.

The high lethality, gruesome death, and likelihood for secondary spread make smallpox a truly fearsome disease, perhaps the most fearsome agent for bioterrorism. Fortunately the disease remains extinct and the remaining stocks of the organism are controlled by only two countries, the United States and Russia (inheritors of the USSR weapons program). Unfortunately, the collapse of the Soviet economic and political structure in the 1990s raised concerns that the Russian government may have lost control of its smallpox inventory [12,21]. The Soviets reputedly produced 20 metric tons [12] of smallpox in weapon form, making it possible that some stocks fell into the hands of terrorists or countries that support terrorism. So far, these fears have not materialized. Hopefully, a terrorist organization equipped with smallpox would hesitate to rerelease an incurable, highly infectious, extinct disease. Aside from the universal condemnation such an act would incur, it would also expose the members of the organization as well as their supporters to dying of smallpox themselves.

Tularemia

The "*tularensis*" of *Francisella tularensis* comes from Tulare County, California where the organism was first discovered to produce a plague-like illness in rodents [43]. The "*Francisella*" honors Dr. Edward Francis who discovered that the deer fly transmitted the microbe to humans causing an illness previously known as deer fly fever but now known as "tularemia" [43]. Originally considered a North American disease, the organism has subsequently been recognized as the cause of large outbreaks in Europe and the former USSR [43,44].

The microbe is a small nonmotile, aerobic, Gram negative, cocco-bacillus, bacterium [44,45], distantly related to the etiologic agents for Q-fever and legionellosis [45]. The organism exists in four subspecies forms or "biovars" [45]. The bacterium normally lives and multiplies in small mammals (voles, mice, rats, squirrels, rabbits, and hares) that serve as the natural "reservoir" of infection [43–45]. The animals acquire the illness through arthropod (ticks, biting flies, and mosquitoes) bites and by contact with a contaminated environment [44]. Most humans become infected by the bite of a tick or a fly, but the illness can also be acquired by handling infected animal tissues; consuming contaminated soil, water, meat, or vegetation; and from inhaling aerosols [43–45]. The microbe is highly infectious; it is believed that as few as ten organisms can cause disease [43]. Unless they take precautions, laboratory workers have a substantial risk of accidentally infecting themselves through direct contact or inhalation of an aerosol [44,45]. Fortunately, there is no human-to-human transmission [43–45].

The disease exists in six clinical forms that vary according to the body site that first comes in contact with the microbe, the virulence of the organism, and the number of infecting organisms [44]. The most common forms of the illness begin with the bite of an arthropod or contamination of a break in the skin; from this "portal of entry" the organism spreads to local lymph nodes producing painful enlargement (glandular tularemia) [44]. Usually, however, the organism also multiplies at the portal of entry resulting in one or more papules that rupture and ulcerate (ulceroglandular) [44]. If the portal of entry is the lining of the eye, the disease is known as "oculoglandular" [44].

If the organism infects the throat through consumption of contaminated food or water it is known as "oropharyngeal" [44]. Inhalation of the organism (as well as secondary spread from another site of infection to the lung) produces a severe lung infection known as "pneumonic" tularemia [43,44]. Sometimes the organism does not produce a local infection, but instead causes a generalized severe form of disease known as "typhoidal" tularemia that can include clinical features of pneumonic tularemia [44].

A panel of experts, known as the Working Group on Civilian Biodefense (WGCB), reviewed the utility of tularemia as a biological weapon and postulated that an attack would most likely come in the form of an aerosol resulting in pneumonic tularemia [44]. Based on their review of the literature [44], the WGCB predicts such an attack would begin with the sudden appearance of large numbers of patients within three to five days of exposure to the aerosol, with some cases occurring as late as two weeks after exposure [44]. The patients would present with pneumonia, remarkable only in terms of the large numbers of patients presenting at the same time [44]. Patients would complain of an abrupt onset of fever, headache, chills, generalized body aches, sore throat, cough, shortness of breath, and chest pain [44]. Chest x-ray evidence of pneumonia would be present in most patients, but delayed in one-quarter to one-half of the patients [44]. Significant impairment may occur despite therapy, surviving untreated patients may experience illness lasting weeks to months [44]. Depending upon the public health response, susceptibility to antimicrobial therapy, and virulence of the weapon, fatality rates could reach 30–60 percent, but might be less than 2 percent [44]. It is possible, however, that in the event of an attack the virulence of tularemia could have been enhanced by laboratory manipulation [44].

Normally the infection can be treated with antimicrobial therapy; regimens employing a daily injection of an aminoglycoside are preferred over oral therapy with doxycycline or ciprofloxacin [43,44]. The utility of antimicrobial therapy in the event of an attack is questionable. The organism has been engineered to be resistant to chloramphenicol and tetracycline [44] and both the United States and the USSR have created biological weapons using aminoglycoside-resistant strains [44]. Nevertheless, in the event of a massive attack, the WGCB recommends either oral doxycycline or ciprofloxacin [44]. In the past, laboratory workers could be immunized against tularemia by scarification with an investigational, live, attenuated vaccine [45]; more recently the FDA has withdrawn this license, so a vaccine is not available [45].

The WGCB speculated that an attack with tularemia could be distinguished from an anthrax attack by the more toxic clinical appearance of inhalational anthrax along with the telltale mediastinal widening exhibited by anthrax [44]. The attack could also be distinguished from an attack with plague by the more virulent clinical course presented by pneumonic plague (see the following text) [44]. The WGCB anticipates that standard bacteriologic laboratory procedures would lead to the quick identification of infections due to anthrax or plague [44]. Unfortunately, because routine procedures do not detect tularemia, the organism could escape identification until a physician requested specific testing [44].

Authorities have projected that the dispersal of 50 kg of tularemia organism over an urban population of 5 million would result in 250,000 casualties and 19,000 deaths [44].

Plague

Synonymous with epidemic deadly contagion, "plague" has great potential to evoke terror as a weapon of bioterrorism. The disease earned its fearsome reputation by causing three deadly pandemics in the sixth, fourteenth, and twentieth centuries [15,46]. The cause of plague, *Yersinia pestis*, is a Gram negative, cocco-bacillus, bacterium that demonstrates a characteristic bipolar (safety pin) staining under the microscope [15,46]. The genus name honors Alexandre Yersin who, in 1894, discovered the etiology of plague in Hong Kong at the beginning of the third and most recent pandemic [15].

Plague is endemic to Europe and Asia; authorities suspect it spread to North America during the most recent pandemic by causing epidemic ("epizootic") infection in North American rodents [15]. The disease normally resides in rodents, where it is transmitted from one animal to the next by the bite of a flea (the "vector" of transmission) [15,46]. One bite can transmit as many as 24,000 organisms [15], but it is estimated that only one to ten organisms are required to infect a person [15]. The oriental rat flea is the classic vector [15] but all kinds of fleas can transmit the illness [15]. When the animal host dies of the disease, the flea leaves the dead host and seeks a new, live host [46]. Normally, the rodent population both maintains and contains the disease, humans experience only sporadic "wild" disease acquired by handling infected tissues or by the occasional fleabite from a rural rodent flea [15]. When massive numbers of infected urban rats die, such as in epizootic infection, the fleas may leave their customary rodent hosts in large numbers to infest human hosts causing an urban outbreak of plague [46]. The urban outbreak can expand to become an epidemic if the disease spreads to the lungs of infected humans ("pneumonic plague"), who in turn transmit the disease through the air by coughing [15,46]. Inhalation of respiratory secretions is the only way epidemic disease can spread from human to human [46].

Most (85–90 percent) patients with wild disease have "bubonic plague" [15] that begins when a flea bite introduces the microbes into the skin, whereupon the organisms transform and begin to produce disease-causing toxins and virulence factors [15]. These factors enable the germs to migrate to the local lymph nodes, where, despite the host defensive mechanisms, the organisms multiply, causing local inflammation and tissue destruction [46]. The patient perceives the illness, at this time, as the abrupt onset of high fever, chills, fatigue, headache, nausea and vomiting, followed by painful swelling of the lymph nodes near the fleabite [15]. The term "bubonic plague" derives from the characteristic swollen lymph nodes, known as "bubos," that arise one to eight days after the fleabite [15,46].

In a minority of wild cases (10–15 percent), the fleabite leads to direct invasion of the blood stream by the *Y. pestis* bacilli producing "septicemic plague" [15]. More commonly (23 percent), the microbes enter the blood stream after multiplying in the local lymph nodes leading to the combination of bubonic and septicemic plague [15]. Septicemia generates an intense generalized inflammatory response ("sepsis"), that can result in shock, multiorgan failure, bleeding into the tissues ("purpura"), impaired blood clotting ("disseminated intravascular coagulation"—"DIC"), impaired breathing ("respiratory distress syndrome"), and gangrene of the extremities [15,46]. The extremity gangrene turns the limbs black, from which the disease gets the name the "black death" [46]. Septicemic plague has a mortality of 50 percent if untreated [46].

Once the microbes enter the bloodstream, they can migrate to other sites, such as the lungs, causing pneumonia [46]. Very few (1 percent) patients with wild disease present with only pneumonic plague [15], more often (9 percent) they present with both bubonic and pneumonic plague [15]. Patients have cough, chest pain, shortness of breath, and a productive sputum [15,46]. The chest x-ray shows a lobar pneumonia [46]. Pneumonic plague has a mortality of 100 percent in untreated patients [46] and 15 percent in treated patients. Pneumonic plague acquired from another human has a higher mortality than wild type disease because the victim has inhaled organisms that have already undergone transformation into the virulent form by growing in another human victim [15].

Normally physicians diagnose the infection by recovering the organism from the bubo, blood, or sputum by using standard bacteriologic methods [12,15,46]. The infection can be confirmed by detecting *Yersinia* antibodies ("serologic assay"), but this is helpful only for retrospective confirmation as it takes time for the patient to develop an immune response [15,46]. Rapid molecular techniques exist to confirm the identity of the organism [15], but these are only available through public health, military, and CDC laboratories [46].

To avoid further transmission, infected patients require strict isolation; for the first four days of therapy for "pneumonic" plague (as well as for a wound draining *Y. pestis*) and for the first 48 hours for all other infections [15]. Therapy is best accomplished with injectable antibiotics (gentamicin) for a minimum of ten days [15,46]. In cases of mild infections or in situations where injectable antibiotics are not feasible, the patient can be treated with either oral doxycycline (or tetracycline) or ciprofloxacin [15,46]. Exposed patients can be protected from acquiring the disease by the preventive ("prophylactic") postexposure oral administration of either doxycycline or ciprofloxacin for seven days [15,46].

A U.S.-licensed, formaldehyde-killed, whole-cell vaccine exists, but the vaccine is reserved for military use and patients with occupational exposure [15]. The vaccine may not be effective against pneumonic plague [15] and it is no longer readily available, having been discontinued by the manufacturer in 1999 [27,46].

Japan, the United States, and the USSR examined the utility of plague as a biological weapon [11,46]. While it is possible, that, like Japan [11], an attacker would use fleas, the result would be the less deadly bubonic plague and would also require sophisticated technology to maintain, infect, harvest, and package such a flea weapon [15]. Instead, experts predict that a plague attack would use aerosolized bacteria causing large numbers of infectious pneumonic plague [15,46]. In 1970, the WHO reported that the discharge of 50 kg of plague over a city of 5,000,000 would cause 150,000 cases of pneumonic plague with 36,000 deaths [46]. Experts project that human illness would begin in one to six days postattack [46] and death would occur in two to six days [46]. A plague attack should become evident by the abrupt presentation of large numbers of people with the pneumonic form in an atypical area for plague [46] and without the typical die-off of urban rodents that occurs before human outbreaks [46].

Viral Hemorrhagic Fevers

In his novel *Executive Orders*, the popular writer Tom Clancy described a fictional bioterrorist attack on the United States by an imaginary country the "United Islamic Republic." In this novel, the attacker used spray cans filled with Ebola virus to create an infectious aerosol and expose people attending trade shows. Although Tom Clancy's novel included the deaths of several thousand Americans due to the Ebola virus, the fictional attack ultimately failed to cause the intended horrific epidemic of hundreds of thousands to millions of deaths. The attack failed because the virus failed to cause human-to-human transmission ("secondary cases") and the telltale clinical features of Ebola virus quickly alerted physicians to the outbreak. Informed of the outbreak, public health officials rapidly instituted strict but effective controls to contain and prevent further spread of the illness. Although entirely imaginary, this novel underlines the weaknesses and successes of such an attack. Even though the enemy successfully collected and propagated the deadly virus, the project required an expensive program to fund, contain, and weaponize the organism. Even though the enemy succeeded in surreptitiously attacking U.S. citizens, causing many deaths and tremendous terror, the outbreak failed to spread because biologic barriers and public health barriers interrupted the human-to-human transmission.

Despite Clancy's optimistic yarn, viral hemorrhagic fevers (HF) pose a serious and credible threat for a successful terrorist attack. Unlike smallpox, these deadly viruses exist in the wild where they can be collected. For example, in 1993, the Aum Shinrikyo religious cult sent a group of 16 cult doctors and nurses to Zaire disguised as a medical mission with the purpose of bringing back samples of Ebola virus for weaponization [17]. Many of the HF organisms can be propagated and harvested from tissue culture in sufficient quantities to prepare infectious materials [47]. Blood harvested from infected patients is highly contagious, but requires direct contact to transmit illness. Unlike anthrax, botulinum, plague, and tularemia, bioterrorists could use this agent without having to first weaponize the organisms and construct a weapon production facility. All that would be required would be for a group of suicidal terrorists to willingly expose themselves to the wild agent and then move through population centers as their illness progressed. While such an act would probably not cause many secondary cases, it would cause terror and prompt a massive public health response.

Viral HF refers to a disparate group of organisms (see Table 5.3) that share common clinical and microbiologic features [47]. HF viruses are simple RNA viruses with lipid envelopes [47]. The virions are susceptible to detergents, acids, and household bleach, but they are stable at neutral pH, particularly in the presence of protein [47]. Because of the protein-enhanced stability, infectious virions are stable in blood and tissue for prolonged periods of time [47]. Virions are also stable as small particle aerosols making it possible to "weaponize" these viruses [47].

The pathologic process underlying viral HF is damage to the microcirculatory (vascular) system resulting in the movement of fluids from the blood into the tissues [47]. The loss of circulating blood volume generates profound shock while the vascular damage and blood clotting abnormalities lead to characteristic bleeding (hemorrhage) into the tissues [47]. As a group HF viruses exhibit a high morbidity and mortality [47] with death rates ranging from 5 to 25 percent or higher [47,48]. Ebola virus outbreaks have had mortality rates as high as 50–90 percent [47,48].

While the precise mix and degree of clinical features varies with the particular illness,* certain features are common to most HF syndromes [47]. Patients usually present with fever, muscle aches (myalgia), and exhaustion (prostration) [47]. They may also have headache, sore throat, abdominal

Table 5.3 Hemorrhagic Fever (HF) Viruses

Hemorrhagic Fevers (HF)			
Arenaviridae	*Bunyaviridae*	*Filoviridae*	*Flaviviridae*
Lassa fever	Rift Valley fever	Marburg virus	Yellow fever
Argentine HF	Crimean–Congo HF	Ebola virus	Dengue
Bolivian HF	Hantavirus		Kyasanur-forest
Brazilian HF	Korean HF		Omsk HF
Venezuelan HF			

Source: Jahrling, P.B., Viral hemorrhagic fevers, in *Medical Aspects of Chemical and Biological Warfare*, Sidell, F.R., Takafuji, E.T., and Franz, D.R., Eds., Office of the Surgeon General at TMM Publications, Borden Institute, Walter Reed Army Medical Center, Washington, DC, 1997, 591–602.

* Unlike the other HF illnesses, the *sin nombre* Hantavirus produces a syndrome characterized by pulmonary edema [47]. Lassa fever patients do not typically develop hemorrhages and hemorrhage is seen in only severe cases of Rift Valley fever [47]. Liver failure is characteristic of Yellow fever and is seen in a small proportion of patients with Crimean-Congo HF, Rift Valley fever, Marburg HF, and Ebola HF [47].

pain, and diarrhea [48]. Characteristically, the physical examination reveals a low blood pressure (hypotension), flushing, and point-like bleeding into the tissues (petechiae) [47]. The hypotension progresses to shock and kidney failure [47]. In nearly all syndromes, the blood cells that normally promote clotting decrease to a varying degree (i.e., a low platelet count) resulting in bleeding tendencies (DIC) [47]. As a consequence, many HF patients develop spontaneous hemorrhages particularly from mucosal surfaces and traumatic injuries (e.g., skin puncture sites for blood samples and administration of intravenous fluids) [47]. Involvement of the liver is also common, and there may be involvement of the nervous system and the lungs [47].

Of the HF viruses, only the Lassa fever virus, the Marburg virus, the Ebola virus, and the Crimean–Congo virus have caused significant outbreaks with person-to-person transmission [48]. Transmission occurs by close personal contact and contact with infected tissue, blood, secretions, and excretions [48]. There is no convincing evidence of transmission through the air [48]. As the outbreak progresses, transmission efficiency becomes increasingly inefficient from case to case, so outbreaks tend to dissipate quickly [48].

The HF viruses infrequently infect humans [47]. For most HF viruses, wild animals, particularly wild rodents, serve as the reservoir of infection [47]. Humans acquire the diseases from close contact with infected animals (e.g., slaughtering and consumption) or by the bite of an arthropod vector (e.g., mosquitoes and ticks) [47]. Because HF are closely linked to reservoir animals and transmitting vectors, the HF viruses are geographically restricted [47]. A travel history to rural sites in an endemic region is a major clue to the etiology of HF [47,48]; on the other hand, travel restricted to urban sites in an endemic region makes the diagnosis unlikely [48]. Bioterrorism should be suspected when large numbers of victims suddenly appear outside of the normal geographic locality for the HF [47].

The major alternative diagnostic considerations for HF are malaria and sepsis, because these two conditions can present with clinical features similar to HF [47,48]. The presence of malaria can be determined by examining blood smears while sepsis can be determined by isolating bacteria from the blood [48]. Laboratory diagnosis of HF can be difficult as the diagnosis is beyond the capability of community laboratories. In most cases viremia is present on admission and can be detected in the serum or plasma by sending the specimen to a public health laboratory or the CDC or the USAMRIID [47]. Blood is infectious and hazardous [47]; because many HF patients develop copious bleeding, HF patients pose a major hazard to care givers [47]. If a physician suspects HF the patient should be isolated and the physician should immediately notify local and state health departments as well as the CDC [48].

In most cases therapy for HF is limited to symptomatic support [47], however patients do not respond well to fluid support and are prone to develop pulmonary edema [47]. Ribavirin reduces Lassa fever mortality [47] and is recommended for Crimean–Congo HF and severe cases of Venezuelan HF, Korean HF, Brazilian HF, Argentine HF, and Bolivian HF viral infections [49]. Acutely infected patients with Argentine HF and Bolivian HF will improve with the administration of antibodies recovered from convalescent patients [47], but this therapy is not available for other HF [47]. With the exception of the Yellow fever vaccine, there are no readily available vaccines with demonstrated efficacy [47,49].

Botulism

Known as agent X before the poison had been purified and analyzed [50], botulinum toxin is the most toxic, naturally occurring, substance known to man [50,51]. Botulinum toxin is also one of the first agents to be exploited as a biological weapon in the modern era [50]. For example, some historians believe that in the spring of 1942, the British used a modified hand grenade containing botulinum toxin to assassinate Reinhard Heydrich, the head of the German Gestapo and Security Service [50]. After the 1991 Gulf War, Iraq admitted to producing enough botulinum toxin to wipe out the entire world population three times over [51]. Fortunately, even though Iraq deployed missiles and bombs containing more than half of their stock of toxin, the Iraqis did not use these weapons [51]. In addition to Iraq, Iran, North Korea, and Syria are believed to have developed or are developing botulinum toxin as a weapon [51].

Immense toxicity apparently does not necessarily equal immense destructive power; on at least three occasions, during the 1990s, the Aum Shinrikyo attacked Japanese and U.S. military sites with aerosolized botulinum toxin but failed to cause disease [51]. In contrast to destructive purposes, highly diluted botulinum toxin has been licensed for the treatment of chronic muscle spasms that distort eye movement (strabismus), cause spasmodic winking (blepharospasm), and cause chronic neck pain and distortion of head positioning (cervical torticollis) [51].*

The bacterium, *Clostridium botulinum*, a spore forming, Gram positive rod that does not tolerate oxygen (obligate anaerobe) produces botulinum toxin [51]. While *C. botulinum* can be purchased from commercial sources, like the American Type Culture Collection, the organism can also be easily recovered from the soil [50,51]. For example, the Aum Shinrikyo cult isolated their strain of *C. botulinum* from northern Japanese soil [51].

"Botulism"—poisoning by botulinum toxin—is a disease of modern technology [50]; it was not readily apparent to medical historians before the introduction of new food preservation methods in the nineteenth century [50]. Because the *C. botulinum* spores tolerate boiling, the spores contaminating foodstuffs can persist when the food is improperly cooked or preserved. If the preservation creates an environment devoid of oxygen, such as occurs in canning, the spores can germinate releasing the toxin [51]. Because the toxin is odorless and tasteless [51], the consumer of the tainted food may not recognize that the food has gotten spoiled. Intoxication, however, can still be avoided by cooking the tainted food, because heating the toxin at 85°C for at least five minutes readily destroys the toxin [27,51].

Although seven botulinum toxins (types A–G) have been described, only four have been identified with human disease (toxin A, 54 percent; toxin E, 27 percent; toxin B, 15 percent; and toxin F, 2 percent of cases, respectively) [51]. The remaining three types (C, D, and G) are known from nonhuman sources, although these types appear to be equally toxic to humans and have been reported to cause rare human cases [51]. Of interest, type A is most commonly found in the western United States, type B in the eastern United States, and type E in Canada and Alaska [50,51]. Toxin typing is important for prescribing the correct neutralizing antitoxin and for epidemiological analysis [51].

Neurotoxins like the botulinum toxin and the plant toxin curare cause paralysis by blocking the transmission of signals across the microscopic gap (synapse) between the nerve cell and the associated muscle cell (neuromuscular junction). Normally, the nerve cell signals the muscle cell to contract by first forming a small bud (synaptic vesicle) on the nerve cell surface that contains the chemical (neurotransmitter) acetylcholine. The vesicle pinches off the nerve cell, crosses the synapse, and then binds and fuses to the muscle cell releasing the acetylcholine into the muscle cell [51]. The released acetylcholine causes muscle contraction by binding to a specific acetylcholine receptor on the muscle fiber [51].

* Therapeutic botulinum toxin (Myobloc® or Botox®) will not work as a weapon because each drug vial contains only a small fraction of the estimated human lethal dose.

On a weight-by-weight basis, botulinum toxin is far more potent than other toxins like curare. Curare blocks neurotransmission by binding to the acetylcholine receptor, physically preventing acetylcholine from binding to the receptor [50,51]. Botulinum toxin, however, multiplies its effect by repeatedly catalyzing the destruction of proteins required to release acetylcholine into the muscle cell [50,51]. Specifically, botulinum toxin is a zinc-dependent metallo-proteinase that enters the nerve cell and cleaves specific proteins that are normally required to promote the fusion of the synaptic vesicle containing acetylcholine with the muscle cell [50,51]. This blocked fusion prevents the release of the acetylcholine into the nerve cell resulting in an uncontracted ("flaccid") muscle paralysis [50,51].

Botulism occurs in three natural forms (food-borne, wound, and intestinal) that rely upon absorption of the toxin across a mucosal (or wound) surface into the blood [51]. The toxin does not penetrate intact skin, so contact botulism does not occur; however, inhalation of aerosolized toxin has occurred as a laboratory accident [50,51] and is the most likely route of administration for a bioterrorism attack [50,51].

Botulism characteristically presents with paralysis of the head and neck muscles that progresses to involve all of the skeletal muscles in a patient with normal mental function and showing no evidence of acute infection such as fever [51]. Depending on the amount of toxin, the extent and pace of paralysis varies from patient to patient [51]. The illness usually begins 12–72 hours after ingestion of tainted food [50,51] when the patient begins to drool and experience difficulty in chewing, speaking, swallowing, and seeing [51]. The paralysis spreads equally to both of the upper limbs, followed by the trunk and then both lower limbs [51]. The paralysis can be severe enough to require mechanical breathing support [50,51]. On physical examination, the physician finds drooping of both eyelids, enlarged and slowly reacting pupils, loss of the gag reflex, inability to hold the head upright, weakness, and diminished deep tendon reflexes [51]. If the patient has food poisoning, the patient may also complain of abdominal pain, nausea, vomiting, and diarrhea. These gastrointestinal symptoms appear to be due to other bacterial products in the spoiled food rather than to the botulinum toxin *per se* [51]. Because recuperation requires regeneration of the neuromuscular junctions, recovery may take weeks to months. During that time, the patient may require extensive nursing care and mechanical breathing support [51].

Intestinal botulism occurs primarily in infants and presents with constipation. Wound botulism occurs with contaminated injuries and has a similar presentation to food-borne botulism except the patient may have a fever due to wound infection [51]. Neither condition is likely to be the result of a bioterrorism attack [51]. A bioterrorism attack could occur through contamination of one or more food products, but this would be an inefficient use of the poison. Botulism is not known to be acquired by contaminated water [51], and this is an unlikely attack method because water purification treatments inactivate the toxin and because poisoning a major water source like a reservoir would require an exceedingly large amount of toxin [51].

On the other hand, experts have projected that in an urban setting, aerosolization of a single gram of toxin could kill more than 1 million people [51]. Although inhalational botulism does not occur in nature, animal experiments and a German laboratory accident in 1962 involving three workers indicate that inhalational botulism will appear similar in all respects to food-borne botulism [50,51]. Regardless of how it is acquired, botulism is not contagious because it is an intoxication rather than an infection [51].

Physicians may misdiagnose the sporadic case of botulism, but the diagnosis becomes increasingly evident as groups of patients present common features of geography, time, and exposure [51]. The diagnosis is confirmed by a "mouse bioassay," meaning the laboratory injects a mouse with a test fluid to determine if the fluid will produce signs of botulism in the mouse. If the animal displays symptoms, then the laboratory confirms the presence of the toxin by adding an antiserum to the fluid to nullify the toxin. The fluid sample could be a sample of the patient's serum or a filtrate of a clinical sample (such as vomitus, stool, or gastric contents) or a filtrate of the suspect food [50]. This assay can detect as little as 0.03 ng* of botulinum toxin and generates a result in one or two days [51]. The assay must be performed before the patient receives antiserum therapy and is available only through select public health laboratories [51]. The assay will not only confirm the diagnosis of botulism but also reveal the toxin type. Finding large numbers of patients with an unusual type of botulism (e.g., A or B from the wrong region or type C, D, F, and G) should prompt the consideration of a terrorist attack [51].

If diagnosed quickly, disease progression can be prevented by administration of the correct antiserum. A horse antiserum to botulinum toxins A, B, and E is available from the CDC [27]. Recipients may develop allergic reactions to the horse serum including shock (anaphylaxis), hives (urticaria), and a generalized inflammatory condition known as "serum sickness" [27,51]. A new antiserum against all seven types of botulinum toxin is under investigation by the U.S. Army; this antiserum has been treated to reduce the likelihood of an allergic reaction [27].

Once botulinum has been established, there is no antidote or therapy for this toxin. With supportive care, often including intravenous feedings and mechanical ventilation, the patient will recover over a period of weeks to months. Because such patients often require prolonged intensive care, authorities fear that a concerted bioterrorism attack with botulinum toxin will quickly overwhelm medical facilities [51].

An investigational pentavalent (ABCDE) botulinum toxoid can be obtained from the CDC to protect high-risk laboratory workers and military personnel [27]. The toxoid, however, does not work after exposure to botulinum toxin [27].

Future Perspectives and Countermeasures

While the weapons bioterrorists could use are fearsome, the weapons bioterrorists have used have been ineffectual and the incidents of bioterrorism have been rare [39].

Writing on behalf of the Monterey Institute of International Studies in a 1999 issue of *Emerging Infectious Diseases* devoted to bioterrorism, Tucker reported that the center had compiled an open source database of all publicly known cases where terrorists sought to use or acquire biological agents. The Monterey Institute recorded only 55 bioterrorist events over the 40 year period from 1960 through 1999, most of which were hoaxes [1]. Tucker notes that over this 40 year period only one bioterrorist attack led to casualties: the Oregon Rajneeshee religious cult caused 751 cases of food poisoning—but no deaths—in their unsuccessful attempt to manipulate local elections [1]. The only other serious incidents during this period also involved a religious cult and also proved ineffectual. The Japanese Aum Shinrikyo cult used botulinum toxin in 1990 and 1993 and anthrax in 1993 to unsuccessfully attack both the Japanese citizenry and the Japanese government [17].

In 1999 Dr. Donald Henderson,† who led the World Health Organization's global smallpox eradication program, commented on the paradox between the potency of bioterrorist weapons and the impotency of bioterrorism. Henderson noted four "academic" explanations for this anomaly [21]:

* In contrast, the estimated lethal dose for injected toxin is 0.09–0.15 μg, for inhaled toxin is 0.70–0.90 μg, and for ingested toxin is 70 μg [41].

† In November 2001, Dr. Henderson was appointed to direct the newly created Office of Public Health Preparedness at the Department of Health and Human Services.

- Because biological weapons have not been successfully used in the past they will not be successfully used in the future.
- Because the use of biological weapons is repugnant, no one will use them.
- The technology of bioterrorism is beyond the reach of the bioterrorist.
- The capacity of biological weapons for causing mass destruction makes the use of these weapons unthinkable.

Dr. Henderson questioned these arguments noting that technological advances, the increasing boldness of terrorists, and the willingness of nations that support terrorism (like Iraq) to produce and deploy biological weapons predicted future disasters [21]. Considering the subsequent 2001 anthrax attack through the U.S. mail, some might consider Dr. Henderson's warnings prophetic. Because the anthrax attack actually resulted in only 22 casualties and 5 deaths, others might consider Dr. Henderson's warnings exaggerated. To this, others might reply that only a prompt massive public health effort succeeded in limiting the 2001 anthrax attack to just 22 casualties.

Perhaps the best approach is to expect that bioterrorism will never lead to massive loss of life and health but still prepare for disaster. In the years following the 2001 attacks, the United States has followed this strategy. Over this period, the United States has not suffered another major attack with a biological weapon. At the same time, the U.S. federal government has prepared for such an attack by creating, in 2003, the "Strategic National Stockpile (SNS)" and in 2004, Project BioShield.

The SNS is a stockpile of vaccines, antimicrobial agents, and medical supplies. Maintained by the CDC and managed jointly by the Department Homeland Security and the Department of Health and Human Services, the SNS is intended for an emergency response to an attack with a biological weapon or a national epidemic [52,53]. The cache contains antimicrobial agents for anthrax, plague, and tularemia as well as enough smallpox vaccine for the entire U.S. population [52]. The SNS has been configured to deliver these supplies to anywhere within the United States or its territories within 12 hours of the decision to deploy the supplies [34].

Despite this remarkable progress, the SNS does not provide blanket protection. The program could be defeated by an attack with an unconventional biological agent—something other than the conventional agents: anthrax, smallpox, tularemia, and plague. The program is not equipped to counter a conventional agent that has been manipulated to be antimicrobial resistant or vaccine resistant [52]. While the stockpile has been configured to counter large attacks—for example, the SNS includes enough drugs to provide the recommended 60 day course of therapy for as many as 20 million anthrax victims—the preparations could still be overwhelmed if an attack generates massive numbers of casualties and exposed individuals. "Holes" also exist in the response plans for specific agents, notably a shortage of anthrax vaccine [52]. Authorities have called for new procedures to promote new drug and vaccine development to counter an attack with likely biological weapons [52]. To meet this demand, the U.S. Congress passed Project BioShield in 2004; this program provided new funding and new procedures for the development of new agents to counter biological weapons [54]. As a consequence, contracts have been awarded for stocks of new anthrax vaccines, anthrax therapeutics, smallpox vaccine, and botulinum antitoxin [54].

In reviewing these preparations, Cohen et al. remind us that there has not been a truly successful attack with biological weapons on a U.S. target [39]; they note that the 2001 anthrax attack had limited casualties and the attack missed the intended targets [39]. From the perspective of Cohen et al., the billions spent on protecting the United States from attack with biological weapons would be better spent on addressing some of the reasons they claim prompt bioterrorism and promote worldwide mortality and morbidity: poverty, hunger, environmental degradation, and misallocation of resources [39].

In preparing for disaster, we are fortunate that the Internet provides ready access to updated information. Appendix A lists Internet resources on bioterrorism.

Appendix A Electronic Resources for Bioterrorism

Educational:

1. www.cdc.gov/ncidod/eid/vol5no4/pdf/v5n4.pdf Electronic issue of the journal *Emerging Infectious Diseases* devoted to the topic of bioterrorism.
2. http://www.globalsecurity.org/wmd/intro/bio.htm GlobalSecruity.org Web site, provides information on the development and deployment of biological weapons as well as other weapons of mass destruction. Provides electronic access to *Medical Aspects of Chemical and Biological Warfare* [1997] Textbook of military medicine, Published by the Office of The Surgeon General, Borden Institute, Walter Reed Army Medical Center, Washington, DC.
3. http://www.idsociety.org/bt/toc.htm Infectious Diseases Society of America directory of electronic links to multiple informational and educational resources.
4. http://www3.niaid.nih.gov/topics/BiodefenseRelated/Biodefense/default.htm National Institute of Allergy and Infectious Disease Bioterrorism Web site describes NAID-sponsored research and provides access to online articles.
5. www.ph.ucla.edu/epi/bioter/bioterrorism.html University of California Los Angeles: electronic library and archives regarding bioterrorism as well as general educational information in support of academic studies on the epidemiology and public health response to bioterrorism.
6. http://www.usamriid.army.mil/education/instruct.htm Provides free access to a number of USAMRIID textbooks, handbooks, and instructional materials, including: *USAMRIID's Medical Management of Biological Casualties Handbook* (also known as the *USAMRIID Blue Book*; J. B. Woods, editor, 6th edition, 2005, published by the U.S. Army Medical Research Institute of Infectious Diseases, Fort Detrick, Maryland).

Response guidance:

1. www.bt.cdc.gov CDC: links to CDC bioterrorism resources, reports of field investigations, and fact sheets.
2. http://www.bt.cdc.gov/bioterrorism/ CDC Emergency Preparedness and Response to Bioterrorism Web site.
3. www.emergency.com/cbwlesn1.htm Emergency Response and Research Institute: specific guidance on how to manage an incident.
4. http://www.interpol.int/Public/Bioterrorism/default.asp Interpol site for bioterrorism information.

Link directories to Web sites and electronic resources:

1. http://www.apic.org/Content/NavigationMenu/PracticeGuidance/Topics/Bioterrorism/Bioterrorism.htm Association for Practitioners of Infection Control: overview of bioterrorism and links to electronic resources.
2. http://ec.europa.eu/health-eu/my_environment/bio_terrorism/index_en.htm European Union directory to electronic resources for the public health response to bioterrorism threats.
3. http://www.nlm.nih.gov/medlineplus/biodefenseandbioterrorism.html MedlinePlus, Health Topic, Biodefense and Bioterrorism: directory to a wide range of electronic resources on bioterrorism.
4. http://bioterrorism.slu.edu St. Louis University Center for the Study of Bioterrorism and Emerging Infections website and link directory.

5. www.hshsl.umaryland.edu/resources/terrorism.html University of Maryland Health Sciences Library directory to electronic resources on bioterrorism, including online textbooks for medical care and emergency response.
6. http://www.cidrap.umn.edu/cidrap/ University of Minnesota, Academic Health Center, Center for Infectious Disease and Research Policy Web site with news and educational links.
7. http://www.usamriid.army.mil U.S. Army Medical Research Institute of Infectious Diseases (USAMRIID) home Web site; offers links to a variety of educational, scientific, public policy, and news items regarding USAMRIID and bioterrorism.
8. www.fda.gov/oc/opacom/hottopics/bioterrorism.html U.S. Food and Drug Administration Bioterrorism Page: provides links to federal Web sites and electronic documents concerning bioterrorism.
9. www.foodsafety.gov/~fsg/bioterr.html U.S. Food and Drug Administration in conjunction with other government agencies Web page on food safety, provides links to Web sites focused on food safety and bioterrorism.
10. http://www.who.int/topics/bioterrorism/en/ World Health Organization Web site for a limited amount of news, information, and links concerning bioterrorism.

News, public policy, and opinion:

1. http://www.fas.org/programs/ssp/bio/index.html Federation of American Scientists Chemical and Biological Arms Control Program: news, public policy, links to electronic documents.
2. www.stimson.org The Stimson Centre: news and views on chemical and biological weapons.

References

1. Tucker JB. Historical trends related to bioterrorism: An empirical analysis. *Emerging Infectious Diseases.* 1999;5(4):498–504 (www.cdc.gov/ncidod/eid/vol5no4/contents.htm).
2. Rotz LD, Khan AS, Lillibridge SR, Ostroff SM, and Hughes JM. Public health assessment of potential biological terrorism agents. *Emerging Infectious Diseases.* 2002;8(2):225–230 (www.cdc.gov/ncidod/EID/vol8no2/01-0164.htm).
3. Associated-Press. Report: Army lab was missing samples. *The New York Times* January 22, 2002; nytimes.com.
4. Stern J. The prospect of domestic bioterrorism. *Clinical Microbiology Reviews.* 1999;5(4):517–522 (www.cdc.gov/ncidod/eid/vol5no4/contents.htm).
5. Cole LA. Learning from inappropriate responses. In: Novick L and Marr JS, eds., *Public Health Issues Disaster Preparedness: Focus on Bioterrorism.* Jones & Bartlett Publishers, Sudbury, MA, 2001, pp. 65–68.
6. Anonymous. Fire department response to biological threat at B'nai B'rith headquarters, Washington, DC Report 114 of the Major Fires Investigation project by Varley-Campbell and Associates, Inc., for the United States Fire Administration, Federal Emergency Management Agency, April 1997. (www.chem-bio.com/resource/tr114.pdf).
7. Henry L. SUN Profile: Harris' troubled past includes mail fraud, white supremacy. *Las Vegas Sun* 1998; www.lasvegassun.com/dossier/crime/bio/harris.html.
8. CDC. Bioterrorism alleging use of anthrax and interim guidelines for management—United States, 1998. *Morbidity and Mortality Weekly Report.* 1999;48(04):69–74.
9. CDC. Update: Investigation of bioterrorism-related anthrax and interim guidelines for clinical evaluation of persons with possible anthrax. *Morbidity and Mortality Weekly Report.* 2001;50(43):941–948.
10. Anonymous. Sacremento man charged with sending anthrax-hoax letters. Department of Justice Press Release, Sacramento Division of the Federal Bureau of Investigation, 11/13/2008 (http://sacramento.fbi.gov/dojpressrel/pressrel08/sc111138.htm).

11. Christopher GW, Cieslak TJ, Pavlin JA, and Eitzen EM. Biological warfare: A historical perspective. *Journal of the American Medical Association.* 1997;278(5):412–417.
12. Kleitmann WF and Ruoff KL. Bioterrorism: Implications for the clinical microbiologist. *Clinical Microbiology Reviews.* 2001;14:364–381.
13. Eitzen Jr, EM and Takafuji ET. Historical overview of biological warfare. In: Sidell FR, Takafuji ET, and Franz DR, eds., *Medical Aspects of Chemical and Biological Warfare.* Office of the Surgeon General at TMM Publications, Borden Institute, Walter Reed Army Medical Center, Washington, DC, 1997, pp. 415–424.
14. Kortepeter MG and Parker GW. Potential biological weapons threats. *Emerging Infectious Diseases.* 1999;5(4):523–527 (www.cdc.gov/ncidod/eid/vol5no4/contents.htm).
15. McGovern TW and Friedlander AM. Plague. In: Sidell FR, Takafuji ET, and Franz DR, eds., *Medical Aspects of Chemical and Biological Warfare.* Office of the Surgeon General at TMM Publications, Borden Institute, Walter Reed Army Medical Center, Washington, DC, 1997, pp. 479–502.
16. Davis CJ. Nuclear blindness: An overview of the biological weapons programs of the former Soviet Union and Iraq. *Emerging Infectious Diseases.* 1999;5(4):509–512 (www.cdc.gov/ncidod/eid/vol5no4/contents.htm).
17. Olson KB. Aum Shinrikyo: Once and future threat? *Emerging Infectious Diseases.* 1999;5(4):513–516 (www.cdc.gov/ncidod/eid/vol5no4/contents.htm).
18. Franz DR, Parrott CD, and Takafuji ET. The U.S. biological warfare and biological defense programs. In: Sidell FR, Takafuji ET, and Franz DR, eds. *Medical Aspects of Chemical and Biological Warfare.* Office of the Surgeon General at TMM Publications, Borden Institute, Walter Reed Army Medical Center, Washington, DC, 1997, pp. 425–436.
19. O'Neal G. Behind the biowarfare "Eight Ball." *USA Today* December 20, 2001;p. 10D.
20. Alibek K. *The Chilling True Story of the Largest Covert Biological Weapons Program, Told from the Inside by the Man Who Ran It.* Random House, Inc., New York, 1999.
21. Henderson DA. Bioterrorism as a public health threat. *Emerging Infectious Diseases.* 1999;4(3):488–492 (www.cdc.gov/ncidod/eid/vol5no4/contents.htm).
22. Friedlander AM. Anthrax. In: Sidell FR, Takafuji ET, and Franz DR, eds., *Medical Aspects of Chemical and Biological Warfare.* Office of the Surgeon General at TMM Publications, Borden Institute, Walter Reed Army Medical Center, Washington, DC, 1997, pp. 467–478.
23. Swartz MN. Recognition and management of anthrax—An update. *New England Journal of Medicine.* 2001;345(22):1621–1626.
24. Inglesby TV, Henderson DA, Bartlett JG, et al. Anthrax as a biological weapon: Medical and public health management. *Journal of the American Medical Association.* 1999;281(18):1735–1745.
25. Salyers A and Whitt D. Bioterrorism (Rapid Response Chapter). *Microbiology: Diversity, Disease, and the Environment.* Fitzgerald Science Press, Inc., Bethesda, MD, 2001 (www.fitzscipress.com).
26. Meselson M, Guillemin J, Hugh-Jones M, et al. The Sverdlovsk anthrax outbreak of 1979. *Science.* 1994;266:1202–1208.
27. Anonymous. Drugs and vaccines against biological weapons. *The Medical Letter.* 2001;43(115):87–89.
28. Russell PK. Vaccines in civilian defense against bioterrorism. *Emerging Infectious Diseases.* 1999;5(4):531–533.
29. Liedtke L. HHS statement on anthrax vaccination. Vol. 2001: Infectious Diseases Society of America and the Centers for Disease Control and Prevention, 2001.
30. Joellenbeck LM, Zwanziger LL, Durch JS, and Strom, BL, eds. Committee to assess the safety and efficacy of the anthrax vaccine, medical follow-up agency. In: *The Anthrax Vaccine: Does It Work? Is it Safe?* Institute of Medicine, National Academy of Sciences, National Academy Press, Washington, DC, 2002 (www.nap.edu).
31. Jernigan DB, Raghunathan PL, Bell BP, et al. Investigation of bioterrorism-related anthrax, United States, 2001: Epidemiologic findings. *Emerging Infectious Diseases,* 2002;8(10):1019–1028.
32. CDC. Update: Investigation of bioterrorism-related anthrax Connecticut, 2001. *Morbidity and Mortality Weekly Report.* 2001;50(48):1077–1079.
33. Weiss R and Eggen D. Additive made spores deadlier: 3 nations Known to be able to make sophisticated coating, *Washington Post,* October 25, 2001; p. A0.

34. Bhattacharjee Y and Enserink M. FBI discusses microbial forensics—But key questions remain unanswered. *Science* 2008;321(22):1026–1027.
35. Kristof ND. Profile of a killer. *The New York Times* January 4, 2002, p. A21.
36. McClain DJ. Smallpox. In: Sidell FR, Takafuji ET, and Franz DR, eds., *Medical Aspects of Chemical and Biological Warfare*. Office of the Surgeon General at TMM Publications, Borden Institute, Walter Reed Army Medical Center, Washington, DC, 1997, pp. 539–559.
37. Henderson DA, Inglesby TV, Bartlett JG, et al. Smallpox as a biological weapon: Medical and public health management. *Journal of the American Medical Association*. 1999;281(22):2127–2137.
38. Stolberg SG and Petersen M. A nation challenged: Bioterrorism; U.S. orders vast supply of vaccine for smallpox. *New York Times*, November 29, 2001.
39. Cohen HW, Gould RM, and Sidel VW. The pitfalls of bioterrorism preparedness: The anthrax and smallpox experiences. *American Journal of Public Health*. 2004;94(10):1667–1671.
40. Casey CG, Iskander, JK, Roper, MH, et al. Adverse events associated with smallpox vaccination in the United States, January–October 2003. *Journal of the American Medical Association* 2005;294(21):2734–2743.
41. Anonymous. FDA approves second-generation smallpox vaccine. U.S. Food and Drug Administrtation, *FDA News*, September 1, 2007.
42. Weinstein, I. An outbreak of smallpox in New York City. *American Journal of Public Health* 1947;37:1376–1384.
43. Evans ME and Friedlander AM. Tularemia. In: Sidell FR, Takafuji ET, and Franz DR, eds., *Medical Aspects of Chemical and Biological Warfare*. Office of the Surgeon General at TMM Publications, Borden Institute, Walter Reed Army Medical Center, Washington, DC, 1997, pp. 503–512.
44. Dennis DT, Inglesby TV, Henderson DA, et al. Tularemia as a biological weapon: Medical and public health management. *Journal of the American Medical Association*. 2001;285(21):2763–2773.
45. Oyston PC, Sjosted A, and Titball RW. Tularemia: Bioterrorism defence renews interest in Francisella tularensis. *Nature Reviews Microbiology*; 2004;2:967–978.
46. Inglesby TV, Dennis DT, Henderson DA, et al. Plague as a biological weapon: Medical and public health management. *Journal of the American Medical Association*. 2000; 283(17):2281–2289.
47. Jahrling PB. Viral hemorrhagic fevers. In: Sidell FR, Takafuji ET, and Franz DR, eds., *Medical Aspects of Chemical and Biological Warfare*. Office of the Surgeon General at TMM Publications, Borden Institute, Walter Reed Army Medical Center, Washington, DC, 1997, pp. 591–602.
48. CDC. Management of patients with suspected viral hemorrhagic fever. *Morbidity and Mortality Weekly Report*. 1988;37 (S-3):1–16.
49. Gilbert DN, Moellering RC, and Sande MA. *The Sanford Guide to Antimicrobial Therapy 2001*. 31st edition, Antimicrobial Therapy, Inc., Hyde Park, VT, 2001.
50. Middelbrook JL and Franz DR. Botulinum toxin. In: Sidell FR, Takafuji ET, and Franz DR, eds., *Medical Aspects of Chemical and Biological Warfare*. Office of the Surgeon General at TMM Publications, Borden Institute, Walter Reed Army Medical Center, Washington, DC, 1997, pp. 643–654.
51. Arnon SS, Schechter R, Inglesby TV, et al. Botulinum toxin as a biological weapon. *Journal of the American Medical Association*. 2001;285(8):1059–1070.
52. Borio LL and Gronvall GK. Anthrax countermeasures: Current status and future needs. *Biosecurity and Bioterrorism: Biodefense Strategy, Practice, and Science*. 2005;3(2):102–112.
53. Anonymous. Strategic National Stockpile. Centers for Disease Control and Prevention (http://emergency.cdc.gov/stockpile/).
54. Russell PK. Project BioShield: What it is, why it is needed, and its accomplishments so far. *Clinical Infectious Diseases* 2007:45(Suppl 1):S68–S72.

Chapter 6

Biological Terrorism: Classification and Manufacture

Mark A. Prelas

CONTENTS

Classification of Agents 80
Future of Biowarfare in the Biotechnology Age 80
Manufacturing Process 81
  Fermentation 81
    Small-Scale Fermentation 84
  Viral Production Process 84
    Small-Scale Use of Fertile Chicken Eggs 84
  Live Tissue 84
    Small-Scale Use of Live Tissue 85
  Live Animals 85
    Small-Scale Use of Live Animals 85
Conclusions 86
References 86
Bibliography 86

Biological agents are living organisms or the toxins generated by living organisms that cause disease in humans, animals, or plants. These agents can be bacteria, viruses, mycoplasma, or toxins as described in Chapter 5. The agent may be lethal or incapacitating.

Biological agents can be produced by four methods. The most common means of producing bacterial agents is by fermentation. Viral agents are most commonly produced by the inoculation of fertile eggs. Both viral and bacterial agents can be produced in live animals or in live tissue. Toxins are derived as a by-product of the growth of a biological organism just as alcohol is a by-product of the growth of yeast. Toxins can also be derived from snakes, insects, spiders, sea creatures, and plants.

Classification of Agents

Biological agents can be used as antipersonnel agents that are effective against humans. They may also be employed as antianimal, antiplant, and antimaterial agents. Antianimal agents are effective against animals. Antiplant agents are live organisms that cause disease or damage to plants. Antimaterial agents cause damage or breakdown of materials such as rubber.

Potential bacterial agents that may be used in a biological warfare include anthrax (*Bacillus anthracis*), plague (*Yersinia pestis*), tularemia (*Francisella tularensis*), salmonella (*Salmonella typhi*), and cholera (*Vibrio cholerae*). There are a host of other bacterial and antimaterial agents that can be used for domestic terrorist attack. There are many other potential bacterial agents as discussed in U.S. Army Medical Research Institute of Infectious Disease, *Biological Casualties Handbook*, 2000. Agents can also be derived from the family of organisms called rickettsiae that cause Q-fever (*Coxiella burnetii*).

Viral agents are composed of DNA (e.g., smallpox) or RNA (viral hemorrhagic fevers such as Ebola, Marburg, and Congo-Crimean) that require living cells to replicate. Examples of other viral agents are dengue, encephalitis (e.g., Venezuelan equine, West Nile, Japanese, Western equine and eastern equine), monkeypox, white pox, Rift Valley fever, Hantaan virus, and yellow fever.

Toxins are poisonous chemicals that are produced by the metabolic activities of living organisms. These agents are organic chemical compounds such as proteins, polypeptides, and alkaloids. Toxins can be categorized in two ways: neurotoxins that affect nerve impulse transmission and cytotoxins that destroy or disrupt cells. Toxins can be derived from bacteria and they can be either exotoxins (poisons that diffuse out of cells) or endotoxins (poisons contained in the cell but are released when the cell disintegrates). Toxins produced by fungi are called mycotoxins. Mycotoxins are exotoxins that include trichothecenes (which may be the source of yellow rain discussed in Chapter 7), aflatoxins (produced by *Aspergillus flavus*) and temorgens (which affect the nervous system). Toxins can be produced from plants such as castor beans (ricin), abrus seeds (abrin), and algae (anatoxin-a from blue-green algae). Finally, a number of toxins are generated by animals, such as batrachotoxin from a frog, palytoxin from soft corals, saxitoxin from shellfish, conotoxins from sea snails, tetrodotoxin from puffer fish, snake venom, and spider venom.

Future of Biowarfare in the Biotechnology Age

Just as the atomic age began in the twilight of the industrial age, we are on the threshold of the biotechnology revolution. The human genome is well in hand and we are beginning to understand the aging process. Dreamers of this age foresee a time when replacement organs can be grown, viruses can be designed to attack diseases such as cancer, and the aging process is slowed down, if not stopped. However, nature always seems to have a balance in that the promise of a technology is countered by its terror.

In his book, *Biohazard*, Ken Alibek relates a conversation with fellow Soviet bioweaponer, Lev Sandakchiev. According to Sandakchiev, it is possible to produce a "chimera virus." Chimera is a mythological beast with the head of a lion, the body of a goat, and the tail of a serpent. To a bioweaponer, it is a virus that takes the property of lethality from one organism and mixes this with the infectious property of another. According to Alibek, one of the goals of the Soviet bioweapons program was to produce a smallpox–ebola weapon. These pioneers in the biotechnology age made substantial progress using crude tools, such as the search for promising mutations in nature when a new epidemic arises, or mutations created in the growth of a large batch of agents in a Soviet bioweapon factory, or perhaps the splicing of genetic material from one agent to another. As the tools of the biotechnology age grow, so do the potential good and the potential mischief. Motivated bioweaponers of the future will likely have the tools to create the "chimera virus." It may take the form of a designer virus that can attack the genetic patterns of a specific individual or a whole ethnic group. If history has taught us one thing, it is that knowledge cannot be stopped, only slowed down. The threshold of the biotechnology age is upon us for good or for evil.

Manufacturing Process

Fermentation

Fermentation is a method of providing nutrients to biological organisms for rapid growth. A simple example of fermentation is the brewing of beer or wine. Here, the biological organism is yeast and the growth of yeast produces alcohol as the by-product. Fermentation is widely used in the pharmaceutical industry as well for production of a number of drugs. The widespread use of this technology, along with basic understanding of the processes involved, make production of biological warfare agents by fermentation rather easy. As a result, it is difficult to isolate or identify a fermentation facility that is designed or used exclusively for the production of biological agents. The home brewing of beer and wine is simple and prevalent and the presence of brewing facilities in a home would be beyond suspicion.

Fermentation can be used to produce lethal bacteria such as anthrax or toxins such as botulinum from the growth of the bacteria *Clostridium botulinum*. Two methods for fermentation can be used. The first is the batch process in which a single fill of nutrients is used and the organisms grow until the nutrients are gone. The second method is continuous fermentation where nutrients are added as organisms are taken out. We will focus on the batch fermentation process because it is easier to implement and lends itself well to the anaerobic (absence of oxygen) fermentation that is required for anthrax and botulinum toxin.

The first step in the batch fermentation process is to acquire a culture of the organism. The nutrients need to be prepared prior to the addition of the organism. The content of the nutrient mixture is highly dependent upon the organism that one wants to grow. In the case of brewing beer, malt is added as the nutrient and hops and grains are added for flavor (see Figure 6.1).

Once the nutrient is ready, the biological organism is added as shown in Figure 6.2 and the container is kept at a certain temperature that encourages growth of the organism. Other environmental conditions may be varied as well.

This basic batch fermentation process can be used for the growth of biological agents in large scale using a fermentor having a greater than 500 L capacity [1,2]. In large-scale production, the first step is to acquire a seed stock of the organism that will be grown. This seed stock can be

Figure 6.1 The author (on the left) and his colleague (Dr. Malcolm Harris) use malt as the nutrient for the fermentation process.

Figure 6.2 The biological organism (in this case yeast) is added to the nutrient. Environmental conditions such as temperature for optimum growth of the organism are then used.

obtained from many sources. For example, the United States has the American Type Culture Collection in Rockville, Maryland. Prior to an incident in April 1995 involving Larry Harris, a member of a white supremacist group in Ohio, it was feasible to order cultures of deadly organisms from the American Type Culture Collection for $35 by simply using an order form with a university letterhead. Mr. Harris tried to order three vials of plague from the American Type Culture Collection catalog. Mr. Harris did not realize that it took at least 30 days for the American Type

Culture Collection to fill an order. He became impatient after two weeks and began to make telephone calls to the American Type Culture Collection. These calls raised suspicions and a subsequent investigation revealed Mr. Harris' plot. As a result, the American Type Culture Collection has implemented strict standards in their ordering process. However, in his book *Biohazard*, Ken Alibek reported that Iraq had picked up strains of anthrax, tularemia, and VEE once targeted by the U.S. biological weapons program for weaponization from the American Type Culture Collection prior to the changes in the ordering process [1]. There are at least 90 other culture collections around the world and most are not as secure as the American Type Culture Collection.

Culture collections obtain their samples of organisms from researchers and from outbreaks of disease in the human and animal populations around the world. The animal and human populations of the world are potential incubators for the growth of biological organisms. Mutations occur in large populations of the organisms and time or outbreaks facilitate the growth of large populations, thus it is important to collect samples from each outbreak to determine if the organism has mutated and to provide a stock of material for the production of a vaccine.

As shown in Figure 6.3, the second step is to put the seed organisms into a small container or flask filled with nutrients and to mix it thoroughly. The organisms start to grow with time. The contents of the flask are then put in a larger container or midsized fermentor and mixed. The organisms are then allowed to grow in the midsized fermentor. As the organisms approach their peak population, the contents of the midsized fermentor are transferred to a larger volume or large-size fermentor with additional nutrients. The organisms are allowed to grow in the large-size fermentor until its population reaches a peak level. At this point in time, the contents of the large-size fermentor are placed in a centrifuge and the contents are separated and concentrated. In a weaponization process, additives are placed in the concentrated materials for performance purposes and the next step in the process is to dry the mixture. Once dried, the material is milled and sized. The resulting milled and sized material is then ready for use or storage. This technology exists. For example, the biological weapons program in the former Soviet Union demonstrated large-scale production of anthrax, smallpox, plague, and other agents [1,2].

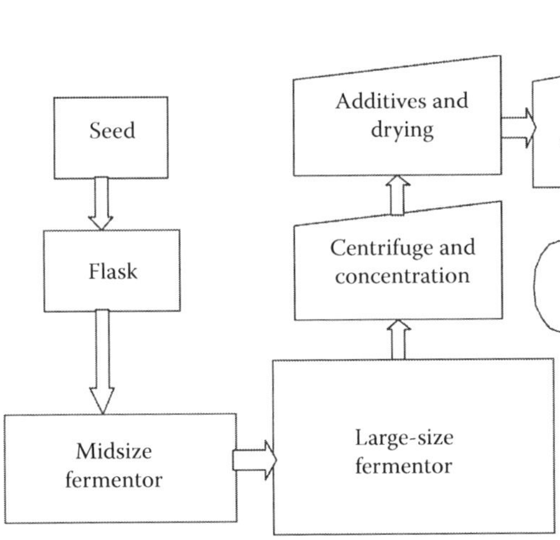

Figure 6.3 Diagram for large-scale fermentation of biological organisms.

Small-Scale Fermentation

The batch fermentation process can be adapted to the small-scale (typically less than 50 L) production of biological organisms. For example, home brewing of beer or wine is very common and equipment necessary to set up a fermentor is easily available. As described above, the process of fermentation used for beneficial biological organisms is the same process that is used for the growth of lethal biological agents. For example, it is feasible to grow *Clostridium botulinum* (the organism that produces botulism toxin) in a garbage can.

Viral Production Process

A viral agent requires the presence of cells to replicate. This requirement makes the viral agent more difficult to cultivate. Several methods are available and are discussed below.

One of the methods used for the production of viral agents is through the use of fertile chicken eggs. In this process, fertile chicken eggs are inoculated with the viral agent from the seed stock. The egg is allowed to incubate until the viral organism population has peaked. The embryo from the egg is harvested and the viral organism is concentrated with a centrifuge. The concentrated material is then collected and additives are mixed with it. The mixture is freeze dried and then this material is milled and sized. These milled and sized materials are then used or stored (see Figure 6.4).

Small-Scale Use of Fertile Chicken Eggs

The use of fertile chicken eggs as a medium for the growth of viral agents can be used on a small scale. This type of small-scale production is used in university-type laboratories. Thus, the expertise for this type of processing is widely available.

Live Tissue

Live tissue may be used for bacteria as well as viral production. The mechanism for the use of live tissue is analogous to that of viral production with fertile chicken eggs (see Figure 6.5).

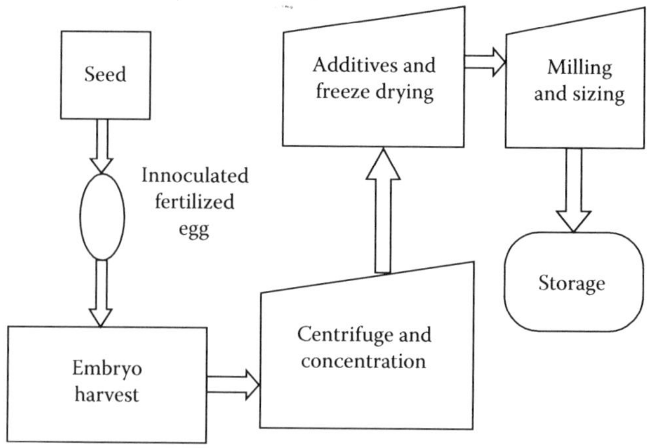

Figure 6.4 Production of viral agents with fertile chicken eggs.

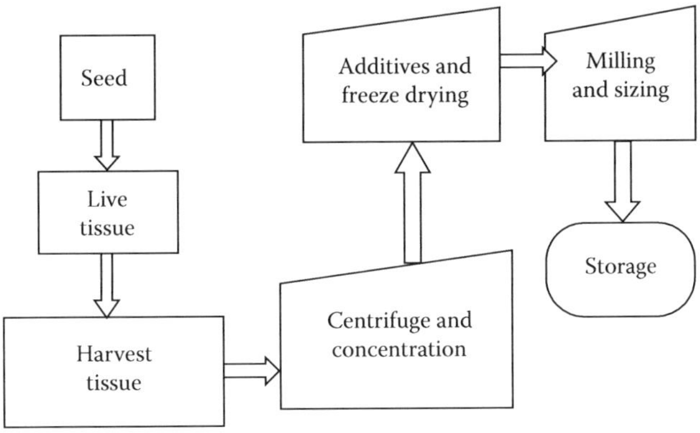

Figure 6.5 The use of live tissue in the growth of biological agents.

Small-Scale Use of Live Tissue

It is feasible to use live tissue to grow biological organisms on a small scale. For example, *Francisella tularensis* (tularemia) can be grown on blood agar plates. Blood agar is a common material used in high school biology laboratories and is widely available. Each plate is capable of producing thousands of organisms.

Live Animals

Live animals can be used to grow both viral and bacterial organisms. The method of using live animals is similar to the use of chicken embryos and live tissue (see Figure 6.6).

Small-Scale Use of Live Animals

Live animals are easily obtained and can be used virtually undetected as a means of incubating lethal biological organisms. Such an operation could occur in rural as well as urban environments.

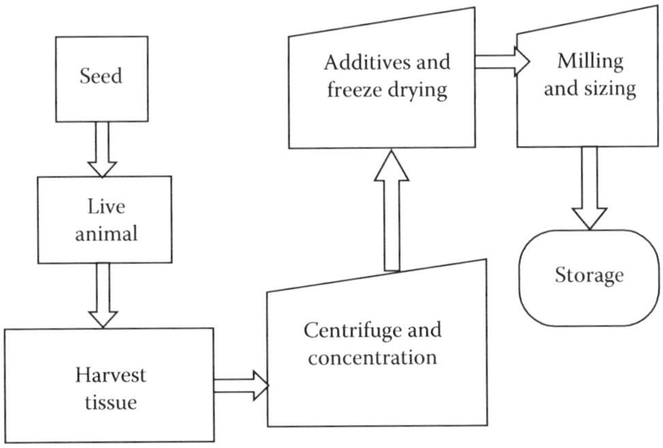

Figure 6.6 Use of a live animal for the production of biological agents.

An example of the use of live animals for the production of lethal organisms would be the inoculation of a sheep with anthrax. The sheep would serve as a host for the growth and production of anthrax. When the disease has nearly run its course, the sheep could be killed and the anthrax-bearing tissue harvested for concentration and drying.

Conclusions

Four methods for the production of biological agents were discussed in this chapter: fermentation, fertile eggs, live tissue, and live animals. The use of these methods on a large scale for the production of biological weapons is very difficult to detect, because these same methods are employed by the legitimate vaccine and pharmaceutical industries. This is why the implementation of the Biological Weapons Convention is so difficult [3]. To detect the production of biological weapons, it would require detailed inspection of vaccine or pharmaceutical production facilities in a signatory country. Because biotechnology and the pharmaceutical industries use proprietary technology and keep trade secrets, the open inspection of these industries could have important strategic and economic consequences. For example, economic espionage, the theft of trade secrets, costs the United States $250 billion per year. The FBI has recently identified 23 countries involved in this practice and the pharmaceutical industry is one of the main targets. Thus countries are not motivated to employ the strict inspection regime that the Biological Weapons Convention would need to become successful.

The only currently available means of addressing the proliferation of biological weapons is through the Australia Group, an informal organization of 30 members. The Australia Group is committed to ensuring that the export of materials and equipment useful for the production of chemical and biological weapons from the member countries is curtailed [4].

To make matters even more interesting, each of the production methods described in this chapter is adaptable to small-scale production and is virtually undetectable. Advancements in biotechnology will only enhance the access to new and more lethal organisms.

In the view of the author, biotechnology will present a more dangerous and complex nonproliferation problem than any other technology for the production of weapons of mass destruction.

References

1. K Alibek. *Biohazard.* New York: Random House, 1999.
2. G Bozheyeva, Y Kunakbayev, and Y Yeleukenov. *Former Soviet Biological Weapons Facilities in Kazakhstan: Past, Present, and Future.* Monterey, CA: Monterey Institute of International Studies, Center for Non-Proliferation Studies, June 1999 (http://cns.miis.edu/pubs/opapers /op1/index.htm).
3. BWC (Biological Weapons Convention). Washington, DC: U.S. Department of State, 1972 (http://www.state.gov/www/global/arms/treaties/bwc1.html).
4. AG (Australia Group), *Fact Sheet Released by the Bureau of Nonproliferation*, Washington, DC: U.S. Department of State, April 1, 2000 (http://www.state.gov/www/global/arms/bureau_np/000401_ag.html).

Bibliography

Center for Defense and International Security Studies (CDISS), 2000 (http://www.cdiss.org/cruise1.htm).

GW Christopher, TJ Cieslak, JA Pavlin, and EM Eitzen, Jr. Biological warfare: A historical perspective. *Journal of the American Medical Association.* 6: 412–418, August 1997.

FAS (Federation of American Scientists). *Biological Weapons* (http://www.fas.org/nuke/guide/usa/cbw/bw.htm).
SM Hersh. *Chemical and Biological Warfare*. Garden City, NY: Doubleday and Company, Inc., 1969.
Militarily Critical Technologies (MCT) Part II. *Weapons of Mass Destruction Technologies (WMD)*. February 1998 (http://www.dtic.mil/mctl).
L Pringle. *Chemical and Biological Warfare: The Cruelest Weapons*. Hillside, NJ: Enslow Publishers, Inc., 1993.
E Regis. *The Biology of Doom*. New York: Henry Holt and Company, 1999.
U.S. Army 1. *Medical Research Institute of Infectious Disease*, 2000 (http://www.biomedtraining.org/materials.htm).
U.S. Army 2. *The Army Tactical Missile System*, Special Text 6-60-30, 2000 (www.army.mil/gunnery/manuals/afom/afom.doc).
RD Walpole. Intelligence related to possible sources of biological agent exposure during the Persian Gulf war, 2000 (http://www.gulflink.osd.mil/library/43917.htm).

Chapter 7

Biological Terrorism: Weaponization and Delivery Systems

Mark A. Prelas

CONTENTS

History of Biological Weapons 90
Munitions 93
Small-Scale Deployment 96
Conclusions 96
Appendix A Calculation of the Mass of Infectious Organisms Required to Produce a Lethal Dose-50 (LD_{50}) in a Volume, V 97
References 98
Bibliography 98

The specter of biological weapons has haunted mankind for nearly a 1000 years. Until recently, biological weapons have been viewed as strategic weapons. As a strategic military tool, biological weapons are very limited. They are highly dependent upon the weather, temperature, wind direction, wind speed, and other factors that cannot be controlled. However, with the proliferation of information that an open society offers, the know-how to develop and use biological weapons is becoming available to individuals. Thus, biological weapons must now be viewed as a much broader threat. Biological weapons have a psychological effect upon people as they can create terror among the masses. This makes biological weapons an ideal tool for terrorism.

We review here the weaponization of biological agents and the delivery systems that were designed for the efficient dispersal of the agents both for military and domestic terrorist attacks.

History of Biological Weapons

We begin our examination of the uses of biological weapons in the pre–World War II era.

- The use of biological agents is believed to have happened much earlier than that recorded in history. One of the first uses of biological agents occurred in 1346 during the siege of the Genoese city of Caffa (located in present day Feodossia, Ukraine). The Tartars, believing that the Europeans were responsible for an epidemic of the plague in Asia, initiated a siege against the Genoese-controlled city. The cadavers of plague victims were catapulted into Genoese city [1]. One of the significant dangers of using biological weapons manifested itself in the siege of Caffa. A few Genoese merchants escaped Caffa by sailing home and took the illness with them. Ships with infected rats arrived from Caffa at the port of Messina, Sicily in 1347, and the disease spread from there. Europe was plunged into an epidemic, and after five years, 25 million people, or about one-third of Europe's people, were killed. The impact of the plague was probably magnified by the superstitions of Europeans who believed that cats, the natural predator of rats, were witches. Cats were killed because of this superstition. This epidemic was referred to as the "black death."
- In 1710, during the war between Russia and Sweden, Russia adopted the Tartar tactic from the siege of Caffa and used the bodies of plague victims to expose Swedish soldiers.
- Perhaps the most effective use of a biological agent in warfare occurred during the French and Indian War of 1776. Sir Jėffery Amherst ordered the use of blankets and handkerchiefs that had been used in a smallpox hospital to be delivered to the Indians loyal to France [2]. An officer who delivered the infected cloth wrote in his journal "I hope it will have the desired effect." Indeed, it may have had its desired effect. Sir Jeffery Amherst was able to take Fort Carlillon due to the weakened state of the Indians and he renamed it Fort Ticonderoga.
- In 1917, during World War I, German agents infected allied horses and cattle with glanders before they were shipped to the European front.

The means of finding effective biological agents and delivering those agents to the enemy is a complex problem. Not until the application of twentieth century science did biological agents become a legitimate military threat. The era from World War II to the present represents the application of twentieth century science to the weaponization of biological agents. As is known from aerosol science (see Chapter 4) particles with a mean distribution of below 5 μm are the most effective way of infecting a human (host) with a biological agent. The weaponization of a biological organism requires

- Good agent properties: virulence, stability to heat, stability in air, stability in humidity, stability to ultraviolet light, can be concentrated, can be dried, can be made into 1–5 μm particles and can survive in aerosol form.
- Munitions: biological agents have to be delivered to the target efficiently.
- Meteorological conditions: atmospheric conditions such as wind speed, wind direction, and humidity need to be optimum. If the wind blows in the wrong direction, the agent will not disperse over the target. If it is raining, then the aerosol washes out of the air.
- Method of dissemination: spray (line source) or explosion (point source).

If the agent is sensitive, an explosion might destroy it. The start of the modern era of the biological weapons began with the Japanese biological weapon program with the formation of Unit 731 between 1937 and 1945. Unit 731 performed experiments on Chinese, Russian, and American prisoners to determine which diseases could best serve as weapons. The program successfully used a biological weapon in 1940. Japan dropped plague-infected fleas on areas in China and Manchuria and caused the outbreak of plague [1,3].

The U.S. program began in 1941, when intelligence indicated that Germany and Japan were involved in biological weapons research. Secretary of War, Henry L. Stimson, requested the National Academy of Science to review the feasibility of manufacturing biological weapons. In 1942, a committee formed by the National Academy of Science concluded that biological weapons were feasible. As a result, George W. Merk was asked by the Secretary of War to form the War Reserve Service. Camp Detrick in Fredrick, Maryland, was chosen as the War Reserve Service's primary site. The site became operational in 1943. In 1944, Dugway proving grounds in Utah was established as a test center for the program. Additionally, a production plant was built in Terre Haute, Indiana. During 1947–1949, small-scale tests of simulated biological agents, *Bacillus globigii* (BG) and *Serratia marscens* (SM), were performed at Camp Detrick. *Serratia marscens* is a harmless bacterium that is easily tracked due to its bright red color. For example, instructors in medical schools used it to demonstrate the transmission mechanisms for infectious diseases. An instructor would put the organism in his or her mouth and then lecture. The organism would be captured on plates covered with nutrients around the room. The next day, the dispersion of SM around the room could be seen on the plates by its characteristic color. *Bacillus globigii* is used as a simulant for anthrax because it too forms a spore-like anthrax, but it is harmless to humans.

In 1950, the U.S. biological weapons program was extended due to the Korean War. An anticrop bomb was developed by 1951 and was placed into production. The U.S. program had looked at 2000 potential plant pathogens. Of those, 551 could be potential threats to our agricultural industry. These include rice blast, late blight of potato, stem rust of wheat, stem rust of rye, southern corn leaf blight, and citrus canker.

In 1953, the Camp Detrick program was expanded and the construction of large-scale production of biological agents was underway. A large-scale production facility was established in Pine Bluff, Arkansas, and it became operational in the same year. By 1954, tularemia was being produced at the Pine Bluff plant.

Soviet Minister Marshal Zhukov added fuel to the fire in 1955 when he stated that the USSR would use chemical and biological weapons in future wars. From 1959 to 1969, the military services submitted requirements for biological weapon munitions including artillery shells, missiles, drones, and other weapons. With emphasis on munitions, the Desert Test Center (DTC) was established at Ft. Douglas, Salt Lake City in 1962. In 1964–1966, the virus and rickettsiae production plants were built at Pine Bluff, Arkansas.

The United States also engaged in simulations, using harmless bacterium, to demonstrate the potential of biological weapons [3,4]. In 1949, attack teams with sprayers introduced SM into the intake vents of the Pentagon's air conditioning system. Had this been a real anthrax attack, half of the military's top command would have been killed. This simulated attack convinced the military that biological weapons were a threat.

To demonstrate the threat to the U.S. population, in April of 1950, the USS *Coral Sea* and USS *K. D. Bailey* sprayed both SM and BG into the wind blowing toward Norfolk, Hampton, and Newport News, Virginia. The tests demonstrated that U.S. coastal cities could be threatened by a biological attack.

In September 1950, about 2 mi off the cost of San Francisco, U.S. Navy ships sprayed SM, BG, and a cloud of fluorescent particles, along a dissemination line of 3 mi length. The material was collected at monitoring stations around the bay area. The fluorescent particles (FP) deposited throughout the city's streets and sidewalks and at night and under ultraviolet light glowed like stars. Traces of SM, BG, and FP were found as far away as 23 mi. If the organism had been anthrax, it would have produced lethal doses in an area of about 50 mi^2.

A series of tests were designed to show that a large-scale attack with biological weapons was feasible. On December 2, 1957, an *AC-119* sprayed an area from South Dakota to International Falls, Minnesota, with FP while a cold air front was moving down from Canada. Particles were detected 1200 mi away in New York State.

A plane flying from Toledo, Ohio, to Abilene, Texas, and a second plane flying from Detroit, Michigan, to Goodland, Kansas, sprayed about 40 lb of FP per minute. Sampling stations on the ground proved that large areas of the country could be attacked with biological weapons.

A jet aircraft equipped with a BG sprayer flew a predetermined pattern near Victoria, Texas. The BG was found as far east as the Florida Keys.

Travelers at the Greyhound Bus terminal in Washington, DC, and the Washington National Airport, Washington, DC, were subjected to BG in October 1965. Scientists walked through the bus terminal and the airport and sprayed the bacterium into the air without being detected. Aerosol traps were placed at strategic points to capture the bacterium as it moved through the air.

A light bulb filled with BG was dropped on the tracks in the New York City subway in June 1966. BG spread throughout the subway system within 20 min. Monitoring of the BG demonstrated that even this small amount of material, had it been anthrax, could have killed thousands of people.

Overall, more than 200 tests were performed to demonstrate the potential of biological weapons. This research culminated between 1964 and 1968 with a series of tests at facilities in the Pacific including the well-known project SHADY GROVE. The tests demonstrated that a single weapon was able to cover 2400 km^2 with 30 percent casualties [3].

President Nixon of the United States renounced the use of biological weapons in 1969. This marked the beginning of the end of the U.S. biological weapons program. Between 1970 and 1972, all biological weapon stocks were destroyed, and, in 1975 President Ford signed the Biological Weapons Convention along with 144 countries.

The biological weapons program in the USSR has been shrouded in secrecy since its inception in the 1920s. The first weapons used were low-flying airplanes with crop sprayers. After World War II, bombers armed with an explosive dispersion system were added. However, until the defection of Vladimir Pasechnik in 1989 and Ken Alibek (formerly Kanatjan Alibekov) in 1992 the full extent of the USSR program was not known [5]. After signing the Biological Weapons Convention in 1972, the USSR developed an extensive program for the production of biological agents in sufficient quantities to load multiple-warhead ballistic missiles and cruise missiles. An extensive network of production facilities were built for the Ministry of Defense under the direction of the Fifteenth Directorate, the Ministry of Medical and Microbiological Industries under the direction of Biopreparat, the Ministry of Health under the Second and Third Main Directorate, and the Ministry of Agriculture under the direction of the Main Directorate for Industrial Production and Scientific Enterprise [5]. Techniques were developed for the weaponization of anthrax (antibiotic resistant), brucella, smallpox, tularemia, Q-fever, glanders, plague, Marburg variant U, Lassa fever, monkeypox, and Ebola. By 1987 the USSR could produce 5000 tons of anthrax per year or 80–100 tons of smallpox per year [5]. Of most concern was the USSR's program to genetically engineer new agents [5].

The Russian government has opened many of the Biopreparat sites to the international community. Dr. Alibek has expressed his concern, however, that many of the sites of the Fifteenth Directorate are still not open to the west for inspection.

Munitions

The weaponization of biological agents requires that they be dispersed by the most effective means possible. Military weapons dispense and disperse their submunitions payload from a primary unit to maximize the spread of the biological agent by the delivery system. The primary unit is the shell, missile, or cruise missile that carries the submunitions (Figure 7.1).

Dissemination of biological agents may be achieved by releasing or discharging the agents from munitions or submunitions by a pressurized gas or an explosive to form an aerosol. The stability of the agent determines if the agent can be released by explosives or by pressurized gas. The submunitions can be of the spherical design, as shown in Figure 7.1, or a Flettner rotor design for wider dispersal patterns. Less sophisticated designs, such as a dart or a cylinder, can be used for a more compact dispersal pattern.

The system does not have to be complex to be of concern. Iraq purchased the widely available R-400 bomb for biological agent dispersal [7]. A diagram of how the R-400 can be adopted for biological agent dispersal is shown in Figure 7.2.

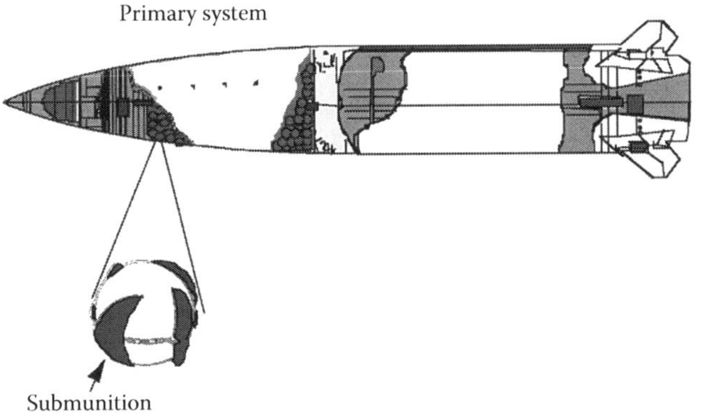

Figure 7.1 Primary system loaded with submunitions. (Data from U.S. Army 2. The Army Tactical Missile System. Special Text 6-60-30, 2000, www.army.mil/gunnery/manuals/afom/afom.doc.)

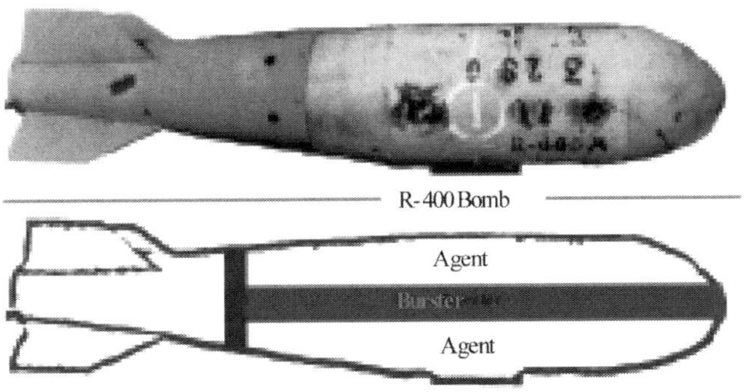

Figure 7.2 Use of an R-400 bomb for biological agent dispersal.

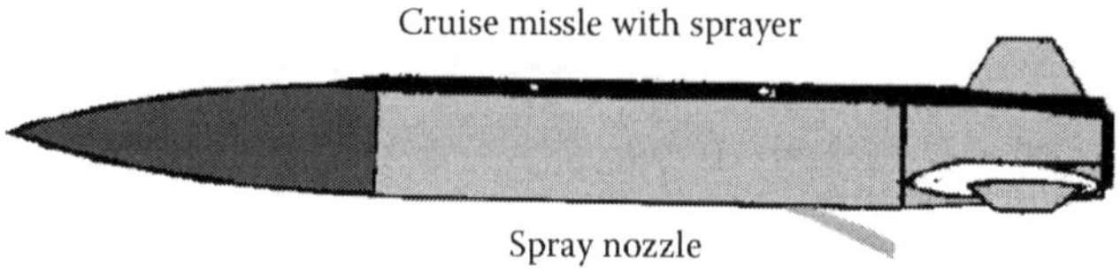

Figure 7.3 A cruise missile equipped with a sprayer (similar to the Russian made TMU-28/B).

It is possible to use sprayers mounted on cruise missiles to disperse biological agents. This method produces a line source and is a very efficient means of disseminating biological agents (see Figure 7.3). Due to the proliferation of cruise missiles, this possibility is very real [8].

Biological agents can be ingested in the gastrointestinal system, they can be introduced into the lungs by aerosols, or the skin may absorb the agent. In modern biological weapons, the dispersal method of choice is by aerosols. Specifically, particles with 1–5 μm diameter are called the primary aerosol. The primary aerosol flows rather easily and a person becomes infected because he or she is breathing at a rate of 10–20 L of air per minute. Each aerosol particle will contain a number of infectious organisms. The goal of dissemination of biological agents is to put as many infectious organisms in the vulnerable areas of the human body as possible. Aerosol particles having diameter in the range of 18–20 μm deposit in the sinus. The sinus is the least infectious area of the pulmonary system. Particles of 15–18 micrometer in diameter can deposit in the throat. The throat is a slightly more infectious area than the sinus. Particles in the range of 7–12 μm in diameter will deposit in the esophagus. This area is more infectious than the throat but is not the most sensitive region. The most infectious area is in the lungs where particles of 4–6 μm deposit in the bronchioles and particles of 1–3 μm deposit in the alveoli. Alveoli are the most vulnerable areas within the lungs. Therefore, an ideal biological weapon would be one that would disperse biological aerosols in the size range of 1–3 μm in diameter. Table 7.1 shows the infective dose of various biological agents. This table also points out whether or not an infected person would transmit the disease to another person by coughing or by other mechanisms [9].

The number of organisms required to cause an infection is the next important factor because it determines the number of aerosol particles that must be deposited. In Table 7.1, the number of organisms required to infect a human host is shown for several biological organisms. In addition, the table indicates if the organism can be passed from a person who is infected to another person.

With the infective dose and assumptions about the number of microorganisms per aerosol particle, one can calculate the amount of aerosol that is required to infect a building of 1 km^2 in area (see Appendix A).

We introduce here the concept of the LD_{50}—lethal dose (LD)—that will kill 50 percent of the exposed population. Biological agents are the most effective weapons (as compared to chemical and nuclear weapons) in terms of the amount of material needed for lethality (see Table 7.2).

Biological weapons can impact a larger area than nuclear or chemical weapons (see Table 7.3). Biological weapons are less expensive than nuclear or chemical weapons.

It is important to note that Table 7.3 assumes ideal weather conditions for the dispersion of chemical and biological agents.

Table 7.1 Infective Dose of an Organism and Potential Transmission from One Person to Another

Disease	*Transmits Human to Human*	*Infective Dose (Aerosol)*
Inhalation anthrax	No	8,000–50,000 spores
Brucellosis	No	10–100 organisms
Cholera	Rare	10–500 organisms
Glanders	Low	Assumed low
Pneumonic plague	High	100–500 organisms
Tularemia	No	10–50 organisms
Q fever	Rare	1–10 organisms
Smallpox	High	Assumed low (10–100 organisms)
Venezuelan equine encephalitis	Low	10–100 organisms
Viral hemorrhagic fevers	Moderate	1–10 organisms
Botulism	No	0.001 μg/kg is LD_{50} for type A
Staph. Enterotoxin B	No	0.03 μg/person incapacitation
Ricin	No	3–5 μg/kg is LD_{50} in mice
T-2 Mycotoxins	No	Moderate

Source: U.S. Army 1. Medical Research Institute of Infectious Disease, 2000, http://www.biomed-training.org/materials.htm.

Table 7.2 Amount of Biological Agent Required to Produce a LD_{50} in a 1 km^2 Area

Agent	*Kilograms of Agent Required to Produce a LD_{50} over 1 km^2*
Anthrax	0.007
Plague	0.00009
SEB	40
Botulinum	60
Ricin	600

Table 7.3 Relative Comparisons of the Destruction Power of Nuclear, Chemical, and Biological Weapons

Parameter	*Nuclear*	*Chemical*	*Biological*
Affected area (mi^2)	~100	~100	~2,000
Human lethality	98 percent	30 percent	Up to 75 percent depending on agent
Residual effect	Six months of radioactive fallout on ~1000 mi^2	3–36 hours over the same area	Potential epidemic depending on agent
Time for effect	Milliseconds	Seconds	Days
Property damage	~40 mi^2	None	None

Small-Scale Deployment

Biological weapons can be successfully deployed on a small scale. For example, in September of 2001, weapons grade anthrax was sent through the mail in envelopes to various broadcasting news channels [10]. The letters also went to U.S. Senators Tom Daschle and Patrick J. Leahy. At the time of this writing, the source of the anthrax was unknown, however it was of a weapon grade comparable to material developed by the United States earlier [11,12]. The particles making up the powder did not have an electrostatic charge and thus did not agglomerate. Material of this quality can be disseminated by a variety of methods. These may include spraying (from a dry powder garden sprayer to a crop duster), airborne release from a container (such as breaking a glass jar), to just throwing it into the air.

A highly infectious agent such as smallpox could be a devastating weapon even on a small scale. Due to the eradication of smallpox in 1972, the natural resistance to the smallpox virus in the human population should be fairly weak. Additionally, smallpox vaccinations given prior to 1972 are probably no longer effective. Officially, there should be only two seed samples of live smallpox virus left in the world, one in the United States and the another in Russia. However, one cannot discount the possibility of the existence of other samples. If a terrorist were to be exposed to smallpox, it would be feasible for that terrorist to infect a planeload of people on a long haul flight while in the infectious stages of the disease. Given the nature of travel across borders today as compared to 1972, it would be very difficult to implement quarantine along with vaccination as a means of containment. There is a potential of spreading smallpox worldwide.

Conclusions

The biological weapons programs of the United States and the former USSR committed substantial resources to the understanding of the science and technology. Biological agents were weaponized. Information from these programs is filtering out into the public domain and is the cause of great concern for the proliferation of biological weapons. There is little doubt that the technology has proliferated to other countries. Even groups, cults, and individuals are beginning to acquire the knowledge. There are recent examples. Aum Shinrikyo tried to deploy anthrax in Japan several times from 1993 to 1995 but failed [5]. In addition, at the time of this writing, *The Times of London* reported that it had discovered documentation in Afghanistan that Al-Qaeda had a keen interest in developing biological weapons [13].

Appendix A Calculation of the Mass of Infectious Organisms Required to Produce a Lethal Dose-50 (LD_{50}) in a Volume, *V*

Consider M (kg) of aerosol infected with biological organisms that is dispersed in a volume [V (m^3)] of air. Using simplifying assumptions, the mass concentration, assuming no settling and other losses, is given by

$$\frac{M}{V}\ (\mathrm{kg/m^3}) \tag{7.A.1}$$

Assuming an average particle diameter of d, the number concentration is

$$N = \frac{M/V}{\pi d^3 \rho/6}\ (\text{number of particles/m}^3\text{ of air}) \tag{7.A.2}$$

where ρ is the average density of the particles in kg/m^3. If each aerosol particle contains J organisms, then the number of organisms per cubic meter of air (N_o) is

$$N_o = NJ\left(\frac{\text{organisms}}{\mathrm{m}^3}\right) \tag{7.A.3}$$

If the volume of air that an average person breathes in per minute is V_b (m^3/minute), the rate of organisms (R_o) that a person breathes in per minute is

$$R_o = N_o V_b\left(\frac{\text{organisms}}{\text{minute}}\right) \tag{7.A.4}$$

A lethal dose-50 (LD_{50}) is the number of organisms that would cause the death of 50 percent of the people receiving that dose. To receive a LD_{50}, an average person would need to accumulate a total of A organisms/LD_{50}. Thus, the multiples of LD_{50} (X) accumulated over an exposure time of T (minutes) is

$$X = \frac{A}{TR_o} \tag{7.A.5}$$

Assuming that X is a single multiple of LD_{50} over the exposure time, one can set Equation 7.A.5 equal to one and then derive Equation 7.A.6 using Equations 7.A.3 and 7.A.2. Equation 7.A.6 is a formula for the required mass of aerosol to infect a given volume of space with one LD_{50} over an exposure time of T using simplified assumptions.

$$M = \frac{A(V/TV_b)(\pi d^3 \rho/6)}{J}\ (\mathrm{kg}) \tag{7.A.6}$$

References

1. L Pringle. *Chemical and Biological Warfare: The Cruelest Weapons*. Hillside, NJ: Enslow Publishers, Inc., 1993.
2. GW Christopher, TJ Cieslak, JA Pavlin, and EM Eitzen, Jr. Biological warfare: A historical perspective. *Journal of the American Medical Association* 6: 412–418, Aug 1997.
3. E Regis. *The Biology of Doom*. New York: Henry Holt & Company, 1999.
4. FAS (Federation of American Scientists). *Biological Weapons* (http://www.fas.org/nuke/guide/usa/cbw/bw.htm, last date accessed on 07/09/09).
5. K Alibek. *Biohazard*. New York: Random House, 1999.
6. U.S. Army 2. The Army Tactical Missile System. Special Text 6-60-30, 2000 (www.army.mil/gunnery/manuals/afom/afom.doc).
7. RD Walpole. Intelligence related to possible sources of biological agent exposure during the Persian Gulf war, 2000 (http://www.gulflink.osd.mil/library/43917.htm).
8. Centre for Defence and International Security Studies (CDISS), 2000 (http://www.cdiss.org/cruise1.htm).
9. U.S. Army 1. Medical Research Institute of Infectious Disease, 2000 (http://www.biomedtraining.org/materials.htm).
10. E Lipton and J Kirk. Months later, scientists know where anthrax outbreak began. *St. Louis Post Dispatch*. December 26, 2001. (http://home.post-dispatch.com/channel/pdweb.nsf/TodayWednesday/86256A0E0068FE5086 256B2E003C2973?OpenDocument&PubWrapper=A-section).
11. WJ Broad. Terror anthrax linked to type made by U.S. *New York Times*, December 3, 2001 (http://www.nytimes.com/2001/12/03/national/03POWD.html).
12. WJ Broad and J Miller. A nation challenged: The investigation; U.S. recently produced anthrax in a highly lethal powder form. *New York Times*, December 13, 2001 (http://query.nytimes.com/search/abstract?res=F20F16FF385B0C708DDDAB0994D9404482).
13. A Loyd. Scientists confirm Bin Laden weapons tests. *The Times*, London, U.K., December 29, 2001.

Bibliography

W Allen. Army tests conducted here in the 1950s showed how biological agent might spread. Zinc cadmium sulfide particles were sprayed from street corners in a city. *St. Louis Post-Dispatch (MO)*, September 20, 2001, p. A10.

General Accounting Office. *Biological Weapons, GAO/NSIAD-00-138*, Effort to reduce former soviet threat offers benefits, poses new risks. April 2000.

General Accounting Office. *Bioterrorism, GAO-01-915* Federal Research and Preparedness Activities. September 2001.

SM Hersh. *Chemical and Biological Warfare*. Garden City, NY: Doubleday and Company, Inc., 1969.

B Lambrecht. Planning for bioterrorism attack takes on a new urgency for U.S. government prepares for worst-case scenario with drills, training. *St. Louis Post Dispatch (MO)*, September 20, 2001, p. A10.

Chapter 8

Biological Terrorism: Sensors and Detection Systems

Tushar K. Ghosh and Mark A. Prelas

CONTENTS

Introduction 100
Detection of Biological Agents in the Environment 101
 Standoff Detection 101
Point Detection 103
 Sampling Devices 104
  Viable Particle-Size Impactors 104
  Virtual Impactors 106
  Cyclone Sampler 107
  Bubblers/Impingers 108
 High Air Volume Collectors 109
 Surface Sampling 109
 Nonspecific Detection 112
  Aerodynamic Particle Sizing 112
  Fluorescent Aerodynamic Particle Sizer 113
  Flow Cytometry 114
  Portable Biofluorescence 116
 Specific Detection Technologies 118
  Mass Spectroscopy-Based Identification 118
 Identification by Targeting at the Molecular Level 123
  Nucleic Acid-Based Identification Systems 124
  Q-PCR 125
  Immunoassay-Based Identification Systems 127

Simultaneous Detection of Multiple Agents 136
NRL Array Biosensors 136
Quantum Dots Multicomponent Detection 136
No-Tag Biosensors 139
Surface Plasmon Resonance 140
Interferometer Biosensors 140
Piezoelectric Crystal Balance 141
Resonant Mirror Biosensors 142
Promising Technologies on the Horizon 143
Charge-Based Deep Level Transient Spectroscopy (Q-DLTS) 143
Up-Converting Phosphor Technology 144
Spectroscopic Methods 144
Cell- and Tissue-Based Biosensors 145
Conclusion 148
References 148

Introduction

The detection of biological agents used for bioterrorism is a challenging task, particularly in the outdoor environment. The shortcomings of the biological agent detection systems became rather obvious during the Persian Gulf War of 1991. A number of pathogens could not be detected immediately because of the limitations and capabilities of the technology that was available at that time. During the Gulf War, 17 research and development systems were deployed to the Gulf region to monitor the air for suspected Iraqi biological warfare agents. Twelve of the 17 systems were mobile and the remaining 5 systems were static, employed at critical logistic facilities. The mobile systems consisted of high-volume air samplers and sensitive membrane antigen rapid test (SMART) identification tickets. The static systems had a commercial aerosol sampler with SMART tickets. The mobile units were mounted on Humvees and on Isuzu Troopers equipped with high-volume XM-2 air samplers. The XM-2 air samplers had low reliability and an unacceptable false alarm rate [1]. Most of these detection systems can be used for domestic applications because of the similarities in the agents that can be employed both in warfare and in terrorism. Although there are similarities in the detection systems for the battlefield and domestic counterterrorism, the needs of domestic counterterrorism differ in several major respects from their battlefield counterpart:

1. Domestic detection systems must deal with a much broader range of agents.
2. The false positive requirements are much more demanding for domestic protection.
3. Detecting an attack in the vast urban population will be extremely difficult.
4. There is much less supporting infrastructure in civilian populations.
5. The detection system must meet the needs of local law enforcement personnel, fire fighters, public health officials, and others who would likely be first on the scene following a biological attack.

The identification of biological organisms within minutes and at the parts per billion to parts per trillion concentration levels is a challenging task. A number of detection systems have been developed since the Persian Gulf War by taking advantage of the advancement in genomics, biotechnology, microengineering, and microcomputers. Although the detection systems for biological agents can be broadly classified as (a) the detection of biological agents in clinical samples and (b) the detection of biological agents in the environment, the difference between the two systems is mainly in the collection of samples. Once a sample is collected (whether from patients or environment), the same methodologies and equipment can be used for specific detection and identification of the biological agents.

Detection of Biological Agents in the Environment

Real-time detection and measurement of biological agents in the environment is daunting. A myriad of microorganisms are present in the environment and each organism has its own signature. Also, the number of biological agents that could be employed in a terrorist attack is much larger compared to the number in biological warfare. Most detection schemes are specific for a particular biological agent. As a result, civilian agencies currently do not have the capability at any level to detect a broad range of biological agents. A number of military units, most notably the Army's Technical Escort Unit, the U.S. Marine Corps Chemical Biological Incident Response Force, and the Army Chemical Corps, presently have some first-generation technology available.

Detection technologies are categorized by their requirement to come in direct physical contact with the biological agent. Depending on the need, the detection system architecture and sensors involved will be different. For early warning of a biological event, a "standoff" detection system may be sufficient. However, to take countermeasures, diagnostic capability would require "point" detection. For early warning, sensitivity of the detection system is not important. The presence of live biological agents needs to be determined. Specificity of the biological agents is not important. This is also true for the control of contaminated environments, determination of decontamination efficacy, and threat assessment. Generally, the concentration level has to be far in excess of the infectious dose limit to infect or kill someone. Determination of dose level will require specific identification of the biological agents, and thus a point detection system would be required. Also, for cleanup and reoccupation of contaminated areas, point detectors will be useful.

Standoff Detection

In a standoff detection system, detection is accomplished from a distance and does not require direct physical contact. Threat scenarios involving releases of biological agents as a line source upwind from the target are likely to happen in the battlefield; however a similar tactic may be used in domestic terrorism. Most of the agents for domestic terrorism can be delivered as aerosols. Therefore, standoff monitors may be aimed at detecting particles of biological nature in distant clouds. Generally, the size range of the biological particles is from 0.5 to 5 μm. Standoff systems can be either active or passive. In active mode, a laser beam is focused on the target and the return energy is continuously analyzed for signature of biological agent. In a passive mode an infrared sensor is used to track, detect, and collect data from particles of biological origin by analyzing their emitted energy.

Standoff detection offers safe, real-time determination of particulates or aerosols in the atmosphere by utilizing lasers, infrared and Raman spectroscopy, and fluorescence [2]. The application of these devices is somewhat limited by their range, which is typically several kilometers. This can limit their use for urban bioterrorism scenarios. However, these devices may be used for monitoring predetermined, high-risk sites or large public gathering places, such as stadiums, for aerosol clouds. Standoff detection is generally based on Light Detection And Ranging (LIDAR) system. A LIDAR system can be operated either in passive or in active mode.

In the passive mode, the backscattering of laser light is utilized to determine the size and spatial distribution of airborne particles. The technique cannot distinguish biological particles from nonbiological particles. It determines the particle size distribution in the cloud, and the abrupt increase of particles in the range from 1 to 5 μm in diameter is monitored. The Los Alamos National Laboratory developed a LIDAR detection system using a 1.55 μm wavelength optically pumped oscillator laser that operates at 100 Hz, with 0.5 J per pulse [3]. It utilizes an InGaAs detector with an 86 percent optical efficiency, a telescope of 75 cm in diameter, and a field view of 150 μrad. The complete unit is mounted on a helicopter and is capable of aerosol tracking and mapping at distances up to 50 km. A typical long-range LIDAR system is shown in Figure 8.1.

When operating a LIDAR system in active mode, the thermal emissions from a given direction are monitored. Fibertek Inc. [4] has developed a short range biological standoff detection system for military use that can be used in active mode. The infrared unit can provide cloud detection, acquisition and tracking capability, while the UV unit provides real-time detection and discrimination between the biological and nonbiological aerosols using ultraviolet laser-induced fluorescence (LIF). The presence of tryptophan is detected. Because all living organisms have tryptophan, identification of specific organisms because of the similarity of their emission spectra is not possible.

Figure 8.1 A long-range LIDAR system. (From Military Analysis Network, http://www.fas.org/man/dod-101/sys/land/lr-bsds.htm.)

The Naval Research Laboratory and Research International [6] have developed a small, model airplane-like, unmanned aerial vehicle (UAV) for standoff detection. The size of UAVs can range from a few inches to a foot and carry sensors on-board capable of downloading data to a ground-based control system. Prototype vehicles have been successfully demonstrated in cities and inside buildings as well as in outdoor terrains. Furthermore, they are reusable and easily transported. In the event of biological agents being released in a building, such vehicles could locate "hot zones" and monitor decontamination efficacy, reducing human exposure and risk. Later, the Naval Research Laboratory developed a remote biosensor using a fiber-optic-based sensor [7]. The complete unit contained an automated fluidics unit for immunoassays, a cyclone sampler, a radio transceiver, and batteries weighing about 4.5 kg, and was loaded on a remotely piloted airplane. This remote biosensor was able to collect bioaerosols in flight, identify them, and transmit back to the ground operator.

Prasad and his coworkers [8] have designed a new eye-safe portable digital LIDAR (PDL) for the detection of biological agents. The detection system consisted of an 8 in. telescope, $<10\,\mu J$/pulse energy at 2.5 kHz, photon counting digital detection, and 2 s averaging. Two tests were carried out at Dugway Proving Grounds. The portable LIDAR system was able to differentiate between natural and unusual clouds, and to track the aerosol cloud location, their wind speed, and direction.

A number of standoff detection systems based on LIDAR have been developed and are undergoing further field testing [9]. The main objective is to make them portable and capable of distinguishing biological agents from other nonbiological agents.

Soldier Biological and Chemical Command (SBCCOM) and Edgewood Chemical and Biological Center (ECBC) are developing a compact LIDAR that is lightweight, ground-based, and is capable of tracking, calculating relative concentrations, and mapping potential biological aerosols. The system still cannot discriminate between the biological and nonbiological aerosols.

The concept behind a Hybrid LIDAR system that is being developed by the Electro Optics Organization Inc. (EOO) and Stanford Research Institute (SRI) is that the IR-LIDAR first scans for suspicious aerosols from an unmanned aerial vehicle (UAV). If something is spotted, the UV system further analyzes the atmosphere for biological agents.

NASA Goddard Space Flight Center developed Micro-Pulse Lidar (MPL) system for monitoring atmospheric cloud and aerosol structures. Currently, Science and Engineering Services, Inc.—SESI manufacturing—have several models (MPL1000 and MPL2000) that can be used in standoff detection systems for biological units. These instruments cannot discriminate between the biological and nonbiological aerosols. All the standoff detection systems described require manual interpretation of raw data.

Point Detection

Point detection refers to testing a sample that has been taken directly from the environment suspected of contamination by biological agents. This may include monitoring of the air/water systems in buildings for general pathogen contamination or contamination by specific biological agents. Although the objective of point detection is to specifically identify and quantify the targeted biological agent, in many situations neither exceptional sensitivity nor exceptional specificity is required. The assessment of the total microbial content may be sufficient to determine contamination and alert personnel to danger. A sharp and unexplainable rise in total microbial count probably should be sufficient to trigger protective action, regardless of whether the specific pathogen can be identified. More precise identification would be important for forensic uses, and for optimal treatment of many agents (e.g., broad-spectrum antibiotics might be prescribed as soon as the agent is identified as bacterial, even if the species is unknown). Depending on the specific needs, a point detection system may contain various components:

1. Sampling devices
2. Nonspecific detection systems
3. Specific detection systems

Sampling Devices

Air sampling of microorganisms is governed by the same principles of collection as other particulates; however, the viability of organisms complicate their collection. The main objective here is to keep the collected microorganisms in a viable state so that subsequent identification steps become easier. Due to this requirement, special handling and processing techniques are necessary, because analytical identification and enumeration of collected organisms are different from other nonbiological particulates. Several points need to be considered in the selection of a sampler for biological agents [10]:

1. A single sampler may not be effective for all types of agents.
2. No sampling device provides 100 percent recovery of bioaerosols.
3. Viability of bioaerosol samples must be maintained in the sampler for subsequent growth and identification.
4. Efficiency of the sampling device depends on the size of a particular organism.
5. Survival and growth of individual organisms depend on the temperature, pH, and nutritional content of the collection media.
6. Samplers must be operated and used according to the manufacturer's specifications.

Most instruments used for the identification of biological agents require a liquid sample. As a result, airborne microbes are extracted from aerosols or particulates in a liquid. This not only is a very efficient method of extracting the microbes, but at the same time, they can be in a concentrated form for direct use in subsequent equipment. Four general types of sampling devices are available to accomplish one or more of these objectives. They are (1) viable particle-size impactors, (2) virtual impactors, (3) cyclone samplers, and (4) bubblers/impingers. Each of these technologies is described below.

Viable Particle-Size Impactors

The viable particle-size impactors usually have multiple stages connected in series or stacked one over another, which is also called a cascade impactor. Each impactor is called an impactor stage and contains a number of precision-drilled orifices. They are arranged in order of cutoff size with the largest cutoff size first. The cutoff size is reduced in each stage by decreasing the nozzle size or the number of nozzles in that stage. The most common type of impactor used for collection of bioaerosol is known as a six-stage Andersen impactor. Each stage contains 400 holes. Immediately below each stage is a petri dish containing agar or other suitable growth medium. Air is typically drawn through the impactor at a rate of 28.7 L/minutes. The jet velocity is uniform in each stage but increases in each succeeding stage due to a decrease in the diameter of holes in consequent stages. When the velocity imparted to the particle is sufficient, its inertia will overcome the aerodynamic drag and the particle will leave the stream of air and deposit on the agar medium. The impaction mechanism is shown in Figure 8.2. Otherwise, the particle continues to travel to subsequent stages. Each succeeding stage will remove the largest particles with the last stage collecting remaining particles. A six-stage Andersen impactor with the nozzle plate and impaction plate is shown in Figure 8.3. Although impactors can be used directly to collect bioaerosols and require no further processing of samples, they have several disadvantages, particularly if employed to collect biological agents used in a terrorist attack. The choice of nutrient has to be microorganism-specific. Not necessarily all the microbes can be grown in one type of nutrients. Also, the incubation period can be anywhere from one to ten days depending on the type of microbes. In the event of bioterrorism, rapid identification, preferably within hours, may be necessary.

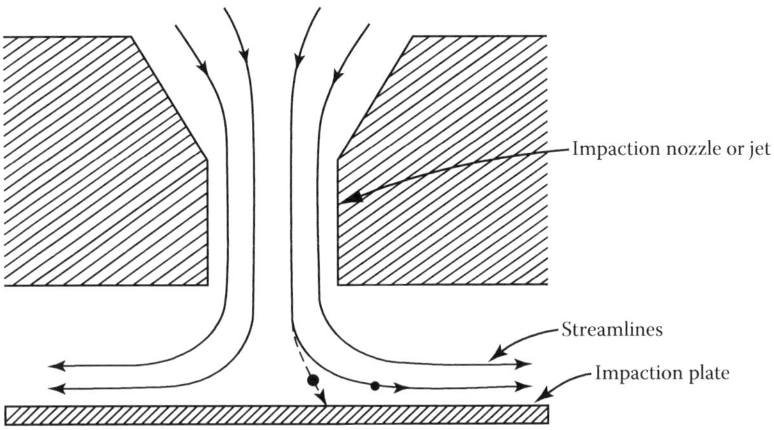

Figure 8.2 Impaction mechanism of particles in an impactor. (From Hinds, W.C., *Aerosol Technology: Properties, Behavior, and Measurement of Airborne Particles*, John Wiley & Sons, Inc., New York, 1982. With permission.)

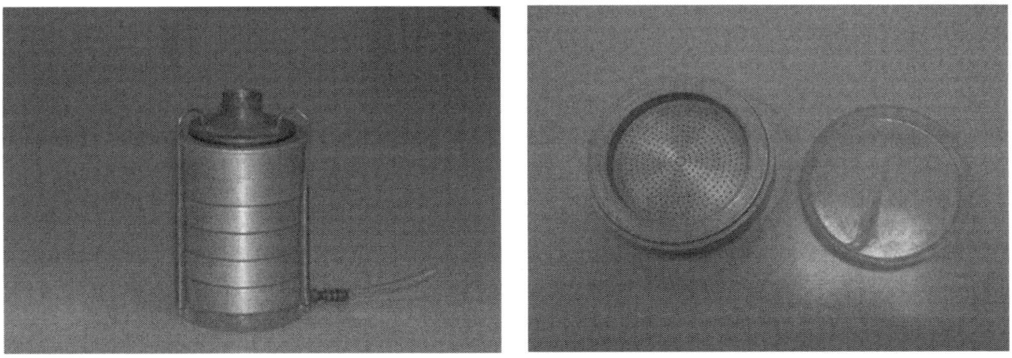

(a) (b)

Figure 8.3 (a) A six-stage Andersen impactor for collection of viable particles from air. (b) A petri dish and an impactor with holes.

Virtual Impactors

A virtual impactor is similar to a viable particle-size impactor, but uses a collection probe instead of a petri dish as its impaction surface. It separates particles by size into two airstreams. The impaction surface is replaced with a virtual space of stagnant or slow-moving air. Large particles are captured in a collection probe rather than impacted onto a surface. The cutoff size of the particles is controlled by controlling the ratio of major to minor flow rate. An accelerating nozzle directs the aerosols toward a collection probe resulting in a diversion of 90° away from the collection probe. This creates a major flow path and a minor flow path. The separation of particles from the air stream takes place at this point. Small particles with low inertia follow the flow streamlines and are carried away readily with the major flow. Large particles with greater inertia deviate from the streamlines and continue moving axially in their forward path down the collection probe with the minor flow. The separation efficiency curve is determined by the ratio of the major and minor flows and the physical dimensions of the nozzle and collection probe.

Particles smaller than the cut size of the impactor remain in both the major and minor flows. But particles larger than the cut size become concentrated in the minor flow (see Figure 8.4).

Several virtual impactors can be stacked one over another. In this way the particles can be concentrated to many times the original concentration before collection. The final stage can then impact the particle stream into a liquid, resulting in a highly concentrated liquid sample. In Figure 8.5, a schematic of a two-stage virtual impactor is shown. Three collection filters and two virtual impactors are assembled in a compact concentric unit with cylindrical symmetry.

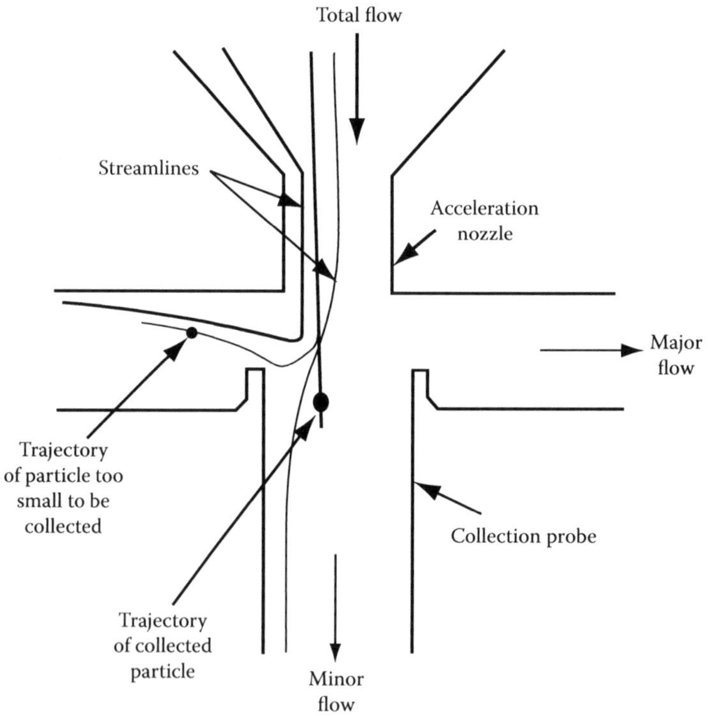

Figure 8.4 A schematic of the flow path inside a virtual impactor (Courtesy of TSI Inc., St. Paul, MN.)

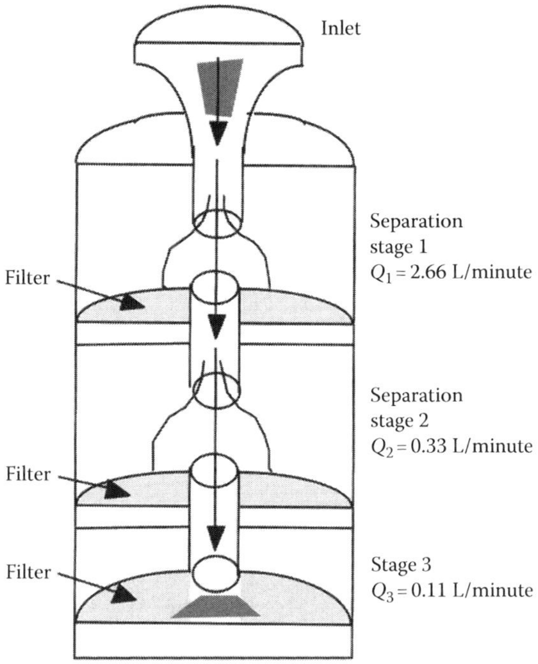

Figure 8.5 Schematic of a two-stage virtual impactor. (Courtesy of TSI Inc., St. Paul, MN.)

The total flow is controlled with a personal air sampling pump and the split at each stage is controlled by a flow orifice.

Virtual impactors can be used to collect and concentrate the particles for direct feeding to other units such as a chemical–biological mass spectrometer (CBMS). Griest et al. [12] collected bioaerosols by an opposed jet virtual impactor for analysis by their CBMS unit. Several modifications to the original design of a virtual impactor have been proposed by various researchers to improve its performance. Gotoh and Masuda [13] have developed an annular jet-type virtual impactor. The new impactor had a better performance compared to the impactor with a rectangular jet because the annular jet has no end, which causes the deterioration of the performance in the rectangular jet-type impactor. To increase the sampling flow of the virtual impactor, Ding et al. [14] developed both multinozzle and longer slit configurations. According to them, a longer slit nozzle increased the inlet flow more effectively than using multiple nozzles.

Cyclone Sampler

In a cyclone sampler, a particle-laden air stream is introduced tangentially near the top of a cylinder. The air stream flows spirally down the chamber following the inner wall, then reverses toward the end and spirals up the center of the chamber and out through the exit. Larger particles are collected on the outer wall due to centrifugal force. Smaller particles follow the airstream that forms the inner spiral and leave the cyclone through the exit tube. The working principle of a cyclone sampler is shown in Figure 8.6. Application of a water spray to the outer walls of a cyclone facilitates particle collection and preservation. Also, a pump may be used to inject liquid into the

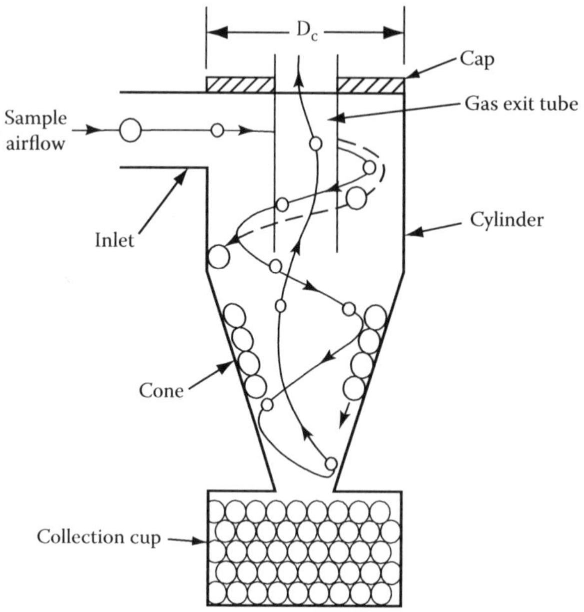

Figure 8.6 Particle collection mechanism in a cyclone sampler. (From Cox, C.S. and Wathes, C.M., *Bioaerosol Handbook*, Lewis Publishers, Boca Raton, FL, 1995. With permission.)

air inlet to wash particles deposited in the inner walls of the chamber into the collection vessel at the bottom. Sometimes a detergent is added to ensure proper wetting of the wall. The air sampling rate can be varied from 75 to 1000 L/minute depending on the size of the cyclone. A cyclone sampler is shown in Figure 8.7.

The samples collected by cyclone samplers can also be in concentrated form and can be fed directly to an instrument for identification. Ligler et al. [7] used a cyclone-type air sampler while testing a remote sensing unit for the analysis of biological agents. The cyclone sampler was able to collect aerosolized bacteria in flight. Griffiths and Stewart [16] compared the performance of five industrially important bioaerosol samplers with that of a glass wet-walled and a cyclone sampler. The test aerosols were *Saccharomyces cerevisiae* and *Penicillium expansum* spores. The cyclone sampler and the Andersen microbial sampler met the basic criteria for a suitable sampler for airborne bioaerosols.

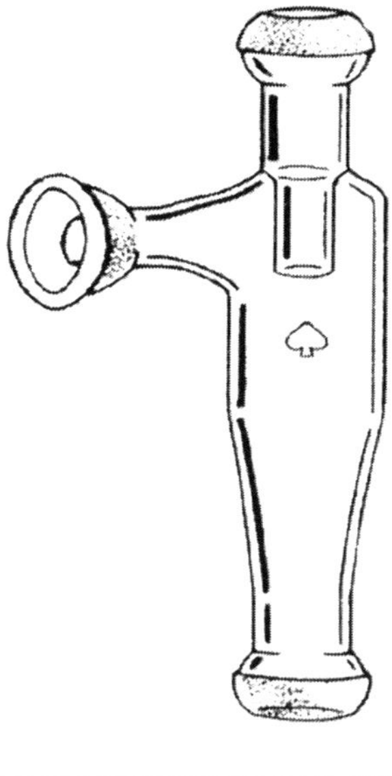

Figure 8.7 A cyclone sampler. (Courtesy of Ace Glass Inc., Vineland, NJ.)

Bubblers/Impingers

In this type of sampler, usually an air jet is impinged into the liquid contained in the sampler. As the air passes through the liquid, the aerosol particles are captured by the liquid surface at the base of the jet. To collect the smallest particles possible, the jet is typically made with a small critical orifice causing the flow to become sonic. The most common type of impinger is called an all-glass impinger

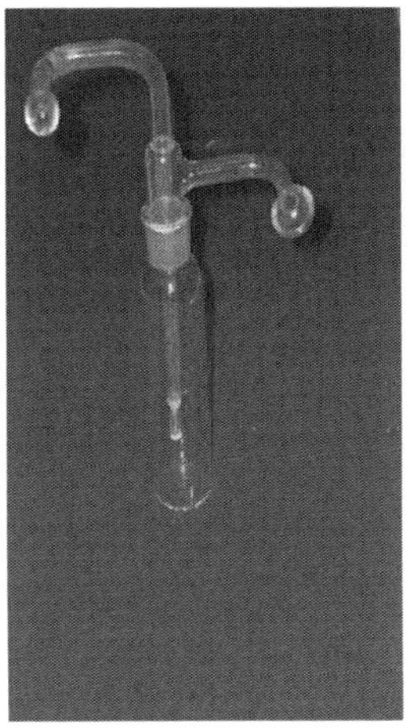

Figure 8.8 An all-glass impinger for collection of airborne microbes.

or AGI-30 (Figure 8.8). The jet is raised to 30 mm above the base of the sampler to minimize the impact of the viable microorganisms with the base of the sampler, and therefore to increase the capture efficiency of viable particles.

Although any of these samplers can be used to collect samples from the atmosphere, prior knowledge of the characteristics of the microorganisms are important to devise a collection strategy or to choose a correct sampler. The environment in which the target microbe exists can significantly affect the physiology of the microbe and their detection procedure. For example, *Bacillus anthracis* that causes anthrax exists as a hard, oval, inactive spore in the atmosphere and is highly resistant to sunlight, heat, and disinfectants. However, in tissue, including blood, it germinates into a rod-shaped vegetative bacillus, actively proliferating and producing its characteristic toxins. Therefore, the detection of *B. anthracis* from air will be different than in the blood. Also, the growth state and gene expression of the collected agents may depend on the growth or collection media. Another issue that should be kept in mind is the very low concentration of these airborne microbes in the environment. Therefore, if a proper sampler is not selected, enough microbes may not be collected by the sampling unit leading to false negative results in subsequent analysis.

High Air Volume Collectors

Most of the collectors described above draw only a small volume of air. One of the main reasons is that the collection liquid can evaporate quickly if prolonged sampling time is used. To overcome this problem, several high air volume collection systems have been developed. Also, most of these collection systems incorporate an automatic detection system to avoid transfer of sample for further processing.

The Lawrence Livermore National Laboratory has designed a two-stage aerosol collector that combined a newly LLNL-designed slit-virtual impactor with a commercial wetted-wall cyclone collector (Research International SASS 2000). The virtual impactor has been optimized to capture particles in the 1–10 μm size range, and the wetted-wall cyclone traps the particles in fluid. The system is capable of handling 2300 L of air/minutes (lpm) utilizing only 4 mL liquid. The sample can be directly analyzed in the system. The LLNL developed immunoassays that are rapid, sensitive, and specific and can detect more than one threat agent simultaneously (i.e., multiplexed) from a single sample using a flow cytometer [17]. Various components of the system are shown in Figures 8.9 and 8.10, and the complete packaged unit is shown in Figure 8.11.

Northrop Grumman (Arlington, VA) has developed a high-volume sampling and detection system for biological agents. It incorporated GeneXpert Technology's PCR system and the unit was designed for screening mail at U.S. Postal Service facilities [18]. A schematic diagram of the system is shown in Figure 8.12.

Surface Sampling

The sampling from a surface for detection of biological agents is challenging. Generally, swabs, tape lifts, or vacuuming of the surface are used for collection of samples. Moistened noncotton

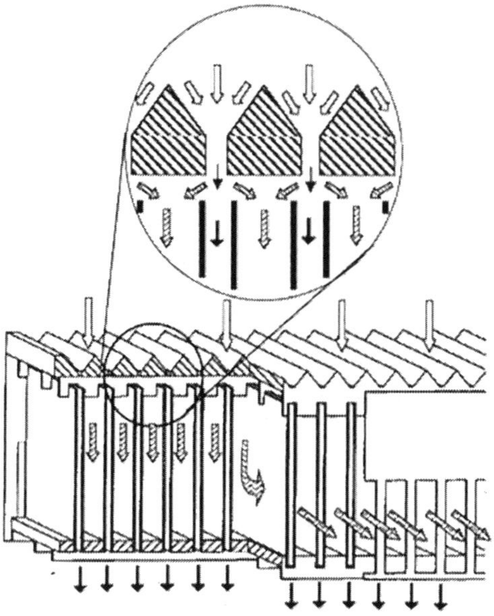

Figure 8.9 A slit-virtual impactor designed by LLNL for sampling high-volume air. (From Bergman, W. et al., *J. Aerosol Sci.*, 36(5–6), 619, 2005. With permission.)

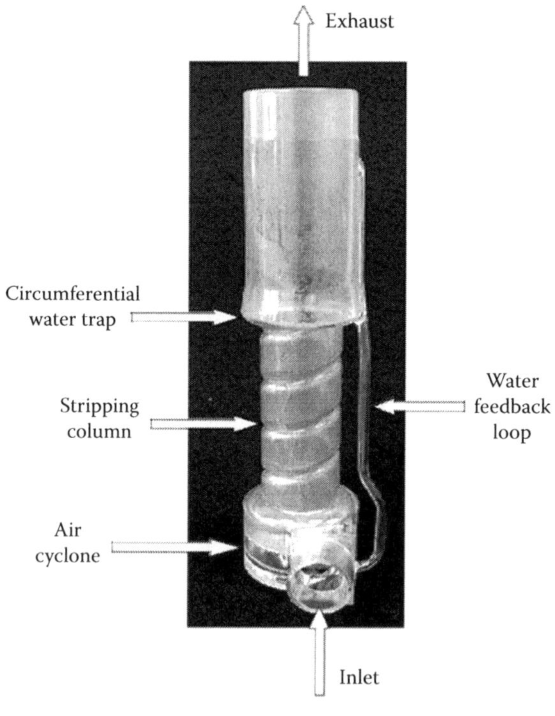

Figure 8.10 A cyclone impactor used by LLNL in their high-volume sampler. (From Bergman, W. et al., *J. Aerosol Sci.*, 36(5–6), 619, 2005. With permission.)

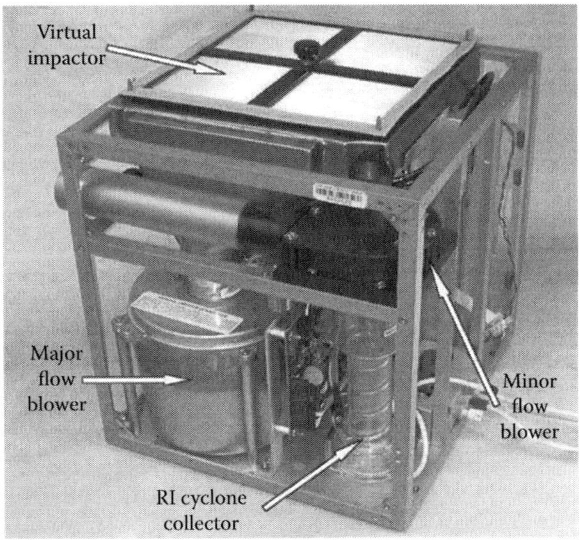

Figure 8.11 Complete assembly of the LLNL high-volume air sampler. (From Bergman, W. et al., *J. Aerosol Sci.*, 36(5–6), 619, 2005. With permission.)

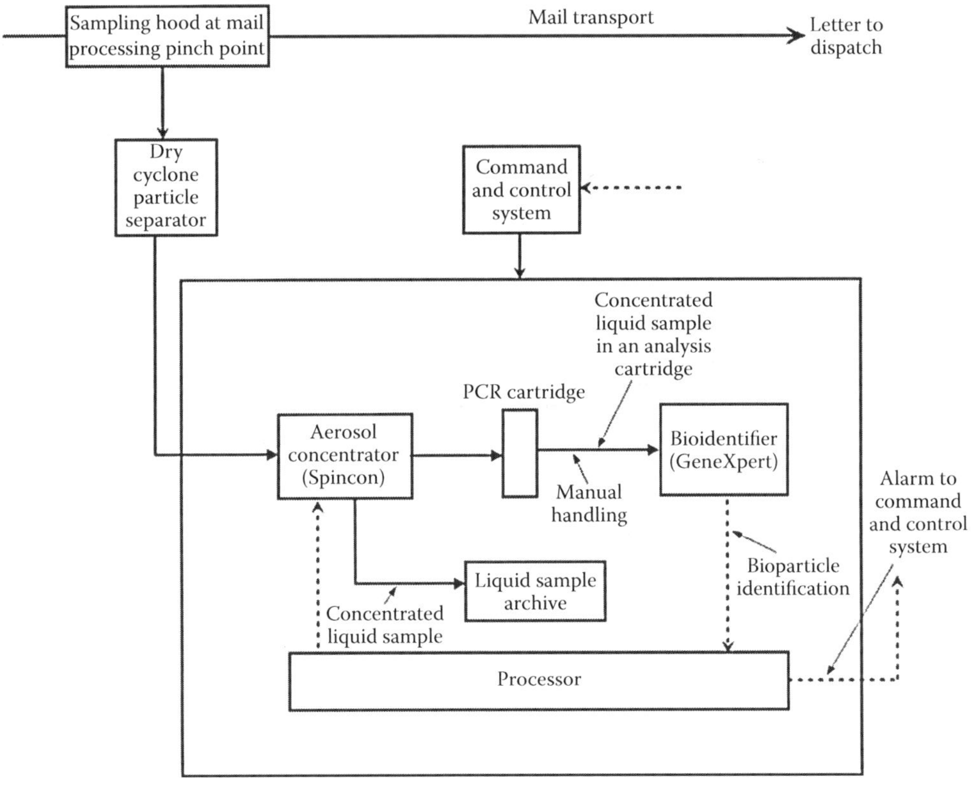

Figure 8.12 A schematic diagram of arrangements for testing bioaerosols in a postal service facility. (Data from Tilles, D.J. et al., Point source biological agent detection system. U.S. Patent 7405073, Issued July 29, 2008.)

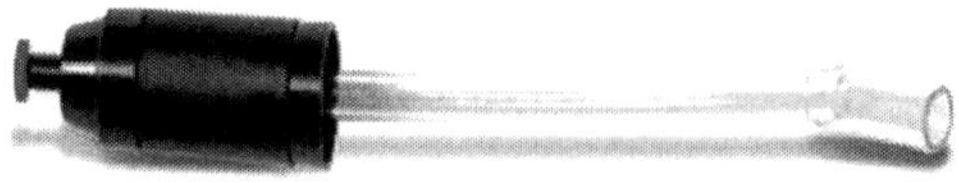

Figure 8.13 A cassette for sampling surface for bioaerosols. (Courtesy of Aerotech, Inc., Pittsburgh, PA, www.aerotech.com.)

(rayon or polyester) wipes or swabs are used to wipe or swab the area. The sample is next sent to a laboratory for analysis. Protocols regarding sample storage, transpiration, etc., which are generally set by the analyzing laboratory must be followed. The collection media must be sterile and used with a sterile wetting agent, such as sterile water, a sterile saline solution, or a sterile phosphate-buffered solution. Swabs are best used for smooth small surface areas that do not have a large accumulation of dust. For larger surface, greater than 98 cm^2 (15.5 $in.^2$), wiping of the surface is recommended.

Sampling of carpet for biological agents is specially problematic. Carpet is listed as one of the nine potential sources of BAs in an occupied space by the American Conference of Governmental Industrial Hygienists ([ACGIH]—Bioaerosols: Assessment and Control, 1999). The porous nature of the carpet may allow the biological agents to penetrate through the carpet and accumulate underneath. Care must also be taken in interpreting the data. The CarpetChek TM system designed by Aerotech laboratories is widely used for sampling from carpet. The sampling probe is shown in Figure 8.13.

The inlet tube should be inserted as deep as possible into the carpet to collect a representative sample of approximately 1 g.

Nonspecific Detection

Nonspecific detection is generally used as a "trigger" to monitor for the presence of biological agents. Generally, a sudden increase in the atmospheric particulates in the size range of 1–5 μm above the background level is monitored. Both the biological and nonbiological particles are counted. However, a more sophisticated detection system can differentiate between the biological and nonbiological particles.

Aerodynamic Particle Sizing

Aerodynamic particle sizing (APS) can be used as a simple trigger for the presence of biological agents and for counting the relative number of particles in specific size ranges. A schematic diagram of an APS system is shown in Figure 8.14. The particle-laden air stream, drawn into the system through a flow nozzle, produces a controlled, high-speed aerosol jet. The air velocity at any point in the flow field stays constant during the measurement period. However, individual particles accelerate at different rates within the jet, based on the size of the particles. Smaller particles accelerate at a higher rate than larger particles because the particle velocity at any given point is inversely proportional to the aerodynamic size of the particle. A laser beam measures the time-of-flight of the individual particles. The beam is split into two parallel beams, and as the particles pass through them, a pair of electrical pulses are produced by forward-scattered light, collected and sensed with a photomultiplier tube. A high-speed clock measures the time between the electrical pulses (time-of-flight). The aerodynamic particle size is calculated with a previously stored calibration curve. Particles are thus counted and sized for a specified sampling period, and results are displayed as a histogram of aerodynamic diameter versus number.

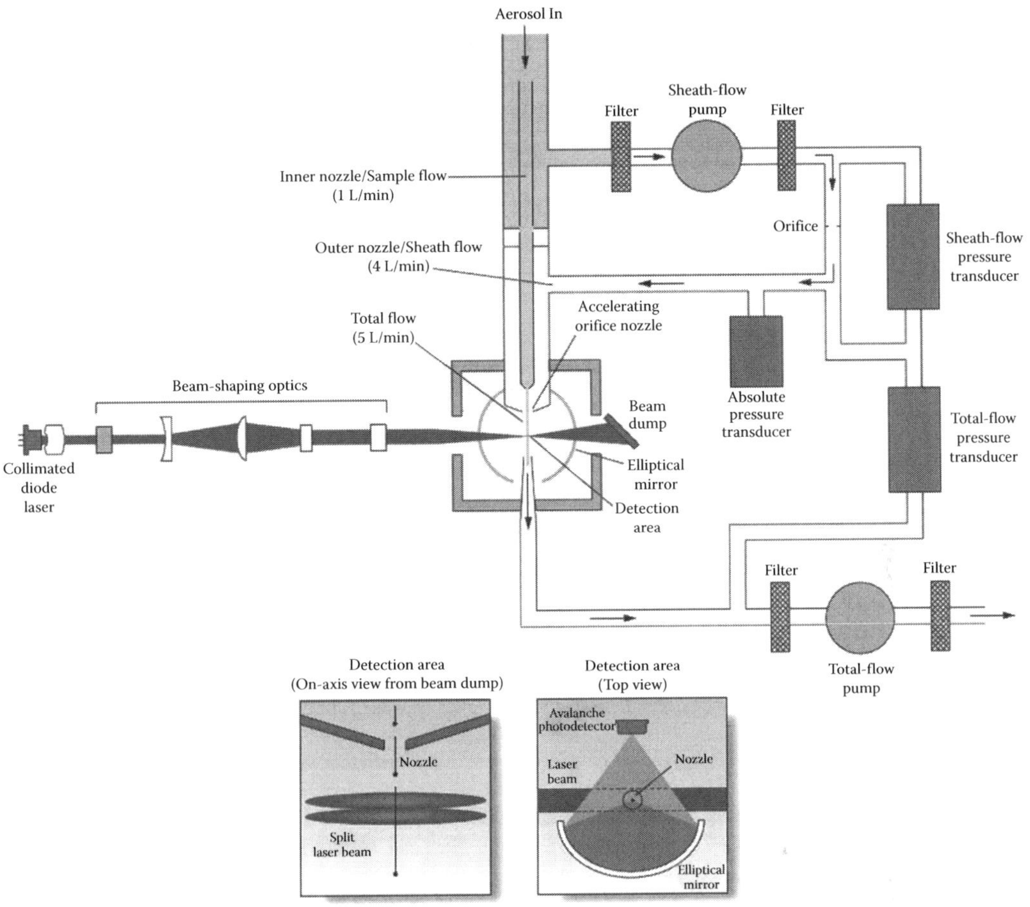

Figure 8.14 Schematic diagram of the APS flow system. (Courtesy of TSI Inc., St. Paul, MN.)

Fluorescent Aerodynamic Particle Sizer

The fluorescent aerodynamic particle sizer (FLAPS) is the modified version of the APS system. An additional laser (blue or ultraviolet) is employed to detect aerosol particle fluorescence in addition to aerodynamic particle size. The second laser beam is located downstream and is perpendicular to the standard dual laser beams. FLAPS examines a concentrated aerosol sample for biological fluorescence and compares this response to background particle size characteristics. Thus, FLAPS can discriminate between the nonbiological and biological aerosols. A FLAPS functions on the principle of flow cytometry technique. The particle size and fluorescence for each particle in an air stream are measured. This permits it to distinguish between biological aerosol particles and nonbiological materials like sand. A HeNe laser provides the size measurements of the respirable particles (0.5–15 μm size range) by the time-of-flight method. Molecular excitation of biological particles for fluorescence measurement is initiated by a HeCd UV laser at 325 nm. Particles containing molecules that are excitable at this wavelength emit light at between 400 and 580 nm. A characteristic fluorescence is suggestive of biological properties inherent with the particle. A schematic diagram of FLAPS system is shown in Figure 8.15.

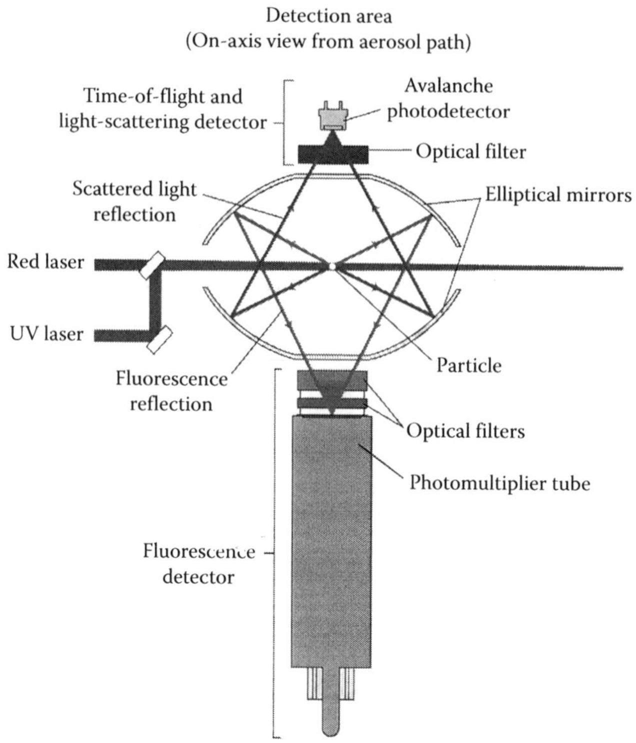

Figure 8.15 A schematic diagram of the FLAPS system. (Courtesy of TSI Inc., St. Paul, MN.)

Recent efforts include employment of UV laser-induced fluorescence (UV LIF) for diagnostic measurement of biological agents. Most of these techniques utilize quadrupled Nd:YAG laser at 266 nm in the ubiquitous tryptophan absorption band from 260 to 290 nm [19–24]. However, a number of researchers have employed UV wavelength at 355 nm [25–28]. The FLAPS developed by Ho et al. [29] measures fluorescence signals of single spores under flow cytometry using UV excitation at 340–360 nm. They later developed a second-generation FLAPS (FLAPS2) that was smaller, power efficient, and field portable. Field testing of FLAPS2 with spores of *Bacillus subtilis var niger* showed that FLAPS technology can measure fluorescence signals from single particles in an aerosol. Eversole et al. [30] at Naval Research Laboratory developed a prototype single particle fluorescent analyzer (SPFA) and compared its performance against a FLAPS in outdoor settings. The SPFA system differentiated between the biological and nonbiological particles using particle size and intrinsic UV fluorescence excited by 266 nm laser pulses. It detected at least 87 percent of the released particles. Individual particle data was also obtained in the visible fluorescence band that could be used for some identification.

Flow Cytometry

Flow cytometry is used to measure certain physical and chemical characteristics of cells or particles as they travel in suspension, one by one, in a fluid stream through a light source. The current flow cytometer consists of a laser, collection optics, electronics, and a computer to translate signals to data. Scattered and emitted fluorescence are measured. A fluorescent dye may be added to cells to

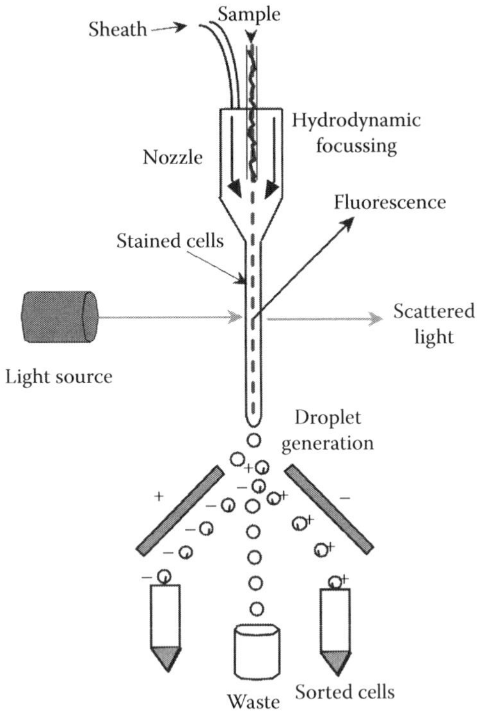

Figure 8.16 Schematic of a flow cytometry system. (Data from www.flow-cytometry.de/start.html.)

measure other characteristics. Because the measurements are made on individual cells, detection of specific organisms in a complex mixture of other biological and nonbiological particles is possible. The modern instruments can make measurements at rates of up to 10,000 particles/s.

In flow cytometry, cells must be sorted physically into a single cell or particle of interest from a heterogeneous population. Cells are aspirated from a sample and ejected one by one from a nozzle in a stream of sheath fluid, which can be any ionized fluid. The cells are then electrically charged and electrostatically deflected to the proper stream. As the cell is intercepted with the laser beam, scattered light and fluorescence signals are generated and measured using appropriate electronics. The process is shown in Figure 8.16.

A laser beam interacts with each individual cell as it passes through a flow cell constructed with optical windows as part of the coaxial arrangement. Excitation of the molecule is accomplished using an argon ion laser at 488 nm, which is close to the absorption maximum of the common fluorochrome fluorescein isothiocyanate (FITC). A more sophisticated system may incorporate a tunable laser to cover a wide range of wavelengths. Laser beams are usually focused to a spot between 10 and 60 μm in diameter and only a few microseconds are required for a cell to travel to this spot. The optical arrangement of a typical flow cytometer is shown in Figure 8.17.

The flow cytometry has widespread application both in medical fields and detecting biological agents [31]. Additionally, flow cytometry technology can provide structural characteristics of biological cells (see Table 8.1). Stopa et al. [32] at U.S. Army Edgewood Research Center worked on development of flow cytometry-based biological detection systems. Their results showed that flow cytometry analyzed aerosol samples effectively, but was dependent on the dye used for staining the

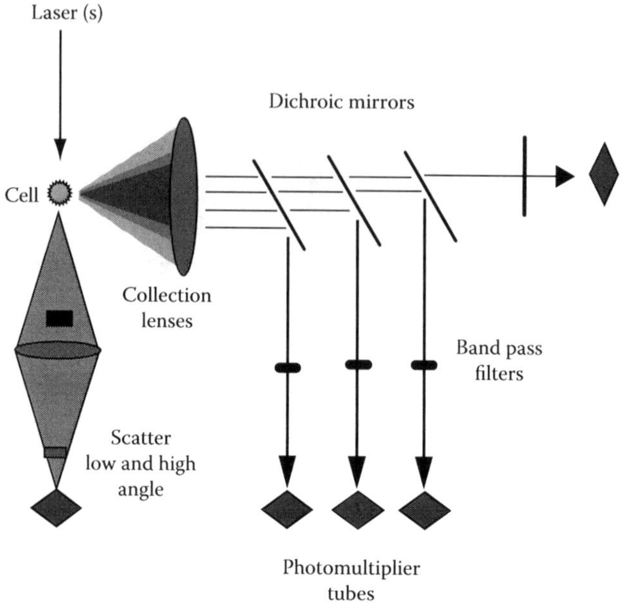

Figure 8.17 A typical optical arrangement of a flow cytometry system. (From www.uwcm.ac.uk/study/medicine/haematology/cytonetuk/introduction_to_fcm/optics.htm. With permission.)

Table 8.1 Structural Characteristics of Biological Agents Measurable by Flow Cytometry

Parameter	*Measuring Method*
Cell size	Extinction or small angle light scattering
Cell shape	Pulse shape analysis
Cytoplasmic granularity	Large angle light scattering, electronic impedance
Birefringence	Polarized light scattering

Source: Biological Detection System Technologies, Technology and Industrial Base Study. A Primer on Biological Detection technologies. Prepared for the North American Technology and Industrial Base Organization, February 2001.

liquid. The samples consisted of liquid impinger fluids collected during 40 releases of four different simulants: *Bacillus subtilis var. niger* (BG spores), *Erwinia herbicola*, MS2 coliphage virus, and ovalbumin. When using the CPO dye the detection reliability was 50 percent, and it increased to 70 percent when the YOYO-1 dye was used.

Portable Biofluorescence

During the Gulf War, a UV-excited fluorescence technique was examined for detection of bioaerosols. The sensor developed based on this technique was called the portable biofluoro-sensor (PBS). The performance was mixed during the Gulf War, however since then, significant improvement

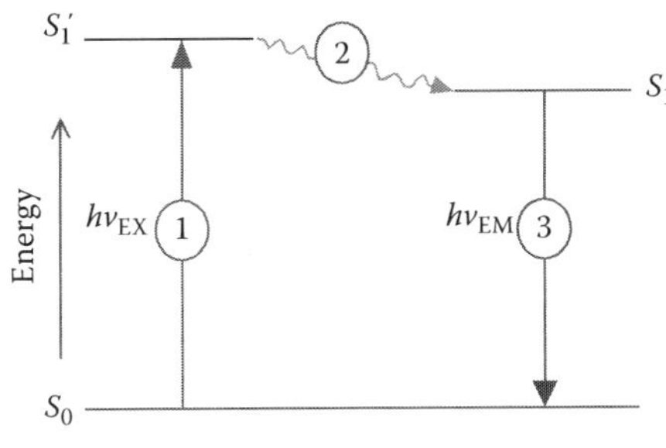

Figure 8.18 Excitation of molecules by a laser.

has been made and it has become more reliable. In this method, tryptophan in BW agents was targeted for detection by the fluorescence approach. Using photon energy in the UV region of the spectrum, tryptophan in the biomolecule is excited. The excited component spontaneously reverts to an unexcited state followed by emission of light at higher wavelengths (Figure 8.18). The emission of light depends upon the specific type of molecular component being irradiated and the excitation wavelength. This provides a unique spectrum for that particular component. This emission spectrum can be used to identify a component in a complex mixture. Because all of the biological agents have a common compound, tryptophan, the biofluorescence approach specifically targets this chemical. A typical spectrum is shown in Figure 8.19.

Biofluorescence techniques may be divided into two categories: (a) primary fluorescence and (b) secondary fluorescence. In the primary biofluorescence method, naturally fluorescent components of the biomaterials, such as tryptophan, are used. The primary approach requires the least amount of analysis time and sample preparation. In the secondary fluorescence method, a special fluorophore (i.e., fluorochrome stain) is added to the sample before UV-irradiation. Such methods do not depend on the existence of a natural fluorophore within the targeted compound. Secondary methods, however, require a longer measurement time. Generally, a filtered, pulsed xenon lamp is used

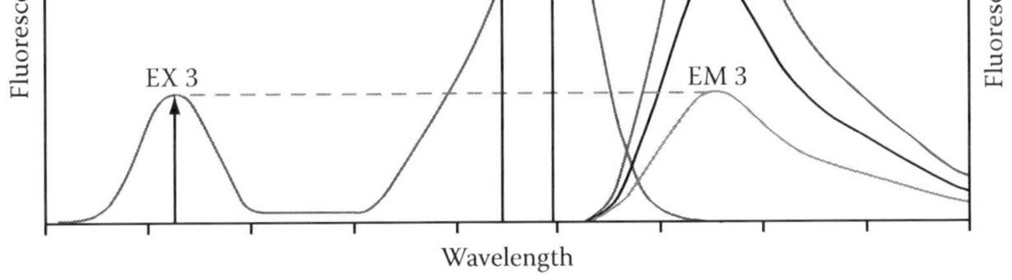

Figure 8.19 A typical emission spectrum from a biofluorescence sensor.

in the 200–285 nm spectral region for excitation. Fluorescence usually occurs between 310 and 360 nm. Fluorescence spectral intensity at several wavelengths is measured with two or more filtered photomultiplier tubes or solid-state avalanche photodiodes. Although both the air and liquid samples can be used, liquid samples provide better efficiency than airborne samples.

The techniques described in this section utilize signals from fluorophores contained within particles of biological origin, mainly tryptophan, and nicotinamide adenine dinucleotide, which is associated with metabolic processes are targeted for signal generation [34]. So far single-wavelength excitation and single-wavelength emission fluorescence have been used for particle analysis [35]. However, the performance of biofluorescence sensors may be increased by acquiring fluorescence emission at several wavelengths [19]. Tjarnhage et al. [36] obtained spectral data from the biological warfare agent simulants at eight different excitation and emission wavelength combinations. The data was collected using a system consisting of a cyclone sampler and a commercial spectrofluorometer. Using this technique, they were able to separate biological from nonbiological particles such as dust and smoke. Also, biological agents could be differentiated from each other using the measured fluorescence signals.

Specific Detection Technologies

Specific detection/identification systems are designed to identify the specific types of biological agents. Most of the methods have been designed for analysis of clinical samples. However, once a sample is collected from the environment, the same instrument can be used to identify the microbes present in the sample. The specific identification systems can be broadly classified as

- Mass spectroscopy-based identification
- Identification by targeting at the molecular level

Mass Spectroscopy-Based Identification

Mass spectrometers (MS) characterize compounds based on their specific mass profiles, following limited fragmentation by an energy source. The mass fraction is next ionized using an ion source. MS uses the difference in mass-to-charge ratio of ionized atoms or molecules to separate them from each other. The biological agents contain lipids or fat, which has a distinctive structure. This provides unique fragmentation patterns that can be used to identify biological agents. Steps involved in MS-based analysis include creation of gas-phase ions, separation of the ions in space or time based on their mass-to-charge ratio, and measurement of the quantity of ions of each mass-to-charge fraction. Therefore, an MS consists of an ion source to create gas-phase ions, a mass selective separator to separate the ions in space or time based on the mass-to-charge ratio, and an ion detector to quantify the ions. The main challenge in MS is creation of gas-phase ions. The separation of ions in space and time is rather standard nowadays. Most of the MS use the time-of-flight method for separation of charged ions. The quantification of ions by their mass-to-charge ratios is accomplished using a quadrupole mass detector.

Laser Pyrolysis

In this method, a particle beam is produced when aerosols expand through a nozzle into a vacuum and is introduced into the mass spectrometer chamber [37,38]. Using multiple lasers, individual

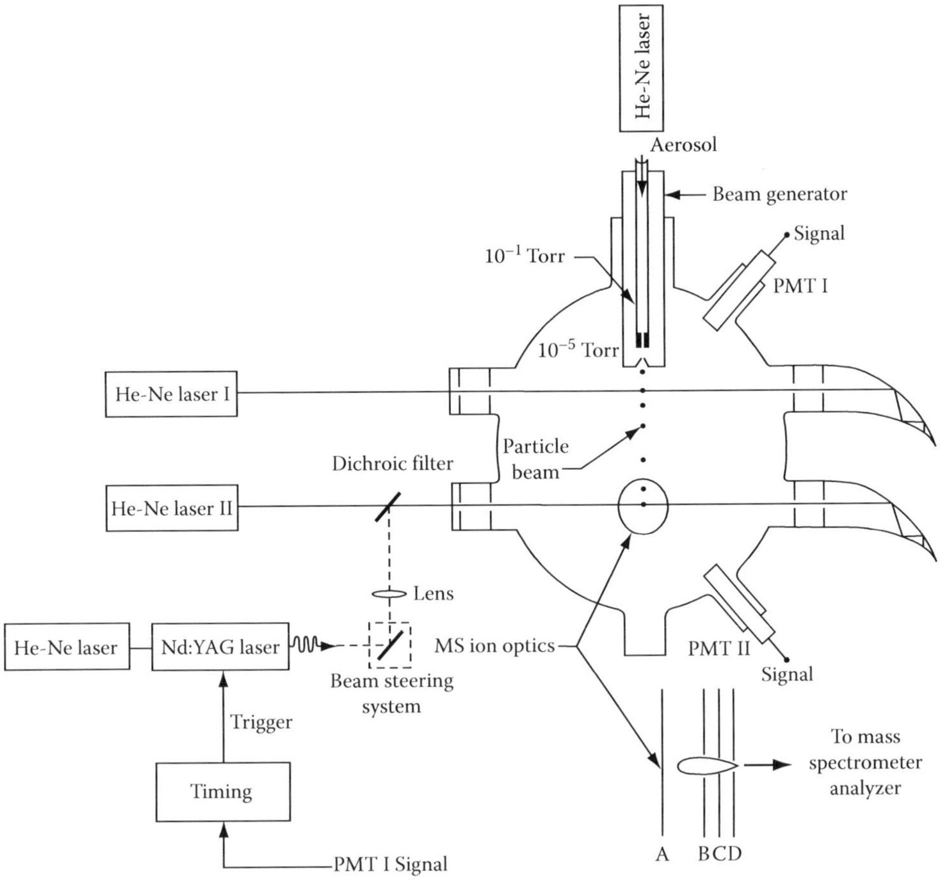

Figure 8.20 Laser pyrolysis MS system. (From Sinha, M.P., *Rev. Sci. Instrum.*, 55(6), 886, 1984. With permission.)

particles are pyrolyzed into small mass fragments and ionized by a laser pulse while in flight in the beam (Figure 8.20). A burst of ions is produced from individual particles after volatilization and ionization by electron impaction in the ion source of the mass spectrometer. The mass spectrometer detector then measures the intensities of the ions. Intensities of different mass fractions are obtained and compared with a library of mass spectral data of different microbes grown under different conditions for identification by comparison. Figure 8.21 shows mass spectra of three different bacteria.

Fast Atom Bombardment

Further improvement in microbial analysis using MS has been achieved by applying fast atom bombardment mass spectrometry (FABMS) [39]. This method works best for polar and higher molecular weight compounds such as peptides and other biomolecules. FABMS utilizes a fast moving beam of neutral atoms targeted toward a metal coated with a liquid

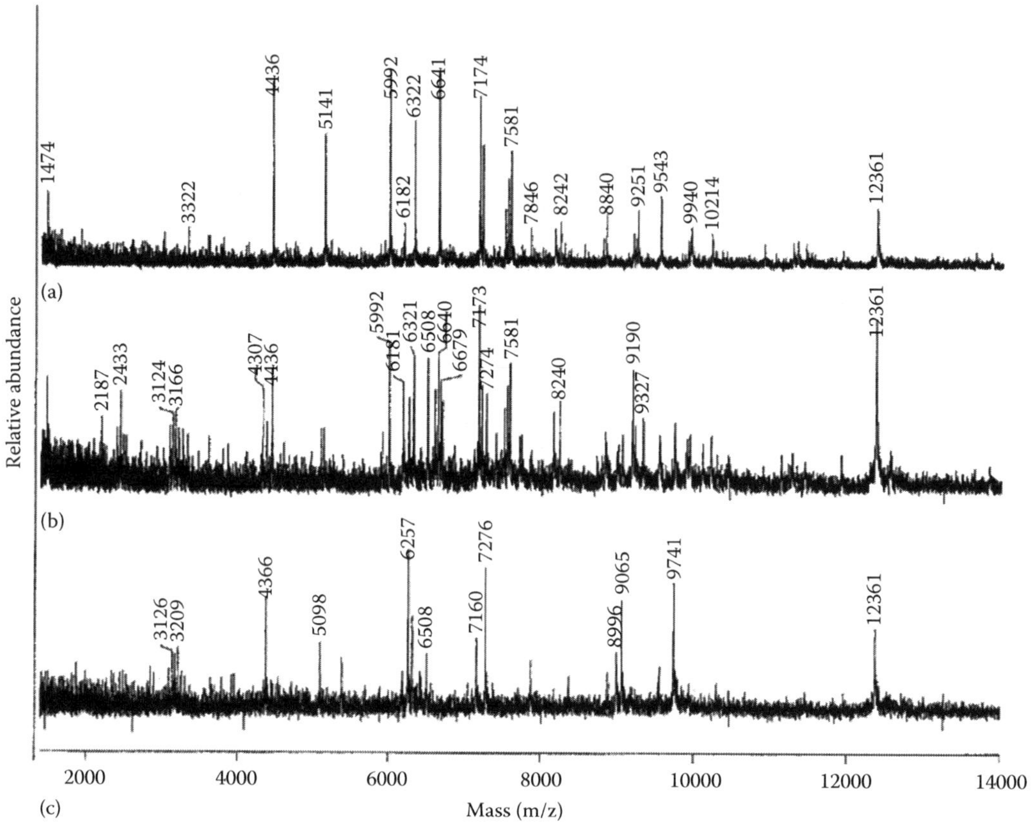

Figure 8.21 MALDI-MS spectra of several bacteria. (From Jarman, K.H. et al., *Anal. Chem.*, 72, 1217, 2000. With permission.)

matrix in which the sample is dissolved. Phospholipids and other polar lipids are selectively desorbed from a lysed bacterium to provide molecular ions. There is no extraction of the lipids involved. The FABMS method can be used in positive or negative ion modes with a selection of matrices. Generally pseudomolecular ions together with some fragment ions having lower mass are formed.

Electrospray Ionization

Electrospray ionization (ESI) is one of the more recent ionization techniques that is finding rapid use in identification of microbes due to their very high sensitivity [40,41]. In this method, a dilute solution of the analyte flows through a stainless steel capillary tube at the rate of about 1 mL/minute. A high negative or positive electric potential in the range of 3–5 kV is applied to the end of the tube. The strong electric field at the end of the capillary pulls the solution into a Taylor cone, and at the tip of the cone, the solution is nebulized into small charged particles (see Figure 8.22).

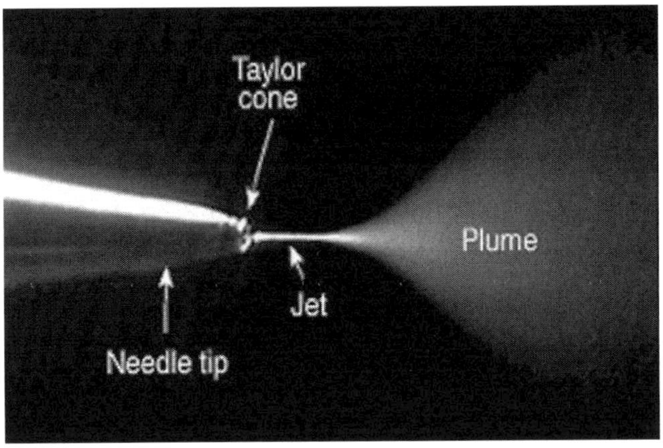

Figure 8.22 Taylor cone.

The charged droplets travel toward the counterelectrode through an evaporation chamber. In this region, solvent evaporates rapidly from their surfaces and they shrink in size. As the droplets get smaller, the electrical surface charge density increases, causing fragmentation due to the repulsive force on the charged droplet, resulting in the formation of a fine mist (particles). A schematic diagram of ESI system is shown in Figure 8.23.

The ions and cluster ions generated from the sample have much greater molecular mass, and therefore, greater momentum than those of the solvent and move toward the target at the end of the inlet region. To assist the evaporation of the droplets and the breaking up of unwanted cluster ions, a drying gas (nitrogen) flows along and past the end of the capillary. The ions then pass

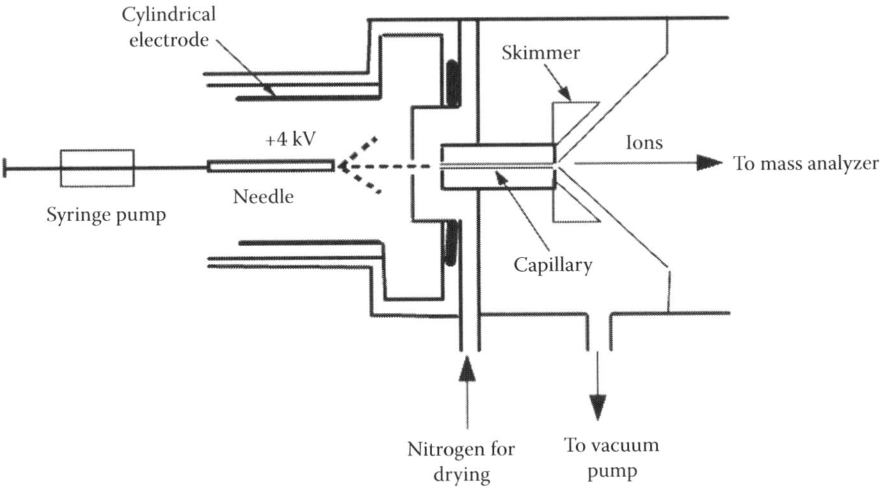

Figure 8.23 Electrospray ionization system (From Gates, P., http://www-methods.ch.cam.ac.uk/meth/ms/theory/esi.html; as reported in http://www.unmc.edu/publichealth/biostatistics/grounds/Lec6-Duan.pdf. With permission.)

through two evacuated regions via a nozzle and a skimmer. These conically shaped holes refine the separation of sample ions from solvent ions on the basis of momentum; however, electrical potentials applied to the nozzle and skimmer also aid in the separation. Finally, sample ions flow into the analyzer of the mass spectrometer where their mass-to-charge ratios are measured by a quadrupole mass detector.

Matrix-Assisted Laser Desorption and Ionization

Matrix-assisted laser desorption and ionization (MALDI) is one of the most successful ionization methods for the mass spectrometric analysis and investigation of large molecules. This technique allows for vaporization and ionization of nonvolatile biological samples from a solid-state phase directly into the gas phase. Various components of an MALDI system are shown in Figure 8.24.

The sample (analyte) is suspended or dissolved in a solid or liquid matrix which strongly absorbs laser light. Matrices are small organic compounds that are cocrystallized with the analyte. The sample is mixed with a matrix at molar ratios of 1,000:1 to 10,000:1 matrix to sample, to assist in the analysis of large, fragile molecules. It seems that the presence of the matrix, spares the analyte from degradation, resulting in the detection of intact molecules as large as 1 million Da mass. The matrix for biological analysis is usually a large organic compound such as 2,5-hydroxybenzoic acid, with certain properties such as high absorption at the laser beam that prevents the decomposition of fragile samples like proteins and oligonucleotides. A detailed review on MALDI ionization mechanisms has been given by Zenobi and Knochenmuss [42].

Upon laser irradiation (usually with a pulsed laser), the matrix absorbs light resulting desorption and ionization of analyte. The ions enter the mass spectrometer, most commonly a time-of-flight mass spectrometer. A spectrum of ion intensity as a function of the travel time is recorded. A library of MALDI mass spectra has been generated for about 100 different pathogens, nonpathogens, and pure known proteins [43].

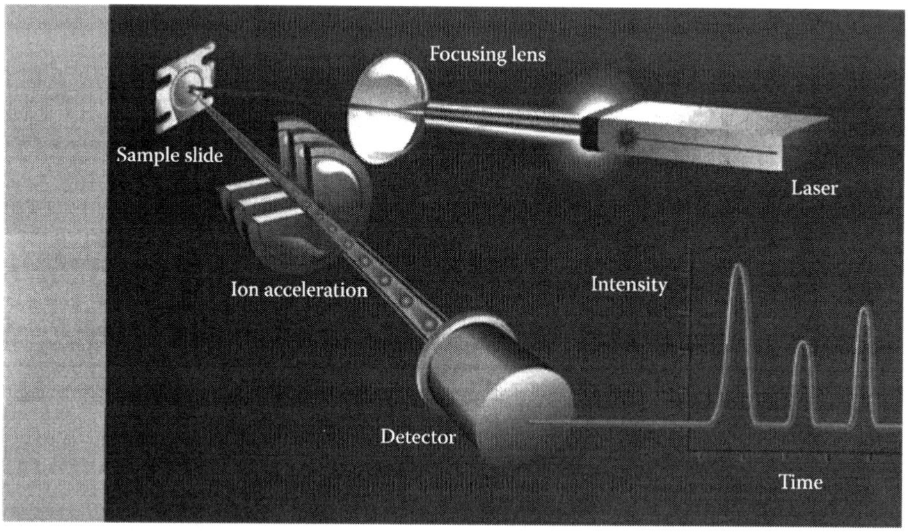

Figure 8.24 Schematic of matrix-assisted laser desorption/ionization time-of-flight mass spectrometry. (Courtesy of Thermo Electron Corporation, Waltham, MA.)

Mass spectrometer based identification of biological agents is becoming a viable tool because of the recent developments that have made these systems fieldable [44]. Snyder et al. [45] used a pyrolysis-gas chromatograph ion mobility spectrometer to discriminate between aerosols of BG spores, EH, and ovalbumin. The Block II Chemical Biological Mass Spectrometer (CBMS) developed by Griest et al. [12] is capable of detecting and identifying both the chemical and biological agents on the battlefield.

Identification by Targeting at the Molecular Level

Biological agents can be in the form of vegetative cells and spores, viruses, and toxins. These agents can be identified by using nucleic acid or immuno-based methods. Also, their products, such as antigens and toxins, can be targeted for identification purposes. An identification scheme will look like the one shown in Figure 8.25.

When identifying biological agents by targeting at a molecular level, a detection system requires two components: (1) a probe and (2) a transducer. A probe deals with how the assay or detection device recognizes the particular target microbe. The transducer technology deals with how the assay or detection device communicates the activity of the probe to the observer. The probe and transducer together determine specificity, sensitivity, and time required to make an identification. Most of the current systems incorporate both the probe and the transducer into a single unit. Probe technologies are generally based on nucleic acids, antibody–antigen binding,

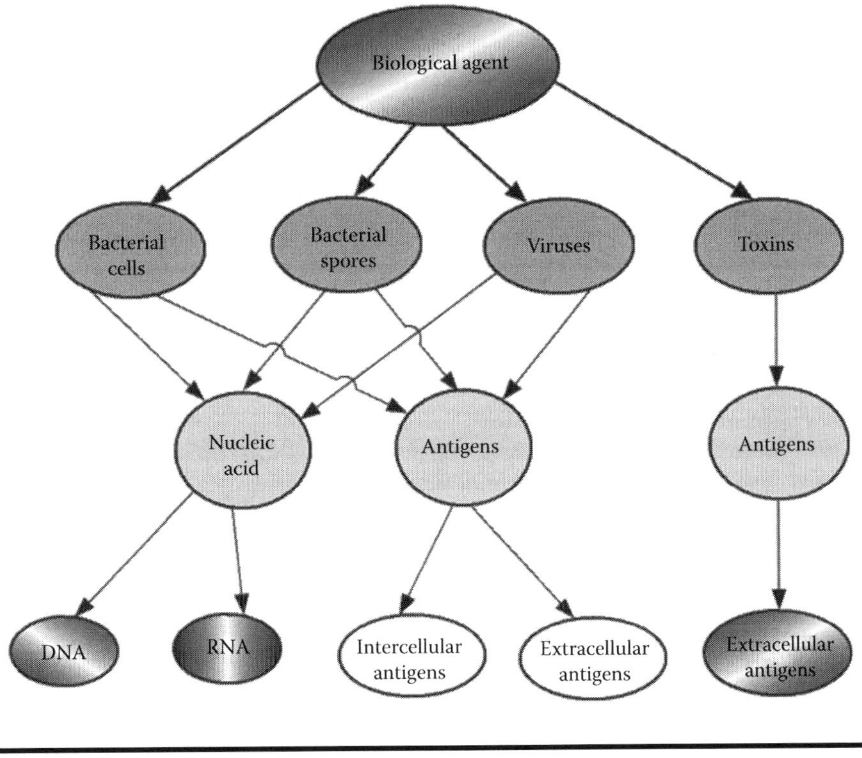

Figure 8.25 Analysis at the molecular level. (From Iqbal, S.S. et al., *Biosens. Bioelectron.*, 15, 549, 2000. With permission.)

and ligand–receptor interactions, whereas main transducer technologies include electrochemical, piezoelectric, colorimetric, and optical systems. The transducer system acquires signals that are unique to the probe system and generate low noise signals that can be further processed without degradation to provide a signal that is related to the microbe concentration.

Nucleic Acid-Based Identification Systems

All living organisms essentially can be discriminated on the basis of nucleic acid (DNA or RNA) sequences unique to that particular organism. Each type of organism has some unique sections of DNA or RNA. The unique DNA structure of each organism can be used to identify pathogens and biological warfare agents. Nucleic acid-based probes capitalize on the extreme selectivity of DNA and RNA recognition. These probes and their binding can be detected directly or by tagging with an easily detected molecule that provides a signal. Therefore, nucleic acid-based detection systems can be divided into two categories: (1) direct target probing with signal amplification and (2) target amplification.

Direct Target Probing with Signal Amplification

The basis of virtually all nucleic acid targeted probe systems is the ability of engineered single strands of RNA or DNA to bind specifically to strands of complementary nucleic acids from pathogens to form stable hybrid complexes. Most systems use sandwich hybridization involving two probes. One probe targets the nucleic acid that is captured by an oligonucleotide capture probe, which is immobilized on a solid support and has sequences complementary to the target. A second oligonucleotide probe, which carries a covalently attached label or reporter molecule, hybridizes to a complementary region on the target for signal generation. The design of the probe can be highly specific if there is a good fit to a pathogen-unique region of the target nucleic acid, or it can provide more generic identification if there is a fit with a region of nucleic acids conserved among several related pathogens. The sensitivity of these hybridization assays for bacteria is between 1,000 and 10,000 colony-forming units. The capture target is detected by virtue of a linked reporter probe labeled with the enzyme alkaline phosphatase. A variety of reporter molecules including radioisotopes, fluorophores, enzymes, or haptens can be used. Among these reporter molecules, enzymes are most widely used, which utilize biotin–streptavidin. The probe is labeled with biotin. The streptavidin–enzyme complex then binds to the biotinylated signal probe and detects presence of the target. The final readout is generally calorimetric.

The time-consuming part of the method is in the sample preparation and the time required to detect the signal. However, the main advantages of nucleic acid-based methods are in their universality, sensitivity and adaptability, and multiplex capabilities for a host of different microbes. Disadvantages of this technology include difficulty in isolation and "clean up" of DNA samples, degradation of the nucleic acid probes, and interference from related sequences or products.

Target Amplification

Nucleic acid-based detection has been greatly improved due to the development of amplification processes for the target organisms in vitro. These amplification processes are capable of generating enormous copies of target nucleic acid from a single copy. The amplification or copying of target nucleic acid is accomplished through the polymerase chain reaction (PCR) [47–51]. PCR involves enzymatic replication of a target region of nucleic acid defined by a set of oligonucleotide primers.

A target DNA sequence can be selectively amplified or enriched to several millions in just a few hours. Within a dividing cell, DNA replication involves a series of enzyme-mediated reactions, whose end result is a faithful copy of the entire genome. A PCR reaction is carried out in the following manner [52]:

- A small quantity of the target DNA is mixed with a buffered solution containing DNA polymerase, oligonucleotide primers, the four deoxynucleotide building blocks of DNA, and the cofactor $MgCl_2$.
- The mixture is heated at 94°C–96°C for one to several minutes during which the DNA is denatured into single strands.
- The mixture is then cooled to 50°C–65°C during which the primers hybridize to their complementary sequences on either side of the target sequence. This may take one to several minutes depending on the probe.
- Finally, the mixture is again heated at 72°C for one to several minutes during which the polymerase binds and extends a complementary DNA strand from each primer.

The DNA sequence between primers doubles after each cycle and millions to billions of copies can be made after less than 30 cycles. Following amplification, the product is loaded into the wells of an agarose gel and an electrophoresis method is used for signal generation.

PCR has become a powerful tool for identification of infectious disease and biological agents [53]. Further modification of the basic PCR method, mainly in the assay technique, has been proposed. These are colorimetric enzyme immunoassays (PCR-EIA) and fluorogenic 5′ nuclease PCR assays. Lawrence Livermore Laboratory has adopted these assays into a miniaturized analytical thermal cycling instrument (MATCI) to shorten the performance time. The PCR-EIA is found to be at least ten times more sensitive than standard PCR and the other methods described above. In Table 8.2, a comparison of these methods for the *Yersinia pestis* agent are given.

Q-PCR

The PCR enzymatic replication is most frequently used for determining the presence/absence of biological agent. Recently, quantitative PCR (Q-PCR) is being used for rapid detection of single

Table 8.2 Comparison of Sensitivity of Various PCR Formats for *Y. pestis*

	Performance Time	*Limit of Sensitivity*	*Specificity (%)*
Standard PCR	2–3 hour	300 copies	100
PCR-EIA	2.5–3.5 hour	30 copies	100
5′ Nuclease PCR	2–3 hour	300 copies	100
MATCI	20–60 minutes	>300 copies	100

Source: Henchal, E.A. and Ibrahim, M.S., Evaluation of polymerase chain reaction assays for identifying biological agents, *NATO ASI Series*, Ser. 1: Disarmament Technologies, Vol. 30 (Rapid Methods for Analysis of Biological materials in the Environment), Stopa, P.J. and Bartoszcze, M.A., Eds., 2000, 239–249. With permission.

pathogen-specific genes. This allows real-time quantification of target genes. Gibson et al. [55] used the RT-PCR technique for simultaneous detection and quantification of gene expression. As noted by Elnifro et al. [56], a sample can be assayed by Q-PCR for the presence of multiple genes/pathogens. This is possible by multiplexing that combines oligonucleotide primers specific for several genes of interest in one PCR reaction. Varma-Basil et al. [57] developed a real-time PCR assay that simultaneously detected four bacterial agents that could be used in bioterrorism (Figure 8.26).

Several Q-PCR-based systems are developed for detection and identification of biological agents [58]. Most of these systems performed rather well in a controlled environments such as research laboratories and hospitals; however, they did not do well in field testing. The GeneXpert Q-PCR DNA detection system (Cepheid, Sunnyvale, CA) and the LightCycler system (Roche Diagnostics GmbH, Mannheim, Germany) have developed detection kits specifically for *B. anthracis* and are commercially available. The GeneXpert system is automated that can process field samples and perform amplifications followed by product detection. Applied Biosystems (ABI, Foster City, CA) offers several 96-well plate format Q-PCR systems and developed several Q-PCR assays including one for *B. anthracis* and variola virus.

Although Q-PCR instruments are very useful in a laboratory, for quick detection, these instruments should be portable and fieldable. Idaho Technology (Salt Lake City, UT) developed a ruggedized advanced pathogen identification device (RAPID), which is portable and fieldable, based on Q-PCR platforms that incorporated the LightCycler technology. This system has been

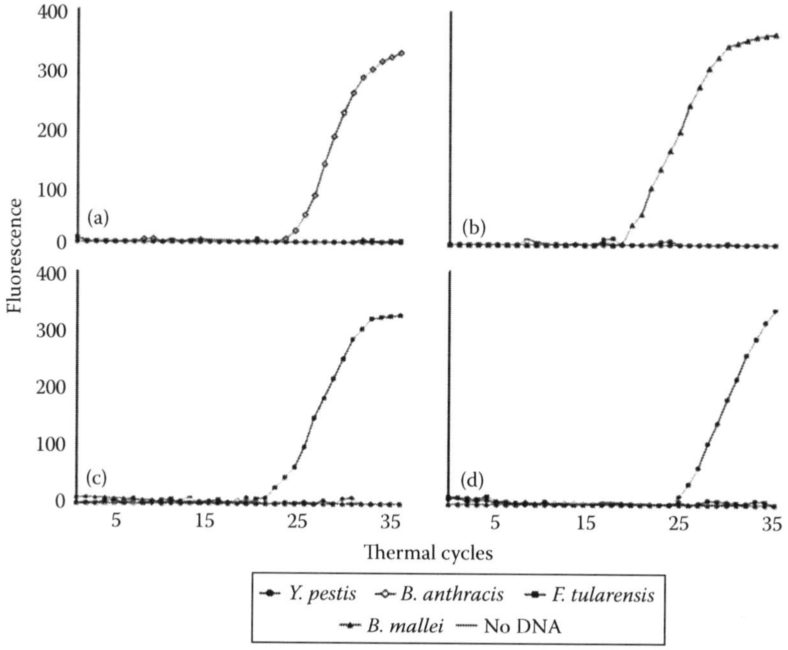

Figure 8.26 Four-color multiplex assay. The results are shown for real-time PCRs containing DNA from different bacterial species, both primer pairs, and a mixture of four differently colored molecular beacons designed to detect all four select agents. (From Varma-Basil, M. et al., *Clin. Chem.*, 50, 1060, 2004. With permission.)

designed for use by military field hospitals and first responders and in other harsher environments. Higgins et al. [59] employed the RAPID system for detecting *B. anthracis* in various buildings. Also, Van Kessel et al. [60] used the RAPID system for detecting *Salmonella* in raw milk. Smiths Detection (Edgewood, MD) developed a commercial version of the handheld advanced nucleic acid analyzer based on the technology developed by the Lawrence Livermore National Laboratory, called BioSeeq, that is portable and can be operated with the heavy gloves of a hazmat suit. BioSeeq uses either a prepared PCR cartridge and preset protocols to analyze samples in the field or individual samples with programmable protocols in a laboratory mode for customized assay designs. The PCR kits in various formats are available for the detection of *B. anthracis, Francisella tularensis, Y. pestis, C. botulinum, E. coli* O157:H7, *Salmonella* spp., *Brucella* spp., *Listeria* spp., dengue virus, orthopox virus, and smallpox [58].

Immunoassay-Based Identification Systems

An immunoassay depends on the highly specific binding (reaction) of antigens with their corresponding antibodies thus forming a complex. In this method, the presence of an analyte is detected and identified based on the antigen–antibody binding reaction. An antibody has a Y shape structure consisting of two heavy chains and two light chains joined by covalent double bonds. The base of the Y is constant among antibodies, while the top of the Y is specific for a particular antigen forming the variable region (see Figure 8.27).

An antigen is a foreign substance that triggers an immune response and may be a lipid, polysaccharide, or protein. The epitope is the site of the antigen, because the antibody does not generally recognize the whole antigen, detected by the antibody. Each antigen may have several different antigenic determinants. The antibody attaches itself to the antigen. Each antibody is specific for one antigenic epitope. The antibody–antigen binding is shown schematically in Figure 8.28.

A number of detection methods have been developed based on the immunoassay technology. These methods are described in the following sections.

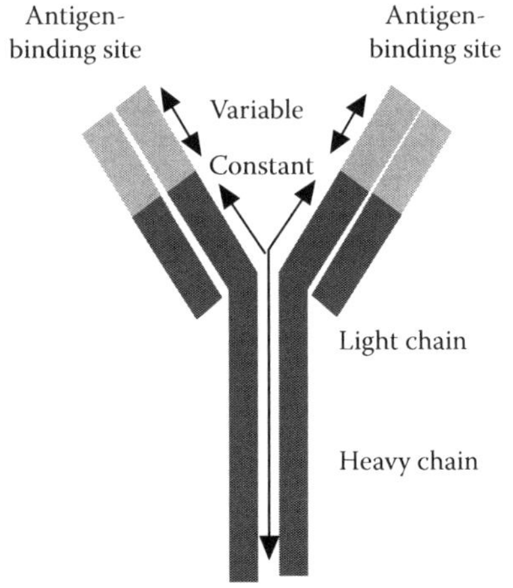

Figure 8.27 Antibody structure. (Data from Antibody structure, www.biology.arizona.edu/immunology/tutorials/antibody/structure.html.)

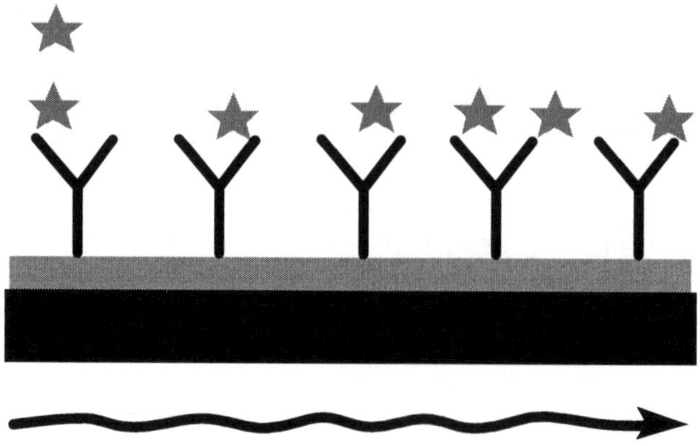

Figure 8.28 Antibody–antigen binding.

Handheld Immunochromatographic Assays

The handheld immunochromatographic assay (HHA) is a simple, antibody-based assay that can be used to identify a variety of biological warfare agents. HHAs are inexpensive and very reliable. HHAs are designed to identify one agent per assay. There are two types of HHAs; the chromatographic type and the flow-through assay type.

In the chromatographic type, a membrane strip is printed with three lines: (1) detector antibody-coated blue latex particles, (2) biological-agent-capture antibody, and (3) a reaction control of antibody directed to the antibody on the blue latex particles. The triple-coated membrane strip is dried and is mounted onto a ticket. To detect the presence of a biological agent, a small portion of liquid sample containing the suspected agent is placed in a well on the assay (Figure 8.29). The solution wicks through the assay where it is successively exposed to different antibodies. If antigen is present, a complex is formed and is captured by the biological-agent-capture antibody

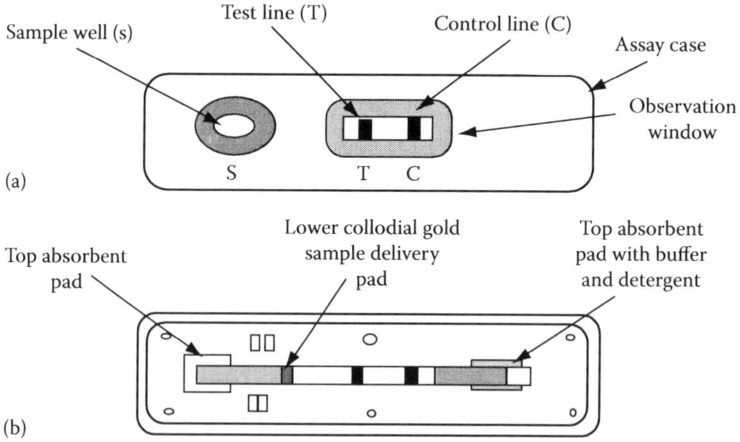

Figure 8.29 A handheld immunoassay ticket: (a) cover on and (b) cover removed.

and a line appears in the test window (T). A line will also appear at the site of the reaction control window (C). Appearance of a line in this region only indicates that the antibodies are behaving properly but is not an indication of exposure to the biological agent. Therefore, a positive assay will have two lines, one in each window. A negative assay will have only one line in the reaction control window (C). On average, it takes 15 minutes to complete the assay. A shorter exposure time could give false negative results and a longer time may give false positives as the labeled antibody can start to flow back down the assay. The colored indications are not permanent and will fade quickly with time. To overcome the lack of sensitivity and occasional false positives of traditional HHAs, the U.S. Army Solider and Biological Command (SBCCOM) and the U.S. Army Research Laboratories are investigating dendrimer-based tickets. So far, a variety of nanostructured polymeric materials have been synthesized and tested. Among them, the rigid, spherical, tree-like dendrimers are the best nanostructured polymers capable of orienting the antibody-binding direction at different surfaces. As a result, HHA tickets have been significantly enhanced, and the detection time has been dramatically shortened.

Flow-Through Assay

Handheld immunoassays can be also carried out in a flow-through mode. The ticket, which is a plastic container, consists of a sample well with an absorbent pad backing to the membrane. To perform a test, the liquid sample suspected of containing the agent is introduced into the sample well. Antigen in the sample is captured on the membrane. A second reagent solution is added to the same sample well and it also flows through the membrane surface. The reagent solution contains an indicator antibody tagged with colloidal gold as an indicating agent. When the tagged antibody binds with the antigen on the membrane surface, a red spot is produced. Generally, a reaction control antibody is bound in a horizontal strip on the membrane, whereas the specific antiagent antibody is bound in a vertical strip. If a red "minus sign" appears every time a test is conducted, it confirms the validity of the test. A red "plus sign" indicates the presence of the biological agent (see Figure 8.30).

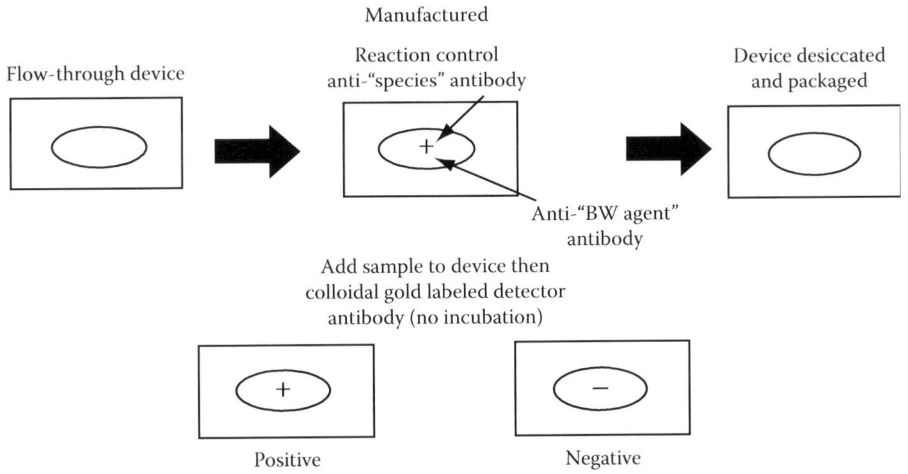

Figure 8.30 A flow-through assay system.

Smart Tickets

The sensitive membrane antigen rapid test (SMART)™ is a registered trademark of New Horizons Diagnostics Corporation. The SMART identification tickets are self-contained, colorimetric, and are based on solid-phase immunofiltration assays designed to be used in conjunction with a liquid interface. SMART tickets are capable of detecting both endospore-forming bacteria and proteinaceous toxins or soluble antigens, including bacteria. The detection is accomplished by targeting the antigen in the sample that binds with antibody tagged with colloidal gold-labeled reagents. Antibodies specific to the agent of interest are conjugated to colloidal gold particles. When concentrated on solid surfaces, these particles can be seen by the naked eye. Labeled antibodies can easily be lyophilized and reconstituted without losing activity or specificity. The presence or absence of the target antigen is indicated colorimetrically. A small red dot appears on the ticket that the user compares with a color chart (see Figure 8.31). The older version of SMART tickets that were used during the Gulf War tends to provide a higher percentage of false positives. The reliability of this method has been improved significantly by employing a lateral flow system. In lateral flow devices, the chemical reagents are separated across the test strip. This lateral design provides fewer false positives in environmentally collected samples. The diagnostic kits are available for anthrax, cholera, ricin, staph enterotoxin, *Y. pestis*, tularemia, and botulism toxin [62].

Electrochemical Luminescence

The ability of certain molecules such as ruthenium (II) tris(2,2′-bipyridine) (Rubpy32+) to emit light or to luminesce has been utilized to detect antibody–antigen binding of the biological agent. If the light is produced by a chemical reaction, it is called chemiluminescence. If the chemiluminescent reaction is initiated by an electrical stimulation of the molecules, it is then called electrochemiluminescence (ECL).

A typical ECL sandwich assay takes place in the following manner. A sample is mixed with a reagent containing biotinylated TSH antibody and a second ruthenium conjugated TSH antibody.

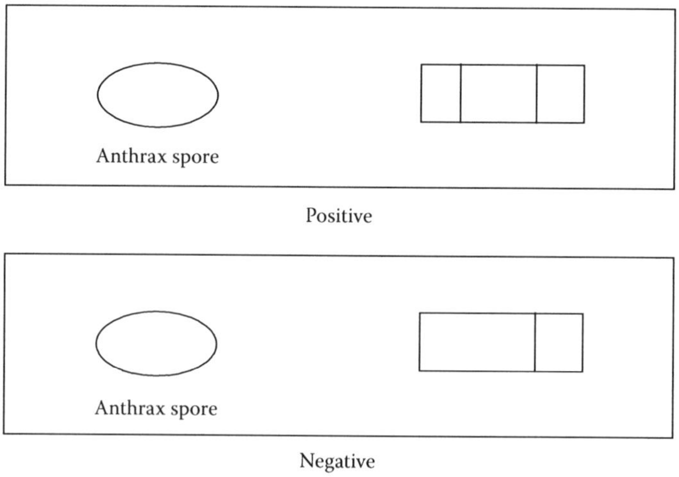

Figure 8.31 A SMART ticket for anthrax detection.

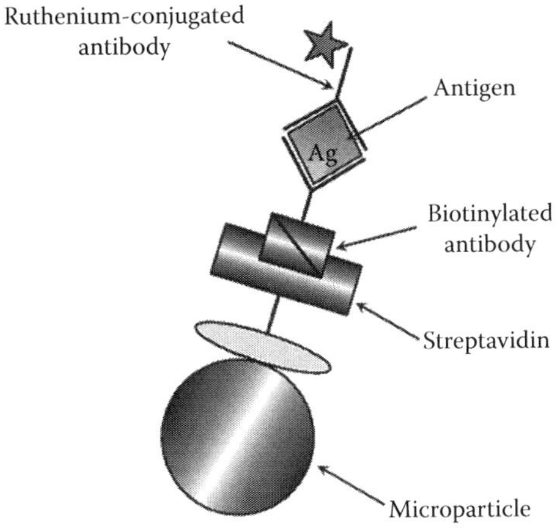

Figure 8.32 Schematic of the electrochemiluminescence assay process. (Courtesy of Roche Diagnostics, Indianapolis, IN, http://us.labsystems.roche.com/ecl/ecltech.htm.)

Antibodies capture the TSH present in the sample in this step. The captured antibody is immobilized on streptavidin-coated paramagnetic microparticles. The biotinylated TSH antibody attaches to the streptavidin-coated surface of the microparticles. The antigen forms a sandwich with these two reagents. The solution is next drawn into the ECL measuring cell along with a buffer solution containing tripropylamine (TPA). A magnet located under the electrode captures the microparticles in a thin, even layer on the electrode's surface. The magnet is removed and voltage is applied to the electrode. The association of TPA and the electrode results in a fast electron transfer reaction. This transfer initiates the excitation of the ruthenium (II) tris(2,2′-bipyridine) (Rubpy32+) molecule which results in a emission of a photon at 620 nm. The ECL reaction occurs only if the antigen is present. This process also regenerates the ruthenium complex, which can perform multiple cycles during the measurement. The result is amplification of the signal. Multiple readings are taken by the photomultiplier tube (PMT) and the readings are integrated and compared to the calibration curve to obtain a quantitative result. Regeneration of the electrode surface is accomplished by controlled variation of the electrode potential. The ECL measuring cell is then ready for another measurement. The process for detecting the biological agent is shown in Figure 8.32. Although the very first measurement takes about 17 minutes, subsequent measurements can be obtained in one minute. A general review of the chemiluminescence immunoassays process was provided by Rongen et al. [63] and Bowie et al. [64]. Yu et al. [65] have used the electrochemiluminescence assay for the detection of biological threat agents. Results of detecting several biological agents by electrochemiluminescence is shown in Table 8.3. Yu et al. [65] concluded that electrochemiluminescence is a sensitive and effective means to detect biological agents from various matrices.

Light-Addressable Potentiometric Sensor

The light-addressable potentiometric sensor (LAPS) consists of an array of semiconductor devices, on top of which the biological agents are immobilized. The LAPS comprises an electrolyte–insulator–semiconductor (EIS)-structure, where a bias potential can be applied between an ohmic contact at the backside of the semiconductor and a reference electrode in the electrolyte.

Table 8.3 Results of Detection of Various Biological Agents by the Electrochemiluminescence Method

Biological Agent	*Detection Limit*
Staphylococcal enterotoxin type-B	0.5 pg/mL
B. *anthracis*	0.001 cfu/mL
Bot A	4 pg/mL
Cholerae toxin B	2 pg/mL
Ricin A chain	0.5 pg/mL

Source: Yu, H. et al., *Biosens. Bioelectron.*, 14(10–11), 829, 2000. With permission.

By illuminating parts of the surface of the device with a beam of light, an electrical potential is generated between thin gold layers on the surface of the insulator located under the membrane filters. Therefore, surface potentials can be measured in a spatially resolved manner by scanning the light pointer across the surface of the device. A number of biochemical events occurring simultaneously on the surface can be measured.

A typical LAPS sandwich assay is shown in Figure 8.33. The complete process may be divided into three stages: (1) reaction stage, (2) separation stage, and (3) detection stage.

In the reaction stage, the labeled antibodies, the sample containing the analyte, streptavidin, and antifluorescein/urease conjugate are combined together to form the first reagent. If antigen is present in the sample, the sandwich reaction occurs in the solution.

The reaction product is transferred onto a nitrocellulose biotinylated membrane filter by filtering the solution through the membrane. The strong affinity of streptavidin for biotin is used to capture and concentrate the reaction complexes onto a biotinylated membrane filter and is called the separation stage (see Figure 8.34)

A labeled antifluorescein urease antibody, which binds to the fluorescein label on the previously captured complex, is filtered through the same membrane. The detection is accomplished by placing this membrane filter into the reader, which contains the substrate urea and the LAPS. Inside the reader, urea is hydrolyzed by urease, producing a pH change due to enzymatic activity at the silicon sensor surface.

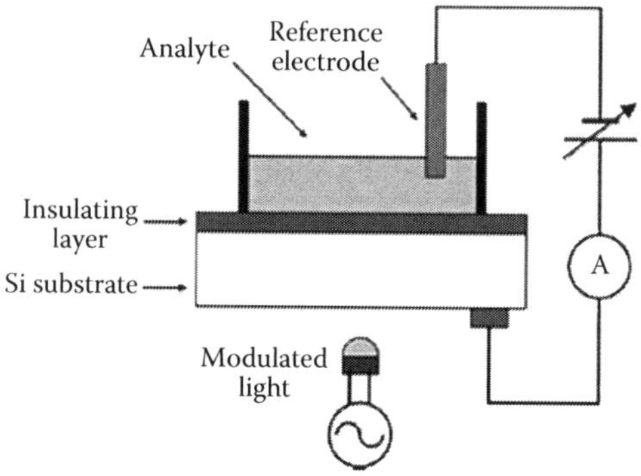

Figure 8.33 A typical LAPS system. (From Yoshinobu, T. et al., *Sensors and Actuators,* B95, 352, 2003. With permission.)

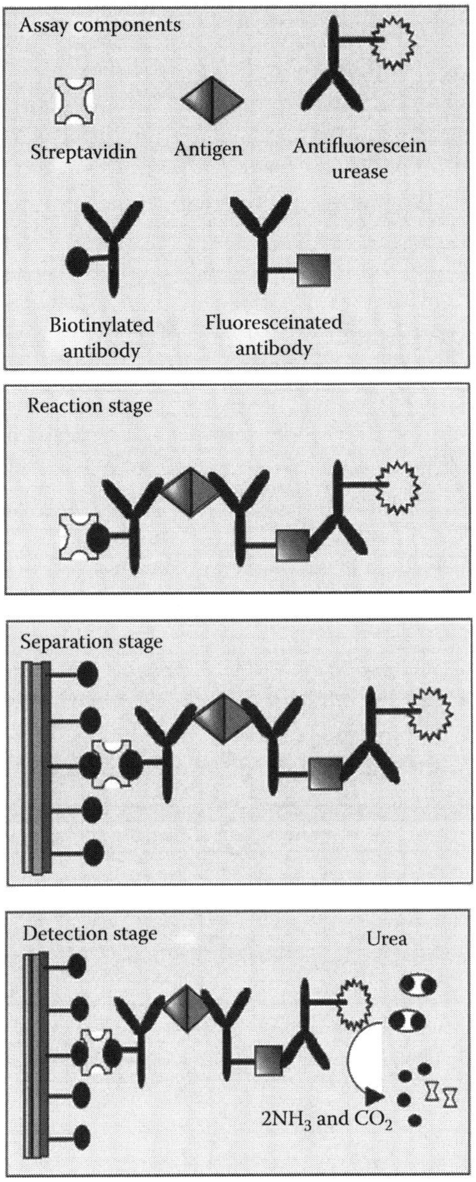

Figure 8.34 Schematic of the LAPS immunoassay process. (Data from Threshold System, Immuno ligand assay system, www.moleculardevices.com/pages/thresh_ila.html. With permission.)

The U.S. Department of Defense has implemented a biological integrated detection system (BIDS) for providing early warning and detection of biological threat agents in a battlefield. In the BIDS, the biological detection system employs a LAPS and a flow-through immunofiltration enzyme-based assay system. As indicated by Uithoven et al. [68], the LAPS system was tested using *B. subtilis* spores in the concentration range of 10^4 to 10^6 cfu/mL. The limit of detection was 3×10^3 cfu/mL for *B. subtilis*.

Fluorescent Evanescent Wave Fiber-Optic Immunosensor

In this technology, antibodies are immobilized on the surface of either a glass optical fiber, a plastic cylindrical waveguide, or a planar waveguide. The antibodies bind fluorescently labeled analytes in a test sample and the antigen–antibody binding is detected using the fluorescent tag approach. The bound label should be within the evanescent wave zone. The input light excites the fluorescently labeled analyte resulting in a fluorescence signal. A fiber-optic waveguide is used to confine and direct light along its length. The basic design of an optical fiber consists of two components—the core and the cladding. Core and cladding differ primarily in the refractive index of the glass. The core's refractive index is slightly higher than the cladding's, thereby creating a boundary for a circular waveguide. The biosensor is created by removing (i.e., etching away) the fiber-clad material and the exposed core glass is coated with an unlabeled capture antibody. The coated fiber core is exposed to the analyte to which a second fluorescently labeled antibody is added. Molecular species can interact with the evanescent wave radiation as the analyte–antibody complex now acts as the cladding or lower refractive index medium. The nature of the evanescent wave is such that it interacts only with the molecular species that lie within its penetration depth. Antigens and fluorescently labeled antibodies form a sandwich immunocomplex with the immobilized antibody. This immunocomplex lies within the evanescent zone, and the evanescent wave interact with the fluorophores and the resulting fluorescence is coupled back into the fiber and can be detected from a distance.

A fiber-optic sensor, in general, will consist of a source of light, a length of sensing (and transmission) fiber, a photodetector, demodulator, processing and display optics, and the required electronics. A schematic diagram of one channel of a multichannel fiber-optic based evanescent wave fluorescence sensor is shown in Figure 8.35. Generally, a near-infrared diode laser is used for the light source. The input fiber light is coupled into the dual-tapered sensing fiber and travels down the tapered fiber length. Tapering the fibers enhances the signal. If the tagged antibody is

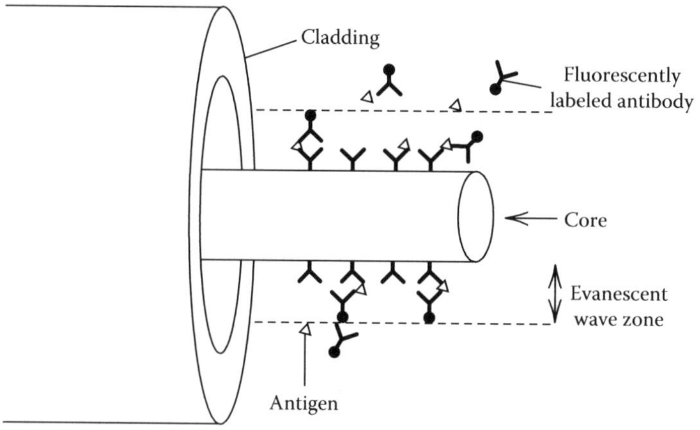

Figure 8.35 Antibodies immobilized onto the exposed core of an optical fiber bind antigens in solution, concentrating them within an evanescent sensing zone. (From McCormack, T. et al., Biomaterials and biosensors, in *Principles of Chemical and Biological Sensor,* Diamond, D., Ed., John Wiley & Sons, Inc., New York, 1998. With permission.)

present, which constitutes the presence of biological agent, or a positive test, the input fiber light excites fluorescence from the special fluorescent dye tag, cyanine 5. Antigen concentration can be determined based on the intensity of fluorescence at a certain point. This fluorescent light travels back down the sensing fiber and is collected by standard return fiber. A schematic diagram of an evanescent wave fiber-optic immunosensor is shown in Figure 8.36.

Research International Corporation has developed a portable automated fiber-optic biosensor, called RAPTOR, for the detection of biological threat agents. It performs rapid (three to ten minutes) fluorescent sandwich immunoassays on the surface of short polystyrene optical probes for up to four target analytes simultaneously. The optical probes can be reused up to 40 times, or until a positive result is obtained, reducing the logistical burden for field operations. Numerous assays for toxins, such as SEB and ricin, and bacteria, such as *B. anthracis* and *F. tularensis*, have been developed (see Table 8.4). Research International has commercialized the RAPTOR, and the development of a second-generation instrument, sponsored by the U.S. Marine Corps, is now in progress [71].

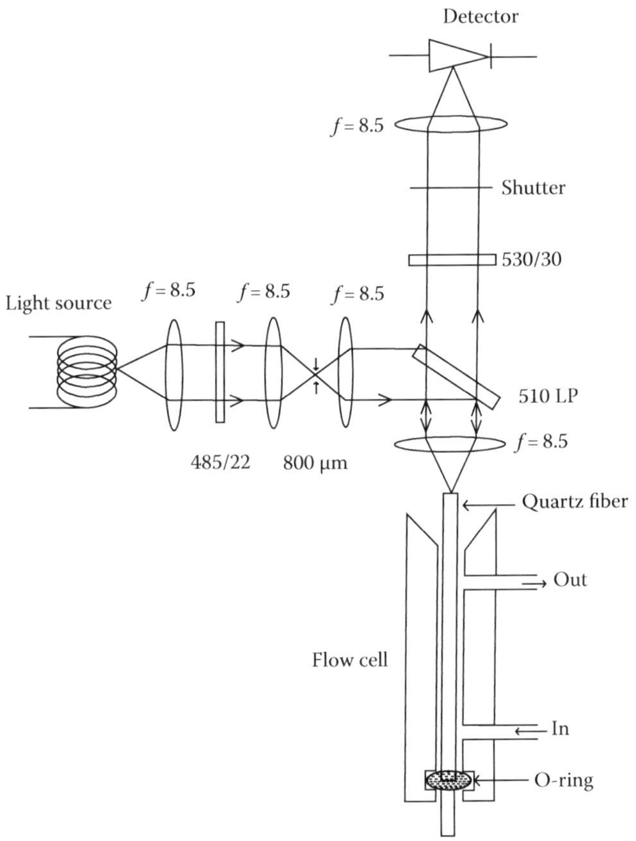

Figure 8.36 Schematic diagram of an evanescent wave immunosensor. (From Rogers, K.R. et al., *Anal. Biochem.*, 182, 353, 1989. With permission.)

Table 8.4 Limits of Detection for Toxins and Pathogens Using a Ten Minute Assay Performed with RAPTOR

Biological Agents	*Type*	*Limit of Detection*
Staphylococcal enterotoxin B (SEB)	Toxin	1 ng/mL
Ricin	Toxin	10 ng/mL
Cholera toxin	Toxin	1 ng/mL
Y. pestis F1	Bacterial surface protein	10 ng/mL
B. anthracis	Gram positive bacterium (vegetative form)	50 cfu/mL
B. globigii	Gram positive bacterium (spore)	5×10^4 spores/mL
Brucella abortus	Gram negative bacterium	7×10^4 cfu/mL
F. tularensis	Gram negative bacterium	5×10^4 cfu/mL
Giardia lamblia	Protozoan cysts	3×10^4 cysts/mL

Source: Anderson, G.P. et al., RAPTOR: A portable, automated biosensor, *Proceedings of the First Conference on Point Detection for Chemical and Biological Defense*, October 2000. With permission.

Simultaneous Detection of Multiple Agents

Although immunoassays generally test for only one analyte per assay, recent advances in assay design and in matrix format have resulted in the development of multiplex assays that can be performed on multiple samples simultaneously by automated systems. The accuracy and sensitivity depend on the antibody quality. The detection limit is generally ~10^5 CFU and is typically lower than with PCR and other DNA-based assays.

NRL Array Biosensors

The Naval Research Laboratory (NRL) of the United States has developed a portable array of biosensors for the detection of multiple agents simultaneously. The proposed system uses total internal reflection fluorescence excitation and planar waveguides coupled with PDMS flow cells to allow simultaneous detection and quantification of multiple target analytes (up to nine currently demonstrated) in multiple samples [72]. The following nine targets were detected by them in a single 3×3 array: Staphylococcal enterotoxin B, ricin, cholera toxin, *B. anthracis* Sterne, *B. globigii*, *F. tularensis* LVS, *Y. pestis* F1 antigen, MS2 coliphage, and *S. typhimurium* (see Figure 8.37). A number of researchers have utilized NRL's array biosensor to detect a variety of agents. Ligler et al. [73] summarized this work and it is provided in Table 8.5.

Quantum Dots Multicomponent Detection

The unique property of quantum dots (QDs), which have the capability to emit multiple fluorescent signals from the same sensing region, can be utilized to simplify the performance of

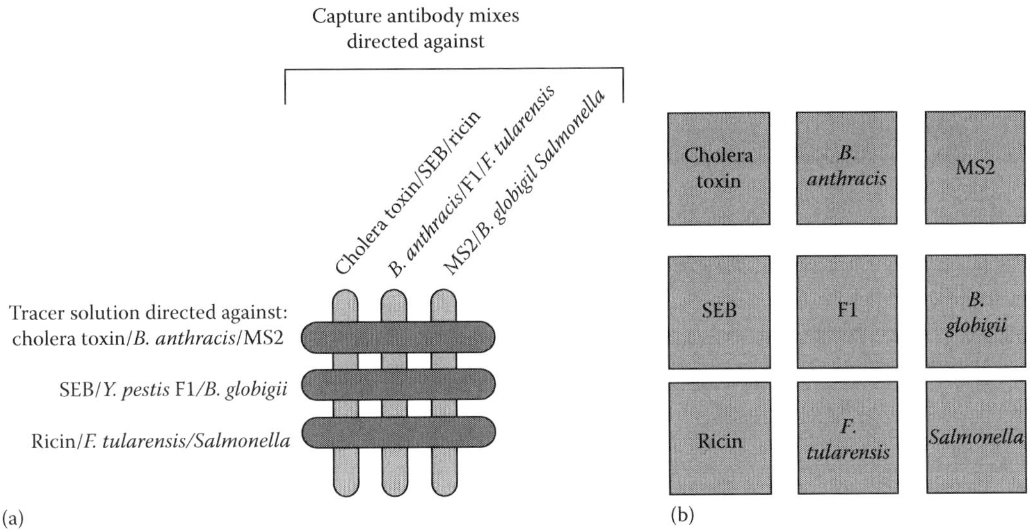

Figure 8.37 Schematic of nine-analyte detection using a 3 × 3 array. (a) Schematic of the antibody mixtures used for capture (above cartoon) and interrogation (left of cartoon); and (b) position of the analyte-specific fluorescent square in the 3 × 3 array with each of the nine analytes tested. (From Taitt, C.R. et al., *Anal. Chem.* 74, 6114, 2002. With permission.)

Table 8.5 Biological Agents Detected by the Naval Research Laboratory's Array Biosensors

Target	*Limits of Detection (LOD)*[a]
Small molecules	
TNT	1–20 ng/mL[b,c]
Deoxynivalenol	0.2 (1–10 ng/g)[d]
Ochratoxin A	0.8 (3.8–100 ng/g)[d]
Aflatoxin B_1	0.3 (0.6–5.1 ng/g)[d]
Protein targets	
Toxins	
SEB	ng/mL[b] (0.1–0.5 ng/mL)[d] (1 ng/mL)[e] (100 ng/mL)[f]
Cholera toxin	1.6 (100 ng/mL)[f]
Botulinum toxoid A	20 (20–500 ng/mL)[d]
Botulinum toxoid B	200 ng/mL
Ricin	8 ng/mL

(continued)

Table 8.5 (continued) Biological Agents Detected by the Naval Research Laboratory's Array Biosensors

Target	*Limits of Detection (LOD)*[a]
Allergens	
Ovalbumin	25 pg/mL[b] (1.3 ng/mL)[d]
Physiological markers	
Y. pestis F1 antigen	25 ng/mL[b,e]
D-dimer	50 ng/mL[b,e]
Bacterial targets	
Br. abortus	3×10^3 cfu/mL[b] (5×10^5 cfu/mL)[f]
F. tularensis	10^5 (7×10^6 cfu/mL)[f]
S. typhimurium	8×10^4 (8×10^4–4×10^5 cfu/mL)[d]
Shigella dysenteriae	5×10^4 (5×10^4–8×10^5 cfu/mL)[d]
Campylobacter jejuni	10^3 (2×10^3–3×10^3 cfu/mL)[d]
Listeria monocytogenes	10^4 cfu/mL
B. globigii	10^5 cfu/mL
B. anthracis	624 (7×10^4 cfu/mL)[f]
E. coli O157:H7	5×10^3 (1×10^4–5×10^4 cfu/mL)[d]
Staphylococcus aureus	~10^6 cfu/mL
Viral targets	
MS2 bacteriophage	10^7 pfu/mL[b]
Vaccinia	10^7–10^8 pfu/mL[b]

Source: Ligler, F.S. et al., *Anal. Sci.*, 23, 5, 2007. With permission.

[a] cfu/mL (colony-forming units/mL); pfu/mL (platform-forming units/mL).

[b] Buffer LOD.

[c] Buffer LOD depends on immunoassay format.

[d] LOD range in food matrices.

[e] LOD range in clinical matrices.

[f] Fixed concentration measured in environmental matrices (not LOD).

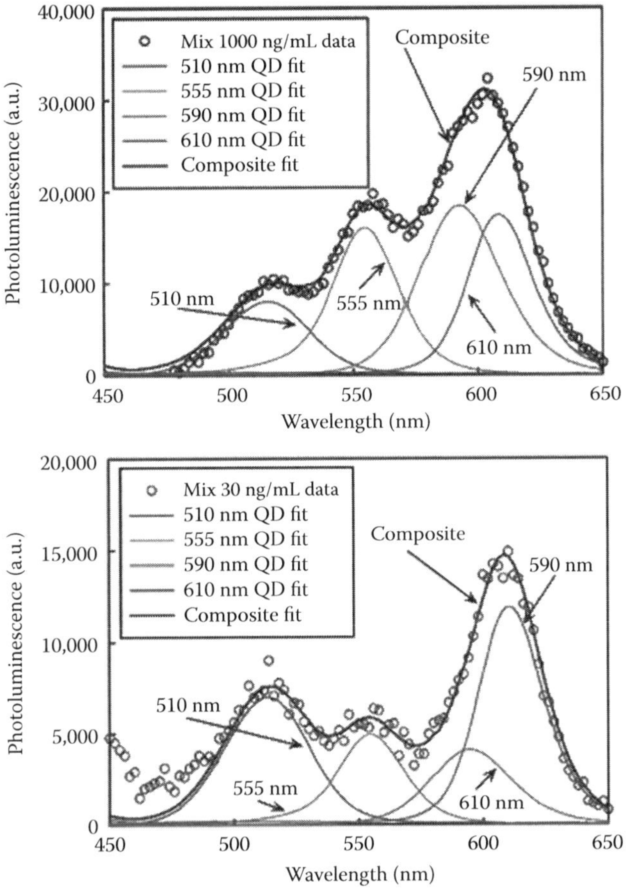

Figure 8.38 Multitoxin assay examining mixes of all four toxins at 1000 ng/mL each toxin (top graph) and 30 ng/mL each toxin (bottom graph) probed with a mix of QD-detection antibody conjugates. Measured values are shown as circles. Both the composite fit and the fit from each of the four individual QD components are displayed. Each data point represents the average of three experiments. (From Goldman, E.R. et al., *Anal. Chem.*, 76, 684, 2004. With permission.)

multiplexed analysis. Goldman et al. prepared bioinorganic conjugates made with highly luminescent semiconductor nanocrystals (CdSe–ZnS coreshell QDs) and antibodies to perform multiplexed fluoroimmunoassays. They detected cholera toxin, ricin, shiga-like toxin 1, and staphylococcal enterotoxin B simultaneously from a single sample in single wells of a microtiter plate. Individual agents were identified by deconvoluting the signal from mixed toxin samples, which also allowed quantification of all four toxins simultaneously (see Figure 8.38).

No-Tag Biosensors

A number of sensors have been developed or are under development that do not need to form a sandwich assay. Antigen–antibody binding is detected directly, so no tag reagent is required.

Advantages to this type of assay include simplification of the analysis process (fewer steps, fewer components), minimized disposable fluid use (no need to carry tag reagent solutions), reuse of sensors after a negative test (minimal disposable use), and a smaller, lighter weight instrument that consumes less power. Examples of no-tag biosensor methods include interferometry, surface plasmon resonance (SPR), piezoelectric crystal microbalance, waveguide coupler, and electrical capacitance. These methods are briefly described below.

Surface Plasmon Resonance

Several biosensors have been developed based on the phenomenon known as surface plasmon resonance (SPR), which is a quantum optical–electrical phenomenon arising from the interaction of light with a metal surface. Under certain conditions, the energy carried by photons of light is transferred to packets of electrons, called plasmons, on a metal's surface [75,76]. Energy transfer occurs only at a specific resonance wavelength of light: the wavelength where the quantum energy carried by the photons exactly equals the quantum energy level of the plasmons.

SPR sensors generally use a 50 nm thick gold coating on a plastic support. Three types of surface structures are used in SPR-based sensors: the surface of a right angle prism, a submicron sinusoidal grating molded into the plastic surface, and an optical waveguide-based system.

Gold is used because it does not oxidize easily, and therefore, the surface chemistry or properties are not affected. The gold is subsequently coated with binding molecules. The binding molecules may be antibodies, DNA probes, enzymes, or other reagents that can react exclusively with a specific analyte.

The coated metal surface interacts with light at a characteristic resonant wavelength that depends upon the molecular composition at the metal's surface. When the coated metal is exposed to a sample that contains the analyte, the analyte binds to the metal through its specific interaction with the binding molecules. As an analyte is bound, the composition at the surface changes, and, consequently, the resonant wavelength shifts. The magnitude of the change in the resonant wavelength is proportional to the amount of binding that takes place, which is proportional to the concentration of the analyte in the sample. In the SPR system, the binding events are monitored in real-time and it is not necessary to label the interacting biomolecules (see Figure 8.39).

Interferometer Biosensors

Several biosensors are developed based on the interferometry principle that measures the change in refractive index on the surface of a planar single mode waveguide. An antibody coating is applied to the waveguide sensor's surface and its binding with the antigen changes the refractive index of the surface layer, which, in turn, alters the velocity of light traveling in the waveguide through its evanescent field interaction. Various types of interferometers are available including Mach–Zehnder, dual mode, and polarization, all of which have a planar architecture. The phase change due to the change in refractive index with respect to a reference light beam is measured. A polarization interferometer utilizes two perpendicular polarized modes of a laser beam to perform the immunoassay. A guided polarized light perpendicular to the surface (TM mode) that has a high degree of evanescent wave interaction with the sensor coating forms the active arm of the interferometer. A horizontally polarized light (TE mode) that does not interact with the coating is the reference arm. Antigen–antibody binding on the surface causes a phase shift to occur between the two light beams. The degree of phase shift is directly proportional to the change in

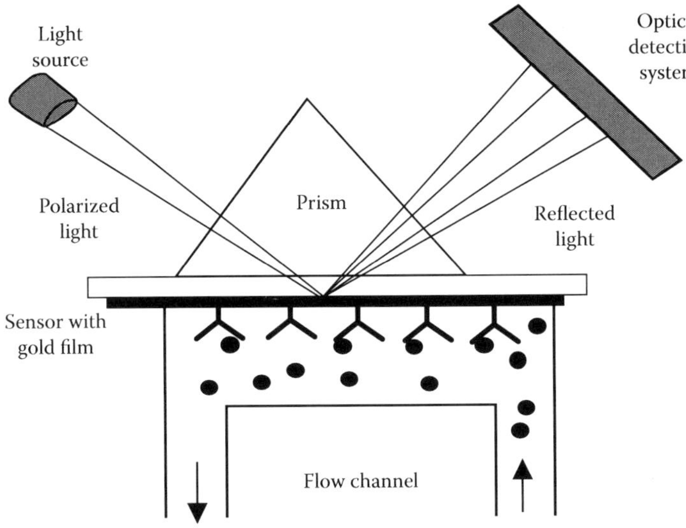

Figure 8.39 Principle of operation of a surface plasmon resonance biosensor. (Courtesy of SPR Basics, www.xantec.com/html/spr.html.)

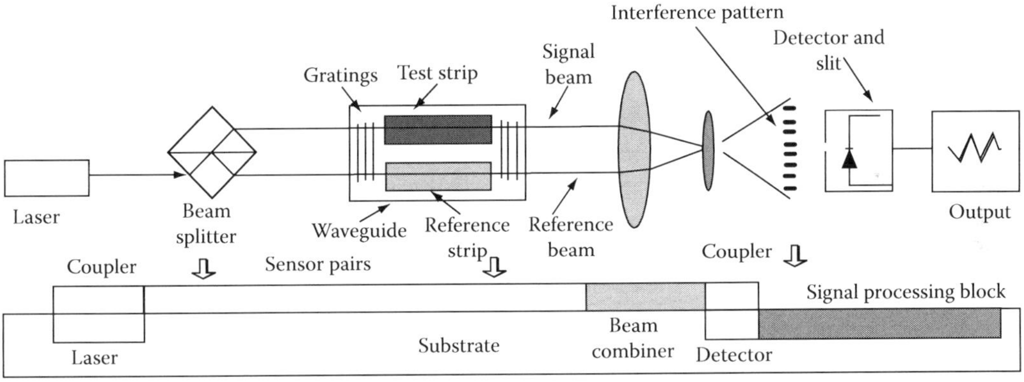

Figure 8.40 Interferometer setup and integration. (From Kim, D. et al., Integrated Bio-Optoelectronic Sensor System, www.ece.gatech.edu/research/GTAC/Sp02PDFHandouts/DaeikKim.pdf. With permission.)

refractive index which, in turn, is related to the degree of antigen–antibody binding. A schematic diagram of an interferometry system is shown in Figure 8.40 [78].

Piezoelectric Crystal Balance

The piezoelectric immunosensor is a very sensitive biosensor capable of detecting antigens in the picogram range. This type of device is believed to have the potential to detect antigens in the gas phase as well as in the liquid phase.

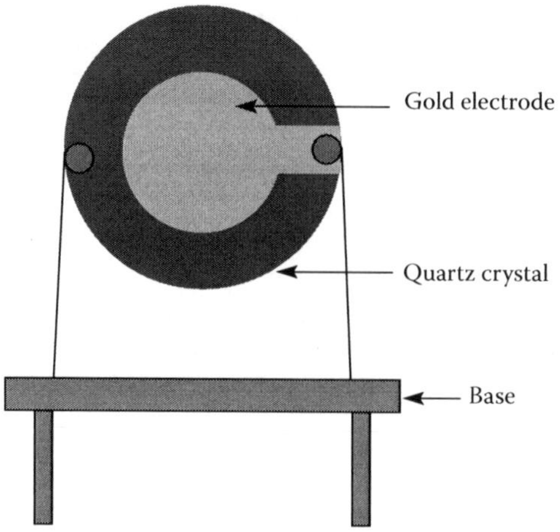

Figure 8.41 Piezoelectric biosensor.

The antibody–antigen binding reaction deposits a small quantity of mass onto the surface of the oscillating piezoelectric crystal. This mass change results in a frequency change, which is measured.

The most frequently used detector crystal for piezoelectric applications is alpha quartz because they are insoluble in water and resistant to high temperatures. Alpha quartz crystals do not lose their piezoelectric properties up to a temperature of 579°C. The resonant frequency of quartz crystal depends on the physical dimensions of the quartz plate and the thickness of the electrode deposited. Although both the AT- and BT-cut crystals are used as piezoelectric detectors, the AT-cut crystal is the most stable for construction of biosensors. The crystals usually take the form of discs, squares, and rectangles (see Figure 8.41).

Kumar [79] constructed a piezoelectric crystal biosensor using a 10 MHz AT-cut quartz crystal with an electrode coating deposited on each side using the sputtering method. The crystal was mounted on a holder with stainless steel leads. A silver composite was used to connect the electrode to the wire. The crystals were 14 mm in diameter, and the electrodes on both sides of the crystal were 8 mm in diameter. Figure 8.42 shows the schematic diagram of a piezoelectric crystal biosensor. A flow cell can be used to introduce the sample, washing liquids, or buffer solutions to the sensing surface. Because no tag reagent is used, the sensor need not be replaced following a negative result. However, after a positive test, the sensor needs to be replaced.

Piezoelectric crystal sensors can be used for both the gas and liquid phases [80]. Detection of biological warfare agents using piezoelectric crystal sensors has been reported by a number of researchers [81]. Carter et al. [82] detected the *Vibrio cholera* bacterium with an antibody-based piezoelectric crystal sensor. Later, they used the same sensor for the detection of ricin.

Resonant Mirror Biosensors

The resonant mirror biosensor combines an SPR sensor with the sensitivity of a waveguide device, creating a highly sensitive, yet simple, device. The resonant mirror biosensor consists of

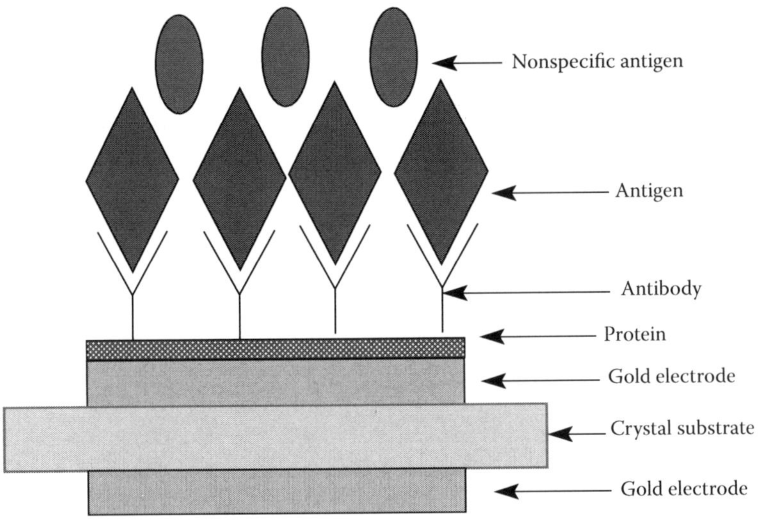

Figure 8.42 Piezoelectric immunoassay. (From Kumar, A., *JOM-e*, 52(10), 2000. www.tms.org/pubs/journals/JOM/0010/Kumar/Kumar-0010.html. With permission.)

four layers: the sensing surface, the high refractive index dielectric resonant layer, the low index coupling layer, and a prism. Polarized laser light illuminates the underside of the sensor surface at angles greater than the critical angle. The light is totally internally reflected and illuminates the detector array. A series of polarizing filters are incorporated such that any light which follows this path is blocked before reaching the detectors. At one angle, called the resonant angle, a component of the light can couple through the low refractive index spacer layer and propagate along the high refractive index guiding layer. The angle where this coupling occurs, the resonant angle, is essentially dependent upon the refractive index at the surface of the sensor within the evanescent field. Hence, changes in refractive index (or mass) will change the resonant angle. So, as mass increases due to the binding at the binding surface, the signal will increase, and as mass decreases at the dissociation surface, the signal will decrease. This change in angle is linear with respect to mass. The fabrication of the resonant mirror is rather simple. Sputtering and ion beam assisted evaporation techniques are used to make the devices. Because of these methods, large quantities of uniform devices can be made inexpensively. A mirror arrangement is shown in Figure 8.43.

Promising Technologies on the Horizon

Charge-Based Deep Level Transient Spectroscopy (Q-DLTS)

Q-DLTS is discussed in Chapter 22 [84]. This unique technology is based on the ability to create a surface with a negative electron affinity by terminating the bonds on a diamond film surface with a halide [85]. This negative electron affinity causes the diamond surface to generate a positive charge which attracts polar molecules. The energy level of the molecule on the surface of the sensor is measured by passing a transient current through the detector. The response of the molecule

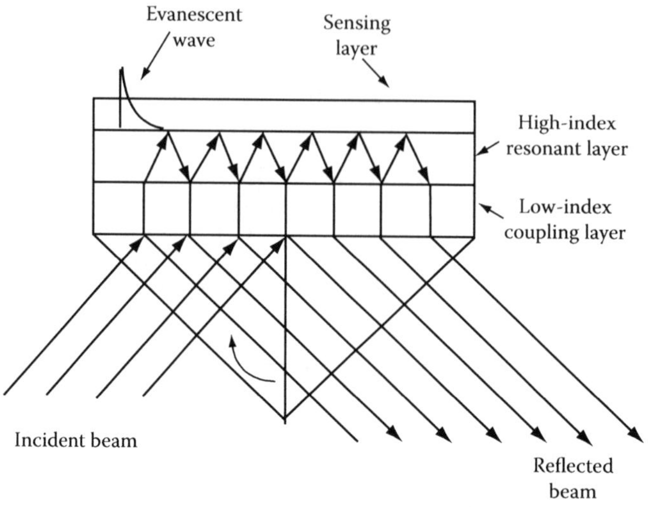

Figure 8.43 Resonance mirror arrangement. (Courtesy of Affinity Sensors, http://www.affinity-sensors.com/faq.html.)

to this transient driver is unique. The method has been used with simple polar molecules. The sensitivity of the Q-DLTS technology is potentially in the subfemtogram level.

Q-DLTS may be adaptable to exiting systems that detect components of biological material such as lipids or may be used to directly detect the antigen.

Up-Converting Phosphor Technology

In this method, the phosphor particles are attached to detection probes, antibodies, or DNA that direct the phosphors to bind to biological agents. Up-converting phosphor materials emit visible light upon excitation with near-infrared light rather than UV light. If the target antigen is present, an infrared diode laser causes the phosphor probe to emit visible light. Some of the advantages of this method are

High sensitivity (single-phosphor particle)
Many colors for multiplexing (ten unique colors currently)
Robust, no photobleaching
Diode laser excitation (compact sensors)

Spectroscopic Methods

Fourier transform infrared spectroscopy (FTIR) and dispersive Raman microscopy can provide rapid identification of biological agents. The vibration of bonds within functional groups are used to identify as well as to quantify the biochemical composition of the molecule. Goodacre et al. [86] used a Bruker IFS28 FTIR Spectrometer equipped with a mercury–cadmium–telluride–liquid nitrogen cooled detector to identify the *E. coli* isolate Ea and the *Proteus mirabilis* isolate Pa. The FTIR spectra of these two bacteria taken in diffuse reflectance mode is shown in Figure 8.44.

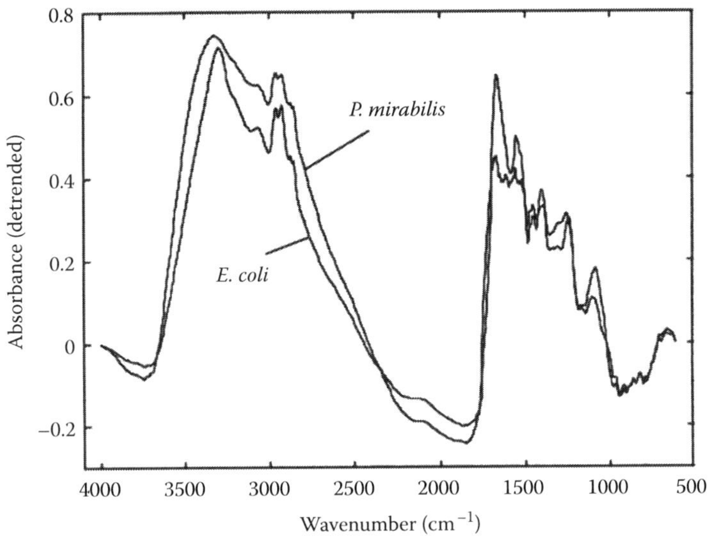

Figure 8.44 FTIR diffuse reflectance absorbance spectra of *E. coli* isolate Ea and *P. mirabilis* isolate Pa. (Data from Goodacre, R. et al., Intelligent systems for the characterization of microorganisms from hyperspectral data. *NATO ASI Series*, Ser. 1: *Disarmament Technologies*, Vol. 30 (Rapid Methods for Analysis of Biological materials in the Environment), Stopa, P.J. and Bartoszcze, M.A., Eds., 2000, 111–136.)

In Raman microscope, a laser illuminates the sample on a substrate and generates Raman scattering. The fingerprints of the sample is matched against a library of known fingerprints. The sample can be precisely identified by point-by-point matching of the fingerprints with the library data at all wavelengths. Dispersive Raman spectra of the same bacteria are shown in Figure 8.45.

Cell- and Tissue-Based Biosensors

Several researchers are utilizing the intrinsic response of a specific cell or tissue to a potentially toxic or foreign substance to identify a biological agent. As noted by Sapsford et al. [87], cell-based sensing can be grouped into two general classes: (1) those relying on inherent cellular physiological processes for detection, or "innate" cell-based sensors; and (2) those using cells that have been genetically engineered or that have had sensing materials introduced into them, i.e., engineered cell-based sensors. These cells produce a signal when they interact with toxic or foreign substances that can be measured by an electrode or an optical detector. The innate cells take advantage of either the electrical excitability of the mammalian cell membrane in response to biological-agent analytes, or chromatophores, which are pigment cells responsible for the brilliant colors of fish, amphibians, and reptiles. Biological agents can induce changes in the appearance of chromatophores or the color, which can be detected by a spectrophotometer. Rider and coworkers [88] have engineered B-lymphocytes expressing a specific membrane-bound antibody receptor, to detect targeted biological agents within minutes. Binding of a bioagent to the cell surface antibodies causes an increase in intracellular Ca levels resulting in the emission of light from the cytosolic aequorin (see Figures 8.46 and 8.47).

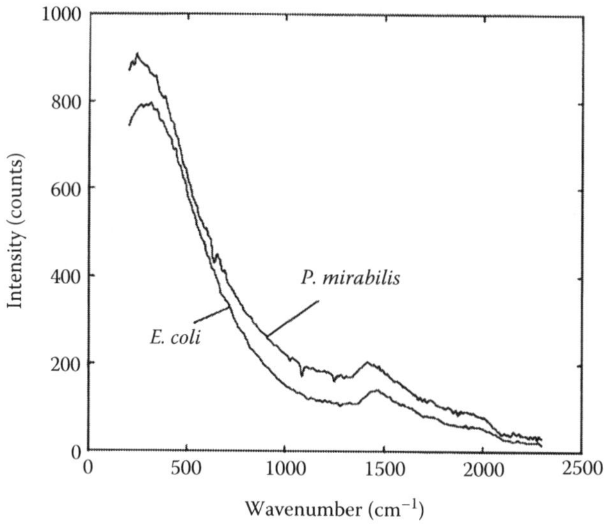

Figure 8.45 Dispersive Raman spectra of *E. coli* isolate Ea and *P. mirabilis* isolate Pa. (From Goodacre, R. et al., Intelligent systems for the characterization of microorganisms from hyperspectral data. *NATO ASI Series*, Ser. 1: *Disarmament Technologies*, Vol. 30 (Rapid Methods for Analysis of Biological materials in the Environment), Stopa, P.J. and Bartoszcze, M.A., Eds., 2000, 111–136. With permission.)

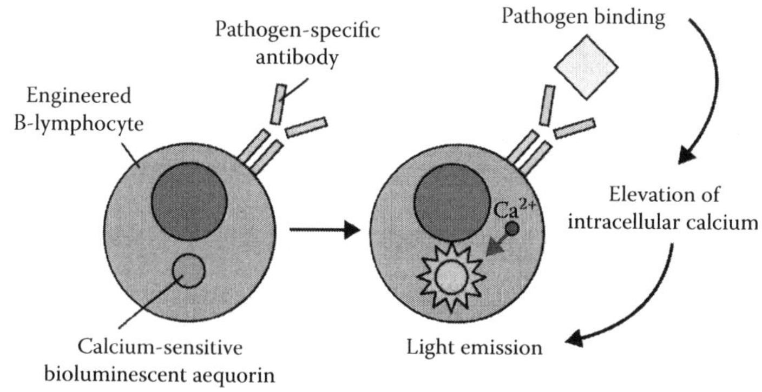

Figure 8.46 The CANARY method (cellular analysis and notification of antigen risks and yields). B-lymphocytes were engineered to express calcium-dependent bioluminescent aequorin in the cytosol as well as pathogen-specific antibodies on the cell surface. Ligation of the antibody by the pathogen causes an elevation in intracellular calcium ions, thus triggering emission of light from the aequorin within seconds of pathogen contact. (From Livingston, A.D. et al., *Genome Biol.*, 6(6), 112, 2005. With permission.)

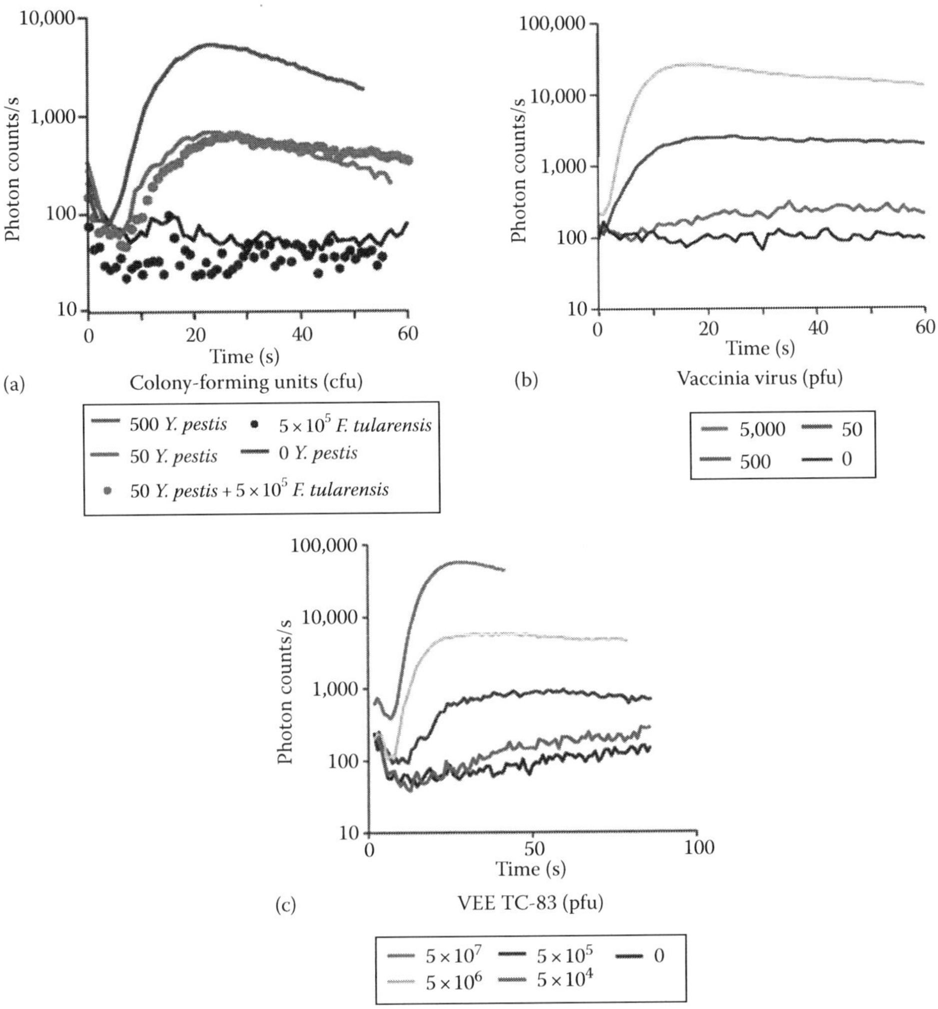

Figure 8.47 Dose response and limit of detection for pathogen-specific B cells. (a) Formalin-inactivated *Y. pestis* or *F. tularensis* (50 μL) were concentrated for 60 s at 10,000 × *g*, then *Y. pestis*-specific cells (20 μL) were added and spun for an additional 5 s. Photon emission was measured in a luminometer. Identical results were obtained with a live, avirulent strain of *Y. pestis*. (b) Vaccinia virus was concentrated and tested with orthopox-specific cells as described in a. (c) Irradiated TC-83 VEE was assayed (without concentration) with VEE-specific cells. (From Rider, T.H. et al., *Science*, 301(5630), 213, 2003. With permission.)

Cell- or tissue-based biosensors are still in the development stage and have not been field tested. However, they still have to overcome the antibody cross-reactivity problems like other antibody-based technologies along with long-term shelf life and maintenance as other cell-based systems.

Conclusion

Following the Persian Gulf War of 1991, significant improvements have been made in the field of biosensors. Not only a number of new techniques have been developed, but also the reliability and accuracy of the previous sensors have been improved considerably. However, it is likely that no one detection technology will meet all civilian needs as the number of potential threat agents for domestic terrorism are significantly larger than that for military use. The challenge with the biological detector is to achieve high sensitivity in the presence of large amount of interfering substances. Interference is generally due to the same physical parameter that is being used for selectivity, such as size, mass, or charge. One option may be to use multiple sensors; however, this can increase the cost significantly. Mobility and fieldability of the biological detection systems are also a major concern. Recently, a number of prototype units have been designed with decreasing size and weight, making them more mobile and fieldable.

References

1. Biological warfare and detection capabilities. www.gulflink.osd.mil/faq_biologic_5jun.htm
2. L Power and W Ellis, Jr. Pathogenic microbe sensor technology. Presented at the Defense Advanced Research Projects Agency Meeting on Bio-surveillance: Providing Detection in the New Millennium. Johns Hopkins University Applied Physics Laboratory, Laurel, MD, February 11, 1998. (As reported in Institute of Medicine. Chemical and Biological Terrorism: Research and Development to Improve Civilian Medical Response. Washington, DC: National Academy Press, 1999).
3. TR Wehner, PD Stroud, and WL May. Lidar detection of biological aerosols. Presented at the International Symposium on Optical Science Engineering, and Instrumentation Program on Remote Sensing, Denver, CO, August 4–9, 1996.
4. Fibertek Inc., www.fibertek.com.
5. Military Analysis Network, http://www.fas.org/man/dod-101/sys/land/lr-bsds.htm
6. R Foch. Micro unmanned vehicle. Presented at the Defense Advanced Research Projects Agency Meeting on Bio-surveillance: Providing Detection in the New Millennium. Johns Hopkins University Applied Physics Laboratory, Laurel, MD, February 11, 1998. (As reported in Institute of Medicine. Chemical and Biological Terrorism: Research and Development to Improve Civilian Medical Response. National Academy Press, Washington, DC, 1999).
7. FS Ligler, GP Anderson, PT Davidson, RJ Foch, JT Ives, O King, D Keeley, G Page, DA Stenger, and JP Whelan. Remote sensing using an airborne biosensor. *Environ. Sci. Technol.* 32(16): 2461–2466, 1998.
8. CR Prasad, HS Lee, IH Hwang, M Nam, SL Mathur, and B Ranganayakamma. Portable digital LIDAR: A compact stand-off bioagent aerosol sensor. *Proc. SPIE-Int. Soc. Opt. Eng.*: *Chem. Biol. Sensing II* 4378: 50–59, 2001.
9. AA Fatah, JA Barrett, RD Arcilesi, KJ Ewing, CH Lattin, and TF Moshier. An Introduction to Biological Agent Detection Equipment for Emergency First Responders. NIJ Guide 101-00, December 2001.
10. KA Robertson, TK Ghosh, AL Hines, SK Loyalka, RC Warder, Jr., and D Novosel. Airborne Microorganisms: Their occurrence and removal. The fifth international conference on indoor air quality and climate, Toronto, Canada, July 29–Aug 3, 1990, *Indoor Air '90*, Vol. 4, Toronto, ON, 1990, p. 567.
11. WC Hinds. *Aerosol Technology: Properties, Behavior, and Measurement of Airborne Particles.* John Wiley & Sons, Inc., New York, 1982.
12. WH Griest, MB Wise, KJ Hart, SA Lammert, CV Thompson, and AA Vass. Biological agent detection and identification by the Block II Chemical Biological Mass Spectrometer. *Field Anal. Chem. Technol.* 5(4): 177–184, 2001.
13. K Gotoh and H Masuda. Development of annular-type virtual impactor. *Powder Technol.* 118(1–2): 68–78, 2001.

14. Y Ding, ST Ferguson, JM Wolfson, and P Koutrakis. Development of a high volume slit nozzle virtual impactor to concentrate coarse particles. *Aerosol Sci. Technol.* 34(3): 274–283, 2001.
15. CS Cox and CM Wathes. *Bioaerosol Handbook.* Lewis Publishers, Boca Raton, FL, 1995.
16. WD Griffiths and IW Stewart. Performance of bioaerosol samplers used by the UK biotechnology industry. *J. Aerosol Sci.* 30(8): 1029–1040, 1999.
17. W Bergman, J Shinn, R Lochner, S Sawyer, F Milanovich, and R Mariella Jr. High air flow, low pressure drop, bio-aerosol collector using a multi-slit virtual impactor. *J. Aerosol Sci.* 36(5–6): 619–638, 2005.
18. DJ Tilles, GA DiFurio, and JC Schmidt. Point source biological agent detection system. U.S. Patent 7405073, Issued July 29, 2008.
19. RG Pinnick, SC Hill, P Nachman, G Videen, G Chen, and RK Chang. Aerosol fluorescence spectrum analyzer for rapid measurement of single micrometer-sized airborne biological particles. *Aerosol Sci. Technol.* 28: 95–104, 1998.
20. SC Hill, RG Pinnick, S Niles, YL Pan, S Holler, RK Chang, J Bottiger, BT Chen, CS Orr, and G Feather. Real-time measurement of fluorescence spectra from single airborne biological particles. *Field Anal. Chem. Technol.* 3: 221–239, 1999.
21. YL Pan, S Holler, RK Chang, SC Hill, RG Pinnick, S Niles, and JR Bottiger. Single-shot fluorescence spectra of individual micrometer-sized bioaerosols illuminated by a 351-or a 266-nm ultraviolet laser. *Opt. Lett.* 24: 116–118, 1999.
22. GW Paris, RA Copeland, K Mortelmans, and BV Bronk. Spectrally resolved absolute fluorescence cross sections for bacillus spores. *Appl. Opt.* 36: 958–967, 1997.
23. YS Cheng, EB Barr, BJ Fan, PJ Hargis, DJ Rader, TJ O'Hern, JR Torczynski, GC Tisone, BL Preppernau, SA Young, and RJ Radloff. Detection of bioaerosols using multiwavelength UV fluorescence spectroscopy. *Aerosol Sci. Technol.* 30: 186–201, 1999.
24. PH Kaye, JE Barton, and E Hirst. Simultaneous light scattering and intrinsic fluorescence measurement for the classification of airborne particles. *Appl. Opt.* 39: 3738–3745, 2000.
25. J Ho. Real-time detection of biological aerosols with fluorescence aerodynamic particle sizer (FLAPS). *J. Aerosol Sci.* 27: S581–S582, 1996.
26. PP Hairston, J Ho, and FR Quant. Design of an instrument for real-time detection of bioaerosols using simultaneous measurement of particle aerodynamic size and intrinsic fluorescence. *J. Aerosol Sci.* 28: 471–582, 1997.
27. LM Brosseau, D Vesley, N Rice, K Goodell, M Nellis, and P Hairston. Differences in detected fluorescence among several bacterial species measured with a direct-reading particle sizer and fluorescence detector. *Aerosol Sci. Technol.* 32: 545–558, 2000.
28. GA Luoma, PP Cherrier, and LA Retfalvi. Real-time warning of biological-agent attacks with the Canadian Integrated Biochemical Agent Detection System II (CIBADS II). *Field Anal. Chem.* 3(4–5): 260–273, 1999.
29. J Ho, M Spence, and P Hairston. Measurement of biological aerosol with a fluorescent aerodynamic particle sizer (FLAPS): Correlation of optical data with biological data. *NATO ASI Series*, Ser. 1: *Disarmament Technologies*, Vol. 30 (Rapid Methods for Analysis of Biological Materials in the Environment), 2000, pp. 177–201.
30. JD Eversole, WK Cary, CS Scotto, R Pierson, M Spence, and AJ Campillo. Continuous bioaerosol monitoring using UV excitation fluorescence: Outdoor test results. *Field Anal. Chem. Technol.* 15(4): 205–212, 2001.
31. HM Davey and DB Kell. A portable flow cytometer for the detection and identification of microorganisms. *NATO ASI Series*, Ser. 1: *Disarmament Technologies*, Vol. 30 (Rapid Methods for Analysis of Biological Materials in the Environment), Eds. PJ Stopa and MA Bartoszcze, 2000, pp. 159–167.
32. PJ Stopa, H Kulaga, P Anderson, and M Cain. Field applications of flow cytometry. *NATO ASI Series*, Ser 1: *Disarmament Technologies*, Vol. 30 (Rapid Methods for Analysis of Biological Materials in the Environment), Eds. PJ Stopa and MA Bartoszcze, 2000, pp. 137–158.
33. Biological Detection System Technologies. Technology and Industrial Base Study. A Primer on Biological Detection technologies. Prepared for the North American Technology and Industrial Base Organization, February 2001.

34. MW Mayo and SC Hill. Fluorescence spectra of bacteria, pollens and naturally occurring background. *Third Workshop for Stand-off Detection for C and B Defence*, Williamsburg, VA, October 1994, pp. 105–112.
35. PP Hairston, J Ho, and R Quant. Design of and instrument for real-time detection of bioaerosols using simultaneous measurements of particle aerodynamic size and intrinsic fluorescence. *J. Aerosol Sci.* 28: 471–482, 1997.
36. T Tjarnhage, M Stromqvist, G Olofsson, D Squirrell, J Burke, J Ho, and M Spence. Multivariate data analysis of fluorescence signals from biological aerosols. *Field Anal. Chem. Technol.* 5(4): 171–176, 2001.
37. MP Sinha. Laser induced volatilization and ionization of microparticles. *Rev. Sci. Instrum.* 55(6): 886–891, 1984.
38. KH Jarman, ST Cebula, AJ Saenz, CE Petersen, NB Valentine, MT Kingsley, and KL Wahl. An algorithm for automated bacterial identification using matrix-assisted laser desorption/ionization mass spectrometry. *Anal. Chem.*, 72(6): 1217, 2000.
39. DN Heller, RJ Cotter, C Fenselau, and OM Uy. Profiling of bacteria by fast atom bombardment mass spectroscopy. *Anal. Chem.* 59: 2806–2809, 1987.
40. University of Melbourne Australia, School of Chemistry, Faculty of Science, http://www.chemistry.unimelb.edu.au/MassSpec/homepage/electrospray.html
41. Electrospray ionization, www.methods.ch.cam.ac.uk/meth/ms/theory/esi.html
42. R Zenobi and R Knochenmuss. Ion formation in MALDI mass spectrometry. *Mass Spectrom. Rev.* 17: 337, 1998.
43. Standing committee on program and technical review of the US Army chemical and biological defense command, NRC. *Review of Mass Spectrometry and Bioremediation Programs of the Edgewood Research*, Development and Engineering Center, National Academy Press, Washington, DC, 1998.
44. JP Dworzanski, WH McClennen, PA Cole, SN Thornton, HLC Meuzelaar, NS Arnold, and AP Snyder. Field-portable, automated pyrolysis-GC/IMS system for rapid biomarker detection in aerosols: A feasibility study. *Field Anal. Chem. Technol.* 1: 295–305, 1997.
45. AP Synder, A Tripathi, WM Maswadeh, J Ho, and M Spence. Field detection and identification of a bioaerosol suite by pyrolysis-gas-chromatograph-ion mobility spectrometry. *Field Anal. Chem. Technol.* 5(4): 190–204, 2001.
46. SS Iqbal. MW Mayo, JG Bruno, BV Bronk, CA Batt, and JP Chambers. A review of molecular recognition technologies for detection of biological threat agents. *Biosens. Bioelectron.* 15: 549–578, 2000.
47. VG Delvecchio, R Redkar, S Cheng, and M Gress. Development of PCR-based assays for the detection and molecular genotyping of microorganisms of importance to biological warfare. *NATO ASI Series*, Ser. 1: *Disarmament Technologies*, Vol. 30 (Rapid Methods for Analysis of Biological Materials in the Environment), 2000, pp. 219–229.
48. M Ibrahim, S Sofi, S Michelle, D Fishel, J Ezzell, and E Henchal. Detection of biological agents using probe-based PCR assays. *Proceedings of ERDEC Science Conference on Chemical and Biological Defense Research*, Maryland, US, Meeting Date 1998, pp. 227–232, 1999.
49. G Franciosa, L Fenicia, C Caldiani, and P Aureli. PCR for detection of Clostridium botulinum typ c in avian and environmental samples. *J. Clin. Microbiol.* 34: 882–885, 1996.
50. BN Clossais, S Minjolle, J Gicquel, R Colimon, and PM Andre. Automated determination of amplified PCR products: Application to HCV viremia detection and quantification. *Cell Biol.* 41: 959–966, 1995.
51. W Beyer, P Glockner, J Otto, and R Boehm. A nested PCR method for the detection of Bacillus anthracis in environmental samples collected from former tannery sites. *Microbiol. Res.* 150(2): 179–186, 1995.
52. MV Bloom. Polymerase Chain Reaction, Access Excellence, The National Health Museum, www.accessexcellence.org/RC/CT/polymerase_chain_reaction.html
53. JE McDade and BE Anderson. Molecular epidemiology: Application of nucleic acid amplification and sequence analysis. *Epidemiol. Rev.* 18: 90–97, 1996.
54. EA Henchal and MS Ibrahim. Evaluation of polymerase chain reaction assays for identifying biological agents. *NATO ASI Series*, Ser. 1: *Disarmament Technologies*, Vol. 30 (Rapid Methods for Analysis of Biological materials in the Environment), Eds. PJ Stopa and MA Bartoszcze, 2000, pp. 239–249.
55. UE Gibson, CA Heid, and PM Williams. A novel method for real time quantitative RT-PCR. *Genome Res.*, 6: 995–1001, 1996.

56. EM Elnifro, AM Ashshi, RJ Cooper, and PE Klapper. Multiplex PCR: Optimization and application in diagnostic virology. *Clin. Microbiol. Rev.* 13(4): 559–570, 2000.
57. M Varma-Basil, H El-Hajj, SAE Marras, MH Hazbon, JM Mann, ND Connell, FR Kramer, and D Alland. Molecular beacons for multiplex detection of four bacterial bioterrorism agents. *Clin. Chem.* 50: 1060–1062, 2004.
58. DV Lim, JM Simpson, EA Kearns, and ME Kramer. Current and developing technologies for monitoring agents of bioterrorism and biowarfare. *Clin. Microbiol. Rev.* 18(4): 583–607, 2005.
59. JA Higgins, M Cooper, L Schroeder-Tucker, S Black, D Miller, JS Karns, E Manthey, R Breeze, and ML Perdue. A field investigation of *Bacillus anthracis* contamination of U.S. Department of Agriculture and other Washington, DC, buildings during the anthrax attack of October 2001. *Appl. Environ. Microbiol.* 69: 593–599, 2003.
60. JS Van Kessel, JS Karns, and ML Perdue. Using a portable real-time PCR assay to detect *Salmonella* in raw milk. J. *Food. Protect.* 66: 1762–1767, 2003.
61. Antibody structure, www.biology.arizona.edu/immunology/tutorials/antibody/structure.html
62. New Horizons Diagnostics Inc., www.nhdiag.com/anthrax.shtml
63. HA Rongen, RM Hoetelmans, V Bult, and WP van Bennekom. Chemiluminescence and immunoassays. *J. Pharm. Biomed. Anal.* 12(4): 433–462, 1994.
64. AR Bowie, MG Sanders, and PJ Worsfold. Analytical applications of liquid phase chemiluminescence reactions—A review. *J. Biolumin. Chemilumin.* 11(2): 61–90, 1996.
65. H Yu, JW McMahon, and TM Campagnari. Detection of biological threat agents by immune magnetic microsphere based solid phase fluorogenic and electro chemiluminescence. *Biosens. Bioelectron.* 14(10–11): 829–840, 2000.
66. T Yoshinobu, MJ Schoning, R Otto, K Furuichi, Yu Mourzina, Yu Ermolenko, and H Iwasaki. Portable light-addressable potentiometric sensor (LAPS) for multisensor applications. *Sensors and Actuators*, B95, 352, 2003.
67. Threshold System. Immuno ligand assay system, www.moleculardevices.com/pages/thresh_ila.html
68. KA Uithoven, JC Schmidt, and ME Ballman. Rapid identification of biological warfare agents using an instrument employing a light addressable potentiometric sensor and a flow through immunofiltration-enzyme assay system. *Biosens. Bioelectron.* 14: 761–770, 2000.
69. T McCormack, G Keating, A Killard, BM Manning, and R O'Kennedy. Biomaterials and Biosensors. In *Principles of Chemical and Biological Sensor*, Ed. D Diamond, John Wiley & Sons, Inc., New York, 1998.
70. KR Rogers, JJ Valdes, and El Defrawi. *Anal. Biochem.* 182: 353–359, 1989.
71. GP Anderson, CA Rowe-Taitt, and FS Ligler. RAPTOR: A portable, automated biosensor. Proceedings of the First Conference on Point Detection for Chemical and Biological Defense, Williamsburg, VA, US, October, 2000.
72. CR Taitt, GP Anderson, BM Lingerfelt, MJ Feldstein, and FS Ligler. Nine-analyte detection using an array-based biosensor. *Anal. Chem.* 74: 6114–6120, 2002.
73. FS Ligler, KE Sapsford, JP Golden, LC Shriver-Lake, CR Taitt, MA Dyer, S Barone, and CJ Myatt. The array biosensor: Portable, automated systems. *Anal. Sci.* 23: 5–10, 2007.
74. ER Goldman, AR Clapp, GP Anderson, HT Uyeda, JM Mauro, IL Medintz, and H Mattoussi. Multiplexed toxin analysis using four colors of quantum dot fluororeagents. *Anal. Chem.* 76: 684–688, 2004.
75. M McDonnell. Biosensors in the detection of biological agents. Uses of Immobilized Biological Compounds, *NATO ASI Series*, Ser E, Vol. 252, 1994, pp. 369–373.
76. RPH Kooyman, J Kolkman, J van Gent, and J Greve. Surface plasmon resonance immunosensors: Sensitivity considerations, *Anal. Chim. Acta* 213: 35–45, 1988.
77. SPR Basics, www.xantec.com/html/spr.html
78. D Kim, MA Brooke, and NM Jokerst. Integrated Bio-Optoelectronic Sensor System, www.ece.gatech.edu/research/GTAC/Sp02PDFHandouts/DaeikKim.pdf
79. A Kumar. Biosensors based on piezoelectric crystal detectors: Theory and application. *JOM*-e 52(10), 2000, www.tms.org/pubs/journals/JOM/0010/Kumar/Kumar-0010.html
80. JL Harteveld, MS Nieuwenhuizen, and ER Wils. Detection of staphylococcal enterotoxin B employing a piezoelectric crystal immunosensor, *Biosens. Bioelectron.* 12(7): 661–667, 1997.

81. MS Nieuwenhuizen, J Harteveld, LN Johannes, and K Gerritse. Detection of staphylococcal enterotoxin B employing a piezoelectric crystal immunosensor. *Proceedings of ERDEC Science Conference on Chemical and Biological Defense Research*, Maryland, MD, US, Meeting Date 1998, pp. 493–501, 1999.
82. RM Carter, MB Jacobs, GJ Lubrano, and GG Guilbault. Piezoelectric detection of ricin and affinity purified goat anti-ricin antibody. *Anal. Lett.* 28: 1379–1386, 1995.
83. Affinity Sensors, http://www.affinity-sensors.com/faq.html
84. VI Polyakov, AI Rukovishnikov, AV Khomich, BL Druz, D Kania, A Hayes, MA Prelas, RV Tompson, TK Ghosh, and SK Loyalka. Surface phenomena of the thin diamond-like carbon films. *Proc. Mater. Res. Soc.* 555: 345, 1999.
85. M Prelas, G Popovici, and LK Bigalow. *Handbook on Industrial Diamond and Diamond Films*, Marcel-Dekker, New York, 1998.
86. R Goodacre, R Burton, N Kaderbhai, EM Timmins, A Woodward, PJ Rooney, and DB Kell. Intelligent systems for the characterization of microorganisms from hyperspectral data. *NATO ASI Series*, Ser. 1: Disarmament Technologies, Vol. 30 (Rapid Methods for Analysis of Biological materials in the Environment), Eds. PJ Stopa and MA Bartoszcze, 2000, pp. 111–136.
87. KE Sapsford, C Bradburne, JB Delehanty, and IL Medintz. Sensor for detecting biological agents. *Mater. Today* 11(3): 38–49, 2008.
88. TH Rider, MS Petrovick, FE Nargi, JD Harper, ED Schwoebel, RH Mathews, DJ Blanchard, LT Bortolin, AM Young, J Chen, and MA Hollis. A B cell-based sensor for rapid identification of pathogens. *Science* 301(5630): 213–215, 2003.
89. AD Livingston, CJ Campbell, EK Wagner, and P Ghazal. Biochip sensors for the rapid and sensitive detection of viral disease. *Genome Biol.* 6(6), 112–117, 2005.

Chapter 9

Biological Terrorism: Consequences and Medical Preparedness

L. David Ormerod

CONTENTS

Introduction 154
Epidemiology of Bioterrorism 156
Utility of Biological Weapons 158
Nature of a Biological Attack 159
Strengthening U.S. Defenses against Biological Weapons 161
  Physician Preparedness 162
  Microbiology Laboratory Preparedness 163
  Infection Control Officer/Hospital Epidemiologist Preparedness 166
  Medical Examiner and Coroner Preparedness 166
  Mortuary Services Preparedness 167
  Reporting a Suspected Bioterrorism Event 168
  Hospital Preparedness 168
  Local Civic Preparedness 170
  State and State Public Health Service Preparedness 171
  Federal Government Preparedness and Operations 175
Conclusions 179
References 180

Introduction

The threat of bioterrorism (BT) occupied a remote corner of the public consciousness until the coordinated terrorist attacks on the United States on September 11, 2001. The use of airplane as a missile did not implicate a weapon of mass destruction, but the fearful loss of life brought home the modern vulnerabilities of even the most technologically advanced nations to terrorism in all its forms. The risk that applied murderous technology could fall into the hands of a well-financed, but relatively unsophisticated enemy was self-evident. It underlined, furthermore, that the open source of scientific knowledge comes with a strategic price, and in the biological arena, the development of BT agents was potentially feasible for some nonstatal, asymmetric terrorists. How do the nation and its populace learn to cope with the threat of deliberately propagated, appalling, epidemic disease?

Let us start by examining the following hypothetical scenario. On December 9, 2002, 20 cases of smallpox are confirmed in Oklahoma and additional cases are suspected in Georgia and Pennsylvania [1]. As smallpox virus was eradicated in 1980, except for two high-security scientific laboratories, it is presumed that a bioterrorist attack has almost certainly occurred, but from where—an international source or domestic? The National Security Council (NSC) meets to plan strategy. Containment must primarily be by vaccination, as there are no useful therapeutic agents, but there are only 12M doses of smallpox vaccine stockpiled. Among the most immediate decisions to be made are to determine whom to vaccinate, where, and how. It is known that smallpox is highly infectious and it is anticipated that one-third of patients will die. What do you tell the public?

By December 15, 2002, there are 2000 cases in 15 states and isolated cases are confirmed in Canada, Mexico, and the United Kingdom. The local medical facilities in the affected areas are overwhelmed, vaccine supplies are dwindling, and social unrest is increasing rapidly. Federal and some state borders are closed, and commerce is disrupted. With the failure of initial containment, how are the local, state, and federal authorities respond to this worsening situation?

The epidemic continues to deteriorate. On December 22, 2002, there are now 16,000 cases in 25 states and 1,000 deaths, and dissemination has occurred to ten foreign countries. The most cogent prediction is that within another three weeks 300,000 people will have become infected by smallpox, of which 100,000 will ultimately die. Vaccine supplies are depleted. There is uncertainty as to whether new cases of infection are being acquired from known infected individuals, from unvaccinated contacts, as the consequence of ineffective vaccine, or perhaps from new bioterrorist attacks. The national economy is badly affected. Food supplies are scarce, populations are increasingly desperate, and the affected states have restricted all nonessential travel. The source of the attack is still unknown. How should the federal government respond?

Although of low probability, this scenario is certainly feasible [2,3]. It was presented in June 2001 as a major exercise in defense preparedness at Andrews Air Force Base, Washington DC, entitled "Dark Winter." Former senior government officials, senior administrators with policy or operational responsibilities in biological weapon (BW) preparedness, and experienced journalists were involved in a two-day planning exercise constructed as a series of mock NSC meetings. Among the study conclusions were that (1) U.S. government leadership was unfamiliar with the consequences and the policy options pursuant to major BW attack; (2) in a situation with limited options, the potential constitutional conflicts that could exist between state and federal interests had not been foreseen; (3) there was incomplete recognition of the centrality of public health and medical expertise in what might well be a prolonged emergency—and this was allied to poor preparedness at all levels; (4) there was a critical lack of surge capacity in the U.S. health system; and (5) because of the potential for social dislocation, the rapid dissemination of accurate information untainted by political constraints is of paramount importance in any response to BT.

The National Response Plan (NRP) integrates federal government domestic prevention, preparedness, response and recovery plans into a single, all-discipline, and all hazards plan (Chapter 27). The NRP provides the structure and the machinery of a national coordinating vehicle in which federal responsibilities and authority are exercised to the limits permitted by state jurisdiction, as well as the operational direction for the federal support of local and state incident managers.

For a century, civilian and military public health officials have been entrusted with the management of public health crises. The All Hazards approach of the NRP, however, creates a unified system that is designed principally for conventional disaster relief, in which public health leadership is very much subsidiary. The activities of local, state, federal, and relief organizations are coordinated under a national incident management command structure in which the health services are secondary players. The NRP structure inserts into epidemic control [4] a bureaucracy designed for the coordinated fire services-hazardous materials (HAZMAT)-emergency medical services-law enforcement dialectic. In a prolonged medical emergency, although the assets of the Federal Response Plan (FRP) will be critical, the decision-making and coordination would be better placed in the hands of experienced medical authorities trained in disaster management, and supported by the FRP hierarchy. However, this reality seems unlikely to be recognized without the tempering of a national disease epidemic with widespread casualties.

Disaster management under the FRP is divided into (a) crisis management under the leadership of the Department of Justice (DOJ) in the guise of the Federal Bureau of Investigation (FBI), and (b) consequence management under the leadership of the Federal Emergency Management Agency (FEMA) and the FEMA Office of National Preparedness (ONP). The recently created Department of Homeland Security (DHS) now has overall supervision, but the FRP remains the controlling instrument in any BT response.

The Department of Health and Social Security (DHSS) is the primary agency for Health and Medical Services pursuant to the FRP Emergency Support Function (ESF) #8. Considerable planning and preparedness development is being fostered through its lead agency, the Centers for Disease Control and Prevention (CDC), the CDC Bioterrorism Preparedness Response Program (BPRP), and the DHHS Office of Emergency Preparedness (DHHS/OEP). The DHS has introduced a new department, the Office of Health Affairs (OHA) under the direction of the DHS Chief Medical Officer. The OHA is responsible for coordinating all federal agencies involved in BT (also Chemical Terriorism (CT) and Nuclear Terrorism (NT)) through its WMD and Biodefense Office, it operates the National Biosurveillance Integration System, and plays a major role in Project Bioshield [5] through its Medical Readiness Office and Medical Countermeasures Division.

The design of the FRP is predicated by the principle that local entities will be the first responders, supplemented as necessary by state resources. Only when state capabilities are exceeded will federal agencies be called upon to supplement the response, recovery, and mitigation phases. All activities ostensibly remain under state control. But in most BT attacks (or natural epidemic infections), there will not be a recognized disaster site, and widespread dissemination across state (and possibly national) borders will often have occurred before the nature of the incident is even suspected. As we shall see later, the FRP introduces structural impediments into BT responsiveness where many of the needs tend to be unique, although where considerable federal involvement may be imperative. Certainly, preparedness at all levels may help to mitigate some of these difficulties.

Preparedness involves a wide range of activities, such as medical system education, developing flexible response plans, the training and equipping of responders with up-to-date technology, and in mitigating community vulnerabilities. Emergency responsiveness in the public health and medical communities has traditionally been limited in scope, capacity, and in integration with other constituencies. As a consequence of the Nunn-Lugar-Dominici Act (1997), extensive educational activities in biodefense preparedness training were formulated by numerous federal sources, that included HHS [6,7], FEMA [8], the Department of Defense (DOD) [9], other federal agencies [10], and nongovernmental organizations (NGOs) [11], but usually on categorical grant programs with a narrow range of activities. The Homeland Security Act (2002) centralized FEMA and certain HHS and DOJ-directed preparedness and response programs under the new DHS.

Within DHS, the Office of State and Local Government Cooperation and Preparedness (SLGCP) is charged with coordinating first responder terrorism preparedness at both the local and state levels and for measuring programmatic performances. The educational programs cover a range of activities, including emergency planning, training, and equipment support, responses to biological (and chemical) attacks, law enforcement, and public health. Many of these programs were initially replicative, poorly designed, and often failed to reach their targeted audience [12]. Since consolidation has been established under the DHS remit, there have been considerable accomplishments within the first responder community in urban and some rural areas. The CDC Coordinating Office for Terrorism Preparedness and Emergency Response (COTPER) is the main vehicle for harmonizing public health responsiveness at local, state, and national levels [13] through an integrated series of offices and divisions. COTPER also manages the Strategic National Stockpile (SNS, see below), and by the training and coordination of the 62 CDC Bioterrorism Preparedness project areas.

Epidemiology of Bioterrorism

The nature of terrorism predicates that no government can reduce to zero the risk to which its population is subject, no matter the magnitude of the financial, administrative, and technical investment. The dangers of BT have been recognized by the defense community for many years, but until recently, the strategic risks were believed small, confined by technical and tactical difficulties, and by the moral opprobrium associated with the deliberate, uncontrolled release of epidemic diseases into the civilian community. Responsible science was also reluctant to invite the problem. As Henderson has said, "until recently, I had doubts about publicizing the subject because of concern that it might entice some to undertake dangerous perhaps catastrophic experiments. However, events have made it clear that likely perpetrators already envisage every possible scenario" [14]. What is the present risk of BT in the United States?

The question has been explored in detail [15–18]. In the early 1970s, more than 100 countries, including the United States, ratified the Biological and Toxin Weapons Convention (1972). The U.S. BW Program was terminated in 1969/1970 and the U.S. stockpile of BWs destroyed [19]. Although most nations complied, a few, notably the former Soviet Union, Iraq, North Korea, Israel, and South Africa, continued to develop BW, and some remain potential sources of "weapons-grade" infective agents for international and national terrorist groups.

The development of BW requires little specialized equipment, and information on the science and technology is openly available. The professional skills can be hired and the processes are indeed generally inexpensive. However, there remain key technical problems that have to be overcome to produce an effective BW, notably the dangers of contamination, considerations of scaling up bench-top production methodologies, technicalities in microbial biology, and difficulties in establishing an effective delivery system—usually some form of aerosolization (Chapter 7). Governments have found it necessary to employ hundreds of scientists to weaponize BW (Chapter 7) as weapons of mass destruction (WMD). The assumption that effective BW is potentially easy to develop is an oversimplification. Unless a terrorist group is technologically sophisticated, the most likely means for terrorists to obtain effective BW is to steal or purchase them from the black market.

The Aum Shinrikyo BT attacks on Matsumoto (1994) and the Tokyo subway (1995) overshadowed the cult's failure to successfully weaponize and disseminate either anthrax or botulinum. However, this domestic development of potential capability in BT in an allied nation-generated shockwaves throughout the U.S. defense community, already alerted by the concomitant danger of the dissemination of insecure BW stockpiles in the former Soviet Union [20], and by Iraq's perceived BW capability [20] and its use of chemical weapons in the Iran–Iraq war of 1980–1988.

The historical record demonstrates only a small but significant terrorist use of biological agents, and almost invariably with unsophisticated weapons. The gradual increase in the number and severity of conventional terrorist attacks and the predilection for more indiscriminate targeting associated with groups motivated by religion, religious cults, or by Christian far right ideology, when contrasted with politically motivated groups, has been interpreted to represent an increased risk to the U.S. population [21]. Although members from across the spectrum of terrorist groups have attempted to acquire BW, very few groups have undertaken long-term programs to develop and use them. For strategic reasons, most terrorist groups indeed operate well below their individual capacities for violence. However, there is recent credible evidence of an interest within Al Qaeda, to manufacture weaponized anthrax and ricin [22]. Ironically, the September 2001 U.S. anthrax attacks using the mail are believed to have a domestic origin and a research laboratory source is suspected. Conventional explosive and chemical terrorism are less-complicated options that will tend to counter the biological risk. This being so, the present obstacles to volume production, the weaponizing process, and the problems afforded by the need to disseminate hazardous infective agents or toxins are likely to become more accessible over time, as scientific knowledge disseminates and technology becomes more readily available.

Currently, terrorist attempts to develop BW are likely to produce agents with limited infectivity that are restricted to use as environmental contaminants indoors. Initial target population exposures would be relatively small. However, the use of a highly contagious agent as a contaminant might still generate a large epidemic if the BW attack goes undetected and if containment measures are not taken. An example of this risk is afforded by a single undiagnosed case of smallpox that was imported into the former Yugoslavia in 1972 and which resulted in 175 cases and 35 deaths. Ten thousand contacts were quarantined in hotels guarded by the military and the entire nation of 20 million people was vaccinated [23]. Moreover, even low technology, biological microevents (e.g., 2001 anthrax attacks) have the potential for producing disease, disability, and death; civil and social unrest; and profound economic disruption.

The uniquely inhuman and random nature of an epidemic attack on civilians has profound implications for the security, commerce, and welfare of our society. It is the use of fully weaponized and optimized BW allied to their skilled dissemination using knowledge of meteorological and microclimatic conditions or of the ventilation systems of buildings, ships, or aircraft that gives BW the potential for use as WMD. Some biological attacks could even have greater potential for loss of life than a nuclear device. This doomsday scenario has engaged the strategic defense community to recommend the drastic enhancement of homeland security against BW. A disseminated BT attack as a "continuation of politics by other means" is quintessentially terrifying and unimaginable to populations long complacent from the historical control of epidemic disease within their midst.

At least for the time being, technological constraints suggest that lower-level BT threats will continue to be the most feasible scenario for U.S. homeland security. However, BWs of mass destruction could be developed by a disciplined terrorist group able to attract biologists and engineers of sufficient caliber, and then with the capability of developing secure larger-scale production capabilities. Alternatively, weaponized biological agents might be obtainable from one of the nation-states that retain BW stockpiles, but there is no evidence that dissemination of weapons-grade BW from these so-called rogue states has occurred, although thefts of stock cultures have been reported [24]. The strategic risks of discovery are a deterrent to those countries, as the international military response would be formidable.

BWs remain a potent intimidatory threat, but to be truly effective in intimidation capability for their use must first be established. Although tactics and strategy may change over time, the leadership of most predominantly secular terrorist groups is deterred by the inherent uncontrollability of hazardous biological agents and the sheer magnitude of the casualties that could result. Epidemics fail to respect ethnic, social, and national boundaries. The public alienation and unprecedented international retaliation would almost invariably be counterproductive [21,25], with the exception perhaps of their limited use against "legitimate" targets, such as in assassinations, attacks on specific buildings, or in agroterrorism (Chapter 11).

There remains a hard core of militant, religiously motivated terrorist groups with authoritarian decision-making structures that may be without such constraints. Their goals are to undermine the foundations of the State, disengage from the secular Western world, and to restore a fundamentalist culture based upon ancient text. Fervid religious belief can provide the moral imperative for indiscriminate terrorism that is unencumbered by secular conscience, this heady mix fostered by economic and political impoverishment. Religious cults, such as Aum Shinrikyo, and domestic Christian right wing or apocalyptic groups that purvey a seditious brew of paranoid, volatile, often racist rhetoric also have a predilection for indiscriminate violence. Domestic loner, "loony" terrorists, such as the Unabomber Ted Kaczynski, might also be free of restraint.

Utility of Biological Weapons

One aspect that tends to be neglected in discussions of the relative risks of BT is a consideration of the strategic and tactical motivations of terrorist groups. It is argued that there is an ineluctable spiral of terrorism lethality [26] that might lead to the proliferation of BW use [27]. Whether BW would further the terrorist objectives is primarily dependent upon the societal consequences of their deployment. This will vary with the nature of the infectious agent used and with the technological sophistication of both the BW and of its dispersal system.

Terrorist violence is typically directed towards targets of symbolic value to the society. Perpetrators generally seek specific political, religious, or social objectives and employ violence to coerce governments to accede to these agendas. The objectives of (bio)terrorism are usually (1) the assassination of prominent citizens, (2) the indiscriminate targeting of the civilian population, (3) economic and commercial disruption, (4) attacks on military facilities, (5) propaganda, and (6) intimidation and blackmail.

The absence of an effective BW dispersal mechanism (Chapter 7) will force terrorists to use infectious biological agents as a contaminant in confined spaces. To produce an optimized weapon, the biological agents generally need to be milled and then aerosolized at a stable particle size of 1–5 μm and dispersed downwind as a continuous release across a front and under optimal climatic conditions. In addition, the BW has to be released at sufficient altitude to spread over but not pass over the target. Given the right weather conditions, BW aerosol may drift for up to a 100 mile and have the capacity to infect the inhabitants of a city in its path. At the higher end of the unsophisticated weapon spectrum, fatalities in the low tens of thousands are feasible, while a more advanced BW could injure hundreds of thousands [17].

The stability of the BW varies considerably with the infectious agent. Anthrax, for example, is quite robust, but viruses tend to be sensitive to such factors as humidity, desiccation, oxidation, air pollution, ultraviolet light, and excessive heat. As wind will disperse and rain will scour an aerosol cloud, BW is not an all-weather option. BW can also be developed to infect agricultural animals and crops (Chapters 11 and 12) or to contaminate food and water supplies.

Nature of a Biological Attack

Most BW cause diseases that already exist in nature and can cause spontaneous outbreaks of disease in the United States or elsewhere, in human and sometimes in animals. There are increasing risks, however, of the malevolent derivation of genetically modified organisms that could have unique virulence or new clinical or epidemiological features. With the exception of diseases produced by certain biological toxins, in which the effects can be similar to chemical release, the onset of disease caused by most BT infections is delayed for a few days and up to several weeks with certain agents—a variable interval known as the incubation period. As the infectious agents themselves are usually odorless and colorless and a well-produced aerosol is invisible, it may be the exception for the BT crime scene to be detected contemporaneously. The initial infectious onslaught will likely be an occult event and there will be no opportunity to ameliorate the consequences of the attack until the subsequent epidemic is detected. The perpetrators may have long fled. Crisis management in a BT context may therefore be very different to other terrorist attacks.

Several clinical patterns of disease presentation (Chapter 5) are possible depending upon the microbial agent utilized, the size of the inoculum, the mode of infection, and the specific immune status of the individual. Aerosol infection is not the usual natural mode of transmission for several of the candidate organisms and this may often result in unusual presentations. There are indeed few clinical features specific to these diseases, at least initially. The nature of these often exotic infections can quite easily be lost among the many conventional diseases that present with fever, malaise, respiratory, gastrointestinal, or neurological complaints in ill individuals. In particular, the early symptoms may be confused with severe influenza. Furthermore, patients are likely to be widely scattered geographically, and even internationally, obscuring the early epidemic pattern.

The front line of BT is therefore the health service. Physicians and other healthcare workers are the "first responders." In the United States, BT attacks will usually be first detected by emergency department physicians and nurses, infectious disease consultants, microbiologists in the hospital or regional reference laboratory, hospital infection control officers, county medical examiners, or by specialists in the public health services. Until recently, medicine has been woefully unprepared for such an eventuality. Despite considerable recent expenditures on public health service and hospital preparedness, considerable anxieties remain about the capabilities of the system. It is imperative to realize that with the majority of contagious BW, there will only be a short window of opportunity before secondary transmission of infection results in further waves of medical casualties. Avoidable delays in diagnosis, treatment, and vaccination containment can have appalling consequences.

The use of unexpected agents, the possibility of multiple, separate BW attacks, or an attack using more than one organism needs to be considered in the strategic assessment. One indicator of an outdoors BT attack may be the concomitant infection and illness of farm and domestic animals from a number of candidate infectious agents. Furthermore, it will often be unclear in the initial stages of a terrorist-introduced epidemic whether an outbreak has a natural or a man-made causation. Intelligence reports or terrorist claims may be helpful. Considerable public health, epidemiological, and federal resources may be necessary to make this distinction.

There are a number of features that may be significant in indicating an intentional causation, although none alone are conclusive [28–30]:

1. Larger epidemics than anticipated, clustering of patients, or an unusual epidemic pattern
2. Increased numbers with unexplained febrile illness or death, especially if rapidly fatal
3. Unusual age distribution, geographic occurrence, or unusual seasonal onset
4. Significantly greater or lower rates of infection from certain areas
5. Epidemiological findings that suggest a common factor such as a location, building, subway, or vessel
6. A single case of disease caused by exotic agent, e.g., smallpox
7. Concomitant human epidemic and animal zoonotic
8. Unusual strains, variants, or antibiotic resistance patterns
9. Separate, noncontiguous outbreaks
10. Simultaneous epidemics with different organisms

As long as BT can be confined to local acts of contamination in a major city, such as the 2001 U.S. anthrax mail attacks, the current improved public health and Metropolitan Medical Response System (MMRS) (see below) capabilities may now be sufficient, although it clearly was not at that time. However, it is obvious to anyone who has visited a U.S. emergency room that a sudden surge of ill patients will rapidly outstrip available capacity in almost all communities. Annual influenza epidemics are obviously handled with difficulty. Add into the equation the widespread contamination of hospital and medical office facilities that may occur early in an epidemic, the hazards to unvaccinated staff, and the risk of subsequent waves of infection, and it is clear that considerable nationwide contingency planning must be put into place to boost infrastructure and to anticipate all possible eventualities [31–34].

During a virulent epidemic, emergency rooms, inpatient facilities, isolation rooms, intensive care and respiratory ventilation facilities, laboratories, pharmaceutical supplies, and morgue facilities may be rapidly overwhelmed. Hospitals and essential services may be incapacitated in the initial attack or, subsequently, the local economy and school systems may cease to function, and hospital staff may be infected or stay at home—75 percent of hospital workers are female and in the modern era many are heads of families who will need to care for children when schools are closed. The "anxious well" may swamp any functioning medical service, and civil panic may complicate disaster management. New ways of delivering emergency care and treating patients in temporary facilities may be needed and arrangements developed for home therapy of the lesser ill and of the recuperating.

As a national priority, the U.S. government has decreed that medical and public health facilities must be strengthened across the country to facilitate the management of unfamiliar epidemics and to accommodate surge capacities, with the enormous implications that such an undertaking entails. The expertise to detect and control an epidemic are primarily provided by the combination of large numbers of medical and public health assets, the latter a loosely affiliated network of more than 3000 federal state and local health agencies, and allied to numerous private sector voluntary and professional health organizations.

The novels, *The Plague,* by Albert Camus [33], and *Blindness,* by José Saramago [34], bear eloquent testimony to such events, and are well worth reading by anyone concerned with preparedness against BT and epidemic infections.

Strengthening U.S. Defenses against Biological Weapons

In recognition of the national vulnerability, considerable enhancements of BT response programs at all levels have been under way since President Clinton's 1995 Presidential Decision Directive, PDD 39. The programs have rapidly accelerated since the World Trade Center attacks. In a 2004 National Security Presidential Directive (NSPD 33/HSPD 10) entitled, "Biodefense for the 21st Century," President G. W. Bush outlined the main features of a coordinated biodefense program based on measures of threat awareness, prevention and protection, surveillance and detection, and response and recovery [35]. The federal government invested $10 billion in the period 2001–2004 to build infrastructure, organization, and skills, such as in the following programs:

- Specific biomedical research, including new anthrax and Ebola virus vaccines
- Enhanced environmental detection technology, health surveillance, and laboratory capabilities
- Radically improved public health infrastructure for all biological (and chemical) hazards, including terrorism
- Improved food, agriculture, and water surveillance and mitigation
- Strengthened intelligence and law enforcement biodefense capabilities
- Improved military biodetection, training, and vaccination
- Expanded international cooperation and interoperability through the State Department
- Established Biowatch—monitoring air over major U.S. cities for BW releases
- Established Bioshield—developing drugs and vaccines against BW agents
- Investment of $4.4 billion to state and local health systems in 2001–2004 period for preparedness enhancements
- Assured smallpox vaccine supply for all citizens, increased national antibiotic cache, and increased funding of the SNS from $51 million to $400 million per annum
- Increased NIH funding for biodefense medical research 30 times to $1.5 billion/year
- Established National Biodefense Analysis and Countermeasure Center at DHS for the study of BW and to provide a BT forensic center

Increasingly, federal funding for antiterrorist efforts is reaching the healthcare community. In FY 2006, more than $4 billion was budgeted for biodefense expenditure under the auspices of the Department of Health and Human Services (DHHS), including NIH $1.8 billion, CDC $1.6 billion, HRSA $0.51 billion, and FDA $0.24 billion. The National Institute of Allergy and Infectious Diseases (NIAID) has been appointed the lead NIH agency for BT research. Other government agencies that received funding for biodefense-related research include DHS, DOD, USDA, the State Department, NSF, and the EPA.

Considerable national benefits have accrued from improved disease surveillance and the increased research into the diagnosis and management of epidemic infectious disease—whether caused by BW candidate agents or by naturally occurring epidemics [36], e.g., severe acute respiratory syndrome (SARS) [37]. There was certainly considerable misinvestment in the early years of the U.S. Bioterrorism Program, but appreciable improvements have occurred with the greater accountability demanded by the DHS [12,38,39]. Specific concerns remain about the overall capabilities of the biodefense program—not in the least because of the deficiencies revealed in the FEMA, public health, and healthcare response to Hurricane Katrina in August 2005.

All states now have a BT plan in place, but the system does remain a work in progress. Important public health deficiencies are still identified in state and local jurisdictions, specifically in coordination with the SNS, with persisting gaps in laboratory capabilities and staffing, and in compliance with the needs of the CDC National Electronic Disease Surveillance System, (NEDSS). Half the states would run out of hospital beds within two weeks in a moderately severe flu pandemic. Moreover, 40 states have a worsening shortage of registered nurses [36], a deficiency that would invariably deteriorate in a prolonged medical crisis.

Confusion still persists within the complex BT response system regarding the roles of various local, state, and federal agencies; the absence of agreed standards or templates on the service performance and capacity levels required of state and local public health departments and hospitals; the absence of adequate surge capacities within healthcare; and the poverty of engagement of the private sector, academia, and other nongovernmental entities [36]. Objective practical testing and practice exercises are far too few. With the October 2007 Homeland Security Presidential Directive (HSPD) 21, entitled, "Public Health and Medical Preparedness," these concerns are beginning to be addressed by the DHS [40]. There is a detailed review available of the present state of BT preparedness [41].

The risk of naturally occurring endemic and epidemic infectious disease remains ever present, with influenzal illnesses the most important mimic. More than 30 previously unknown infectious diseases have been identified since the early 1970s [42], including SARS coronavirus (2003); H5N1 influenza virus (avian flu: 1997); Hantavirus (1993); HIV (AIDS: 1982); and Ebola virus (1977).

Physician Preparedness

There has, until recently, been poor involvement of healthcare professionals and healthcare facilities in disaster preparedness [43] in the face of conflicting responsibilities, as the strategic risks of BT were thought insufficient to justify the considerable investment required to mitigate a major BW attack. The accurate and rapid diagnosis of these usually unfamiliar diseases by all physicians has to be a principal target. There needs to be a high level of suspicion as well as a high level of knowledge of putative agents, yet many physicians have had no training currently to identify BW exposure. Although there have been improvements among the emergency medicine and primary care communities, hospital-based access to physician training is uneven [44] and physicians' general self-assessments of BT preparedness (as well as a sometimes uncertain sense of professional obligation to treat during epidemics) reveal that physician preparedness remains a major hurdle [45].

Training is being institutionalized in schools of medicine and schools of nursing. Courses are being established by county, state, and national medical societies. Preparedness is being recognized at specialist board certification/recertification, and for state licensure. The Association of American Medical Colleges (AAMC) has convened a health education coalition on BT in partnership with CDC and the American Medical Association (AMA) to develop educational materials in BT for healthcare professionals. The American College of Emergency Physicians (ACEP) is conducting courses for its crucial constituents. An eight-hour Department of Justice (DOJ) technician-hospital provider training course is available through the National Domestic Preparedness (NDP) office in designated cities. Almost all assessments of physician preparedness at this time are based upon self-assessments.

Several syndromic disease patterns should raise the possibility of BT in the differentiation from endemic infections (Chapter 5): a fulminant disease process; acute severe pneumonia or respiratory distress; a febrile encephalopathy; acute neuromuscular symptoms; unexplained fever associated with a rash; fever with bleeding from mucous membranes (coagulopathy); unexplained acute icteric (jaundice) syndromes, or massive diarrhea with dehydration. The clustering of cases is particularly significant. On first suspicion, the correct response is to immediately contact the public health department disease prevention and control office on a 24-hour, 7-day-week basis. Many physicians are currently unfamiliar with the appropriate lines of communication in the event of seeing a patient with a suspicious disease pattern. Extensive databases and national expertise can be accessed in an emergency by telephone at 1-800-424-8802.

Three major volunteer organizations can mobilize medical professionals in emergencies to enhance the surge capacity. The Surgeon General's Office manages the Medical Reserve Corps (MRC), a branch of the Citizen Corps that is organized into community-based units. The Health Resources and Services Administration (HRSA) runs a state-based program called the National Emergency System for Advance Registration of Volunteer Health professionals (NESAR-VHP). Disaster Medical Assistance Teams are designed to supplement responses at disaster sites, and can be variously sponsored by a safety agency, public health organization, major medical center, NGOs, and other organizations, upon signing a memorandum of agreement with the National Disaster Medical System (NDMS). Local and state medical societies may play a role in organizing local physicians. Volunteer physician credentialing was identified as an important unresolved issue during the response to Hurricane Katrina and potential solutions are being investigated by DHS.

Microbiology Laboratory Preparedness

There are 158,000 laboratories in the United States that serve the medical community and consequently might be involved in a BW attack. Automated microbial identification systems that are used routinely in medicine perform poorly on BW agents. Specific testing is therefore necessary. Biosafety facilities are minimally required to culture these organisms and many smaller facilities are lacking them. Most hospital and private clinical laboratories are Level A facilities that are expected to be able to rule out BT pathogens [46].

Guidelines for a network of sentinel laboratories are being devised under the auspices of the American Society for Microbiology (ASM) and the CDC whereby BT preparedness planning [47] becomes an integral part of the standard hospital disaster plan. Currently, specific guidelines are available for excluding anthrax, plague, tularemia, brucellosis, Q fever, botulism toxin, *Burkholderia mallei* (glanders) and *B. pseudomallei* (melioidosis), unidentified viruses, and staphylococcal enterotoxin B. Based upon accreditation of their highly infectious agent capability, facilities, policies, and procedures, sentinel labs are designated, as either advanced sentinel clinical laboratories or basic sentinel clinical laboratories, and their roles are defined. Sentinel labs use standard microbiology protocols according to published guidelines to "rule out or refer." It is not the role of sentinel laboratories to identify suspected highly infectious pathogens.

Comprehensive rules for the handling, investigation, specimen selection, and the transport and storage of all suspected BT and other highly infectious agents are also promulgated, including the formal use of biological safety cabinets in negative pressure rooms [47]. Larger microbiology laboratories are being encouraged to enhance their instrumentation and skill levels to allow greater testing within community laboratories—a critical element to save time and money, and to increase surge capacity during any infectious disease outbreak. Microbiology laboratories are considered partners and in selected cases are registered sentinel members of a national BT laboratory network.

Specimens from suspected BT-related cases are to be submitted to the state public health laboratory, which will then determine their appropriate management—with the exception of potential smallpox samples that must be transported directly to the Biosafety Level 4 laboratory at CDC. State health departments coordinate the transportation of samples, maintaining safety and quality.

The Laboratory Response Network (LRN) for BT was established in 1999 with federal funding as a secure integrated computer network of approximately 150 laboratories: members of APHL; CDC; the CDC Rapid Response and Advanced Technology Laboratory (RRAT); the CDC

Environmental Health Laboratory for Chemical Terrorism (EHLCT); FBI; DOD; the state and major local public health laboratories; the nation's major clinical laboratories; and certain international laboratories [41]. Each laboratory in the LRN has been assigned an operative designation A to D, according to the progressively more stringent levels of safety, containment, and technical proficiency required at successive levels (see Table 9.1). A major role of the LRN is to investigate samples in a distributed fashion to ameliorate surge issues. The Network also provides emergency assistance and support through the pooling of resources and personnel based upon cooperative

Table 9.1 Hierarchical Organization of the Laboratory Response Network for Terrorism

Lab Level	*Biosafety Level*	*Capabilities*	*Sites*
A	BSL-2	Rule out specific agents	Clinical labs
		Early detection of cases	Sentinel labs
		Forward specimens in LRN	
B	BSL-3 recommendation	Rule in specific agents	Selected state/or BSL-2 with isolate and identify county labs
	BSL-3 practices	Antimicrobial sensitivities	Veterinary, food, environment labs
C	BSL-3	Provide surge capacity PCR assays	Selected state public health labs
		Molecular typing	
		Toxicity testing	
D	BSL-4	Probe for universal agents	CDC; USAMRIID
		All level (A-C) testing	
		Smallpox isolation	
		Negative stain EM for smallpox virus	
		Molecular typing	
		Validate new assays	
		Detect genetic recombinants	
		Provide specialized reagents	
		Bank isolates	
		Considerable surge capacity	

Source: Modified from Sehulster, L. and Chinn, R.T.W., Guideline for Environmental Infection Control in Health-Care Facilities, 2007, Recommendations of CDC and the Healthcare Infection Control Practices Advisory Committee (HICPAC), http://www.guideline.gov/summary/summary.aspx?ss=15&doc_id=3843 (accessed November 28, 2007).

agreements. All parts of the LRN have appropriate procedures related to chain-of-custody issues and the collection, preservation, and shipment of specimens. BW testing reagents are to be supplied by the CDC, although there have been significant supply problems [36].

Routine hospital and private laboratories must be alert to the risks associated with highly infectious biological agents. The qualifications, supervision, and experience of microbiology staff are variable across the United States, and hence their capability to suspect or detect unusual infectious agents. Inadvertent deterioration in less-utilized skills has resulted from the economies necessitated by managed care. One factor likely to enhance the early detection of BW pathogens is the renewed emphasis on close professional relationships between clinicians and microbiologists in the routine diagnosis of serious infection. The importance of professional training for microbiological staffs in BW is reflected in the training programs and materials that have been devised by federal agencies such as the CDC and by professional organizations, which include AAMC, the Infectious Disease Society of North America (IDSNA), the National Laboratory Training Network (NLTN), the Association of Public Health Laboratories (APHL), and the National Association of Clinical Laboratory Scientists (NACLS). Outcome measures need to be incorporated, as in the laboratory proficiency testing administered by the College of American Pathologists (CAP). Still, microbial biosafety issues remain a problem in many laboratories.

Large clinical microbiology laboratories are required to develop a BT preparedness plan to anticipate all eventualities. If a possible BT agent is grown or detected, phone calls must be placed immediately to the following individuals: the responsible physician; the microbiology laboratory director, supervisor, and manager; infection control officer; local health department; state health department; the laboratory director on call, the clinical pathologist on call; the chief of infectious diseases; and the hospital director. The laboratory director is responsible for putting the contingency plan into operation as soon as a BT event is suspected. The plan should include:

- Risk analysis check list for the laboratory
- Vaccination policies and list of OSHA (Occupational Safety and Health Administration) safety measures, including personal protective clothing
- Postexposure vaccination, drug prophylaxis, and prospective care policies
- FBI chain-of-command and evidence documentation for isolates
- Measures to ensure security of and to limit access to isolates
- Standard BT candidate agent protocols [49]
- Use of universal precautions and containment facilities, e.g., biosafety cabinets
- Autoclaving or incineration of infected material; instrument disinfection protocols
- Ongoing preparedness training program descriptions
- Levels of stock supplies and sourcing of emergency supplies
- Storage and emergency sourcing of packaging materials; training in specimen transportation in accordance with IATA (UN 6.2) packaging regulations; utilization of secure courier systems
- Location of state and federal reference laboratories with round-the-clock contact numbers
- Location of nearest laboratory capable of confirmatory identifications
- Official log of hospital, local government, law enforcement, and EMS contact numbers
- Policy establishing an official administrative spokesman for all inquiries

The methodologies of dealing safely with BT pathogens are very labor intensive. The provision of surge capacity is also a critical issue, provided largely through the LRN and major military and federal assets. National investment in an efficient and safe system for the identification of highly infective pathogens is currently inadequate. At the local hospital level, busy laboratories on tight budgets must maintain routine operations and yet develop complex capabilities necessary to support the rapid, accurate, and safe diagnosis of rare dangerous pathogens [50]. As samples can be safely disinfected by autoclaving, the dissemination of new PCR techniques to afford rapid diagnosis is a high priority [48].

Infection Control Officer/Hospital Epidemiologist Preparedness

There are substantial risks that hospitals can become major venues for contagious disease transmission during epidemics. The infection control community is responsible for hospital environmental control and in assuring the safety from infection within the facility of patients, staff, and the public [48]. Infection control officers also work closely with the department of infectious disease in coordinating the hospital emergency response to epidemics. These professionals are involved in many aspects of hospital operations, not least in studying local patterns of infective disease, in conjunction with the hospital epidemiologist. The first suspicions of an unnatural BW attack as distinct from natural events may emerge from this kind of local institutional review.

Early suspicion is of paramount importance as three of six categories. Biological agents (smallpox, plague, and the viral hemorrhagic fevers) are transmissible from person to person. The safety of the hospital and its staff are critical if the hospital is to continue functioning. Vaccination, prophylactic drug treatment, and postexposure protocols must be in place, together with a hospitalwide plan for their implementation. The families of hospital and other frontline workers should also be treated prophylactically for several very practical considerations, including ring-fencing of the home situation that could otherwise undermine the response.

Other responsibilities include the development and enforcement of the use of universal precautions; the establishment of protocols for mass patient isolation; procedures for the appropriate use of disease-specific protective equipment (PPE) including respiratory isolators, gloves, gowns, and masks; formal policies for institution, staff, and patient security; the provision of dedicated patient housing, closed ventilation systems, plumbing, and waste disposal; and predetermined plans for triage, patient transportation, cleaning, decontamination, sterilization, discharge management, and postmortem care [51].

The infection control officer, infection control committee chairman, or designate, is empowered to rapidly implement preventive and containment measures in response to an infectious disease outbreak. Considerable challenges are inherent in the likely scenario of a BT response to unfamiliar diseases in a situation with large numbers of severely ill infectious patients and a scarcity of equipment and resources. Droplet and airborne infection control practices are disease- and situation-specific (Chapter 5), and require appropriate infrastructure, heavy commitments of skilled nursing, and considerable personal protective equipment (PPE) and logistical resources. These activities are unavoidably time consuming and make considerable demands upon all involved [52]. There is also the same, unmet need for education and training in BT threats among infection control and hospital epidemiologist professionals as among other hospital constituencies. Only 56 percent of infection control practitioners who responded to a recent survey had received any BT preparedness training [53].

Medical Examiner and Coroner Preparedness

The U.S. medicolegal death investigation systems vary considerably from state to state in their organizational and jurisdictional structures. The medical examiners and coroners (ME/Cs) who run this system occupy an important position in the national surveillance of unusual causes of infectious disease mortality, given their state-derived statutory authority to investigate suspicious, sudden, or unexplained deaths. They see, for example, fatalities that have not been examined by other physicians or emergency departments and persons dying without a confirmed diagnosis. Autopsies are an effective method of obtaining accurate etiologies in deaths caused by infectious disease or by toxic exposure, and should be undertaken in all cases of death of uncertain cause where there is a possibility of an infective (or toxic) etiology. Postmortem examination may reveal characteristic findings, such as hemorrhagic mediastinitis in pulmonary anthrax, or may indicate the route of exposure. Autopsy also assures a thorough laboratory investigation of suspected terrorism-related cases by the submission of optimal specimens into the LRN via the local state public health laboratory. ME/Cs are also skilled in preserving medicolegal evidence.

The role of ME/Cs in BT preparedness has recently been reviewed and extensive recommendations made as to how to incorporate their skill set into BT disaster surveillance and management [54]. The public health systems must prospectively inform the regional ME/Cs of infectious disease outbreaks within their jurisdiction. In common with all other medical first responders, education and training programs are needed that are directed to the specific and separate needs of medical examiners and coroners [55]. Protective equipment and procedures must be put in place. In addition, improved autopsy facilities are required in many facilities to ensure that prospectors are protected from dangerous infectious disease. Robust communications with hospitals, emergency personnel, and local and state health departments must be established. Mass BW casualty planning must be undertaken in each jurisdiction, and must necessarily involve the local mortuary services.

Mortuary Services Preparedness

The general principles and best practices of managing large numbers of infective mass casualties are reviewed in a 2005 Capstone document [56]. The ME/C retain all mass fatality management (MFM) decision-making authority, sign all death certificates, must identify assets required to process remains, and relay the equipment and personnel needs of the emergency response under their jurisdiction to the state ME/C and to the local emergency manager (LEM). They are statutorily responsible to the FBI for evidence gathering from the remains of suspected terrorism-related cases. Local law enforcement is responsible for securing the mortuary facilities and associated family assistance centers (FAC).

The ME/C is responsible for creating an infrastructure of purpose-built teams to accomplish the potentially extraordinary workloads. Secured facilities, supplementary staffing (forensic pathologists, death investigators, remains handlers, and scribes), and equipment may be available on memoranda of agreements with morticians and funeral directors, MMRS units, hospitals, private industries (e.g., PPE, refrigerated trucks for the storage of remains, transportation, and decontamination equipment), etc. Extensive state ME/C and DHS federal assets are available as needed. Disaster Mortuary Operational Response Teams (DMORT) are available at DHS with a full-service mobile morgue. VA, DHHS, DOD, and Red Cross assets may be useful in supplementing the mortuary activities [56]. Appropriate organism and disease-specific precautions must assure that further spread of infection is avoided.

There are eight phases of incident-specific caseload management: (1) notification; (2) evaluation and incident-specific planning; (3) remains and possessions recovery; (4) holding morgue operations; (5) secure transportation and temporary storage; (6) morgue operations, such as performing autopsies, identification of remains by fingerprint, forensic dental, anthropological methods, or by

DNA recovery, and in running the FAC; (7) transportation and temporary storage; and (8) final disposition (state-enforced cremation is required for some infected corpses). At each step in the process, proof of evidentiary continuity is required. Embalming will often be inappropriate for biologically contaminated remains.

Reporting a Suspected Bioterrorism Event

It is likely that the first suspicion of a possible BT attack will occur among hospital professional staff. It will usually be inappropriate to await diagnostic confirmation, because the consequences of delay may be very serious should an epidemic be later confirmed. This is a 24-hours-a-day, 7-days-a-week responsibility. The case for notification should be developed by the Infection Control Officer in consultation with infectious disease specialists, clinicians, and the laboratory director. The notification of suspicious findings must include the hospital administration, DHS, CDC, FBI, and local and state public health authorities. Criteria include

1. One or more cases diagnosed with
   a. Suspected smallpox or anthrax
   b. An uncommon agent or disease occurring without explanation, e.g., *Burkholderia mallei* or *pseudomallei*, pulmonary anthrax, or plague
   c. A microbial isolate with markedly atypical features
   d. Illness suspected from aerosol, food, or water sabotage
2. One or more clusters of unexplained illness

The state governor is responsible for declaring a state of emergency. The DHS/CDC and FBI will coordinate the decision as to whether to declare a suspected bioterrorist attack.

Hospital Preparedness

U.S. Hospitals have all-hazards disaster management plans in place in accordance with the Joint Commission on Accreditation of Healthcare Organizations (JCAHO). These are required to be tested (and modified, as a consequence) by at least one tabletop exercise or major drill per annum. These plans are tailored to the needs and assets of each community by means of local hazard vulnerability analyses. They are coordinated with the emergency medical services, law enforcement, fire department, and local government. The standards also establish requirements for staff training and familiarization with the plan. Disaster management planning remains a continuing process and considerable effort is being made to incorporate planning for catastrophic incidents, including BT.

Hospital biodefense is being funded federally through the HRSA's National Bioterrorism Hospital Preparedness Program that has, unfortunately, proven to be spread too thinly to make many systematic improvements. Business constraints on hospital activities in this highly regulated and managed care environment make hospitals reluctant partners in BT preparedness. U.S. hospitals remain largely unaccountable to public officials and they just cannot afford unfunded BT mandates. Major system limitations persist, particularly in the areas of communications, hospital security, decontamination procedures, and in the paucity of realistic methods with which to test real-time functionality.

Hospital preparedness, therefore, remains a notable bottleneck in BT response planning. Problems are consistently encountered in internal and external communications; in security;

decontamination; staffing, staff training, staff protection; and with inadequate training levels combined with nonobjective performance evaluations [57]. Any of these failures can seriously impair BT responsiveness. In contemplating BW mass casualties, hospitals need to plan for circumstances in which their facilities may well be overrun by a sustained demand for sophisticated healthcare. Surge capacity issues [58] include unresolved problems in the emergency provision of beds, isolation capacity, healthcare personnel, pharmaceutical caches, PPE, and decontamination facilities, and with psychosocial health, communication, and information technology implications. Planners need to consider that patients may have to be cared for in unconventional but secure alternative sites close to the main facility. Hospitals may need to quarantine, divert incoming patients, or evacuate. Home care may have to be organized for some patients. Coordinated lockdowns may be necessary to regain control of difficult situations. Maximum utilization has to be maintained, to be supplemented by regional, state, and federal assets. Around-the-clock, multiple shift capabilities with additional expansion of selected hospital operations must be provided for. It has to be taken into consideration that personnel may be unavailable, perhaps part of the epidemic, and skilled, temporary replacements should be sourced in advance. Shortage areas such as RNs, laboratorians, and pharmacy are especially problematic. New staff shortages and organizational difficulties can also be expected during the disease outbreak.

Outside aid will probably be essential. Important components of hospital BW planning [31,59,60] include:

- Hospital disaster plans to include BW responses.
- Telephone connections and Internet access may be swamped. Therefore, intercom systems, secure radio, and electronic communications to public health services, EMS, local and state government, law enforcement, regional health assets, CDC, FEMA, and the local media are needed.
- Emergency department personnel, infectious disease and infection control specialists, microbiologists, and the medical and nursing staffs are to be alerted on the detection of unusual infectious disease manifestations.
- Planning for efficient internal communications, with a dedicated staff, phones, FAX, an organized system of hospital runners, dedicated secure Internet connections, and in-built communications redundancy.
- Medical surveillance and epidemiology infrastructure in place.
- BW infection control and microbiology protocols incorporated.
- Pharmaceutical and antibiotic reserves to be actively monitored; standing plans to increase surge capacity.
- Maintenance of rosters of essential emergency personnel; organization of volunteer personnel; up-to-date listings of volunteer physicians, retired medical and nursing professionals and medical students; with consideration of an annual familiarization course.
- Dedicated decontamination facilities, with planning for rapid enhancement in trailers, tents, canopies, or large open areas.
- Plans for hospital lockdown; disposal of contaminated material; additional mortuary facilities; auxiliary power; increased fuel storage capacity; and enhanced security utilizing contracted private security personnel.
- PPE training. Supplies will need to be rapidly augmented. Level C equipment (splash protection with air-purifying respirators) will be appropriate for most incidents, controlled by OSHA standards. Chemoprophylaxis and vaccinations—to include families of hospital staff.

- Medical and pharmaceutical stockpiles including antibiotics, antitoxins, ventilators, and other supplies; emergency sourcing in place.
- Mental health resources to treat family members of casualties and to care for the corps of responders.
- Regional planning for all health facilities to work as a team and to increase surge capacity. This may include the exclusive use of certain facilities as fever hospitals; for patient triage; for the transfer of patients between institutions; and for the use of emergency make-shift facilities as hospitals, e.g., hotels, civic halls, or sporting arenas, with other facilities used to conduct screening and prophylaxis. Veterans administration facilities will be an integral part of regional planning under the VA 4th Mission. The U.S. military and several states (including CN, NC, and NV) possess manned mobile hospital facilities. These emergency planning concepts are part of the DOD-proposed Modular Emergency Medical System (MEMS) [9].
- Rigorous, repetitive training and drills necessary to maintain preparedness. It will usually be best to contract for expert programs including systematic follow-up exercises rather than establish local educational activities.
- Hospital Incident Management Command Center that is familiar with local, state, and federal disaster planning.

The DHHS OEP developed a federal MMRS in response to the lessons learned from the Aum Shinrikyo 1995 sarin attack on the Tokyo subway. Now under the DHS, the MMRS provides structure for an integrated response to mass casualty events that utilizes medical, public health, law enforcement, EMS, fire service, and other professionals to support local resources, The MMRS coordinates the mass casualty preparedness of member cities to CBN terrorism, epidemic disease outbreaks, natural disasters, and large-scale hazardous material incidents, $32 million in grants were awarded for MMRS preparedness projects in FY 2007. Concentrating on major cities, 124 have received training and testing programs to build upon existing local emergency response programs. However, the avoidance of state and county institutions has drawn criticism on the basis that wider dissemination of skills throughout their jurisdictions should be fostered.

One of the difficulties of establishing true hospital BW preparedness is the current inadequacy of federal funding for both the private and public hospital sectors. Considerable further federal support will be necessary for a system already constrained by managed care, unremunerated indigent care, and by numerous unfunded federal and state mandates if hospital BT preparedness is to be cogently addressed. The indemnification of private entities (including hospitals) in a disaster is tied to the presidential authority to declare a national emergency.

Local Civic Preparedness

Local preparedness will determine the consequences over the first few days of any disaster response—until the full weight of state and federal resources are mobilized. Before the state governor declares an emergency, the mayor has full controlling authority, and provides an essential component of the response thereafter. Good planning must prevent jurisdictional conflicts that are otherwise all too likely. Each local authority is encouraged to develop a current, comprehensive, all-purpose disaster management plan remove, to be maintained on file at the State Emergency Management Agency (SEMA).

There are approximately 3,000 local public health departments in the United States and 75 percent serve populations of 50,000 or fewer [61]. The median local health department employs

13 staff with a mean size of 67 employees. In only 16 states, mostly in the east and southeast, local health departments are run as offices of the State Department of Health [61]. The majority, however, are agencies of local government, and as a consequence, state health authorities have little leverage to improve them. Communications between the two entities may be minimal. Staffing levels are commonly pared back with inadequate resources and little or no spare capacity.

It is obvious that federal and state investments are necessary at this level [62,63]. Local and regional training courses must be arranged and the numbers of professional personnel and the provision of equipment markedly enhanced. Another substantial need is to establish secure two-way communications into the BW Internet-based networks and to enhance bilateral information flows. Local health departments are to be integrated systemically within regional disaster planning; familiarity with the local community is an invaluable asset. Involvement in disseminating information to the local general public, in disease surveillance, and in mass vaccinations is an essential part of the local BT response.

Cognizant of the structural deficiencies in the local public health services, a strong civic infrastructure [64], comprising individuals, voluntary associations, social service organizations, faith-based groups, chambers of commerce, women's clubs, Rotary, etc., may be critical to managing a mass health emergency. Local agencies are highly motivated to protect the communities they serve. During the 1947 smallpox outbreak in New York City, for example, private volunteers helped staff of free vaccination clinics in 12 hospitals, 84 police precincts, and every public and parochial school in the city, helping to vaccinate 6.3 million persons in four weeks, 5 million in the first two weeks.

Municipal leadership is expected to plan for the potential consequences of BW attack in the face of more pressing political realities that take general precedence. Coordination has to be fostered between the public health services, healthcare facilities, and healthcare professionals on one hand and the local fire, EMS, law enforcement, transportation, the Red Cross, and personnel management services on the other if the local disaster relief organization is to be adapted to incorporate epidemic healthcare emergencies [12,65]. Local mutual assistance agreements between adjacent municipalities and counties enhance overall responsiveness.

State and State Public Health Service Preparedness

Before the turn of this century, the U.S. public health services had suffered from at least 30 years of deferred maintenance [66]. The system was antiquated, grossly underfinanced, underequipped, and understaffed. Traditionally, the source of funding for local levels of the public health service comes from state and local government. The state of disarray was summarized in a 1988 Institute of Medicine report, entitled, "The Future of Public Health" [67]. The Stafford Report subsequently led to a systematic attempt to improve the service, and there has now been more than a decade of enhanced investment at both the federal and state levels. The development of a twenty-first century comprehensive public health service is still undermined by limited availability of funds at the local level (outside of the MMRS) [68] and by the absence of objective and verifiable "optimally achievable measures for preparedness"—as have been formalized for the first responder community [69]. This will likely change, as national public health performance standards are under consideration as the result of HSPD 21.

All the states have organized their disaster response capabilities under a State Emergency Management Agency (SEMA), with responsibilities for emergency preparedness within state borders, and for developing the state emergency plan. In a few states, the SEMA is under the authority of the state's National Guard and which takes care of the facility. Until recently, SEMA had a traditional disaster approach and state health departments had largely been excluded from the planning process. The twenty-first century state disaster plan now coordinates all state and local responders in a unified disaster response.

The State Governor has full authority within the State, and federal assets cannot be deployed in emergencies until requested by the Governor. However, when the President declares a national emergency under the Stafford Act, the Governor cedes leadership under the Incident Command System (ICS) to the Federal On-Scene Coordinator (FOSC), which in the case of a BW attack will generally be the FEMA OSC. State and local authorities are well represented in the unified command structure. A strong case can be made for developing a modified command structure to accommodate the realities of a biological event where there may be no disaster "site."

To be prepared for a bioterrorist attack, state and local organizations need to have a number of core capabilities within a coordinated regional and national public health system, and a governance structure that has never previously existed, for which there are very few historical exemplars. To create such a system, considerable infrastructural and personnel investments are required, and reinforced through regional agreements with the private sector, academia, and NGOs. Relatively moderate amounts of federal funding under the CDC Public Health Preparedness and Response for Bioterrorism program have so far reached below the level of the state agencies, with the notable exception of the MMRS; 95 percent of the new federal funds have so far been committed to repairing the most broken parts of the system. Indeed, the states have generally left it to the federal government to invest in biodefense in their jurisdictions. Many public health experts believe that the current levels of BT funding fall far short of the investment needed to achieve the minimum preparedness requirements [36,70–72]. Interstate differences in capabilities [73] are an operational issue that necessitates an immediate fix [74]. Median state public health expenditure is currently only $31 per person per annum, compared with $690 for K-12 education, $215 for higher education, and $96 for the prison service [36]. As with all programs, dependent on federal funding for their development, sustainability is a concern, and these programs have already experienced cuts before many basic preparedness goals could be met [36].

The strongest argument for building up the state public health infrastructure as a primary component of the national defense strategy against BW attack (presumably a rare event) is that it will also be an invaluable asset to combat the spectrum of national health problems. The 1918 influenza epidemic killed 40M people worldwide, and there can be no doubt that pandemics will occur in the future. The HIV epidemic also serves as an example where better public health preparedness would have led to earlier containment measures. A public health system is needed that endows a network of reference microbiology laboratories and of epidemiologists, that establishes effective, proactive disease surveillance at the local level, and coordinates training and health-related communications across the state, and also to relevant jurisdictions such as the veterinary, agriculture, and food safety services. Education of the general public is an important criterion in BT preparedness [63].

The system is being reengineered to provide a framework around which the consequences of a bioterrorist attack or of a natural epidemic can be managed effectively, and one to which federal and state emergency assets can easily be integrated. Telecommunication enhancements have been required at all levels of the public health system to coordinate its responsiveness and to interconnect with its response partners. The state public health laboratories provide a robust backbone for the LRN. The goal is to be able to identify, rapidly and safely, almost all BW and naturally infective agents internally in each of the 50 states and the capital territory. The physical upgrading of facilities, the provision of up-to-date diagnostic molecular biology equipment and a full complement of state laboratory personnel, and embedding improved training programs have been provided at considerable expense. As the public health personnel are aging, the CDC Infectious Disease Fellowship Program has been a useful source of trained replacement manpower.

A 1999 General Accounting Office (GAO) Report [70] recorded that the majority of state public health departments had no professional epidemiologist at the time to conduct active surveillance of infectious disease occurrences. Half had insufficient staff to conduct regular surveillance of endemic infectious diseases, such as hepatitis C virus and *Streptococcus pneumonia* [71]. Epidemiological investigations seek to determine when, where, and how exposure to dangerous pathogens take place, and whether infection is still occurring. The magnitude of any epidemic threat is determined by measuring the numbers of proven cases and by estimating attack rates and the epidemic curve. The anticipated response to treatment and containment measures can then be assessed and judged against finite results. Timely decisions on vaccination campaigns, mass antibiotic distribution, isolation, quarantine, control of transportation, closure of public places, and the emergency provision of services are heavily dependent on timely, robust epidemiological data.

It is especially important that the implications and limits of epidemiologic data are clearly understood by the nonspecialist, disaster managers. The National Electronic Disease Surveillance System (NEDSS) has been developed to integrate and standardize the surveillance of infectious disease [35]. It promotes fast, accurate standards-based electronic reporting as part of the CDC Public Health Information Network (PHIN). NEDSS incorporates an Internet-based platform that is directly accessible to medical and public health professionals, and provides electronic access to laboratory results (ELR), public health messaging, and centralized access to multiple health information databases. Timely and comprehensive data is thereby available across the network. Not all states are yet compliant.

The Health Alert Network (HAN) is a high-speed electronic Internet CDC platform that supports communications between local, state, and federal assets as a portal for standardized public health training with distance-based learning technologies.

The Epidemic Information Exchange System (Epi-X) is a secure system with round-the-clock coverage to report and discuss preliminary information concerning disease outbreaks and other events related to BT across jurisdictions [72]. Epi-X provides a rapid means of contact with key officials, real-time access to expert opinion, and a secure conduit for patient-related data. It constitutes an important component of a proactive surveillance system designed to provide early identification of BW events. Both NEDSS and Epi-X run on the HAN system. The established PulseNet network is also available to compare the investigational "fingerprinting" of organisms across the United States and Europe.

A number of limited syndromic and symptom surveillance prototypes are operational [75]. Prospective real-time data can be collated electronically from such sources as emergency rooms, reports from physicians, sentinel hospitals and coroners, hospital admissions, ambulance runs, numbers of index laboratory tests, and pharmacy sales of certain medications. The possibility of assuring a more sensitive infectious disease surveillance system is being assessed against the substantial costs, lack of selectivity, and deviation of public health effort [13,76]. More local intensive "situational awareness" may also afford more sensitive detection [75].

Early indices of unusual infections must always be followed with active surveillance and epidemiological investigation, and with policy decisions regarding interventions. Until recently, there has been no standard method of epidemiological reporting, and much of which had been by mail. The 1999 GAO Report [70] quoted, as an example, the fact that CDC was using over 100 data systems in monitoring health events with common hardware and software incompatibilities. The adoption of standardized systems throughout the public health community has been a major goal of the biodefense planning.

The general public must be treated as a key partner in the medical and public health response to BT [77]. Information sharing is most effective if undertaken close to home and supplemented with national information management. A population informed as to its hidden dangers and advised how it can best care for it in emergencies is more likely to support advice during an epidemic. The importance of rapid, authoritative, honest, and most importantly consistent public communications with the public in any ongoing disaster cannot be overestimated. Operational communication planning is strategically very important.

In addition to federal agencies, state and local BT response planning needs to involve the following entities:

- Public health agencies
- City/county/state government
- School systems
- Emergency management agency
- Environmental agencies: fire, health, water, air quality, consumer safety
- Health organizations: hospitals, urgent care centers, physicians, nursing homes, custodial care facilities, home healthcare providers, pharmacies, poison control centers, mental and occupational health centers
- Local emergency planning committee
- National Guard
- Private sector: trade and business organizations, industry, labor
- Public information office
- Public safety: fire, police
- Public works/sanitation
- Transportation systems
- Volunteer organizations, e.g., Red Cross
- Veterinarians

The CDC emphasizes the importance of jurisdictional contingency planning in the following areas, followed by multiple operational performance assessments from hands-on exercises, and subsequent amendments:

- Ensure emergency response plan is authorized by governmental jurisdiction
- Identify facilities suitable for emergency operations centers
- Identify alternative treatment facilities
- Plan for evacuation and relocation of individuals and agencies
- Roster of laboratories capable of handling specimens
- Roster of medical facilities capable of handling casualties
- Roster of veterinary laboratories capable of handling specimens
- Roster of veterinary facilities capable of handling infected animals
- Guidelines for addressing environmental decontamination issues
- Safety guidelines for workers dealing with infected people or animals
- Mutual aid agreements with surrounding jurisdictions, including VA and military installations
- Procedures for assisting special populations needing medical care during emergency
- Capabilities for incident stress counseling for victims and response personnel
- Protocols for decontamination of patients on arrival at treatment facility

- Protocols for decontaminating mass casualties (mainly chemical/toxin attack)
- Protocols for instituting mass isolation within a health facility
- Procedures for organizing and coordinating volunteers during a disaster
- Tested plans for instituting mass vaccination or medication distribution from the National Pharmaceutical Stockpile (NPS), including prioritizing first responders and medical/healthcare providers

Federal Government Preparedness and Operations

Where possible, domestic preparedness should rely on existing systems of all-hazards management, whereby an effective federal response capability has developed over the last 15 years and been honed by considerable experience. The deployment of federal assets to support the local and state emergency management response and the requirements of FBI investigations are common to all terrorism responses. The unique aspects of a biological attack, however, include the initial absence of a crime scene, casualty implications that are difficult to assess initially, an emergency that can continue to expand exponentially should an epidemic develop, the unique complexity of medical consequence management, and the profound degree of nationwide economic and social dislocation possible.

In the aftermath of the September 11, 2001 attacks, President George W. Bush formed the DHS under the auspices of the Homeland Security Act of 2002. The homeland security functions of 22 disparate federal agencies, previous erstwhile partners in the National Response Plan, were matrixed into the DHS. Within the new directorate, the component agencies should be better able to analyze threats and intelligence, protect critical infrastructure, and coordinate responses to future emergencies including those presented by biological threats. DHS is working to build a comprehensive National Incident Management System (NIMS) upon the current disaster management system promulgated by FEMA. The FRP, the National Contingency Plan, the U.S. Government Interagency Domestic Terrorism Concept of Operations Plan, and the Federal Radiation Emergency Response Plan are to be consolidated in the near future into a single all-hazard plan. Until this happens, the FRP, under FEMA leadership, remains the controlling program for biological agent preparedness and consequence management; other agencies are involved according to ESF needs.

As argued previously, the command structure ought to reflect the fact that this is primarily a medical and public health crisis within a disaster. The ICS [78] for a BT event ought ideally to reflect this reality. Important lessons were learned in the recent limited anthrax attacks via the mail system, in that CDC found itself isolated from the ICS and the involved public health authorities had occasion to purposely bypass the command structure in efforts to obtain information from a number of federal agencies [79]. Again in the Hurricane Katrina disaster, an ineffective ICS undermined the medical response. Further insights were gained from the 2000 TOPOFF exercise centered around a fictional BW plague attack on Denver [80]. The lack of familiarity of the medical leadership with the ICS and the reluctance of public health officials to give advice in the absence of solid scientific data despite a burgeoning epidemic were identified as major command and control problems. This study also recognized the likely imperative that political leadership will be necessary to provide moral and legal authority when highly consequential decisions have to be taken.

Federal resources are deployed only after the declaration of an emergency by the state governor, advised by the state Office of Emergency Management. A manifest disaster (such as 9/11) permits the president to unilaterally declare an emergency. A presidential declaration under the Stafford act activates the FRP and a Federal Coordinating Officer (FCO) is appointed to lead the response. Emergency Preparedness Liaison Officers (EPLO) assist the state and federal agencies in the assignment of specialized and strategic federal assets. The FBI and FEMA are likely to be mobilized simultaneously in BT to coordinate disaster management functions. Exceptionally, assets might be predeployed if intelligence suggests the likelihood of an attack.

The overall operations of the NRP [8,81] are considered in Chapters 27 and 29. This section will emphasize the role of the health and medical services response in a BT attack. Before the nature of the attack is discerned, large numbers of infections may already have occurred across widespread jurisdictions. At this stage, the de facto leadership is held by the public health services and by local governments. The leadership for further consequence management will transfer to FEMA on the declaration of an emergency. It is crucial to retain the authority of mayors and state governors in the command and control operations at all stages of the response.

The consequences of the outbreak are primarily limited by the timely and successful medical treatment of victims and by the containment of the epidemic—both are fundamentally medical and public health matters, although the logistics of this response rightly remain the responsibility of the FRP. The actions of FEMA are guided by the FRP and the by the 1997 Terrorism Annex. ESF #8 empowers the DHSS to fulfill the public health and medical requirements identified by state and local governments through the HHS executive agent, the Assistant Secretary for Health (ASH) and the Principal Deputy Assistant Secretary for Health (PDASH). The HHS OEP is the action agent coordinating and facilitating the ESF#8 response. The HHS regional health administrators (RHAs) are the operating agents. Under the FRP, each supporting federal agency contributes to the overall response, but retains control over their own resources and personnel. FEMA may activate an Emergency Support Team (EST) that provides an HQ interagency coordinating team to facilitate the deployment of federal assets. The Catastrophic Disaster Response Group (CDRG) is an interagency advisory resource.

The HHS Emergency Operations Center (EOC) will be activated within 12 hours of notification. The command and control structure is based upon ICS principles. A predesignated EOC core staff and affiliates (including the Assistant Secretary of Defense [Health Affairs], DOD, the Undersecretary for Health-VA, and the Director of FEMA) will be supplemented by federal partners and other high-level agencies and NGOs as appropriate. Special expert advisory groups will be assembled for consultation with the EOC as needed. Support agencies are put on alert and communication networks are activated.

A self-supporting ESF#8 Management Support Unit (MSU) will be deployed to the regional ESF#8 to provide long-distance emergency communications. FEMA will also mobilize its central and regional resources, on which the DHSS will have senior representation. FEMA determines which agencies will need to be represented on its Joint Operations Center (JOC) Command Group, on the Consequence Management Group (JOC CMG), and on the Joint Information Center (JIC) staff. The complex nature of the FRP command structure is discussed in Chapter 10 and federal partners under ESF#8 is listed in Table 9.2.

The initial federal asset dispatched to the incident site(s) is the FEMA Emergency Response Team-Advance Element (ERT-A), a team that initially supports the state EOC and identifies suitable facilities in which to set up operations. A Regional Operating Center (ROC) is formed by the FEMA Regional Director to coordinate the early response—to be replaced, if warranted, by an interagency ERT. The FCO, State Coordinating Officer (SCO), ERT, the RHA (DHHS Regional Health Administrator), federal agency regional representatives, and state and local liaison officers are organized as the Disaster Field Office (DFO).

Table 9.2 Federal Partners under FRP ESF#8

DHS	
DHHS OEP	Federal Emergency Management Agency
Department of Justice	Food and Drug Administration
National Domestic Preparedness Office	National Security Council
Federal Bureau of Investigation	Department of State
Office of Justice programs	Department of Energy
Department of Agriculture	Department of Defense
Department of Transportation	General Services Administration
Department of Veterans Affairs	U.S. Postal Service
National Communication System	Agency of International Development

The HHS RHA establishes a regional ESF#8 office as a coordinating center (CC). The CC interfaces with other ESF#8 assets, with state and local public health agencies, and with medical authorities. To assist state and local governments, regular assessments of need are performed, issues are prioritized, and repeated strategic analyses undertaken involving the following areas (the responsible HHS agencies are noted):

- Health and medical needs: Office of Public Health and Science (OPHS)/OEP/National Disaster Medical System (NDMS)—deploy assessment teams
- Health Surveillance: CDC—monitoring field investigations, advice
- Medical care personnel: OPHS/OEP/NDMS—disaster medical assistance teams (DMATs) and National Guard/Military/VA teams
- Drugs, supplies, and medical equipment: OPHS/OEP/NDMS—SNS guided by a CDC SNS Technical Advisory Response Unit (TARU), commercial sourcing
- Drug safety: Federal Drug Administration (FDA)—surveillance for unsafe products and equipment
- Biological hazard consultation: CDC—field investigations, treatment consultations, decontamination
- Patient evacuation: OPHS/OEP/NDMS—DOD resources
- In-hospital care: OPHS/OEP/NDMS—intensive care, regional and national networks
- Worker health/safety: CDC—decontamination, prophylaxis, treatment
- Public health information: CDC
- Mental healthcare: Substance Abuse and Mental Health Services Administration (SAMHSA)
- Victim identification/mortuary services: OPHS/OEP/NDMS
- Veterinary services: OPHS/OEP/NDMS—assist veterinary authorities

The regional ESF#8 Coordinating Center will develop and update medical assessments and provide situation reports called SITREPS to the CDRG, EST, JOC, JIC, other ESF EOC, the support federal agencies, state authorities, and other organizations on a need-to-know basis. The CC will mobilize preestablished local reserves and access other regional resources. The Joint Regional Medical Planning Office (JRMPO) or other entity designated by the DOD Defense Coordinating Officer (DCO) will assist requests for the use of a variety of military assets that are pertinent to the early management of a BT response.

The national HHS EOC will (1) activate the DOD support network, (2) alert NDMS resources on a standby basis, (3) mobilize regional NDMS Federal Coordinating Centers (FCC) to obtain bed availability reports from participating nonfederal hospitals, (4) alert the Global Patient Movement Requirement Center (GPMRC) to collate bed availability, (5) alert the HHS Supply Service Center (SSC), the Defense Logistics Agency (DLA), and other preidentified sources of medical supplies, (6) alert national communications and transport agencies, and (7) obtain weather forecasts and geographic information from ESF#5. Real-time data are acquired and analyzed systematically from local ESF#8, FEMA DFO, from various federal officials at the scene, the state governor, state health officials, state EMS, state disaster authorities, and regional assets.

To facilitate urgent manpower and facility needs, the national HHS EOC can mobilize the regional MMRS and deploy mobile NDMS units called Disaster Medical Assistance Teams (DMATs) to enhance triage, patient care, and patient transportation capabilities. Veterans Administration assets, including hospitals, Emergency Medical Response Teams (EMRTs) and Medical Emergency Radiological Response Teams (MERRT) can be accessed through the VA Emergency Management Strategic Healthcare Group (EMSHG). National Guard units can be activated under Title 36 by the state governor and under Title 10 by the U.S. president.

Substantial military assets can be obtained under Title 10 status when requested by a state governor or by a lead federal agency. Skilled reaction teams and medical, transportation, supply, security, engineers, or public affairs units can be provided. However, it remains an important consideration that dependence on the military should be considered as a last resort because of potential conflicting responsibilities. The Joint Task Force-Civil Support (JTF-CS) is the focus of BW consequence management requests to the military.

Air transportation requests are routed via state authorities to regional ESF#8 and on to the NDMS OSC (on-scene commander). When appropriate, patients will be transferred out to relieve local facilities. Patient transfers are coordinated via GPMRC via a system of collection points and utilizes the 375th Aeromedical Evacuation Squadron based at Scott AFB. Logistical air support is provided by the Department of Agriculture and by other resources. Considerable human resources and materiel can thereby be transported into the area, as long as the airspace remains open.

An early issue in epidemic management is the availability of sufficient logistical supplies to treat the burgeoning numbers of infected and exposed patients. CDC has established the SNS as a national repository of antibiotics, chemical antidotes, vaccines, antitoxins, life-support medications, intravenous medications, ventilators and airway maintenance supplies, and medical/surgical items. The stockpile includes smallpox and anthrax vaccines, botulinum antitoxin, "millions" of treatment doses for anthrax, plague, and tularemia, Tamiflu (Oseltamivir) and Relenza (Zanamivir) for influenza, and substantial stocks of other antivirals. A "push pack" of medical materiel will be transported to the local site anywhere within the United States within 12 hours of federal authorization. How a pandemic 50-state requirement is to be managed is currently under advisement. The VA manages the pharmaceutical stockpile inventory. Additional pharmaceuticals are stored at manufacturers' warehouses in the Vendor Managed Inventory (VMI) program. Planning is incorporated into state and local preparedness plans to manage and distribute the supplies on arrival.

FEMA and each partner agency in the Health and Medical Services Emergency Response have structured operational plans related to biodefense (see Chapters 10 and 27). Much of the logistical management is common to all disasters and therefore, coherent institutional experience is readily available within DHS and FEMA. After a BW attack, there may be unfamiliar difficulties in the real-time assessment of the status of the epidemic and in the prolonged intensive response that may be required. There is a particular challenge of providing major supplementation of medical and nursing manpower. Alternative medical facilities may have to be set up and manned from scratch in short order to enhance surge capacity, and perhaps to replace contaminated facilities. A small army of support personnel will also be required in the midst of an epidemic. Treatment and disease containment may have to be undertaken across the United States and in foreign countries. Indeed, as much effort may have to be expanded in infection containment as in patient care.

Civilian communications assume considerable importance—as exemplified by New York Mayor Giuliani after the 2001 World Trade Center terrorism. It is crucial to have communications strategies in place and to disseminate prompt, consistent, and accurate information. Finally, the legal ramifications of many issues in the consequence management of BT and epidemic biological agents must be resolved. Such issues include the emergency licensing of out-of-state professionals; exemption of certain mandated professional and institutional standards; HIPAA; exemption of certain public security information from open records laws; compulsory vaccination; population-based prophylactic drug distribution; travel restriction; isolation; quarantine; closure of businesses and public spaces; conflict with interstate commerce laws; enforced evacuation; the emergency appropriation of medical and other facilities; mass fatality management; the role of the military and reserves; and questions of local, state, and federal authority. The legal framework for biological disaster management needs to be brought up-to-date with some urgency.

Conclusions

On January 10, 2002, President Bush signed the $2.9 billion Terrorism Appropriations Bill to enhance funding in biodefense. The monies are being invested in comprehensive preparedness readiness at state and local levels. Infectious disease surveillance and investigation, hospital mass casualty management, public health laboratories, and communication and reporting capabilities are to be improved. Administratively, the funding is divided into three programs: (1) CDC—for public health preparedness; (2) HRSA—for regional hospital planning; and (3) HHS OEP—to support the MMRS—80 percent of the U.S. population will then be covered by MMRS. Other funding includes further support for the stockpiling of antibiotics ($650 million), to establish and maintain a dedicated BT workforce at CDC, to continue to develop the new CDC Rapid Response and Advanced Technology Laboratory (RRATL), expand the CDC Epidemiologic Intelligence Service (EIS), expand other CDC and National Institutes of Health (NIH) facilities, to expand vaccine programs, and stockpile a national supply of smallpox vaccine by autumn 2002. There are substantial increases in applied and basic science BW-related research, and in efforts to develop better detection and monitoring technology (by DOD) and to improve environmental detection methods for biological agents (by EPA).

Most of the infrastructure and training created to bolster the national capabilities in disaster management will enhance the public health services. The BT preparedness of the medical and public health systems will radically improve U.S. capabilities in infectious disease containment. The complexity of the NRP command and control system, however, is not optimal and has failed substantially at the 1984 Los Angeles Olympics, at hurricanes Hugo, Andrew, and Katrina, and during the 2001 anthrax attacks. The NRP has yet to manage a major biological epidemic, and the command structure would appear ill suited to manage responses to BT. The DHS is currently overhauling the national emergency response plan and it is hoped that the need for the medical leadership of BT responsiveness will be recognized.

The strengthening of relationships between healthcare assets and law enforcement, fire departments, and other local, state, and federal agencies will engender future preparedness benefits. New vaccine development for candidate BW agents and their strategic use will provide the single most cost-effective intervention [82]. Efficient electronic communications will continue to integrate the medical elements of the response and interface them with the local, state, and federal emergency management communities and with the general public. It is hoped that a flexible national system will evolve that will be capable of responding efficiently to the most dire of BT doomsday predictions. The level of preparedness at all levels, including the general population, will ultimately determine outcomes in infective epidemics.

Preparedness for a BW event must be tested at all levels. Considerable expenditure is required on new technology and facilities, in enhancing the workforce, and in the provision of comprehensive educational and training programs. Quite aside from the potential for major loss of life and the profound societal consequences of a major BT attack or major natural epidemic, the economic case for biopreparedness is also convincing. A recent study estimated the potential economic impact of a bioterrorist attack as $477 million per 100,000 persons exposed to a brucellosis weapon and $26.2 billion per 100,000 persons exposed to an anthrax attack [83]. As "Dark Winter" has illustrated, the consequences of a poorly mitigated smallpox attack could be devastating.

References

1. T O'Toole, M Mair, and TV Inglesby. Confronting biological weapons. Shining light on "Dark Winter." *Clinical Infectious Diseases* 34:972–983, 2002. Internet: www.journals.uchicago.edu/cgi-bin/resolve?CID020165 (accessed December 2, 2007).
2. DA Henderson. Looming threat of bioterrorism. *Science* 283:1279–1282, 1999. Internet: http://cas.bellarmine.edu/tietjen/ecology/looming_threat_of_bioterrorism.htm (accessed December 2, 2007).
3. DA Henderson, TV Inglesby, and JG Bartlett. Smallpox as a biological weapon: Medical and public health management. Working Group on Civilian Biodefense. *JAMA* 281:127–137, 1999. Internet: http://jama.ama-assn.org/cgi/content/full/281/22/2127 (accessed December 2, 2007).
4. TB Cole. When a bioweapon strikes, who will be in charge? *JAMA* 2000:284:944–948. Internet: http://jama.ama-assn.org/cgi/content/full/284/8/944 (accessed December 2, 2007).
5. JW Runge. Statement for the record Jeffrey W. Runge, MD Chief Medical Officer Office of Health Affairs before the U.S. House of Representatives Committee on Appropriations Subcommittee on Homeland Security "Bioterrorism preparedness and role of DHS Chef Medical Officer," March 29, 2007. Internet: http://www.dhs.gov/xnews/testimony/testimony_117528 0009133.shtm (accessed November 20, 2007).
6. Department of Health and Human Services. Health and Medical Support Plan for the Federal Response to Acts of Chemical/Biological (C/B) Terrorism: Final Interim Plan. Washington, DC: Government Printing Office, 1996. Internet: bioterrorism.slu.edu/bt/key_ref/FEMA/C-BHMPlan.pdf (accessed December 2, 2007).
7. CDC Strategic Planning Group. Biological and Chemical Terrorism: Strategic Plan for Preparedness and Response. *Morbidity and Mortality Weekly Report* 2000:49(RR-4):1–14. Internet: http://www.cdc.gov/mmwr/preview/mmwrhtml /rr4904a1.htm (accessed December 2, 2007).
8. Federal Emergency Management Agency. Federal Response Plan. Washington, DC: Government Printing Office, 2003. Internet: www.au.af.mil/au/awc/awcgate/frp/frpbasic.pdf (accessed December 2, 2007).
9. Department of Defense. Improving Local and State Agency Response to Terrorist Incidents Involving Biological Weapons. Washington, DC: Government Printing Office, 2000. Internet: http://www.chem-bio.com/resource/2000/bwirp_interim_plan_guide.pdf (accessed December 2, 2007).

10. Anonymous. United States Government Interagency Domestic Terrorism Concept of Operations Plan. Washington, DC: Government Printing Office, 2001. Internet: http://www.fas.org/irp/threat/conplan.html (accessed December 2, 2007).
11. F Cilluffo, S Cardash, and G Lederman. Combating Chemical, Biological, Radiological, and Nuclear Terrorism: A Comprehensive Strategy. Washington, DC: Center for Strategic and International Studies, 2001. Internet: www.911investigations.net/IMG/pdf/doc-343.pdf (accessed December 2, 2007).
12. AE Smithson and L-A Levy. Ataxia, the Chemical and Biological Warfare Threat and the US Response. Stimson Center Report No. 35. Washington, DC: Henry L Stimson Center, 2002. Internet (accessed March 10, 2002). Internet: http://www.stimson.org/?SN=CB20020111235 (accessed December 2, 2007).
13. Anonymous. Coordinating Office for Terrorism Preparedness and Emergency Response (CG). Internet: www.cdc.gov/maso/pdf/COTPERfs.pdf (accessed November 20, 2007).
14. DA Henderson. Bioterrorism as a public health threat. *Emerging Infectious Diseases* 4:488–492, 1998. Internet: www.cdc.gov/ncidod/eid/vol4no3/mcdade.htm (accessed December 2, 2007).
15. RA Falkenrath, RD Newman, and BA Thayer. *America's Achilles Heel, Nuclear Biological, and Chemical Terrorism and Covert Attack.* Cambridge, MA: MIT Press, 1998.
16. J Lederberg, ed. *Biological Weapons: Limiting the Threat.* Cambridge, MA: MIT Press, 1999.
17. N Gurr and B Cole. *The New Face of Terrorism. Threats from Weapons of Mass Destruction.* London, U.K.: Tauris, 2000.
18. J Miller, S Engelberg, and W Broad. *Germs, Biological Weapons and America's Secret War.* New York: Simon & Schuster, 2001.
19. E Regis. *The Biology of Doom.* New York: Henry Holt, 1999.
20. CJ Davis. Nuclear blindness: An overview of the biological weapons programs of the former Soviet Union and Iraq. *Emerging Infectious Diseases* 5:509–512, 1999. Internet: http://www.cdc.gov/ncidod/EID/vol5no4 /davis.htm (accessed December 2, 2007).
21. B Hoffman. *Inside Terrorism.* London, U.K.: Indigo, 1998.
22. AK Cronin. Terrorist Motivations for Chemical and Biological Weapons Use: Placing the Threat in Context. Congressional Research Service, 2003. Internet: www.fas.org/irp/crs/RL31831.pdf (accessed December 1, 2007).
23. F Fenner, DA Henderson, I Arita, Z Jezek, and ID Ladnyi. *Smallpox and Its Eradication.* Geneva, Switzerland: World Health Organization, 1988.
24. JB Tucker and KM Vogel. Preventing the proliferation of chemical and biological weapon materials and know-how. *The Nonproliferation Review* 7:88–96, 2000. Internet: cns.miis.edu/pubs/npr/vol07/71/tucker71.pdf (accessed December 2, 2007).
25. RA Falkenrath. Confronting nuclear, biological, and chemical terrorism. *Survival* 40(3):43–65, 1998.
26. W Laquer. *The New Terrorism: Fanaticism and the Arms of Mass Destruction.* Oxford, U.K.: Oxford University Press, 1999.
27. GH Christopher, TJ Cieslak, JA Pavlin, and EM Eitzin. Biological warfare. A historical perspective. *JAMA* 278:412–417, 1997.
28. SL Weiner. Strategies of biowarfare defense. *Military Medicine* 152: 25–28, 1987.
29. DL Noah, AL Sobel, SM Ostroff, and JA Kildrew. Biological warfare training: Infectious disease outbreak differentiation. *Military Medicine* 163:198–201, 1998.
30. United States Army Medical Research Institute of Infectious Diseases. *Medical Management of Biological Casualties Handbook* (the Blue Book), 4th edn. Fort Detrick, MD: USAMRIID, 2001. Internet: biotech.law.lsu.edu/blaw/bluebook/Bluebook_htm.htm (accessed December 2, 2007).
31. B Brown and AJ Meltzer. Medical response to biological terrorist attack. In: *Countering Biological Terrorism in the U.S.: An Understanding of Issues and Status.* Siegrist DW and Graham JM, eds. Dobbs Ferry, NY: Oceana Publications, 1999, pp. 117–126.
32. MT Osterholm. The medical impact of a bioterrorist attack: Is it all media hype or clearly a potential nightmare? *Postgraduate Medicine* 106(2):121–130, 1999. Internet: http://www.postgradmed.com/issues/1999/08_99/osterholm.htm (accessed December 1, 2007).
33. A Camus. *The Plague.* Gilbert S, trans. New York: Vintage, 1975.
34. J Saramago. *Blindness.* Pontiero G, trans. San Diego, CA: Harcourt Brace, 1977.

35. Anonymous. Fact sheet: President Bush signs Biodefense for the 21st Century. National Security Presidential Directives—NSPD-33. Internet: http://www.fas.org/irp/offdocs/nspd/biodef.html (accessed November 26, 2007).
36. Trust for America's Health. Ready or Not? Protecting the Public's Health from Diseases, Disasters, and Bioterrorism, 2006. Internet: http://www. healthyamericans.org/reports/bioterror06/ (accessed November 26, 2007).
37. JE McDade. Addressing the potential threat of bioterrorism value added to an improved public health infrastructure. *Emerging Infectious Diseases* 5:591–592, 1999. Internet: http://www.cdc.gov/ncidod/EID/vol5no4/mcdade.htm (accessed December 1, 2007).
38. NJ Rabkin. Combating Terrorism: Linking Threats to Strategies and Resources. Testimony to the Subcommittee on National Security, Veterans Affairs, and International Relations, House Committee on Government Reform, July 26, 2000. Washington, DC: General Accounting Office, 2000. Internet: www.gao.gov/archive/2000/ns00218t.pdf (accessed December 2, 2007).
39. Executive Office of the President, Office of Management and Budget. Annual Report to Congress on Combating Terrorism, May 18, 2000. Internet: www.whitehouse.gov/omb/legislative/nsd_annual_report2001.pdf (accessed October 19, 2008).
40. Anonymous. Public Health and Medical Preparedness. Homeland Security Presidential Directive/HSPD-21. Internet: http://www.fas.org/irp/offdocs/nspd/hspd-21.htm (accessed November 21, 2007).
41. N Khardori, ed. *Bioterrorism Preparedness: Medicine—Public Health—Policy*. Hoboken, NJ: Wiley-VCH, 2006.
42. L Duckworth. Super agency to tackle threat of holiday diseases. *Independent* (newspaper). London, U.K., January 11, 2002.
43. JE Waeckerle. Domestic preparedness for events involving weapons of mass destruction. *JAMA* 283:252–254, 2000. Internet: http://jama.ama-assn.org/cgi/content/extract/283/2/252 (accessed December 2, 2007).
44. RW Niska and CW Burt. Training for Terrorism-Related Conditions in Hospitals: United States, 2003–04. Advance Data from Vital and Health Statistics; no 380. Hyattsville, MD: National Center for Health Statistics, 2006. Internet: http://www.cdc.gov/nchs/data/ad/ad380.pdf (accessed December 1, 2007).
45. GC Alexander and MK Wynia. Ready and willing? Physicians' sense of preparedness for bioterrorism. *Health Affairs* 22:189–197, 2003. Internet: http://content.healthaffairs.org/cgi/content/full/22/5/189 (accessed November 29, 2007).
46. JW Snyder and W Check. Bioterrorism Threats to our Future. The Role of the Clinical Microbiology Laboratory in Detection, Identification, and Confirmation of Biological Agents. Washington, DC: American Academy of Microbiology and American College of Microbiology, 2001. Internet: http://www.asm.org/Academy/index.asp?bid=2159 (accessed December 2, 2007).
47. American Society for Microbiology. Sentinel Level Clinical Laboratory Guidelines. Internet: http://www.asm.org/Policy/index.asp?bid=6342 (accessed November 28, 2007).
48. L Sehulster and RTW Chinn. Guideline for Environmental Infection Control in Health-care Facilities, 2007. Recommendations of CDC and the Healthcare Infection Control Practices Advisory Committee (HICPAC). Internet: http://www.guideline.gov/summary/summary.aspx?ss=15&doc_id=3843 (accessed November 28, 2007).
49. JW Snyder, ed. Cumitech 33: *Biological Agents Associated with Bioterrorism*. Washington, DC: American Society for Microbiology, 2000.
50. MJR Gilchrist. The progress, priorities, and concerns of public health laboratories. In: *Biological Threats and Terrorism: Assessing the Science and Response Capabilities*. Knobler SL, Mahmoud AAF, and Pray LA, eds. Washington, DC: National Academy Press, 2002, pp. 160–165.
51. APIC Bioterrorism Task Force and CDC Hospital Infections Program Bioterrorism Working Group. Bioterrorism Readiness Plan: A Template for Healthcare Facilities. Internet: http://bioterrorism.slu.edu/key_ references/BioPlan.pdf (accessed December 2, 2007).
52. RW Grow and L Rubinson. The challenge of hospital infection control during a response to bioterrorist attacks. *Biosecurity and Bioterrorism: Biodefense Strategy Practice, and Science* 1:215–220, 2003. Internet: http://www.upmc-biosecurity.org/website/resources/publications/2003_orig-articles/2003–09–15-hospitalinfectcontrol.html (accessed November 28, 2007).

53. BN Shadel, T Rebmann, B Clements, JJ Chen, and RG Evans. Infection control practitioners' perceptions and educational needs regarding bioterrorism: Results from a national needs assessment survey. *American Journal of Infection Control* 31:129–134, 2003. Internet: premierinc.com/quality-safety/—/downloads/Btsurvey ICPajic0503.pdf (accessed November 28, 2007).
54. KB Nolte, RL Hanzlick, DC Payne, et al. Medical examiners, coroners, and biological terrorism. A guidebook for surveillance and case management. *MMWRRR* 53(RR08):1–27, 2004. Internet: http://www.cdc.gov/mmwr/preview/mmwrhtml/rr5308a1.htm (accessed November 28, 2007).
55. KB Nolte, SS Yoon, C Pertowski (letter). Medical examiners, coroners, and bioterrorism. *Emerging Infectious Diseases* 6:559–560, 2000. Internet: http://www.cdc.gov/ncidod/eid/vol6no5/nolte_letter.htm (accessed December 2, 2007).
56. U.S. Army Research Development and Engineering Command and Department of Justice Office for Domestic Preparedness. Capstone Document: Mass Fatality Management for Incidents Involving Weapons of Mass Destruction, 2005. Internet: http://www.ecbc.army.mil/hld/dl/MFM Capstone August 2005.pdf (accessed November 29, 2007).
57. JN Rubin. Recurring pitfalls in hospital preparedness. Internet: http://www.homelandsecurity.org/journal/articles/rubin.html (accessed November 21, 2007).
58. SJ Phillips and A Knebel, eds. Mass Medical Care with Scarce Resources. A Community Planning Guide. Internet: www.ahrq.gov/research/mce/mceguide.pdf (accessed November 30, 2007).
59. Johns Hopkins Center for Civilian Biodefense Studies. Enhancing bioterrorism preparedness and response post-September 11: Interim actions for the medical and public health community, 2002.
60. ASA Lister. An Overview of the U.S. Public Health System in the Context of Emergency Preparedness. Congressional Research Service, 2005. Internet: www.fas.org/sgp/crs/homesec/RL31719.pdf (accessed December 2, 2007).
61. TL Milne. Countering bioterrorism threats: Local public health perspectives. In: *Biological Threats and Terrorism: Assessing the Science and Response Capabilities*. Knobler SL, Mahmoud AAF, and Pray LA, eds. Washington, DC: National Academy Press, 2002, pp. 176–178.
62. MR Fraser and VS Fisher. *Elements of Effective Bioterrorism Preparedness: A Planning Primer for Local Public Health Agencies*. Washington, DC: National Association of County and City Health Officials, 2001. Internet: www.kdheks.gov/han/download/response_plan.pdf (accessed December 2, 2007).
63. P Quinlisk. Combating terrorism: Federal response to a biological weapons attack. Testimony to the Subcommittee on National Security, Veterans Affairs, and International Relations, House Committee on Government Reform, July 23, 2001. Serial 107-99, 127-34. Washington, DC: Government Printing Office, 2001. Internet: bulk.resource.org/gpo.gov/hearings/107h/81593.pdf (accessed December 2, 2007).
64. Working Group on Community Engagement in Health Emergency Planning, University of Pittsburgh Center for Biosecurity. Community engagement: Leadership tools for catastrophic health events. *Biosecururity and Bioterrorism* 5:8–24, 2007. Internet: http://www.upmc-biosecurity.org/website/focus/community_engage/2007_working _group/full_report.html (accessed November 28, 2007).
65. ER Taylor. Are We Prepared for Terrorism Using Weapons of Mass Destruction?: Government's Half Measures. Cato Institute Policy Analysis No. 387. Washington, DC: Cato Institute, 2000, pp. 1–19. Internet: http://www.cato.org/pubs/pas/pa-387es.html (accessed December 2, 2007).
66. J Gibson. Assessing state and territorial health departments. In: *Biological Threats and Terrorism: Assessing the Science and Response Capabilities*. Knobler SL, Mahmoud AAF, and Pray LA, eds. Washington, DC: National Academy Press, 2002, pp. 173–176.
67. Committee for the Study of the Future of Public Health, Institute of Medicine. The Future of Public Health. Washington, DC: National Academies Press, 1988.
68. U.S. General Accounting Office. Combating Terrorism: Need to Eliminate Duplicate Federal Weapons of Mass Destruction Training: Report to Congressional Requesters. March 2000. Washington, DC: GAO, 2000. Internet: www.gao.gov/archive/2000/ns00064.pdf (accessed December 2, 2007).
69. Committee on Assuring the Health of the Public in the 21st Century. The Future of the Public's Health in the 21st Century. Washington, DC: National Academies Press, 2002.
70. U.S. General Accounting Office. Emerging Infectious Diseases: Consensus on Needed Laboratory Capacity Could Strengthen Surveillance, February 1999. Washington, DC: GAO, 1999. Internet: www.gao.gov/cgi-bin/getrpt?GAO/HEHS-99-26 (accessed December 2, 2007).

71. MT Osterholm. Bioterrorism: Our Frontline Response, Evaluating U.S. Public Health and Medical Readiness. Testimony to the Subcommittee on Public Health, Senate Committee on Health, Education, Labor, and Pensions, March 25, 1999. S/HRG 106-21, 68-72. Washington, DC: Government Printing Office, 1999. Internet: books.google.com/books?isbn=0756700345... (accessed December 2, 2007).
72. Bioterrorism Preparedness and Response Program. National Bioterrorism and Response Initiative: Overview and General Information about the Initiative. Atlanta, GA: Centers for Disease Control and Prevention, 2000.
73. G Pezzino, MZ Thompson, and M Edgar. A multi-state comparison of local public health preparedness assessment using a common, standardized tool. National Network of Public Health Institutes, Illinois Public Health Institute, Kansas Health Institute, and Michgan Public Health Institute, 2006. Internet: www.astho.org/pubs/NNPHIreport.pdf (accessed November 21, 2007).
74. Trust for America's Health. Shortchanging America's Health 2006. A State-by-State Look at How Federal Public Health Dollars Are Spent. Internet: http://healthyamericans.org/reports/shortchanging06/ (accessed November 21, 2007).
75. National Academy of Sciences. Global Infectious Disease Surveillance and Detection: Assessing the Challenges. Finding Solutions Workshop, Summary and Assessment. Internet: http://books.nap.edu/catalog/11996.htm (accessed November 28, 2007).
76. AE Smithson. A review of federal bioterrorism preparedness programs from a public health perspective. Testimony to the Subcommittee on Oversight and Investigations, Committee on Energy and Commerce, October 10, 2001. Washington, DC: Government Printing Office, 2002. Internet: http://www.yale.edu/lawweb/avalon/sept_11/testimony_027.htm (accessed December 2, 2007).
77. TA Glass and M Schoch-Spana. Bioterrorism and the people: How to vaccinate a city against panic. *Clinical Infectious Diseases* 34:217–223, 2002. Internet: http://www.journals.uchicago.edu/CID/journal/issues/v34n2/011333/011333.html (accessed October 19, 2008).
78. PA Erickson. *Emergency Response Planning for Corporate and Municipal Managers.* San Diego, CA: Academic Press, 1999, pp. 82–102.
79. JL Geberding. Lessons learned: The challenges and opportunities. In: *Biological Threats and Terrorism: Assessing the Science and Response Capabilities.* Knobler SL, Mahmoud AAF, and Pray LA, eds. Washington, DC: National Academy Press, 2002, pp. 149–152.
80. T Inglesby, R Grossman, and T O'Toole. A plague on your city: Observations from TOPOFF. *Clinical Infectious Diseases* 32:436–445, 2001. Internet: http://www.journals.uchicago.edu/doi/abs/10.1086/318513 (accessed December 2, 2007).
81. PH Benwell-Lejeune. Federal cooperation. In: *Countering Biological Terrorism in the U.S.: An Understanding of Issues and Status.* Siegrist DW and Graham JM, eds. Dobbs Ferry, NY: Oceana Publications, 1999, pp. 85–100.
82. PK Russell. Vaccines in civilian defense against bioterrorism. *Emerging Infectious Diseases* 5:531–533, 1999. Internet: http://www.cdc.gov/ncidod/EID/vol5no4 /russell.htm (accessed December 1, 2007).
83. AF Kaufman, MI Meltzer, and GP Schmidt. The economic impact of a bioterrorist attack: Are prevention and postattack intervention programs justifiable? *Emerging Infectious Diseases* 3:83–94, 1997. Internet: http://www.cdc.gov/ncidod/eid/vol3no2/kaufman.htm (accessed December 1, 2007).

Chapter 10

Biological Terrorism: Preparation for Response—What the Government Can Do in Defending the Homeland

Marion C. Warwick

CONTENTS

Introduction 186
Perspectives on the Use of Biological Agents as Weapons...187
History of Biological Warfare 187
Weaponizing Process 188
Biological Weapons..189
Role of the U.S. Government...190
Role of the Military 191
Federal Agencies 191
Designation of an Overall Authority 192
Role of State and Local Governments..193
Prevention...193
Deterrence 193
Preemption 194

Release and Transmission 194
Airborne Transmission 194
Waterborne Transmission 195
Foodborne Transmission 196
Zoonotic and Agricultural Transmission 196
Zoonotic 196
Agricultural 197
Other Releases 198
Secondary Transmission 198
Response 200
Surveillance for Bioterrorism 200
Immediate Detection Technology 200
Surveillance through Monitoring Illness 201
Syndromic Surveillance 201
Information Sources Needed for Disease Surveillance 203
Outbreak Investigation 204
Coordination of Outbreak and Criminal Investigations 205
Laboratory 206
Mass Medical Care 207
Skeletal Staffing of Hospitals 207
Workforce Shortage in the Medical Field 207
Need for Infection Control Plans at Hospitals 207
Regional Planning 208
Planning for the Arrival of Federal Support 208
Mass Distribution of Emergency Medications 209
Prioritization of Vaccine Recipients 210
Handling Mass Mortalities 210
Psychological Distress 211
Communications 212
Communication between Responding Agencies 212
Public Information 212
Future Directions 213
Training 213
Training for the General Public 215
Research 215
General Research Needs 215
Vaccines 216
Genomics 218
Conclusions 218
Acknowledgments 219
References 220

Introduction

The field of response to bioterrorism is developing so rapidly that, at best, this chapter will serve as a snapshot of the state of preparedness at the point in time just after the attacks on the World Trade Center and the Pentagon, and the establishment of the U.S. Office of Homeland Security.

This chapter begins with some background and explanation of the particular threats posed by the use of biological agents in warfare or terrorism and introduces the importance of an efficient government response. From there, the discussion proceeds in a chronological order following the issues raised by a bioterrorism (BT) attack: prevention and deterrence, counteraction of each method of release and transmission, and the various elements of response that will be needed after an attack. This chapter ends with training, research, and conclusions, because they build on an understanding of the threats, and look forward to proactively mitigating them.

Perspectives on the Use of Biological Agents as Weapons

Epidemic disease evokes a primordial quality of dread disproportionate to that provoked by threats of equal magnitude from other causes [1]. Perhaps part of the reason for this is that infectious diseases have plagued mankind since antiquity [2]. They have played a pivotal, though often overlooked, role in the history of mankind, and there is no reason to believe that they will not continue to influence our history [3]. Today, human immunodeficiency virus (HIV), malaria, polio, measles, tuberculosis (TB), and other communicable diseases are threatening to cause massive individual suffering on an order of magnitude sufficient to threaten societal disruption in large parts of Africa and Asia [4]. At the same time, worldwide changes in societal practices, demographic patterns, and travel are enabling the emergence of new pathogens to which humans are immunologically vulnerable [5]. Given the delicate balance between the human race and microbes (mankind's historic enemy), why would anyone think to use biological agents as weapons?

Those who develop biological weapons have asked whether it, "is worse to die from a disease… than from bullets, bombs, or nuclear radiation?" and have argued that dying from disease is a "natural way of dying" [6]. In the sense that infectious diseases can cause death when deployed; they are no different from other weapons. However, mankind's repugnance of poison and unseen killers makes the use of biological agents particularly inhumane, and the use of an instrument that has historically been mankind's enemy seems to place the user on the side of the inhuman. Furthermore, unlike other weapons, infectious diseases are alive, and hence not fully under the control of the person who wields them. Once released, they may spread and have effects reaching far beyond the original intent of those releasing them [7].

History of Biological Warfare

In spite of these concerns, biological pathogens, or living microorganisms that cause disease, have been used since antiquity as weapons [8]. Biological warfare has been defined as "the use of microorganisms and toxins, generally of microbial, plant, or animal origin, to produce disease and death in humans, livestock and crops" [9]. From a military point of view, paying attention to infectious diseases makes sense. Until the Russo–Japanese war, illness claimed more casualties in battle than inflicted by wounds of war [10].

The United States started its biological weapons program during World War II when it was believed that enemy states were developing them [11,12]. Countries known to have had biological weapons programs include Japan [13], England [14], the former Soviet Union [15], South Africa [16], and North Korea [17]. Other countries suspected of past or present bioweapon development include Iran, Syria, Egypt, Libya, Israel, and China [18]. Though the United States stopped its program in 1972, the Soviet Union's biological weapons program expanded throughout the 1980s and 1990s, and until recently [19]. Iraq was suspected of having a biological weapons program until the second Iraq War [20,21].

Today, widespread biotechnology and vaccine manufacture, requiring similar skills as for the production of biological weapons, increase the available facilities and the pool of expertise required for the manufacture of biological weapons. In addition, the Internet and encryption technology are decreasing the barriers to the production of weapons of mass destruction (WMD) by making knowledge available and allowing criminals and terrorists to communicate efficiently and anonymously [22]. However, the production of effective, biological agents as weapons may require better equipment and facilities than those usually available to small domestic groups [23].

Weaponizing Process

Weaponizing is the process of modifying living microorganisms to create deadly tools of war or terrorism [24] that differ from naturally occurring diseases in some important characteristics. Biological weapons programs go through many stages to achieve such a final product [25,26]. Out of thousands of possibilities, organisms with characteristics of durability and lethality are selected [27]. Biological weapons programs working independently in different countries have tended to select the same organisms, as there are a limited number of microbes that are both lethal and hardy enough to survive in the environment. Selecting the disease is not enough; diseases may have many strains that vary in their lethality. The Aum Shinrikyo cult responsible for the sarin gas attack in Tokyo in 1995 had also attempted releases of anthrax, which failed partly because they used a nontoxic strain of anthrax [28].

Once selected, the organisms are cultured in large quantities [29]. The fermenting tanks used for this stage vary in size from desktop models to huge vats several stories in height [30]. Whatever the size of production, the organisms in this wet form are not viable in the environment for long, are difficult to deploy, and therefore must be converted to a dry form for efficient use. Converting actively metabolizing organisms into a dry, inactive form while also maintaining their viability is technically difficult [31]. Some programs have used freeze drying for this process. For aerosol dispersion, microorganisms are more effective if milled down to a particle size of between one and five microns. At this size, they can evade the human upper respiratory tract defenses and be deposited in the lung when deployed.

The product at this stage is a deadly weapon, but it can be made even more deadly by removing electrostatic charges [32]. Small charged particles tend to clump together or be drawn to dust fragments in the air. If the tiny particles are coated or mixed with inert material to remove the electrostatic charges, they can linger, suspended in the air, for longer periods of time and avoid clumping together. Once pathogens have gone through this weaponizing process, they can infect exposed populations much more efficiently and in low dosages [33]. They may also cause different forms of disease. For instance, 95 percent of naturally occurring anthrax causes skin disease, in which the organism enters the body through damaged skin. But anthrax that has been weaponized through all these steps can more easily cause the inhalational form of the disease. Weaponized microorganisms must be handled carefully, to prevent illness among those working with them, and must be stored properly.

Various methods of dissemination are tested to ensure that the microorganisms are able to withstand the dissemination process and remain viable enough to cause disease when the target is exposed. Most biological warfare programs test releases on animals [34], but human testing has also been performed. During World War II, some American conscientious objectors volunteered for testing in lieu of fighting [35], and a small unit in Japan tested its weapons on prisoners of war [36]. If "cocktails," or multiple biological agents, were released simultaneously, the resulting mixture of diseases would make investigation of the outbreaks more confusing and difficult [37].

Biological Weapons

A list of diseases known to have been weaponized is presented in Table 10.1 [38]. Of the known weaponized agents, smallpox and anthrax pose the greatest threats [39], but for different reasons: smallpox is so contagious that its mortality rate of 30 percent kills large numbers of people; anthrax is not contagious, but can have a mortality rate as high as 90 percent in its inhalational form, and it is very durable in the environment.

TABLE 10.1 CDC's List of the BT Diseases of Most Concern

Disease	*Biological Agent*
Category A—High priority agents	
Smallpox	Variola major
Anthrax	*Bacillus anthracis*
Plague	*Yersinia pestis*
Botulism	Toxin of *Clostridium botulinum*
Tularemia	*Francisella tularensis*
Hemorrhagic fevers	Filoviruses: Ebola, Marburg
	Arenaviruses: Lassa, Junin, and others
Category B—Second highest priority agents	
Q fever	*Coxiella burnetii*
Brucellosis	*Brucella* species
Glanders	*Burkholderia mallei*
Venezuelan, and eastern and western equine encephalomyelitis	Alphaviruses
Typhus	*Rickettsia prowazekii*
Ricin toxin	From castor beans
Epsilon toxin	*Clostridium perfringens*
Staphylococcal enterotoxin B	*Staphylococcus* species
Foodborne or waterborne disease agents	*Salmonella, Shigella dysenteriae, E. coli 0157:H7, Vibrio cholerae*, and *Cryptosporidium parvum*
Category C—Emerging pathogens	
Pathogens that could be engineered for mass dissemination, such as Nipah virus, hantaviruses, tick-borne hemorrhagic fevers, and others	

Source: Data from CDC (Centers for Disease Control and Prevention). *Morb. Mortal. Wkly. Rep.*, 49(RR-4), 5, April 21, 2000.

Smallpox has changed the course of history several times [40]. "Approximately 500 million people died of smallpox in the century that just ended. This compares with 320 million deaths during the same period as a result of all military and civilian casualties of war, cases of swine flu during the ruinous 1918 pandemic, and all cases of AIDS worldwide [41]." In his book, *Scourge: The Once and Future Threat of Smallpox* [42], Jonathan Tucker describes the ten year campaign which resulted, in 1979, in the first-ever eradication of a disease. This was a major triumph for public health and for humanity. Jeffrey Koplan, director of the Centers for Disease Control and Prevention (CDC), has commented, "It's almost inconceivable that the incredible international human effort that went into eradicating smallpox could be overturned by malicious human acts…People subsumed all their differences working side by side to eradicate smallpox—Russians, Americans, Brazilians, Indians. In East Africa, wars were literally put on hold, and truces held, while everyone went into the field to get this done. It's such a painful thing to consider that someone could use smallpox for a negative purpose, particularly when you are aware that it could cause hundreds of millions of deaths [43]."

Today there are only two internationally legal repositories of the smallpox virus: at research facilities in CDC in Atlanta, and in Vector, Koltsovo, Russia. However, weaponized smallpox is known to have existed in Russia in large quantities (contrary to the Biological and Toxin Weapons Convention) as recently as 1992 [44].

Smallpox victims develop an extremely painful rash and a high fever. As smallpox is caused by a virus, antibiotics will not help. Antiviral medications do exist today, but as they were invented after smallpox had been eradicated, it is not known whether they would be effective against smallpox, though it is thought that one of them, Cidofovir, might be effective [45]. Smallpox is treated supportively (i.e., intravenous fluids, bed rest, and care of any complications that develop) without specific therapy, but today's supportive therapy may improve survival rates over those seen in the past.

The chief threat of smallpox is that it is contagious and that it spreads rapidly. It was eradicated in the last century by giving vaccine to everyone who had been in contact with a new case, as soon as the case was discovered. Contrary to most vaccines, the smallpox vaccine is effective even if given a few days after exposure to the disease. (This is a good example of how public health functions: not in treating individuals who are ill, but in interventions among well persons to prevent disease in the population). The production of vaccine has recently been accelerated, which will greatly improve our ability to cope with an outbreak. Controlling the spread of disease will be a first priority in response to a smallpox outbreak.

The signs and symptoms of the other BT diseases have been described elsewhere [46–49]. Biological weapon agents have unique differences from chemical and nuclear WMD. First, there is a time lag between release and symptoms, resulting in difficulty determining that an event has occurred as well as in uncovering the perpetrator and finding evidence of attribution [50]. Second, there is potential for secondary transmission, causing expanding and unpredictable waves of new cases. Third, biological agents can be genetically manipulated, possibly leading to the creation of entirely new diseases.

Role of the U.S. Government

A 2001 GAO report [51] describes the federal agencies that have received funding for BT. Condensed descriptions from this report, along with a few other sources, have been included throughout this chapter as extracts (distinguished from the text by smaller font size) under the section most suitable, to demonstrate the breadth and complexity of government programs for BT.

> Against BT, both in prevention and response, the government, as opposed to private citizens, must take the lead role. Though it is important that citizens understand and

support the government, prevention involves international diplomacy, covert intelligence, research, and law enforcement, all governmental functions. Following a BT attack, needs would quickly overwhelm the resources of local hospitals, facilities, and supplies. The response to a large BT attack would require capabilities and expertise beyond the scope of any locality. Coordination of local, state, and federal governments is needed to both develop and deploy the assets to contain and control a biological disaster.

The public can contribute to the preparation for BT by becoming informed about the threats posed by BT, and supporting and advising the government in planning efforts. Knowledge can help individuals become mentally prepared; some may want to offer their services voluntarily in the event of an outbreak. An educated public will also help create the political will necessary to combat terrorism.

Role of the Military

That biological warfare could be employed against military or civilian targets, overseas or in the homeland, raises questions about what role the military should have in defense of the homeland, and how it can best reorganize to meet new threats. The role of the military in civilian defense is limited by the Posse Comitatus Act of 1878, passed after the Civil War to restrict the government's ability to use the military in keeping civil order. However, a 1984 disaster-relief law allows troops to respond to a national disaster at the President's order if they operate under the direction of the Federal Emergency Management Agency (FEMA) [52]. Other experts argue that in a crisis situation, predelegated legal authority may allow for military enforcement of civil laws even without special authorization from either the president or Congress [53]. If the homeland is attacked by foreign powers, it seems reasonable for the military to respond in defense. New doctrines, concepts, definitions, and strategies will need to be developed and articulated as the military adapts to its mission of civil support [54].

Several military units are working on plans to provide support to civil authorities in a terrorist incident: the U.S. Army Medical Research Institute for of Infectious Diseases (USAMRIID), the U.S. Army Soldier Biological and Chemical Command, the Director of Military Support, and the Joint Task Force for Civil Support (JTF-CS). The Joint Task Force for Civil Support (JTF-CS), part of U.S. Joint Forces command, is responsible for command and control of Department of Defense (DOD) Forces responding under the Federal Response Plan. JTF-CS engages in exercises, works with the Office of Emergency Preparedness (OEP) to develop plans for medical support to an incident, and with FEMA to plan the deployment of Force Packages, or military response units that could also respond to an incident [55].

The Chemical Biological—Rapid Response Force (CBRRF) is a U.S. Marine Corps asset, which can deliver technical expertise and equipment to the scene of a chemical or biological incident [56].

Other contributions of the military are described under the "Surveillance," "Mass Medical Care," and "Research" sections.

Federal Agencies

More than 40 federal agencies have been involved in BT planning and could be involved in response to an attack [57].

The complexity of coordination that will be required of these agencies is daunting [57]. Many GAO reports have described duplicative and uncoordinated government spending for BT [59,60].

In order for these multiple resources to become assets, they must be coordinated capably and efficiently.

Designation of an Overall Authority

Several important congressional reports, including the Gilmore Commission [61], the Hart, Rudman Report [62], and others [63,64], have strongly recommended designation of an office with a high level of authority to help solve the problems of incoordination and duplication of effort. This was accomplished in October 2001, with the creation of the Office of Homeland Security [65]. This new office may be able to provide the direction needed to streamline government planning to eliminate duplication and to cover all aspects of BT preparation.

U.S. government plans for BT response have developed through a series of legislation and directives [70], and are given below:

- The Executive Order 12656, Assignment of Emergency Preparedness Responsibilities, November 1988, designates the National Security Council (NSC) as the principal forum for emergency policies. FEMA is to provide advice to the NSC based on coordination with other agencies at the federal, state, and local levels.
- The Federal Response Plan & Terrorism Incident Annex, April 1992, breaks down portions of emergencies into categories, and assigns responsibility for each to various agencies. Under this plan, Health and Human Services (HHS) is the lead agency responsible for the medical and public health response to BT.
- Presidential Decision Directive 39, June 1995, directs federal agencies within their areas of responsibility to reduce vulnerabilities, deter and respond to terrorism and WMD.
- Presidential Decision Directive 62, May 1998, clarifies the roles of agencies further, addresses cyber security, and establishes the Office of the National Coordinator for Security, Infrastructure Protection, and Counterterrorism to take the lead in developing guidelines for crisis management.
- The CONPLAN (Concept of Operations Plan), January 2001, provides overall guidance to agencies at all three levels of government on how the federal response will be coordinated.
- The National Security Presidential Directive-1 (NSPD-1), February 2001, designates the NSC Principals Committee as a forum for considering policy that affects national security and establishes the NSC Policy Coordination Committee to develop and implement policies for multiple agencies.

Under these directives, the Federal Bureau of Investigation (FBI) is designated as the lead federal agency during the crisis phase and FEMA as the lead federal agency during the consequence phase of an event. These phases are meant to overlap and occur simultaneously.

> Under the Federal Response plan, described earlier, HHS has the lead responsibility for medical and public health response to emergencies and terrorist incidents. A Special Assistant for Bioterrorism has recently been appointed within HHS to coordinate BT activities across the department [71]. The HHS oversees five agencies that are given the responsibility to prepare for BT. The Agency for Healthcare Research and Quality (AHRQ), the Food and Drug Administration (FDA), and the National Institutes of Health (NIH) are mainly focused on research. The OEP and the CDC are focused mainly on consequence management [72].

Within CDC, the Bioterrorism Preparedness and Response Program (BPRP) coordinates BT planning internally and also administers BT funding for state health departments, which in turn, assist local health departments in BT planning and response. As federal authority among different federal agencies has been consolidated in the Office of Homeland Defense for WMD, one report has recommended that the BPRP, responsible for coordinating BT planning among the units within CDC, should be placed within the Office of the Director of CDC, and be given budgetary authority [73].

Role of State and Local Governments

Any BT outbreak on American soil would necessarily take place in a local jurisdiction somewhere; the local government would be responsible for handling the situation until help from state and federal governments arrives. The threats, resources, and capabilities of local governments vary widely. One thing they do have in common is a variety of agencies that could assist: most localities have fire, police, and public health departments, hospitals, and an office of the American Red Cross. The challenge local governments face is coordinating the work of these agencies. Most disciplines have close relationships with their state and federal counterpart agencies, but work very little with other agencies outside of their discipline, even though they are in the same locality. However, an effective response from local governments will require local integration across the nation to streamline response and maximize capabilities across disciplinary lines.

States have further assets that can assist in an emergency, such as National Guard troops and state emergency management agencies. The governor of a state can declare a state emergency, and can request the president to declare a national emergency. State agencies coordinate between their counterpart agencies in federal and local levels of government and can offer assistance to local agencies when requested. State agencies face the same challenges of integration between agencies and disciplines described for federal and local governments.

Prevention

Deterrence is designed to prevent the development of a BT attack through creating disincentives; preemption stops a BT attack in process before any harm can occur.

Deterrence

Congress has passed legislation to deter the development of biological weapons. In 1989, the Biological Weapons Act was passed, which made the possession, sale, or manufacture of a biological substance "for use as a weapon" illegal [74]. In 1991, American companies were prohibited from commercial transactions with countries suspected of developing biological weapons, and in 1996, it became illegal to threaten to develop biological weapons. In 1997, 24 organisms and 12 toxins became designated as "restricted," requiring a permit to possess them [75].

Preventing programs from developing biological weapons would be ideal if it could be done. The Biological and Toxin Weapons Convention of 1972 [76] was meant to discourage nations from manufacturing biological weapons by international convention. As of December 2000, there were 143 states parties and 18 signatories to the Convention [77]. This has been controversial, and in 2000 and 2001 the United States was the sole nation holding up negotiations [78]. Some argue that treaties that cannot verify compliance are ineffective [79], that weapons inspections in Iraq failed to uncover existing programs, that positive scientific exchanges would be more effective [80], and that instituting more intrusive inspections would place confidential U.S. technological advances in jeopardy [81]. Proponents argue that abandoning an international agreement ratified by 110 nations with no other mechanism in place seems unwise [82,83], and that enforcement may be an alternative way to strengthen the treaty [84].

Another concern is an estimated 70,000 research scientists and technicians formerly employed in the biological weapons programs of the former Soviet Union, who either lost their jobs or became underemployed [85] when these programs were dismantled. Their expertise would be desirable to those trying to develop biological weapons programs [86]. Opportunists may include transnational criminal organizations and others who would be willing to sell to the highest bidder, whether they are state or nonstate actors [87]. There is also the possibility that biological samples from these programs may have been available to interested parties [88] through bribery or smuggling [89]. The United States has funded programs to find alternative work for those scientists [88,90], and this funding should be continued.

Preemption

Preemption requires identification and location of an attack or delivery system and the capacity to disrupt it [91]. The roles of both foreign and domestic intelligence communities are critical in this regard, and mechanisms to provide better intelligence sharing and combined analysis are needed [92].

Release and Transmission

Before an organism or toxin can cause disease in a human, it must enter the body. Intact skin is an excellent barrier; therefore, handwashing alone [93] may be highly effective in reducing the threat from specific BT agents, such as cutaneous anthrax. Organisms can enter the human body through any orifice, but the most likely portals of entry for BT are the nose (inhalation), the mouth (ingestion), and a break in the skin. Manufacturers of biological weapons are faced with the dilemma of releasing their product into the environment in such a way that humans will either inhale it, ingest it, or encounter it on a break in the skin. Different methods of release have been studied to achieve this purpose; each method or technology has inherent difficulties and advantages. Prevention and response plans must be tailored specifically to meet each method of transmission: air, water, food, zoonotic, agricultural, and others. Aside from an initial release, the prevention of subsequent spread of agents that are transmitted from person to person is also critical, and will require special planning.

Airborne Transmission

The airborne transmission route is often the most feared because of the potential for large numbers of casualties in both humans and animals [94,95]. However, as sunlight kills most organisms, and turbulent or high winds disperse the concentration of agents released in the air, airborne transmission is highly dependent on weather conditions. A clear, calm night with a slow steady air current [96] and an inversion with a layer of cold air trapping the release near the ground [97] are the best conditions for an airborne release in the outdoors. Biological weapons could be released into the outside air by handheld or other single point devices, or moving sources such as trucks and airplanes with modified spraying equipment.

To produce the small particles of one to five microns required to cause inhalational disease, specialized spraying equipment or other alterations would have to be retrofitted to airplanes. Air intake and air conditioning systems [98], or the internal air currents in subways could also be used to spread disease. The risk of a successful biologic attack by airborne transmission could be decreased by establishing procedures to limit access to items for specialized spraying, and by mandating standards for security of air-intake systems in public buildings, businesses, and private homes. Measures could include hepa filters, irradiation, and securing access. Until monitoring systems to detect the presence of pathogens in the air are available, there is little else that can be done to protect against an airborne release.

> The Environmental Protection Agency (EPA) is responsible for the nation's air quality, and has capabilities for sampling and identifying environmental contaminants. It also plays a role in decontamination and long-term remediation. The EPA has 220 on-scene coordinators trained to respond to a hazardous material spill affecting the environment [99].

Waterborne Transmission

A safe water supply [100] in the United States has resulted in the near elimination of deadly waterborne diseases, such as typhoid, cholera, and diarrhea, that still threaten many areas of the world. The three main elements of this system are supply, treatment, and distribution. Physical points of vulnerability include dams, aqueducts, pumping stations, and intake areas. Controlling human access to vulnerable points is difficult, but could be improved by incorporating intrusion sensors into existing disaster monitoring systems and increasing fences and other physical barriers. Because many portions of the water system are automated, measures must also be taken to guard against cyber attack.

Water supplies are difficult to contaminate because large quantities of contaminants would be required to obtain lethal concentrations and because chlorine kills most pathogens. Nevertheless, water systems may still be vulnerable to those biologic organisms for which only a small infective dose is required. If panic or anxiety is the goal, changing the color or taste of the water supply may be sufficient without actually introducing a toxic substance or achieving a lethal level of contamination [101].

One approach to improve water safety could focus on building greater versatility, redundancy, and interconnectedness into the system, so that if one unit failed or became contaminated, water could be channeled from other units. Because existing water systems have evolved independently and are often fragmented, developing more broadly connected regional systems would require new collaboration, perhaps through mutual aid agreements for various assets such as water, equipment, and repair response. Other efforts should focus on better monitoring devices for biological pathogens and toxins, and treatments capable of responding to them. Advances in water treatment technologies could be more widely applied, including sequential treatment in series when needed, to achieve a higher level of contamination removal [102].

Currently, most public health communicable disease programs do not routinely collect information on the water supply of persons with waterborne diseases, either at home or at work, yet this could be important for detecting problems related to a water source, whether municipal or private.

Closer coordination between environmental and public health agencies could allow collection of this data and could further improve control of waterborne diseases.

> The EPA is the lead agency for protection of the nation's water supply. For a BT incident involving the water supply, the EPA would work with CDC to design a response appropriate to each situation. The EPA is coordinating with the CDC to develop staff training for the biological aspects of its WMD response, and is creating methods to assess the vulnerability of water supply systems in conjunction with the Department of Energy (DOE) and the American Water Works Association Research Foundation [99].

Foodborne Transmission

The largest outbreak of BT to date was foodborne, perpetrated in 1984 by a religious group that hoped to cause enough temporary illness in the community to influence local elections. They did not succeed, though 751 persons became ill through eating from salad bars contaminated with *Salmonella typhimurium*, a common foodborne illness [103]. Fortunately, cooking kills most pathogens and deactivates many toxins.

> The FDA's Center for Food Safety and Applied Nutrition is responsible for the safety of the food supply. In a collaborative effort, the CDC, the FDA, the U.S. Department of Agriculture (USDA), and nine state health departments have developed a program called FoodNet which provides more timely information on the occurrence of diseases that are likely to be foodborne. The CDC has also collaborated with the FDA and the USDA on another program called PulseNet, designed to improve the capability of state and federal laboratories to distinguish between subtypes of foodborne bacteria to better characterize the extent of a given outbreak [104].
>
> The FDA's Center for Food Safety and Applied Nutrition, responsible for monitoring and labeling the nation's food supply, has been preparing for BT involving food as a vector. It has developed a procedures manual used by health department workers in the investigation of foodborne outbreaks [104].
>
> The FDA's Center for Toxicological Research conducts research regarding the detection of various proteins in the food supply, including methods to determine their toxicity. The Center could bring this diagnostic capability to support a BT incident affecting the food supply. The Center has been developing training materials in conjunction with FEMA and Arkansas public health officials [105].

Zoonotic and Agricultural Transmission

Zoonotic

Many of the BT agents are zoonotic diseases, that is, they can infect both animals and humans and transmission can occur between species. Thus, even if their occurrence is eliminated in humans, a reservoir of disease can remain among animals and wildlife that can be difficult to eradicate and will likely remain a potential source of infection for humans. Examples include anthrax [106], plague [107], tularemia [108], some of the viral encephalitides, brucellosis, and Q fever. To date animal and human health issues have been handled by separate government agencies that have little knowledge of each other's work. Effective BT planning will necessitate a coordinated approach between these agencies, even to the level of integrating data systems. Better integration of agencies with the responsibilities for veterinary and medical public health should be encouraged to address outbreaks that can affect both animals and humans [109].

West Nile disease is viral encephalitis spread to humans by infected mosquitoes, which also feed on horses and birds. Its spread across the country, tracked by testing of samples from birds and mosquitoes, reveals a slow progression westward, arriving in St. Louis in October 2001 [110], two years after it was first identified in New York City. Compared to other diseases, West Nile virus may not cause many fatalities, but because of its presence in the environmental ecosystem, it is here to stay.

Infected insects have been used as biological weapons. Though less effective than other methods [111], infected fleas can be grown in large quantities which cause disease when disseminated [112]. Because fleas infect rats, controlling rats helps to decrease the incidence of fleaborne diseases. Plague is an example of a BT disease spread by fleas in its naturally occurring form. Many local and state health departments have existing mosquito and rat control programs, which would help to control the spread of some zoonotic diseases if they were ever released. Further study has been recommended to determine the effectiveness of these programs, and to identify new interventions [113].

Agricultural

Biological agents can be targeted specifically to affect crops and livestock to undermine economic progress and stability [114]. Countries are dependent on agriculture for food and economic health. In the spring of 2001, when an outbreak of foot and mouth disease occurred in the United Kingdom, "over 3.9 million livestock were slaughtered and an estimated 119,131,446 pounds [$172,621,465] in indemnity payments were made during the campaign to eradicate foot and mouth disease" [115].

A recent Harvard University report lists recommendations for the USDA in improving the safety of animals and plants for BT attacks on four different levels [116]:

1. Organism level. The USDA should be ready to supply vaccines for all (the most dangerous) foreign animal diseases.
2. Farm level. The USDA should set up a Biosecurity Training Program to counter the threat of diseases and pests at the farm level.
3. Sector level. The USDA should invest more resources in disease detection, surveillance, and diagnostic technologies. Examples include creating linked animal–human disease databases, developing more rapid diagnostic tests for foreign animal diseases, upgrading Plum Island (see the following text) to BL-4 (Biosafety level 4 is the highest level of safety, requiring laboratorians to wear protective gear and masks, and special circulation and treatment of air), and establishing a contingency network of veterinarians.
4. National level. The USDA should be ready to deal with the public reaction to a serious food scare, and it should have the budgetary means to proceed with fast and efficient recovery.

These recommendations are similar to what is needed for human health.

> The USDA has an important role to play in the defense of attacks on plants and animals. The USDA monitors the Plum Island Animal Disease Center in New York, a research center with the laboratory diagnostic capability to detect unusual diseases in animals and plants. The USDA also houses the Animal and Plant Health Inspection Service, responsible for responding to the veterinary side of outbreaks of zoonotic disease. This Service has begun to develop educational materials and training programs for the recognition of biological weapons agents [117].

> The FDA's Center for Veterinary Medicine regulates food additives and drugs given to animals, whether agricultural or domestic. In this capacity, the FDA has been collaborating with veterinary diagnostic laboratories and state officials to increase preparedness regarding risks to the food supply that could arise from biological terrorism directed against plants or animals [118].

Other Releases

Biological organisms can be engineered to corrupt materials such as the rubber in tires or synthetic materials, asphalt, and other kinds of plastics. These could cause both disruption and economic loss.

> The U.S. Department of Transportation (DOT) oversees all civilian air, sea, and land transport within the United States, and also coordinates the safety of pipeline facilities. Through its National Response Center, staffed and housed by the Coast Guard, it serves as the point of contact for information regarding any oil or other WMD materials released from transportation systems into the environment, and houses the National Response Team, a coordinating body composed of representatives from 16 federal agencies with responsibilities for response to an environmental emergency [119].

Secondary Transmission

If disease can spread beyond the site of initial release, carried to others by those infected from the first exposure, then it is said to be communicable or to have secondary transmission. Diseases with secondary transmission, such as pneumonic plague and smallpox, could spread outward in expanding waves, magnifying the initial release. To control communicable diseases, the treatment of individual patients needs to be combined with approaches to decrease transmission among the public. Strategies have been defined to decrease transmission from individual patients for both plague and smallpox, and would include wearing masks and taking antibiotics for plague [107], and vaccination and respiratory isolation with hepa masks and negative air pressure rooms for smallpox [120–122].

Measures to decrease transmission on a larger scale are more difficult to agree upon. The first major exercise of the federal response plan was called TOPOFF (for top officials) in May 2000, and simulated an expanding outbreak of plague. State public health officials who participated later made these observations:

> The process of isolating patients until they are no longer contagious and identifying close contacts is typically straightforward. Isolation, however, was not possible during this exercise. The hospitals had too many patients and worried-well persons and too few health-care workers and empty rooms to permit isolation of pneumonic plague patients. As a result, an executive order was issued quarantining all persons in metropolitan Denver in their homes.
>
> However, quarantining two million persons is not simple. Essential workers must be identified, be given prophylaxis and protective barriers, and be permitted to do their jobs. Other members of the community can stay in their homes only a few days before they need fresh supplies of food. Therefore, a one-time, blanket quarantine order is unlikely to be successful and cannot be enforced unless these and many other issues are addressed. The hospitals were quite demanding in their requests for

reinforcements, and we made great efforts to assist them. However, by day three of the exercise it became clear that unless controlling the spread of the disease and triage and treatment of ill persons in hospitals receive equal effort, the demand for health-care services will not diminish. This was the single most important lesson we learned by participating in the exercise [123].

In another federal exercise called "Dark Winter" in June 2001 [124], senior officials over the course of two days walked through the major simulated decision points that could occur during a smallpox outbreak as it expanded rapidly to many states through person-to-person transmission. The exercise generated Congressional hearings, and together with its timing just prior to the attacks on the World Trade Center, was influential in mobilizing government planning for smallpox and discussions on quarantine. A summary of "lessons learned" through interviews of the participants and Congressional testimony included the following points [124]:

1. Senior decision makers trained in national security and defense matters are unfamiliar with issues surrounding BT attacks.
2. A lack of information systems with real-time data in the medical and public health communities would confront decision makers with many uncertainties.
3. An insufficient supply of smallpox vaccine would limit options to control an outbreak, and could cause disagreement about disposition of existing vaccine.
4. The medical care system lacks capacity to handle a sudden increase in patients.
5. Decision makers will require advice from public health leaders regarding quarantine or other measures to control the spread of an outbreak. There is little experience and few resources available to understand the potential effects of various countermeasures, particularly quarantine.
6. A smallpox outbreak may bring out tensions between federal and state governments, which would have different priorities in response. For instance, states may want access to vaccine, control over quarantine measures, and control over their National Guard assets. The federal government may want to reserve vaccine for the military or for national outbreak control, to standardize quarantine criteria nationwide, and to federalize the National Guard.

Notes from the script of the Dark Winter exercise contain a good summary of federal legislation regarding quarantine [125]. According to Congressman Christopher Shays, commenting on lessons learned from the Dark Winter exercise, "Should a contagious biological weapon be used, containing the spread of disease will present significant ethical, political, cultural, operational, and legal challenges" [126].

What measures would actually be useful for controlling the spread of a localized outbreak and what they would cost society are points that need study and public discussion. People seeking to flee an epidemic could also spread it; control of an outbreak might require forcible restraint of citizens. The need for enforcement of quarantine, if it were medically recommended, would raise difficult issues on how to enforce it, and how to balance the interests of the health of the public versus individual civil liberties [127]. To prevent these decisions from being made rapidly and arbitrarily in a crisis situation, the ramifications of quarantine need to be thought through in advance to provide maximum protection of civil liberties and maximum containment of the epidemic.

Although quarantine has not been invoked for many years, diseases with secondary transmission are not new, and have traditionally been the province of public health. In the United States, CDC has coordinated their control through specific programs for each disease or groups of diseases, such as AIDS, TB, hepatitis, diarrheal diseases, vector-borne diseases, and others.

Response

Effective response to a BT attack requires planning by individual agencies, integration of plans with other agencies, and different levels of government. These are described in a chronological manner from detection and surveillance, to outbreak investigation, medical care of ill persons, psychological distress, and preventive treatment to protect the exposed.

Surveillance for Bioterrorism

The longer time lag between release and symptoms is perhaps the most distinguishing feature of biologic agents. With a chemical or nuclear release, casualties are immediate, obvious, and may be massive. After the release of a biologic weapon, life would go on as normal for several days during the incubation period of the disease before people began to become ill; there would be no disaster scene to respond to. However, early detection in this setting becomes of paramount importance because substantial decreases in death or major morbidity may be achieved if medication or vaccination is given soon enough after exposure. One model estimates that if 50,000 persons were infected with anthrax, 5,000 deaths would result if preventive therapy were started immediately; whereas 32,875 deaths would result if treatment were started six days after release [128]. The economic consequences would parallel these findings, with an estimated $14–22 billion saved in medical costs if preventive therapy were started immediately, versus $320 million to $1 billion saved if treatment were delayed for six days after the release [129].

Immediate Detection Technology

It would be convenient if technology existed to detect the presence of a bioweapon in the air, water, or food when it was initially released. This would make it easier to apprehend the perpetrator, provide an opportunity to stop the release, and to prevent disease from developing among those who were exposed.

> The Defense Advanced Research Projects Agency (DARPA), a research arm of the DOD, is working on methods to detect, diagnose, and treat BT and other infectious diseases through many ways, including genetic sequencing. One of these research projects is to develop a diagnostic method that would detect disease in an individual before symptoms occur [130].
>
> The Department of the Treasury oversees the U.S. Secret Service, responsible for protecting the president, his family, and other heads of state. The U.S. Secret Service has been developing a biological agent detector and improving its laboratory capacity to detect biological and chemical agents [131].
>
> The DOD has created Civil Support Teams, mobile units capable of testing for the presence of deadly chemicals and biological agents in the field. The teams can be in the field within four hours of deployment anywhere in their area of service. From 1999 to 2001, Congress authorized in sequential years 10, then 17 more, and then five additional Civil Support Teams. Six teams are currently certified, ready for service. These units are federally funded and trained, but report to the governor of the state they are located in. They are light mobile units. Their mission is to rapidly detect harmful agents in the environment, assess the extent of an incident, and identify measures for decontamination or amelioration [132].

Surveillance through Monitoring Illness

As environmental detection devices for biological agents are at present mostly in the research stage (unlike devices for the detection of chemical agents), the first sign of a BT attack would likely be illness in victims [133]. In a setting where large numbers of persons are exposed, some persons will develop symptoms earlier than others will. These cases, if they are detected early enough, may allow an investigation and response to be initiated in time to protect others who have been placed at risk through exposure [134].

The current systems for monitoring communicable diseases have enabled health departments for years to track trends for the major communicable diseases of public health significance, including TB, syphilis, AIDS, diarrheal diseases, and others. Under these reporting processes, the data is available for analysis several weeks after the onset of illness. Most current systems require a definitive laboratory diagnosis to ensure the accuracy of data. Systems require physicians or laboratories to submit data on each case of a reportable illness, frequently done by mailing paper forms to local health departments [135], which are subsequently forwarded through state health departments to CDC. The time delays in these surveillance systems make them inadequate for a BT incident. There is a need for basic communications infrastructure in public health. A CDC survey of city and county health departments in 1999 found that 20 percent lacked e-mail capabilities and over half did not have continuous high-speed Internet access [136].

The international capacity to detect outbreaks is even more deficient [137], though progress is underway through the World Health Organization and other groups. ProMED is an international electronic listserv, moderated within the International Society for Infectious Diseases, that posts reports of disease outbreaks among plants, animals, or humans [138], and provides a forum for scientific discussion which can assist discovery of outbreaks and their causes. The Infectious Disease Society of America hosts a similar listserv for infectious disease physicians and public health practitioners to exchange information [139]. There are also unique isolated projects. An animal disease surveillance project in Africa is underway to monitor and report zoonotic diseases [140].

Syndromic Surveillance

Syndromic surveillance for BT has been recommended to provide earlier detection of an outbreak [141]. Instead of collecting data about diseases that have been definitively diagnosed, syndromic surveillance monitors the numbers of persons presenting with clusters of symptoms that could be expected in the very early phases of illness caused by the weaponized BT agents. If there was an effective release of a BT agent, many people would have similar symptoms within a short period of time. Symptom patterns might appear to be nonspecific, such as the upper respiratory or gastrointestinal symptoms, which are seen everyday in medical clinics. Such problems are often treated without a definitive diagnosis. However, if a larger number of persons than those recorded in past seasons were to become ill with similar symptoms within a short period of time, this increase would only be detected by a system that monitored for such syndromes. At this time, hospitals neither collect nor monitor this sort of data in an ongoing or timely way.

The way hospitals are organized to care for patients provides an example of some of the issues that need to be resolved in order for hospital care to become a good source of BT surveillance data. For rapid information on illness in humans, monitoring hospitals is a logical place to start because hospitals process large numbers of ill persons. Yet hospitals do not report data on communicable diseases in incoming patients. Such reporting is seen as the job of physicians and laboratories after patients have been seen and properly diagnosed, thus assuring accurate data.

An incidental benefit to a syndromic surveillance system is that it could also detect naturally occurring outbreaks. It is likely that outbreaks are being missed under the current system. An example of an outbreak which was missed under current reporting systems but which could have been detected under a syndromic surveillance system is the cryptosporidiosis outbreak in Milwaukee [142]. In this incident, although an estimated 403,000 persons developed transitory diarrheal illness, the outbreak was not detected by public health authorities. The reasons are no surprise to those working in public health communicable disease programs. Most persons probably did not visit a doctor; of those who did, few were probably tested; of those tested, cryptosporidium may have been overlooked as it is not usually included in routine laboratory panels for diarrheal illness; and those patients that were tested and appropriately diagnosed may not have been reported to the health department [143]. Health department authorities became alerted to the outbreak because a pharmacist reported his observation that all the over-the-counter antidiarrheal medications were sold out. This outbreak could have been detected earlier by monitoring data from over-the-counter pharmaceutical sales or by syndromic reporting of the numbers of patients presenting with diarrhea.

In a time when market forces, led by federal reduction of medical payment for Medicare and Medicaid, are forcing hospitals to struggle to stay in business, it is unreasonable to request that hospitals provide additional data to government agencies on the rates of diseases, whether those data is in paper forms or computer reports. Yet effective surveillance would require not only that this be done, but also that it be done in a timely and ongoing manner.

One way to do this without taking additional time from hospital staff would be to monitor the streams of data which hospitals generate in the course of patient care (personal communication, M. Williams, St. Louis County Health Department and T. Bailey, Department of Infectious Diseases, Washington University School of Medicine, 2000). For instance, when chest x-rays are ordered in evaluating patients with respiratory infections (a possible an early sign of some BT agents), monitoring the numbers of chest x-rays ordered per number of patients seen would be a possibility for this sort of monitoring. It could be arranged to identify other computerized data, i.e., the number of prescriptions for antibiotics per number of patients seen that could suggest the early symptoms of a BT event. If such systems were in place, they could also provide useful information for routine hospital planning, such as for scheduling personnel or ordering supplies. The alerts of potential BT events generated by this system would need to go to authorities within the hospital or the local health agency, which have the responsibility to investigate local outbreaks and take measures to control them. Local authorities would alert state and federal officials if a BT event were suspected [144].

For a system like this to be effective, many unique agreements would need to be negotiated. Because hospitals are often private entities, it is not possible to negotiate one agreement that would apply to all hospitals. Instead, individual agreements may need to be made with each hospital system. Likewise, hospitals have different data systems, so software solutions for reporting may need to be individually tailored to each hospital system. It is possible that standards for electronic medical records would enable the collection of timely syndromic surveillance data without compromising patient confidentiality. If privacy concerns were satisfied, electronic medical record databases could open the door to epidemiologic research and consequent medical advances, which have never been possible before.

> The Texas Department of Health, in collaboration with CDC and their National Guard (the 6th *Civil Support Team), is developing an early detection system based on interpreting electronic data from medical centers in the light of past experience from archival data. They estimate that this system would add* 24–72 hours to their response time through earlier detection of a BT event [145].

Information Sources Needed for Disease Surveillance

A robust surveillance system requires diverse sources of input in addition to hospitals, because early signs of attack could manifest elsewhere. For disease among humans, surveillance should include data sources affected at places where ill people might go. Sales of pharmaceuticals, emergency room visits, hotline phone calls, Web site visits, emergency medical service calls, urgent care visits, and physician's offices are some of the places to be monitored for increases in the rates of illness that surpass expected rates, based on past experience. Other sources include emergency department utilization, numbers of hospital admissions, intensive care unit occupancy, physician's database searches [146], unexplained deaths, ambulance runs, 911 calls, poison control center calls, and absenteeism in work sites and schools [147].

A BT event might be targeted to cause disease among animals or plants or could do so among animals or plants as an unintended consequence. Therefore, information from agricultural sources, veterinarians, veterinary laboratories, zoos, and departments of wildlife and conservation should be included. Local health agencies would be the appropriate recipient of data on human health; for animals and plants, corresponding data is collected by different governmental agencies.

However, the scope of data sources could potentially be much wider. Because some communicable diseases require certain environmental conditions that are detectable from the air, remote sensing data from satellites could identify times and places where these diseases could exist in the environment, or could monitor for disease in plants. Rose, Huq, and Lipp describe colloquia in which "scientists in the fields of climatology, meteorology, microbiology, medicine, ecology, epidemiology, oceanography, and space science [are collaborating] to study how natural climate variability affects occurrence and prevalence of pathogenic microorganisms, vectors, and disease outcomes" [148]. This interdisciplinary work will require long-term monitoring of disease parameters, including mining archival health data, and will lead to a better understanding of the relationships between our environment and human health. It is possible that surveillance data monitored for climate research could also detect BT events, and it is equally likely that advances in understanding of this field could generate unforeseen possibilities for protection and response.

For each of these sources of information, issues corresponding to those described for hospitals would need to be identified and resolved. Many of the parties which would need to be included in such a system have not viewed themselves a part of a disease surveillance system before relationships need to be established, legal authority agreed upon between different agencies and levels of government, computer systems designed both to collect and analyze this information, protection of individual privacy ensured, and a mechanism established to feed this information to persons who need to know and with the authority to act on it. It would be reasonable for data from all sources to be monitored centrally. An outbreak among animals can be a sentinel event signaling the risk of an outbreak for humans, as diseases can cross species. Climate and the environment may influence microorganisms in ways that are only now beginning to be discovered. There is a need for greater understanding of these interrelationships. At present, it is not clear what agency would be capable of coordinating and interpreting data from all these resources, or how subsequent investigation and interventions would be arranged. A unit should be designated to integrate disease data from many diverse sources, to begin to interpret their relationships, and to identify early warning signs of a disease outbreak among plants, animals, and humans. This unit will also need a mechanism to initiate investigation and control measures. Some federal funding has been allocated to study this problem among the civilian community. An office within CDC has been designated for BT surveillance. However, nationally, a unified, effective system to deal with this complex and critical problem is still a distant prospect. A high level of authority and priority will be essential in developing an effective surveillance system for communicable disease outbreaks and for BT.

Outbreak Investigation

One of the charges of public health is to watch over and monitor the rates of disease in the population. At the local, state, and federal levels, authorities follow trends in communicable diseases and look for ways to decrease their incidence. The CDC is the national agency for public health, working directly with all state health agencies, which, in turn provide oversight for local health department programs related to the control of communicable diseases. The CDC would provide guidance for the public health investigation and control of a BT outbreak.

When an outbreak is suspected, several processes begin. Case definitions are determined and increased surveillance is started to find as many cases as possible. Every case may add to the cumulative body of evidence, eventually pointing to the source of the outbreak. Records of hospitals and emergency rooms may be sought, a national advisory may be issued, and, at times, the public may be notified through the news media. Background rates of the disease are determined to see if the situation is indeed a rise above the normal rate. As suspected cases are found, environmental and human samples may be sent for laboratory analysis. As information begins to come in, various hypotheses are generated. Often, a questionnaire is designed, specific to the outbreak situation, to standardize interviews of persons and allow for statistical analysis.

It is often possible to prevent further transmission even before the cause of an outbreak has been determined, if a factor or exposure is found to be related to disease. A classic example is the closure of the Broad Street pump, in eighteenth century London, which stopped a cholera outbreak before there was an understanding of microorganisms. The pump was shut down simply because it was noted that persons who obtained their water from that pump had a much higher rate of disease.

Epidemiology is the basic science that gives public health tools for these activities. Epidemiologists are experienced in distinguishing a real increase from apparent increases in rates of disease, in conducting statistical analyses sometimes necessary to do this, in applying the various techniques needed to collect and interpret data, and in the methods to investigate and control outbreaks when they occur. These skills have enabled investigators to track down unknown diseases and find the causes of new outbreaks, like Hanta virus [149].

There is a need for many more trained epidemiologists at all levels of public health [150]. For nearly two decades funding shortages and hiring freezes for communicable disease programs in local and state public health departments have left these departments with skeletal crews with haphazard ability to detect outbreaks [151]. Epidemiologists are a critical defense in detecting all outbreaks, including BT events. Finding persons with these skills can be difficult. More students of public health specialize in law or management, which offer the possibility of more lucrative jobs in the private sector, than specialize in epidemiology, which requires more science and statistics. Even students specializing in epidemiology may graduate without training in infectious disease epidemiology or outbreak investigation. The CDC has a two-year training program called the Epidemic Intelligence Service (EIS), which enrolls about 70 persons every year. However, few health departments can afford to hire these persons at the salaries that graduates of either of these training programs would expect. If funding were available and designated for health departments to hire trained epidemiologists [152], schools of public health might encourage more students to obtain these skills. A trained public health staff nationwide would greatly improve public health response capabilities for detection of all health problems as well as BT preparation.

Although it is improving, there has been a divergence between the fields of private and public medicine; few physicians are on the faculties of schools of public health, and medical school curricula have tended to teach little about public health. Few physicians have been trained to be epidemiologists. To effectively control disease, better coordination must occur between the medical community (taking care of individual patients) and the public health community (concerned with trends of disease in the population). These two fields would be more effectively integrated if there were more physician epidemiologists who can speak face to face as equals with both groups.

> The CDC has been preparing a national BT response-training plan, a crisis communications plan, and has been providing assistance to state and local health departments in many areas of BT preparedness. The CDC has created a Web site with information on the BT diseases for physicians, public health workers, and the general public [153].

Coordination of Outbreak and Criminal Investigations

In a suspected terrorist event, public health outbreak investigation staff and law enforcement officials will find themselves working side by side. Public health staff may be called upon to submit reports to local police, the state highway patrol, or the FBI. Public health staff need to be familiar with the rules for evidence, to ensure their ability to testify under oath that all evidence or samples have been collected, stored, and examined properly. Likewise, law enforcement personnel are not accustomed to a concurrent need for witnesses to receive prophylactic medication or undergo laboratory testing. They also may not know how to assist in a public health outbreak investigation. These law enforcement personnel need to become familiar with measures to prevent transmission of illness, and the circumstances when various interventions would and would not need to be applied. Government staff working in different services need to learn about each other's work to develop a coordinated approach to outbreak and criminal investigations. There are also spectra of privacy and dissemination of information issues, which have different legal implications for the medical and law enforcement communities, that need to be addressed.

Some progress has been made. In January 2000, a group of law enforcement and public health officials met to discuss which parts of their work in a BT investigation could be shared. Their report [154] identifies portions of information from interviews that could be exchanged, and how and when information would flow between agencies and levels of government most smoothly. In addition, they recommended that law enforcement and public health professionals form joint working groups and develop personal relationships, recommendations that are being followed across the nation.

Outbreaks due to BT agents have international implications as well, as the use of a BT agent violates the Biological Toxin and Weapons Convention. Negotiating an additional protocol to this convention that would establish standards for evidence handling and procedures for investigating outbreaks would be useful in handling the international implications resulting from a BT attack [155]. A BT attack would be grounds for retaliation. If it was possible to identify the aggressor through previously negotiated mechanisms, the support of an international court of law would lend credence to the cause of an aggrieved nation or could clear a nation from suspicion.

> The FBI is the lead federal agency for the crisis management of a WMD incident. The FBI has established and trained a WMD coordinator in each of its 56 field offices. The FBI has the ability to coordinate the deployment of a Domestic Emergency Support Team to assist field offices with technical advice in the management of a WMD event. Through four regional meetings with CDC, the FBI is assisting to prioritize the needs of the public health community. The FBI is working with CDC to develop a secure, Web-based communication system between CDC and state health departments called Epi-X, which will give health departments access to health-related information without compromising law enforcement sensitive information [156].

The FDA's Office of Regulatory Affairs would have responsibility for the investigation of a BT attack that targets any product regulated by the FDA. It maintains a 24 hour emergency hotline and has established a notification system with the FBI for bioterrorist events [157].

Laboratory

Whether a suspicious outbreak is a BT event or a naturally occurring outbreak, the need for rapid, accurate diagnosis of the causative agent is essential; laboratories are critical in confirming the presence or absence of a pathogen, in human samples or in the environment. Laboratory analysis can also identify unique characteristics of an organism, making it possible to distinguish between separate outbreaks of the same disease and track how outbreaks are spreading. The scientific expertise of laboratorians is essential, as well as laboratory facilities and equipment, and computerized communication to forward results of testing. Currently, there is a shortage of trained microbiologists; in addition, legislation passed in 1998 lowered educational standards, and has increased the potential that BT pathogens could be overlooked or that lab accidents could occur [158].

Cost cutting in the medical care system has resulted in fewer laboratory tests being conducted for diagnosis and patient care [159]. However, laboratories can only test samples that they receive. Disincentives to ordering clinical tests must be changed so that physicians are encouraged to use more routine laboratory testing as a part of patient care. This is especially important during influenza season, because some of the BT diseases can look like influenza in their early stages.

Most laboratory work for the diagnosis of human diseases is handled by private laboratories. However, there are quite a number of rare diseases for which reagents and facilities are only available at CDC. Smallpox, for instance, because it is airborne and highly contagious, requires Biosafety level 4 (BSL4) facilities; CDC is one of the few BSL4 laboratories in the nation. The capabilities of state public health laboratories vary, but clearly a network of laboratories capable of testing for the BT diseases throughout the country would be valuable both for improved response time and for increasing the national capacity to handle large numbers of samples.

Through funding from CDC, this capacity now exists for the diagnosis of most of the BT diseases at state laboratories throughout the country, instead of being located exclusively at federal agency headquarters. However, adding more laboratories, increasing the capability of existing laboratories, and collaboration between food, water, veterinary [160], and private laboratories could increase the national laboratory capacity further. Currently there are few mechanisms for exchange of information between state laboratories, or between private laboratories in the same region or state; an exchange that could facilitate early recognition of an outbreak [159]. Laboratories need BT response plans with measures to handle a massive influx of specimens, packaging of some specimens to higher level laboratories, and mechanisms to handle increased numbers of inquiries from patients, families, and the news media [161].

The Hazardous Materials Response Unit within the FBI conducts research on laboratory evidence of attribution for biological material. It has also worked with the CDC to develop laboratory protocols that include the chain of custody necessary for a criminal investigation, and to assist the CDC in developing its Laboratory Response Network for BT [162]. The USAMRIID would provide back up to CDC for confirmation of the diagnosis when identifying BT agents and would also work with the FBI in a terrorist incident [163].

Mass Medical Care

Hospitals face a host of problems, which tend to prevent even their participation in the emergency planning process for BT: among these, decreases in financial revenues [164] and workforce capacity [165], and increases in regulatory demands [166], leave them with few administrative resources for emergency planning. Reductions have occurred in major sources of income for hospitals from Medicare, Medicaid managed care, and tight private coverage contracts. There is little financial margin left over for unfunded projects such as emergency planning. Hospitals are facing a growing number of federal regulatory demands: billing system accuracy, safer needles, greater patient privacy, limitations on medical devices, and medical and medication error reduction. Creating industry standards for both WMD preparedness and regional planning could level the playing field by requiring all hospitals to comply. A 2001 Chemical and Biological Institute report [167] recommended that a federal task force be formed to identify the barriers to hospital participation in the BT planning process, and propose some workable solutions. This report also recommended that federal grants should be extended to hospitals for planning and for participation in regional emergency planning.

Skeletal Staffing of Hospitals

Increased competition among hospitals and a constant effort to improve cost efficiency have caused hospitals to trim their staff and facilities until they are operating near to full capacity as often as possible. This has resulted in a national trend toward decreasing surge capacity in hospitals and medical facilities, that is, their ability to expand capacity to meet a sudden need for hospital care. This is unfortunate in the face of an increasing threat for BT, or even an unexpected large natural outbreak. In 1999, a routine Influenza season caused an increase in the volume of patients large enough to deplete the hospital resources in many regional areas, forcing them to close their doors to new patients [168]. Hospitals can prepare to increase their surge capacity by maintaining lists of retired workers and arranging for contingency use of alternate care sites. However, a mass casualty BT event is likely to overwhelm even such enhanced resources very quickly.

An important factor to consider in emergency planning is that the majority of hospital and healthcare workers are females (many are heads of households), and have responsibilities in the home, taking care of family members. If these persons were to continue reporting to work over the relatively long period of time that a bioterrorist incident would require, hospitals would need to plan for the care of the staff's family members [169].

Workforce Shortage in the Medical Field

There are workforce shortages in every area of the healthcare industry [170], including physicians, nurses, pharmacists, food service workers, housekeepers, and office staff. The shortages are broad in scope and likely to be long term. The same changing demographics, which will result in more patients in future years, are also likely to result in fewer healthcare workers in a profession that has been traditionally dominated by younger individuals. In addition, there has been a change in the image of healthcare professions as careers; they have been seen as less attractive; and fewer persons are entering the workforce in the health professions.

Need for Infection Control Plans at Hospitals

Hospitals need plans that accommodate the differences in medical care required for various BT agents. The Association for Professionals in Infection Control has created standards for infection control measures, which define specific precautions healthcare workers should apply in caring for victims of BT agents [171]. Diseases, which have the capacity for secondary transmission (the spread of disease from infected persons to individuals not exposed to the initial release), may require measures for isolating large numbers of patients for healthcare and possibility quarantine for healthcare personnel and others exposed to these patients. Diseases treated with ventilatory support [172] may require collaboration between hospitals to develop plans for acquiring ventilators, bedspace, and staff to care for these patients. Ideally, specific plans would be delineated for each ward and personnel for each type of emergency. Preexisting agreements with hotels or like facilities to handle housing of massive numbers of ill or quarantined persons will be needed, along with all the attendant needs of hospital care, such as meals, bedding, and laundry.

> The Agency for Healthcare Research and Quality (AHRQ), under the oversight of HHS, supports research designed to improve healthcare through improved quality and reduced costs, which has included research on ways to improve the preparedness of both healthcare providers and institutions in response to a BT attack. Its research projects specific to BT have included information and decision support systems [173].

Regional Planning

For effective care of mass casualties, it would be optimal to triage patients external to the hospitals receiving them [174]. "Effective triage can reduce system stress by separating the worried well, the potentially exposed, and the sick, and sending them to the appropriate care facility, which may include self-medication in the home" [175]. Triage of patients to different facilities implies regional planning, a rare occurrence in today's competitive healthcare field, but which will be essential to maximize the limited assets of hospitals [176].

Some regulations, requiring hospitals to treat any ill person who arrives at their facility, do not contain a provision for regions to designate hospitals to receive either "uninfected" or "infected" patients—a measure that could decrease the regional transmission of infectious diseases during an outbreak situation. There needs to be a capability to waive these regulations for emergencies, to facilitate prehospital triage of patients [168] to prevent patients with communicable diseases from exposing healthcare workers and other patients to the risk of infection [177].

Planning for the Arrival of Federal Support

Even if federal assets are made available, planning for their arrival will need to be done by staffs overwhelmed with many other responsibilities. During the TOPOFF exercise in Denver, hospitals lacked the staff to keep track of either the numbers of patients they had received or their available bedspace [178]. There was also a lack of coordination in how that information was reported to public health workers [179], who needed to decide where to send federal medical relief workers. Arrangements also needed for the housing, food, and other needs for relief workers. For any large incident, state and local governments may become overwhelmed with the logistical and resource arrangements that will be needed to support federal assets [180].

> The OEP, within HHS, coordinates a national system for medical care called the National Disaster Medical System (NDMS), which includes participation from the DOD, with the Department of Veterans Affairs (VA), FEMA, state and local governments, and the private sector. This system coordinates all federal supplemental

medical care, which could be brought either to a local incident involving civilians within the United States or to military personnel evacuated from foreign sites, whether the cause of illness is from natural disasters or intentional harm. The NDMS system includes specialized teams of medical personnel called Disaster Medical Assistance Teams (DMAT), and mobile teams which are self-sustaining for an initial 72 hours to provide specialized assistance to a disaster. Specific teams address mortuary needs, psychological needs, surgical needs, and other needs. These teams can also provide primary care if local facilities become overwhelmed. Four teams called National Medical Response Teams (NMRS) are trained to respond to events involving WMD. The OEP has conducted training exercises to enhance the adaptability of these teams in working with DOD and DOE and in integrating efforts with local personnel in response to emergency events [181].

Mass Distribution of Emergency Medications

The window of opportunity for the administration of treatments, vaccinations, or remedies for the weaponized disease agents of BT can be as small as within 24 hours of developing symptoms. For that reason, everything possible must be planned in advance to streamline the delivery process of pharmaceuticals as efficiently as possible. The creation of a national pharmaceutical stockpile has made planning for mass treatment or prophylaxis much easier. Problems with stockpiling medications are numerous and complex. Medications expire, so it is necessary to have a rotating supply of items, and inventories may be subject to taxation. Because pharmaceutical companies and hospitals keep low inventories and operate on a "just in time" basis, it is likely local supplies of antibiotics would be depleted in days by a large-scale BT event [182]. Local jurisdictions should keep a cache of supplies, with state and federal support, to serve until the arrival of the federal supplies [183].

The CDC's National Pharmaceutical Stockpile Program (NPSP), has negotiated a contract through the VA to solve some of these problems. The pharmaceuticals that would be needed for the agents considered to pose the greatest threat have been prioritized, doses and amounts needed have been calculated, rotating supplies have been arranged, and storage facilities have been designated. The NPSP is solidifying arrangements with each state for receipt of the materiel. Most states involve their health and public safety departments for this task. Each state must coordinate with the CDC on plans for reception, make internal plans for transport and security, and coordinate with local jurisdictions [184]. Local jurisdictions are responsible for on-site distribution of medication to the public. Guidelines need to be delineated for local communities on standards for receipt of the NPSP, preincident training of volunteers, and identification of characteristics recommended for physical distribution sites.

The VA is under contract with CDC to rotate, store, protect, and transport the stockpile. The OEP has made similar contracts with the VA for medical supplies for the four National Medical Response Teams responsible for responding to WMD incidents. The VA assists in training civilian medical personnel who staff the National Disaster Medical System in WMD response. VA hospitals participate in local community emergency planning activities and sometimes deploy to presidentially declared national emergencies [185].

The FDA has been working with the CDC on facilitating the safe use of investigational drugs in an emergency setting and safe labeling for pharmaceuticals in the

National Pharmaceutical Stockpile Program. Though the task does not fall under its usual responsibilities, the FDA has been compiling a list of medications that would be effective in a BT attack, along with information on manufacturers, inventories, suppliers, and lead time for producing the drugs [186].

The Department of Commerce, through the Office of Law Enforcement Standards, provides standards and user guides for equipment such as respirators, and decontamination and detection devices used by persons working in criminal justice and public safety to make sure they are safe and effective. This office also assists DOD and Department of Justice (DOJ) in preparing a Standardized Equipment list of technical equipment considered essential for responding to terrorist attacks [187].

Prioritization of Vaccine Recipients

Influenza is a vaccine-preventable disease responsible for a large number of deaths every year among the elderly and persons with certain chronic diseases [188]. These persons should have priority to receive the influenza vaccine if there is a delay in the supply, which happened in 2000 [189] and 2001 [190]. Because vaccines are distributed through the private sector, which has little incentive to prioritize recipients, in most states there is no mechanism to assure that influenza vaccine gets preferentially to those who need it the most. Similarly, a potential issue in the distribution of BT pharmaceuticals is the prioritization of risk groups in the face of limited supplies. Should vaccine or medication be reserved for just those known to be exposed? What about healthcare workers who encounter ill persons in their work? If a large expanding outbreak is in process, it could be important to ensure the safety of those who keep power and water supplies functioning, and the safety of fire, police, and emergency workers, the National Guard, the military, and others. These decisions will require hard choices, planning, and forethought.

Handling Mass Mortalities

Mass casualty events from a BT attack would result in new problems, requiring new plans. Bereaved families will have varying requests for disposition of bodies and effects of the deceased. These will have to be balanced with the need for preservation of evidence required to build a legal foundation for subsequent prosecution. For instance, legal requirements may indicate that testing and sampling be documented for each victim—an impossibility in a mass casualty situation where the number of victims greatly overwhelms testing and storage capacity. Cities do not maintain morgue space for large numbers of casualties, so alternative arrangements should be made.

Discussions need to occur between hospital staff, medical examiners, and law enforcement, so that in a BT event the needs of each discipline can be addressed under constraints of both time and resources. Procedures also need to be in place for handling the personal property of victims, autopsy reports, and samples. Eventually, these discussions may require legislation to clarify procedures for mass casualties.

Death notification should occur as rapidly as possible, and be handled by professionals with training and experience [191]. It could be useful to consolidate the responsibility for notification of family members of the deceased, and associate this task with some provision of bereavement counseling for them, but this is unlikely to happen unless it is planned. Providers of counseling and psychological care for the bereaved need to be identified in advance and plans made for how these arrangements will be activated. The many different agencies offering services and compensation for victims should share information to simplify the paperwork required of victims and to streamline their benefits process [192].

Psychological Distress

Among the persons presenting for care in the wake of a mass casualty event will be persons with symptoms due to psychological causes, some of which can become long term. Six months after the bombing of the Oklahoma City federal building in 1995, 34 percent of survivors had posttraumatic stress disorder (PTSD), and 23 percent major depression [193]. The numbers of psychological victims will likely increase according to the intensity of the stress (including the numbers of physical victims, surprise, lack of preparation, tired or deficient leadership, and the inexperience of psychiatric teams). Many of these features are likely to be present in a BT attack [194]. Distinguishing between the physical and psychological victims will be neither trivial nor easy, and some persons may fall into both categories. Symptoms of psychological distress can overlap with the signs of early illness from many of the BT agents: fatigue, headache, muscle aches, joint pain, and nausea or vomiting [195].

Irrespective of the cause of the patient's symptoms, pain and distress are real and must be treated. Based on the numbers of psychological casualties in the sarin gas attack in Tokyo, there may be as many as four psychological casualties for every physical casualty in a large mass casualty incident [196]. These psychological victims should be included in disaster planning [197], and provisions made for diagnosis and care for these psychological victims. Five years after the 1995 sarin gas attack in Tokyo, in 2000, out of 191 victims who responded to a survey, many still had lingering psychological effects, including depressed mood (13 percent), flashback experiences (13 percent), and physical symptoms such as fatigue (16 percent), stiff muscles (15 percent), and headache (10 percent) [198].

Following the Oklahoma City bombing, it was found that 76 percent of the people who later developed PTSD had shown early symptoms within one day of the bombing, and 94 percent within one week. In psychological terms, these early symptoms are called "avoidance" and "numbing," and include going out of the way to avoid thinking about the event, an inability to feel love, and a sense of pointlessness in thinking about the future [199]. Although some studies have found that early symptoms have low predictive value for long-term effects [200], systems to look for these symptoms could provide a way for the identification of some persons who could benefit from early intervention. Groups who have been found to be at greater risk for developing PTSD include females, those with concurrent significant physical injuries, and those with major concurrent negative events in their lives [199]. Because it is likely that the number of psychiatric casualties will exceed the physical casualties, planning for psychiatric care is essential.

Healthcare workers and those responding to an event may themselves become psychological casualties [201] and may be at higher risk than others [202]. Disaster plans should include ongoing measures for monitoring psychological stress among workers and arrangements for persons who need help to receive it in a timely manner, both to prevent worsening of acute symptoms and decrease the risk of subsequent psychological consequences. A program in the Air Force, which encouraged staff to seek mental health services, if they needed them, reduced suicides by 50 percent [203].

Training and exercise scenarios for emergency responders should include actor victims who have been trained to demonstrate signs of psychiatric distress, and should teach responders in the prevention and mitigation of psychiatric distress [204]. Victims should be broadly defined to include first responders. Victims should be rapidly identified, quickly given access to information and services, sources of funding, and the qualifications of those providing services [205].

Mental health professionals need to be involved in the preparation for response to mass casualty events. Research is needed on the effectiveness of critical incident stress debriefing, a method of psychiatric intervention which has advocates and doubters among mental healthcare professionals [201].

The Office of Justice Programs (OJP), in some cases, can provide direct assistance to victims of terrorism, such as funding for the provision of mental health treatment. The JTF-CS and the NDMS, previously mentioned, also have psychiatric care units [206]. The Substance Abuse and Mental Health Services Administration (SAMHSA), under the auspices of HHS, is responsible for behavioral health issues [207]. The American Red Cross also offers many services that address psychological needs.

Communications

Communication between Responding Agencies

During a BT incident, there will be a need for rapid and accurate communication between responders at local, state, and national levels, between agencies with different functions, and private sector agencies such as hospitals and clinics [208]. The Health Alert Network, a program administered to state and local health departments through CDC, has enabled many local health departments to obtain computers with Internet access, an essential infrastructure for rapid communication necessary during an infectious disease outbreak. Many agencies are setting up procedures both to operate and to receive notifications at night. The TOPOFF exercise revealed that there is a need for communications equipment to be compatible (currently some responding agencies have communications equipment that operates on limited and noncompatible frequencies), and for redundancy of methods in case some means of communication fail [209].

It would be useful to develop the capacity for online communication connecting all the various agencies responding to an emergency. Such a system would provide, according to the needs of each participating agency, access to information about when and where events occurred, which agencies were involved in the response, what steps were being taken by which agencies, the names of contact persons within organizations, maps, and a mechanism to share other pertinent data. Such a computer system would decrease the confusion in an emergency and enhance the ability of all those involved to respond promptly and effectively. The system might be tailored to existing emergency response systems already in use, so that each agency would see a screen that looked familiar to them, but that would enhance their system by allowing them access to appropriate parts of the larger developing picture. Confidentiality of data across institutional lines, assurance of appropriate access to this system, computer logistics, and assignments of responsibility for this system are examples of the issues that would need to be resolved.

The OEP, housed within the HHS, has conducted both preparedness and research activities. It has also worked on enhancing systems for communication during disasters [181].

Public Information

In a BT incident, the victims would not be the only intended targets of the attack; presumably, terrorists intend to instill fear and disrupt society. Because biological weapons are unfamiliar to most people, their use carries additional potential for panic and fear. How the media handles such an event will have critical implications for public reaction. In the midst of enormous public interest, a balance should be sought between providing immediate information and validated, accurate information. If multiple experts give variations in opinion, the public will need an authoritative source for medical information, and a way to correct rumors [210]. As always, balanced, accurate media coverage with a sensitivity to context is an art; a BT attack would test the mettle of both reporters and the public.

The media may help the public to assist in controlling the disaster by identifying where and when the release may have occurred, determining who may have been exposed, and relaying information to others regarding interventions such as medications, vaccines, or measures individuals can take to protect themselves from disease. The pivotal role of the media dictates that advance planning of this process should occur to a detailed level to ensure maximum accuracy and efficiency.

A government report on media relations in WMD [211] has recommended that all levels of government engage the media before a crisis, that plans include designating mental health experts with media experience who could convey sound advice to the public in a crisis, that the public be informed about best- and worst-case scenarios, and what the government is doing to resolve the situation. Other recommendations included identifying "validators," who can provide good information and "credible sources," and who are skilled at conveying information to the public, targeting news appropriately for different audiences, and providing methods for two-way communication to correct misinformation, such as hotlines and Web sites.

Future Directions

Training

A part of developing new response procedures is to train those who would need to participate in them. Because BT is a new threat, many persons who would be called upon to respond may require training about what BT is, and what the symptoms, diagnosis, and treatment of weaponized agents are, before they are ready to assimilate training on their role in response plans.

Many stand-alone programs have been developed for training, but a longer term approach would institutionalize BT training, as required material, with specific standards for training and recertification of diverse professionals: healthcare professionals, lawyers, public health professionals, first responders, policy makers, research scientists, agricultural workers, veterinarians, and others. Institutionalized training will require defining basic knowledge requirements for each category of professionals so that these can be included in the training curricula for each of these groups [212]. If these components were also to be included in certification requirements for relicensing, for example, it would be assured that working professionals were updated both currently and on an ongoing basis as this field progresses. A useful report recommending this approach in specific terms has been developed on this subject for those working in the emergency medical system [213]. This approach could allow for the reallocation of money currently being spent in possibly redundant training programs [214].

> The DOJ, through the FBI, is the lead federal agency for crisis management of any terrorist incident in the United States. Its Office of Justice Programs (OJP) has overseen programs to provide first responders with training, equipment, technical assistance, and exercises [215]. Most of the Domestic Preparedness Program previously responsible for these was transferred from the DOD to the DOJ in October 2000 [56]. This program has several components providing expertise to help train civil emergency responders at the local, state, and federal levels in responding to incidents

involving WMD or high-yield explosives. The DOD [216] has worked with the OEP on the creation of the Metropolitan Medical Response System (MMRS), described in the following text, and has coordinated yearly tabletop exercises designed to test major components of local response plans. Its Expert Assistance Program includes a WMD helpline to assist in nonemergency planning, a Web site, a hotline for immediate access to technical expertise during an incident, and a database with information about chemical agents, biological agents, detection devices, and personal protective equipment.

FEMA [217] is the lead federal agency in managing the consequence phase of a terrorist attack. It supports training at the state and local levels for emergency planners and officials in other agencies with a role in emergency response. It funds grants for state agencies to develop terrorism annexes to existing disaster plans, which can be used by states in different ways to fit needs specific to each state, such as training, conducting exercises, or other planning activities. FEMA funds training provided through the Emergency Management Institute and the National Fire Academy, and maintains databases on WMD agents meant to serve as a resource guide for response. FEMA is collaborating with DOD and DOJ on updating the Standardized Equipment List which first responders use in purchasing their supplies. Together with the National Emergency Management Association, FEMA is creating a self-assessment tool for government agencies to detect areas for improvement in their emergency plans. A baseline survey using this tool in 1998 reported areas that states could improve on in their plans and equipment for response to a terrorist incident.

The Metropolitan Medical Response System (MMRS), overseen by the OEP, has trained senior staff in local first response agencies, health agencies, hospitals, and trainers in 120 cities, and provides funding for equipment and other projects [218]. This program contracts collectively with local agencies that have, in many instances, not worked together closely in the past, to improve the integration of local plans for response to a WMD incident. The OEP has collaborated with the Institute of Medicine to conduct research on developing assessment and performance measures to improve these MMRS programs nationwide. These programs initially tended to be weighted toward public safety responders: fire, police, and emergency management [219]. The OEP was overseeing a project in Charlotte, North Carolina, in 2001, to enhance the healthcare system contribution to this process, including community healthcare systems, medical providers, and the public health system.

Through the Office of State and Local Domestic Preparedness Support, the OJP [220] has provided funding to 120 larger metropolitan areas for emergency equipment and training targeted to the first responder community: fire, emergency medical, and public safety personnel. The office also conducted a survey to assist local communities in determining their risks and needs and to obtain an overall picture of the comparative preparedness of the metropolitan areas. The OJP has directed one-day exercises in 52 cities, in which personnel from public health, fire, law enforcement, and emergency management agencies worked through a bioterrorist incident from its incubation period through its conclusion, requiring personnel to address quarantine, mass mortalities, medical surveillance, and patient tracking.

The CDC provides oversight for several hospitals and universities engaged in research and training for BT preparedness [221]. The OEP [222] provides management staff and funding for the U.S. Public Health Service Noble Training Center in

Alabama, a center training first responders in responding to a WMD incident. The center is also developing training materials on WMD response for physicians, nurses, and emergency medical technicians.

Training for the General Public

Training for the general public should be balanced to promote knowledge, without creating a sense of fear, and should begin prior to a BT attack. Education should raise awareness of the principles of infectious diseases, and the strengths and weaknesses of biological warfare. Public participation is essential in implementing disease control measures for any disease. Dissemination of information to the public in advance has been recommended as an effective way to decrease panic and mitigate psychological stress during a real event as it removes the element of surprise [223,224]. Understanding the mechanisms of disease transmission and how to protect oneself on an individual level would also alleviate individual personal unease because it gives direction for action [225]. If people know beforehand that they might need to do nothing in particular for a BT attack except to follow public health recommendations on the news, this could help prevent an atmosphere of panic. Individuals who washed their hands frequently, avoided crowds, and stayed at home could possibly decrease the spread of agents with secondary transmission.

There are also opportunities for the public to plan participation in a large disaster: volunteers will be needed to help with the distribution of the NPSP, or could receive training in how to provide basic interventions to psychiatric victims to help prevent later psychiatric effects [226]. Agencies providing services to victims could benefit from working together to recruit, screen, and train volunteers to assist in responding to a BT attack [227].

Research

General Research Needs

The Defense Science Board has recommended creating (1) a database of "signatures" of the biological warfare agents, (2) small diagnostic tools capable of immediately detecting all agents in the database, and (3) a computerized system for alerting defense and public health responders to the possibility of an outbreak [228]. Scientific collaboration on discovering relationships between climate and human health have been mentioned previously.

There is a need for understanding potential effects of various quarantine measures or mass prophylaxis measures on the control of disease, and their cost in lives and dollars. Study of the quarantine measures should address "implementation authority, enforcement, logistics, financial support, and psychological ramifications" [229]. The more thoroughly these issues are resolved in advance, the safer our civil liberties will be. Research is also needed on the causes for low public trust and how better trust could be restored [230].

In addition to planning and training, many agencies are involved in research projects. The DOE [231] houses a chemical and biological national security program, which conducts research related to BT as part of a larger mandate to reduce the danger from WMD. It has an analysis component, which postulates the value of projected research through simulation models. Its technology development component conducts advanced research on detection methods, modeling capabilities, decontamination procedures, and methods for both attribution and medical countermeasures based on molecular biological studies. Its Domestic Demonstration and Application programs are developing future operational systems based on the integration of existing technology for specific applications.

The DOD has for years been involved in the research and treatment of unusual diseases, including tropical infectious diseases and those caused by agents of biological warfare. USAMRIID is the lead institution for these activities [232]. Research projects include developing vaccines, therapeutics, and databases for assistance in diagnostic procedures. The institute is equipped with a biosafety level 4 laboratory, one of the few in the world in which researchers can study dangerous airborne pathogens safely. The USAMRIID is collaborating with the NIH on developing an anthrax vaccine, and also collaborating with other military agencies in developing plans for potential support to civil authorities following a terrorist incident.

The OJP has research programs which collaborate with the FBI's, Technical Support Working Group, and the Office of State and Local Domestic Preparedness Support to determine the agents that terrorists are most likely to use [233].

The Technical Support Working Group is an interagency body chaired by the DOD and the DOE that has been working since 1987 on accelerating the development of technologies to combat terrorism [234]. The National Institutes of Health (HHS) is composed of 27 separate institutes and centers, and additionally funds research in private facilities nationwide [235]. The FBI, through its Hazardous Materials Response Unit, conducts research on the identification of biological agents directed toward developing capabilities for attribution of an event, to person, group, or geographical region. Some of this research was conducted by the Massachusetts Institute of Technology and some by the U.S. Army Soldier Biological and Chemical Command [162].

Vaccines

Anthrax vaccine is an example of an effective pharmaceutical that could be used in an outbreak situation to protect persons from exposure or to decrease the length of time exposed persons would need to take protective antibiotics [236]. Production of this vaccine has been delayed because its sole supplier, Bioport, has had difficulties meeting FDA standards [237]. Unfortunately, problems with the supply of anthrax vaccine are not unique. The vaccine industry has had difficulties resulting in shortages of many vaccines [238]: meningitis, tetanus toxoid, yellow fever, and others. Because they do not bring in large revenues, pharmaceutical companies have less incentive to produce vaccines than some of their other products. In view of the lack of economic incentive for their development in the private sector, government oversight and funding for vaccine research and production should be considered. Vaccines could also be potentially powerful tools against BT, another endeavor that would require federal funding.

While a shortage of these vaccines is worrisome in this country, medical care in America is available to unvaccinated persons who become ill, and the presence of a majority of vaccinated persons in communities have a tendency to keep outbreaks from spreading. In the developing world, a lack of vaccines results in much suffering and mortality from preventable causes. Measles, preventable by vaccine, kills nearly 1 million children each year in the developing world; childhood vaccines that cost just a few cents each could save an estimated 3 million lives a year [239]. There is a need for research and development of new vaccines, both for diseases that cause tremendous mortality worldwide and for the BT diseases. Jack Woodall, the founder of ProMED, has proposed an international transparent scientific collaborative effort to develop vaccines against the BT diseases [238]. Research on vaccines could also decrease the risk of BT by employing experienced scientists from the dismantled Russian biological weapons program. Furthermore, if research could result in vaccines and other measures for the prevention of infectious diseases that currently plague the developing world, it is possible significant savings in lives could occur, also resulting in strengthened economies and increased political stability.

The subject of global poverty and disease is worth a mention. A recent article in *The Economist* argues that while it may be too glib to attribute the root causes of terrorism to poverty and disease in the developing world, nevertheless, there is likely a correlation between rates of illness in countries and political instability, and that reducing the rate of infectious diseases in the developing world may result in fewer states which could offer a safe haven for terrorist groups. The article holds that every country bears responsibility for appropriating their own resources toward some measure of healthcare for their citizens, yet calculates even that with a judicious use of funds; some countries simply do not have enough money. While acknowledging that corrupt officials often divert donated funds, the article suggests that the dire need should motivate wealthier global citizens to persist in trying to help. It calculates that with proper use of funds, if every citizen in the developed world would contribute monies worth approximately less than two tanks of gas for most cars that "a colossal number of lives could be saved, and immeasurable suffering relieved." [240]. These are complex issues, but the stakes are high and one cannot afford to ignore them.

The National Institute of Allergy and Infectious Diseases (NIAID) is an NIH institute that houses a program conducting research on diagnostic methods, vaccines, and therapeutic medications for the BT diseases [241]. Its research has been focused on smallpox, developing early detection methods, extending the shelf life of existing vaccine, preventing complications from the smallpox vaccine, and developing new therapeutic medications for smallpox. It also formed a working group on anthrax vaccines collaborating with the USAMRIID and other agencies to develop and test a new anthrax vaccine [242].

The FDA's Center for Biologics Evaluation and Research conducts research to ensure both the efficacy and safety of vaccines against the BT diseases, including anthrax, smallpox, and plague. The FDA's Center works with CDC and DOD to establish a system of lot numbers and surveillance activities that would detect adverse side effects from vaccines. The FDA's Center for Devices and Radiological Health has been evaluating for safety a device intended to detect anthrax in humans, and is developing processes for allowing the use of investigational devices such as those in an emergency situation. The FDA's Center for Drug Evaluation is developing corresponding processes for allowing the use of investigational medications in an emergency situation.

Because many of the BT diseases do not affect humans naturally, it is often not possible to conduct studies on vaccines, devices, or medications for these diseases using human data as is usually done. In an emergency situation such as a BT attack in which no other diagnostic methods or therapy may be available, the use of investigational methods that have not been previously studied in humans may be the only option to protect exposed persons. To solve this problem, the FDA is working with NIH, CDC, and other agencies to develop standards for the use of animal and laboratory data in licensing diagnostic devices and pharmaceuticals for emergency use in protecting the public from a BT attack. Because there may be no natural market for these vaccines, medications, and diagnostic devices, this work is dependent on government funding for its research [243].

The CDC also conducts its own research on anthrax, smallpox, and other BT diseases. The DOT is conducting research on improving metropolitan area responses to WMD incidents in local mass transit systems [119].

Genomics

Because biological agents are living organisms, they have the potential for genetic alteration. Organisms could be genetically altered to be antibiotic or vaccine resistant, have enhanced aerosol and environmental stabilities [244], elude standard detection and diagnostic methods [245], or evolve into new diseases after therapeutic treatment is administered for their first phase [246]. Genetic modulators could be produced to cause anything from mood changes to altered functioning of the immune system. If this possibility has not been ignored by those in the business of weaponizing biological agents [247], neither are those in this country unaware of how to deal with new diseases. New diseases such as Legionnaires' disease [248] and Hanta virus [249] have been identified in the past and will continue to be identified. Nevertheless, new diseases would impose further difficulties in dealing with a biologic attack. The method of transmission would have to be identified to prevent further spread of disease, a method of laboratory diagnosis would have to be found to identify which persons have been affected by the outbreak, and effective treatments found. However, our advancing understanding of the genomic technologies, which have the potential to make biowarfare more deadly, may also provide the hope for new solutions. If an increased understanding of the immune system, and its interactions with genetic modulators resulted in effective and rapid response measures, it could serve as a major deterrent to BT in general. Solutions could enable discoveries in diagnostics and treatments to be so rapid they would "render biological warfare or terrorism an obviously futile as well as morally unacceptable act" [250].

The NIAID, an agency of the NIH, has a large research program conducting research on the genomics of the BT diseases and how they affect the pathogenesis of disease. Identification of the genomic sequences of the BT diseases will pave the way for new diagnostic methods and therapeutics for diseases [251].

Conclusions

Recommendations and ideas for action have been placed throughout this chapter as they fit into each topic of discussion. Rather than a summary of points covered in this chapter, these conclusions suggest trends that may be beneficial in developing defenses against BT, and some perspectives on thinking about the subject.

First, knowledge is key to conquering the threat of BT. The public and those working in all levels of government need to understand the threat of BT and what measures would be effective to protect the population. All components of society (individual agencies; federal, state, and local levels of government; and various disciplines) have unique characteristics, assets, and challenges that will present different opportunities for progress in this multifaceted field. Widespread knowledge of problems and potential solutions will allow each entity to make progress as their own situation allows.

Many separate and fragmented systems need to become integrated and work together on common goals. The nation's public health system, lacking in basic infrastructures such as electronic communications systems and trained staff, must now forge closer or even new relationships with many entities: the medical community to track disease in humans; the veterinary, wildlife, and agricultural communities to track disease in animals and plants; the intelligence community to track threats and investigate outbreaks; and the public safety and military communities to plan response. Further, ultimate solutions will depend on new advances in genetics, immunology, laboratory science, technology, and epidemiology, and will involve international collaboration. This alignment of purpose throughout the government and the private sector is unlikely to occur without informed leadership, entrusted with broad powers. Public support will be critical to create the political will for this integration, which will need to cut some redundant programs to fund other areas that are lacking.

The government's electronic communications should reflect these relationships. There is a need for a more integrated infrastructure for the appropriate exchange of information across agency lines, levels of government, the medical and veterinary communities, research institutions, and private industry. This would greatly enhance the ability of the United States both to detect an outbreak and mobilize a coordinated response. This electronic network should be secure, maintain individual and agency confidentiality, and be adaptable. Epidemiologists throughout the process should participate in the interpretation of data so that trends are spotted rapidly.

However, the scope of this problem is larger than any one country. As BT programs were started because of international conflict, solutions to the threat they pose must also be international in scope. Negotiation of treaties and conventions will help clarify expectations and standards. International collaboration also needs to deepen in other areas, including law enforcement and scientific exchange. An appreciation for the medical problems in the developing world, with research into vaccines and other measures to stem the worldwide toll of communicable diseases, would help stabilize the world economy, provide work for underemployed scientists with dangerous skills, and advance the medical knowledge of mankind. Finally, the roots of conflict are often economic. It is possible that if affluent countries can apply some of their resources to alleviating disease and poverty abroad, less of that disease and poverty will be brought back home from other countries, one way or another.

Acknowledgments

Paul Fennewald, the Jefferson City FBI Office, reviewed the manuscript concerning the role of law enforcement in response to a BT event. Thaddeus Zajdowicz, MD, Office of the Joint Task Force for Civil Support, reviewed it regarding the role of the military. Eddie Hedrick, Director of Infection Control, University of Missouri Hospitals, Columbia, reviewed it for hospital planning and infection control. Their reviews were very important and very much appreciated. The CDC Health Alert Network and Epi-X updates have been of noteworthy assistance in the scientific and public health areas. The Physicians Online Web site provided the views of physicians in practice. The weekly electronic *Homeland Security Newsletter*, published by the ANSER Institute for Homeland Security, provided many sources for this chapter. (Some of these sources have not been attributed in the references section to the newsletter through my own filing errors). This online journal provides an ongoing, balanced account of issues related to homeland security, describing federal activities and legislation influencing the governmental process, and advances in science and technology, and it is highly recommend for anyone interested in this subject. Finally, the assessments and conclusions are my own and are not to be considered those of the Missouri Department of Health and Senior Services or the University of Missouri, Columbia.

References

1. A Camus. *The Plague*. New York: Vintage Books, a Division of Random House, 1948.
2. FF Cartwright and MD Biddiss. *Disease and History*. New York: Dorset Press, 1972.
3. A Karlin. *Man & Microbes: Disease and Plagues in History and Modern Times*. New York: G.P. Putnam's Sons, 1995.
4. U.S. National Intelligence Council; The global infectious disease threat and its implications for the United States NIE, January 2000, p. 46. <<http://www.odci.gov/nic/>> accessed 1/14/02.
5. L Garrett. *The Coming Plague, Newly Emerging Diseases in a World out of Balance*. New York: Farrar, Straus & Giroux, 1994.
6. E Regis. *The Biology of Doom. The History of America's Secret Germ Warfare Project*. New York: Henry Holt and Company, 1999, pp. 221–222.
7. T Mangold and J Goldberg. *Plague Wars, the Terrifying Reality of Biological Warfare*. New York: St. Martin's Press, 1999, p. 214.
8. GW Christopher, TJ Cieslak, JA Pavlin, and EM Eitzen. Biological warfare: A historical perspective. *JAMA* 278(5): 412–417, 1997.
9. EJ DaSilva. Biological warfare, bioterrorism, biodefence and the biological and toxin weapons convention. *EJB: Electronic Journal of Biotechnology* 2(3): 1, December 15, 1999. <<http://ejb.ucv.cl/content/>> accessed 1/14/02.
10. H Gold. *Unit 731 Testimony*. Tokyo: Yen Books, 1996, p. 17.
11. SH Harris. *Factories of Death, Japanese Biological Warfare, 1932–45, and the American Cover-Up*. New York: Routledge, 1994, pp. 152–157.
12. E Regis. *The Biology of Doom. The History of America's Secret Germ Warfare Project*. New York: Henry Holt and Company, 1999, pp. 24–113.
13. E Regis. *The Biology of Doom. The History of America's Secret Germ Warfare Project*. New York: Henry Holt and Company, 1999, p. 86.
14. E Regis. *The Biology of Doom. The History of America's Secret Germ Warfare Project*. New York: Henry Holt and Company, 1999, p. 201.
15. T Mangold and J Goldberg. *Plague Wars, the Terrifying Reality of Biological Warfare*. New York: St. Martin's Press, 1999, pp. 41–52.
16. T Mangold and J Goldberg. *Plague Wars, the Terrifying Reality of Biological Warfare*. New York: St. Martin's Press, 1999, pp. 215–282.
17. T Mangold and J Goldberg. *Plague Wars, the Terrifying Reality of Biological Warfare*. New York: St. Martin's Press, 1999, pp. 322–334.
18. M Leitenberg. An assessment of the biological weapons threat to the United States. *Journal of Homeland Defense* 2000. <<http://www.homelanddefense.org/journal/Articles/Leitenberg.htm>> accessed 1/8/01.
19. K Alibek and S Handelman. *Biohazard, The Chilling True Story of the Largest Covert Biological Weapons Program in the World—Told from Inside by the Man Who Ran It*. New York: Dell Publishing, 1999.
20. J Miller, S Engelberg, and W Beard. *GERMS, Biological Weapons and America's Secret War*. New York: Simon & Schuster, 2001, p. 125.
21. T Mangold and J Goldberg. *Plague Wars, the Terrifying Reality of Biological Warfare*. New York: St. Martin's Press, 1999, pp. 283–321.
22. RA Falkenrath, RD Newman, and BA Thayer. *America's Achilles' Heel: Nuclear, Biological and Chemical Terrorism and Covert Attack*. Cambridge, MA: The MIT Press, 1998, p. 175.
23. RA Falkenrath, RD Newman, and BA Thayer. *America's Achilles' Heel: Nuclear, Biological and Chemical Terrorism and Covert Attack*. Cambridge, MA: The MIT Press, 1998, p. 153.
24. K Alibek and S Handelman. *Biohazard, The Chilling True Story of the Largest Covert Biological Weapons Program in the World–Told from Inside by the Man Who Ran It*. New York: Dell Publishing, 1999, p. 281.
25. E Regis. *The Biology of Doom. The History of America's Secret Germ Warfare Project*. New York: Henry Holt and Company, 1999.
26. M Leitenberg. An assessment of the biological weapons threat to the United States. *Journal of Homeland Defense* 15–16, 2000. <<http://www.homelanddefense.org/journal/Articles/Leitenberg.htm>> accessed 1/8/01.

27. K Alibek and S Handelman. *Biohazard, The Chilling True Story of the Largest Covert Biological Weapons Program in the World–Told from Inside by the Man Who Ran It.* New York: Dell Publishing, 1999, pp. 18–20.
28. PJ Boyer. The Ames Strain, How a sick cow in Iowa may have helped to create a lethal bioweapon. *The New Yorker.* November 12, 2001, p. 72.
29. E Regis. *The Biology of Doom. The History of America's Secret Germ Warfare Project.* New York: Henry Holt and Company, 1999, pp. 55–57.
30. K Alibek and S Handelman. *Biohazard, The Chilling True Story of the Largest Covert Biological Weapons Program in the World –Told from Inside by the Man Who Ran It.* New York: Dell Publishing, 1999, p. 118.
31. DR Franz. Presentation on bioterrorism to media representatives sponsored by the Missouri Department of Health and Senior Services and CDC, August 2001.
32. PJ Boyer. The Ames Strain, How a sick cow in Iowa may have helped to create a lethal bioweapon. *The New Yorker.* November 12, 2001, pp. 69–70.
33. RA Falkenrath, RD Newman, and BA Thayer. *America's Achilles' Heel: Nuclear, Biological and Chemical Terrorism and Covert Attack.* Cambridge, MA: The MIT Press, 1998, p. 152.
34. E Regis. *The Biology of Doom. The History of America's Secret Germ Warfare Project.* New York: Henry Holt and Company, 1999, p. 123.
35. E Regis. *The Biology of Doom. The History of America's Secret Germ Warfare Project.* New York: Henry Holt and Company, 1999, p. 166.
36. H Gold. *Unit 731 Testimony.* Tokyo: Yen Books, 1996.
37. Interview with Dr. Ken Alibek. *Journal of Homeland Security* September 28, 2000. *Homeland Security Newsletter.* «http://homelandsecurity.org/bulletin/currentbulletin.htm» accessed 7/13/01.
38. CDC (Centers for Disease Control and Prevention). Biological and chemical terrorism: Strategic plan for preparedness and response. *MMWR* 49(RR-4): 5–6, April 21, 2000.
39. DA Henderson. The looming threat of bioterrorism. *Science* 283:1279–1283, February 26, 1999.
40. JB Tucker. *Scourge: The Once and Future-Threat of Smallpox.* New York: Atlantic Monthly Press, 2001.
41. MT Osterholm and J Schwartz. *Living Terrors, What America Needs to Know to Survive the Coming Bioterrorist Catastrophe.* New York: Delacorte Press, 2000, p. 17.
42. JB Tucker. *Scourge: The Once and Future Threat of Smallpox.* New York: Atlantic Monthly Press, 2001, pp. 45–122.
43. R Preston. Dept of amplification: Updating the small pox vaccine. *The New Yorker.* January 17, 2000, p. 27.
44. R Preston. The demon in the freezer. *The New Yorker.* July 12, 1999, p. 46.
45. DR Franz, PB Jahrling, AM Friedlander, DJ McClain, DL Hoover, WR Bryne, JA Pavlin, GW Christopher, and EM Eitzen. Clinical recognition and management of patients exposed to biological warfare agents. *JAMA* 278(5): 405, August 6, 1997.
46. J Chin. Ed. *Control of Communicable Diseases Manual,* 17th ed. Washington, DC: American Public Health Association, 2000.
47. USAMRIID (U.S. Army Medical Research Institute of Infectious Diseases). *Medical Management of Biological Casualties Handbook,* 4th ed. February, 2001.
48. R Zajtchuk. Editor in Chief. *Textbook of Military Medicine. Part I. Medical Aspects of Chemical and Biological Warfare.* Published by Office of the Surgeon General, Department of the Army, Washington, DC, 1997, pp. 467–677.
49. DR Franz, PB Jahrling, AM Friedlander, DJ McClain, DL Hoover, WR Bryne, JA Pavlin, GW Christopher, and EM Eitzen. Clinical recognition and management of patients exposed to biological warfare agents. *JAMA* 278(5): 399–411, August 6, 1997.
50. RA Falkenrath, RD Newman, and BA Thayer. *America's Achilles' Heel: Nuclear, Biological and Chemical Terrorism and Covert Attack.* Cambridge, MA: The MIT Press, 1998, p. 244.
51. GAO (General Accounting Office). Report to Congressional Committees. Bioterrorism, Federal Research and Preparedness Activities. GAO-01-915, September 2001, p.78.
52. MT Osterholm and J Schwartz. *Living Terrors, What America Needs to Know to Survive the Coming Bioterrorist Catastrophe.* New York: Delacorte Press, 2000, pp. 158–159.

53. RJ Larsen and RA David. Homeland defense: State of the union. *Journal of Homeland Security.* <<http://www.homelandsecurity.org/journal/Articles/article/cfm?article=13>> accessed 6/8/01.
54. M Dobbs. Homeland security: New challenges for an old responsibility. *Journal of Homeland Defense* <<http://www.homelanddefense.org/journal/Articles/Dobbs.htm>> accessed 3/19/01.
55. GAO (General Accounting Office) Report to Congressional Committees. Bioterrorism, Federal Research and Preparedness Activities. GAO-01-915, September 2001, pp. 41–43.
56. GAO (General Accounting Office) Report to Congressional Committees. Bioterrorism, Federal Research and Preparedness Activities. GAO-01-915, September 2001, p. 45.
57. Center for Nonproliferation Studies. Monterey Institute of International Studies. Clinical and Biological Weapons Resource Page. <<http://www.cns.miis.edu/research/cbw/domestic.htm>>. accessed 10/12/01.
58. J Heinrich. Bioterrorism, Coordination and Preparedness. Testimony before the Subcommittee on Government Efficiency, Financial Management, and Intergovernmental Relations. Committee on Government Reform. House of Representatives. GAO 02-129T, 2001, pp. 21–22.
59. J Heinrich. Bioterrorism, Coordination and Preparedness. Testimony before the Subcommittee on Government Efficiency, Financial Management, and Intergovernmental Relations. Committee on Government Reform. House of Representatives. GAO 02-129T, 2001, pp. 7–11.
60. J Miller, S Engelberg, and W Beard. *GERMS, Biological Weapons and America's Secret War.* New York: Simon & Schuster, 2001, p. 358.
61. Second Annual Report to the President and the Congress of the Advisory Panel to Assess Domestic Response Capabilities for Terrorism Involving Weapons of Mass Destruction. <<http://www.rand.org/organization/nsrd/terrpanel>> accessed 1/14/02.
62. Road Map for National Security: Imperative for Change, Phase III Report of the United States Commission on National Security in the 21st Century. March 15, 2001. <<http://www.homelandsecurity.org/sugg_reading/Phase_III_Report.pdf>> accessed 1/14/02.
63. RJ Larsen and RA David. Homeland defense: State of the union. *Journal of Homeland Security.* <<http://www.homelandsecurity.org/journal/Articles/article/cfm?article=137>> accessed 6/8/01.
64. GAO (General Accounting Office) Report to Congressional Committees. Combating Terrorism, Selected Challenges and Related Recommendations. GAO-01-822, September 2001, p. 41.
65. Executive Order Establishing Office of Homeland Security. October 12, 2001. <<http://www.whitehouse.gov/news/releases/2001/10/print20011008–2.html>> accessed 10/12/2001.
66. M Moodie, J Ban, C Manzi, MJ Powers, J Jaworski, S Kishinchand, and R Wyman. Bioterrorism in the United States: Threat, Preparedness, and Response. Chemical and Biological Arms Control Institute. 2001. <<http://www.cbaci.org>> accessed 1/08/02. *Homeland Security Newsletter.* <<http://homelandsecurity.org/bulletin/currentbulletin.html>> accessed 8/03/01.
67. E Smithson, Prepared statement before the Senate Committee on Governmental Affairs Subcommittee on International Security, Proliferation and Federal Services. October 17, 2001, p. 2.
68. JS Gilmore, III. Hearing of the Committee of Government Affairs. U.S. Senate. Responding to Homeland Threats. Is Our Government Organized for the Challenge? September 21, 2001. <<http://www.senate.gov/~gov_affairs/092101witness.htm>> accessed 09/28/01.
69. GAO (General Accounting Office) Report to Congressional Committees. Combating Terrorism, Selected Challenges and Related Recommendations. GAO-01-822, September 2001, pp. 14–15.
70. GAO (General Accounting Office) Report to Congressional Committees. Combating Terrorism. Selected Challenges and Related Recommendations. GAO-01-822, September 2001, pp. 131–136.
71. HHS (Health and Human Services). HHS names physician to coordinate anti-bioterrorism initiatives. *HHS News.* July 10, 2001. <<http://www.hhs.gov/news/press/2001pres/20010710a.html>> accessed 07/16/01.
72. GAO (General Accounting Office) Report to Congressional Committees. Bioterrorism, Federal Research and Preparedness Activities. GAO-01-915, September 2001, p. 48.
73. M Moodie, J Ban, C Manzi, MJ Powers, J Jaworski, S Kishinchand, and R Wyman. Bioterrorism in the United States: Threat, Preparedness, and Response. Chemical and Biological Arms Control Institute. 2001, p. 196. <<http://www.cbaci.org>> accessed 1/08/02. *Homeland Security Newsletter.* <<http://homelandsecurity.org/bulletin/currentbulletin.html>> accessed 8/03/01.

74. L Garrett. *Betrayal of Trust; the Collapse of Global Public Health.* New York: Hyperion Books. 2000, p. 539.
75. L Garrett, The nightmare of bioterrorism. *Foreign Affairs* 80(1): 82, January–February 2001.
76. Convention of the Prohibition of the Development, Production and Stockpiling of Bacteriological (Biological) and Toxin Weapons and on their Destruction, U.S. Department of State Archives. April 10, 1972. <<http://www.state.gov/www/global/arms/treaties/bwc1.html>> accessed 1/14/02.
77. M Whelis. Investigating disease outbreaks under a protocol to the biological and toxin weapons convention. *Emerging Infectious Diseases* 6:6, November–December 2000. <<http://www.cdc.gov/ncidod/EID/vol6no6/wheelisohtm>> accessed 11/20/00.
78. FAS Public Interest Report. Controlling biological weapons: It's time for action. *Journal of Federation of American Scientists* 53(5): 2, 2000. <<http://www.fas.org/faspir/v53n5.htm>> accessed 01/02/01.
79. L Garrett. *Betrayal of Trust; the Collapse of Global Public Health.* New York: Hyperion Books, 2000, p. 498.
80. DR Franz and R Zajtchuk. Biological terrorism: Understanding the threat, preparation, and medical response. *Disease-a-Month* 46: 2, February 2000.
81. SM Block. The growing threat of biological weapons. *American Scientist* 89(1): 8, January–February 2001.
82. Biological Weapons Convention, Stop the clock, support the ban. *The Economist* June 14, 2001.
83. SM Block. The growing threat of biological weapons. *American Scientist* 89(1): 9, January–February 2001.
84. J Miller, S Engelberg, and W Beard. *GERMS, Biological Weapons and America's Secret War.* New York: Simon & Schuster, 2001, p. 317.
85. L Garrett. *Betrayal of Trust; the Collapse of Global Public Health.* New York: Hyperion Books, 2000, pp. 505–507.
86. MT Osterholm and J Schwartz. *Living Terrors, What America Needs to Know to Survive the Coming Bioterrorist Catastrophe.* New York: Delacorte Press, 2000, p. 110.
87. B Roberts. Ed. *Hype or Reality? The "New Terrorism" and Mass Casualty Attacks.* Alexandria, VA: Chemical & Biological Arms Control Institute, 2000, p. 275.
88. L Garrett. *Betrayal of Trust; the Collapse of Global Public Health.* New York: Hyperion Books, 2000, p. 513.
89. MT Osterholm and J Schwartz. *Living Terrors, What America Needs to Know to Survive the Coming Bioterrorist Catastrophe.* New York: Delacorte Press, 2000, pp. 111–112.
90. R Lugar. Nunn-Lugar: A tool for the new U.S.-Russian strategic relationship. Carnegie Nonproliferation Conference. *Homeland Security Newsletter.* June 2001, pp. 4–9. <<http://homelandsecurity.org/bulletin/currentbulletin.html>> accessed 6/22/01 <<http://www.usinfo.state.gov/topical/pol/arms/stories/01061901.htm>> accessed 06/22/01.
91. RA Falkenrath, RD Newman, and BA Thayer. *America's Achilles' Heel: Nuclear, Biological and Chemical Terrorism and Covert Attack.* Cambridge, MA: The MIT Press, 1998, p. 249.
92. RA Falkenrath, RD Newman, and BA Thayer. *America's Achilles' Heel: Nuclear, Biological and Chemical Terrorism and Covert Attack.* Cambridge, MA: The MIT Press, 1998, pp. 265–267.
93. CDC (Centers for Disease Control and Prevention). CDC Guidelines for handwashing and environmental control. <<http://www.cdc.gov/ncidod/hip/GUIDE /handwash_ pre.htm>>.
94. A Kohnen. Responding to the Threat of Agroterrorism: Specific Recommendations for the United States Department of Agriculture. BCSIA Discussion Paper 2000-29. ESDP Discussion Paper ESDP-2000-4. John F. Kennedy School of Government, Harvard University, October 2000. *Homeland Security Newsletter.* <<http://homelandsecurity.org/bulletin/currentbulletin.html>> accessed 10/12/01.
95. HL Hinton. Combating Terrorism: Considerations for Investing Resources in Chemical and Biological Preparedness. Testimony before the Committee on Governmental Affairs, U.S. Senate. GAO-02-162T, October 17, 2001, pp. 9–10. *Homeland Security Newsletter.* <<http://homelandsecurity.org/bulletin/currentbulletin.html>> accessed 10/19/01.
96. MT Osterholm and J Schwartz. *Living Terrors, What America Needs to Know to Survive the Coming Bioterrorist Catastrophe.* New York: Delacorte Press, 2000, p. 75.
97. WHO (World Health Organization). Health Aspects of Chemical and Biological Weapons: Report of a WHO Group of Consultants. 1970, p. 87.

98. E Regis. *The Biology of Doom. The History of America's Secret Germ Warfare Project.* New York: Henry Holt and Company, 1999, p. 117.
99. GAO (General Accounting Office) Report to Congressional Committees. Bioterrorism, Federal Research and Preparedness Activities. GAO-01-915, September 2001, pp. 76–77.
100. RG Luthy. Safety of Our Nation's Water. Testimony before the U.S. House of Representatives, Committee on Science. Hearing on H.R. 3178 and the Development of Anti-Terrorism Tools for Water Infrastructure. November 14, 2001.
101. RG Luthy. Safety of Our Nation's Water. Testimony before the U.S. House of Representatives, Committee on Science. Hearing on H.R. 3178 and the Development of Anti-Terrorism Tools for Water Infrastructure. November 14, 2001, p. 4.
102. RG Luthy. Safety of Our Nation's Water. Testimony before the U.S. House of Representatives, Committee on Science. Hearing on H.R. 3178 and the Development of Anti-Terrorism Tools for Water Infrastructure. November 14, 2001, p. 5.
103. TJ Torok, RV Tauxe, RP Wise, JR Livengood, R Sokolow, S Mauvais, KA Birkness, MR Skeels, JM Horan, and LR Foster. A large community outbreak of salmonellosis caused by intentional contamination of restaurant salad bars. *JAMA* 278(5): 389–395, August 6, 1997.
104. GAO (General Accounting Office) Report to Congressional Committees. Bioterrorism, Federal Research and Preparedness Activities. GAO-01-915, September 2001, pp. 58–59.
105. GAO (General Accounting Office) Report to Congressional Committees. Bioterrorism, Federal Research and Preparedness Activities. GAO-01-915, September 2001, pp. 59–60.
106. TV Inglesby, DA Henderson, JG Bartlett, MS Ascher, E Eitzen, AM Friedlander, J Hauer, J McDade, MT Osterholm, T O'Toole, G Parker, TM Perl, PK Russell, and K Tonat. Anthrax as a biological weapon, medical and public health management. *JAMA* 281(18): 1735–1745, May 12, 1999.
107. TV Inglesby, DT Dennis, DA Henderson, JG Bartlett, MS Ascher, E Eitzen, AD Fine, AM Friedlander, J Hauer, JF Koerner, M Layton, J McDade, MT Osterholm, T O' Toole, G Parker, TM Perl, PK Russell, M Schoch-Spana, and K Tonat. Consensus statement: Plague as a biological weapon; medical and public health management. *JAMA* 283(17): 2281–2290, May 3, 2000.
108. DT Dennis, TV Inglesby, DA Henderson, JG Bartlett, MS Ascher, E Eitzen, AD Fine, AM Friedlander, J Hauer, M Layton, SR Lillibridge, JE McDade, MT Osterholm, T O'Toole, G Parker, TM Perl, PK Russell, and K Tonat. Consensus statement: Tularemia as a biological weapon; medical and public health management. *JAMA*, 285 (21), 2763–2773, June 6, 2001.
109. HL Hinton. Combating Terrorism: Considerations for Investing Resources in Chemical and Biological Preparedness. Testimony before the Committee on Governmental Affairs, U.S. Senate. GAO-02-162T, October 17, 2001, p. 11. *Homeland Security Newsletter.* <<http://homelandsecurity.org/bulletin/current bulletin.html>> accessed 10/19/01.
110. W Allen. West Nile virus is found in St. Louis area, officials say. *St. Louis Post-Dispatch*, A-section, October 6, 2001.
111. T Mangold and J Goldberg. *Plague Wars, the Terrifying Reality of Biological Warfare.* New York: St. Martin's Press, 1999, p. 36.
112. E Regis. *The Biology of Doom. The History of America's Secret Germ Warfare Project.* New York: Henry Holt & Company, 1999, p. 112.
113. L Garrett. *The Coming Plague, Newly Emerging Diseases in a World out of Balance.* New York: Farrar, Straus & Giroux, 1994, p. 615.
114. EJ DaSilva. Biological warfare, bioterrorism, biodefence and the biological and toxin weapons convention, *EJB: Electronic Journal of Biotechnology* 2(3): 1, December 15, 1999, ISSN: 0717-3458; <<http://ejb.ucv.cl/content/vol2/issue3/full/2/2.pdf>> accessed 1/14/02.
115. University of Georgia, College of Veterinary Medicine. *Southeastern Cooperative Wildlife Disease Study Briefs* 17(3): 3, October 2001.
116. Kohnen. Responding to the threat of agroterrorism: Specific recommendations for the United States Dept. of Agriculture. BCSIA Discussion Paper 2000-29, ESDP Discussion Paper ESDP-2000-04, John F. Kennedy School of Government, Harvard University, October 2000, pp. 36–37. *Homeland Security Newsletter.* <<http://homelandsecurity.org/bulletin/currentbulletin.html>> accessed 10/12/01.

117. GAO (General Accounting Office) Report to Congressional Committees. Bioterrorism, Federal Research and Preparedness Activities. GAO-01-915, September 2001, p. 36.
118. GAO (General Accounting Office) Report to Congressional Committees. Bioterrorism, Federal Research and Preparedness Activities. GAO-01-915, September 2001, p. 59.
119. GAO (General Accounting Office) Report to Congressional Committees. Bioterrorism, Federal Research and Preparedness Activities. GAO-01-915, September 2001, p. 72.
120. JF English, MY Cundiff, JD Malone, JA Pfeiffer, M Bell, L Steele, and JM Miller, Bioterrorism Readiness Plan: A Template for Healthcare Facilities. Association of Professionals in Infection Control [APIC] and the BT Group in the CDC. April 1999, pp. 27–29.
121. DA Henderson, TV Inglesby, JG Bartlett, MS Ascher, E Eitzen, PB Jahrling, J Hauer, M Layton, J McDade, MT Osterholm, T O'Toole, G Parker, T Perl, PK Russell, and K Tonat. Consensus Statement: Smallpox as a biological weapon; medical and public health management. *JAMA* 281(22): 2127–2137, June 9, 1999.
122. CDC (Centers for Disease Control and Prevention). Vaccinia [Smallpox] Vaccine, Recommendations of the Advisory Committee on Immunization Practices [ACIP]. *MMWR* 50(RR-10), June 22, 2001.
123. RE Hoffman and JE Norton. Lessons learned from a full-scale bioterrorism exercise. *Emerging Infectious Diseases*, 6:6, November–December 2000. «http://www.cdc.gov/ncidod/eid/vol6no6/hoffman.html» accessed 12/1/00.
124. T O'Toole and T Inglesby. Shining light on Dark Winter, *Biodefense Quarterly* 3:2, Autumn 2001. «http://www.hopkinsbiodefense.org/darkwinter.html» accessed 1/7/02.
125. Dark Winter Exercise Script. «http://www.hopkins-biodefense.org» accessed 1/14/02.
126. Congressman C. Shays. Combating terrorism: In search of strategy, priorities and leadership. National Governors Association Conference, July 2001. *Homeland Security Newsletter*. «http://homelandsecurity.org/bulletin/currentbulletin.html» accessed 7/20/01.
127. MT Osterholm and J Schwartz. *Living Terrors, What America Needs to Know to Survive the Coming Bioterrorist Catastrophe*. New York: Delacorte Press, 2000, pp. 159–161.
128. RA Falkenrath, RD Newman, and BA Thayer. *America's Achilles' Heel: Nuclear, Biological and Chemical Terrorism and Covert Attack*. Cambridge, MA: The MIT Press, 1998, p. 155.
129. AF Kaufman, MI Meltzer, and GP Schmid. The economic impact of a bioterrorist attack: Are prevention and postattack intervention programs justifiable? *Emerging Infectious Diseases* 3(2): 12, 1–17, April–June 1997. «http://www.cdc/gov/EID/vol3no2/kaufman.htm» accessed 8/5/98.
130. GAO (General Accounting Office) Report to Congressional Committees. Bioterrorism, Federal Research and Preparedness Activities. GAO-01-915, September 2001, pp. 40–41.
131. GAO (General Accounting Office) Report to Congressional Committees. Bioterrorism, Federal Research and Preparedness Activities. GAO-01-915, September 2001, p. 74.
132. GAO (General Accounting Office) Report to Congressional Committees. Bioterrorism, Federal Research and Preparedness Activities. GAO-01-915, September 2001, p. 42.
133. Committee on R&D Needs for Improving Civilian Medical Response to Chemical and Biological Terrorism Incident, Institute of Medicine, *Clinical & Biological Terrorism Research Development to Improve Civilian Medical Response*. Washington, DC: National Academy Press, 1999, pp. 65–66. «http://books.nap.edu/books/0309061954/html/65.html» accessed 1/8/02.
134. RA Falkenrath, RD Newman, and BA Thayer. *America's Achilles' Heel: Nuclear, Biological and Chemical Terrorism and Covert Attack*. Cambridge, MA: The MIT Press, 1998, p. 154.
135. P Quinlisk. Testimony before the Subcommittee on National Security, Veterans Affairs, and International Relations, Committee on Government Reform, U.S. House of Representatives. July 23, 2001. «http://www.house.gov/reform/ns/107th_testimony/council_of_state_and_territorial.htm» accessed 7/27/01.
136. SG Stolberg and J Miller. Bioterror role an uneasy fit for disease centers. *New York Times*, November 11, 2001, front page.
137. L Garrett. *The Coming Plague, Newly Emerging Diseases in a World out of Balance*. New York: Farrar, Straus & Giroux, 1994, pp. 592–620.
138. *ProMED* Web site: «http://www.isid.org/isid/index.html» accessed 6/29/01.
139. *Emerging Infectious Diseases* Website: «http://www/idsociety.org/EIN/TOC.htm» accessed 1/7/02.
140. Preslar. Animal disease surveillance project: Recent advances. *Journal of Federation of American Scientists* 53(5): 15, September–October 2000.

141. E Smithson, Prepared statement before the Senate Committee on Governmental Affairs Subcommittee on International Security, Proliferation and Federal Services, October 17, 2001, p. 5.

142. WR MacKenzie, NJ Hoxie, ME Proctor, MS Gradus, KA Blair, DE Peterson, JJ Kazmierczak, DG Addiss, KR Fox, JB Rose, and JP Davis. A massive outbreak in Milwaukee of cryptosporidium infection transmitted through the public water supply. *New England Journal of Medicine* 331:3, July 21, 1994.

143. GAO (General Accounting Office) Report to the Chairman, Committee on Agriculture, Nutrition, and Forestry, U.S. Senate. Food Safety: CDC is working to address limitations in several of its foodborne disease surveillance systems. GAO-01-973, September 2001, p. 7. *Homeland Security Newsletter.* «http://homelandsecurity.org/bulletin/current bulletin.html» accessed 10/12/01.

144. M Moodie, J Ban, C Manzi, MJ Powers, J Jaworski, S Kishinchand, and R Wyman. Bioterrorism in the United States: Threat, Preparedness, and Response. Chemical and Biological Arms Control Institute. 2001, pp. 40–42. «http://www.cbaci.org» accessed 1/08/02. *Homeland Security Newsletter.* «http://homelandsecurity.org/bulletin/currentbulletin.htm» accessed 8/30/01.

145. L Gaunt and SE Kornguth. The University of Texas Biological and Chemical Countermeasures Program. *Journal of Homeland Security* September 21, 2001. «http://www.homelandsecurity.org/journal/SciTech/univtexas.cfm» accessed 9/21/01.

146. V Jormanainen, J Jousimaa, I Kunnamo, and P Ruutu. Physicians' database searches as a tool for early detection of epidemics. *Emerging Infectious Diseases* 7(3): 474–476, May–June, 2001.

147. M Moodie, J Ban, C Manzi, MJ Powers, J Jaworski, S Kishinchand, and R Wyman. Bioterrorism in the United States: Threat, Preparedness, and Response. Chemical and Biological Arms Control Institute. 2001, pp. 37–39, «http://www.cbaci.org» accessed 1/08/02. *Homeland Security Newsletter.* «http://homelandsecurity.org/bulletin/currentbulletin.htm» accessed 8/30/01.

148. JB Rose, A Hug, and EK Lipp. Health, climate and infectious disease: A global perspective. American Academy of Microbiology, 2001, p. 1. «http://www.asmusa.org/acasrc/pdfs/climate2.pdf» accessed 1/7/02.

149. L Garrett. *The Coming Plague, Newly Emerging Diseases in a World out of Balance.* New York: Farrar, Straus & Giroux, 1994, pp. 528–549.

150. M Moodie, J Ban, C Manzi, MJ Powers, J Jaworski, S Kishinchand, and R Wyman. Bioterrorism in the United States: Threat, Preparedness, and Response. Chemical and Biological Arms Control Institute. 2001, pp. 61–64. «http://www.cbaci.org» accessed 1/08/02. *Homeland Security Newsletter.* «http://homelandsecurity.org/bulletin/currentbulletin.htm» accessed 8/3/01.

151. L Garrett. *The Coming Plague, Newly Emerging Diseases in a World out of Balance.* New York: Farrar, Straus & Giroux, 1994, p. 605.

152. M Moodie, J Ban, C Manzi, MJ Powers, J Jaworski, S Kishinchand, and R Wyman. Bioterrorism in the United States: Threat, Preparedness, and Response. Chemical and Biological Arms Control Institute. 2001, p. 64, «http://www.cbaci.org» accessed 1/08/02. *Homeland Security Newsletter.* «http://homelandsecurity.org/bulletin/currentbulletin.htm» accessed 8/3/01.

153. GAO (General Accounting Office) Report to Congressional Committees. Bioterrorism, Federal Research and Preparedness Activities. GAO-01-915, September 2001, p. 53.

154. NDPO/DOD, Criminal and Epidemiological Investigation Report. Held on January 19–21, 2000. DTIC SBCCOM Biological Wartime Improved Response Program, December 2000.

155. M Whelis. Investigating disease outbreaks under a protocol to the biological and toxin weapons convention. *Emerging Infectious Diseases* 6:6, November–December 2000. «http://www.cdc.gov/ncidod/EID/vol6no6/wheelisohtm» accessed 11/20/00.

156. GAO (General Accounting Office) Report to Congressional Committees. Bioterrorism, Federal Research and Preparedness Activities. GAO-01-915, September 2001, pp. 70–71.

157. GAO (General Accounting Office) Report to Congressional Committees. Bioterrorism, Federal Research and Preparedness Activities. GAO-01-915, September 2001, p. 60.

158. JW Snyder and W Check. Bioterrorism threats to our future; the role of the clinical microbiology laboratory in detection, identification, and confirmation of biological agents. American Academy of Microbiology and the American College of Microbiology. 2001, p. 11. *Homeland Security Newsletter.* «http://www.homelandsecurity.org/bulletin/current_bulletin.htm» accessed 8/17/01.

159. JW Snyder and W Check. Bioterrorism threats to our future; the role of the clinical microbiology laboratory in detection, identification, and confirmation of biological agents, American Academy of Microbiology and the American College of Microbiology. 2001, p. 6. *Homeland Security Newsletter.* <<http://www.homelandsecurity.org/bulletin/current_bulletin.htm>> accessed 8/17/01.
160. M Moodie, J Ban, C Manzi, MJ Powers, J Jaworski, S Kishinchand, and R Wyman. Bioterrorism in the United States: Threat, Preparedness, and Response. Chemical and Biological Arms Control Institute. 2001, p. 78. <<http://www.cbaci.org>> accessed 1/08/02. *Homeland Security Newsletter.* <<http://homelandsecurity.org/bulletin/currentbulletin.htm>> accessed 8/3/01.
161. JW Snyder and W Check. Bioterrorism threats to our future; the role of the clinical microbiology laboratory in detection, identification, and confirmation of biological agents, American Academy of Microbiology and the American College of Microbiology, 2001, p. 5. *Homeland Security Newsletter.* <<http://www.homelandsecurity.org/bulletin/current_bulletin.htm>> accessed 8/17/01.
162. GAO (General Accounting Office) Report to Congressional Committees. Bioterrorism, Federal Research and Preparedness Activities. GAO-01-915, September 2001, p. 70.
163. GAO (General Accounting Office) Report to Congressional Committees. Bioterrorism, Federal Research and Preparedness Activities. GAO-01-915, September 2001, p. 43.
164. R Pollack. Commentary—Facing the fragility of health in America. Health Forum, June 2000 <<http://www.healthforum.com/HFPubs/asp/ArticleDiplay.asp/PubID=&ArticleID=15828&Keyword=Work>> accessed 1/7/02.
165. Workforce Supply for Hospitals and Health Systems: Issues and Recommendations Developed by the AHA Strategic Policy Planning Committee—Approved as a Statement of interim positions by the AHA Board of Trustees, January 23, 2001. American Hospital Association. <<http://www.aha.org/workforce/advocacy/WorkforceB0123.asp>> accessed 1/7/02.
166. Patients or Paperwork: The Regulatory Burden Facing America's Hospitals. American Hospital Association. <<http://www.aha.org/ar/Advocacy/paperworkreport/asp>> accessed 1/7/02.
167. M Moodie, J Ban, C Manzi, MJ Powers, J Jaworski, S Kishinchand, and R Wyman. Bioterrorism in the United States: Threat, Preparedness, and Response. Chemical and Biological Arms Control Institute. 2001, p. 174. <<http://www.cbaci.org>> accessed 1/08/02. *Homeland Security Newsletter.* <<http://homelandsecurity.org/bulletin/currentbulletin.htm>> accessed 8/3/01.
168. E. Smithson. Prepared statement before the Senate Committee on Governmental Affairs, Subcommittee on International Security, Proliferation and Federal Services, October 17, 2001, p. 6.
169. M Moodie, J Ban, C Manzi, MJ Powers, J Jaworski, S Kishinchand, and R Wyman. Bioterrorism in the United States: Threat, Preparedness, and Response. Chemical and Biological Arms Control Institute. 2001, p. 101. <<http://www.cbaci.org>> accessed 1/08/02. *Homeland Security Newsletter.* <<http://homelandsecurity.org/bulletin/currentbulletin.htm>> accessed 8/3/01.
170. JD Bentley. Challenges for hospitals, strategic policy planning, American Hospital Association. Presentation at the 2nd National Symposium on Medical and Public Health Response to Bioterrorism: Public Health Emergency & National Security Threat, Washington DC, November 28–29, 2000.
171. JF English, MY Cundiff, JD Malone, JA Pfeiffer, M Bell, L Steele, and JM Miller. Bioterrorism Readiness Plan: A Template for Healthcare Facilities, Association of Professionals in Infection Control [APIC] and the BT Group in the CDC. April 1999.
172. SS Arnon, R Schechter, TV Inglesby, DA Henderson, JG Bartlett, MS Ascher, E Eitzen, AD Fine, J Hauer, M Layton, S Lillibridge, MT Osterholm T O'Toole, G Parker, TM Perl, PK Russell, DL Swerdlow, and K Tonat. Botulinum toxin as a biological weapon, medical and public health management. *JAMA* 285(8): 1059–1070, February 28, 2001.
173. GAO (General Accounting Office) Report to Congressional Committees. Bioterrorism, Federal Research and Preparedness Activities. GAO-01–915, September 2001, p. 48.
174. A Mass Casualty Care Strategy for Biological Terrorism Incidents, Neighborhood Emergency Help Center. Prepared in response to the Nunn-Lugar-Domenici Domestic Preparedness Program by the Department of Defense. May 1, 2001. <<http://www2.sbccom.army.mil/hld/downloads/bwirp/nehcgreenbook.pdf>> accessed 1/7/02.

175. M Moodie, J Ban, C Manzi, MJ Powers, J Jaworski, S Kishinchand, and R Wyman. Bioterrorism in the United States: Threat, Preparedness, and Response. Chemical and Biological Arms Control Institute. 2001, p. xvi. <<http://www.cbaci.org>> accessed 1/08/02. *Homeland Security Newsletter.* <<http://homelandsecurity.org/bulletin/currentbulletin.htm>> accessed 8/3/01.
176. AE Smithson and LA Levy. Ataxia: The Chemical and Biological Terrorism Threat and the U.S. Response. The Henry L. Stimson Center, Report No. 35. October 2000, p. 309. <<http://www.stimson.org/>> accessed 1/8/02.
177. L Hinton. Combating Terrorism: Considerations for Investing Resources in Chemical and Biological Preparedness. Testimony before the Committee on Governmental Affairs, U.S. Senate. GAO-02-162T, October 17, 2001, p. 11. *Homeland Security Newsletter.* <<http://homelandsecurity.org/bulletin/current bulletin.htm>> accessed 10/19/01.
178. GAO. Testimony before the Committee on Veterans' Affairs, House of Representatives. Homeland Security. Need to consider VA's role in strengthening federal preparedness. GAO-02-145T, October 15, 2001, p. 8. *Homeland Security Newsletter.* <<http://homelandsecurity.org/bulletin/currentbulletin.htm>> accessed 10/19/01.
179. RE Hoffman and JE Norton. Lessons learned from a full-scale bioterrorism exercise. *Emerging Infectious Diseases*, 6(6): 2, November–December 2000. <<http://www.cdc.gov/ncidod/eid/vol6no6/hoffman.htm>> accessed 12/1/00.
180. L Hinton. Combating Terrorism: Considerations for Investing Resources in Chemical and Biological Preparedness. Testimony before the Committee on Governmental Affairs, U.S. Senate. GAO-02-162T, October 17, 2001, pp. 9–10. *Homeland Security Newsletter.* <<http://homelandsecurity.org/bulletin/current bulletin.htm>> accessed 10/19/01.
181. GAO (General Accounting Office) Report to Congressional Committees. Bioterrorism, Federal Research and Preparedness Activities. GAO-01-915, September 2001, pp. 62–66.
182. MT Osterholm and J Schwartz. *Living Terrors, What America Needs to Know to Survive the Coming Bioterrorist Catastrophe.* New York: Delacorte Press, 2000, pp. 130–131.
183. M Moodie, J Ban, C Manzi, MJ Powers, J Jaworski, S Kishinchand, and R Wyman. Bioterrorism in the United States: Threat, Preparedness, and Response. Chemical and Biological Arms Control Institute. 2001, pp. 109–110. <<http://www.cbaci.org>> accessed 1/08/02. *Homeland Security Newsletter.* <<http://homelandsecurity.org/bulletin/currentbulletin.htm>> accessed 8/3/01.
184. GAO (General Accounting Office) Report to Congressional Committees. Bioterrorism, Federal Research and Preparedness Activities. GAO-01-915, September 2001, pp. 53–54.
185. GAO (General Accounting Office) Report to Congressional Committees. Bioterrorism, Federal Research and Preparedness Activities. GAO-01-915, September 2001, p. 75.
186. GAO (General Accounting Office) Report to Congressional Committees. Bioterrorism, Federal Research and Preparedness Activities. GAO-01-915, September 2001, pp. 57–58.
187. GAO (General Accounting Office) Report to Congressional Committees. Bioterrorism, Federal Research and Preparedness Activities. GAO-01-915, September 2001, p. 38.
188. CDC (Centers for Disease Control and Prevention). Prevention and control of influenza. *MMWR* 50(Rr-04), April 20, 2001. <<http://www.cdc.gov/mmwr/preview/mmwrhtml/rr5004al.htm>> accessed 1/7/02.
189. CDC (Centers for Disease Control and Prevention). Updated recommendations from the advisory committee on immunization practices in response to delays in supply of influenza vaccine for the 2000–01 season. *MMWR* 49(39): 888–892, October 6, 2000. <<http://www.cdc.gov/mmwr/preview/mmwrhtml/mm4939a3.htm>> accessed 1/7/02.
190. CDC (Centers for Disease Control and Prevention). Delayed influenza vaccine availability for 2001–02 season and supplemental recommendations of the advisory committee on immunization practices. *MMWR* 50(27): 582–585, July 13, 2001. <<http://www.cdc.gov/mmwr/preview/mmwrhtml/mm5027a3.htm>> accessed 1/7/02.
191. U.S. Dept. of Justice, Office of Justice Programs, Office for Victims of Crime. Responding to Terrorism Victims: Oklahoma City and Beyond. October 2000, NCJ 183949, p. 31.
192. U.S. Dept. of Justice, Office of Justice Programs, Office for Victims of Crime. Responding to Terrorism Victims: Oklahoma City and Beyond. October 2000, NCJ 183949, p. 32.

193. CS North. The course of post-traumatic stress disorder after the Oklahoma City bombing. Proceedings of the International Conference on the Operational Impact of Psychological Casualties from Weapons of Mass Destruction, Bethesda, MD, July 25–27, 2000. *Military Medicine* Suppl. 166(12): 51, December 2001.
194. S Noy. Prevalence of psychological, somatic, and conduct, casualties in war. Proceedings of the International Conference on the Operational Impact of Psychological Casualties from Weapons of Mass Destruction, Bethesda, MD, July 25–27, 2000. *Military Medicine* Suppl. 166(12): 31–32, December 2001.
195. RH Pastel. Collective behaviors: Mass panic and outbreaks of multiple unexplained symptoms. Proceedings of the International Conference on the Operational Impact of Psychological Casualties from Weapons of Mass Destruction, Bethesda, MD, July 25–27, 2000. *Military Medicine*, Suppl. 166(12): 44–45, December 2001.
196. JA Romano and JM King. Psychological casualties resulting from chemical and biological weapons. Proceedings of the International Conference on the Operational Impact of Psychological Casualties from Weapons of Mass Destruction, Bethesda, MD, July 25–27, 2000. *Military Medicine* Suppl. 166(12): 21–22, December 2001.
197. EJ Lord. Exercises involving an act of biological or chemical terrorism: What are the psychological consequences? Proceedings of the International Conference on the Operational Impact of Psychological Casualties from Weapons of Mass Destruction, Bethesda, MD, July 25–27, 2000. *Military Medicine*, Suppl. 166(12): 34–35, December 2001.
198. N Kawana, S Ishimatsu, and K Kanda. Psycho-physiological effects of the terrorist sarin attack on the Tokyo subway system. Proceedings of the International Conference on the Operational Impact of Psychological Casualties from Weapons of Mass Destruction, Bethesda, MD, July 25–27, 2000. *Military Medicine*, Suppl. 166(12): 23–26, December 2001.
199. CS North. The course of post-traumatic stress disorder. Proceedings of the International Conference on the Operational Impact of Psychological Casualties from Weapons of Mass Destruction, Bethesda, MD, July 25–27, 2000. *Military Medicine*, Suppl. (12): 51–52, December 2001.
200. Committee on R&D Needs for Improving Civilian Medical Response to Chemical and Biological Terrorism Incident, Institute of Medicine, *Clinical & Biological Terrorism Research and Development to Improve Civilian Medical Response*. Washington, DC: National Academy Press, 1999, p. 166.
201. Committee on R&D Needs for Improving Civilian Medical Response to Chemical and Biological Terrorism Incident, Institute of Medicine, *Clinical & Biological Terrorism Research and Development to Improve Civilian Medical Response*. Washington, DC: National Academy Press, 1999, p. 168.
202. Human Behavior and WMD Crisis/Risk Communication Workshop—Final Report. Co-sponsored by Defense Threat Reduction Agency, Federal Bureau of Investigation, U.S. Joint Forces Command. March 2001, p. 27. *Homeland Security Newsletter*. <<http://homelandsecurity.org/bulletin/currentbulletin.htm>> accessed 7/20/01.
203. Human Behavior and WMD Crisis/Risk Communication Workshop—Final Report. Co-sponsored by Defense Threat Reduction Agency, Federal Bureau of Investigation, U.S. Joint Forces Command. March 2001, p. 34. *Homeland Security Newsletter*. <<http://homelandsecurity.org/bulletin/currentbulletin.htm>> accessed 7/20/01.
204. C Di Giovanni. Pertinent psychological issues in the immediate management of a weapons of mass destruction event. Proceedings of the International Conference on the Operational Impact of Psychological Casualties from Weapons of Mass Destruction, Bethesda, MD, July 25–27, 2000. *Military Medicine*, Suppl. 166(12): 59–60, December 2001.
205. U.S. Dept. of Justice, Office of Justice Programs, Office for Victims of Crime. Responding to Terrorism Victims: Oklahoma City and Beyond. Oct 2000, NCJ 183949, p. 30.
206. GAO (General Accounting Office) Report to Congressional Committees. Bioterrorism, Federal Research and Preparedness Activities. GAO-01-915, September 2001, p. 69.
207. U.S. Department of Health & Human Services, Disaster Mental Health, Substance Abuse and Mental Health Services Administration: The Center for Mental Health Services. <<http://www.mentalhealth.org/cmhs/EmergencyServices/default.asp>> accessed 1/7/02.

208. M Moodie, J Ban, C Manzi, MJ Powers, J Jaworski, S Kishinchand, and R Wyman. Bioterrorism in the United States: Threat, Preparedness, and Response. Chemical and Biological Arms Control Institute. 2001, pp. 135–142, <<http://www.cbaci.org>> accessed 1/08/02. *Homeland Security Newsletter.* <<http://homelandsecurity.org/bulletin/currentbulletin.htm>> accessed 8/3/01.
209. GAO. Testimony before the Committee on Veterans' Affairs, House of Representatives. Homeland Security. Need to consider VA's role in strengthening federal preparedness. GAO-02-145T, October 15, 2001, p. 11. *Homeland Security Newsletter.* <<http://homelandsecurity.org/bulletin/currentbulletin.htm>> accessed 10/19/01.
210. C Quigley. Dual-edged sword: Dealing with the media before, during, and after a weapon of mass destruction event. Proceedings of the International Conference on the Operational Impact of Psychological Casualties from Weapons of Mass Destruction, Bethesda, MD, July 25–27, 2000. *Military Medicine*, Suppl. 166(12): 56–58, December 2001.
211. Human Behavior and WMD Crisis/Risk Communication Workshop—Final Report. Co-sponsored by Defense Threat Reduction Agency, Federal Bureau of Investigation, U.S. Joint Forces Command. March 2001. *Homeland Security Newsletter.* <<http://homelandsecurity.org/bulletin/currentbulletin.html>> accessed 7/20/01.
212. B Roberts. *Hype or Reality? The "New Terrorism" and Mass Casualty Attacks.* Alexandria, VA: Chemical & Biological Arms Control Institute, 2000, p. 260.
213. Developing Objectives, Content and Competencies for the Training of Emergency Medical Technicians, Emergency Physicians, and Emergency Nurses to Care for Casualties Resulting from Nuclear, Biological, or Chemical Incidents, Final Report, April 2001. Office of Emergency Preparedness and American College of Emergency Physicians. JHS July 2001.
214. E Smithson. Prepared statement before the Senate Committee on Governmental Affairs Subcommittee on International Security, Proliferation and Federal Services. October 17, 2001, pp. 4–5.
215. GAO (General Accounting Office) Report to Congressional Committees. Bioterrorism, Federal Research and Preparedness Activities. GAO-01-915, September 2001, pp. 67–68.
216. GAO (General Accounting Office) Report to Congressional Committees. Bioterrorism, Federal Research and Preparedness Activities. GAO-01-915, September 2001, pp. 39–45.
217. GAO (General Accounting Office) Report to Congressional Committees. Bioterrorism, Federal Research and Preparedness Activities. GAO-01-915, September 2001, pp. 78–80.
218. GAO (General Accounting Office) Report to Congressional Committees. Bioterrorism, Federal Research and Preparedness Activities. GAO-01-915, September 2001, pp. 65–66.
219. M Moodie, J Ban, C Manzi, MJ Powers, J Jaworski, S Kishinchand, and R Wyman. Bioterrorism in the United States: Threat, Preparedness, and Response. Chemical and Biological Arms Control Institute. 2001, pp. 160–161. <<http://www.cbaci.org>> accessed 1/08/02. *Homeland Security Newsletter.* <<http://homelandsecurity.org/bulletin/currentbulletin.htm>> accessed 8/3/01.
220. GAO (General Accounting Office) Report to Congressional Committees. Bioterrorism, Federal Research and Preparedness Activities. GAO-01-915, September 2001, pp. 67–69.
221. GAO (General Accounting Office) Report to Congressional Committees. Bioterrorism, Federal Research and Preparedness Activities. GAO-01-915, September 2001, p. 49.
222. GAO (General Accounting Office) Report to Congressional Committees. Bioterrorism, Federal Research and Preparedness Activities. GAO-01-915, September 2001, p. 62.
223. S Noy. Prevalence of psychological, somatic and conduct casualties in war. Proceedings of the International Conference on the Operational Impact of Psychological Casualties from Weapons of Mass Destruction, Bethesda, MD, July 25–27, 2000. *Military Medicine*, Suppl. 166(12): 31–32, December 2001.
224. Human Behavior and WMD Crisis/Risk Communication Workshop—Final Report. Co-sponsored by Defense Threat Reduction Agency, Federal Bureau of Investigation, U.S. Joint Forces Command. March 2001, pp. 49–50. *Homeland Security Newsletter.* <<http://homelandsecurity.org/bulletin/current bulletin.htm>> accessed 7/20/01.
225. M Dobbs. A renaissance for U.S. civil defense? *Journal of Homeland Security*, July 2001, p. 6. <<http://www.homelandsecurity.org/journal/Articles/Dobbs_July01.html>> accessed 7/06/01.

226. JP Revel. Meeting psychological needs after Chernobyl: The Red Cross experience. Proceedings of the International Conference on the Operational Impact of Psychological Casualties from Weapons of Mass Destruction, Bethesda, MD, July 25–27, 2000. *Military Medicine*, Suppl. 166(12): 19–20, December 2001.
227. U.S. Dept. of Justice, Office of Justice Programs, Office for Victims of Crime. Responding to Terrorism Victims: Oklahoma City and Beyond. October 2000, NCJ 183949, p. 33.
228. Protecting the Homeland, Report of the Defense Science Board, 2000 Summer Study Executive Summary. Office of the Undersecretary of Defense for Acquisition, Technology, and Logistics. Vol. 1, pp. 13–14. *Homeland Security Newsletter*. «http://homelandsecurity.org/bulletin/currentbulletin.htm» accessed 5/18/01.
229. L Hinton. Combating Terrorism: Considerations for Investing Resources in Chemical and Biological Preparedness. Testimony before the Committee on Governmental Affairs, U.S. Senate. GAO-02-162T, October 17, 2001, p. 11. *Homeland Security Newsletter*. «http://homelandsecurity.org/bulletin/currentbulletin.htm» accessed 10/19/01.
230. Human Behavior and WMD Crisis/Risk Communication Workshop—Final Report. Co-sponsored by Defense Threat Reduction Agency, Federal Bureau of Investigation, U.S. Joint Forces Command. March 2001, p. 14. *Homeland Security Newsletter*. «http://homelandsecurity.org/bulletin/currentbulletin.htm» accessed 7/20/01.
231. GAO (General Accounting Office) Report to Congressional Committees. Bioterrorism, Federal Research and Preparedness Activities. GAO-01-915, September 2001, pp. 46–47.
232. GAO (General Accounting Office) Report to Congressional Committees. Bioterrorism, Federal Research and Preparedness Activities. GAO-01-915, September 2001, pp. 42–43.
233. GAO (General Accounting Office) Report to Congressional Committees. Bioterrorism, Federal Research and Preparedness Activities. GAO-01-915, September 2001, p. 68.
234. RA Falkenrath, RD Newman, and BA Thayer. *America's Achilles' Heel: Nuclear, Biological and Chemical Terrorism and Covert Attack*. Cambridge, MA: The MIT Press, 1998, p. 312.
235. GAO (General Accounting Office) Report to Congressional Committees. Bioterrorism, Federal Research and Preparedness Activities. GAO-01-915, September 2001, pp. 60–62.
236. CDC (Centers for Disease Control and Prevention). Use of anthrax vaccine in the United States: Recommendations of the Advisory Committee on Immunization Practices. *MMWR* 49(RR-15): 14, December 15, 2000.
237. S Block. The growing threat of biological weapons. *American Scientist*, 89(1): 6–7, January 4, 2001. «http://www.sigmaxi.org/amsci/articles/olarticles/bloclpl.html» accessed 01/04/01.
238. J Woodall. The vaccines for peace proposal, motivating the production of vaccines against dual-threat agents. Sabin Vaccine Report IV-2, Fall 2001, p. 6.
239. S Flanders. In the shadow of AIDS, a world of other problems. *The New York Times*, June 24, 2001.
240. Poverty and sickness; terrorism is not the only scourge. *The Economist*, 351:8253, December 22, 2001, p. 10.
241. GAO (General Accounting Office) Report to Congressional Committees. Bioterrorism, Federal Research and Preparedness Activities. GAO-01-915, September 2001, pp. 61–62.
242. GAO (General Accounting Office) Report to Congressional Committees. Bioterrorism, Federal Research and Preparedness Activities. GAO-01-915, September 2001, pp. 54–58.
243. GAO (General Accounting Office) Report to Congressional Committees. Bioterrorism, Federal Research and Preparedness Activities. GAO-01-915, September 2001, pp. 56–57.
244. T Mangold and J Goldberg. *Plague Wars, the Terrifying Reality of Biological Warfare*. New York: St. Martin's Press, 1999, p. 373.
245. B Roberts. *Hype or Reality? The "New Terrorism" and Mass Casualty Attacks*. Alexandria, VA: Chemical & Biological Arms Control Institute, 2000, p. 196.
246. Inside the Soviet Union's Biowarfare Program: Interviews with Dr. Ken Alibek and Dr. Sergei Popov. *Journal of Homeland Security* 01(01): 22–24, June 2001.
247. J Miller, S Engelberg, and W Beard. *GERMS, Biological Weapons and America's Secret War*. New York: Simon & Schuster, 2001, p. 310.
248. CDC (Centers for Disease Control and Prevention). Legionnaires disease—United States. *MMWR* 26: 300, 1997. «http://www.cdc.gov/mmwr/PDF/wk/mm4603.pdf» accessed 1/7/03.

249. L Garrett. *The Coming Plague, Newly Emerging Diseases in a World out of Balance*. New York: Farrar, Straus & Giroux, 1994, pp. 528–549.
250. CM Fraser and MR Dando. Genomics and future biological weapons: The need for preventive action by the biomedical community. *Nature Genetics* Published online October 22, 2001. DOI: 10.1038/ng 763. p. 17.
251. GAO (General Accounting Office) Report to Congressional Committees. Bioterrorism, Federal Research and Preparedness Activities. GAO-01-915, September 2001, p. 61.

Chapter 11

Agroterrorism: Agroeconomic Bioterrorism

Keith A. Hickey

CONTENTS

Introduction 234
Agroeconomic Systems and Vulnerabilities 235
    Point Attacks on the Food Supply Chain 235
    Distributed Attacks on the Agroeconomic System 236
    Descriptions of the Plant/Animal Disease Process 236
Psychological and Economic Terrorism 237
    The Psychology of Terrorism and the Terrorist 237
    Economic Terrorism 238
Agroeconomic Protection and Response Hierarchy 239
Technologies in Agroeconomic Terrorism Planning and Response 241
    Bioterrorism Detection and Analysis 241
    Geographic Information Systems and Remote Sensing Technology 241
    Time Series Analysis and Risk Assessments 243
    Bioterrorism Response Modeling and Bioinformatics 244
Conclusions 245
Case Study 1: Genetically Modified Organisms 246
Case Study 2: Hoof and Mouth Disease 247
References 249
Bibliography 250

Introduction

Agroeconomic bioterrorism is bioterrorism conducted against economic and agricultural commodities such as animals/livestock, food crops and other derivative products and systems (e.g., cotton, wool, leather, milk, wood, food distribution systems, etc.). Because the attacks are not conducted against people directly, the inevitable effects are economic damage that requires a widespread geographical consideration. Society cares about 100 people, but it does not care about 100 animals, 100 trees, 100 food plants, and the like. Agroeconomic targets are systems involving complexity and are widespread in scope. Local (focal) or point attacks can cause significant economic damage, primarily through psychological or societal reactions to the perception of risk and danger. Distributed (or multifocal) attacks on the agroeconomic base of food crops or animal livestock require both similar and significantly different considerations than do bioterrorism or biowarfare directed at people. The response to agroeconomic bioterrorism is, by necessity, multidisciplinary involving

- Spatial–temporal analysis of relationships (systems theory, operations research, and spatial econometrics)
- Environmental biophysics for the physical propagation of toxins and pathogens in water, dust, or air (soil science, hydrogeology, aerosol microphysics, and meteorology)
- Epidemiology and disease propagation modeling (plant pathology, veterinary medicine, entomology, and demography)
- Information and communication systems (geographical information systems, common databases, communication, and reporting networks or pathways)

The U.S. agroeconomic system has a dedicated system of expert and professional response to naturally occurring plant and animal diseases and pests known as the Animal and Plant Health Inspection Service (APHIS) of the United States Department of Agriculture (USDA). Specialized research capabilities are available through the USDA Agricultural Research Service (ARS). Bioterrorism and biowarfare against agroeconomic systems would activate these teams to respond in a manner similar to naturally occurring outbreaks. In fact, often the difficulty is in recognizing a deliberate attack and the identity of the attacker as opposed to a spontaneous outbreak. The teams of the APHIS are highly trained and are experienced with responding to naturally occurring threats to the agroeconomic system. "The Veterinary Services (VS) unit has an Emergency Programs staff which coordinates efforts to prepare for and respond to outbreaks of exotic animal diseases. The staff is assisted in its efforts by Federal and State field veterinarians, animal health technicians, and disease specialists" (APHIS Web page: www.aphis.usda.gov). In addition, the National Animal Health Reporting System (NAHRS) is a joint effort of the U.S. Animal Health Association (USAHA), the American Association of Veterinary Laboratory Diagnosticians (AAVLD), and the USDA APHIS. The NAHRS is voluntary and considered to be one part of a comprehensive, integrated animal health surveillance system in the United States.

Similarly, the Plant Protection and Quarantine (PPQ) unit of APHIS has the responsibility regarding outbreaks of plant diseases. "The American plant safeguarding system is focused on preventing the entry and establishment of invasive plant pests in the form of insects, plant diseases, noxious weeds, and other injurious organisms" (Safeguarding American Plant Resources, USDA-APHIS-PPQ July 1, 1999).

As opposed to accidental invasions, the intentional introductions of exotic invasive species may differ in the following ways: (1) use of nontraditional pathways, (2) increase of the probability of survival of the pest in-transit, (3) widespread dissemination of the disease from disparate foci, (4) use of highly virulent strains, (5) high rates of inoculums, (6) introduction into remote areas, (7) targeting of susceptible natural environments, (8) release of multiple species simultaneously, and (9) precise timing of releases to coincide with maximal colonization potential [1].

In addition to foreign terrorists or enemies, who are interested in the destruction or economic disruption of the United States, there are dedicated domestic ecoterrorist groups such as the Animal Liberation Front (ALF) and the Earth Liberation Front (ELF) whose principle call to arms, and agenda is the disruption of the U.S. agribusiness system. Predominantly, these groups are anticapitalist and anarchist, and their primary aims are to target the economy and attack corporate property. In general, with exceptions, they do not advocate direct violence toward people. For a further discussion, see "Psychological and economic terrorism" section as well as the two case studies "Genetically modified organisms" and "Hoof and mouth disease."

"Since the September 11, 2001 attacks, all USDA personnel at U.S. at ports of entry, food inspection facilities, and research labs and buildings, are currently on a heightened state of alert. At ports of entry, personnel are conducting intensified product and cargo inspections of travelers and baggage to prevent the entry of animal or plant pests and diseases." "We are examining our responsibilities—looking at our short and long term needs to ensure USDA continues to protect America's food supply and agriculture against pests and disease of any kind," says Agriculture Secretary Ann M. Veneman. "We stand ready—and are making sure that we are prepared, coordinated, and able to respond should we ever face an emergency" ("Agricultural Biosecurity," USDA Q&As 10/25/01).

This heightened awareness of the dangers of agroterrorism has facilitated cooperative efforts between various government agencies. It has been recognized that the U.S. agricultural infrastructure is extremely vulnerable to a terrorist attack by a biological weapon [2]. The 9/11 Commission Report emphasized the failures of organization and communication when dealing with a terrorist threat. The USDA, Department of Health and Human Services, Food and Drug Administration (FDA), the Department of Homeland Security (DHS), and the Federal Bureau of Investigation (FBI) through the Strategic Partnership Program Agroterrorism (SPPA) initiated cooperation with the states and the private sector to protect agricultural commodities and the nation's food supply from terrorist threats (Release No. 0279.05 July 26, 2005 USDA: www.usda.gov). This initiative provides for vulnerability assessments of critical infrastructure and key resources to facilitate prevention, surveillance, communication, emergency response, and recovery efforts.

"The feasibility of an agroeconomic attack hinges on three factors" [2]:

1. The technical ability to acquire and deploy a bioagent.
2. An interest in sickening or killing animals or crops as a means to its goal.
3. A desire to do so using the bioagent.

Agroeconomic Systems and Vulnerabilities

Point Attacks on the Food Supply Chain

Attacks on the food supply chain can be from many sources including poisons, toxins, or contaminants of a biological, chemical, or radiological nature. Point attacks on centralized facilities involve considerations of access and biosecurity. Crop-dusting planes as dispersal units of biological or chemical agents, insertion of cyanide into drugs such as Tylenol, contaminating food-processing plants, and anthrax-contaminated letters are examples of point attack vulnerabilities. Surveillance and inspections, access control, sophisticated packaging, automated handling systems, food and mail irradiation to kill microbes, and other local biosecurity measures [3] to prevent security breaches and the introduction and movement of infectious diseases or toxins can reduce the risk of point attacks.

Distributed Attacks on the Agroeconomic System

In contrast, distributed attacks on the agroeconomic system would not typically involve chemical or radiological contaminants because of dispersal issues for large areas. Biological agents would be the terrorist weapon of choice to cause a widespread economic disruption. Biosecurity involving access control becomes difficult and impossible to implement because of the size and the scope of the agribusiness industry, that is primarily conducted in rural areas. Given the difficulty in implementing security, a widespread attack, especially in food crops, is not as easy to conduct as it would appear because of the natural barriers in crop disease propagation, and the rapid response and disease containment provided by plant pathologists in commercial crops, and animal health inspectors and veterinarians in commercial livestock.

"It has been known for a long time that many naturally occurring microorganisms and toxins are potential biological weapons against people, and crops with many examples of deliberate infections or infestations including rinderpest virus in cattle, glanders and anthrax in horses, African swine fever virus and the Colorado potato beetle" [1]. Plant diseases as bioweapons such as rusts, blight, smuts, and the like were also heavily studied in the former Soviet Union, as were easily transmissible animal diseases such as hoof and mouth disease, rinderpest, and African swine fever. As many as 10,000 Soviet bioweapons researchers at the Soviet Union's Biopreparat were working solely on antiagricultural bioweapons projects [1]. The New York Academy of Sciences [1] has the most complete detailed survey of potential bioterrorist threats against the United States and the world agricultural systems.

A tool used to assess the vulnerabilities within a system or infrastructure to an attack is the CARVER plus Shock method (FDA—An Overview of the Carver plus Shock Method for Food Sector Vulnerability Assessments, 7-18-07). CARVER is an acronym for a set of attributes used to evaluate the attractiveness of a target for an attack along with the seventh attribute for the modified Shock attributes of a target. These attributes are

Criticality—measure of the public health and economic impacts of an attack
Accessibility—ability to physically access and egress from the target
Recuperability—ability of a system to recover from an attack
Vulnerability—ease of accomplishing the attack
Effect—amount of direct loss from an attack as measured by a loss in production
Recognizability—ease of identifying the target
Shock—combined heath, economic and psychological impacts of an attack

Federal agencies, such as the Food and Safety and Inspection Service (FSIS) and the Food and Drug Administration (FDA), have used this method to evaluate the potential vulnerabilities of farm-to-table supply chains of various food commodities. The method can also be used to assess the potential vulnerabilities of individual facilities or processes.

Descriptions of the Plant/Animal Disease Process

Plant pathology is the study of plant disease. Veterinary medicine is similarly related to the study of animal disease. "Disease is the result of a dynamic interaction between an organism (plant, animal, or human) and its environment. This interaction results in abnormal physiological and often morphological or neurological changes in the organism. The expression of a disease by a host is called a symptom. The actual visualization of the pathogen is called a sign. Signs and symptoms relate to the presence of a disease. One characteristic that all symptoms share is that some aberrant function, growth pattern, or physiological dysfunction affects the well-being of the organism. Therefore, disease may occur at any level of organization within an organism.

There are four elements in the propagation of disease—a susceptible host, a virulent pathogen, a favorable environment, and the amount of time under consideration. Most disease problems are caused by biotic pathogens or living agents. These agents include viruses, mycoplasmas, bacteria, fungi, protozoa, nematodes, and parasites. The term environment is general and includes obvious factors such as temperature and moisture as well as interactions between the pathogens and other competing microorganisms (the biological environment). The cause of disease need not be restricted to infectious agents, such as viruses, bacteria or fungi, but may also be caused or enabled by nutritional or genetic disorders (Wyllie, Thomas D., Plant Pathology Course Notes, University of Missouri-Columbia, 1995). In the case of bioterrorism against commercial plants and animals, the health status and environmental conditions of the organism involved radically affect the degree of success of the bioattack.

Psychological and Economic Terrorism

The Psychology of Terrorism and the Terrorist

The psychology of agroeconomic bioterrorism has some significant differences from the psychology of either warfare or the use of weapons of mass destruction in terrorist attacks against human targets. While all terrorism attacks are short-term tactical missions against limited targets conducted with a longer range strategic goal of government destabilization or motivating societal or policy changes, agroeconomic bioterrorism can instill the same desired fear, panic, and the loss of confidence without the direct loss of human life. In fact, the long-term effects and psychological damage inflicted by an agroeconomic attack might be significantly greater because of long lasting and more widely distributed economic hardships without the natural national anger and a sense of purpose often generated by the loss of human life.

An early example of agroeconomic warfare was demonstrated in the classic Peloponnesian War between Athens and Sparta. During the initial phases (431–425 BC), the Spartans used a ravaging war against the Athenian land to draw out the Athenians from their walls into pitched battle. Ravaging crops, especially the permanent olive trees and grape vines, was a psychological and economic attack and an affront to the spiritual and religious life of the Greek polis. However, the reality of the farmland devastation by the Spartans proved to be more difficult in practice than in symbolism, and their hopes for a quick and decisive war were dashed [4].

The only effective antidote to the psychological effects of bioterrorism is knowledge through familiarization, education and training, and the perception, confidence, and reality of governmental expertise and ability to deter future attacks and restore the country to health and normalcy in a reasonable time frame. The psychological effects of terrorism are the perceived loss of power and control by both the individual and the government to protect themselves.

"Because it is effective and cheap (and sponsorship can be disguised or denied), terrorism increasingly will be a weapon of choice for extremists and rogue states. Whereas politically motivated terrorism appears to be in decline, terrorism carried out in the name of religion is increasingly ascendant. Religious zealots exhibit few self-imposed constraints" [1]. Ecoterrorism is a form of religious zealotry and extremism with the worship of "Mother Earth."

"Terrorism is an act composed of at least four crucial elements" [5]:

1. An act of violence against plant, animal, or human
2. A motive or goal
3. Perpetuated against innocent persons
4. Staged to be played before an audience whose reaction of fear and terror is the desired result

The categories of persons who commit terrorism are criminals, crusaders, and crazies [6]. The profile of an agroeconomic bioterrorist would likely fall into the crusader category except when done by state-sponsored terrorism. Attacking crops, animals, and economic commodities does not cross the potential barrier to killing humans. Although personal gain could be a motivation, it is much more likely that idealism with a desire for prestige and recognition within a collective cause is the most likely motivation.

An example is the ecoterrorist movement including the Earth Liberation Front (ELF) and Animal Liberation Front (ALF), which over the past decade have conducted many violent and destructive acts including arson and vandalism especially in the states of California, Oregon, and Washington. By destroying property alone, the group regards their work as "nonviolent, direct actions." Acts have been committed against logging, agriculture, affluent homes, and vehicles (SUVs), as well as animal research facilities and researchers.

"The motivations for agroeconomic bioterrorism can include" [2]

1. The profit motive such as commodity speculation.
2. Anti-genetically modified organisms (anti-GMO) or other ecoterrorist extremist idealism.
3. The psychological barrier is often lower when the target is animals, plants, or economic as opposed to the taking of human life.
4. Agricultural targets are "soft targets" with relatively low security, easily attacked with limited financial or technological resources, and it is hard to detect and prosecute the attacker.

Economic Terrorism

Past incidents of large-scale disease outbreaks show the financial impact of an outbreak includes not only the cost of the lost agricultural products, but also the cost of the disrupted trade, and even societal change and instability [2]. "For any fool-proof system, there is a fool who is bigger than the proof" (Edward Teller, 1980, University of Missouri-Columbia College of Engineering Croft Lecture). These words show the basis of insurance in the world of business. Insurance rates are the price of risk as estimated from current assumptions and future predictions of economic conditions, wars, natural disasters, and terrorism. In rapidly changing times and with risk uncertainty, insurance companies will raise their premiums for coverage or will back away from insuring the risk until predictability returns.

Risk to the insurers and liability vulnerability to natural or man-made disasters is spread among the various insurance companies by a process of reinsurance. Terrorist attacks on September 11, 2001 and the following anthrax bioterror attacks have significantly raised the uncertainty of insurance risk estimates leading to upheavals in the property and casualty insurance of businesses and difficulties in the reinsurance industry (Economic Perspectives of Terrorism Insurance May 2002, Chairman Jim Saxton(R-NJ) Joint Economic Committee, U.S. Congress). The U.S. government responded to the needs in terrorism insurance with the Terrorism Risk Insurance Act (TRIA), signed into law on November 26, 2002. It was designed as a temporary measure to allow time for the insurance industry to develop their own solutions and products to insure against acts of terrorism. The Act has been extended under the Terrorism Risk Insurance Program Reauthorization Act through December 31, 2014. TRIA is a U.S. government reinsurance facility to provide reinsurance coverage to insurance companies following a declared terrorism event. In 2007, losses from the act must exceed $100 million to trigger the recovery. The cap on assistance is $100 billion per year.

An early study on the economic impacts of the September 11, 2001 attacks yielded ten tentative conclusions [7]. Relevant conclusions for this presentation included:

- An increased unemployment rate and decreased gross domestic product (GDP) trend.
- Diffusion of the decrease in activity in one sector of the economy (e.g., airline, travel) into other sectors of the economy more rapidly than in past recessions.
- A consumer confidence decline with decreased consumer spending increasing the probability and possible severity of a recession through early 2002, higher oil prices not likely to be a major problem unless military or terrorist actions disrupt oil supplies.
- Increased probability and possible severity of a recession in most other nations, especially major U.S. trading partners, such as Canada and Mexico, as well as the United States.
- Unlikely to have a major impact on agricultural prices in the short run, however, an international recession would reduce the demand for U.S. exports and could result in downward pressure on agricultural prices.
- The United States and other major nations must use lower interest rates, increased government spending, or decreased taxes to encourage economic growth. The effectiveness of lower interest rates may be very limited.

It is clear that acts of terrorism through both actual economic assault and perceptions of risk can have magnified effects throughout the United States and the rest of the world through complex economic relationships of consumer confidence and the global trade and finance markets.

Agroeconomic Protection and Response Hierarchy

"The threat of an agroterrorist attack can be countered on four levels" [2]:

1. At the organism level, through animal or plant disease resistance.
2. At the farm level, through facility management techniques designed to prevent disease introduction or transmission.
3. At the agricultural sector level, through USDA disease and response procedures.
4. At the national level, through policies designed to minimize the social and economic costs of a catastrophic disease outbreak.

Kohnen's paper [2] discusses in depth the threat of agroterrorism and a comprehensive strategy to counter it. "The Office International des Epizooties (OIE), also called the World Organization for Animal Health, is an intergovernmental organization with 155 member countries. The OIE maintains a list of transmissible diseases which have the potential for very serious and rapid spread, irrespective of national borders, which are of a serious socioeconomic or public health consequence and which are of major importance in the international trade of animals and animal products. List A diseases could severely damage the U.S. agricultural market, since an outbreak of one of these diseases is internationally recognized as grounds for export embargo" [2]. An example of a List A animal disease is hoof and mouth disease (HMD).

"Vaccines exist for most of the List A diseases, though they are not generally used except to control an emerging outbreak. Vaccines can keep animals from acquiring diseases, but in most cases they do not keep animals from being carriers. A cow vaccinated against HMD can carry the disease in her throat tissues for two and a half years after exposure. Also, a vaccinated animal cannot be distinguished from an infected one; the titers are the same" [2]. An even more sobering thought is the spread of the HMD into the wildlife population, such as deer, where population numbers have skyrocketed in recent years. An effort to eradicate the disease epidemic in both the commercial livestock bases of pigs, cattle, and sheep as well as the deer population could reach monstrous level. This is why the genetic efforts in vaccine production and vaccine quality is so exciting. Incorporating a vaccine into both a feed plant for animal food-stock and into forage crops for the wildlife would be critical. In addition, it would be beneficial to have a vaccine available where the titers for infected and vaccinated animals could be easily distinguished.

"Comparable to the OIE for animal export guidelines, the International Plant Protection Convention (IPCC) sets international standards for plant export guidelines. The IPCC has 111 member countries, each of which submits its own plant import restrictions" [2]. "Plant pathogen resistance include herbicides, to eliminate weeds, and pesticides, to control insect pests. Virus-resistant plant varieties reduce the need for insect control as a means of stopping virus transmission" [2].

At the farm level there is excitement (and fear) in genetically modified organisms (GMO) or biotech crops. Biotech methods may rapidly create new resistant crops that significantly increase crop yield with a reduced cost in herbicides and pesticides, and without the laborious Mendelian plant breeding initiatives that have previously increased crop yields. Unfortunately, there are concomitant concerns with genetic diversity from the resulting monocultures, food quality, and the like that have led to controversy, both within the agricultural industry between farmers and agribusiness, between countries and with environmental activist groups.

"In animal production at the farm level, intensive farming of livestock animals and broilers is efficient; it allows farmers to raise more animals with fewer resources. The increased density of animals per farm heightens the epidemiological risk. The trend toward larger farms is unlikely to change in the foreseeable future" [2].

"At the sector level, there is the USDA disease detection and response mechanism. The organization and duties of APHIS were previously discussed. A detection/surveillance system using satellite tracking systems (remote sensing) for crop distress is being developed by ARS. By combining various field measurements such as reflectance with Global Positioning System (GPS) information, the system (in reality a Geographic Information System—GIS) can pinpoint problems within fields. This system provides a rapid response and integration of available information concerning crop diseases and crop stress" [2]. The technology and beneficial applications of remote sensing and GIS will be discussed in more detail in a later section.

Similarly, the sector response to animal diseases needs rapid diagnostic capabilities. Some of the state-of-the-art genetic tests and diagnostic detection technologies will be discussed in a later section.

At the national level, the USDA as well as other federal agencies have the responsibility to eliminate the perception of risk as well as the actual risk. The study of perceived risk, and the psychological and public relations implications have a long and interesting history [8,9]. Often, federal "deep pockets" are the most essential elements in rapid eradication of the threat and compensation to the directly economically injured.

Technologies in Agroeconomic Terrorism Planning and Response

Bioterrorism Detection and Analysis

The general identification methods of bioagents from either bioterrorism or biowarfare include [5]

1. Isolation of the etiologic agent by culture (possible in one to two days for some agents)
2. Detection of toxin by mass spectroscopy, animal inoculation, or other methods
3. Antibody detection (specific immunoglobulin M, IgM, may appear within three days)
4. Antigen detection via enzyme immunoassay or other sensitive assay methods
5. Genome detection employing DNA probes
6. Detection of metabolic products of the infectious or toxic agent in clinical specimens

"Detector systems and methodologies are rapidly evolving and represent an area of intense interest within the research and development community. The principal difficulty in detecting or remote sensing of bioagent aerosols stem from differentiating the artificially generated bioagent cloud from the background of organic matter normally present in the atmosphere" [10]. The key problems in laboratory-grade diagnostic detection is the cost, portability, complexity, sensitivity, specificity, and speed of diagnosis. Modern biotechnology approaches have made significant progress in the detection of bioagents.

"Polymerase Chain Reaction (PCR) is a fast, inexpensive technique for making an unlimited number of copies of any piece of DNA. Sometimes called molecular photocopying, PCR has had an immense impact on genetic research. The powerful duplication ability of PCR allows genetic and molecular analysis using small amounts of cells or tissues" [11].

DNA-based computer chips are being developed to detect and identify biological pathogens to begin to address the issues of rapid diagnosis and wide specificity and sensitivity (Moore, Samuel K., Making chips, *IEEE Spectrum* March 2001, pp. 54–60). Sandia National Laboratory in conjunction with Lawrence Livermore National Laboratory have developed a broad-spectrum bioagent detector that is briefcase-sized and emphasizes improved sensitivity, and rapid response time. The microfluidic, chip-based modules use a capillary electrophoresis detector with three analysis trains; DNA amplification to identify bacteria and viruses using PCR; immunoassays to identify bacteria, viruses, and toxins; and protein signatures to identify toxins (BioBriefcase, Sandia Corporation, April 2008).

DNA microarrays are used to study gene activity or expression, and diagnose diseases. Gene expression shows the subset of genes in a cell actively making proteins. These researchers have adapted existing tools—semiconductors, inkjet printers, and flat panel displays—to the manufacture of these DNA microarrays. Active electronic elements in the microarrays are used to manipulate and sense DNA. Microarrays can perform experiments with thousands of genes simultaneously. Bioagent detectors can be based on different technologies including DNA-based detectors, mass spectrometry, antibody-based tests, and sensing of chemicals and bacteria using indicators and synthetic compounds that change state when exposed.

Geographic Information Systems and Remote Sensing Technology

A geographic information system (GIS) is a combination of computer technologies that integrate massive databases of spatial data, and provides a display and query interface for building and analyzing spatial relationships. GIS uses geography and computer-generated maps as an interface for integrating and assessing massive amounts of location-based information [12]. On the ESRI ArcUser site www.esri.com, applications of GIS have been developed for public safety, disease tracking, and emergency response that allows public safety personnel to effectively plan for emergency response, determine mitigation priorities, analyze historical events, and predict future events. GIS can also be used to get critical information to emergency responders upon dispatch or while on route to an incident to assist in tactical planning. Spatial–temporal analysis can improve organizational integration of data and information allowing, better decisions based on time and spatial relationships as well the visualization of data. GIS can manage and portray spatial data for epidemiological modeling of disease diffusion in a susceptible population in space and time, as well as overlaying biometeorology influences of stresses of heat and weather, soil type, topology, and so on [13].

In emergency response situations, quick and accurate information is the key. Moreover, flexible systems are needed to respond to new, unexpected threats. Integrated, comprehensive databases and communication networks are essential. Breakdowns in uniform response and coordination between separate responder units and organizations are the first casualty of information and decision support systems that are not properly designed.

APHIS and the Centers for Epidemiology and Animal Health (CEAH) have the Veterinary Services (VS) Atlas Spatial Data Library, which is a geographic data library to provide geographic data layers that have been processed for immediate use in maps and for spatial analysis. This access to preformatted data will simplify common spatial tasks related to surveillance, epidemiologic investigations, environmental analyses, and emergency response activities. The Center for Animal Disease and Information and Analysis (CADIA) has a link to analysis information with GIS and spatial analysis for geospatial analysis. The actual benefit of the integration of spatial technologies through a GIS is the improved situation awareness from the remote sensing components along with the predictive modeling capabilities and decision support that results from the integration of databases in time and space.

Remote sensing obtains data from a sensor at a distance far away from the measured phenomena. Usually, the data measured from the sensor is from the electromagnetic radiation spectrum either directly, or indirectly, from reflection or reradiation. The electromagnetic spectrum (EM) measurement can include light, thermal (heat), radar, and the like or a combination of the various EM spectrums or bands to provide a multispectral composite image [14,15]. "Remote sensed data can be collected using either passive (only receive a signal) or active (send/receive signals) remote sensing systems. Suborbital (airborne) and satellite remote sensing systems can provide fundamental biological and/or physical (biophysical) information directly, without having to use other surrogate or ancillary data" [15]. Remote sensing imaging capabilities and data processing include image interpretation and analysis, classification methods, morphological function and elevation modeling, and transformational analyses. These biophysical parameters can be used in a site-specific environmental biophysics analysis [16].

Given an environmental dataset geo-referenced in a GIS, spatial statistics can be performed for an understanding of spatial processes and an investigation of the important spatial statistical variable of spatial autocorrelation. Spatial statistics can be used to characterize and identify differences in variables across space and their significance in quantitative geography [17–20]. When observations are irregular in time space, the variogram sample estimator can be used to estimate spatial variance. There is a relation between the variogram and the autocovariance function [17,20]. A good introduction to the concepts and utilization in practice of spatial statistics is given in [18,20].

The integration of physical data obtained from remote sensing systems including GPS within a GIS framework can be critical to advancements in plant breeding field trials evaluating crop yield and resistance. "A central problem confronting a plant breeder when comparing genotypes in a field trial is that the yield of a genotype is markedly affected by the condition, particularly the soil moisture and fertility, of the plot in which the genotype is sown. Comparison problems increase with separation between plots and lead to the conclusion that marked soil variations occur which tend to make adjacent tree or plot yields alike. This has major repercussions in the replication and randomization statistics in agricultural field trials. The non-uniformity of conditions over the trial is sometimes referred to as within-trial heterogeneity or 'fertility' trials. Heterogeneity or fertility trends result in spatial correlation between plots, so a useful statistic for examining the within-trial heterogeneity is the spatial autocorrelation coefficient" [21]. "The main purpose of spatial analysis is to estimate genotypic effects and their standard error of differences. Resulting estimates of genotype effects from spatial analysis to reduce variability showed increased precision as the within-trial heterogeneity increased compared to standard incomplete block analysis" [21].

"For plant breeders, the strength of a GIS system is its capacity to provide information on test locations that can be used in supporting the analysis of genotype × environment interactions. For example, temperature, relative humidity, dew point and dew duration, and wind direction and velocity all have important and direct influences on plant disease epidemiology. Recent insights into the relationship between meteorological conditions and disease intensity allow simulation (using long-term meteorological records) of the intensity and frequency of specific diseases or, in some cases, disease vectors (e.g., insect carriers). Mapping the extent and intensity of crop diseases allows characterization of test locations, as well as production areas. Characterization of production areas assists in the setting of research priorities. A GIS can provide temporal (frequency/intensity) and spatial information supporting research efforts" [21]. Similarly, real-time remote sensing data from satellites is available for input to a GIS for use by natural resource managers such as precision agricultural professionals, who will use the data to more accurately determine what portions of land received precipitation and determine where best to apply agricultural chemicals.

Time Series Analysis and Risk Assessments

Most time critical decisions or strategic predictions are not made in an environment of absolute certainty, but are instead made with incomplete information and involve statistical analysis or estimates of the current state or predicted future state of a system. The National Plant Board (NPB) in its recommendations to the USDA APHIS stated "The pest risk analysis process should be continuously improved, expanded, and implemented. The quest for efficiency and transparency requires development of pest risk analysis models that incorporate and standardize levels of information needed to perform the risk analysis. Cost–Benefit analysis models should be used to incorporate social sciences and economic theory into the risk management process" [22]. Techniques of risk analysis and risk assessment have long been used in the aerospace and nuclear technology industries [23,24]. Preliminary hazards analysis (PHA), event tree analysis (ETA) and fault tree analysis (FTA), and consequence analysis (CA) have been used to identify accident sequences and describe the consequences of the accident.

Specialized environmental risk assessment methodologies have application in the context of bioterrorism risk assessment especially in the environmental transport of diseases and toxins. Previous work has been done in aerosol transport, environmental and food pathway transport of radionuclides, pollution studies, and soil transport of contaminants [25–32].

In addition to the standard risk assessment and analysis, the issues of measurements and estimates made over time and space have been studied in the context of time series analysis. Standard analysis of variance (ANOVA) and regression analysis techniques contained in common statistics packages such as SAS, SPSS, S-PLUS, and the like for providing estimates, and accessing the sources of variability [33] have to be expanded or modified in the case of time series analysis

[17,34]. S-PLUS has built-in time series analysis algorithms as well as being extensible with its built-in matrix processing. SAS and SPSS have routines that perform basic time series analysis, SAS/ETS and SPSS Trends. For the case of multivariate time series analysis, a matrix approach is absolutely necessary [17,34].

For cost–benefit analysis, economic and financial relationships and quantities that vary in space and time and have spatial–temporal correlation are studied in the context of econometric and spatial econometric analysis of time series. Econometrics and spatial econometrics often has some specialized characteristics and assumptions that differ from standard time series analysis [35,36].

Bioterrorism Response Modeling and Bioinformatics

Information quality and uniformity is critical in emergency planning and emergency management response. Different data sources (e.g., data acquisition from satellite sensors such as radar, thermal, GIS, and GPS) often have different datasets measuring some, but not all, of the same parameters and with various degrees of accuracy. Information from various sources both in time and space can be integrated (fused) into a single database with a combined accuracy superior to any one single dataset. This process is called multiple sensor integration (MSI) or multisensor data fusion [37] and has been highly developed in the military as part of situation awareness, especially for tactical aerospace state estimation in target tracking and for decision support systems. Classical and modern techniques for analyzing signals include Fourier spectra, statistical properties of time series, correlation functions, spectral density functions, and time series modeling [38].

Likewise, Bioinformatics seeks to make sense of a bewildering amount of data through computational and database techniques. "Biology in the 21st century is being transformed from a purely laboratory-based science to an information science as well. The information includes comprehensive global views of DNA sequence, RNA expression, protein interactions, or molecular transformations. Increasingly, biological studies begin with the study of huge databases to help formulate specific hypotheses or design large-scale experiments. In turn, laboratory work ends with the accumulation of massive collections of data that must be sifted. These changes represent a dramatic shift in the biological sciences" [39].

"As molecular biology works toward characterizing the genetic basis of biological processes, mathematical and computational sciences are beginning to play an increasingly important role; they will be essential for organization, interpretation, and prediction of the burgeoning experimental information" [40]. These mathematical and computational sciences include

- Object-oriented computer languages for information parsing and pattern matching in DNA sequences such as Perl, Bioperl, or Scheme [39,41,42].
- Data-mining techniques [43] involving database construction issues as well as multivariate statistical analysis (principal components, factor analysis, etc.) and decision making [17,44].
- Categorical time series analysis [17] for estimating the spectral envelope of a DNA sequence using the nucleotide alphabet to find coding and noncoding signal segments.
- Mathematical and statistical genetic analysis, such as linkage analysis to map genes and computational methods to predict protein structure, which is critical for the protein function [40,45].

To make sense of this overwhelming amount of data, a user-friendly human interface to the various databases is needed. Moreover, in a rapidly changing technological environment, this human interface should be easily modifiable to incorporate and investigate new paradigms of computation and new algorithms, i.e., the interface should be a rapid prototyping system. Because of the highly multidimensional characteristics of the data and the necessary algorithms to process it, the interface should include, at a bare minimum, embedded or easily added vector and matrix operation constructs. Several processing environments include these capabilities including S-PLUS, Mathematica, MATLAB®, and the like. Mathematica [46–48] and S-PLUS [49,50,27] are two of the most useful environments for processing interfaces to large databases such as generated in GIS, remote sensing, and bioinformatics.

A discussion of Mathematica as a front-end user interface to a GIS database and rapid prototyping system will be given. Mathematica is a programming language as well as a comprehensive symbolic computation system. As a higher level language, projects developed using the resources of Mathematica can be developed much quicker than similar projects using FORTRAN or C, albeit with a computational overhead and reduction of computational speed. Mathematica inherently contains several characteristics that aid programming in the rapid prototyping environment including [48]

- Mathematical formula and algorithms
- Pattern matching capabilities
- Simple manipulation of structured data (lists, vectors, and matrices)
- Modularization for organizing larger programs
- Object-oriented elements to make code development easier
- Traditional procedural programming in the style of FORTRAN and C

These elements, in addition to built-in graphical and display tools, allow the rapid development of processing algorithms to control the large GIS system with its massive database and allow the interface processing and display of the desired data. This kind of system would be a significant aid in the optimized use of GIS data for modeling and emergency response.

Conclusions

Agroeconomic bioterrorism is a real threat in the present world. The agroeconomic system in the United States is large, diverse, and of critical economic importance. It has both inherent safety mechanisms and dangerous vulnerabilities. The USDA and the U.S. agricultural response system (APHIS and ARS) of plant pathologists, veterinarians, and other professionals are (and always will be) underfunded and understaffed for the magnitude of the threat that they face—both naturally occurring pests and diseases as well as deliberately introduced threats. However, they have real-world experience and procedures dealing with natural disease outbreaks in plants and animals.

The agricultural system is relatively unprotected, but a bioterrorist would have to attack the agricultural system over a wide geographical area and coordinated with an assault on many different plant or animal systems to have a truly devastating effect on the diverse U.S. economy. Although this is not impossible to implement for a well-trained, well-funded bioterrorist group, it certainly is not trivial for a casual effort.

The anthrax bioattack shows the difficulty in coordinating a dispersed and distributed attack with massive casualties and yet it also shows the relative ease that a bioattack can be carried out to inflict psychological and economic damage much greater and widespread than the real injuries. The September 11, 2001 terrorist attack shows the propagation of economic effects from one economic sector and one geographic location throughout the linked economy to other sectors and other geographic locations. One truly lives in a complex global and networked economy with all the sophistication and benefits that it brings, as well as the potential risks entailed when it fails. The U.S. agroeconomic system is a vital and vulnerable part of that global economy.

Case Study 1: Genetically Modified Organisms

Genetically modified organisms (GMOs), or Biotech crops, generate significant passion and controversy between several special interest groups with agendas at several levels. With that passion comes the motivation for activism, extremism, and even ecoterrorism against agribusiness. It is hoped that with perceived adequate regulation and enhanced consumer education that biotech foods will gain acceptance in consumer markets. Resistance to food derived from GMO is especially high in Europe where as many as 80 percent are opposed. The potential economic and environmental benefits from biotech crops are significant with increasing crops yields that will benefit the world food supply, while reducing the environmental assault of large-scale use of herbicides and pesticides. The U.N. Development Program (UNDP) agency came out with a report in 2001 in support of biotech foods in the effort to stem world hunger. An example of a GMO is "Golden Rice" that has been modified to contain beta carotene to combat vitamin A deficiencies in Asia that lead to blindness. Opponents such as Bio-Justice that are opposed to genetic engineering have called golden rice a "Frankenfood."

In addition to biotech food, research in plant-based genetic-derived products such as vaccines and human disease therapies are ongoing. These vaccines and therapies have the potential to generate public relations, "good will," that may aid the biotech food markets by association.

The most widely noted case of biotech crops generating controversy is in the case of the genetically modified corn known as Starlink. "StarLink had won government approval as animal feed but not as food for humans. It cross-pollinated widely contaminating 430 million bushels of corn, and triggering nationwide recalls of taco shells, corn chips and other foods" (Elias, Paul, "Molecular Pharmers hope to raise human proteins in crop plants," AP release, *St. Louis Post Dispatch*, 10-28-01). This is an example of how significant economic damage can be accomplished through a bioassault even without endangering human life.

Biotech corn is another example of a GMO that has been modified using the *Bacillus thuringiensis* to provide natural pest resistance. "Plant genetic engineering refers to the transfer of foreign DNA which codes for specific genetic information, from a donor species into a recipient plant species by means of a bacterial plasmid, virus, or other vector. A segment of DNA that codes for a desirable trait is inserted into the plant genotype where it replicates and is expressed in the new plant genotype. This is similar to the plant breeder backcross method in which desirable genes are transferred to a recipient genotype by a succession of crosses. The difference is that the plant breeder can employ the backcross only among species that are cross-fertile, whereas the molecular biologist is not limited to obtaining the DNA from a donor plant species that is cross-fertile with the recipient plant species" [51]. "The use of Bt corn was developed as a way of providing corn with natural resistance to some pests, particularly the European corn borer and to a lesser extent the corn earworm, the southwestern corn borer, and the lesser cornstalk borer" (Research Q&A: Bt Corn and Monarch Butterflies, Agricultural Research Service, Web page: www.ars.usda.gov). The use of pesticides with Bt corn was enormously reduced with significant positive environmental benefits. The Bt varieties of corn are currently approximately 20 percent of the U.S. corn crop.

Bt corn has been controversial in the public press because of potential threats to monarch butterflies and possible human allergic reactions. These allegations were refuted in 2001 by studies from EPA and USDA on monarch butterflies, and CDC for the alleged allergic reactions.

In the past, the Mexicans have been angered that unlabeled U.S. imports had transferred modified genes including the Bt gene to local corn, even though planting genetically modified crops is banned in Mexico. The danger is that genetically modified strains could displace or contaminate the valuable Mexican genetic diversity resource stockpile of wild varieties of corn (Stevenson, Mark, "Accidental spread of modified corn is seen as cultural attack," AP release, *St. Louis Post Dispatch*, 1-1-02). Genetic diversity is an important issue for plant breeding and evolutionary adaptation [52,53]. Diversity is essential for species survival in space and time, by adaptation to specific environments. Genetic diversity has a leading role in competition, symbiosis and parasitism, impact of climate, absorption of nutrients, and the effect of nutritional deficiencies. The importance of wild relatives for breeding is important for the improvement of crops by wild genes for disease and pest resistance. One advantage of gene transfer through genetic engineering is by opening up tertiary (distantly related) gene pools [52].

The only thing certain is that controversies associated with GMO will continue for the near future. The recent rise in energy costs, especially oil, as well as concerns on the quality assurance of imported foodstuffs have highlighted a complex network relationship of linked economies. Food safety, transportation, fertilizers, biofuels, climate concerns, international trade, and higher food prices and starvation in third world countries have all shown these linked tendencies. The importance and potential disruptive characteristics of the increasingly higher profile agroeconomic system have now been demonstrated. This psychological pressure point could be exploited in acts of psychological and economic terrorism.

It is in the political agenda of certain environmental activist groups to continue the hysteria of imagined threats while ignoring the benefits associated with biotech foods in addressing real-world hunger. Real problems should be addressed as they come along (which they always will in the real world) with a rational and thoughtful analysis backed with technical expertise.

Case Study 2: Hoof and Mouth Disease

Hoof and mouth disease (HMD) is a naturally occurring disease that affects hoofed animals including domesticated economic livestock such as cattle, swine, and sheep as well as wildlife such as deer. The disease is rarely fatal to the infected animal but can destroy the economic productivity of a herd and because of the highly infectious nature of HMD, it can rapidly spread throughout an entire region by infected animals, noninfected carriers such as humans, by air transmission, and within various animal species. The outbreak of HMD in February of 2001 in Britain has shown the economic dangers of a widespread epidemic including direct economic damage in the destruction of livestock herds as well as ancillary economic damage in other areas such as a reduction in tourism through travel restrictions and security to prevent the disease from spreading from region to region or from country to country.

In the case of HMD disease, vaccination of herds is not usually performed due to the difficulty in differentiating between an infected animal and a vaccinated animal. Vaccinated animals are banned from export sales, which is a significant consideration in most large-scale livestock producers. With a HMD outbreak, quarantines and an embargo will also cause widespread economic disruption.

The United States has been free from HMD disease since 1929 but the economic dangers of an outbreak could be catastrophic to the pork and beef industries. An outbreak would potentially be even more difficult to eradicate than previous U.S. outbreaks, due to the proliferation of deer wildlife that has exploded in recent years due to significant conservation efforts. A resident endemic infectious population in wild deer would be disastrous to the domesticated herds, and livestock breeding or large-scale confinement production areas.

Vaccines can keep animals from acquiring diseases, but in most cases, they do not keep animals from being carriers. A cow vaccinated against HMD can carry the disease in her throat tissues for two and a half years after exposure. Moreover, a vaccinated animal cannot be distinguished from an infected one; the titers are the same [2]. An even more sobering thought is the spread of the HMD into the wildlife population, such as deer, where population numbers have skyrocketed in recent years. An effort to eradicate the disease epidemic in both the commercial livestock bases of pigs, cattle, and sheep as well as the deer population could reach monstrous levels. This is why the genetic efforts in vaccine production and vaccine quality is so exciting. Incorporating a vaccine into both a feed plant for animal food-stock and into forage crops for the wildlife would be critical.

In addition, it would be beneficial to have a vaccine available where the titers for infected and vaccinated animals could be easily distinguished. Subunit vaccines such as viral coat protein put into forage crops have the potential to accomplish that goal. "Easy, inexpensive methods of vaccination are crucial to the prevention of animal diseases in rural regions of the world" [54].

Currently, the United States is in the process of relocating the Plum Island Animal Disease Research Laboratory, New York, to a new site in the interior of the United States. The new National Bio and Agro-Defense Facility currently has five states under consideration (Georgia, Kansas, Mississippi, North Carolina, and Texas). The economic development and technical prestige of hosting the new laboratory are significant but questions have been raised about the possible safety concerns of contagious disease containment at a nonoffshore site. In August 2007, HMD was found at two farms at Surrey, Great Britain. The HMD was tied to a release due to biosecurity breaches at British animal research laboratories. The HMD outbreak luckily was rapidly contained without a severe economic impact.

Would a potential terrorist consider HMD? Domestic ecoterrorists with an animal rights or antimeat agenda as well as foreign enemies would consider the livestock industry a prime target for economic disruption. In April of 2001, People for the Ethical Treatment of Animals (PETA) cofounder Ingrid Newkirk expressed hope that HMD, which devastated the British cattle industry, would come to the United States; "It will bring economic harm only for those who profit from giving people heart attacks" (Richard Berman, *USA Today*, November 1, 2001). Recent environmental extremist attacks in 2008 have included "nonviolent chemical warfare" by the Sea Shepherds against the Japanese factory ship *Nisshin Maru* to harass and obstruct the whaling industry, as well as firebombing attacks in California against biomedical researchers who conduct animal experiments.

Russian cyber-attacks (whether state organized or spontaneous groups) against the Georgian Internet infrastructure have also been conducted in 2008 in conjunction with the shooting war. Attacks on computer networks affecting the telecommunications, transportation, command, and control, and emergency response aspects of the agroeconomic system could also be coordinated with biological assaults.

Groups that defend the use of force as a tool in social justice movements see the use of force as a morally righteous tactic to stop perceived atrocities in animal research, and animal exploitation such as whaling. The ends justify the means is a philosophy that often has an appeal to the highly charged emotional states of passionate extremists. Calling it "ecodefense" not ecoterrorism is their rationale and justification for environmental extremism. Antiglobalism, anticapitalism, anarchism, extreme enviro-activism, and extreme animal-activism are all motivating factors that could lead to the psychological and economic attacks of agroeconomic terrorism.

References

1. TW Frazier and DC Richardson. Editors. *Food and Agricultural Security: Guarding Against Natural Threats and Terrorist Attacks Affecting Health, National Food Supplies, and Agricultural Economics.* New York: New York Academy of Sciences, Vol. 894, 1999.
2. A Kohnen. Responding to the Threat of Agroterrorism: Specific Recommendations for the United States Department of Agriculture, BCSIA Discussion Paper 2000-29, ESDP Discussion Paper ESDP-2000-04. John F. Kennedy School of Government, Harvard University, Cambridge, MA. October 2000.
3. Bovine Alliance on Management and Nutrition (BAMN). *An Introduction to Infectious Disease Control on Farms (Biosecurity),* BAMN Publications, 2001.
4. V Hanson. *A War Like No Other.* New York: Random House, 2005.
5. CC Combs. *Terrorism in the Twenty-First Century,* 2nd ed. Upper Saddle River, NJ: Prentice Hall, 2000.
6. F Hacker. *Crusaders, Criminals, Crazies: Terror and Terrorism in Our Time.* New York: W.W. Norton & Company, 1976.
7. DB Schweikhardt. An Assessment of the Economic Impacts of the September 11 Terrorist Attacks: Ten Tentative Conclusions, Staff Paper No. 01-41, Department of Agricultural Economics, Michigan State University, East Lansing, MI, October 2001.
8. S Plous. *The Psychology of Judgment and Decision Making,* New York: McGraw-Hill, 1993.
9. HW Lewis. *Technological Risk.* New York: W.W. Norton and Company, 1990.
10. NATO (North Atlantic Treaty Organization). *Handbook on the Medical Aspects of NBC Defensive Operations, AmedP-6(B),* Part II—*Biological, FM 8–9.* Departments of the Army, the Navy, and the Air Force. February, 1996.
11. JL Witherly, GP Perry, and DL Leja. *An A to Z of DNA Science.* New York: Cold Spring Harbor Laboratory Press, 2001.
12. Introduction to ArcGIS I. GIS Education Solutions (Course Training Set). ESRI Educational Services, Redlands, CA, 2001.
13. MS Meade and RJ Earickson. *Medical Geography,* 2nd ed. New York: Guilford Publication, 2000.
14. JB Campbell. *Introduction to Remote Sensing,* 2nd ed. New York: Guilford Publication, 1996.
15. JR Jensen. *Introductory Digital Image Processing: A Remote Sensing Perspective,* 2nd ed. Upper Saddle River, NJ: Prentice Hall, 1996.
16. GS Campbell and JM Norman. *Environmental Biophysics.* Heidelberg: Springer-Verlag, 1998.
17. RH Shumway and DS Stoffer. *Time Series Analysis and Its Applications.* New York: Springer, 2000.
18. PA Rogerson. *Statistical Methods for Geography.* Thousand Oaks, CA: Sage Publications, 2001.
19. Y Pannatier. *Variowin: Software for Spatial Data Analysis in 2D.* New York: Springer, 1996.
20. AS Fotheringham, C Brunsdon, and M Charlton. *Quantitative Geography: Perspectives on Spatial Data Analysis.* Thousand Oaks, CA: Sage Publications, 2000.
21. RA Kempton and PN Fox. Editors. *Statistical Methods for Plant Variety Evaluation.* London, U.K.: Chapman and Hall, 1997.
22. National Plant Board. Safeguarding American Plant Resources: A Stakeholder Review of the APHIS-PPQ Safeguarding System. USDA-APHIS-PPQ. July 1, 1999.
23. EJ Henley and H Kumamoto. *Reliability Engineering and Risk Assessment.* Englewood Cliffs, NJ: Prentice Hall, 1981.
24. NJ McCormick. *Reliability and Risk Analysis.* Burlington: Academic Press, 1981.
25. SE Jorgensen, Editor. *A Systems Approach to the Environmental Analysis of Pollution Minimization.* Boca Raton, FL: Lewis Publishers, 2000.
26. TB Borak, Editor. *Applications of Probability and Statistics in Health Physics.* Madison, WI: Health Physics Society, 2000.
27. SP Millard and NK Neerchal. *Environmental Statistics with S-PLUS.* Boca Raton, FL: CRC Press, 2001.
28. PS Levy and S Lemeshow. *Sampling of Populations: Methods and Applications,* 3rd ed. New York: John Wiley & Sons, 1999.
29. GM Pierzynski, JT Sims, and GF Vance. *Soils and Environmental Quality,* 2nd ed. Boca Raton, FL: CRC Press, 2000.
30. MMR Williams and SK Loyalka. *Aerosol Science: Theory and Practice.* Oxford, U.K.: Pergamon Press, 1991.

31. LL Sanders. *A Manual of Field Hydrogeology*. Upper Saddle River, NJ: Prentice-Hall, 1998.
32. M Eisenbud and T Gesell. *Environmental Radioactivity*, 4th ed. Burlington: Academic Press, 1997.
33. J Neter, MH Kutner, CJ Nachtsheim, and W Wasserman. *Applied Linear Statistical Models*, 4th ed. New York: WCB/McGraw-Hill, 1996.
34. GC Reinsel. *Elements of Multivariate Time Series Analysis*, 2nd ed. New York: Springer, 1997.
35. M Fujita, P Krugman, and A Venables. *The Spatial Economy*. Cambridge, MA: The MIT Press, 2000.
36. F Hayashi. *Econometrics*. Princeton, NJ: Princeton University Press, 2000.
37. E Waltz and J Llinas. *Multisensor Data Fusion*. Norwood, MA: Artech House, 1990.
38. R Shiavi. *Introduction to Applied Statistical Signal Analysis*, 2nd ed. Burlington: Academic Press, 1999.
39. AD Baxevanis, BF Ouellette, and BF Francis. Editors. *Bioinformatics: A Practical Guide to the Analysis of Genes and Proteins*, 2nd ed. New York: John Wiley & Sons, 2001.
40. ES Lander and MS Waterman. Editors. *Calculating the Secrets of Life*. Washington, DC: National Research Council, National Academy Press, 1995.
41. HM Deitel, PJ Deitel, TR Nieto, and DC McPhie. *Perl: How to Program*. Upper Saddle River, NJ: Prentice Hall, 2001.
42. M Watson. *Programming in Scheme*. New York: Springer, 1996.
43. J Han and M Kamber. *Data Mining: Concepts and Techniques*. Burlington: Academic Press, 2001.
44. KP Yoon and C-L Hwang. *Multiple Attribute Decision Making*. Thousand Oaks, CA: Sage Publications, 1995.
45. K Lange. *Mathematical and Statistical Methods for Genetic Analysis*. New York: Springer, 1997.
46. S Kaufmann. *A Crash Course in Mathematica*. Basel, Switzerland: Birkhauser Verlag, 1991.
47. PT Tam. *A Physicist's Guide to Mathematica*. Burlington: Academic Press, 1997.
48. R Maeder. *The Mathematica Programmer*. Chestnut Hill, MA: AP Professional, 1994.
49. WN Venables and BD Ripley. *Modern Applied Statistics with S-PLUS*, 3rd ed. New York: Springer, 1999.
50. A Krause and M Olson. *The Basics of S and S-PLUS*, 2nd ed. New York: Springer, 2000.
51. JM Poehlman and DA Sleper. *Breeding Field Crops*, 4th ed. Ames, IA: Iowa State University Press, 1995.
52. OH Frankel and AHD Brown. *The Conservation of Plant Biodiversity*. Cambridge, U.K.: Cambridge University Press, 1995.
53. D Briggs and SM Walter. *Plant Variation and Evolution*, 3rd ed. Cambridge, U.K.: Cambridge University Press, 1997.
54. DJ Bourgaize, R Thomas, and RG Buiser. *Biotechnology*. Boston, MA: Addison-Wesley, 2000.

Bibliography

RM Bourdon. *Understanding Animal Breeding*, 2nd ed. Upper Saddle River, NJ: Prentice Hall, 2000.

DC Coleman and DA Crossley. *Fundamentals of Soil Ecology*. Burlington: Academic Press, 1996.

PJ Fellows. *Food Processing Techology: Principles and Practice*. Crystal City, VA: Ellis Horwood Limited, 1988.

JC Frauenthal. *Mathematical Modeling in Epidemiology*. Heidelberg: Springer-Verlag, 1980.

N Gershenfeld. *The Physics of Information Technology*. Cambridge, U.K.: Cambridge University Press, 2000.

PJ Kramer and JS Boyer. *Water Relations of Plants and Soils*. Burlington: Academic Press, 1995.

JW Polderman and JC Willems. *Introduction to Mathematical Systems Theory*. New York: Springer, 1998.

DL Streiner and GR Norman. *PDQ Epidemiology*, 2nd ed. Philadelphia: B. C. Decker Inc., 1998.

Chapter 12

Agroterrorism: Attributes and Implications of High-Impact Targets in U.S. Agriculture

Katie Thompson

CONTENTS

Introduction 252
Choosing Agroterrorism 252
The Agroterrorism Landscape: What Is It 252
Making the Choice 254
Money 254
Lethality 256
Biology 256
Risk 257
Summary 257
Choosing the Target 257
Money 257
Financial Damage 257
Profit 259
Other Factors 260
Summary of Targets 261
Livestock 261
Crops 262
Choosing the Weapon 263
Summary: Our Choices 264
Bibliography 265

Introduction

Terrorism is first and foremost a crime. As with any crime, the choices and actions of the criminal boil down to three things: Means, motive, and opportunity. In this chapter, I will look at how these features combine to increase the likelihood that specific aspects of U.S. agriculture and the U.S. food supply will become—rather, are—a terrorist target of choice.

I will also discuss what choices we can make about prevention, preparation, and response to an agroterrorist action. Because we have limited resources to apply to these concerns, it is essential to set priorities and act on them. Those priorities should take into account the agroterrorism targets and weapons most likely to have a high impact on U.S. agriculture. Some of the potential agroterrorism scenarios lead to irreversible consequences; there will be no second chance.

In media interviews about my agroterrorism novel, I am consistently asked this question: Aren't I just giving ideas to terrorists? My answer: Absolutely not. That scenario, and the considerations of target and weapon choices in this chapter, is for the rest of us. The terrorists already know. Indeed, they are miles ahead of us. We need to catch up, and focus, before our actions in safeguarding our national assets become irrelevant.

Choosing Agroterrorism

The Agroterrorism Landscape: What Is It?

Agroterrorism has been loosely defined to encompass terrorist threats to any target involving agricultural products. This sloppy definition, however, lumps together two distinct industries with different—and often conflicting—needs and concerns. One industry (which will be referred to here specifically as "agriculture") produces renewable raw materials. The second industry ("food processing") *processes* those raw materials. In fact, there are additional secondary industries such as energy and construction that also depend on agriculture.

These industries are typically mutually exclusive in identity of practitioners, source of financing, influences on the industry, drivers of profitability, technology, ownership, regulatory concerns, and other criteria.

A farmer who produces corn will not have the same business plan (or banker or customer or insurer or taxes or annual cycle) as an ingredient producer who buys corn to make corn syrup, or a food producer who buys corn syrup to make cookies, or an energy company that buys corn to make ethanol. They only have one thing in common: The handling of commoditized and in some cases brand-name raw materials. Table 12.1 shows examples of industries that use agricultural products.

Thus describing the study or issue of agroterrorism simply as "food defense" is unsuitable, and lumping these distinct industries together to assess their appeal and vulnerability to terrorists is inappropriate.

Agroterrorism is more accurately defined as terrorism applied to agriculture. Agriculture, as illustrated by the U.S. Department of Agriculture (USDA), is the commercial practice of production of renewable raw materials from living organisms: plants, animals, fungi, and microbes. The criterion of commercial function is essential. The lawn or garden in a private home, for example, is not considered agriculture; it is gardening. In contrast, acres of lawn grown and harvested in footwide strips as a commercial product—a "turf farm"—are indeed agriculture. In other words, U.S. agriculture is a large collection of businesses that produce renewable raw materials.

Table 12.1 Examples of Secondary Uses of Agricultural Products

Raw Material Produced by Agriculture	*Processed Form Produced by Secondary Industry*	*Secondary Industry*
Corn	Syrup	Food industry
Corn	Ethanol	Energy industry
Soybean	Oil	Construction industry (paint)
Trees	Pulp	Paper industry
Trees	Lumber	Construction industry

The USDA tracks the commercial output (i.e., livestock and crops) of the 2.1 million such businesses in the United States. A typical grain farm business of 1000 acres may net only a modest profit margin—if any—for the producer, but the value of the grain produced and sold each year by that farm could top $500,000. Thus the economic impact of this sector is significant. Table 12.2 lists products for which the USDA gathers data and forms projections.

These definitions of agriculture and agroterrorism results in two profound implications when performing a terrorism risk assessment: (1) these are businesses; and (2) these businesses depend heavily on biological processes. For a certain kind of criminal, there is some appeal in the prospect of damaging as many as 2.1 million businesses using a weapon that reproduces itself. There is

Table 12.2 Products Tracked by the USDA

Plants	Grains, oilseeds, legumes	Corn, wheat, barley, oats, lentils, peas, rice, sorghum, peanuts, soybeans, dry edible beans, canola, sunflower, Austrian winter peas
	Tree nuts	Pecans, almonds, hazelnuts, walnuts
	Tree fruits	Apricots, sweet cherries, pears, prunes, papayas, citrus fruit, peaches, bananas, apples, oranges
	Other fruits	Guavas, grapes
	Vegetables and tubers	Potatoes, sweet potatoes, taro
	Other crops	Hay, sugarcane, cotton, tobacco, maple syrup, sugar beet, hops, olives, coffee, ginger root, cut flowers, potted flowering plants, honey, mushrooms, mustard seed, peppermint, pickles, pumpkins, spearmint oil
Animals	Livestock	Beef cattle, dairy cattle, hogs, sheep, bison, milk, cheese, butter, whey, mink, mohair, wool
	Poultry	Chicken, turkeys, eggs
	Fish	Catfish, trout

additional appeal in the fact that, due to the structure of the U.S. agricultural marketplace, a suitably chosen target in U.S. agriculture could generate significant low-risk profit opportunities for the agroterrorist or their sponsor.

Making the Choice

The choice of target and weapon ultimately depends on the goals and capabilities of the terrorist: What is their budget? Is it an individual, or a group? Do they want to kill people, or damage an economy? How much risk are they willing to take? In other words, as with any crime, the agroterrorist must decide or act upon his means, motive, and opportunity. Table 12.3 compares these attributes for four different examples of terrorism.

The four biggest differences between agroterrorism and other forms of terrorism are money, lethality, biology, and risk.

Money

By definition, agroterrorism is an attack against U.S. businesses. In addition to the costs of response and cleanup that accompany a destructive terrorist event, an agroterrorism attack will result in direct losses to the attacked businesses, indirect costs to the businesses due to industrywide effects, including market value of the products, and opportunity costs. The duration and distribution of the attack may also lead to permanent shifts in the industry. A year-long foot-and-mouth disease (FMD) outbreak in the United States, for example, could lead to a permanent reduction of the U.S. livestock industry as other countries step into the marketplace.

There is a second financial aspect of agroterrorism: profit potential. Because an agroterrorism event is essentially economic terrorism, the markets will have a response. Because the products in question are commodities traded on major exchanges, there is opportunity for an interested party to take an equity position. In other words, an agroterrorist—or an entity made aware of an impending strike against a major commodity—could place their orders, speculating that prices will go up (or down).

The general public is only peripherally aware of the unique and counterintuitive nature of commodity trading. Commodities markets are highly liquid; traders may buy and sell enormous amounts of grain on a daily basis; there are active exchanges worldwide; extreme leverage is used; and most significantly for this subject, money can be made not only when prices rise, but also when prices fall. Table 12.4 lists some of the major commodity exchanges and some of the commodities traded on each exchange.

Consider this hypothetical example of a midsize commodities trading client, placing trades following his assessment of some news or information: At 6:45 a.m., the client uses his online trading software to place an electronic order for 100 "contracts" (500,000 bushels) of corn, speculating that prices will fall. At 9:30 a.m. Chicago time, the markets open. By 10:15 a.m., prices have indeed dropped, by 10¢ per bushel. The client has earned $50,000. At 10:16 a.m., he places the electronic order to cash out. At 10:17 a.m., he goes to check on his other accounts, where he has placed similar unspectacular, midsize orders with brokers at commodity exchanges in China, Brazil, and London.

Larger traders and institutional investors such as hedge funds may buy or sell 2000 or more contracts (10 million bushels) at a time, thus financially significant trades do not necessarily raise red flags. Price swings of 10¢ per bushel—or more—in one day are not uncommon, and a news or weather event can and does cause prices to hit daily limits (up or down) for multiple days in a row.

Thus, advance knowledge of an agroterrorism event could be worth millions of dollars to speculators in the commodities markets. Those speculators may be the perpetrator of the agroterrorism event, his sponsors, or clients who buy the advance information from him.

Table 12.3 Comparison of Four Types of Terrorism

	Agroterrorism	*Chemical Terrorism*	*Bioterrorism*	*Other Terrorism*
Specific example	FMD outbreak	Sarin gas attack	Smallpox outbreak	Bombing of public building
Target	Cattle or hogs	Humans	Humans	Building
Weapon	FMD virus	Sarin gas	Smallpox virus	Explosives
Means				
Public access to weapon	+++	–	–	+
Technical skills required	0	++	+++	+++
Ease of use	+++	–	–	–
Cost of execution	–	+	++	+
Personnel required	One	Few	Multiple	Multiple
Motive				
Duration of assault	Months to years	Hours	Weeks	Seconds
Media appeal	Low	High	High	High
National economic impact	+++	–	+	–
Profit potential	+++	0	0	0
Antihuman	No	Yes	Yes	Yes
Opportunity				
Candidate locations	Rural farm	Urban area	Urban area	Urban area
Risk of capture during attack	0	+++	++	++
Risk from weapon	0	+++	++	++

Table 12.4 Major International Commodity Exchanges

Exchange	*Location*	*Major Commodities Traded*
Chicago board of trade	Chicago	Corn, soybeans, oats, ethanol, rice, wheat
Chicago mercantile exchange	Chicago	Corn, wheat, oats, rice, soybeans, lumber, wood pulp, feeder cattle, lean hogs, live cattle, butter, milk
Minneapolis grain exchange	Minneapolis	Wheat
Dalian commodity exchange	Dalian, China	Corn, soybeans, palm oil
London international financial futures exchange	London	Coffee, corn, sugar, wheat
Brazilian mercantile and futures exchange	Sao Paolo, Brazil	Cattle, coffee, cotton, sugar, corn, soybeans
National commodity and derivatives exchange	Mumbai, India	Soybeans, sugar

Lethality

According to the definition of agroterrorism used in this chapter, agroterrorism is not primarily directed at humans, and it is not typically associated with human deaths. Instead, the biggest benefits of agroterrorism to a criminal are related to money, biology, and risk. As a consequence, criminals interested in lethal consequences may choose other weapons.

However, the lack of lethality is also a benefit of this mode of terrorism. Lack of lethality also leads to a lack of media interest, and diminished public interest, which in turn lowers the risk to the agroterrorist: There is likely to be slower and less response time in the event of an agroterrorism event, and there is less public funding for or interest in prevention, preparation, or response.

Biology

Biology-derived weapons suitable for use in agroterrorism have several advantages, including ease of use, ability to replicate, presence in natural environments, lack of effect on humans (including terrorists), and difficulty in detection. Numerous pathogenic viruses are stable enough to be transported in a crude medium (in wet mud, for example) and can be harvested from the sources of infection without risk to the human carrier, and without fear of detection.

Very little knowledge of biology is required to handle some biological agents suitable as agroterrorism weapons. In addition, a weapon used in an agroterrorism event does not need to be a pathogen at all. For example, herbicide-resistant weed seed could be spread by air over selected fields, such as in top production areas, or in fields producing seed for the next year's grain crops.

Genetic engineering may enhance the range or consequences of a pathogenic or pest repertoire. However, current and emerging pathogens and pests—including viruses, bacteria, fungi, insects, parasites, protozoa, and other miracles of biology—will continue to provide a fruitful source for potential crises for years to come.

Risk

By definition, agroterrorism events are directed toward agricultural entities. This reduces the risk to the agroterrorist by narrowing the host range of the weapon he carries: Noxious weed seed, a devastating cattle virus, or an emerging corn fungus is not going to cause the terrorist anxiety for his/her own health.

In addition, the general public (and the legislators they elect) is largely unaware of the financial structure, impact, or day-to-day activities of the agriculture industry, and certainly uninitiated in the financial complexities of the commodities markets. Thus, the risk to an agroterrorist of prevention, detection, or capture is diminished due to minimal public interest in the target, and due to minimal public awareness of or interest in the immediate consequences (e.g., effect on farmers or commodities markets) of the terrorist event.

Summary

The nature of agroterrorism—an assault on the vulnerable businesses of the U.S. agriculture industry—makes it an appealing target and weapon combination for terrorists who may choose to inflict long-term damage. This type of attack may demand little investment, time, risk, or expertise, and can be executed by an individual working alone. There is also the potential for significant profit. These features make agroterrorism different from other modes of terrorism.

In this chapter, I will look closer at some of these features of agroterrorism. I will examine some of the targets and weapons that, if embraced by a terrorist—or other criminal—would result in the greatest impact on U.S. agriculture.

Choosing the Target

Not all agriculture targets are the same. Having chosen agroterrorism as a general mode, the criminal must focus on one or a few targets. The highest impact target will be one that represents a significant financial and strategic stake in the industry: high dollar production, large production costs and commitment, ripple effect on other products, key global market position, and open production facilities in multiple areas.

In contrast, an attack on a niche product produced in a single region would not have the same impact. A low-impact example would be deliberately accessing a greenhouse full of parsley in rural Vermont and infesting it with a virus that causes stem rot. This would be agroterrorism, but it would not trigger a national trade ban, nor likely spread to surrounding states within days, lead to millions of dollars of crop destruction, provide an avenue for profit for the agroterrorist, or change the structure of U.S. agriculture.

Using this basis for comparison, the primary products of U.S. agriculture can be considered for their suitability as a target.

Money

Financial Damage

In addition to the damages of outbreak or infestation control, cleanup, and recovery, each agriculture product has a level of production that could be disrupted and a national inventory that could be at risk of destruction. Inventory destruction could be as a preventative, control measure, or due to actual or potential exposure. The major commodities also have national values determined by trading on commodity exchanges, value that can change substantially in response to news, or suspicion of news. Thus the value of a farm or ranch inventory can (and does) change significantly without a single item of crop or livestock in that respective state being attacked or even at direct risk.

For crops, inventory is determined on an individual basis. Grain farmers do not typically save grain to use as seed for the next year's crop. Instead, high-quality (or hybrid) grain produced specifically for use as seed is purchased from seed companies each year. Grain stored on a farm is thus harvested crop awaiting sale, and will not return into cultivation. The majority of this grain may be sold before harvest of the following year's crop, and moved to regional storage facilities to await final use and processing. Harvested grain in inventory, in other words, is destined for destruction in most cases, and not for continuous growth.

In contrast, livestock producers frequently maintain breeding stock. An annual inventory of cattle taken in January thus sums up new production (animals prepared for market since the last inventory), breeding animals (animals maintained from year to year), and young animals not yet ready for market. The entire inventory is in a state of continuous growth, and thus more vulnerable to biological agents such as viruses that benefit from the active growth of a host for their amplification.

Four products dominate U.S. agriculture: cattle, hogs, corn, and soybeans. Table 12.5 lists the value and national distribution of the major U.S. agricultural products. An agroterrorism attack would have by far the greatest impact if one or more of these four products were the target.

Indeed, it would be impossible to attack only one of these four targets without significantly influencing the others, as all four are tightly interlinked.

Table 12.5 Values of Annual Production and Inventory in the United States

Agricultural Product	*Value (Billions)*	*U.S. Production Area (Number of States)*
Livestock inventory		
Cattle (1/1/08)	$95.4	50
Hogs (2007)	$4.7	50
Sheep (1/1/08)	$0.84	33
Crop production (2007)		
Corn	$52.1	41
Soybeans	$26.8	31
Potatoes	$3.2	49
Tomatoes	$0.9	21

Source: From U.S. Department of Agriculture National Agricultural Statistics Service (USDA NASS) reports: Annual Summary of Crop Production; Agricultural Prices; Census of Agriculture; Crop Value; Farms, Land in Farms, and Livestock Operations. http://www.nass.usda.gov. With permission.

Corn and soybeans, for example, are rotational crops, meaning that a farmer will usually switch between them each year to maintain soil fertility. A field planted with corn one year will be planted with soybeans the next year, then corn, then soybeans, and so on. Farmers own and maintain the equipment, chemicals, and storage to handle both types of crop.

Cattle and hogs are also interlinked, but in a different way: Both consume significant amounts of grain as feed, and both are major meats in the marketplace. They compete for feed, and for sales. For example, destruction or quarantine of part of the U.S. cattle inventory would drop the price of feed (due to lower demand), and raise the price of pork as a food (due to lower supply).

Thus, as a result of the feed relationship, all four are linked: cattle, hogs, corn, and soybeans. If part of the cattle inventory were removed, again for example, not only would the price of pork rise, but a drop in prices of feed means a drop in prices of corn and soybeans. Depending on the timing of the shift in cattle inventory, the amount of corn and soybeans planted for the following year could also shift, leading to a multiyear effect (either up, or down) on grain prices.

Cattle, hogs, corn, and soybeans are by far the major products of U.S. agriculture, and their production and market prices are interlinked. These four products would be the most appealing targets for an agroterrorist with an interest in damaging U.S. agriculture.

Profit

When considering which products of U.S. agriculture are the most desirable targets for an agroterrorist, it is useful to consider which products may provide opportunity for simultaneous profit.

Not all U.S. agriculture products are traded on commodity exchanges. Only the major crops that are widely bought and sold have been officially selected for such generic, relatively anonymous transactions. Many products are tracked by the USDA—such as broccoli, tomatoes, taro, ginger root, carrots, and goats—but are not bought and sold at exchanges such as the Chicago Board of Trade. Vegetables, fruits, nuts, and other smaller-volume or niche products are sold privately. In contrast, cattle, hogs, corn, and soybeans are widely traded on the major international exchanges.

This changes the opportunity for a criminal to profit from agroterrorism attack against particular targets. An agroterrorist targeting the tomato crop in California fields, for example, may stir public interest because these products are closer to the consumer. However, they will not have access to the ability to profit from shifts in the market price of tomatoes. Those prices may indeed shift, and people in the vegetable industry may make or lose money, but there is not a mechanism for a member of the general public to "buy in." In contrast, with minimal paperwork, most members of the public can open a brokerage account and trade commodities.

Another way to think of this distinction is as if the different products were each a "company." For example: "Tomatoes, Inc." would be a company with $900 million in revenues last year, but it would be a privately held company and outsiders could not share in the profits. In contrast, "Corn, Inc." would have $52.1 billion in revenues, and would be a publicly held company, so anyone worldwide with a brokerage account could buy and sell "shares" (contracts for a set number of bushels or pounds).

As with the trading of stocks, trading of commodities is monitored by a regulatory agency. Stock trading is monitored by the Securities Exchange Commission (SEC), and commodities trading are monitored by the Commodities and Futures Trading Commission (CFTC). Trading of a specific stock is limited to one or few exchanges authorized by the company. However, commodities trading can be performed on a network of international exchanges, and daily trading volumes are substantial and essentially without limits.

Consider this example: Shares in Microsoft are traded on the New York Stock Exchange, and there are only a certain number of shares available. On the other hand, contracts (5000 bushel units) of corn can be traded on exchanges in Chicago, London, Brazil, and China, and the volume of trade only depends on the number of interested parties. This makes monitoring of suspect trades a greater challenge.

If an agroterrorist—or their sponsor—is interested in financial gain, this feature could affect their decision about targets.

Other Factors

Candidate agroterrorism targets also have a range of practical differences. For example, some targets are freely accessible to the general public, and may be shipped nationwide via the U.S. Interstate system, while others are locked away in secured facilities and do not travel far. Table 12.6 compares access and movement of major U.S. agricultural products.

Another consideration is the duration of the attack. While an agroterrorism attack may not have the drama of an explosion, it has endurance. Rubble from an explosion can be removed over a period of weeks or months, but a live virus or microbe may take years to remove. This amplifies the cost and burden of the attack.

Recovery times can also be slow, even after biological agents are neutralized or removed. Table 12.7 compares the times required for replacement of breeding stock or crop. One difference between agricultural products and machine parts built in a factory is the pace of biology. A bombed-out factory can add on extra shifts to rebuild and resume operations. However, it is not possible to add extra shifts to speed up some biological processes. Despite modern methods of biotechnology, rebuilding a national herd or national crop will simply require substantial time for

Table 12.6 Access and Movement of Potential Targets in U.S. Agriculture

Agricultural Product	*Open Access*	*Interstate Movement*
Livestock		
Cattle	+	+
Hogs	–	+
Poultry	–	–
Sheep	+	+
Crops		
Corn	+	+
Soybeans	+	+
Potatoes	+	+
Tomatoes	–	+

Table 12.7 Time Required to Restock Agricultural Populations

Agricultural Product	*Cycle Time*
Livestock	
Cattle, dairy	3 years
Hogs	2 years
Sheep	2 years
Crops	
Corn	1 year
Soybeans	1 year
Potatoes	1 year
Tomatoes	4 months

planting, breeding, growth, and harvest. Furthermore, loss of breeding-age livestock will require additional time for female animals to reach reproductive age. Thus an agroterrorism attack on livestock would require more years of recovery time than an attack on crops.

Another feature that may be of interest to an agroterrorist is the position of the crop in the international marketplace, and the U.S. share of—and stability in—that market. Commodities such as cattle, hogs, corn, and soybeans are currently produced, bought, and sold around the world. Brazil, for example, now produces more soybeans than the United States. Any interruption in U.S. production of crops or livestock would boost prices and encourage increased production in other nations. It cannot be assumed that the United States would be able to resume previous production levels. Any net increase in global production will have a negative effect on price, thus a temporary loss of market share could become permanent.

These attributes, financial and otherwise, combine to make a target more or less appealing to a potential criminal.

Summary of Targets

The crop or livestock species chosen as a target by an agroterrorist must offer benefits to that criminal or their cause. The most significant features of U.S. agriculture are the high financial stakes and the interlinked relationships of the top commodities. A high-impact agroterrorism attack will by definition focus on one of the top four commodities: cattle, hogs, corn, and soybeans. An attack on any one of these four will have significant ripple effects on the remaining three.

Livestock

There are large populations of animals in the United States that are raised and tended but not for agricultural purposes, such as, for example, dogs and cats. An attack against those populations would have social impact, but not the financial and industrial impact of an attack against animals raised for agricultural purposes (cattle, hogs, sheep, etc.). This business aspect is a key part of the definition of agroterrorism. Within this pool, cattle and hogs are by far the most significant financially and geographically. The national inventory of these animals also has a substantial effect on the prices of the major crops due to their consumption of feed.

Cattle and hogs are linked in production and commodities marketing relationships, and are also linked biologically. Some potential agroterrorism weapons will target both cattle and hogs. In contrast, most major crop pathogens do not cross over between the top crops (corn and soybeans).

Crops

The United States is a major global producer of corn and soybeans. The value of the U.S. corn crop is at an all-time high. Figure 12.1 shows the change in the value of the U.S. corn crop over the history of the USDA. Soybeans are produced in several other countries, but the United States has an advantage in corn production due to several features of biology. Corn productivity, for example, is enhanced by the cooler nights found in the U.S. grain belt. Thus more major corn production areas are in the United States than in other countries. In contrast, wheat is produced in many other countries than the United States; the United States only produces about a tenth of global production.

An agroterrorism weapon directed against a major crop would, once released, be potentially able to spread to other countries. However, a weapon directed against corn would have a greater impact on the United States than on other countries.

The primary crop target in U.S. agriculture is corn. Damage to the U.S. corn crop would have the greatest direct and indirect financial impact, and offer the largest potential trading profits to the terrorist and affiliated parties. Production, sales, use, and price of the crop are interlinked with the other three major commodities—cattle, hogs, and soybeans—and would affect their

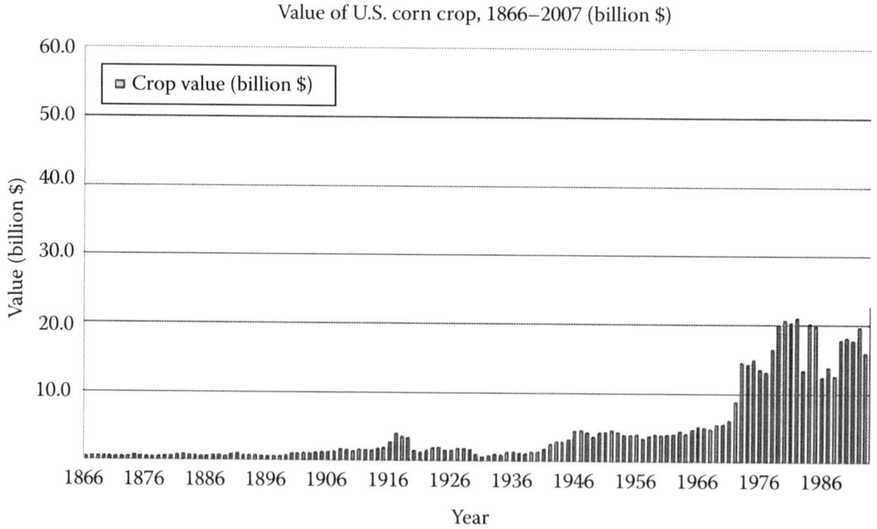

Figure 12.1 U.S. corn crop value. (From National Agricultural Statistics Service, United States Department of Agriculture, www.nass.usda.gov.)

production, sales, use, and price. The United States has a unique edge in global corn production, and would suffer the most from damage to the global corn crop.

The challenge for the U.S. public and decision makers is staying focused on the high-impact targets. There are only a limited number of these major targets: cattle, hogs, corn, soybeans. These targets are not likely to change in the foreseeable future.

Choosing the Weapon

There are only four high-impact targets in U.S. agriculture, but there is a tremendous variety and number of weapons available for the interested agroterrorist. The repertoire of available weapons will continue to change as new biological agents are discovered, and new methods of cultivation and distribution are developed. The challenge for the criminal is choosing—or modifying or creating—a weapon that will be useful and effective at reaching his goals.

However, nothing new needs to be discovered or developed for the arsenal to be explosive. There are already some obvious and major high-utility weapons that are ready to use, such as FMD virus. Table 12.8 lists some examples of biological agents that could be utilized as weapons against the major targets.

Utility is a function of the nature of the biological agent, and the current political and financial landscape. In other words, the result of the biology of the agent may not be as severe as the trade consequences of the agent. Bovine spongiform encephalitis (BSE), for example, causes more severe disease in cattle than does FMD. However, FMD spreads more rapidly, and there are a set of international trade consequences already in place as a result. Thus the impact of an FMD outbreak would be more significant to U.S. agriculture than an outbreak of BSE.

Table 12.8 Examples of Potential Agroterrorism Weapons against Major Crops and Livestock

	Example	
Pathogens	Cattle, hogs: FMD virus, exotic vesicular stomatitis virus	
	Hogs: Nipah virus encephalitis, swine vesicular disease virus, African swine fever virus	
	Corn: corn stunt	
	Soybeans: soybean rust	
Pests	Insects	Grains: Mediterranean cereal cyst nematode, Mexican corn cyst nematode, corn ground beetle, gray corn weevil
	Weeds	Soybean: yellow witchweed

Source: From World Organization for Animal Health (OIE) report: Diseases Notifiable to the OIE. http://www.oie.int; U.S. Department of Agriculture Animal and Plant Health Inspection Service (USDA APHIS) reports: Cooperative Agricultural Pest Survey Program (CAPS) National Pests of Concern; Agricultural Select Agent and Toxin List. http://www.aphis.usda.gov. With permission.

Table 12.9 Comparison of Three Candidate Agroterrorism Weapons

	Anthrax	*FMD*	*BSE*
Agriculture target	Cattle	Cattle, hogs, sheep	Cattle
Profit potential	–	+++	–
Financial impact	+	+++	+
Availability of agent	+	+++	–
Ease of preparation	–	+++	–
Ease of delivery	–	+++	–
Self-perpetuation	–	+++	–
Trade ban trigger	No	Yes	Yes
Human pathogen	Yes	No	Yes
Risk to user	Yes	No	No
Weapon appeal index	3	10	1

Practical considerations are important, as well. Can the agent be acquired easily by the terrorist? Does the terrorist require advanced training or equipment? Can an amateur do the job alone, or is a team of experts required? Together, these considerations change the relative value of a weapon to a criminal who wants to focus on a high-impact target in U.S. agriculture. Table 12.9 compares three well-known potential agroterrorism weapons.

As with the choice of targets, the choice of weapons may be influenced by the potential for profit. Any biological agent that has the potential of wide, and especially, rapid, spread can have an impact on the commodities markets. Discovery of widespread herbicide-resistant weed seed in spring as crops are developing.

Different categories of biological agent can be suitable as weapons against the agricultural targets of cattle, hogs, corn, and soybeans. These include viruses (against livestock), bacteria, and fungi.

Because the targets are also systems, not just organisms, there are also weapons that may be of high utility by attacking the system of production, not just by attacking the organism. Weeds resistant to current herbicides, for example, could reduce yields due to interference with crop growth. Indeed, it may be possible to kill the majority of weeds in a field and allow harvest. However, weed seed could contaminate the harvested grain, limiting the ability of a grower to sell the contaminated grain, or limit the range of possible buyers, thus inflicting significant financial damage and logistic problems.

Summary: Our Choices

As a society, institution, or individual, we have to set effective priorities to deal with agroterrorism. Budgets, political results, and public attention are finite and are not sufficient to provide complete protection from every agroterrorism scenario. As with any decision maker—whether politician or CEO or homeowner—we have to decide where to invest our limited resources. A homeowner, for example, must decide: Fix the leaky roof or fix the leaky ice maker? This requires the decision maker to set priorities (in this case, to protect the home).

Examination of candidate agroterrorism weapons and targets highlights two key features of agroterrorism. First, there is a very limited pool of high-impact targets. Second, there is a much larger and less definable potential pool of weapons (with some notable exceptions). These features and the impossibility of total protection suggest that attention be focused on the high-impact targets, and consequently on selected high-impact actions that will help deal with a range of assaults on those targets, regardless of weapons used.

For example, pushing cattle producers and the cattle industry to stockpile important genetics (e.g., as frozen embryos) would facilitate faster restocking of the national herd after any crisis, regardless of the agroterrorism weapon used. Furthermore, knowledge that this "insurance" is in place would cushion the impact on the marketplace, and give pause to global competitors in the event of an agroterrorism crisis that threatens or damages the national cattle inventory.

Actions like these—target-specific but not weapon-specific—address the problems generated by a variety of agroterrorism attacks.

One of the notable exceptions to this focus on targets instead of weapons is the FMD virus. This weapon has obvious potential appeal to an agroterrorist, and would yield major consequences for the entire set of four high-impact targets (cattle, hogs, corn, and soybeans). It is also reasonable to devote attention to FMD as a specific weapon because there are indeed valuable FMD-specific options to pursue: Completion of FMD vaccine improvement and reevaluation of international agreements on FMD-specific trade bans, for example.

Even within this set of actions, priorities are important. Should money and effort be invested trying to *prevent* or *neutralize* an agroterrorism attack (e.g., by training more crop scouts and veterinarians to detect emerging diseases), or *preparing* for an attack (e.g., by mandatory stockpiling of cattle embryos), or effectively *responding* to an attack (e.g., by training disaster response teams) on U.S. agriculture?

Unfortunately, all of these things need to be done. Perhaps a better question is why more money and effort is not being invested to protect and insulate these high-impact targets.

Bibliography

Chicago Board of Trade (CBOT), http://www.cbot.com

Chicago Mercantile Exchange (CME), http://www.cmegroup.com

Congressional Research Service (CRS) report: Agroterrorism: Threats and Preparedness, March 12, 2007.

Dalian Commodity Exchange, http://www.dce.com.cn

London International Financial Futures and Options Exchange (LIFFE), http://www.euronext.com

Minneapolis Grain Exchange (MGEX), http://www.mgex.com

National Commodity and Derivatives Exchange, http://www.ncdex.com

U.S. Department of Agriculture National Agricultural Statistics Service (USDA NASS) reports: Annual Summary of Crop Production; Agricultural Prices; Census of Agriculture; Crop Value; Farms, Land in Farms, and Livestock Operations. http://www.nass.usda.gov

U.S. Department of Agriculture Animal and Plant Health Inspection Service (USDA APHIS) reports: Cooperative Agricultural Pest Survey Program (CAPS) National Pests of Concern; Agricultural Select Agent and Toxin List. http://www.aphis.usda.gov

World Organization for Animal Health (OIE) report: Diseases Notifiable to the OIE. http://www.oie.int

Chapter 13

Nuclear Terrorism: Nature of Radiation

William H. Miller

CONTENTS

Introduction 267
Amount of Radioactivity 268
Radiation Shielding 268
Radiation Dose 269
Radioactive Half-Life...270
Summary 270
Radioactivity and Radiation 270

Introduction

When defining ionizing radiation, one might consider four important factors:

1. How much—what amount of radioactivity is present?
2. How far will the radiation travel—what kind of containment or shield will stop the radiation?
3. How will it affect me—what is the dose from this radiation to the human body?
4. How long will it be around—what is the radioactive half-life?

Amount of Radioactivity

Radioactivity is a measure of the rate at which radioactive nuclei disintegrate. It is simply a matter of counting how many of them have decayed, emitting their radioactive particles or waves, in a given amount of time.

As with all measurements, we have a plethora of qualities to define the amount of radioactivity. Moreover, as with many of our measuring systems, we have both "traditional" units and new International System of Units (SI units). The original units are referenced to the curie (Ci), named in honor of Madam Curie. A curie is 3.7×10^{10} (37 billion) radioactive disintegrations per second, or approximately the radioactivity of a gram of radium, one of the naturally radioactive elements with which Madam Curie did her research. For many applications of radiation in medicine or industry, the curie is a relatively large quantity, and so the units of mCi (1/1000th) and μCi (1/1,000,000th) are utilized. On the other hand, a nuclear reactor contains millions of curies of radioactivity and units of kCi (1000) and MCi (1,000,000) are sometimes used. Although the unit of the curie is being supplemented with the newer SI unit, it is still very much in common use.

The "new" SI unit becquerel (Bq) is named after Henri Becquerel, the discoverer of radioactivity. It is defined as only one disintegration per second. Thus, it is much, much smaller than the Ci. Multiples of becquerels are the kBq (1000), MBq (1,000,000), etc. These units are summarized in Table 13.1.

Radiation Shielding

To understand radiation shielding, it is necessary to differentiate between radioactive material and radioactive particles or emissions. Radioactive material is any material that contains some number of radioactive nuclei. Thus, radioactive materials can be anything, and in fact everything is radioactive to some small degree due to naturally occurring radioactivity in our environment.

Table 13.1 Various Units of Radioactivity

Curies	*Becquerel or Disintegrations/s*
1 MCi	3.7×10^{16}
1 kCi	3.7×10^{13}
1 Ci	3.7×10^{10}
1 mCi	3.7×10^{7}
1 μCi	3.7×10^{4}
Becquerels or Disintegrations/s	*Curies*
1 Bq	2.7×10^{-11}
1 kBq	2.7×10^{-08}
1 MBq	2.7×10^{-5}
1 GBq	0.027

When the radioactive nuclei decay, they give off particles or waves that fly out of the nucleus and away from the radioactive material.

To contain the radioactive material, one must simply put it in a vessel that will hold the material and not let it escape. On the other hand, shielding the radioactive particles or waves that they emit is a different matter and depends upon the type of emission. For particles that have a charge on them (like beta or alpha particles), the concept of range is used. The range is the distance beyond which a charged particle cannot penetrate. For example, less than 1 cm of plastic is needed to stop all beta particles emitted from a typical radioactive material. For uncharged particles (neutrons) or electromagnetic radiation (gamma rays or x-rays) the concept of half-value layer (HVL) is used. The HVL is the thickness of shield needed to stop one-half of the radiation that is trying to pass through it. A second HVL stops one-half of what is left, one-half of one-half, or one-fourth of the radiation, etc. A centimeter of lead will stop about one-half of the gamma rays at a typically energy of 1 MeV emitted from a radioactive material.

The task of containing radioactive material and radioactive emissions is thus a two-step process: (1) containing the radioactive material so that it is not distributed around the environment and (2) stopping the radioactive emissions they give off.

Radiation Dose

Radiation exposure and dose define the effect of radioactive emissions (particles or electromagnetic radiation) when they leave the substance containing radioactive nuclei and are then absorbed by the material that receives the dose. Although an engineer might be concerned about the dose to the metal in the reactor vessel in a nuclear power plant, most often we define dose to tissue, e.g., the human body. This dose can then be related to the possibility of adverse effects.

Once again there are numerous units to define this quantity. The older units are the Roentgen (radiation exposure measured as charge deposited per unit volume of air), the rad (radiation dose measured in energy absorbed per unit mass), and the rem (Roentgen equivalent man, or equivalent dose to tissue, depending upon the type of radiation involved). Technically they all have precise scientific definitions, but for most cases are all approximately equivalent. Thus a Roentgen of radiation is approximately equivalent to a rad of dose which is usually equal to a rem of equivalent dose. These units are relatively large compared to typical dose from natural background radiation or even the additional doses experienced by workers in a nuclear power plant or radiologists in a hospital. Again the use of "milli-" is used, i.e., mR or mrad or mrem, designating 1/1000 as much.

The new SI units are the grey (Gy) and sievert (Sv) which are both 100 times larger than the rad or rem, respectively. This is all summarized in Table 13.2.

Table 13.2 Radiation Dose

Exposure	*Dose*	*Dose Equivalent*
1 R	~1 rad	~1 Rem[a]
	~0.01 Gy	~0.01 Sv[a]

[a] Usually an equality, depending upon type of radiation.

Radioactive Half-Life

One interesting feature of radioactive material is that it becomes smaller and smaller as time goes by. Because it is decaying, it is self-destructing, and becoming less over time. The rate at which this occurs is defined as the half-life, or the amount of time that it takes for one-half of the radiation to decay. Unfortunately, two half-lives do not eliminate it (i.e., one-half decaying and then the second one-half decaying), but rather the half-life always refers to how much is left NOW. Thus, one half-life reduces the radioactivity by one-half; two half-lives by one-half of one-half or one-fourth; three half-lives by one-eighth; etc. Thus, radioactivity is never zero, but continues to get diminishingly small as time passes. Radioactive nuclei have half-lives that range from fractions of a second to billions of years. The radioactive material introduced into the body for a medical diagnostic procedure might have a half-life of a few hours so that it decays away to negligible levels in a day or so. At the other extreme, some of the naturally radioactive nuclei in our environment have half-lives of billions of years. The reason that they are still around is that they have not had enough time to decay to negligible levels since the earth was formed.

Summary

In summary, we have the following definitions:

- Radioactivity—how much of it is there?
  - Curie—3.7×10^{10} radioactive decays per second
  - Becquerel—1 radioactive decay per second
- Shielding—how far will the radiation travel?
  - Range—maximum penetration distance for charged particles
  - Half value layer—amount of material that will stop one-half of uncharged radiation
- Dose—how will it affect me?
  - Roentgen—a measure of the charge created in a volume of air by radiation
  - Rad—a measure of the energy deposited per unit mass or dose
  - Rem—roentgen equivalent man, equivalent dose depending upon type of radiation
  - Gray—100 rads; also 1 J of deposited energy per kilogram of material
  - Sievert—100 rems, equivalent dose
  - Radioactive half-life—how long will it be around?
  - Half-life—the amount of time for one-half of the radioactivity to decay away

Radioactivity and Radiation

The term "radiation" means many different things. Sunlight, the heat from a fire, radio waves, radar, microwave ovens, and radiation emitted from nuclear phenomena are all forms of radiation. These are separated into two types: ionizing radiation and nonionizing radiation. The radiation emitted from the decay of unstable nuclei is of the former type, i.e., ionizing radiation. Simply put, ionizing radiation has sufficient energy to separate an orbital electron from an atom, nonionizing radiation does not. On the scale of electromagnetic radiation, nonionizing radiation covers the energy spectrum from low energy waves of sonar and shortwave radio through medium energy wave of microwaves and radar and up through the energy of visible waves. Above that, electromagnetic radiation achieves enough energy to cause ionizations. This type of radiation is the subject of this chapter.

All nuclei are made up of combinations of protons and neutrons. For most of the lighter elements there is a one-to-one ratio of neutrons to protons (i.e., helium with 2 neutrons and 2 protons, carbon with 6 and 6, sulfur with 16 and 16). As elements get heavier and heavier, the neutron-to-proton ratio increases to about 1–1.5 (i.e., uranium with 146 neutrons and 92 protons). In general, when these ratios are maintained, the nucleus is stable nonradioactive, and emits no radiation. For some nuclei, however, the nucleus was created with an unstable ratio (i.e., uranium-238, potassium-40, and other naturally occurring radioisotopes). Other nuclei have their ratio altered by radiation coming in from outer space (hydrogen-3 or tritium, carbon-14, and other cosmogenic isotopes). Finally, nuclei are altered by human activities like the fissioning of nuclear fuel resulting in isotopes such as strontium-90, iodine-135, and many, many others. Radioactive decay is simply the attempt of a nucleus to move from a proton-to-neutron ratio that is unstable to a proton-to-neutron ratio that is stable.

To obtain this stable ratio, radioactive nuclei emit particles. The common ones are beta particles (electrons emitted from the nucleus), positrons (positively charged electrons), and alpha particles (a helium nucleus). Beta particles are emitted from nuclei that have too many neutrons to be stable, positrons from nuclei that have too many protons, and alpha particles from heavy, unstable nuclei. After emitting one of these particles, the resulting nucleus is a new element that is usually left with an excess amount of energy. This excess energy is emitted as electromagnetic radiation called gamma rays. Another common form of electromagnetic radiation is x-rays, which emanate from the orbital electrons of an atom that are transitioning from one energy level to another. The other common radioactive particle is the neutron which is largely the product of nuclear fission inside a working nuclear reactor and is not commonly emitted by radioactive materials.

Chapter 14

Nuclear Terrorism: Radiation Detection

William H. Miller

CONTENTS

History of Radiation Detection 273
Detector Systems 274
Detector Systems in Response to Nuclear Terrorism 275

History of Radiation Detection

Human bodies are not able to detect ionizing radiation, either from particles or electromagnetic waves. Human senses are sensitive only to a narrow band of the electromagnetic spectrum—visible light in a nonionizing radiation band—and ionizing radiation is more energetic at lower wavelengths. Although radiation is easy to detect with appropriate instruments and at very, very low levels, the human body is unable to detect even the lethal doses of radiation.

When radioactive substances were first discovered, the harmful effects of large amounts of radiation were not known and detection instrumentation was not considered. Many scientists who studied radioactivity were exposed to harmful amounts. When x-rays began to be used by doctors, many reported that patients who were exposed to x-rays suffered burns. In 1896, the physicist Elihu Thompson deliberately exposed his finger to x-rays so that he could accurately report on the phenomenon of x-ray burns. Thomas Edison was experimenting with x-rays in 1896 when one of his assistants became fatally ill from overexposure to radiation. In 1906, Henri Becquerel, the discoverer of radioactivity, was accidentally burned by a radioactive substance he was carrying in his pocket. When Pierre Curie heard of Becquerel's injury, he taped a radioactive substance to his own arm to observe the injuries it would cause.

Henri Becquerel discovered a method of detecting radiation as far back as 1896. He found that the invisible electromagnetic rays and particles from ionizing radiation would affect silver emulsions in photographic plates just like light rays would. As a result, photographic film has often been used to measure radioactivity.

Film is used for medical x-ray images and for film badges used for measuring personnel dose. The use of x-ray and film to diagnose a broken bone or look for a tumor is familiar to most. For personnel dose measurement, a person who might be exposed to radiation wears a film badge that contains a small bit of photographic film. It is referred to as a dosimeter. The film is covered by a layer of material, such as paper or plastic, that prevents light from reaching the film but allows the radiation to pass through. After use, the film is slipped out of the dosimeter and developed. The extent of darkening on the developed film can be translated into a measure of the total amount of radiation received by the person wearing the dosimeter.

Another of the first systems to be used to detect the charge created by ionizations is the scintillation counter. In a scintillation detector, the energy of the charged particles created by ionizations excites the scintillator molecules. As they de-excite they emit this radiation in the visible spectrum. The simplest system thus uses the eye to detect the flashes of light from the scintillator in a darkened room. Today, photocathodes and photomultipliers are used to electronically detect these light pulses and record them in appropriate counters and spectrometers. A variation of the scintillation detector is liquid scintillation counting, where the sample (usually in the form of a liquid) is introduced directly into the vials containing the liquid scintillation media. Thus, the radioactive nuclei and their emissions are in direct contact with the detection medium. This is particularly useful for detecting very small amounts of weakly penetrating radiation.

The task of manually counting scintillation flashes visually was often the task of graduate students, and Geiger was one such student of Rutherford's. Seeking an automated way to detect radiation, he helped to develop the Geiger–Mueller (GM) tube.

Detector Systems

Ionizing radiation, by definition, has the capability of knocking off electrons from atoms. Many detector systems allow us to detect this radiation by detecting the charge of these electrons.

In the GM counter, an electric potential is set up between a cylindrical detector wall and a center electrode passing through the center of the cylinder. A gas is used as the detection medium in this cylinder and the negatively charged electrons that are released by ionizing radiation in the gas are collected on the center electrode. This creates an electronic pulse that can easily be detected by relatively simple electronic circuit. The simplicity of this system, its low cost (as few as a few hundred dollars) and reliability have made it the most utilized radiation monitoring system.

The GM counter is also the basis for a family of gas-filled detectors that work on basically the same principle. These include ionization chambers (free air chambers, Bragg–Gray chambers, pocket ionization chamber), proportional counters (P-10 gas chambers, 2-pi windowless detectors, fission chambers, BF_3 filled detectors), and GM-based detectors (cylindrical chambers, pancake probes, end-window tubes).

Since the development of gas-filled detectors and scintillation detectors, a variety of new detection media have been developed for specific applications. A family of solid-state detectors is used for spectroscopy (i.e., determining the energy of radiation). Intrinsic (high purity) germanium detectors are used almost exclusively for gamma-ray spectroscopy. These systems are much more expensive than gas-filled or scintillation detectors, but provide very high energy resolution gamma-ray spectra. The output from these detectors can allow simultaneous quantification of 25 or more radioactive isotopes. Other solid-state detectors include diodes for alpha and beta charged particle detection. These diodes are usually small, coin-sized detectors. Newer solid-state materials include CdTe, CdZnTe, HgI_2, and diamond.

Other miscellaneous detectors include neutron detectors, which are variations on many of the systems mentioned above. They incorporate isotopes which strongly interact with neutrons (such as boron-10, lithium-6, helium-3, and uranium-235) in the detection medium. Thermoluminescent dosimeters are used as personnel monitors, performing the same function as film badges. These are small chips of compounds (LIF:Mg, $CaSO_4$:Mn, CaF_2, and CaF_2:Mn) that store the energy of radiation as they absorb it. This energy is released as light when the chip is heated, giving a measure of the sum of radiation absorbed.

Detector Systems in Response to Nuclear Terrorism

To respond to potential terrorist activities involving radioactive materials, first responders should have a basic, portable, handheld, battery-operated survey meter. This survey meter should include several different probes (detector types) for different functions. First, a standard survey GM tube would be used for general background radiation levels. A GM pancake probe would be important to assess contamination on surfaces or on "swipes" (a piece of paper a few square centimeters in size that is rubbed over a contaminated surface to remove and detect loose contamination). An alpha probe would be included to detect alpha radiation since the GM detectors are sensitive only to gamma rays and beta particles.

Air monitoring to detect airborne radioactive particles would be accomplished using a particulate filter and some sort of air pump. By passing potentially contaminated air through the filter, radioactive particles are captured that are subsequently detected with the GM pancake probe mentioned above. Thus, a basic survey meter would be sufficient to alert first-responders to potentially dangerous levels of external radiation and to radioactive contamination, as well as to airborne radioactive material that could lead to internal radiation doses. This information would be essential to keep citizens away from radiation areas and to give emergency workers general guidance on their ability to work in the area without receiving dangerous amounts of radiation dose.

Other systems for first responders include self-alarming personnel dosimeters. These are based upon either GM or ionization chambers and include electronic circuitry to alarm when an individual is entering a high radiation level. They are often capable of recording total dose and some include a pancake-type module for surface contamination or swipe counting.

Beyond this simple system, more sophisticated instrumentation should be available at regional universities, nuclear power plants, hospitals, etc. These systems would help to more precisely determine the types of radioactive contamination, quantify the radioactive isotopes involved, and detect radioactivity at lower levels for cleanup efforts. This instrumentation should include high resolution gamma-ray spectroscopy systems, liquid scintillation counters, and charged particle spectrometers.

Beyond the regional level, the federal government can provide assistance with National Laboratory personnel through the Radiological Assessment Program. Similarly, the Federal Radiological Monitoring and Assessment Center can respond with the teams of individuals. Both programs include complete analytical instrumentation, sophisticated radiation detection equipment including all of the systems mentioned above, aircraft-based air monitoring systems, and mitigation and clean-up support.

Chapter 15

Nuclear Terrorism: Radiation Detectors—Applications in Homeland Security

Tushar K. Ghosh, Mark A. Prelas,
and Robert V. Tompson, Jr.

CONTENTS

Introduction 278
Detection of Radiation 279
Classification of Detectors 280
Personal Dosimeters........ 281
Pocket Dosimeter 281
Film Badge 284
Thermoluminescent Dosimeter........ 284
Digital Electronic Dosimeter........ 285
Survey Meters 286
MicroR Meter, with Sodium Iodide Detector........ 287
Radionuclide Identifiers........ 288
Liquid Scintillation Counter........ 290
Proportional Counters........ 291
Neutron REM Meter, with Proportional Counter........ 292
Fast Neutron Recoil Nucleus Detectors........ 292
Radiation Detection Portal Monitors 295
Spectroscopic Portal Monitors 295

Mobile and Transportable Systems 296
Compliance Levels 299
Demonstration of Compliance 301
Future Directions for Radiation Detection 301
References 304

Introduction

The basic working mechanisms of radiation detectors are discussed in Chapter 14. For homeland security and counterterrorism, detectors are necessary to detect the alpha, beta, gamma radiations, and neutrons. A single detector is not capable of detecting all four radiations; however, detectors that can detect the alpha, beta, and gamma radiations are available. As a result, multiple detectors may be necessary to protect sensitive areas such as airports, seaports, and other port of entries in the United States. For determining radiation doses to individual, decontamination, criminal investigations it may be necessary to identify specific radioisotopes involved in the terrorist attacks. The type of radioisotopes involved in an attack can be identified from the energy spectrum associated with the emissions of various radiations and their energy levels. In this chapter, various types of radiation detectors applicable to homeland security are discussed. Figures 15.1 and 15.2 show the daunting tasks of inspecting cargos and shipments coming to the United States, and also their movements worldwide. However, there are several megaports in the world (Figure 15.2) that can be redesigned for inspection of cargos and shipments.

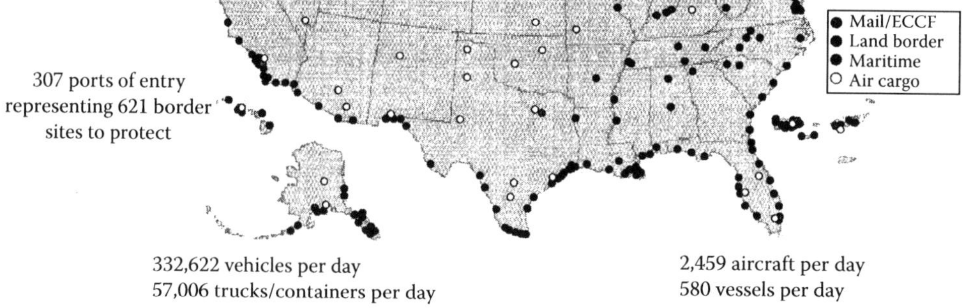

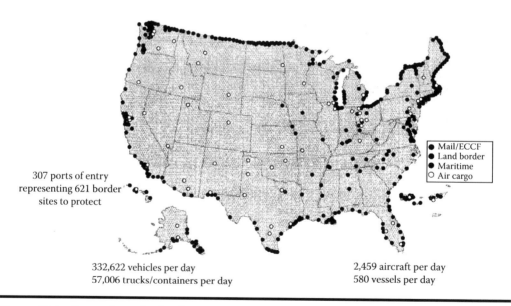

Figure 15.1 Ports of entries in the United States. (From Ely, J. and Kouzes, R.T., Spies, lies, and nuclear threats. Pacific Northwest National Laboratory, PNNL-SA-45766, Health Physics Society Annual Meeting, Washington, DC, July 2005. With permission.)

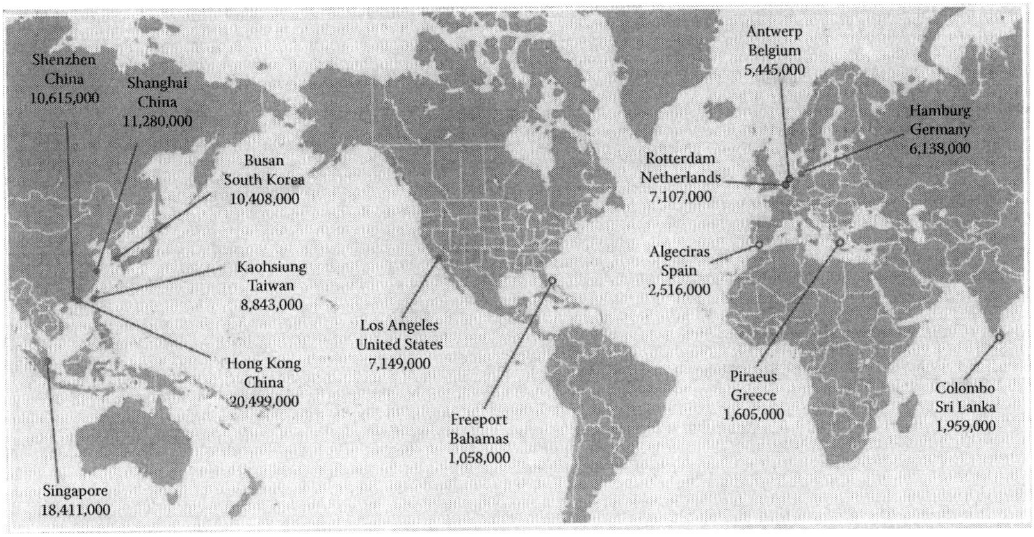

Figure 15.2 Megaports around the world. (From Ely, J. Radiation detection for homeland security: Past, present and future. Pacific Northwest National Laboratory, PNNL-SA-50411, Health Physics Society Annual Meeting, Washington, DC, June 2006. With permission.)

Detection of Radiation

The design of radiation detection systems depends on the type of radiation from a radionuclide. In general, radiation can be grouped into two categories:

- Directly ionizing radiation
- Indirect ionizing radiation

The directly ionizing radiation involves charged particles that have significant electric fields, which can interact directly with the electric fields of the electrons present in materials. These interactions can result in exchange of energy, which may be substantial enough to directly ionize (remove one or more electrons from) the materials that the charged particles are interacting with. Two types of charged particle radiation that are of particular interest are alpha radiation resulting from the decay of nuclear material via the emission of alpha particles and beta radiation resulting from the decay of nuclear material via the emission of beta particle.

The second category, indirect ionizing radiation, involves neutral particles that can interact with the electrons in a material only in an indirect manner. Such interactions can still result in the exchange of energy and the ionization of the materials that the neutral particles are interacting with. Two types of neutral radiation are of particular interest. Neutrons are neutral components of the atomic nucleus that can be emitted by a variety of nuclear processes, and gamma rays are energetic photons that are emitted from the nuclei of excited species as they settle into lower energy states.

Classification of Detectors

Radiation detectors may be classified in a number of ways. They can be categorized based on the radiation detected:

- Alpha detectors
- Beta detectors
- Gamma detectors
- Neutron detectors

Another way to categorize them is as follows:

- Handheld or portable detectors
- Laboratory detectors

The most common handheld, portable detectors are

- Geiger counter, with Geiger–Mueller (GM) tube or probe
- MicroR meter, with sodium iodide detector
- Portable multichannel analyzer
- Ionization (ion) chamber
- Neutron REM meter, with proportional counter

The following instruments are considered laboratory detectors:

- Liquid scintillation counters
- Proportional counter
- Multichannel analyzer system

The U.S. Department of Homeland Security Domestic Nuclear Detection Office (DNDO) is mandated by Congress to set Technical Capability Standards, and implement a Test and Evaluation program, to provide performance, suitability, and survivability information, and related testing, for preventive radiological/nuclear (rad/nuc) detection equipment in the United States. DNDO intends to meet these responsibilities by establishing the Graduated Rad/Nuc Detector Evaluation and Reporting (GRaDER) program.

Based on the technical capability necessary, DNDO has divided the detection systems into following six categories with the objective to develop standards for the equipment and also for the training of the users or operators [3].

- Category 1—Alarming Personal Dosimeters or Pagers
- Category 2—Survey Meters
- Category 3—Radionuclide Identifiers
- Category 4—Radiation Detection Portal Monitors
- Category 5—Spectroscopic Portal Monitors
- Category 6—Mobile and Transportable Systems

Various instruments available under these categories are discussed next.

Personal Dosimeters

1. Pocket dosimeter
2. Film badge
3. Thermoluminescent dosimeter (TLD)
4. Digital electronic dosimeter

Pocket Dosimeter

Pocket dosimeters are direct-reading dosimeters for exposure to x-rays and gamma-rays. As the name implies, they are commonly worn in the pocket and are generally of the size and shape of a fountain pen. These dosimeters work on the principle of ionization of the gas, inside the active volume of the chamber, when a radiation incident occurs. Several detection systems including GM counters work on this principle—ionization of gas. The ionization chamber is described below.

Ionization Chambers

The ionization chamber consists of an anode and a cathode. In some instruments, the outer chamber wall serves as the cathode. The potential difference between the anode and the cathode is in the range 100–500 V. The optimum voltage depends on the chamber size and a number of other factors. Various shapes of the electrodes in the chamber have been proposed and are shown in Figure 15.3. However, the shapes for GM detector or proportional counter are generally well established. In most designs, the outer chamber wall (the cathode) is a cylinder or sphere while the anode is usually rod shaped.

The sensitivity of ionization chamber may be greatly enhanced by using the following design (Figure 15.4). It contains a well detector inside a hollow tubular anode. The sample can be positioned in the center of the chamber.

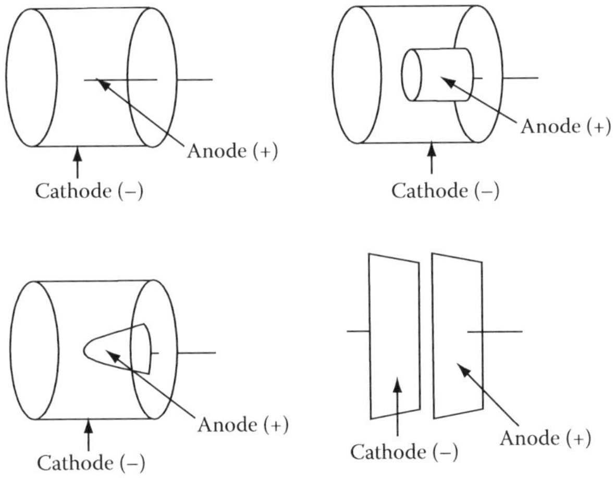

Figure 15.3 Shapes of ionization chambers. (From Oak Ridge Associated University, Ionization Chamber, http://www.orau.org/ptp/collection/ionchamber/introionizationchamberr.htm.)

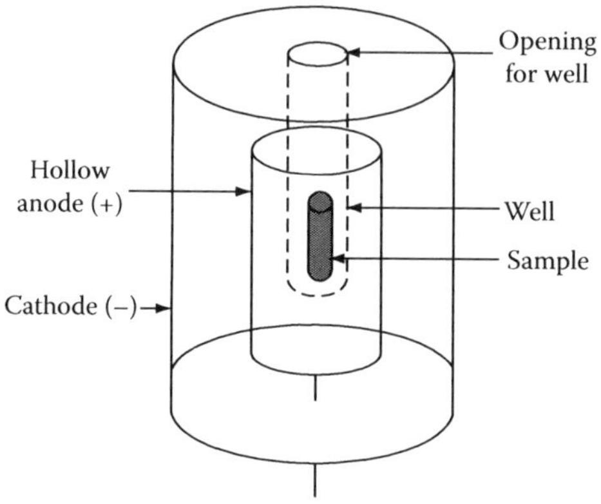

Figure 15.4 Design to enhance sensitivity of ionization chamber. (From Oak Ridge Associated University, Ionization Chamber, http://www.orau.org/ptp/collection/ionchamber/introionizationchamberr.htm.)

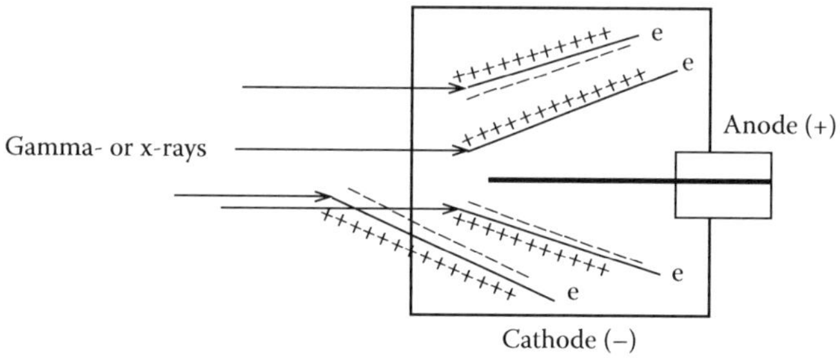

Figure 15.5 Working mechanism of ionization chamber. (From Oak Ridge Associated University, Ionization Chamber, http://www.orau.org/ptp/collection/ionchamber/introionizationchamberr.htm.)

As shown in Figure 15.5, charged particles, alpha or beta, produced through interaction with radiation traverse the gas inside the ionization chamber. The particles should have sufficient energy to penetrate the detector wall. For electrons, gamma- or x-rays, energy is transferred via the photoelectric effect, Compton scattering, or pair production. Most of these gamma- or x-ray interactions occur in the wall of the detector, but some also occur in the chamber fill gas.

The movement of the charged particles through the chamber ionizes the atoms or molecules of the chamber gas, i.e., create ion pairs. This mechanism is shown in Figure 15.6.

The electric field created by the potential difference between the anode and the cathode causes the negative member (electron) of each ion pair to move to the anode while the positively charged gas atom or molecule is drawn to the cathode. The external electrical circuit measures the ion chamber's current which is then correlated to radioactivity or dose. The photograph of a pocket dosimeter and its schematic is shown in Figure 15.7.

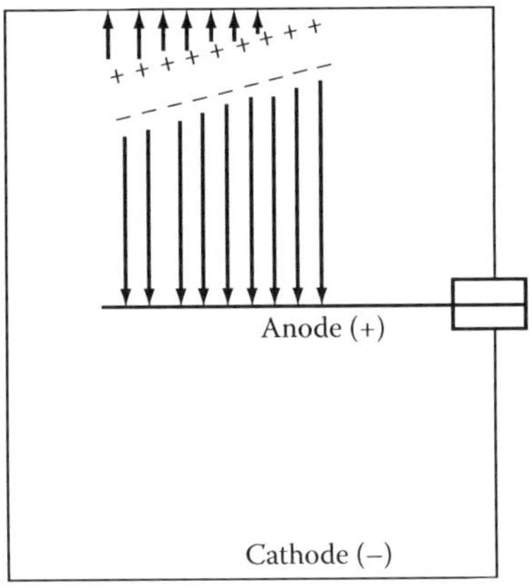

Figure 15.6 Electric field created by potential difference. (From Oak Ridge Associated University, Ionization Chamber, http://www.orau.org/ptp/collection/ionchamber/introionizationchamberr.htm.)

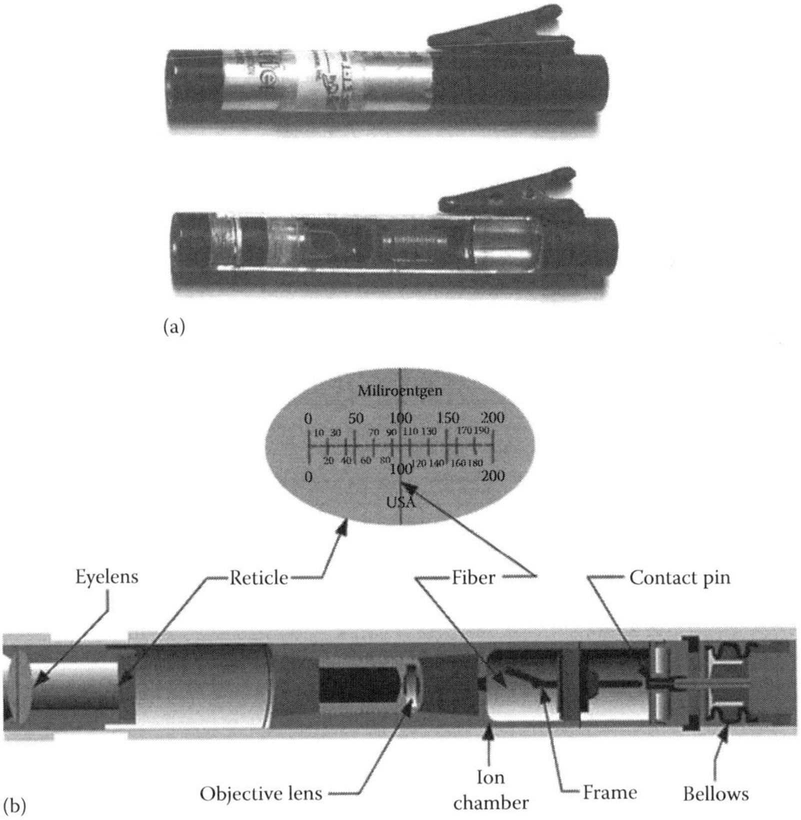

Figure 15.7 Pocket dosimeter: (a) photograph and (b) a schematic drawing. (From NDT Resource center, http://www.ndt-ed.org/EducationResources/CommunityCollege/RadiationSafety/radiation_safety_equipment/pocket_dosimeter.htm. With permission.)

Film Badge

Film badges are commonly used to measure and record radiation exposure due to gamma-rays, x-rays, and beta particles. The film contains a photographic emulsion, silver halide (generally silver bromide) mounted in a plastic container. When a photon, released by incident radiation, interacts with the film emulsion, it undergoes a photoelectric or Compton interaction. The electron that is released deposits its energy altering some of the silver halide grains. During development of the film, these altered grains are reduced to metallic silver. The optical density of the developed film is compared to unexposed film for the entrance of the beta particles or other electrons. The badge holder contains an open window to allow radiation exposure due to beta particles. The badge may also contain three metallic filters, mainly copper, cadmium, and aluminum, placed in different portions of the case to help distinguish among higher energy photons. Films are generally designed to respond to a specific energy range. Metallic filters attenuate the gamma energy to the specific energy level of the film. The film badge can measure the total or whole body, air kerma. A typical commercial film badge from Stanford Dosimetry is shown in Figure 15.8.

Thermoluminescent Dosimeter

The thermoluminescent dosimeter (TLD) is designed to measure doses from x-, beta, and gamma radiations. In a TLD, electrons excited by the photon energy get trapped in the higher energy state until the crystal is heated to a specific temperature. This specific temperature is called the Curie temperature. When heated to the Curie temperature, the electrons return to the valance state releasing the extra energy in the form of visible light photons. The most common crystals used in the TLD in the form of powder are lithium fluoride (LiF), lithium tetraborate ($Li_2B_4O_7$), and manganese-activated calcium fluoride (CaF_2:Mn). Various components of a TLD unit are shown in Figure 15.9.

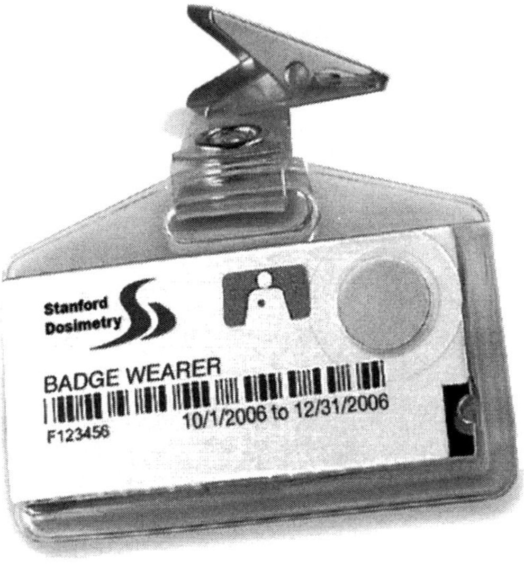

Figure 15.8 A personal dosimeter from Stanford Dosimetry. (From Dosimetry Badge Service, Stanford Dosimetry, LLC, http://www.stanforddosimetry.com/badge_service.html. With permission.)

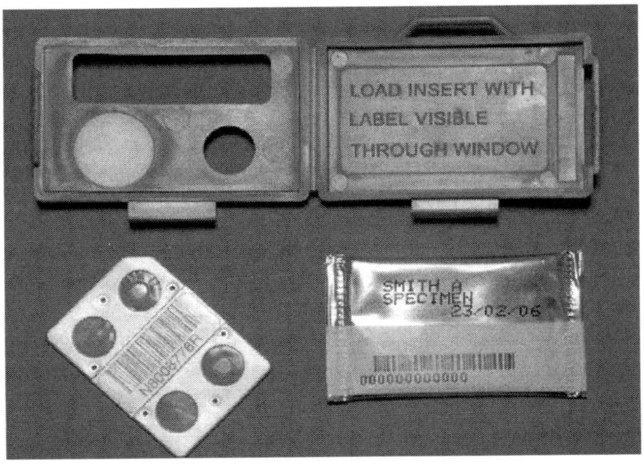

Figure 15.9 Components of TLD. (From Personal Dosimetry Service Radiation Protection Division, Centre for Radiation, Chemical and Environmental Hazards Health Protection Agency, Chilton Didcot Oxon OX11 0RQ, www.hpa.org.uk. With permission.)

Digital Electronic Dosimeter

A number of electronic, digital radiation dosimeters are available in the market. The DHS also prefers this type of personal dosimeters as they cannot only show the data readily in easily readable format, but also can sound alarm when set to a predetermined dose level. One such digital dosimeter is Model PDM-117 electronic pocket dosimeter (EPD) from Cone Instrument (Figure 15.10) that uses semiconductor detectors which are sensitive to gamma- and x-rays of 20 keV and above.

Digital dosimeters are also available for both the neutron and gamma doses. A Thermo Scientific digital dosimeter (Figure 15.11) that contains a photodiode CsI(TL) scintillation detector senses gamma-emitting radioactive materials and provides a useful indication over the range

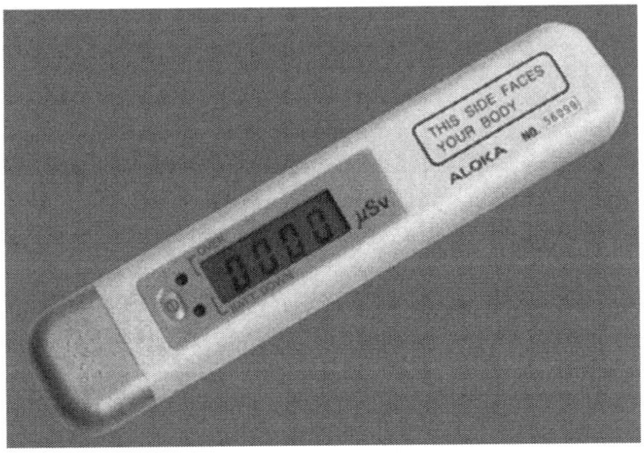

Figure 15.10 Electronic pocket dosimeter. (From Cone Instrument, http://www.coneinstruments.com/CIcatsub1.asp?cat_id = 763. With permission.)

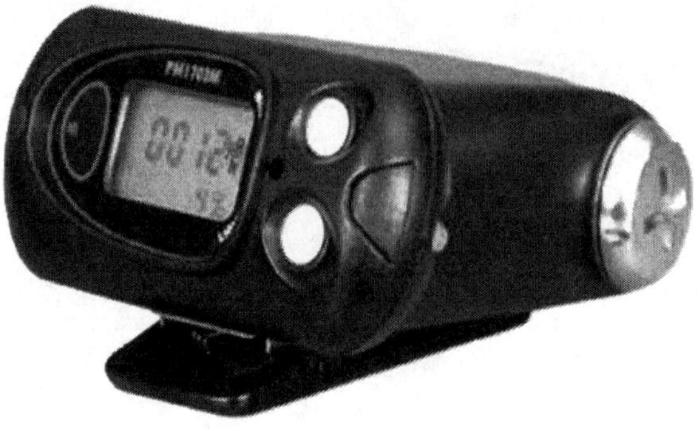

Figure 15.11 Digital dosimeter from Thermo scientific. (Data from Thermo Scientific, http://www.thermo.com/com/cda/resources/resources_detail/1,,200208,00.html?fromPage = search.)

of 0.01–50 μSv/h (10–5000 μR/h) and a neutron detector, a LiI(Eu) scintillator, that is sensitive to neutrons between thermal and 14 MeV.

Survey Meters

Survey meters are used to locate contamination or detect radioactive material. A number of survey meters are available in the market, however, the two most common types of survey instruments used for the detection of ionizing radiation use GM-pancake probe and scintillation (NaI) probe. A typical GM survey meter is shown in Figure 15.12. Although pancake probes are widely used with GM detectors, there are two other design of the probes available: Side Window (cylindrical) and End Window.

The primary function of the pancake GM is the detection and measurement of beta-emitting surface contamination. It also responds to alpha particles and gamma rays. The primary application of the side window GM is the measurement of gamma exposure rates. Nevertheless, its wall can be thin enough to permit higher energy betas (>300 keV) to be counted. Like any GM detector, the end window GM responds to gamma rays. Nevertheless, the end window GM is most

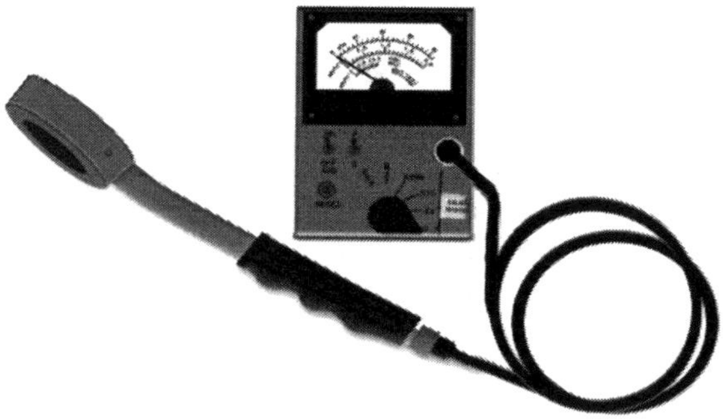

Figure 15.12 A GM counter with a pancake probe.

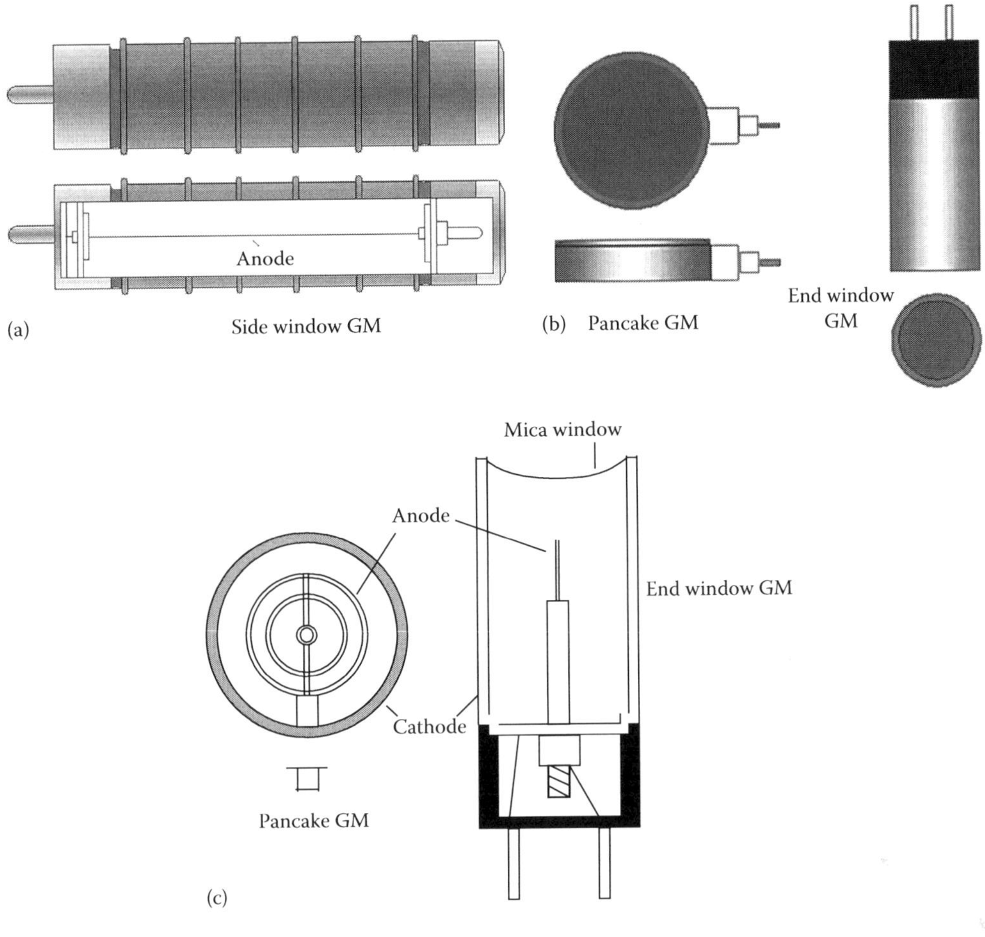

Figure 15.13 Various types of Geiger Mueller (GM) detectors: (a) side window probe, (b) pancake and end window probes, and (c) construction details of pancake and end window probes. (From Oak Ridge Associated Universities, Geiger Mueller (GM) detectors, http://www.orau.org/ptp/collection/GMs/introgms.htm.)

commonly used to count beta activity. The end window GM can also be used to count alpha particles. The basic structure of various probes used in a GM counter is shown in Figure 15.13, and probes available commercially are shown in Figure 15.14.

MicroR Meter, with Sodium Iodide Detector

MicroR meters are designed to measure low-level gamma radiation. Common readout units of MicroR meters are microroentgens per hour (μR/hour) or counts per minute (cpm), and are capable of reading in the range of 0–5000 μR/hour. These meters use a solid crystal of sodium iodide, 1″ × 1″ NaI(TI) scintillator and create a pulse of light when radiation interacts with it. This pulse of light is converted to an electrical signal by a photomultiplier tube (PMT). The pulse of light is proportional to the amount of light and the energy deposited in the crystal. A speaker can be

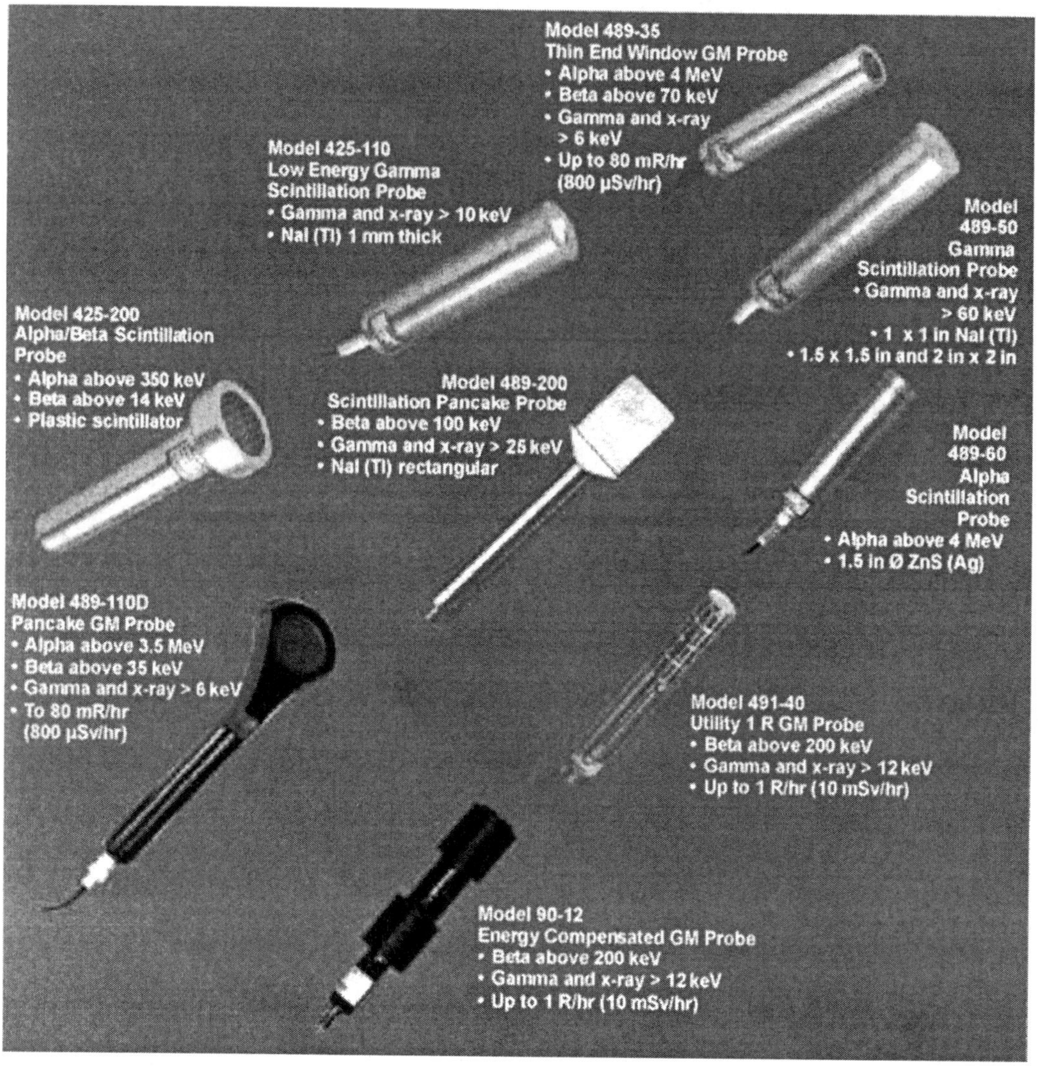

Figure 15.14 Victoreen GM and scintillation probes. (From Radiation Management Services, Fluke Biomedical, http://www.imagingequipment.co.uk/pdf/RS4p8.pdf, www.flukebiomedical.com/rms. With permission.)

incorporated in the meter so that the pulses can give an audible click, a useful feature when looking for a lost source. Special plastic or other inert crystal "scintillator" materials are also used in place of sodium iodide. The front panel of a Ludlum Model 19 MicroR meter is shown in Figure 15.15.

Radionuclide Identifiers

A sodium iodide crystal and a PMT, coupled with a multichannel analyzer (MCA) can be used for identifying radionuclides. A number of handheld units are available in which gamma-ray data libraries and automatic gamma-ray energy identification procedures are incorporated. As a result,

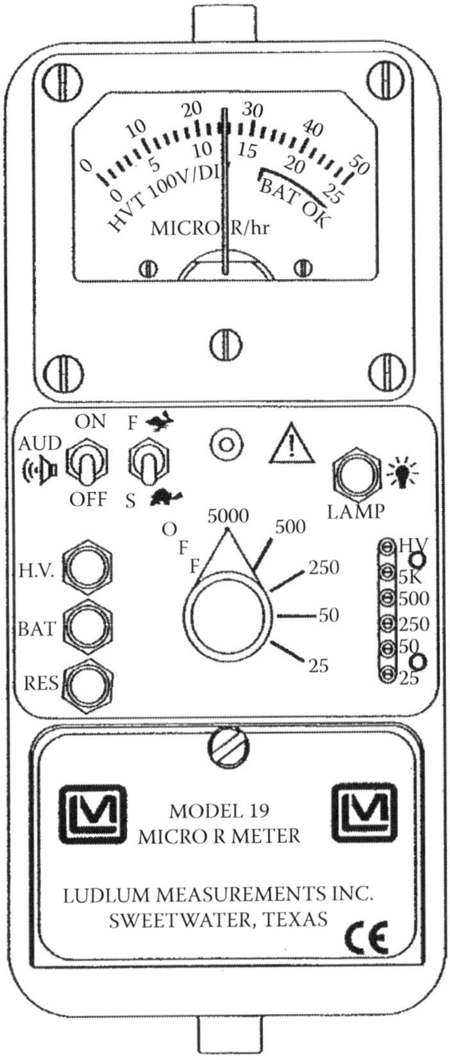

Figure 15.15 The front panel of the widely used Ludlum microR survey meter.

these handheld instruments can automatically identify and display the type of radioactive materials present. The interaction of the alpha, beta, or gamma radiation with the detector material produces electrical pulses of various amplitudes that are proportional to the energy deposited in the detector. The MCA converts these analog pulses to digital values and adds the numerical values in corresponding channels. The resulting energy spectrum represents the probability distribution of the detected radiation as a function of the energy.

These pulses are sorted according to their height by the MCA. This is equivalent to sorting the particles according to their energy. An MCA can be set to do this in the pulse-height analyzer (PHA) mode. The MCA can also scan a whole energy range and record the number of pulses they count in each of the channels. These instruments can be used for identifying gamma emitters and their concentration in a sample, and are often referred to as gamma spectrometers. This is done by comparing the emitted gamma energy with the built-in library of gamma energy corresponding to a particular radionuclide.

Liquid Scintillation Counter

A liquid scintillation counter (LSC) is a traditional laboratory instrument for measuring very low-level radioactivity. It contains two opposing PMTs as shown in Figure 15.16 that view a vial that contains a sample and liquid scintillator fluid, generally called a cocktail, which act as the detector. When the sample emits a radiation (often a low-energy beta), it interacts with the cocktail emitting a pulse of light. If both PMTs detect the light in coincidence, the count is tallied. With the use of shielding, cooling of PMTs, energy discrimination, and this coincidence-counting approach, very low background counts can be achieved. Current LSC units consist of an automatic sample changer allowing multiple sample analyses without operator intervention after each sample, automatic data acquisition, data reduction, and storage.

The cocktail is a mixture of organic solvents; an emulsifier which ensures proper mixing of aqueous samples in the organic solvents; and a fluor, a substance which has the capability of fluorescing when excited by the radioactive substance. Figure 15.17 provides an illustration of interaction of the emitted radiation with the cocktail. The cocktail may be bought directly from several manufacturers. Toluene, dioxane, benzene, and xylene are used to be the solvents of choice. Later, pseudocumene (1,2,4-trimethylbeneze) was tried. However, a number of new generation environmental friendly, safe solvents have been proposed recently. The most common primary scintillator or fluor is diphenyl oxazole (PPO). Bis-MSB, together with POPOP is the secondary scintillators used in most cocktails. Most common surfactant used for emulsification is Triton-X-200 (from Rohm and Haas).

The amplitude of the electrical pulse is converted into a digital value and the digital value, which represents the beta particle energy, passes into the analyzer where it is compared to digital values for each of the LSC's channels. The energy of the radiation or the amount of radioactive material dissolved in the cocktail is quantified.

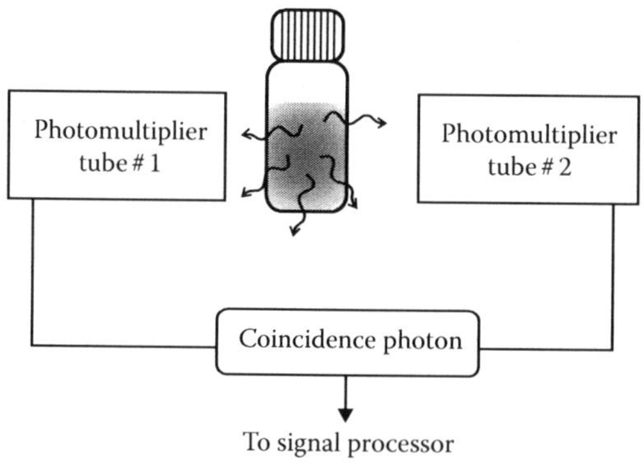

Figure 15.16 The counting protocol of the liquid scintillation counter.

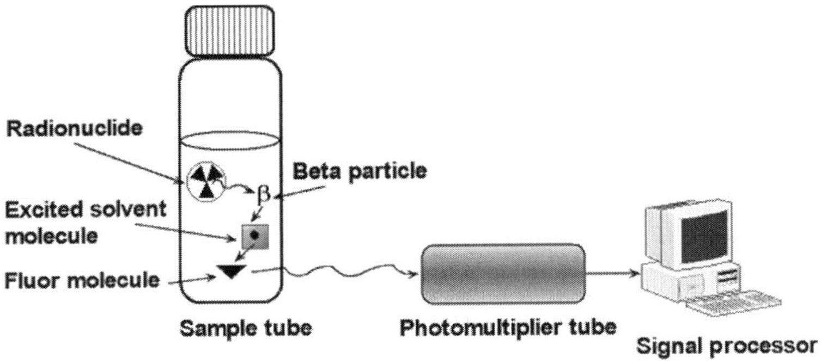

Figure 15.17 Liquid scintillation working mechanism and counting process.

Proportional Counters

Proportional counters are used for quantifying alpha and beta activity, for neutron detection, and to some extent for x-ray spectroscopy. The pulses produced by a proportional counter are larger than those produced by an ion chamber, therefore, are generally operated in the pulse mode (ion chambers usually operate in the current mode). Also, it is possible to distinguish the larger pulses produced by alpha particles from the smaller pulses produced by beta or gamma rays. Three types of proportional counters have been proposed for measuring alpha, beta, tritium, and neutrons.

1. Gas flow proportional—with window (e.g., laboratory alpha–beta counters)
   —windowless (e.g., tritium measurements)
2. Air proportional (alpha counting only)
3. Sealed proportional (e.g., BF_3, He-3 neutron detectors)

The size of the pulse in a proportional counter depends on two things: (1) operating voltage—the higher the operating voltage, the larger each avalanche becomes and the larger the pulse, and (2) energy deposited in the detector gas—the greater the energy deposited in the detector gas by an incident particle of radiation, the larger the number of primary ion pairs, the larger the number of avalanches, and the larger the pulse.

Fill Gas

A number of fill gases are in use in proportional counters. Generally, the proportional gas does not contain oxygen, because electrons heading toward the anode will combine with the electronegative oxygen. In this way negative ions will be picked up by oxygen preventing electron flow and an avalanche of electrons. The result is that the pulse is probably too small to exceed the threshold setting and be counted.

Air is sometimes used as a proportional gas for alpha counting. However, air is not suitable for beta counting. Use of air in the proportional counter allows the use of a thin window when counting alpha particles without the need for a gas-flow system. However, it is essential that the air be dry. In high-humidity conditions, air proportional counters are prone to generating spurious pulses.

For beta counting, the fill gas in a proportional counter (and a GM detector) is usually a noble gas because noble gases are not electronegative and are inert chemically toward detector components. Of the noble gases, argon is the most widely used because of its low cost, but krypton and xenon have also been explored, particularly for low-level x-rays or gamma rays. Methane, propane, and ethylene can also serve as a fill gas, but they have the disadvantage of being flammable.

For dose calculation, a fill gas equivalent to human tissue is used, which is a mixture of 64.4 percent methane, 32.4 percent carbon dioxide, and 3.2 percent nitrogen.

A quench gas is added to prevent the proportional counter from acting like a GM detector. A small amount of methane or CO_2 can act as the quench gas. The quench gas preferentially absorbs the photons, but unlike the fill gas (e.g., argon), it does so without becoming ionized. P-10 gas is the most widely employed gas for gas flow proportional counters. It is a mixture of 90 percent argon and 10 percent methane.

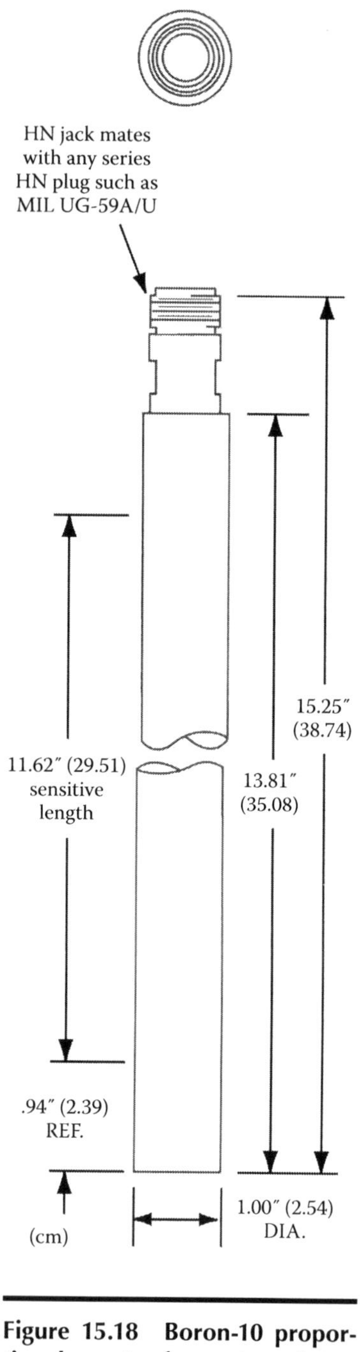

Figure 15.18 Boron-10 proportional counter for neutron detection. (From GE Energy, Boron-10 Proportional Counter, http://www.gepower.com/prod_serv/products/oc/en/reuter_stokes/security_safeguards/boron10.htm. With permission.)

Neutron REM Meter, with Proportional Counter

A boron trifluoride or helium-3 proportional counter tube is a gas-filled device that, when a high voltage is applied, creates an electrical pulse when a neutron radiation interacts with the gas in the tube. The absorption of a neutron in the nucleus of boron-10 or helium-3 causes the prompt emission of a helium-4 nucleus or proton, respectively. These charged particles can then cause ionization in the gas, which is collected as an electrical pulse, similar to the GM tube. The basic design of a neutron detector from GE is shown in Figure 15.18. These neutron-measuring proportional counters require large amounts of hydrogenous material around them to slow the neutron to thermal energies. Other surrounding filters allow an appropriate number of neutrons to be detected and thus provide a flat-energy response with respect to dose equivalent. The design and characteristics of these devices are such that the amount of secondary charge collected is proportional to the degree of primary ions produced by the radiation. Thus, through the use of electronic discriminator circuits, the different types of radiation can be measured separately. For example, gamma radiation up to rather high levels is easily rejected in neutron counters.

Fast Neutron Recoil Nucleus Detectors

Elastic scattering of fast neutrons with light nuclei leads to the transfer of some of the fast neutrons' kinetic energy to the

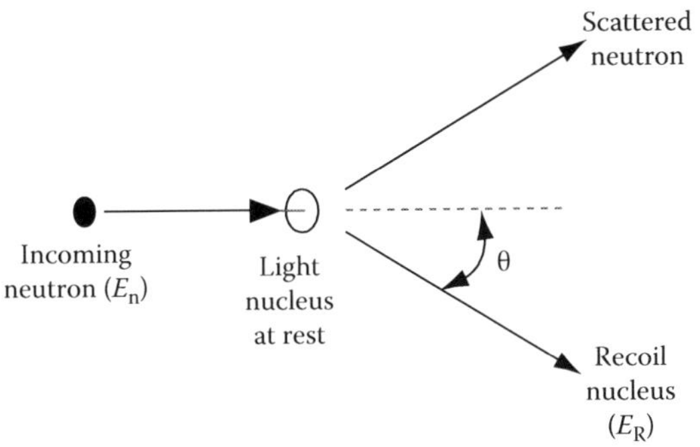

Figure 15.19 Neutron scattering event in the laboratory system.

light nuclear (Figure 15.19). In this reaction, the fast neutron strikes the light nucleus. The fast neutron loses energy and the light nucleus gains energy.

If sufficient energy is transferred from the neutron to the light nucleus to break the chemical bonds, which hold the detector material together, the light nuclei will recoil. The recoil nuclei will then behave much like a charged particle (e.g., proton or alpha) slowing down in the detector material. The process of slowing down will cause ionization and will lead to the formation of ion pairs in the material. As previously discussed, ionization can be used in several ways for detection. For example, the charge can be collected and counted. Another possibility is to use the ions to promote the production of photons, which can be collected and counted (see discussion on scintillators).

Light nuclei, in an elastic scattering event with a neutron, can come off the reaction with a significant fraction of the neutron's initial energy. The governing equation of the recoil nucleus energy is given by [13]:

$$E_R = \left[4A/(1+A)^2\right]\cos^2\theta E_n \tag{15.1}$$

where

A is the mass of light nuclear/neutron mass
E_n is the incoming neutron kinetic energy in laboratory system
E_R is the recoil nucleus kinetic energy in laboratory system
θ is the scattering angle of recoil nucleus in the laboratory coordinate system

The maximum possible recoil energy occurs when the angle θ is zero. Thus, we can calculate the maximum energy transfer from a neutron to a light nuclear using Equation 15.1 (Table 15.1).

The maximum energy transfer ratio (METR) tells us the maximum amount of energy that the neutron can transfer to the light nuclei in a recoil reaction. For example, if a 1 million eV neutron strikes a carbon nucleus, the maximum recoil energy the carbon nucleus will have is 0.284 million eV. Not all reactions will result in the carbon nucleus having the maximum recoil energy. There will be a distribution of energies for the recoil carbon nuclei. The energy distribution of the carbon nuclei is related to the scattering angle Θ in the center-of-mass coordinate system [13]

Table 15.1 Maximum Energy Transfer Ratio (METR) = $E_R/E_n = 4A/(1 + A)^2$

Light Nuclei	A	METR
Hydrogen	1	1
Deuterium	2	0.889
Helium 3	3	0.750
Helium 4	4	0.640
Carbon	12	0.284
Oxygen	16	0.221

$$P(E_R)=\left[(1+A)^2/A\right]\left[\sigma(\Theta)/\sigma_s\right](\pi/E_n) \tag{15.2}$$

where

$P(E_R)$ is the probability function for the light nuclei to have a recoil energy of E_R
$\sigma(\Theta)$ is the differential scattering cross section in the center-of-mass coordinate system
σ_s is the scattering cross section

The detection efficiency (ε) of recoil type detectors for a single species is [13]

$$\varepsilon = 1 - \exp(-N\sigma_s d) \tag{15.3}$$

where

N is the number density of the light atom in the detector material
d is the path length of the neutron through the detector

For example, if you choose the detector material to be a 5-cm diamond crystal and you wanted to measure neutron energy of 1 million eV, the detector efficiency would be about 99 percent. A diamond-based neutron sensor would be an ideal recoil-type neutron detector. The ideal recoil detector would use a single crystal medium made up of one type of light nuclei at high density. You would want the charge being generated by the interaction of the recoil nuclei with the detector media to be able to flow quickly to a collector with minimal charge losses. You would want the detector to have very low thermal as well as other sources of noise. Diamond meets all of these criteria; however, this is an advanced concept for which the state of the art will be discussed at the end of the chapter.

Quite a bit of work has been done on proton recoil detection systems. The proton recoil systems are usually complicated by the presence of carbon because the proton-rich media are organic. Often times these types of detectors use scintillation methods because organic materials are not good at transporting electrons or ions to collectors.

The discrimination of neutrons and gamma in recoil-type detectors is straightforward through pulse height discrimination.

Radiation Detection Portal Monitors

The Department of Homeland Security (DHS) is responsible for providing radiation detection capabilities at U.S. ports of entry. On April 15, 2005, the National Security Presidential Directive 43/Homeland Security Presidential Directive 14, Domestic Nuclear Detection (April 15, 2005) allowed, within DHS, the establishment of Domestic Nuclear Detection Office (DNDO), whose duties include acquiring and supporting the deployment of radiation detection equipment. Customs and Border Protection (CBP) under DHS continues its traditional screening function at ports of entry to interdict dangerous nuclear and radiological materials through the use of radiation detection equipment, including portal monitors. The Pacific Northwest National Laboratory (PNNL), one of the Department of Energy's (DOE) national laboratories, manages the deployment of radiation portal monitors for DHS. The radiation portal is specifically designed to detect low energy gamma rays and neutron emissions, a combination that is characteristic of weapons-grade plutonium and highly enriched uranium.

The radiation portal monitors provide passive, nonintrusive means to screen trucks and other conveyances for the presence of the nuclear and radiological materials. These systems are capable of detecting various types of radiation emanating from nuclear devices, dirty bombs, special nuclear materials, natural sources, and isotopes commonly used in medicine and industry. A variety of portal monitors have been developed to meet various needs (see Figures 15.20 and 15.21).

Spectroscopic Portal Monitors

Sodium iodide detectors can be incorporated in radiation portal monitors (Figure 15.22). These systems will allow the positive identification of radioactive isotopes for the resolution of alarms, and improved rejection of naturally occurring radioactive material (found in cargo such as kitty litter, tile, and fertilizer).

Figure 15.20 A radiation portal monitor for inspection of trucks. (From RadSentry™ Security Portals for SNM and Other Radionuclides, CANBERRA, http://www.canberra.com/pdf/Products/Systems_pdf/C30008-RadSentry-SS.pdf. With permission.)

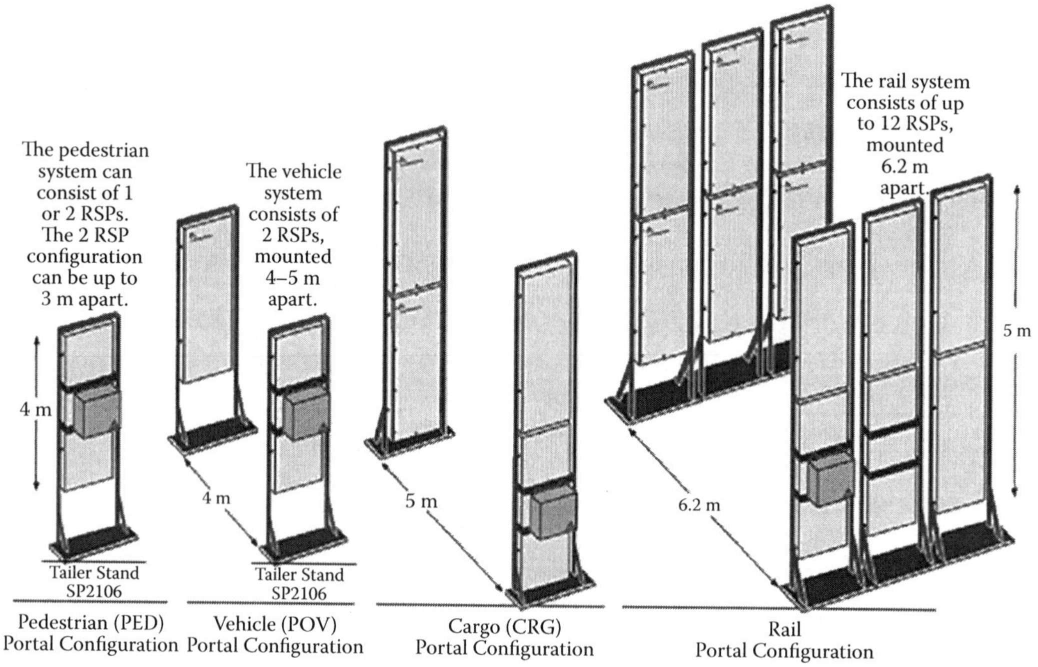

Figure 15.21 Large area gamma-ray scintillators, sensitive to photons from 25 to 3000 keV and large volume He-3 neutron detectors with albedo neutron cavity for optimum neutron capture. (From RadSentry™ Security Portals for SNM and Other Radionuclides, CANBERRA, http://www.canberra.com/pdf/Products/Systems_pdf/C30008-RadSentry-SS.pdf. With permission.)

CANBERRA has developed a germanium (Ge) spectroscopic portal (ASP) monitor. This system has been adapted for secondary screening of cargo containers. Germanium detectors are 15–25 times better than sodium iodide scintillators (FWHM). The CANBERRA system can be operated in three different modes—pass through, intermittent wait-in, and targeted wait-in. In pass through mode, vehicle speeds can be about 5 mph (8 kph). Intermittent pass through requires the vehicle to be stopped manually at fixed intervals (e.g., four stops at 14 ft spacing for 30 s-each). This mode provides better sensitivity and position information. In the targeted mode, the inspection is carried out at a single location.

Mobile and Transportable Systems

This portable radiation-detection device is mounted to a truck chassis and is designed to scan cargo containers on the ground or on trucks, especially at seaports (Figure 15.23).

Radionuclides that these portals shall be able to identify are given below. These radionuclides should be detected at the reference speed (portals) or collection interval (fixed) as required [16]:

- Unshielded: ^{57}Co, ^{60}Co, ^{67}Ga, ^{99}mTc, ^{131}I, ^{133}Ba, ^{137}Cs, ^{192}Ir, ^{201}Tl, ^{233}U, ^{235}U, ^{238}U, plutonium*, ^{241}Am, ^{237}Np.
- Natural materials: Natural sources (such as potash, granite, and ceramic tile) will be used to test monitors for the ability to identify the isotopes ^{40}K, ^{226}Ra, and ^{232}Th.

Figure 15.22 Interior view of the prototype spectroscopic portal monitor constructed at PNNL. (From Radiation Portal monitors, Pacific Northwest National Laboratory, http://rdns-group.pnl.gov/projects.stm (McCormick, K.R. et al., Spectroscopic radiation portal monitor prototype, *2005 IEEE Nuclear Science Symposium Conference Record,* Piscataway, NJ, N14-4, 2005, 292–296. With permission.)

- Shielded by materials that are typical of inspected containers: ^{60}Co, ^{131}I, ^{133}Ba, ^{137}Cs, ^{192}Ir, ^{238}U, plutonium*, ^{237}Np
- Monitors shall identify either weapons-grade plutonium or reactor-grade plutonium (>12 percent ^{240}Pu)

List of radionuclides that handheld devices should be capable of identifying are given below. The radionuclides of greatest interest and those most likely to be encountered are listed below in four different categories:

- Nuclear materials: ^{233}U, ^{235}U, ^{237}Np, Pu*
- Medical radionuclides: ^{18}F (PET), ^{67}Ga, ^{99m}Tc, ^{111}In, ^{123}I, ^{125}I, ^{131}I, ^{133}Xe, ^{201}TI
- Industrial radionuclides: ^{57}Co, ^{60}Co, ^{133}Ba, ^{137}Cs, ^{192}Ir, ^{241}Am
- Naturally occurring radioactive materials (NORM): ^{40}K, ^{226}Ra (in equilibrium with daughters), ^{232}Th and decay products, ^{238}U and decay products

The instrument shall be able to identify the following radionuclides within the times indicated after exposure to the radionuclide:

- Unshielded, in one minute: ^{111}In, ^{133}Xe, ^{99m}Tc, ^{201}TI, ^{67}Ga, ^{125}I, ^{123}I, ^{131}I, ^{18}F(PET)
- Behind 3 mm steel shielding, in two minutes: ^{235}U, ^{238}U, ^{57}Co, ^{241}Am, ^{237}Np

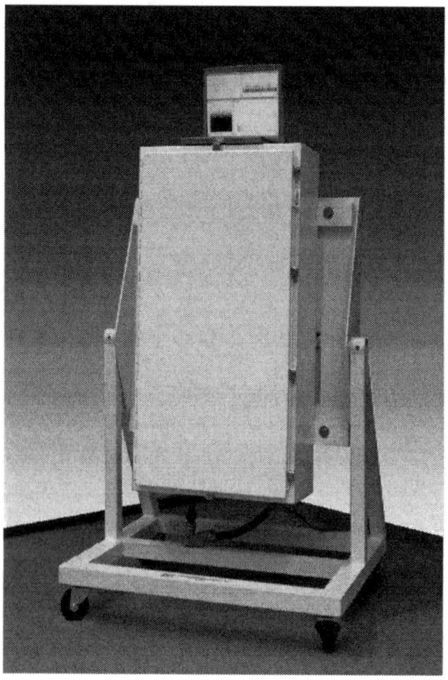

Figure 15.23 The adaptable radiation area monitor (ARAM). (This was developed by scientists and engineers at Lawrence Livermore National Laboratory and licensed to Textron Defense Systems, Wilmington. https://publicaffairs.llnl.gov/news/news_releases/2008/NR-08-10-01.html. With permission.)

- Behind 5 mm steel shielding, in two minutes: Pu*, ^{233}U, ^{133}Ba, ^{40}K, ^{226}Ra, ^{232}Th, ^{137}Cs, ^{60}Co, ^{192}Ir.
- – * >6 percent ^{240}Pu

As described earlier in the chapter, a number of radiation detection systems are available. The DNDO, working with American National Standard Institute, has developed various standards, protocols, and certification processes for these radiation detection systems. These standards are given below [3]:

a. ANSI N42.32-2006 American National Standard Performance Criteria for Alarming Personal Radiation Detectors for Homeland Security
b. ANSI N42.33-2006 American National Standard for Portable Radiation Detection Instrumentation for Homeland Security
c. ANSI N42.34-2006 American National Standard Performance Criteria for Hand-Held Instruments for the Detection and Identification of Radionuclides
d. ANSI N42.35-2006 American National Standard for Evaluation and Performance of Radiation Detection Portal Monitors for Use in Homeland Security
e. ANSI N42.38-2006 American National Standard Performance Criteria for Spectroscopy-Based Portal Monitors Used for Homeland Security
f. ANSI N42.43-2006 American National Standard Performance Criteria for Mobile and Transportable Radiation Monitors Used for Homeland Security

Compliance Levels

The DNDO categorized the instrument performance by different compliance levels. This information is quoted directly from the DNDO report verbatim. The compliance levels are

- Level 0—Equipment has not been tested, the test results are not available or the test results do not meet the minimum subset of the ANSI/Institute of Electrical and Electronic Engineers (IEEE) standards as set forth below in each category
- Level 1—Equipment partially meets the ANSI/IEEE standards and demonstrated specified performance compared to selected key sections of the standards
- Level 2—Equipment fully meets the ANSI/IEEE standards
- Level 3—Equipment fully meets Level 1 or Level 2, and also satisfies the requirements of the applicable published government-unique technical capability standards

The Department adopted several ANSI/IEEE standards against which to test and evaluate radiation detection instruments. Listed below are the equipment categories and corresponding ANSI/IEEE N42 test standards that a given type of instrument must meet to satisfy each described level. Additional levels may be designated once government-unique technical capability standards are approved and published, and government testing is completed using the new standards.

a. **Category 1**—Alarming Personal Dosimeters or Pagers. ANSI N42.32-2006 American National Standard Performance Criteria for Alarming Personal Radiation Detectors for Homeland Security.
   Level 0—Equipment is not tested, or test results not available, or does not meet the minimum subset of the ANSI standards for the levels listed below
   Level 1—The instrument meets all the ANSI N42.32 requirements, except one or more of the following:
   - Functionality test (Section 5.7 ANSI N42.32-2006)
   - Vibration alarm (Section 5.9 ANSI N42.32-2006)
   - Explosive atmosphere (Section 5.14 ANSI N42.32-2006)
   - ANSI N42.42 Data format (Section 5.16 ANSI N42.32-2006)
   - Vibration test (Section 9.1 ANSI N42.32-2006) and meets the following modified requirements, in lieu of the original ANSI requirements:
     - Time to alarm needs to be ≤4 s, does not need to respond to ^{241}Am (Section 6.3 ANSI N42.32-2006) (^{241}Am will be replaced by ^{57}Co or 122 keV x-rays for the NVLAP accreditation program)
     - Temperature range needs to be from 0°C to 50°C (Section 7.1 ANSI N42.32-2006)
   - Does not need to meet cold temperature start-up requirement (Section 7.5 ANSI N42.32-2006)

   Level 2—The instrument meets all the ANSI N42.32 requirements.
   Level 3—The instrument meets all the government-unique technical capability standards requirements, when published.

b. **Category 2**—Survey meters. ANSI N42.33-2006 American National Standard for Portable Radiation Detection Instrumentation for Homeland Security.
   Level 0—Equipment is not tested, or test results not available, or does not meet the minimum subset of the ANSI standards for the levels listed below

Level 1—The instrument meets all the ANSI N42.33 requirements, except the following:

- Functionality test (Section 5.5 ANSI N42.33-2006)
- Vibration (Section 5.7 ANSI N42.33-2006)
- Batteries replaced without tools (Section 5.11 ANSI N42.33-2006)
- Explosive atmosphere (Section 5.10 ANSI N42.33-2006)
- ANSI N42.42 Data format (Section 5.12 ANSI N42.33-2006)
- Cold temperature start-up (Section 7.5 ANSI N42.33-2006)
- Vibration test (Section 9.1 ANSI N42.33-2006)
- Meets the following modified requirements, in lieu of the original ANSI requirements:
  - Instruments do not need to meet the accuracy test for exposure rates lower than 100 μR/hour (Section 6.2 ANSI N42.33-2006);
  - Instruments do not need to meet the photon energy response for ^{241}Am (Section 6.3 ANSI N42.33-2006) (^{241}Am will be replaced by ^{57}Co or x-rays of 122 keV for the NVLAP accreditation program)
  - Instruments do not need to meet the variation of response with angle of incidence for ^{241}Am (Section 6.5 ANSI N42.33-2006) (^{241}Am will be replaced by ^{57}Co or x-rays of 122 keV for GRaDER program)
  - Temperature range needs to be from 0°C to 50°C (Section 7.1 ANSI N42.33-2006)

Level 2—The instrument meets all the ANSI/IEEE N42.33 requirements.

Level 3—The instrument meets all the government-unique technical capability standards requirements, when published.

c. **Category 3**—Radionuclide identifiers. ANSI N42.34 2006 American National Standard Performance Criteria for Hand-Held Instruments for the Detection and Identification of Radionuclides.

Level 0—Equipment is not tested, or test results not available, or does not meet the minimum subset of the ANSI standards for the levels listed below.

Level 1—The instrument meets all the ANSI N42.34 requirements, except the following:

- Interface communication (Section 5.5 ANSI N42.34-2006)
- User interface (Section 5.6 ANSI N42.34-2006)
- Connection to external DC power (Section 5.8 ANSI N42.34-2006)
- Explosive atmosphere (Section 5.11 ANSI N42.34-2006)
- Cold temperature start-up (Section 7.5 ANSI N42.34-2006) and meets the following modified requirements, in lieu of the original ANSI requirements
- Response time ≤2 s (Section 6.2 ANSI N42.34-2006)
- Single radionuclide identification requirements will be limited to the following list of radionuclides— ^{235}U, ^{238}U, ^{239}Pu, ^{241}Am, ^{192}Ir, ^{137}Cs, ^{60}Co
- (Section 6.6 ANSI N42.34-2006)
- Simultaneous radionuclide identification—identify one of the two radionuclides (Section 6.7 ANSI N42.34-2006)
- Radionuclide identifications in ≤5 min (Sections 6.6 and 6.7 ANSI N42.34-2006)
- Over-range—instrument does not need to recover in 30 min (Section 6.17 ANSI N42.34-2006)
- Temperature range needs to be from 0°C to 50°C (Section 7.1 ANSI N42.34-2006)

Level 2—The instrument meets all the ANSI N42.34 requirements.

Note—Testing laboratories need to base the 50 μR/hour exposure rate on the radionuclide of interest. If source used for testing has impurities (e.g., ^{241}Am impurity in a RGPu source) then the exposure rate for testing needs to be produced by the radionuclide of interest and not the impurities present in the source. This applies to Category 3 only.

Level 3—The instrument meets all the government-unique technical capability standards requirements, when published.

d. **Category 4**—Radiation Detection Portal Monitors—To be published (TBP). ANSI N42.35-2006 American National Standard for Evaluation and Performance of Radiation Detection Portal Monitors for Use in Homeland Security.
Level 0—Equipment is not tested, or test results not available, or does not meet the minimum subset of the ANSI standards for the levels listed below
Level 1—To be published in an update on this site
Level 2—The instrument meets all the ANSI N42.35 requirements
Level 3—The instrument meets all the government-unique technical capability standards requirements, when published

e. **Category 5**—Spectroscopic Portal Monitors—ANSI N42.38-2006 American National Standard Performance Criteria for Spectroscopy-Based Portal Monitors Used for Homeland Security.
Level 0—Equipment is not tested, or test results not available, or does not meet the minimum subset of the ANSI standards for the levels listed below
Level 1—TBP in an update on this Web site
Level 2—The instrument meets all the ANSI N42.38 requirements
Level 3—The instrument meets all the government-unique technical capability standards requirements, when published.

f. **Category 6**—Mobile and Transportable Systems (No Subset Anticipated; Level 1 does not apply.)—ANSI N42.43-2006 American National Standard Performance Criteria for Mobile and Transportable Radiation Monitors Used for Homeland Security.
Level 0—Equipment is not tested, or test results not available, or does not meet the minimum subset of the ANSI standards for the levels listed below;
Level 1—TBP in an update on this Web site.
Level 2—The instrument meets all the ANSI N42.43 requirements.
Level 3—The instrument meets all the government-unique technical capability standards requirements, when published.

Demonstration of Compliance

The Compliance Level designation may be attained based upon either of the following:

- New test data from DNDO-accepted or NVLAP-accredited laboratories using existing ANSI/IEEE consensus standards
- New government test data using government-unique standards for certain categories of equipment

Future Directions for Radiation Detection

Improvements in neutron detection techniques have only been incremental during the last few decades when compared to charged particle detection and gamma detection. The reason is that neutrons are very difficult to detect. The bulk of the improvements have occurred with

Table 15.2 Compounds for Future Radiation Detectors

Material	*Band Gap (eV)*	*Density (g/cm^3)*	*Comments*	*Space/Medical/General Applications*
InSb	0.17	5.66	Narrow band gap, three times better energy resolution than Si	High-resolution x-ray astronomy (He_3 temperatures), XRF
InAs	0.35	5.68	Narrow band gap, two times better energy resolution than Si	High-resolution x-ray astronomy (He_3 temperatures), XRF
AlSb	1.62	4.26	Theoretically the best all-round performer	Room temperature Si replacement, compact planetary spectrometers
PbO	1.9	9.8	Highest *Z*, γ-ray detection	Compact γ-ray planetary detectors/radio-guided probes
cBP	2.0	2.9	Thermal neutron detection	Spacecraft in-orbit neutron monitor, neutron capture therapy
i-B_4C	2.0	2.51	Thermal neutron detection, cross section ~4000 barns, third hardest material	Spacecraft in-orbit neutron monitor, neutron capture therapy
III-N			High temperature ceramics, chemically inert, stable, range of band gaps	High temperature applications, planetary surfaces, solid-state lighting
InN	2.0 (0.7)	6.81	High effective hole mass, high *Z*	Compact γ-ray spectrometer for planetary rovers
GaN	3.4	6.15	High-mobility, high-speed applications	Solar x-ray monitors, penetrators, synchrotron applications
c-BN	6.1	3.48	Neutron detection, extremely radiation hard, second hardest material	Planetary surface neutron monitor, nuclear pile detectors
AlN	6.2	3.25	Widest band gap, radiation hard	Solar blind x-ray monitors, well logging
CdMnTe	2.1	5.8	γ-Ray detection, inexpensive replacement for CdZnTe	γ-Ray astronomy, low cost γ-ray imagers/PET detectors, well logging

Table 15.2 (continued) Compounds for Future Radiation Detectors

Material	*Band Gap (eV)*	*Density (g/cm³)*	*Comments*	*Space/Medical/General Applications*
4H-SiC	3.2	3.2	All-round radiation detection (p, n, γ) in extreme environments, radiation hard	Planetary surface x-ray spectrometer, solar flame monitor, nuclear reactors
TlBr	2.68	7.56	High *Z*, γ-ray detection	γ-Ray astronomy/radio guided probes, well logging
Diamond	5.4	3.52	High temperature, hardest material, chemically inert, radiation hard, robust, stable	Detectors for hot corrosive atmospheres, solar flare monitors, hadron therapy, tissue equivalent detectors

Source: Owens, A. and Peacock, A., *Nucl. Inst. Meth. Phys. Res. Sect. A: Accelerators, Spectrometers, Detectors Assoc. Equipment*, 531(1–2), 18, September 21, 2004. With permission.)

Note: The prefixes c, i, and 4H identify a particular crystal structure, i.e., cubic, icosahedral, and four-plane hexagonal, respectively. Apart from AlSb and CdMnTe, which could become the workhorses of room temperature x- and gamma-ray spectrometry, each material has great potential in a specific area. Even though diamond, SiC, and TlBr are already under investigation, we include them here for future development because of their immaturity.

scintillation detection through the reducing noise, better photon collection designs, better optical detection, and better modeling. Various materials suggested for radiation detectors are given in Table 15.2.

Proportional counters have also seen improvements by using lower noise housings (carbon fiber), better electronics, and better modeling. One can only expect a continuation of incremental improvements in the scintillation and proportional counting methods.

Neutron detection is poised for significant gains in the area of recoil detectors. The main emphasis area for future research is to develop solid-state-based radiation detectors. The two main goals are in the development of semiconductor-based detector materials and the growth of crystals of these semiconductor materials.

A strategy that has been pursued on an international scale is solid-state thermal neutron detectors in which coatings of neutron-to-alpha conversion materials (e.g., boron-10 and Li-6) are placed in various configurations on semiconductor materials [18,19]. These types of detectors are typically limited in efficiency to a range of about 2–5 percent/cm^2 because of the limited thickness of the converter layer. With advanced three-dimensional design of the convertor layer and semiconductor substrate, [2] has projected a possible efficiency of 75 percent/cm^2.

Fast neutron detection using solid-state devices is also promising. As described earlier, a recoil-type detector using a large single crystal diamond would approach a detection efficiency of 99 percent for 1 MeV neutrons. Such detectors would have applications in nuclear threat detection systems.

Although a number of neutron detectors are available in the market, they are not sensitive enough for nuclear threat detection systems. Nuclear threat detection technologies typically rely on the measurement of characteristic gamma rays and neutrons to identify and detect potential special nuclear material (SNM) or other materials of interest. Currently of most concern in the nuclear threat detection community is the detection of highly enriched uranium (HEU) as this SNM can be difficult to detect; especially when shielded. Typically, the passive and active techniques are used to monitor and detect SNM. Passive techniques are predominantly reliant upon the detection of the 186 keV gamma-ray line from ^{235}U. However, due to self-shielding in HEU, only the outer surface of the material contributes to the output of the characteristic radiation [19]. Further, this characteristic gamma-ray line is attenuated by a factor of 1000 when shielded by just 5 mm of lead [20]. Because of the challenges introduced by shielding, active interrogation techniques are widely used in material detection and identification. In active interaction techniques, pulsed beams of high-energy photons or neutrons are used to trigger the release of characteristic radiation signatures from the material(s) of interest [21] (see also [22,23] for some examples of methods being used and developed). Even with the initial success and practical utilization of some of these techniques (i.e., the deployment of radiation portals and the implementation of the advanced spectroscopic portal (ASP) [24,25]) there remains a great need for improved detection technologies which are portable, robust, and can be used, to resolve alarms and definitively verify the presence of SNM despite cluttered environments or intentional countermeasures like "shielding" [26]. Based on these criteria, a single-crystal diamond radiation detector could prove to be an ideal candidate to solve this nuclear threat detection need. Such a detector would likely be robust, portable, low-cost, and capable of operating at room temperature with a high intrinsic efficiency (i.e., no big backpacks). To develop this new advanced platform for nuclear threat detection needs, a multifaceted effort to produce large-size, single-crystal diamond on an industrial scale must be made. Even though there has been some recent progress made on the production of single-crystal diamond [27,28], the largest single-crystal substrates are still limited to approximately 10 mm in diameter [27,29].

Isberg et al. [30] and Schmid et al. [31] studied the characteristics of homoepitaxial CVD single-crystal diamond from Element Six (E6, formerly known as De Beers Industrial Diamonds). Isberg et al. [30] reported on the viability of CVD single-crystal diamond to be used for electronic devices. The electron and hole mobilities were observed of 4500 and 3800 cm^2/Vs, respectively, at room temperature, with charge collection distances of more than 10 cm at 1 V/μm [32]. Schmid et al. [31] demonstrated neutron data collection for single-crystal, diamond-based, radiation particle sensor for 2.5, 14.1, and 14.9 MeV incident neutrons. The energy resolutions of neutrons were found to be suitable for spectroscopic purposes. Furthermore, the x-ray and gamma-ray measurements have shown that the high linear attenuation coefficient of diamond at room temperature can, potentially, translate into high detection efficiency for fissile materials [31]. Kaneko et al. [33] also investigated CVD single-crystal diamond as a radiation particle detector. Results using a ^{241}Am source of 5.486 MeV alpha particles have shown that CVD diamond has higher ionization energy (16.1 eV) than HPHT type IIa diamond (13.1 eV). Thus, the potential of CVD diamond is promising, even though the presence of defect and impurity energy levels in the forbidden band gap currently makes it somewhat less than ideal [33].

References

1. J Ely and RT Kouzes. Spies, lies, and nuclear threats. Pacific Northwest National Laboratory, PNNL-SA-45766, Health Physics Society Annual Meeting, Washington, DC, July 2005.
2. J Ely. Radiation detection for homeland security: Past, present and future. Pacific Northwest National Laboratory, PNNL-SA-50411, Health Physics Society Annual Meeting, Washington, DC, June 2006.

3. Department of Homeland Security, DNDO GraDER Guidance Notice, http://www.dhs.gov/xres/programs/gc_1218723613030.shtm
4. Oak Ridge Associated University, Ionization Chamber. http://www.orau.org/ptp/collection/ionchamber/introionizationchamberr.htm
5. NDT Resource center. http://www.ndt-ed.org/EducationResources/CommunityCollege/RadiationSafety/radiation_safety_equipment/pocket_dosimeter.htm
6. Dosimetry Badge Service, Stanford Dosimetry, LLC. http://www.stanforddosimetry.com/badge_service.html
7. Personal Dosimetry Service Radiation Protection Division, Centre for Radiation, Chemical and Environmental Hazards Health Protection Agency, Chilton Didcot Oxon OX11 0RQ. www.hpa.org.uk
8. Cone Instrument. http://www.coneinstruments.com/CIcatsub1.asp?cat_id = 763
9. Thermo Scientific. http://www.thermo.com/com/cda/resources/resources_detail/1,,200208,00.html?fromPage=search
10. Oak Ridge Associated Universities, Geiger Mueller (GM) detectors. http://www.orau.org/ptp/collection/GMs/introgms.htm
11. Radiation Management Services, Fluke Biomedical. http://www.imagingequipment.co.uk/pdf/RS4p8.pdf, www.flukebiomedical.com/rms
12. GE Energy, Boron-10 Proportional Counter. http://www.gepower.com/prod_serv/products/oc/en/reuter_stokes/security_safeguards/boron10.htm
13. GF Knoll. *Radiation Detection and Measurement*, 3rd Ed., John Wiley & Sons, New York, 2000, ISBN 0-471-07338-5.
14. RadSentry™ Security Portals for SNM and Other Radionuclides, Canberra. http://www.canberra.com/pdf/Products/Systems_pdf/C30008-RadSentry-SS.pdf
15. Radiation Portal monitors. Pacific Northwest National Laboratory. http://rdnsgroup.pnl.gov/projects.stm (K McCormick, D Stromswold, J Ely, J Schweppe, and R Kouzes. Spectroscopic radiation portal monitor prototype. *2005 IEEE Nuclear Science Symposium Conference Record*, N14-4, 2005, pp. 292–296.)
16. Oak Ridge National Laboratory, ANSI and IEC Standards for Radiation Detection Instrumentation. ORNL Report No. P04-121468.
17. A Owens and A Peacock. Compound semiconductor radiation detectors. *Nuclear Instruments and Methods in Physics Research Section A: Accelerators, Spectrometers, Detectors and Associated Equipment* 531(1–2): 18–37, September 21, 2004.
18. RJ Nikolića, CL Cheungb, CE Reinhardta, and TF Wangc. Roadmap for high efficiency solid-state neutron detectors. *Proceedings of SPIE*, Vol. 6013: Optoelectronic Devices: Physics, Fabrication, and Application II, J Piprek, Editor, p. 601305 (October 25, 2005) (last accessed 11/12/08, http://spiedl.aip.org/dbt/dbt.jsp?KEY=PSISDG&Volume=6013&Issue=1#P601305000001).
19. D McGregor and RS Klann. High-efficiency neutron detectors and methods of making same. International Patent Application No. PCT/US2003/034436, Publication No. WO/2004/040332, (May 13, 2004) [last accessed 11/12/08; http://www.wipo.int/pctdb/en/wo.jsp?IA=US2003034436&wo=2004040332&DISPLAY=STATUS].
20. CE Moss, CA Goulding, CL Hollas, and WL Myers. Linear accelerator-based active interrogation for detection of highly enriched Uranium. *17th International Conference on Application of Accelerators in Research and Industry*, Denton, TX, November 12–16, 2002. J.L. Duggan and I.L. Morgan, Eds. American Institute of Physics, Malville, NY, 2003.
21. CE Moss, CL Hollas, GW McKinney, and WL Myers. Comparison of active interrogation techniques. *IEEE Transactions on Nuclear Science* 53: 2242–2246, 2006.
22. RF Radel, RP Ashley, GL Kulcinski, and the UW-IEC Team. Detection of highly enriched uranium using a pulsed IEC fusion device. U.S.-Japan IEC Workshop on Small Plasma and Accelerator Neutron Sources, May 22–24, 2007, Argonne National Laboratory, Argonne, IL.
23. CE Moss, CA Goulding, CL Hollas, and WL Myers. Neutron detectors for active interrogation of highly enriched Uranium. *IEEE Transactions on Nuclear Science* 43: 1677–1681, 2004.
24. DHS news release. Homeland Security Officials Unveil Latest Radiation Technology to Secure our Nation's Seaports. April 25, 2006. http://www.cbp.gov/xp/cgov/newsroom/news_releases/archives/2006_news_releases/042006/04252006.xml

25. Testimony of Michael Chertoff, Secretary United States Department of Homeland Security, Before the United States House of Representatives Subcommittee on Homeland Security Committee on Appropriations, February 8, 2007. http://www.dhs.gov/xnews/testimony/gc_1170955671500.shtm.
26. The Department of Homeland Security. R&D Budget Priorities for Fiscal Year 2008. Opening Statement by VS Oxford (Director DNDO, DHS) before the House Science Committee Subcommittee on Technology and Innovation. March 8, 2007.
27. R Bogue. Diamond sensors: The dawn of a new era? *Sensor Review* 27: 288–290, 2007.
28. ST Lee and Y Lifshitz. The road to diamond wafers. *Nature* 424: 500–501, 2003.
29. Sumitomo Electronic USA, Inc. http://www.sumitomoelectricusa.com/scripts/products/ts/hs_mat6.cfm
30. J Isberg, JH Hammersberg, E Johansson, T Wikstrom, DJ Twitchen, AJ Whitehead, SE Coe, and GA Scarsbrook. High carrier mobility in single-crystal plasma-deposited diamond. *Science* 297: 1670–1672, 2002.
31. GJ Schmid, JA Koch, RA Lerche, and MJ Moran. A neutron sensor based on single crystal CVD diamond. *Nuclear Instruments and Methods in Physics Research A* 527: 554–561, 2004.
32. K Kobashi. R&D of diamond films in the Frontier Carbon Technology Project and related topics. *Diamond and Related Materials* 12: 233–240, 2003.
33. JH Kaneko, T Tanaka, T Imai, Y Tanimura, M Katagiri, T Nishitani, H Takeuchi, T Sawamura, and T Iida. Radiation detector made of a diamond single crystal grown by a chemical vapor deposition method. *Nuclear Instruments and Methods in Physics Research A* 505: 187–190, 2003.

Chapter 16

Nuclear Terrorism: Dose and Biological Effects

William H. Miller and Robert Lindsay

CONTENTS

Radiation Dose: Natural and Manmade 307
Biological Effects of Radiation 308
Immediate (or Acute) Effects 309
Delayed Effects 309
Radiation Detection 310
Credible Terrorist Threats Involving Radiation 311
References 312

Radiation Dose: Natural and Manmade

Everything in the world is radioactive to some extent, and always has been. The ocean, the land, the air, and our food all expose us to small amounts of natural background radiation. This is because unstable isotopes that give off or emit ionizing radiation are found everywhere. Our exposure comes from terrestrial elements such as potassium, thorium, uranium, and radium. In addition, much of the earth's natural background radiation is in the form of gamma radiation that comes from outer space.

The radiation amounts differ according to one's location on the earth. Different places on the earth have different amounts of rocks and minerals such as uranium, just like we find deposits of coal, copper, or lead in different locations. In the United States some of the best known deposits of uranium are found in New Mexico, Utah, Wyoming, and Colorado. In some parts of India and Brazil there are also high amounts of background radiation from their rocks and minerals. In these places in India and Brazil, the radiation dose rate exceeds the safety limit that the U.S. government has set as the maximum limit outside of nuclear power plants.

A person living in Kerala, India, receives about 1300 mrems of natural background radiation each year. In the United States, Colorado has one of the highest averages of about 500 mrems per year. To an individual who lives near granite rock formation can increase the background by as much as 100 mrems per year.

Various building materials such as bricks, wood, and stone also emit natural background radiation. People who live in brick homes are exposed to between 50 and 100 additional mrems per year and in wooden homes between 30 and 50 mrems yearly. Cosmic rays from outer space are another large contributor of natural background radiation. Many of the cosmic rays are filtered out by the atmosphere. At higher elevations, there is less atmosphere shielding the radiation coming in from outer space. Generally, exposure increases by about 1 mrem per year for every 100 ft increase in elevation, which is another cause for the higher radiation levels in a state like Colorado. An airplane trip across the United States will expose a person to about 2 mrems of radiation because of the high altitude.

Natural background radiation is also found in plants, animals, and people. Living things are made up of radioactive elements such as isotopes of carbon and potassium. We get about 25 mrems of radiation from the food and water we eat and drink each year. Our bodies harbor more than 5×10^{20} radioactive atoms. About one-half of the radioactivity is in the form of potassium-40, a naturally radioactive form of potassium. Most of the rest of our body's radioactivity comes from carbon-40 and tritium (hydrogen-3).

Still, more radiation is received from man-made sources, primarily from the medical sources for the diagnosis and treatment of disease. We also get small amounts from coal and nuclear power plants and also from the residuals of nuclear weapons testing in the 1950s.

On the whole, the average person in the United States receives 360 mrems per year from all sources: 300 mrems from natural sources and 60 mrems from man-made sources. The natural dose includes 200 + mrems per year from radon, 40 from internal sources, 26 from space, and 28 from the ground. Man-made radiation includes 40 mrems per year from medical x-rays, 14 from nuclear medicine procedures, and the rest from consumer products, nuclear power plants, and other industrial sources.

Biological Effects of Radiation

The effect of radiation on humans has been studied in great detail to set exposure limits for radiation workers. The survivors and the victims of the two nuclear explosions in Japan during 1945 as well as victims of the Chernobyl and other nuclear accidents have been carefully studied. Expert groups (ICRP, BEIR) and the biological results of the exposures have been extensively documented [1]. The cancer treatment programs have enunciated further information where the planned damage to malignant cells as well as the unwanted radiation to healthy tissue is carefully monitored [2].

The result of high doses of radiation is fairly clear and well understood but the effect of low levels of radiation is still controversial and leads to much speculation and reporting in the media. Most regulations are based on conservative extrapolation from the results of high exposures.

The biological effects of radiation can be better understood by differentiating between

1. Deterministic effects which can be directly linked to the dose
2. Nondeterministic or stochastic effects

It also helps to distinguish between immediate and delayed effects.

Radiation detectors are based upon the fundamentals of ionization. In a gas-filled detector, ionization of the gas leads to free electrons that are collected by an electric field and registered by simple electronic counting systems. The Geiger–Mueller tube is of this variety and is the most common detector in use today. These detector systems are available in portable configurations for a few hundred dollars.

In scintillation detectors, the ionization of atoms and the freeing of electrons lead to the production of a small flash of light that can be recorded by a photomultiplier tube and associated electronics. For analytical measurements, solid-state detectors such as intrinsic germanium are in common use. These systems are capable of not only measuring the quantity of radiation, but also identifying the radioactive element from which they came. These systems are capable of quantifying as many as 20–30 individual radioactive species in a single sample with sensitivities at the parts per million to parts per billion level.

Credible Terrorist Threats Involving Radiation

The National Council on Radiation Protection and Measurements (NCRP) Report No. 138 (2001), "Management of Terrorist Events Involving Radioactive Material" provides critical insights into credible terrorist threats. This report provides a consensus of existing and proposed recommendations from federal agencies and scientific bodies and was drafted by an expert committee of NCRP scientists, consulting federal, and state officials.

Based upon the study of the effects of the nuclear blasts in Japan in World War II and having examined the effects of subsequent nuclear weapons testing and the accidental release of radiation from disasters such as Chernobyl, a strong body of knowledge exists about radiation effects and how to minimize them. Short of the use of a nuclear weapon, the spread, or threat of a spread, of some amount of radioactive material probably will cause public concern far in excess of the actual or potential damage to a community or its people.

NCRP Report No. 138 suggests that a terrorist organization is more likely to release a small amount of radioactivity, possibly with an explosion, than it is to obtain and use a nuclear weapon. With the release of small amounts of radioactive material, the necessary containment and cleanup may be well within the capability of public agencies. Such an event could be "catastrophic but manageable."

> When an explosive device is used to disperse radioactive materials, the paradigm shifts. Treatment of casualties is more difficult because of the contamination and the complications associated with other trauma.…The debris from the event and other normally harmless materials will be contaminated. The affected area may be much larger than the immediate scene of the crime. The radiological threat, invisible and uncertain in terms of long-term health impacts, will engender considerable public fear and concern.
>
> At the most basic level is the fact that one of terrorism's chief aims is psychological: to induce fear in a population. Such fear is further compounded when "invisible toxins," such as radiation are involved. People can neither see nor sense the presence of radiation, but they know that it is potentially hazardous.
>
> It must be noted emphatically that radioactive contamination (whether internal or external) is never immediately life threatening and therefore, a radiological assessment or decontamination should never take precedence over significant medical conditions.

For limited releases of radioactive material, people in the area can reduce their exposure by taking shelter in homes or other buildings for hours or a few days until the radiation levels decline.

Ventilation systems using outside air should be shut off and eating contaminated foods should be avoided. Radioactive dust can be washed off of the skin and contaminated clothing should be abandoned to reduce external exposures.

The report places emphasis on the need for public authorities and scientists to be attentive to the psychosocial effects of terrorism involving the dispersal of radioactive material.

References

1. C Herman. *Health Physics*, 3rd edn., McGraw-Hill, New York (1996).
2. TD Jones. *Proceedings of the Thirty-Second Annual Meeting of the National Council on Radiation Protection and Measurements*, Proceedings no. 18, Implications of new data on radiation cancer risk. *Health Phys.* 73(5), 838–839 (1997).

Chapter 17

Nuclear Terrorism: Nuclear Weapons

Sudarshan K. Loyalka

CONTENTS

Introduction 313
History 313
Effects 314
Weapons Technology 315
Summary 318
Bibliography 319

Introduction

Nuclear weapons are the ultimate means of destruction, and humanity can ill afford the acquisition of such weapons by terrorists. These weapons are a recent phenomenon, but they have spread widely among nations. There are legitimate fears that terrorists could acquire or build such weapons. In this chapter, we briefly review the history of such weapons, their effects, and the fundamental technology.

History

The Neutron was discovered in 1932. The following years witnessed intense studies of its properties and interactions with matter. This neutral particle, about 2000 times the mass of an electron, is scattered and absorbed by different materials, with the nature and rate of reaction determined by the nuclei of the host material and the energy of the neutron. Neutrons can also split (fission) some nuclei (the fissile isotopes such as Th-233, U-235, and Pu-239), and release energy in the process as kinetic energy of the fission products and the beta, gamma, and other radiations. New neutrons (two to three on average) are also released in fission, thus providing the basis for a chain reaction. This chain reaction can be sustained (each successive generation has the same number of neutrons), or multiplied (each successive generation has more neutrons), and it can be used for explosive release of energy. Fission of 1 kg of U-235 or Pu-239 releases an energy equivalent to that obtained in an explosion of about 20 kT of TNT.

WWII imperatives led to the Manhattan Project in the United States, and construction, testing, and use of first nuclear weapons in 1945. These detonations were as follows:

Test: July 16, 1945, Trinity (NM), Pu-239, 5 kg, 19 kT of TNT
  Implosion, efficiency = 19 percent

Combat Use: August 6, 1945 (Hiroshima). U-235, 49 kg, 17 kT of TNT
  Gun (1000 ft/s), efficiency = 2 percent, Known as "Little Boy"
  August 9, 1945 (Nagasaki), Pu-239, 5 kg, 20 kT of TNT
  Implosion, efficiency = 20 percent, Known as "Fat Man"

There has been no other combat use of nuclear weapons, but there have been many other detonations, both above ground and underground. The fission bombs have been surpassed with vastly more powerful (~50 MT, 1 MT = 1000 kT) hydrogen or thermonuclear bombs where a fission bomb is used to create a fusion reaction. The announced detonations since 1946 include

United States (Fission: 1946, 48, 51–62, 63-underground;
  Thermonuclear: 10/31/52, Eniwetok, 10.4 MT; 2/28/54, Bikini, 15 MT)
  5/20/56, Bikini, Several MT)
U.S.S.R. (Fission: 8/29/49, Thermonuclear 8/12/53, many other tests)
United Kingdom (10/3/52—Fission and Thermonuclear)
France (2/13/60—Fission and Thermonuclear)
China (1964—Fission and Thermonuclear)
India (1974, May 1998, Fission and possibly Thermonuclear)
Pakistan (May 1998, Fission, U-235 gun type)
North Korea (October 2006, Fission, Pu-239)

It is also widely accepted that Israel has produced and stockpiled nuclear weapons and that South Africa had also produced nuclear weapons and perhaps detonated one. Many other nations have pursued nuclear weapons technology clandestinely at one time or another, and several may be currently doing so.

Nuclear weapons are comparatively compact, and these can be delivered by airplanes, missiles, ships, barges, or even trucks. There is speculation that suitcase-size nuclear weapons exist.

Effects

A one-half ton (TNT) explosive damages an area in about 150 ft radius (e.g., explosion near the Murrah Building in Oklahoma City, or near the U.S. Embassy in Nairobi). By contrast a 20 kT nuclear explosive annihilates an area (people, animals, structures) in a 2-mi radius. A 20 MT thermonuclear bomb can annihilate an area in a 10-mi radius. Volcanic eruptions and asteroids can have still larger impacts. Suspected asteroid impact 62.5 million years ago was perhaps about 100,000 MT, and it may have led to dinosaur extinction.

In a nuclear explosion, the weapon material and surrounding air (and the suspended soil and other material if it were to be a surface or near-surface explosion) reach an extremely high temperature of millions of degrees almost instantaneously. This results in large thermal radiation (as distinct from ionizing radiation) and consequent immediate thermal burns on the living, and fires. The thermal radiation travels at the speed of light, it is absorbed/attenuated by structures, clothing, etc., but its effect is felt almost instantaneously. This is followed by shock waves (in a matter of few seconds) and immediate (within a minute) and delayed (after a minute) effects of ionizing radiation discussed elsewhere in this book. For example, at Hiroshima and Nagasaki approximately 50 percent of the damage was by the blast and shock, about 35 percent by the thermal radiation, and the remainder was by radiation, both immediate and delayed. The effect of the shock (pressure/compression) was more significant on structures, while radiation was more damaging to the living.

The effects of nuclear explosions will vary depending upon the height at which an explosion occurs, the weather conditions, the terrain, the structural details (distribution of buildings, the materials they are made of), the population (the age and gender distribution), and the time of the day (whether people are outdoors or indoors, and the clothing they wear).

The use of a thermonuclear weapon for terrorism purposes is unthinkable. First, one requires a fission bomb to trigger a thermonuclear explosion, and second a fission bomb can in itself wreak so much havoc that no terrorists would need to go beyond the acquisition of fission bombs for any purpose they might have. A fission bomb is really an ultimate weapon in war, and certainly an ultimate in terror.

Weapons Technology

The nuclear weapons technology was born in wartime, and many practical aspects of it have been since well guarded (classified) not only by the United States but by other nations also. Many Manhattan Project documents, and the subsequent nuclear literature, however, provide considerable insights into the basic technology.

Each fission of U-235 or Pu-239 releases about 190 MeV of energy. Thus, approximately 1.5×10^{23} fissions (that is fissions from about 50 gm of U-235 or Pu-239) are required to produce a 1 kT TNT explosion. A larger explosion will require many more fissions. These fissions must be achieved while the weapon is still intact, as the expansion (explosion) leads to a rapid cessation of neutron multiplication, and hence fission. The Los Alamos Primer describes the underlying neutronics.

In a simplified picture, we note that for any given mass, the neutron multiplication factor (the ratio of neutrons in a generation to a previous generation) can be written as

$$k = \frac{\text{Neutrons produced}}{\text{Neutrons absorbed} + \text{neutrons lost due to leakage}}$$

and is a measure of the criticality of the mass ($k > 1$, supercritical; $k = 1$, critical; $k < 1$, subcritical; $k \geq 1$ is needed to sustain a chain reaction). The associated rate equation can be written as

$$\frac{\mathrm{d}n(t)}{\mathrm{d}t} = \frac{k-1}{\ell} n(t) + s(t)$$

where

$n(t)$ is the number density of neutrons (#/cm^3)

ℓ is known as the neutron lifetime (~10^{-6} s)

s (#/cm^3 s) is a source of neutrons

The factor k is approximately expressed as

$$k = \frac{\nu N \sigma_f}{N\sigma_a + B_g^2/(3N\sigma_{tr})}$$

where

ν is the average number of neutrons produced in a fission

σ (cm^2) is known as the cross section for interaction with neutrons

subscripts f, a, t, and tr indicate fission, absorption, total, and transport cross sections, respectively

N indicates the number density of the nuclei (#/cm^3) in the mass, and is obtained as

$$N = \frac{0.6023 \times 10^{24} \rho}{M}$$

where

ρ is the density of the mass (gm/cm^3)

M is the molecular weight (gm/gmol). B (cm^{-2}) is known as the geometric buckling, and is a function of the geometry

For a spherical mass of radius R (cm), this is expressed as

$$B_g = \frac{\pi}{R + 0.7104/(N\sigma_{tr})}$$

Thus the factor k can be written as

$$k(R) = \eta \left(1 + \left(\frac{\pi}{R + \dfrac{0.7104}{N(R)\sigma_{tr}}} \right)^2 \frac{1}{3N^2(R)\sigma_{tr}\sigma_a} \right)^{-1}$$

where

$$\eta = \frac{\nu\sigma_f}{\sigma_a}$$

and is known as the "eta" factor. This would be the value of k if the mass were infinite and thus there was no loss of neutrons due to leakage. Note that for a fixed mass, N is a function of R through its dependence on density, and

$$N(R) = \frac{0.6023 \times 10^{24}}{M} \rho_0 \left(\frac{R_0}{R} \right)^3$$

ρ_0, R_0, are, respectively the initial density and radius of the sphere. N will increase with a decrease in R, as $1/R^3$. Thus given a mass, k depends on R in an inverse fashion.

The rate of energy (the power, P) release in fissions is approximately expressed as

$$P = G_f (N\sigma_f)(vn)\left(\frac{4\pi}{3} R^3 \right)$$

where

G is the energy release (~190 MeV) per fission
v is the speed of neutrons (cm/s)

The product vn is referred to as the neutron flux, and corresponds to neutron path length per unit time. Parameters appropriate to fast (~2 MeV) neutrons and Pu-239 have the approximate values:

$$\eta = 3.0$$

$$\sigma_a = 1.87 \times 10^{-24}\,\text{cm}^2, \quad \sigma_{tr} = 6.0 \times 10^{-24}\,\text{cm}^2$$

$$\ell = 10^{-6}\,\text{s}$$

Together with

$$\rho_0 \approx 15.5\ \text{gm/cm}^3$$

as the normal density of the Plutonium, one finds that for $k = 1$,

$$R \approx 7.0\ \text{cm}$$

This corresponds to a mass of about 22 kg. Refined theory and calculations, with results confirmed by experiments (the Jezebel assembly), show that:

$$R \approx 6.285\ \text{cm}$$

which corresponds to a mass of about 16 kg. This value is substantially reduced if the mass were to be surrounded by suitable reflecting materials such as U-238 and beryllium.

The basic principle then is to

1. Start with a subcritical mass, or masses (which do not sustain a chain reaction because of a larger proportionate leakage of neutrons from the mass as compared to fission) of the fissile material. This mass is usually spherical or cylindrical in shape, and is encased in Uranium-238, beryllium, or some other materials that reflect neutrons or aid in compression. The reflection reduces the required U-235 or Pu-239 mass by about 50 percent.

2. Rapidly compress this mass using chemical explosives or a gun-type system in which one mass is fired into another. The compression leads to an increase in the density of the fissile material decreasing the neutron mean free path (the mean distance a neutron travels before interaction), and thus fissions become comparatively more favored over neutron leakage from the material. During the compression a stage is reached where a chain reaction can be sustained, and as the compression progresses the number of neutrons and fissions, and hence energy release, can double or more with each incremental increase in time (of the order of 10^{-6} s, a microsecond, the "neutron lifetime"). The energy release doubles with progressively shorter increments of time, since as the compression progresses the mean free path becomes smaller and smaller, and thus the mean free time for fission becomes shorter. Since the released energy will lead to expansion (thermal and pressure), the weapon will start losing its ability to sustain a chain reaction as the expansion progresses, and certainly by the time it reaches its original size again. Thus during the compression or assembly phase (the chemical detonation), neutrons are injected at a proper time with an external neutron source, so that the desired number of fissions, and hence energy release, is achieved during the compression and expansion phases combined. Much of the energy release occurs during the last few time increments of the 50 or so fission generations (or the time increments), and thus the criticality should be maintained for as long as possible. The assembly must occur in a fashion that avoids premature detonation (that is release of energy sufficient to cause disassembly, but not sufficient otherwise) by stray neutrons (e.g., those associated with natural, spontaneous production in Pu-240, which is present in small amounts with Pu-239 in the processed material). This requires use of guns that fire at very high speeds (1000 m/s) or rapid (~ a microsecond) and symmetric implosions through shock waves generated by use of chemical explosives. Generally, guns are sufficient for U-235 weapons, but implosion is needed for Pu-239 weapons.

The early fission weapons used polonium (an alpha emitter) and beryllium (which emits a neutron on alpha absorption) to generate neutrons. These materials were initially placed at the center of the sphere, presumably separated by a foil that absorbs alpha particles and prevents an exposure of beryllium to these. The foil is ruptured at an appropriate time in the implosion, leading to neutrons that initiate the explosion. Neutrons can however also be generated through interactions of hydrogen isotopes or other isotopes in small electricity-driven devices (accelerators) that are used these days, for example, in oil exploration.

Fission weapons are characterized by small size; the explosive part is only a few centimeters in diameter. Power density is extremely high, and explosion time is a few microseconds. Commercial nuclear reactors, on the other hand, are large with cores that are approximately 12 ft in diameter. Their power density is low. Also, energy is produced over a long period of time. Design safeguards protect against power excursions.

Summary

Nuclear weapons inflict vast damage, and must not be allowed in the hands of terrorists or irresponsible parties. Seven nations have announced nuclear detonations and many other nations have the capabilities to produce/announce nuclear detonations on short notice. Some are surely working toward acquiring the capability. The fundamentals of crude nuclear weapons production are reasonably well understood and publicized. The available public knowledge base has increased since nuclear weapons were first produced and used in 1945. Still, nuclear weapon design and assembly is not a task for amateurs as many complicated practical and technical details are involved. The task is less difficult however, for a large, well-organized, and well-financed terrorist organization.

Bibliography

GI Bell and S Glasstone. *Nuclear Reactor Theory*. Krieger Publishing Company, Melbourne, FL, 1974.

AC Brown and CB MacDonald. *The Secret History of the Atomic Bomb*. (1977, it includes the Smyth Report which is an official history of the U.S. efforts, 1940–1945, completed before the trinity test).

RL Garwin and G Charpak. *Megawatts and Megatons*. Knopf, Chicago, IL, 2001.

S Glasstone. *The Effects of Nuclear Weapons* (U.S. Govt. sponsored, first published 1950; 1964).

Los Alamos Scientific Laboratory. *Project Y: The Los Alamos Story*. Tomash Publishers, Los Angeles, CA, 1983 (includes U.S. Govt. sponsored *Toward Trinity* by D. Hawkins and *Beyond Trinity* by E.C. Truslow and R.C. Smith).

A McKay. *The Making of the Atomic Age*. Oxford University Press, New York, 1984.

W Meyer, SK Loyalka, W Nelson and RW Williams. The homemade nuclear bomb syndrome. *Nuclear Safety* 18: 427, 1977.

H Morland. *The Secret that Exploded*. Random House, New York, 1986.

Reactor Physics Constants. ANL-5800 (U.S. Govt., 1963).

R Rhodes. *The Making of the Atomic Bomb*. Touchstone Books, New York, 1992.

R Serber. *The Los Alamos Primer* (U.S. Govt., first published as LA-1, April 1943; declassified 1965; annotated book, 1992).

Chapter 18

Nuclear Terrorism: Threats and Countermeasures

Sudarshan K. Loyalka and Mark A. Prelas

CONTENTS

Introduction 321
Threats 322
Materials 322
Expertise 323
Targets and Means of Delivery 324
Countermeasures 324
Protect Nuclear Weapons 324
Protect Nuclear Materials 326
Control Nuclear Transfers 326
Protect Nuclear Expertise 326
Destroy Nuclear Infrastructure 326
Upgrade Intelligence Programs 327
Summary 327
References 327
Bibliography 328

Introduction

There is little question now that some terrorist groups are keenly working toward acquiring nuclear weapons, and are also considering attacking/sabotaging nuclear installations. We discuss here the plausibility of these threats and how governments and industry might effectively respond to prevent such terrorism.

Threats

Motivations for nuclear terrorism exist, both in large terrorist groups and in some states. There is likely to be a greater move toward nuclear threats as terrorists exhaust other means and tactics, and as they become more experienced, sophisticated, and knowledgeable. Nuclear threats are plausible as together with motivations, materials and expertise for making crude weapons may be acquired, means for delivery may be available, attacks on nuclear installations or their sabotage may be feasible, and nuclear weapons may be stolen or purchased. Again, in these discussions we will focus on fission weapons.

Materials

The principal issue in assembling fission weapons is with the availability of a few kilograms of "weapons grade" U-235 and Pu-239 metals or their oxides.

Uranium occurs naturally, and it is mined in many places in the world. This natural Uranium is composed of 99.3 percent U-238 and only 0.7 percent U-235. U-238 can undergo fission with energetic neutrons, but it also absorbs neutrons significantly, leading to substantially negative impact on the chain reaction and overall fission process, and the requisite mass (one needs larger mass to reduce leakage comparatively). In the case of weapons, Uranium must be "enriched" in U-235 content to 20 percent and above, and preferentially 90 percent and above. This is generally accomplished by conversion of natural uranium to a gaseous hexafluoride form, followed by the use of an electromagnetic, diffusion, centrifugation, nozzle flow, or laser process.

Acquisition of natural Uranium by terrorists should be straightforward. The enrichment technologies are however generally both sophisticated and expensive, given the small mass difference between U-235 and U-238. Abdul Qadeer Khan, considered the father of Pakistan's nuclear weapons program, admitted on February 4, 2004 to supplying plans for the ground up development of nuclear weapons beginning with plans for enrichment technology, models of working centrifuges (used for uranium enrichment), suppliers of materials, and schematics of a Chinese nuclear warhead design. The "Khan network" is known to have provided its "nuclear weapon kit" to Libya, Iraq, Iran, North Korea, and perhaps to other countries as well. Much of the technical information was put on CDs (many nonproliferation experts are concerned that these CDs can be easily copied and distributed to anyone). This incident is widely seen as the beginning of the "second nuclear age." This marks the first time that the enrichment technology, warhead design, and supplier network information has been out of state control and security [1].

The world came to know of the "Khan Network," when Libya made a surprise announcement in December of 2003 that it had a nuclear weapons program which it was going to abandon.

Iran has been under international scrutiny since August 2003, when reports emerged stating that Iran was purchasing nuclear weapons technology from Pakistan. Much has been learned about the Iranian nuclear program since. For example, the Iranian program has built P1 (first generation) centrifuges and P2 (second generation) centrifuges. The P1 centrifuge is based on a 40 year old European technology that uses aluminum rotors which are capable of achieving rotational speeds of 64,000 revolutions per minute (RPM). The P2 uses steel rotors which have a higher RPM and are more efficient for isotope separation. The third generation, which Iran may be working on, is used by Europe and the United States. This design uses composite materials (carbon fiber), which are capable of even higher RPM.

Pu-239 is not available naturally (although some of it certainly was produced at one time in the natural reactor in Gabon, millions of years ago). Rather it is produced, together with its higher isotopes some of which are a weapon maker's nightmare, through absorption of neutrons in U-238, and subsequent radioactive decays (transmutations), and processing of irradiated Uranium. The neutron irradiation can be carried out in neutron accelerators and nuclear reactors. In the Manhattan project, such reactors were constructed using natural uranium and graphite or heavy water. Many such reactors are now in commercial use, and these, and other reactors that slightly use enriched Uranium (two to four percent U-235), do produce Pu-239. But this plutonium is also contaminated with Pu-240 which produces neutrons by itself (spontaneous fissions), and is not good for weapons purposes. The weapons grade Plutonium should have five percent or less of Pu-240, and should be mostly Pu-239 to prevent premature explosions of weapons (in a Plutonium-based weapon, implosion is necessary to counter premature disassembly due to neutrons produced by Pu-240). This purity could be realized by short term irradiation of U-238 in research (or commercial) reactors and appropriate processing of the irradiated material. One might also use other neutron generators, e.g., accelerators, to irradiate natural Uranium, and obtain Pu-239. But this latter route is not a very effective way to produce kilogram quantities.

Diversion and theft of U-235 and Pu-239 from national nuclear weapons programs as well as the fuel cycle (manufacture, shipment, use, and reprocessing) associated with research and commercial nuclear reactor plants is the main vulnerability. Fresh commercial reactor nuclear fuel is enriched only to two to four percent in U-235, and is not an issue. The used fuel contains Pu-239, but it is radioactive and is also heavily contaminated with Pu-240. Terrorists could disperse radioactivity in such fuel by using chemical explosives, but separation of Pu-239 from this fuel for an effective fission weapon will be very difficult. There are some research reactors that use 93 percent U-235 or so enriched Uranium fuel (known as Highly Enriched Uranium-HEU), and there are also commercial reactor plants that use Pu-239 based fuel. Fresh fuel here could provide sufficient quantities of weapons grade U-235 or Pu-239.

Of course, an actual weapon could also be stolen, diverted, or purchased. Although all nuclear nations have safeguards, the sheer number of weapons stockpiled by the major nuclear nations, and political instabilities of some other nations that have smaller stocks, do not provide strong assurances against such eventualities.

Up until 1991, the security of nuclear stockpiles and weapons know-how was not a significant concern. However, it quickly became a concern when the Soviet Union collapsed. The Soviet Union had accumulated between 140 and 160 tons of plutonium and a considerably larger inventory of HEU [2]. Under the circumstances of a collapsing economy, the once elite weapons designers of the Soviet Union were facing poverty and hardship. The security of nuclear materials and the potential for the migration of know-how to rogue states was of great concern to many in the West [3].

Expertise

The actual design of a workable explosive requires sophisticated analysis and synthesis, is a work for serious professionals, and is classified. The metallurgy and machining of various materials and components, work with explosives, electronics, neutron sources, and radiation also require equipment and experienced scientists and engineers. Powerful computers are now ubiquitous. Sophisticated computer programs that deal with neutronics, fluid dynamics, heat transfer, and structural issues are also widely available.

It appears that three to five scientists and engineers, with diverse expertise in nuclear physics and engineering, metallurgy, explosives, and electronics are the minimum that would be needed. This team would need access to computers, good laboratories, machine shops, and testing facilities.

The expertise can be developed or acquired while a group is pursuing acquisition of the material. The dissolution of some national nuclear weapons programs has created a large pool of unemployed or disaffected weapons specialists, and some of them could be recruited.

Targets and Means of Delivery

Targets of nuclear terrorism would be large cities and infrastructure, private and public. Nuclear weapons are rather compact, and could be delivered by air, water, or land. Of these, the last two may be more attractive to terrorists as barges/ships can be sailed into harbors, and trucks/trains can be driven into cities or near other defense/government facilities and other industry with smaller likelihood of detection. One could also transport parts of a weapon at different times to thwart detection, and then assemble the weapon at the site.

Nuclear installations (manufacturing and storage facilities, nuclear power plants, and research reactors) and shipments (raw material, fresh fuel, and used fuel) are all plausible targets for acquisition of nuclear material, or attacks that could lead to release of radioactivity from these installations or activities. Nuclear power plants are often located in remote areas and research reactors contain relatively small amount of radioactive material. Neither are likely to undergo a nuclear explosion except in special circumstances, but chemical explosions/fires or plane crashes at these sites can cause great difficulties, and eventual release of radioactivity and harm.

Countermeasures

Countermeasures against the nuclear threats must be general as well as very specific. Both short-term and long-term steps are needed, and these must be vigorously implemented. The greatest concern is with respect to acquisition of the weapons grade nuclear material, and spread of technology that makes its production possible given natural Uranium. There are concerns with the spread of expertise of weapon making, but given the large number of trained scientific and technical personnel and scientific/industrial facilities and laboratories these days, there is only so much that can be done in this area. In the short run the countermeasures must do the following.

Protect Nuclear Weapons

All nuclear nations safeguard their nuclear weapons, but there is unevenness that must be addressed. To safeguard nuclear weapons, a number of Arms Control treaties have been developed. We will describe a few of these and their interlinks and implications to nuclear security.

After the Cuban missile crisis, both the United States and the USSR realized the folly of a nuclear arms race. Even though the earliest efforts to limit nuclear arms met with little success, it did lay the groundwork for the future. The issue early on was how to achieve comprehensive disarmament. At the Geneva-based Eighteen-Nation Disarmament Committee in January 1964, the United States proposed that the number and characteristics of the strategic nuclear offensive and defensive delivery systems be decoupled from the comprehensive disarmament proposals. By 1966, China developed nuclear weapons, and both the USSR and the United States were engaged in the development of antiballistic missile systems. In 1967, it became clear that the nuclear arms race was unmanageable and President Johnson and Premier Kosygin indicated a willingness to reengage in arms control discussions. By July 1, 1968 the Non-Proliferation Treaty was signed and the United States and the USSR agreed to initiate discussions on the limitation and reduction of both strategic nuclear weapons delivery systems and defense against ballistic missiles. The Strategic Arms Limitation Talks (SALT I) occurred from November 1969 to May 1972. SALT I ended when both the United States and the USSR signed the Anti-Ballistic Missile treaty on May 26, 1972 and developed the Interim Agreement on Strategic and Offensive Arms (agreed to begin talks for a more comprehensive nuclear arms treaty) which led to the SALT II talks and the signing of the SALT II treaty on June 18, 1979. The SALT II treaty would have limited nuclear delivery vehicles (missiles, bombers, and air to surface antiballistic missiles) to 2400 units. The treaty was not brought to the senate for ratification, but both countries agreed to abide by the provisions. President Reagan stated that the USSR was not in compliance with SALT II in 1986 and asked to USSR to join with the United States in mutual restraint. One of the major issues with SALT II was verification, a theme that persists to this day. Arms control made progress in the 1980s through the Intermediate-Range Nuclear Forces (INF) Treaty that was signed on December 8, 1987. The START I treaty was undertaken with regard to strategic offensive arms in Article VI of the Treaty on the Non-Proliferation of Nuclear Weapons of July 1, 1968; Article XI of the Treaty on the Limitation of Anti-Ballistic Missile Systems of May 26, 1972; and the Washington Summit Joint Statement of June 1, 1990. The START I treaty was signed in Moscow on July 31, 1991. With START I, the United States and Russia agreed to reduce strategic nuclear warheads to 6000 [4]. In December 1991, the USSR disbanded and became the Commonwealth of Independent States. On May 7, 1992, each of the Commonwealth States that housed nuclear weapons agreed along with the United States to abide by START I in the Lisbon Protocol. START II was designed to reduce the level of strategic nuclear warheads to 3500 and was signed on January 3, 1993. However, START II has not been ratified by the United States but has been ratified by Russia. Another milestone treaty was The Comprehensive Nuclear Test-Ban Treaty (CTBT), which halts nuclear testing. CTBT was signed on September 24, 1996 but was rejected by the U.S. senate in 1999. The reason being that nuclear deterrence is still an important component of the U.S. strategic arms package. Nuclear weapons are complex systems that require extensive testing. Without testing, the current nuclear inventory would age and there would be no mechanism for developing replacements.

When the USSR dissolved and the CIS was established, the future of the treaties that served as the foundation of arms control came into question. The first issue was how to deal with START I because some of the states other than Russia in the CIS housed nuclear weapons. The Lisbon Protocol was initiated to assure that these states still agreed to START I. Additionally, these states agreed to transfer control of the nuclear weapons on their territory to Russia. The next issue was to deal with the security of nuclear materials and with the large number of Former Soviet Union (FSU) scientists engaged in the nuclear weapons enterprise. One of the first steps was the creation of the International Science and Technology Center (ISTC) by President Bush in 1992. The goal of the ISTC was to support FSU scientists engaged in the production of nuclear, chemical, and biological weapons in projects for peaceful uses and economic development. The United States, Japan, and the EC committed 75 million dollars to initiate the program. In addition, the (George) Soros Foundation provided a large amount of money to support FSU scientists. Soros eventually started the International Science Foundation to support FSU scientists and this project eventually evolved into the Civilian Research Development Fund. To safeguard FSU nuclear stockpiles the Nunn–Lugar bill supported efforts to foster Russian warhead dismantlement, work on surplus fissile material disposition options, lab-to-lab cooperative nonweapons projects with Russian nuclear scientists, and support of the Russian highly enriched uranium purchase agreement. In addition, the United States provided funding to the Mayak Production Association for the construction of a plutonium storage facility. The goal of these efforts and others was to help Russia to secure its nuclear materials stockpile. To date, the program has been successful in a number of areas. It has provided support to critical FSU scientists to secure the scientific know-how for the production of nuclear weapons and in addition, it has helped Russia with funding to develop better methods of nuclear stockpile stewardship.

Under the leadership of the Bush administration, the U.S.–Russia Strategic Offensive Reductions Treaty was signed on May 24, 2002. This landmark agreement reduced the number of strategic nuclear warheads to between 1700 and 2200. This reduction is lower than the reduction goals of the START III talks, but unlike START III, the U.S.–Russia Strategic Offensive Reductions Treaty will allow for the storage of nuclear materials from old warheads.

Although the two nations are reducing their stockpiles, some other nations are building theirs though not up to the same levels. These large numbers lead to possibilities that some weapons are not fully accounted for, and that there can be unrecognized theft from storage or during weapon transfers. The best strategy here is to reduce nuclear stockpiles, account for all weapons, and share and adopt good security practices.

Protect Nuclear Materials

All nuclear material from mining to its eventual disposal must be fully accounted for and guarded by public agencies in all nations. The weapons grade material (HEU and Pu-239) must receive the highest level of protection. High level of protection should be provided to fresh nuclear fuel. Irradiated fuel, in most instances, is self-protected, but it would contain Pu-239, and because such fuel can itself be a source of release and a terrorist tool due to its radioactivity content, it also deserves a similar level of protection. The greatest difficulty in this area has been reported with respect to transitions that have occurred with the dissolution of the former Soviet Union, and extensive material stocks that had existed and that are not fully accounted for.

Control Nuclear Transfers

Transfer of nuclear material to unstable states, or states that are prone to cooperation with terrorists, must be stopped.

Protect Nuclear Expertise

There is a vast difference in the theory and practice of weapons technology, and the greater emphasis here must be on ensuring that terrorists do not get access to the technology or the experienced practitioners in the field. Dual use technology should be clearly identified, and its commerce regulated. All present and former weapons scientists should be provided some stable financial support so that they do not find it necessary to help terrorists because of financial hardships.

Destroy Nuclear Infrastructure

Israel destroyed the Osiriak reactor in Iraq in 1981 to prevent what it viewed as the development of a nuclear weapons infrastructure in Iraq. There have been reports of assassinations of some nuclear weapon experts also. These are obviously strong measures, and have not been used widely.

Upgrade Intelligence Programs

Nuclear weapons materials and technology can be acquired in parallel, and often under the disguise of legitimate peaceful work. Intelligence programs should be reviewed, and capabilities developed not only for providing support toward prevention of thefts, and the like, but also to anticipate and constraint dual use operations.

In the long run, all the aforementioned steps will need to be strengthened. Regulations, intelligence, and interdiction (emergency response) are essential to prevent nuclear material from reaching the hands of terrorists. In the United States, the Department of Energy, the Nuclear Regulatory Commission, and the Defense Department have the primary responsibilities for regulating the nuclear material and activities. Other nations have similar organizations that deal with this issue. The International Atomic Energy Agency based in Vienna, Austria provides international regulations and oversight, and cooperation among different nations. In a sense, the very extraordinary nature of nuclear threat has fostered national and international regulation from the beginning and it continues to date. There is a need to strengthen the regulations, and also to ensure some minimum uniform compliance with them globally. The international community must engage more strongly in nuclear arms control and nuclear arms reduction. It must jointly ensure reduction of nuclear terrorist threat worldwide by cooperating in regulation, intelligence, and interdiction.

Summary

Nuclear terrorism could comprise attacks against nuclear installations, and dispersal of radioactive materials from storage, shipment, nuclear reactor fuel, and the like through use of conventional explosives and other means, as well as acquisition and use of nuclear weapons. The threat of fission weapon construction/acquisition and use by terrorists has become more credible with the spread of nuclear technology and international instabilities and dynamics. Given the material, a crude bomb could possibly be built by a small team of scientists and engineers with diverse experience. Protection of weapons and highly enriched Uranium and Pu-239 require the highest level of understanding and international cooperation. Regulations, intelligence, and interdiction on a national as well as on a global level can provide the needed safeguards.

References

1. Christopher Oren Clary, *The A. Q. Khan Network: Causes and Implications*, Master of Arts in National Security Affairs Thesis, Naval Post Graduate School, Monterey, CA, December 2005 (http://www.fas.org/irp/eprint/clary.pdf last accessed 9/2008).
2. World Plutonium Inventories, 1999. *Bulletin of the Atomic Scientists*, 55(5), 71 (http://www.thebulletin.org/issues/nukenotes/so99nukenote.html).
3. M Prelas. Soviet High-Tech Bonanza. Christian Science Monitor, 02/03/1992, (http://www.csmonitor.com/cgi-bin/getasciiarchive?tape/92/feb/day03/03181).
4. Strategic Arms Reduction Treaty (START I). U.S. Department of State, (http://www.state.gov/www/global/arms/starthtm/start.html).

Bibliography

P Leventhal and Y Alexander. *Nuclear Terrorism, Defining the Threat.* Pergamon, Washington, DC, 1986.
P Leventhal and Y Alexander. *Preventing Nuclear Terrorism.* Lexington Books, Lexington, MA, 1987.
Nuclear Proliferation Problems, SIPRI. MIT Press, Cambridge, MA, 1974.
Nuclear Proliferation and Safeguards. Office of Technology assessment, Congress of the United States, Praeger Publishers, New York, 1977.
Stockholm International Peace Research Institute. *Safeguards against Nuclear Proliferation, a SIPRI Monograph.* MIT Press, Cambridge, MA, 1975.

Chapter 19

Chemical Terrorism: Classification, Synthesis, and Properties

Dabir S. Viswanath and Tushar K. Ghosh

CONTENTS

Classification 330
Choking Agents 331
Blood Agents 334
Blister Agents 334
Nerve Agents 334
Incapacitating Agents 335
Tear Agents (Lacrimators) 335
Vomiting Agents (Sternutators) 335
Defoliants, Desiccants, Soil Sterilants, and Plant Growth Inhibitors 335
Emerging Agents 335
Explosives and IEDs 339
Synthesis 340
Mustard 341
Sarin 341
Properties of Chemicals 342
Molecular Weight 342
Boiling Point 350
Density 350

Vapor Pressure 350
Volatility 352
Enthalpy of Vaporization 352
Advantages and Disadvantages of Chemical Weapons 352
Advantages 352
Disadvantages 352
References 353

Classification

The word "chemical" itself creates uneasiness, if not total fear, but the combination of the words "chemicals" and "terrorism" can be deadly. Chemical terrorism is attack on human life and destruction of property using chemicals. Chemicals used for this purpose can temporarily incapacitate or kill human beings, destroy property, or do all at the same time. Many chemicals serve both useful and destructive purposes. A chemical used for chemical terrorism is defined as a chemical substance that could be "employed" because of its direct toxic effect on humans, animals, and plants. A toxic chemical can be defined as any chemical which through its chemical reaction on living processes may cause death, temporary loss of performance, or permanent injury to people, animals, or plants. The term "employed" means that the chemical is dispersed or transported to the site where this toxic effect is created. Various types of ammunition and equipment have been designed for their dispersal. The Chemical Weapons Convention (CWC), Article 2, paragraph 1 defines "chemical weapons" as [1]

1. "Chemical Weapons" means the following, together or separately:
    a. Toxic chemicals and their precursors, except where intended for purposes not prohibited under this Convention, as long as the types and quantities are consistent with such purposes
    b. Munitions and devices, specifically designed to cause death or other harm through the toxic properties of those toxic chemicals specified in subparagraph (a), which would be released as a result of the employment of such munitions and devices
    c. Any equipment specifically designed for use directly in connection with the employment of munitions and devices specified in subparagraph (b)

The word "plants" is not specifically used in the above definition. However the UN document on the definition of chemical warfare and toxic chemicals published in 1969 defines chemical warfare agents as "chemical substances, whether gaseous, liquid or solid, which might be employed because of their direct toxic effects on man, animals and plants." It is appropriate to include plants because chemicals can be used to destroy crops, which may lead to economic loss, fear, and panic among the general population. We know that this is the case from the Vietnam War where Agent Orange, a phenoxy herbicide, was used to defoliate the crops. It is estimated that 19 million gal of this herbicide was used by the United States. However, it turned out to be a carcinogen, and many people were affected and developed soft tissue sarcoma, non-Hodgkin lymphoma, Hodgkin disease, lung and respiratory cancer, prostrate cancer, multiple myeloma, and others.

Several chemicals that can be used for a terrorist attack are commercial chemicals or intermediates. It is well known that a chemical explosive, such as trinitrotoluene (TNT or dynamite) can be used for blasting off obstacles when building bridges or to bring down old buildings, but at the same time it can be used for destructive purposes. We have witnessed the destructive power of ammonium nitrate and fuel oil (both of them are available commercially) in the bombing of the Federal Building in Oklahoma City on April 19, 1995. It not only killed innocent people but also destroyed property. Such terrorist attacks can also bring down the morale of the people and loss of trust in their government. On March 20, 1995 in the Tokyo subway system two persons boarded different trains in Tokyo's main lines between 8:09 and 8:13 a.m., and planted packages, plastic containers filled with sarin and wrapped in newspapers. These containers were punctured with a needle-tipped umbrella. Twelve persons lost their lives, over 5500 were injured, and more than 26 stations were closed. More than anything, this incident produced a tremendous psychological effect on the people of Japan, and made them think that such attacks in other parts of the country may occur and many lost confidence in the government's ability to protect its citizens. The recent Iraq war bears testimony for the use of chemicals by terrorists in the form of IEDs which has killed more U.S. soldiers compared to deaths in the actual combat.

Chemical weapons, warfare agents, or simply chemicals used in terrorist activities can be broadly classified as follows:

- Choking agents (asphyxiating)
- Blood agents or systemic poisons
- Blister agents (vesicants)
- Nerve agents
- Incapacitating agents
- Penetrating agents
- Tear agents (lacrimators)
- Vomiting agents (sternutators)
- Defoliants, desiccants, soil sterilants, and plant growth inhibitors
- Emerging agents
- Explosives and IEDs

A list of these agents is given in Table 19.1. The two-letter code names (e.g., GA = Tabun) of these agents are also given in this table. The two-letter code name is mainly used to identify the agents and it has nothing to do with the chemical formula or the chemical properties of the agent. Several of these agents can persist in the environment for longer periods of time and can cause secondary contamination if proper protection is not taken. In Table 19.1, the persistence data for these agents are given at two temperatures. Most of these agents will eventually degrade in the environment; however, as discussed in Chapter 21, most of these chemical agents can be destroyed by heating.

Choking Agents

These chemicals irritate eyes and throat, and when inhaled, can lead to pulmonary edema, resulting in death from lack of oxygen. Phosgene and chlorine are classified as choking agents. Phosgene has a number of industrial uses in manufacturing various commercial products. Phosgene hydrolyses rapidly, and is used in the production of compact discs, lightweight eyeglasses, and shatterproof glasses. These products are made from polycarbonate resin, which is synthesized from phosgene that is used as a monomer in the synthesis steps. Foams, paints, fibers, and adhesives

Table 19.1 Chemical Warfare Agents That Can Also Be Used for Chemical Terrorism

Type	*Name*	*Code*	*Chemical Formula*	*Persistence 70°F–90°F (hour)*	*Persistence 40°F–60°F (hour)*	*Action*
Choking	Phosgene	CG	$COCl_2$	0.5	1	Rapid
	Diphosgene	DP	$C_2Cl_4O_2$	0.5–3	1–4	Rapid
Nerve	Tabun	GA	$C_2H_5OPO(CN)N(CH_3)_2$	24–48	48–96	Very rapid
	Sarin	GB	$CH_3PO(F)OCH(CH_3)_2$	0.5–24	24–36	Very rapid
	Soman	GD	$CH_3PO(F)OCH(CH_3)C(CH_3)_3$	24–48	48–96	Very rapid
	VX	VX	$(C_2H_5O)(CH_3O)P(O)S(C_2H_4)$ $N[C_2H_2(CH_3)_2]_2$	240–720	720–2160	Rapid
Blood	Hydrogen cyanide	AC	HCN	0.25–.5	0.5–1	Very rapid
	Cyanogen chloride	CK	$CNCl$	0.25–.5	0.5–1	Rapid
	Arsine	SA	AsH_3	0.08–.25	0.25–.5	Delayed
Blister	Distilled mustard	HD	$(ClCH_2CH_2)_2S$	24–48	48–96	Delayed
	Nitrogen mustard	HN-1	$(ClCH_2CH_2)_2NC_2H_5$	24–48	48–96	Delayed
	Nitrogen mustard	HN-2	$(ClCH_2CH_2)_2NCH_3$	24–36	48–72	Delayed
	Nitrogen mustard	HN-3	$N(CH_2CH_2Cl)_3$	48–72	96–144	Delayed
	Phosgene oxime	CX	CCl_2NOH	2–4	3–6	Immediate

	Lewisite	L	$ClCHCHAsCl_2$	18–36	48–72	Rapid
	Mustard lewisite	HL		24–36	48–72	Delayed
	Ethyldichloroarsine	ED	$C_2H_5AsCl_2$	1–2	2–3	Immediate
Blister	Methyldichloroarsine	MD	CH_3AsCl_2	2–4	4–8	Rapid
Vomiting	Diphenyl-dichloroarsine	DA	$(C_6H_5)_2AsCl$	1–2	2–4	Very rapid
	Adamsite	DM	$C_6H_4(AsCl)–NH)C_6H_4$	1–2	2–4	Very rapid
	Diphenylcyanoarsine	DC	$(C_6H_5)_2AsCN$	1–2	2–4	Very rapid
Riot	Chloroacetophenone	CN	$C_6H_5COCH_3Cl$	1–2	2–3	Instant
	Chloroacetophenone in chloroform	CNC		1–2	2–3	Instant
	Chloroacetophenone and chloropicrin in chloroform	CNS		1–2	2–3	Instant
	Chloroacetophenone in benzene and carbon tetrachloride	CNB		1–2	2–3	Instant
	Bromobenzylcyanide	CA	$BrC_6H_4CH_2CN$	24–48	48–96	Instant
	O-Chloro-benzylmalononitrile	CS	$ClC_6H_4CHC(CN)_2$	168–336	168–336	Instant
Incapacitating	Bz	BZ		240–480	720–1440	Delayed

Source: http://www.fas.org/nuke/guide/intro/cw/chem-table.htm. With permission.

are made from polyurethanes, in which the diisocyanate monomers are made using phosgene. Phosgene is also used in making isocyanate intermediates used in the manufacture of pharmaceuticals and agricultural chemicals.

Blood Agents

These are cyanide compounds, the principal one being hydrogen cyanide. Hydrogen cyanide is a colorless liquid that boils at 26°C. The main exposure route is through inhalation. Both gaseous and liquid hydrogen cyanide, as well as cyanide salts in solution, can be harmful and absorbed through the skin. Cyanide compounds are more toxic than phosgene, but evaporate very fast making them difficult to use in warfare because there are problems in achieving sufficiently high concentrations outdoors. However, the concentration of hydrogen cyanide may rapidly reach lethal levels if it is released in confined spaces making it a potent agent for terrorism.

Preparation of CN: Blood Agent. 2-Chloro-1-phenylethanone, 2-chloroacetophenone, a-chloroacetophenone, phenacyl chloride, chloromethyl phenyl ketone (C_8H_7ClO) can be prepared by reacting benzene with 2-chloro acetyl chloride in the presence of a Friedel–Craft catalyst anhydrous aluminum chloride. After the reaction, the mixture is washed in cold water, then sodium hydroxide. Then the mixture is treated with methylene chloride to extract the product. Excess benzene is evaporated, and methylene chloride is also evaporated. The dry powder is further purified by crystallization in hexane.

Blister Agents

These are chemicals that can cause blistering of the skin and extreme irritation of the eyes and lungs. These chemicals incapacitate rather than kill human beings but can kill in large doses. The basic agent is mustard gas. It was extensively used during World War I. Mustard gas is diphosgene, and causes shortness of breath (lung irritant), nausea, and blindness. Later a number of modifications were made to mustard gas to make it more toxic and lethal. These are nitrogen mustard and Lewisite. They undergo slow hydrolysis making them more persistent in the environment and in any fluid.

Nerve Agents

Nerve agents are the most poisonous synthetic chemicals, and they inhibit the vital enzyme activity, specifically of cholinesterase, which is essential for the proper functioning of the nervous system. They disrupt the normal functioning of the nervous system. All nerve agents belong chemically to the group of organophosphorus compounds. They are stable and easily dispersed and have rapid effects both when absorbed through the skin and via respiration. For example, vapor from three drops of a nerve agent can kill a person in four minutes.

- V-series nerve agents, developed in the 1950s, are similar to, but more advanced than, G-series agents. This class includes VE, VG, VM, VS, VR, and VX. These agents are more toxic and more persistent than the G-agents and present a greater skin hazard. They are used for long-term contamination of territory. Nerve agents are organophosphorus esters related to insecticides. They are liquid under normal conditions, and are colorless and odorless.

Incapacitating Agents

Several chemicals in smaller doses can incapacitate a human being for a short time. Incapacitating agents are usually defined as chemical agents that produce reversible disturbances in the central nervous system that disrupt cognitive ability. The agent BZ, which was used by the military in the past but now is used in pharmacology where it is known as QNB, is a cholinergic blocking compound and produces many effects similar to those of atropine, such as mydriasis, drying of secretions, heart rate changes, and decreased intestinal motility. BZ at high doses can lead to confusion, disorientation, and disturbances in perception (delusions, hallucinations) and expressive function (slurred speech) within an hour of exposure. These symptoms are similar to high doses of atropine.

Tear Agents (Lacrimators)

These chemicals cause tears in the eyes and irritation to the skin. They can also be harmful to the respiratory tract. Even in low concentrations, they cause pain in the eyes and flow of tears and make it difficult to keep the eyes open. These substances are chloroacetophenone (CN), *ortho*-chlorobenzylidenemalononitrile (CS), and dibenz (*b,f*)-1,4-oxazepine (CR). The agent CN was the most widely used tear gas; however, recently it has been replaced by CS. At present CS is probably used most widely worldwide as tear gas for riot control. At room temperature, these tear gases are white solid substances. They are stable when heated and have low vapor pressure. Consequently, they are generally dispersed as aerosols.

Vomiting Agents (Sternutators)

As the name indicates, they cause nausea and vomiting. They can also induce cough, headache, and nose and throat irritation. Adamsite (DM) is the most common vomiting agent. It is normally a solid, but upon heating, it first vaporizes and then condenses to form aerosols. Adamsite is dispersed as an aerosol. Under field conditions, vomiting agents can cause great discomfort to the victims. However, indoors, they can cause serious illness or death. Symptoms include irritation of eyes and mucous membranes, coughing, sneezing, severe headache, acute pain and tightness in the chest, nausea, and vomiting. DM has been noted to cause necrosis of corneal epithelium in humans. The human body will detoxify the effects of mild exposures within 30 minutes of evacuation. Severe exposures may take several hours to detoxify and minor sensory disturbances may persist for up to one day.

Defoliants, Desiccants, Soil Sterilants, and Plant Growth Inhibitors

Although we will not discuss the compounds in this category, it is important to note that these chemicals can be used for terrorist activities indirectly. Agent Orange used in Vietnam is an example. They can destroy crops, reduce the fertility of the soil, remove water from the soil, and inhibit plant growth.

Emerging Agents

Many chemicals are considered out of date, and some countries are always on the lookout for more toxic chemicals. The ability to synthesize these chemicals has increased due to better communications through the Internet, enhanced computer modeling, advances in synthetic organic chemistry, and various political considerations.

The new type of chemical weapons will not kill or do any major damage to the human system but would temporarily incapacitate. We saw the use of such chemicals in the recent Moscow Theater incident where the Chechen rebels were subdued by the Russian military. These chemicals are called "calmative or incapacitants or malodorants." It is suspected that the Russians used a fast-acting opiate called Fentanyl. Fentanyl is $C_{22}H_{28}N_2O$. It is *N*-(phenylethyl-4-piperidinyl) propionanilide, phentanyl.

Table 19.2 shows a list of toxic chemicals and precursors designated as chemical warfare agents by the Chemical Weapons Convention (CWC). They are listed under three categories: Schedule 1, 2, and 3 based on the level of their toxicity. The following guideline has been recommended by the CWC in defining a schedule category for a chemical [1].

Table 19.2 List of Toxic Chemicals and Precursors

Schedule 1
A. Toxic chemicals
O-Alkyl (less than or equal to C_{10}, incl. cycloalkyl) alkyl (Me, Et, *n*-Pr, or *i*-Pr)-phosphonofluoridates
Sarin: *O*-isopropyl methylphosphonofluoridate [107-44-8]
Soman: *O*-pinacolyl methylphosphonofluoridate [96-64-0]
O-Alkyl (less than or equal to C_{10}, incl. cycloalkyl) *N,N*-dialkyl (Me, Et, *n*-Pr, or *i*-Pr) phosphoramidocyanidates
Tabun: *O*-ethyl *N,N*-dimethylphosphoramidocyanidate [77-81-6]
O-Alkyl (H or less than or equal to C_{10}, incl. cycloalkyl) *S*-2-dialkyl (Me, Et, *n*-Pr, or *i*-Pr)-aminoethyl alkyl (Me, Et, *n*-Pr, or *i*-Pr) phosphonothiolates and corresponding alkylated or protonated salts
VX: *O*-ethyl *S*-2-diisopropylaminoethylmethyl phosphonothiolate [50782-69-9]
Sulfur mustards
2-Chloroethylchloromethylsulfide [2625-76-5]
Mustard gas
Bis(2-chloroethyl)sulfide [505-60-2]
Bis(2-chloroethylthio)methane [63869-13-6]
Sesquimustard
1,2-Bis(2-chloroethylthio)ethane [3563-36-8]
1,3-Bis(2-chloroethylthio)-*n*-propane [63905-10-2]
1,4-Bis(2-chloroethylthio)-*n*-butane [142868-93-7]
1,5-Bis(2-chloroethylthio)-*n*-pentane [142868-94-8]
Bis(2-chloroethylthiomethyl)ether [63918-90-1]
O-Mustard
Bis(2-chloroethylthioethyl)ether [63918-89-8]

Table 19.2 (continued) List of Toxic Chemicals and Precursors

Schedule 1

Lewisites

Lewisite 1: 2-Chlorovinyldichloroarsine [541-25-3]

Lewisite 2: Bis(2-chlorovinyl)chloroarsine [40334-69-8]

Lewisite 3: Tris(2-chlorovinyl)arsine [40334-70-1]

Nitrogen mustards

HN1: bis(2-chloroethyl)ethylamine [538-07-8]

HN2: bis(2-chloroethyl)methylamine [51-75-2]

HN3: tris(2-chloroethyl)amine [555-77-1]

Saxitoxin [35523-89-8]

Ricin [9009-86-3]

B. Precursors

Alkyl (Me, Et, *n*-Pr, or *i*-Pr) phosphonyldifluorides

DF: methylphosphonyldifluoride [676-99-3]

O-Alkyl (H or less than or equal to C_{10}, incl. cycloalkyl) *O*-2-dialkyl (Me, Et, *n*-Pr, or *i*-Pr)-aminoethyl alkyl (Me, Et, *n*-Pr, or *i*-Pr) phosphonites and corresponding alkylated or protonated salts

QL: *O*-ethyl *O*-2-diisopropylaminoethylmethylphosphonite [57856-11-8]

Chlorosarin

O-Isopropyl methylphosphonochloridate [1445-76-7]

Chlorosoman

O-Pinacolyl methylphosphonochloridate [7040-57-5]

Schedule 2

A. Toxic chemicals

Amiton:

O,O-Diethyl *S*-[2-(diethylamino)ethyl] phosphorothiolate [78-53-5] and corresponding alkylated or protonated salts

PFIB:

1,1,3,3,3-Pentafluoro-2-(trifluoromethyl)-1-propene [382-21-8]

BZ:

3-Quinuclidinyl benzilate [6581-06-2]

B. Precursors

Chemicals, except for those listed in Schedule 1, containing a phosphorus atom to which is bonded one methyl, ethyl, or propyl (normal or iso) group but not further carbon atoms, e.g., methylphosphonyl dichloride [676-97-1]

Dimethyl methylphosphonate [756-79-6]

(continued)

Table 19.2 (continued) List of Toxic Chemicals and Precursors

Schedule 2
Exemption
Fonofos: *O*-Ethyl *S*-phenyl ethylphosphonothiolothionate [944-22-9]
N,N-Dialkyl (Me, Et, *n*-Pr, or *i*-Pr) phosphoramidic dihalides
Dialkyl (Me, Et, *n*-Pr, or *i*-Pr) *N,N*-dialkyl (Me, Et, *n*-Pr, or *i*-Pr)-phosphoramidates
Arsenic trichloride [7784-34-1]
2,2-Diphenyl-2-hydroxyacetic acid [76-93-7]
Quinuclidine-3-ol [1619-34-7]
N,N-Dialkyl (Me, Et, *n*-Pr, or *i*-Pr) aminoethyl-2-chlorides and corresponding protonated salts
N,N-Dialkyl (Me, Et, *n*-Pr, or *i*-Pr) aminoethane-2-ols and corresponding protonated salts
N,N-Dimethylaminoethanol [108-01-0] and corresponding protonated salts
N,N-Diethylaminoethanol [100-37-8] and corresponding protonated salts
N,N-Dialkyl (Me, Et, *n*-Pr or *i*-Pr) aminoethane-2-thiols and corresponding protonated salts
Thiodiglycol: bis(2-hydroxyethyl)sulfide [111-48-8]
Pinacolyl alcohol: 3,3-dimethylbutane-2-ol [464-07-3]
Schedule 3
A. Toxic chemicals
Phosgene: carbonyl dichloride [75-44-5]
Cyanogen chloride [506-77-4] (2851.00)
Hydrogen cyanide [74-90-8] (2811.19)
Chloropicrin: trichloronitromethane [76-06-2]
B. Precursors
Phosphorus oxychloride [10025-87-3]
Phosphorus trichloride [7719-12-2]
Phosphorus pentachloride [10026-13-8]
Trimethyl phosphite [121-45-9]
Triethyl phosphite [122-52-1]
Dimethyl phosphite [868-85-9]
Diethyl phosphite [762-04-9]
Sulfur monochloride [10025-67-9]
Sulfur dichloride [10545-99-0]
Thionyl chloride [7719-09-7]
Ethyldiethanolamine [139-87-7]
Methyldiethanolamine [105-59-9]
Triethanolamine [102-71-6]

Source: Preparatory Commission for the Organization for the Prohibition of Chemical Weapons PC-V/B/WP.10, February 22, 2001. http://www.opcw.nl/guide.htm. With permission.

Explosives and IEDs

Explosives and IEDs have been a greater threat to the U.S. military compared to other chemical weapons. Well-known chemical compounds in this class have been used, and scientists are finding newer and more powerful chemical agents. We will discuss some of these in this section.

The common explosives can be classified as military explosives such as TNT (trinitrotoluene), RDX (**R**oyal **D**emolition e**X**plosive, the chemical name for RDX is 1,3,5-trinitro-1,3,5-triazine), HMX (**H**igh **M**elting e**X**plosive, it is also known as octogen and cyclotetramethylene-tetranitramine), PETN (pentaerythritoltetranitrate, its chemical name is 3-nitrooxy-2,2-bis(nitrooxymethyl)propyl nitrate), CL20; explosive compositions such as Amatol, Comp A-3, Comp B, Comp C-4, Cyclotol, Detasheet, H-6, HBX-1, LX-10, LX-17, Octol, PBX-9404, PBX-9501, PE 4, Pentolite, Semtex-H, Tritonal; peroxide compounds, and a number of new chemicals.

It is reported that replacing carbon atoms by silicon in some explosives results in compounds that are highly sensitive and have much higher explosive strength. The report mentions that these compounds exploded with a touch with a spatula, and they are three times more sensitive than the parent compound. FOX-7 (1,1-diamino-2,2-dinitroethylene) is similar to HMX but more powerful compared to HMX. The Swedish Defense Research Agency synthesized this chemical in the late 1990s.

Guidelines for Schedule 1

1. The following criteria shall be taken into account in considering whether a toxic chemical or precursor should be included in Schedule 1:
   a. It has been developed, produced, stockpiled, or used as a chemical weapon as defined in Article II
   b. It poses otherwise a high risk to the object and purpose of this Convention by virtue of its high potential for use in activities prohibited under this Convention because one or more of the following conditions are met
      i. It possesses a chemical structure closely related to that of other toxic chemicals listed in Schedule 1, and has, or can be expected to have, comparable properties
      ii. It possesses such lethal or incapacitating toxicity as well as other properties that would enable it to be used as a chemical weapon
      iii. It may be used as a precursor in the final single technological stage of production of a toxic chemical listed in Schedule 1, regardless of whether this stage takes place in facilities, in munitions, or elsewhere
   c. It has little or no use for purposes not prohibited under this Convention

Guidelines for Schedule 2

2. The following criteria shall be taken into account in considering whether a toxic chemical not listed in Schedule 1 or a precursor to a Schedule 1 chemical or to a chemical listed in Schedule 2, part A, should be included in Schedule 2:
   a. It poses a significant risk to the object and purpose of this Convention because it possesses such lethal or incapacitating toxicity as well as other properties that could enable it to be used as a chemical weapon
   b. It may be used as a precursor in one of the chemical reactions at the final stage of formation of a chemical listed in Schedule 1 or Schedule 2, part A

c. It poses a significant risk to the object and purpose of this Convention by virtue of its importance in the production of a chemical listed in Schedule 1 or Schedule 2, part A
d. It is not produced in large commercial quantities for purposes not prohibited under this Convention

Guidelines for Schedule 3

3. The following criteria shall be taken into account in considering whether a toxic chemical or precursor, not listed in other Schedules, should be included in Schedule 3:
a. It has been produced, stockpiled, or used as a chemical weapon
b. It poses otherwise a risk to the object and purpose of this Convention because it possesses such lethal or incapacitating toxicity as well as other properties that might enable it to be used as a chemical weapon
c. It poses a risk to the object and purpose of this Convention by virtue of its importance in the production of one or more chemicals listed in Schedule 1 or Schedule 2, part B
d. It may be produced in large commercial quantities for purposes not prohibited under this Convention

In Table 19.2 numbers in square brackets show the CAS (Chemical Abstracts Service) Registry numbers, a unique way of identifying chemical substances. There is no significance to these numbers, but are an unambiguous computer-language description of a compound's molecular structure. A precursor is a chemical that can be chemically combined with another substance to form a chemical substance—in this case a chemical warfare agent. Many precursors are controlled through international efforts but have other commercial uses as well. Therefore it is possible to obtain these precursors and use them to make toxic chemicals.

Synthesis

In this section we will discuss the synthesis steps of a few representative chemicals. The manufacturing facilities generally required are available to any country with a good chemical industry infrastructure. The major equipment required in all cases include mainly reaction vessels, agitators as most of the manufacturing is carried out in a batch process, heat exchangers or condensers, pumps, valves, storage tanks, controllers and measuring equipment (for measuring temperature, pressure or vacuum, toxic gas detectors, flow meters, etc.), balances, and analytical equipment. In all cases, materials of construction are important, as most of the chemicals handled are highly corrosive. Some materials of construction used in these plants are glass-lined vessels, tantalum, graphite, titanium, zirconium, and alloys of some of these metals. The materials of construction are expensive items in the manufacture of these toxic chemicals.

Many chemicals like phosgene and hydrogen cyanide can be procured directly, as they have several commercial uses. Toxic chemicals like mustard gas (most of the vesicants) can be prepared easily, and the technology is well known. Nerve gas is more complicated to synthesize, and in many cases fairly precise control of variables such as temperature is required. These chemicals need more sophisticated technologies. Of the several nerve gases, tabun (*O*-ethyl-dimethylamidophophoylcyanide, GA) is the easiest to manufacture. Most advanced countries think that tabun is out-of-date, and look for other nerve gases. We shall now take specific cases as examples and outline the synthesis procedure.

Mustard

Bis(2-chloroethyl)sulfide, a heavy oily liquid, is made by Levinstein process. It consists of bubbling dry ethylene into sulfur monochloride at 35°C with previously prepared mustard facilitating the reaction. The reaction is

$$S_2Cl_2 + 2CH_2{:}CH_2 \rightarrow (ClCH_2CH_2)_2S + S$$

The nitrogen mustards are a series of chloroalkyl amines, the most active being tris(2-chloroethyl) amine ($N(C_2H_4Cl)_3$) and methyl-bis(2-chloroethyl)amine ($CH_3N(C_2H_4Cl)_2$). These nitrogen mustards are highly active vesicants. The nitrogen mustards are prepared by the reaction of thionyl chloride with the appropriate ethanolamine.

$$RN(CH_2CH_2OH)_2 + 2SOCl_2 \rightarrow RN(CH_2CH_2Cl)HCl + 2SO_2 + HCl$$

Sarin

Sarin ($C_4H_{10}FO_2P$) is methylphosphofluoridic acid 1-methylethyl ester or isopropylmethane-fluorophosphonate. Its Chemical Abstracts Service registry number is 107-44-8. It was discovered in 1938 by Gerhard Schrader, the German chemist, during World War II, but fortunately was not used. It is an organophosphate, a class of chemicals used as pesticides, and it was during the synthesis of pesticides that sarin was accidentally discovered. These organophosphates are highly toxic and stable. It has been replaced by other substances such as VX Sarin, one of most deadly compounds in the weapons arsenal. Closely related to sarin is a compound referred to as GF, or cyclohexyl sarin. GF is also a colorless and odorless liquid.

Large-scale combat use of sarin has not occurred, although its use is strongly suspected in an Iraqi attack on the village of Birjinni on August 25, 1988 (samples collected from the site four years later showed the expected breakdown products of sarin). It is not known with certainty whether or not sarin was used in the Iran–Iraq war. On March 20, 1995, the Aum Shinrikyo released sarin in the Tokyo subway, killing 12 and injuring 5500 people in the first documented terrorist use of chemical weapons. Sarin was produced and stockpiled in large quantities by both the United States and the Soviet Union.

Reesor et al. [3] discuss several routes for the synthesis of sarin. According to Reesor et al., the direct conversion of phosphorous trichloride to methylphosphonic dicholoride, and its subsequent conversion to sarin is a safer method. The formation of aluminum phosphorous chloride or modified APC is the first step in the process. The dichloride is converted into difluoride, and finally to sarin.

A second route for isopropyl methylphosphanofluoridate is the reaction of dicyclohexylamine salt of *O*-isopropyl hydrogen methylphosphonothioate with picryl fluoride [4]. Both Reesor et al. and Boter and Van Den Berg [4] describe the experimental details for the preparation of alkyl methylphosphonofluoridates.

One method that is followed in the manufacture of sarin is the DHMP (dimethyl hydrogen phosphite) process, although other processes have replaced this process. In the DHMP process, phosphorous trichloride and methanol are reacted to give dimethyl phospite. On further heating, dimethyl phosphite is converted to methyl phosphonate. This mixture called "pyromix" is chlorinated using chlorine and phosphorous trichloride to yield methylphosphonic dichloride. This is then fluorinated to yield the difluoride, which combines with dichloride to yield sarin.

During the different stages corrosive and toxic chemicals such as HCl, methyl chloride, oxychloride, and others are formed. The last stage can take place in missiles during flight, as the reactants are far less dangerous than the product so that they can be stored separately. The reaction scheme is shown below as an illustrative example [5].

$$PCl_3 + 3CH_3OH \rightarrow (OCH_3)_2POH + CH_3Cl + 2HCl$$

$$(OCH_3)_2POH \rightarrow (CH_3)PO(OCH_3)(OH)$$

$$(CH_3)PO(OCH_3)(OH) + 2PCl_3 + Cl_2 \rightarrow CH_3P(O)Cl_2 + 2POCl_3 + CH_3Cl + 2HCl$$

$$CH_3P(O)Cl_2 + 2HF \rightarrow CH_3P(O)F_2 + 2HCl$$

$$CH_3P(O)Cl_2 + CH_3P(O)F_2 + 2(CH_3)_2CHOH \rightarrow 2CH_3FP(O)OCH(CH_3)_2 + 2HCl$$

A number of countries are capable of producing these chemical agents because the precursor chemicals are easily available or dual use chemicals. In Table 19.3, the various aspects for their manufacture are summarized.

Properties of Chemicals

Knowledge of the properties of chemicals is important to measure the effectiveness of chemical compounds. We will discuss some simple properties and how they can tell us the effectiveness of chemical compounds. Various physical and chemical properties of chemical agents are given in Table 19.4 [6].

Molecular Weight

Molecular weight is found by adding the atomic weights of all the elements in that compound. Molecular weight can provide the following important information regarding a chemical.

Stability: Higher molecular weight compounds are less stable compared to lower molecular weight compounds. A stable compound persists in the environment for a longer period of time compared to an unstable compound.

Protection: Gas masks and other equipment are used for protection. Based on molecular weight, higher molecular weight materials can be filtered more easily compared to lower molecular weight materials. For example it is difficult to adsorb substances like CO and ammonia using activated carbon filters. We should of course hasten to add that filtration of the materials depends on the properties of the filtering material.

Estimation of unknown properties: Molecular weight helps to estimate unknown properties to a fair amount of accuracy. For example, if we wish to find the boiling point of a substance, we can plot boiling points of some known substances of similar chemical nature and extrapolate or interpolate to get the boiling point using the molecular weight of the substance in question.

Table 19.3 Various Manufacturing Aspects of Chemical Agents

Technology Manufacturing Processes	*Sufficient Technology Level*	*Export Control Reference*	*Critical Materials*	*Unique Test, Production, and Inspection Equipment*
O-Alkyl (≤C_{10}, incl. cycloalkyl) alkyl (Me, Et, *n*-Pr, or *i*-Pr) phosphonofluoridates Example: Sarin (GB) *O*-isopropyl methylphosphonofluoridate	Sovereign States: capable of annual production of approx. 100 tons Subnational: capable of producing any amount	CWC; WA ML 7; USML XIV	Phosphorus trichloride; DF; DC; hydrogen fluoride; isopropanol	Needs expensive corrosive-resistant equipment such as hastelloy or silver
O-Alkyl (≤C_{10}, incl. cycloalkyl) alkyl (Me, Et, *n*-Pr, or *i*-Pr) phosphonofluoridates, Example: Soman (GD) *O*-pinacolyl methylphosphonofluoridate	Sovereign States: capable of annual production of approx. 100 tons Subnational: capable of producing any amount	CWC; WA ML 7; USML XIV	Phosphorus trichloride; DC; hydrogen fluoride; pinacolyl alcohol	Needs expensive corrosive-resistant equipment such as hastelloy or silver
O-Alkyl (≤C_{10}, incl. cycloalkyl) *N,N*-dialkyl (Me, Et, *n*-Pr, or *i*-Pr) phosphoramidocyanidates Example: Tabun (GA) *O*-ethyl *N,N*-dimethylphosphoramidocyanidate	Sovereign States: capable of annual production of approx. 200 tons Subnational: capable of producing any amount	CWC; WA ML 7; USML XIV	Phosphorus oxychloride or phosphorus trichloride; sodium cyanide; dimethlyamine; ethyl alcohol	None identified
O-Alkyl (H or ≤C_{10}, incl. cycloalkyl) Me, Et, *n*-Pr, or *i*-Pr)-aminoethyl alkyl (Me, Et, *n*-Pr, or *i*-Pr) phosphonothiolates and corresponding alkylated or protonated salts, e.g., VX	Sovereign States: capable of annual production of approx. 200 tons Subnational: capable of producing any amount	CWC; WA ML 7; USML XIV	QL; sulfur or DC if Amiton-like process is used	Inert atmosphere high-temperature methylation equipment (QL process)

(*continued*)

Table 19.3 (continued) Various Manufacturing Aspects of Chemical Agents

Technology Manufacturing Processes	*Sufficient Technology Level*	*Export Control Reference*	*Critical Materials*	*Unique Test, Production, and Inspection Equipment*
Phosphonochloridates, chlorosarin: *O*-isopropyl methylphosphonochloridate	Sovereign States: capable of annual production of approx. 300 tons Subnational: capable of producing any amount	CWC; WA ML 7; USML XIV	DC	Glass-lined reactors
Sulfur mustards:	Sovereign States: capable of annual production of approx. 500 tons Subnational: capable of producing any amount	CWC; WA ML 7; USML XIV	Sulfur monochloride or sulfur dichloride or thiodiglycol	None identified
Lewisites (L): L1: 2 chlorovinyldichloroarsine L 2: bis(2-chlorovinyl)chloroarsine L 3: tris(2-chlorovinyl)arsine	Sovereign States: capable of annual production of approx. 500 tons Subnational: capable of producing any amount	CWC; WA ML 7; USML XIV	Arsenic trichloride	None identified
Nitrogen mustards: HN1: bis(2-chloroethyl) ethylamine HN2: bis(2-chloroethyl) methylamine HN3: tris(2-chloroethyl) amine	Sovereign States: capable of annual production of approx. 500 tons Subnational: capable of producing any amount	CWC; WA ML 7; USML XIV	HN 1: ethyl diethanolamine HN 2: methyl diethanolamine HN 3:triethanolamine	Glass- or enamel-lined equipment

Amiton: *O*,*O*-diethyl *S*-[2-(diethylamino)ethyl] phosphorothiolate and corresponding alkylated or protonated salts	Sovereign States: capable of annual production of approx. 500 tons Subnational: capable of producing any amount	CWC; WA ML 7; USML XIV	None	Normally made in solution, extraction equipment
PFIB: 1,1,3,3,3-pentafluoro-2-(trifluoromethyl)-1-propene	Sovereign States: capable of annual production of approx. 2000 tons Subnational: capable of producing any amount	CWC; WA ML 7; USML XIV	None	Needs expensive corrosion resistant equipment such as hastelloy or silver
Phosgene: carbonyl dichloride	Sovereign States: capable of annual production of approx. 2000 tons Subnational: capable of producing any amount	CWC (exempted from WA ML); USML XIV	None	Corrosion resistant equipment
Cyanogen chloride	Sovereign States: capable of annual production of approx. 2000 tons Subnational: capable of producing any amount	CWC (exempted from WA ML); USML XIV	None	None identified
Hydrogen cyanide	Sovereign States: capable of annual production of approx. 5000 tons Subnational: capable of producing any amount	CWC (exempted from WA ML); USML XIV	None	None identified

(continued)

Table 19.3 (continued) Various Manufacturing Aspects of Chemical Agents

Technology Manufacturing Processes	*Sufficient Technology Level*	*Export Control Reference*	*Critical Materials*	*Unique Test, Production, and Inspection Equipment*
Alkyl (Me, Et, *n*-Pr, or *i*-Pr) phosphonyldifluorides DF: methylphosphonyldifluoride	Sovereign States: capable of annual production of approx. 200 tons Subnational: capable of producing any amount	CWC; AG List; WA ML-7; CCL Cat 1E	DC; hydrogen fluoride	Production equipment made of hastelloy or other high nickel alloys; silver
Alkyl (Me, Et, *n*-Pr, or *i*-Pr) phosphonylchlorides, DC: methylphosphonyl dichloride (this material, rather than DF, is the fundamental building block of a significant portion of G and V agents)	Sovereign States: capable of annual production of approx. 400 tons Subnational: capable of producing any amount	CWC; AG List; WA ML-7; CCL Cat IE	Thionyl chloride or phosgene or phosphorous pentachloride Dimethyl methylphosphonate (DMMP)	Glass-lined vessels Glass-lined distillation columns
O-Alkyl (H or $\leq C_{10}$, incl. cycloalkyl) *O*-2- dialkyl (Me, Et, *n*-Pr, or *i*-Pr)-aminoethyl alkyl (Me, Et, *n*-Pr, or *i*-Pr) phosphonites and corresponding alkylated or protonated salts Example: QL	Sovereign States: capable of annual production of approx. 200 tons Subnational: capable of producing any amount	CWC; AG List; WA ML 7; CCL Cat 1E	TR (diethyl methylphosphonite) KB (2-(*N*,*N*,diethylamino) ethanol). Similar esters and amino alcohols	Waste treatment incinerators Distillation columns High-temperature methylation equipment

Source: Section IV Chemical Weapons Technology. www. fas.org/irp/threat/metc 98-2/p2sec04.pdf
Note: CWC: Chemical Weapon Convention; USML: U.S. Munitions List; CCL: Commodity Control List; AG: Australia Group.

Table 19.4 Physical and Chemical Properties of Chemical Agents

Agent	*MW*	*State at 20°C*	*Odor*	*Liquid Density (g/cc)*	*BP(°C)*	*VP(mmHg)*	*Volatility (mg/m³)*	ΔH_V *(cal/g)*
Tabun	162.3	Colorless to brown liquid	Faintly fruity; none when pure	1.073 at 25°C	240	0.037 at 20°C	610 at 25°C	79.56
Sarin	140.1	Colorless liquid	Almost none when pure	4.86	158	2.9 at 25°C 2.10 at 20°C	22,000 at 25°C 16,090 at 20°C	80
Soman	182.18	Colorless liquid	Fruity; camphor when impure	1.022 at 25°C	198	0.4 at 25°C	3,900 at 25°C	72.4
Cyclo-sarin	180.2	Liquid	Sweet; musty; peaches; shellac	1.133 at 20°C	239	0.044 at 20°C	438 at 20°C	90.5
VX	267.38	Colorless to amber liquid	None	1.0083 at 20°C	298	0.0007 at 20°C	10.5 at 25°C	78.2 at 25°C
V_X	211.2	Colorless liquid	None	1.062 at 20°C	256	0.007 at 25°C 0.004 at 20°C	75 at 25°C 48 at 20°C	67.2
Distilled Mustard HD	159.08	Colorless to pale yellow liquid	Garlic or horseradish	1.27 at 25°C 1.27 at 20°C	217	0.072 at 20°C	610 at 20°C	94
Nitrogen mustard HN-1	170.08	Dark liquid	Fishy or musty	1.09 at 20°C	194	0.24 at 25°C	1,520 at 20°C	77
Nitrogen mustard HN-2	156.07	Dark liquid	Soapy (low concentrations); fruity (high)	1.15 at 20°C	75 at 15 mmHg	0.29 at 20°C	3,580 at 25°C	78.8
Nitrogen mustard HN-3	204.54	Dark liquid	None, if pure	1.24 at 20°C	256	0.0109 at 25°C	121 at 25°C	74

(continued)

Table 19.4 (continued) Physical and Chemical Properties of Chemical Agents

Agent	*MW*	*State at 20°C*	*Odor*	*Liquid Density (g/cc)*	*BP(°C)*	*VP(mmHg)*	*Volatility (mg/m³)*	*ΔH$_V$ (cal/g)*
Phosgene oximedichloro-foroxime	113.94	Colorless solid or liquid	Sharp, penetrating	—	53–54 at 28 mmHg	11.2 at 25°C (solid) 13 at 40°C (liquid)	1,800 at 20°C	101 at 40°C
Lewisite	207.35	Colorless to brownish	Varies; may resemble geraniums	1.89 at 20°C	190	0.394 at 20°C	4,480 at 20°C	58 at 0°C–190°C
Mustard–Lewisite mixture	186.4	Dark, oily liquid	Garlic	1.66 at 20°C	<190	0.248 at 20°C	2,730 at 20°C	58–94
Phenyl dichlorarsine	222.91	Colorless liquid	None	1.65 at 20°C	252 to 255	0.033 at 25°C	390 at 25°C	69
Ethyl dichlorarsine	174.88	Colorless liquid	Fruity, but biting; irritating	1.66 at 20°C	156	2.09 at 20°C	20,000 at 20°C	52.5
Methyl dichlorarsine	160.86	Colorless liquid	None	1.836 at 20°C	133	7.76 at 20°C	74,900 at 20°C	49
Hydrogen cyanide	27.02	Colorless gas or liquid	Bitter almonds	0.687 at 20°C	25.7	742 at 25°C 612 at 20°C	1,080,000 at 25°C	233
Cyanogen chloride	61.48	Colorless gas or liquid	Pungent, biting; can go unnoticed	1.18 at 20°C	12.8	1,000 at 25°C	2,600,000 at 20°C	103
Arsine	77.93	Colorless gas	Mild garlic	1.34 at 20°C	−62.5	11,100 at 20°C	30,900,000 at 20°C	53.7 at −62.5°C
Phosgene	98.92	Colorless gas	New-mown hay; green corn	1.37 at 20°C	7.6	1.173 at 20°C	4,300,000 at 7.6°C	59
Diphosgene	197.85	Colorless gas	New-mown hay; green corn	1.65 at 20°C	127–128	4.2 at 20°C	45,000 at 20°C	57.4

Adamsite	277.57	Yellow to green solid	None	1.65 at 20°C (solid)	410	Negligible	Negligible	80
Diphenylcyanoarsine	255.0	White to pink solid	Bitter almond–garlic mixture	1.334 at 35°C	350	0.0002 at 20°C	2.8 at 20°C	71.1
BZ	337.4	White crystal	None	1.33	320	0.03 at 70°C	0.5 at 70°C	62.9
Chloroaceto-phenone	154.59	Solid	Apple blossoms	1.318 at 20°C (solid)	248	0.0041 at 20°C	34.3 at 20°C	98
Chloroaceto-phenone in chloroform	128.17	Liquid	Chloroform	1.40 at 20°C	60–247	127 at 20°C	n/a	n/a
Chloroaceto-phenone and chloropicrin in chloroform	141.78	Liquid	Flypaper	2	60–247	78 at 20°C	610,000 at 20°C (includes solvent)	n/a
Chloroacetophenone in benzene and carbon tetrachloride	119.7	Liquid	Benzene	1.14 at 20°C	75–247	Variable; mostly solvent vapor	n/a	n/a
Bromobenzylcyanide	196	Yellow or solid liquid	Soured fruit	1.47 at 25°C	Decomposes at 242	0.011 at 20°C	115 at 20°C	79.5 at 20°C
O-Chlorobenzyl malonitrile	188.5	Colorless solid	Pepper	1.04 at 20°C	310–315	0.00034 at 20°C	0.71 at 25°C	53.6
CR	195.25	Yellow powder in solution	Burning sensation	—	335	0.00059 at 20°C	0.63 at 25°C	—
Chloropicrin	164.38	Liquid	Stinging; pungent	1.66	112	18.3 at 20°C	165,000 at 20°C	—

Source: Air Force Manual No 355-7, Potential Military Chemical/Biological Agents and Compounds, December 1990, Washington, DC 1.27.
Note: MW: molecular weight; BP: boiling point; ΔH_V: heat of vaporization.

Boiling Point

Boiling point is the temperature at which a substance boils at 1.013 bar pressure. This temperature is termed as the normal boiling point. Boiling point tells us the ability of a compound to vaporize and therefore the evaporation rates. Higher boiling compounds are less volatile compared to lower boiling compounds. Therefore higher boiling compounds persist longer compared to lower boiling compounds. An estimate of the boiling point also throws some light on the rate of decontamination.

Density

Density is defined as mass/volume. It is the mass of a substance contained in a unit volume. It is found by weighing a known volume of the substance at a particular temperature and dividing the mass by the volume. It is generally expressed as gm/cc or gm/cm^3. When this number is compared to the density of water, the number is called specific gravity. We say that the specific gravity of mercury is 13.6, and this indicates that mercury is 13.6 times heavier than water.

Liquid density is a measure of the effectiveness of a chemical substance as toxicity is expressed in terms of units of mass. The chemical efficiency of munitions is defined as

$$\mu = \text{mass of the filling/total mass of the munitions.}$$

Therefore a chemical of a higher density has a higher efficiency for a given mass of the munitions. Densities are also useful to find out whether the particular chemical floats or sinks in water. This is useful again in decontamination with water and subsequent disposal of the chemical.

Vapor Pressure

This is a very important property of the chemical. It is the pressure exerted by a liquid or a vapor when the two are in equilibrium at a particular temperature. Lower boiling substances have a higher vapor pressure and vice versa. Higher vapor pressure indicates higher evaporation rates. Chemicals therefore must have reasonable vapor pressure to be useful. Liquids and solids can be atomized and disseminated in the gaseous phase. When the toxic chemical is dispersed in the gaseous phase, the effectiveness of the chemical also depends on a number of factors such as wind speed and direction, atmospheric temperature, solar radiation, and conditions of the area such as hills, vegetation, etc.

It is very important to have knowledge of the vapor pressure at different temperatures particularly for the storage and transport of the toxicants. However the toxicity of the chemicals makes it very difficult to experimentally determine the vapor pressure at different temperatures, particularly at higher temperatures. However in the range of temperature where the vapor pressure does not exceed 760 mm of Hg, vapor pressures can be estimated using the relation

$$\text{Ln } P = a + (b/T)$$

where

P is the vapor pressure in mm of Hg

T is the absolute temperature in Kelvin (K)

The two constants, *a* and *b*, in the equation can be estimated using two values of *P*. Table 19.5 gives the values of the constant for some specific compounds. It is recommended that these constants be used with caution, and for pressures below 760 mm of Hg.

The vapor pressure of some of the common explosives is shown in Figure 19.1 [7]. The vapor pressure of commonly used explosives such as RDX is very low and this poses a problem in detecting these chemicals when they are concealed as packages, checked baggage, roadside bombs, etc.

Table 19.5 Vapor Pressure Constants

Chemical Compound	*a*	*b*
Tabun	21.548	-7287.4
Sarin	21.008	-5941.1

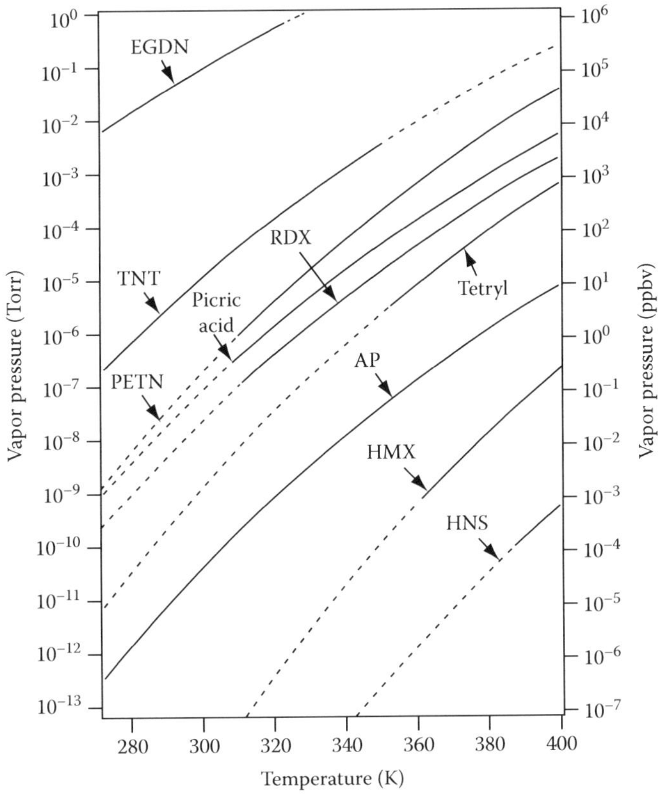

Figure 19.1 Vapor pressure–temperature data of various explosives. (From Moore, D.S., *Rev. Sec. Instrum.*, 75(8), 2499, 2004. With permission.)

Volatility

Volatility is defined as the mass of a chemical in vapor per unit volume of air at a given temperature. Volatility depends on the boiling point, vapor pressure, and temperature. It is calculated using the ideal gas equation, and is given by

$$m = 15826P \times \mathrm{MW}/T$$

where

m is the volatility in mg/m^3
P is the vapor pressure in mm of Hg
MW is the molecular mass of the chemical
T is the temperature in K

This relation shows that as molecular mass increases volatility increases. However the effect of temperature and pressure are related in the sense that when the temperature increases vapor pressure increases. The increase or decrease of volatility depends on the temperature–pressure relation.

Enthalpy of Vaporization

This is the amount of heat required to vaporize a unit mass of a chemical at a given temperature and at its vapor pressure. The enthalpy of vaporization of water at 298.15 K is 540 cal/g. This value indicates the ability of a substance to volatilize.

Advantages and Disadvantages of Chemical Weapons

Advantages

Chemical warfare agents exhibit unique qualities compared to conventional weapons. Effect of chemical weapons can be severe and rapid and they have the enormous capability to inflict casualties. They may be difficult to detect at times because of their low concentrations in the environment. Effective detectors are lacking both when the substance is used and when it is stored. Also it is difficult to judge terrorists' capabilities, because a number of precursor chemicals that can be used to produce chemical terrorism agents have dual use. Many chemicals can be bought or shipped as commercial chemicals. An example is thiodiglycol used in the manufacture of mustard gas, which can also be procured for making ammonium nitrate. A dedicated and skilled chemists can synthesize most of these agents. With the current sophistication of computer chemical modeling, a good chemist can work out strategies for synthesizing more toxic chemicals starting from the currently available chemical structures. Compared to a nuclear weapon, the manufacturing cost of chemical agents are relatively low, and in most cases require low technology.

Disadvantages

The major disadvantages are that the manufacturing processes demand good control of variables, and the chemicals are corrosive.

References

1. Texts of the chemical weapons convention. http://www.opcw.org/cwcdoc.htm
2. Preparatory Commission for the Organization for the Prohibition of Chemical Weapons PC-V/B/WP.10, February 22, 2001. http://www.opcw.nl/guide.htm
3. JB Reesor, BJ Perry, and E Sherlock. The synthesis of highly radioactive isopropyl methylphosphonofluoridate (sarin) containing P^{32} as tracer element. *Can J Chem* 38:1416–1427, 1960.
4. HL Boter and GR Van Den Berg. Organophosphorous compounds III. *Recueil* 85:919–927, 1966.
5. Sarin Home page. www.chem.ox.ac.uk/courses/firstyearonline/week02/sarin1.htm
6. Air Force Manual No. 355-7, Potential Military Chemical/Biological Agents and Compounds December 1990, Washington, DC 1.27.
7. DS Moore. Instrumentation for trace detection of high explosives. *Rev Sci Instrum* 75(8):2499–2512, 2004.

Chapter 20

Chemical Terrorism: Toxicity, Medical Management, and Mitigation

L. David Ormerod

CONTENTS

Introduction 356
Hazards from Chemical Weapons 356
Routes of Exposure 357
Environmental Considerations 358
Signs Suggestive of a Chemical Attack 359
Advice to Civilians Involved in a Chemical Release 359
Protection of First Responders 360
Organization of Rescue Operations after CW Attack 361
Decontamination of Casualties 362
Chemical Weapon Poisoning and Management 363
    Nerve Agents 363
    Vesicating (Blistering) Agents 366
    Blood Agents (Cyanides) 367
    Choking Agents (Lung Irritants) 367
    Psychotomimetic Agents 368
    Toxin Agents 368
Long-Term Consequences of CW Exposure 369
Syndromic Medical Management 369

Medical Forensic Samples 369
Logistics of the Health Services Response to a Civilian Chemical Attack 374
References 376

Introduction

Toxic chemicals are defined as "any chemical which, through its chemical action on life processes can cause death, temporary incapacitation, or permanent harm to humans or animals" [1]. Since the late nineteenth century, industrial production and scientific investigation have continued to generate exponential increases in the number of chemical substances identified, many toxic to humans, animals, or plants. Currently as many as 500,000 U.S. commercial products pose physical or health hazards [2]. In 1999, the Environmental Protection Agency (EPA) estimated that approximately 850,000 facilities in the country were working with hazardous chemicals, a figure which places in some perspective the perennial risk of hazardous material (HAZMAT) release due to mishaps in chemical manufacturing and storage, from industrial accidents, as a result of transportation accidents, or from accidents at home. In the United States where there is an effective regulatory and legal environment, most chemical spills are small with few casualties [3]. HAZMAT response guidelines, training, and equipment have been standardized by the National Fire Academy (NFA) and the Federal Emergency Management Agency (FEMA) to facilitate efficient and effective management of hazardous chemical accidents [4].

However, there are newly perceived terrorist threats to the U.S. homeland utilizing chemicals. These may occur as the consequence of the illicit acquisition of chemical military weapons from the international CW stockpile, the "homespun" development of chemical weapons by nonstatal terrorist groups, or the opportunistic release of industrial chemicals against the civilian population. Dissemination of these chemical agents to terrorist groups is a risk that international conventions are seeking to avoid. The supply of unique or unusual chemical precursors can perhaps be interdicted with some assurance, but a number of important precursors used in the synthesis of chemical weapons have multiple usages (Chapter 19 and Table 24.2) in conventional industries reducing the chances of effective oversight.

Hazards from Chemical Weapons

There are three main hazards from chemical weapons (CW); Inhalation, Absorption and Ingestion. The most important risk is inhalational absorption. A contact hazard from skin and eye exposure is important with certain chemicals and there is a less frequent risk from chemical ingestion. The methods of dissemination that might be employed with any chemical are selected in accordance with their physicochemical properties. Chlorine and phosgene gases were the first form of mass chemical attack, but subsequent CW agents have been liquids or solids at normal temperature and atmospheric pressure. Liquids are much easier to manufacture, store, and transport than gaseous agents.

It is important to have an understanding of the physical nature of the most likely chemical threats. It should be appreciated, for example, that mustard "gas" and the nerve "gases" are not gases, but are in fact liquids. Liquid CW agents are usually dispersed as aerosols (a cloud of suspended microscopic droplets) or as vapor (the gaseous form of a substance at a temperature lower than its boiling point at a given pressure). Other methods of dissemination are as a spray or liquid to be deposited under the effect of gravity upon people or surfaces. Mixed physical forms can be generated by explosive dispersal or by mechanical means. Pyrotechnic dissemination can only be undertaken for heat-resistant and noncombustible agents with low boiling points. The physical properties of the CW may indeed change during propagation if the agent evaporates or condenses. The vapors of CW are heavier than air and so will tend to concentrate under gravity into depressions, basements, etc. However, vapor and aerosol clouds have low settling velocities and the rate of deposition depends principally on chemical and physical forces that bind to specific surfaces, such as soil.

The persistence of a CW agent is inversely proportional to its volatility. The more volatile a chemical, the more quickly it evaporates from contaminated surfaces and the greater is the danger from its vapor. There is an arbitrary division created between nonpersistent chemicals that vaporize in less than 24 hours, e.g., phosgene, sarin, and hydrogen cyanide, and those with a liquid hazard persisting for longer than this threshold, e.g., mustard agent and VX. Environmental factors modify these considerations. The most important losses from a vapor or aerosol cloud result from low-level atmospheric turbulence. Militarily, it is advantageous to consider nonpersistent agents if it is planned for military forces to occupy the area and to use persistent agents for territory denial.

There are universal terms that provide comparative values of CW toxicity [5]. The ED_{50} and the ID_{50} denote the quantities of liquid agent exposure in μg, mg, or g quantities that will predictably cause effects (E) or incapacitation (I) in 50 percent of a group. The LD_{50} is the mean exposure that kills 50 percent of a group. Because of differences in absorption, the ED_{50} and LD_{50} are site specific with regard to inhalational or surface exposures, and ocular absorption through the conjunctival mucous membranes may sometimes be significantly greater than through the dry skin surface. The toxicities of riot control CW are expressed as TC_{50}, the concentration that will induce a noticeable effect in 50 percent of exposed persons, and as the IC_{50}, that gives the concentration that is intolerable to 50 percent of individuals. Such values are estimated healthy adult values.

Comparison of the amounts of CW exposure as aerosol, vapor, or gas is achieved by use of the concentration time product, or Ct. The agent concentration expressed as mg/m^3 is multiplied by the time of exposure in minutes [5]. For example a sarin Ct product of 100 mg minutes/m^3 could have resulted from a one-minute exposure at a concentration of 100 mg/m^3 or a four-minute exposure at 25 mg/m^3, and both will have the same effects. For most CW, an approximately linear relationship is observed (Haber's law), without accounting for differences in rates and depth of respiration, or for ill health. Several of the CWs are exceptions at low concentrations when there is some metabolic detoxification of the agents. Children and the elderly are populations at particular risk. Several factors are common to children that make them especially vulnerable [6,7]: higher respiration rates increase respiratory exposure; high vapor densities closer to the ground cause higher exposures; the larger surface-to-mass ratio and more permeable skin enhance systemic absorption; and the lesser degrees of keratinization in childhood skin make it more vulnerable to vesicant and corrosive agents. Other factors may further compound the risks to children as they may lack the cognitive and physical abilities to flee, are more easily frightened into immobility, may be difficult to isolate in personal protective devices, and, when injured, are more vulnerable to dehydration and shock from vomiting and diarrheal fluid losses.

The physicochemical characteristics of the major CW agents are given in Table 19.4.

Routes of Exposure

The lungs are usually the primary organ of exposure to CW agents. The massive pulmonary surface area that is specialized for gaseous exchange affords the main site of poisoning, and the lungs are frequently injured directly by the chemicals. Volatile and lipophilic agents readily cross respiratory epithelium and obtain equilibrium concentrations in the blood. Furthermore, aerosolized particles of 1–6 μm in diameter are retained within the lungs and continue to be absorbed even after the individual is removed from exposure. Fine particles of <0.6 μm in size will not be retained unless they are able to volatilize within the lung. Particles of size 5–10 μm are retained in the nose, sinuses, and throat from where they may be swallowed and add an ingestion component to the poisoning [6]. Protection from nonpersistent agents is primarily with the use of respirators combined with adequate skin protection.

Skin absorption of CW for most agents is several orders of magnitude less than for respired vapors, and its effects are usually delayed. Many CW agents are hydrophobic, lipophilic chemicals, and are readily absorbed on skin contact, especially in the moist axillary and inguinal areas, and after sweating. Skin absorption can be the primary route of poisoning when exposed to high vapor concentrations in the immediate vicinity of a release site if individuals are equipped only with respiratory protection. Protection from skin-active agents requires a combination of respirators, protective footwear, and dermal and ocular protective clothing. Poorly volatile persistent agents such as VX or vesicant agents are effective by persistent contamination of the environment and clothes.

Oral ingestion can occur from contaminated water and food, by swallowing contaminated respiratory mucus, or by hand–mouth contact [8]. Alimentary poisoning leads to delayed symptoms and increased systemic effects. Chemical attacks can also be perpetrated by the deliberate or incidental spiking of drinking water or foodstuffs. Particle size is unrelated to exposure levels in surface and gastrointestinal contamination.

If large quantities of agent are used, and even a spray of widely varying droplet size, lethal levels of vapor will rapidly accumulate, while the large droplets will settle onto victims or contaminate contact surfaces [9]. Furthermore, highly reactive compounds such as nerve agents and cyanides penetrate and permeate through clothing and latex rubber, necessitating the manufacture of protective equipment from specialized materials. The effectivity of agents is generally greatest within confined indoor spaces.

Environmental Considerations

A slight breeze of about 3–4 mile/hour at night, or close to dawn or dusk, is optimal for the outdoors release of CW agents. Particulate behavior within a cloud is discussed in Chapter 4. The chemical cloud passes along the axis of wind travel from a point or line release and is spread laterally by diffusion, wind shear and turbulence, and by terrain variations that may both disperse the CW or trap it in depressions. The cloud layer closest to the ground travels slowest because of friction. As the density of the CW causes a tendency to settle, the cloud travels in a fashion similar to ocean waves breaking upon the shoreline [10]. Thermal activity on warm sunny days will tend to disrupt a CW cloud during daylight hours. Dynamic processes of evaporation and condensation occur as the cloud travels. Agents that are subject to hydrolysis are susceptible to degradation in wet/humid environments. Rain will scour CW clouds and minimize their dissemination.

Cityscapes present a confusing terrain of urban canyons in which an agent might be remarkably persistent near the ground or mixed by turbulence over extensive vertical heights between tall buildings. Road and pavement surfaces may absorb CW and be vaporized subsequently on heating. Agent fatality predictions are generally based upon open-field use and are likely unreliable in urban settings. Building air conditioning systems and vertical cavities such as elevator shafts and stairwells introduce novel considerations.

Signs Suggestive of a Chemical Attack

At the scene of sudden medical casualties of uncertain cause, initial responders need to be especially alert to any signs suggestive of a CW attack. Many agents are odorless and the chemical/vapor cloud may be invisible. This decision making is critical if first responders are not to become secondary casualties of the event. In the Aum Shinrikyo attack on the Tokyo underground that utilized relatively small amounts of low-grade sarin, at least 10 percent of the emergency service personnel and medical staff became mild casualties themselves [9,11]. A more substantial attack would undoubtedly have led to responder fatalities. The most significant indication of a major chemical release is the simultaneous development of similar symptomatologies among a group of people at a single locale [12]. However, the fundamental first principal in the HAZMAT response is that first responders must delay entry into the area until the risks are assessed and adequate protection is obtained. Indeed, counterintuitively as it might seem, civilians must be prevented from rushing in to rescue the victims.

Other indications of a possible chemical release [12,13] are:

- Mass casualties in the absence of trauma—especially with respiratory, neurological, or gastrointestinal symptoms.
- Casualties distributed in a cluster pattern consistent with agent dissemination, or with an unusual age distribution.
- Lower attack rates in either indoors or outdoors.
- Unusual liquid droplets on vegetation; oily film on water.
- Discolored vegetation.
- Numerous dead animals, birds, and fish.
- Lack of insect life—it may be easiest to determine insect kill on the surface of water.
- Exposed individuals reporting unusual odors or tastes, but some are odorless and tasteless.
- Reported muffled small explosions or dispersing mists.
- Abandoned spray devices or dispersal ordinance containing liquids.
- Civilian panic.
- Location of suspected release inconsistent with a chemical's normal use.

Advice to Civilians Involved in a Chemical Release

Certain precautions can be taken in the event of a CW attack, or alternately in an industrial accident [10,13–16]. CW can act very quickly, often within a few seconds, although symptoms can be delayed at lower prevailing concentrations. Individuals will have very little time to respond to an attack unless they are alerted by events upwind. Outdoors, the impact near the source will be immediate with the lethal cloud perhaps reaching its maximal extent within the first hour. For an indoor release, the spread of the agent throughout the building will likely occur within minutes.

If involved in an outdoors exposure, an attempt should be made to evacuate calmly. Hyperventilation increases exposure. Escape into the nearest building and immediate decontamination by removing clothes and showering will usually be the best option to reduce exposure, and can reduce exposures by 75 percent or more. Contaminated clothes should be isolated in a sealed bag or container. Emergency personnel may be able to provide emergency field shelters with positive pressure ventilation and CW absorptive filters. If there are no buildings available, escape is advisable in an upwind direction from the release site after determination of the wind direction. If this is not possible, escape should be crosswind avoiding dips and hollows where chemical agents may accumulate. Escape in a vehicle should only be made if shelter is not available and according to available directions from emergency personnel, away from residual mists and anticipating that there may be many others with the same motivation. The vehicle windows should be rolled up, the vents closed, and the air conditioning/heater turned off. Buildings offer ten times the protection of a vehicle.

If inside, and involved in an indoors chemical release, the building should be evacuated according to chemical attack plans specific to the building while minimizing passage through the contaminated area. Otherwise, windows and doors should be opened to breathe fresh air. If open windows are not accessible, the building should be evacuated by stairs to the street or roof.

If inside and the buildings are in the path of an outdoors toxic cloud, people are usually best advised to stay indoors in interior rooms and on upper floors, if possible, as this afford protection from CW in liquid form, and partial protection from aerosols and gases. The air conditioning and heating units must be turned off. Windows and doors should be sealed with plastic tape or damp towels, tap water must be avoided, and sojourn established on higher floors to await instruction from rescuing authorities. Shelters must be evacuated immediately, if it is declared safe to do so, as the residual level of chemical may then be higher than outdoors.

The use of rubberized raincoats, boots, mittens, thick plastic sheets, etc. provides some protection against residual chemical cloud in the event of an evacuation. Baby cots and children can be covered in blankets. Eye-sealing goggles and scuba gear should be worn if available. Return to the building must occur only on the advice of emergency authorities as extensive decontamination may first be necessary.

Once clear of the contaminated area, all external apparel should be removed and left outside. Immediate showering and vigorous scrubbing with soap and water should be undertaken and symptomatic individuals need to be rushed to available medical attention. All exposed individuals must be triaged.

Protection of First Responders

Local fire service and HAZMAT crews, emergency medical services, and police are at risk of direct contamination at the incident site, quite possibly with high concentrations of the CW. The precise nature of the chemical poisoning and the precise risks will likely not be known. Respiratory and personal protection equipment (PPE) is obligatory and a worst case scenario will initially be assumed.

A positive pressure self-contained breathing apparatus (SCBA), preferably certified by NIOSH for CBRN, with a Level A protective suit is required to manage several of the major CW agents, and this apparatus, although available in specialist units, is not standard issue to most fire, EMS, and police departments. In illicit, serious chemical releases, monitoring results will be needed to permit lesser degrees of protection [10,16,17]. Large U.S. urban conurbations will ultimately be equipped with automated detection equipment for the major CW agents as soon as reliable equipment is available.

The use of PPE in chemical attacks will usually entail the provision of (1) a prefitted, pressure-demand, full-facepiece, SCBA, or a pressure-demand supplied air respirator with escape SCBA; (2) a fully encapsulating vapor-protective and chemical-resistant suit; (3) inner chemical-resistant gloves; and (4) chemical-resistant safety boots and shoes. Radio communication is necessary when wearing such protection. A detailed discussion of the use of PPE for the variety of CW protection scenarios is found in Chapter 26.

Traditional HAZMAT operations are based upon adjacent-site decontamination of relatively small numbers of casualties with procedures that are considerably time and labor consuming. With mass casualties, compromises have to be made. Efforts must be concentrated initially upon the most contaminated and the sickest individuals before triage is undertaken and these individuals are transported to hospital. It is important that all emergency and decontamination data accompany each patient to hospital. Decontamination, resuscitative and emergency care, and triage are the main initial objectives.

Extensive emergency decontamination facilities are also going to be required at each health care institution receiving patients. In the Tokyo subway sarin attack, 75 percent of the casualties made their own way to medical attention, bypassing the overburdened on-scene decontamination processes. Hospital first responders, including front-line hospital security, can easily be exposed to CW agent concentrations emanating from contaminated casualties and from field equipment. Rapid emergency decontamination before entering the hospital facility will be necessary for all but the most severely ill (who should be cordoned in special facilities and cared for by fully protected staff until resuscitation permits adequate decontamination).

Less rigorous protection is generally required for hospital first responders—such as Level C equipment [18,19] comprising less expensive barrier materials and a full-facepiece with air purifying cannister-equipped respirator. Body fluids such as blood, vomitus, urine, fecal material, and tracheal aspirate have to be treated as potentially dangerous according to universal precautions. Work in PPE equipment is arduous and prone to heat stress. Regular rest periods must therefore be incorporated for all PPE-equipped personnel. Training in equipment use is necessary, and fatalities can result from improper mask-use [20].

Organization of Rescue Operations after CW Attack

In most situations involving chemical attacks, the responsibility for initial crisis management will fall upon local emergency assets, particularly HAZMAT teams (see Chapter 27). State and federal authorities will rarely be involved unless there is prior warning and these assets mobilized prospectively. The National Fire Academy (NFA) has adopted an incident analysis process, GEDAPER, comprising seven steps:

- Gathering information
- Estimating course and harm
- Determining strategic goals
- Assessing tactical options and resources
- Planning and implementation of actions
- Evacuating
- Reviewing

Terrorist CW attacks provide first responders with very serious exposure risks to unfamiliar dangerous chemicals, unique emergency management problems, and an extraordinary mass casualty burden. The absence of official DOT or UN symbol identifiers or other documentary evidence in chemical terrorism is inconsistent with traditional HAZMAT experience, where this safeguard is usually present in chemical spills. Emergency planning is based upon known vulnerabilities and hazard identifications that permit reasonably accurate risk predictions, but which will obviously not be available in most terrorist attacks. The lack of familiarity with CW agents and of chemical releases in such normally low-risk locations as public gathering places present new conundrum that must be recognized if first responders are to avoid becoming casualties. Hazardous materials frequently require different levels of protection and necessitate different protective equipment, skills, and operational approaches. In the absence of good indications as to the nature of the threat, the appropriate decisions may at first be unclear.

Regardless of the incident, the first step is to collect all available information as quickly as possible before going any further. A formal institutionalized discipline is operant in the emergency responder community under the leadership of an Incident Commander working within an Incident Command System [16]. Protocols call for an initial thorough assessment and analysis of the incident site from a safe distance, with observation of the ambient conditions. The first priority is to keep all others away and to avoid approaching the victims until full protection is assured. Obtaining immediate assistance from the Regional Poison Center may assist the Incident Commander in his decision making. Secure cordons are established to delimit (1) the exclusion (hot) zone in which anyone leaving is assumed to be contaminated; (2) the contamination reduction (warm) zone in which decontamination is performed; (3) the support/clean (cold) zone; and (4) a perimeter cordon for crowd control. The formally designated layout of work zones ensures that dirty and clean zones are understood by everyone. A safe refuge for contaminated individuals is set up to reduce the chances of secondary recontamination and to set the stage for triage, decontamination, and medical treatment.

However, it is only by ascertaining the identity (and physical properties) of the substance that has been released that an effective outer perimeter can be established, neutralization plans formulated, decontamination procedures entertained, emergency medical treatment plans made, and environmental preservation precautions taken. Safe distances may be determined using the DOT Emergency Response Guidebook [21], by consulting a commercial reference source such as Chemtrec [22], or by using other reference sources.

In recent years, the unfamiliarity of local responders with the management of CW attacks in many major U.S. locales and in all smaller and rural entities has received urgent and extensive investment. In 1998, the Center for Domestic Preparedness opened a national training center for CBRN terrorism training for the nation's diverse community of emergency responders at Anniston, Alabama [23], where training occurs with "live" CW. Hands-on training programs for first responders are also available at the U.S. Army's Edgewood Chemical Biological Center at the Aberdeen Proving Ground, Maryland [24]. Other training programs in chemical preparedness for first responders are available through multiple sources, including DHS, FEMA, EPA, NFA, and DOJ.

Decontamination of Casualties

Precise recommendations for civilian mass casualty decontamination in the field and on hospital presentation have yet to be established [25]. High decontamination capacity is one of the factors that may reduce the consequences of a CW attack. Hospital decontamination must be performed away from the emergency room if contamination and closure of the facility is to be prevented. All clothing and personnel effects must be removed outdoors using extreme care not to transfer CW agent to the skin, and then stored in labeled, sealed biohazard bags. Ideally, this should occur within the containment zone. Severely contaminated individuals must be decontaminated as a matter of extreme urgency within a matter of minutes. Immediate self-decontamination may be feasible if facilities happen to be available. Copious eye irrigation with suitable available nontoxic fluids and scrubbing with soap and water by protected attendants will remove surface contamination from most CW agents. Solutions of baking soda and sodium thiosulfate may hydrolyze residual CW agents [26]. Bleach solutions should not be used. Oily persistent agents, e.g., VX, may require the use of alcohol, acetone, paraffin, or other solvents. Vesicant (blister agents) contamination of hair or beard is best managed by cutting or shaving of the hair. Military forces have access to commercial decontaminants, formulated for field use with specific CW types [10,26,27]. Pure metals and strong corrosives require dry powder decontamination and gentle brushing or vacuuming before water is applied [28]. The water authorities must be notified immediately about contaminated wastewater produced by the decontamination process.

Ill individuals require concomitant decontamination, medical resuscitation, and treatment. Decontamination of these individuals can be a difficult process, but must be achieved to reduce further poisoning, prevent injury to the medical staff, and avoid contamination of the facility. Dead individuals also require decontamination. Substances that have already reacted with the skin are generally inaccessible to decontamination regimens and may lead to further systemic poisoning. Asymptomatic individuals with perceived mild exposure might be treatable by sending the accompanied person home to take an immediate shower with scrubbing before reporting to a separate triage center away from the incident site [29,30]. Observation holding areas can also be used.

The decontamination of equipment and the environment is a complex problem, in the preserve of the specialist. It must be appreciated that nerve and vesicant agents penetrate and permeate many different types of material such as plastics, paint, and rubber, from which the agents can be released over relatively long periods of time. Resistant paints and materials are used militarily. Contaminated sites may need to be cordoned off for a long period as the area is environmentally decontaminated. Building decontamination from a CW is a problem fraught with problems of public acceptance.

Chemical Weapon Poisoning and Management

Nerve Agents

Thousands of tons of VX and the similar agent, VR, had been stockpiled as CW by numerous nations toward the end of the twentieth century, but are now being progressively destroyed. Several properties had suggested their utility as chemical weapons. The nerve agents are stable compounds, soluble in water, and easily dispersed. As liquid or vapor, these are highly toxic on respiratory, mucosal, cutaneous, and gastrointestinal exposures. Other than certain toxins, VX agent is the most toxic chemical known (see Table 20.1), and as little as 1 mg can be lethal to an adult. Symptoms from the inhalation of vapor or aerosol occur within seconds or minutes of exposure, and death is often rapid. Cutaneous absorption is typically delayed from several minutes to a few hours. The nerve agents bind to the enzyme cholinesterase which is a crucial enzyme present at nerve terminals. When cholinesterase is inhibited, acetylcholine (a nerve transmitter agent active within the synaptic cleft between nerve junctions) is not broken down and therefore it accumulates, generating an unmodulated overstimulation.

There are two kinds of acetylcholine receptors—(a) muscarinic receptors found in smooth involuntary muscle, in secretomotor fibers to secretory glands, and in the central nervous system; and (b) nicotinic receptors that are mainly distributed at the motor end plates of skeletal voluntary muscle. The symptom complex of nerve agent toxicity [31] is somewhat variable depending on the

Table 20.1 Estimated Chemical Weapon Toxic Exposure Limits

Agent	*Effect*	*Ct_{50} (mg minutes/m^3)*	*Liquid on Skin*
Nerve agents			
Tabun (GA)	Miosis	~2–3	
	Death	200–400	50–60 mg/kg
Sarin (GB)	Miosis	~3	
	Death	100–200	20–25 mg/kg
Soman (GD)	Miosis	~2–3	
	Death	50–70	4–5 mg/kg
VX	Death	10–50	<0.1 mg/kg
Vesicant agents			
Distilled HD	Eye	12–200	
Mustard	Pulmonary	100–200	
	Erythema	200–1,000	10 µg
	Death	1,500 inhalation	100 µg/kg
		10,000 skin	
Lewisite (L)	Erythema	>1,500	10–15 µg
	Death	~1,500 inhalation	40–50 mg/kg
Phosgene oxime (CX)	Eye	(?) 200	
	Erythema	(?) 2,500	
	Death	(?) 3,200	
Choking agents			
Phosgene (CG)	Pulmonary	>1,600	
	Death	3,200	
Blood agents			
Hydrogen cyanide (AC)	Death	2,500–5,000	
Cyanogen chloride (CK)	Death	11,000	

Source: Adapted from Chemical Casualty Care Division, U.S. Army Medical Research Institute of Chemical Defense, *Medical Management of Chemical Casualties Handbook*, 3rd ed., USAMRICD, Aberdeen Proving Ground, MD, 1999.

Note: ? means values are yet to be verified from multiple studies.

route and rate of systemic poisoning and also varying between specific nerve agents. Knowledge of severe nerve agent poisoning in human is limited, but there is considerable data on poisonings from the closely related organophosphate pesticides. Incomplete syndromes are common. Symptoms of initial poisoning include: (1) increased salivation and nasal discharge; (2) miotic pinpoint pupils (that also impair night vision); (3) blurred near vision associated with ocular pain; (4) bronchospasm and respiratory distress; (5) nausea and dizziness; (6) headache; and (7) marked tiredness, hallucinations, and slurred speech. Greater exposures become more and more incapacitating. The symptoms of advanced nerve agent poisoning [29] include:

- Intractable salivation, lacrimation, micturition, and defecation.
- Excessive sweating.
- Severe muscular weakness and tremors.
- Coughing, difficulty in breathing, cyanosis, and apnea.
- Abdominal pain, nausea, and vomiting.
- Anxiety, confusion, convulsions, and coma.

Severe poisoning by nerve agents may cause pronounced muscular symptoms. Death is due to acute respiratory failure related to central effects on the brain and to paralysis of the respiratory muscles. Oxygen supplementation should be given at an early stage. Toxicity data for the nerve agents is shown in Table 20.1 and contrasted with other CW agents.

Atropine is the principal antidote for organophosphate poisoning. It acts by binding reversibly to muscarinic acetylcholine receptors. The action of acetylcholine at these receptors is blocked militating against the increased acetylcholine receptor barrage. Atropine is given to adults at a dosage of 4–6 mg I/M or I/V statim, repeated in 2 mg I/M or I/V increments as needed over several days—titrated against the decrease in bronchial secretion, bronchial constriction, and in improvements in blood gas analysis results. Diazepam 10 mg slow I/V is given in severe poisoning for its anticonvulsant action.

Oximes, of which there are several, e.g., 2-PAM (pralidoxime) and HI-6, possess a –CH=NOH group and can (a) reactivate bound cholinesterase, and (b) bind to unbound nerve agent (A)

$$\mathrm{RCH=NOH+EA \rightarrow RCH=NOA+EH}$$

$$\mathrm{RCH=NOH=AX \rightarrow RCH=NOA+HX}$$

The combination of atropine and oxime therapy is markedly synergistic. However, acetylcholinesterase bound to nerve agent can fairly rapidly become covalently bound in an irreversible process known as "aging"—this mainly occurs with soman poisoning. The dosage of pralidoxime is 1–2 g I/V over 5–20 minutes; the dose may be repeated every four to six hours until nicotinic signs resolve. Neither atropine nor pralidoxime is very effective against Central Nervous System (CNS) signs. Obidoxime is the most effective oxime against tabun poisoning. The military prepares these antidote agents as autoinjectors suitable for personal emergency use. In severe cases of nerve agent poisoning, however, antidotal treatment will be insufficient by itself for survival.

Ventilatory support will be needed for patients with impending respiratory failure and is likely to be required for several days until cholinesterase levels are functionally restored. A patient under optimal intensive care from the onset of symptoms may recover from doses as high as 100 times the LD_{50}. The availability of mechanical ventilators is likely to be at a premium after a major nerve agent attack even with the equipment supplementation available through the National Stockpile.

Carbamates can be used as a prophylactic pretreatment. Carbamylated acetylcholinesterase cannot combine with the nerve agent, and hydrolysis slowly restores the native enzyme. Prophylactic oral pyridostigmine can be maintained on a 30 mg eight-hourly schedule for several days aimed at protecting about a third of the blood cholinesterase, although it crosses the blood–brain barrier poorly and offers little protection from the CNS effects; it is stopped immediately should poisoning occur. Partial brain cholinesterase protection can be established prophylactically however using a combination of two centrally acting drugs, the carbamate, physostigmine, and the anticholinergic, scopolamine. This is mainly a military usage.

Vesicating (Blistering) Agents

The blistering and tissue-injuring agents are highly reactive, persistent compounds that combine with numerous biological molecules, notably acting as alkylating agents. These agents can cause severe damage to the lungs, eyes, skin, and other tissues. The two main groups of vesicants are the mustards and the dichlorarsine derivatives. The mustards contain at least two 2-chloroethyl groups, attached either to thioether residues (sulfur mustards) or to amine residues (nitrogen mustards). Although mustard agent is readily soluble in organic solvents, it is only minimally soluble in water, in which it slowly hydrolyzes. Sulfur mustard is another CW that readily crosses the skin and mucous membranes; it interacts with the skin and causes significant tissue damage over a wide range of exposures.

Decontamination that occurs more than a minute or two following adequate exposure will reduce but cannot prevent skin damage. If available, neutralizing chemicals such as chloramine solutions or neutral absorbing powders, such as Fuller's earth, are useful (but not in the eyes) in removing residual agent prior to water decontamination. The contamination of hair or beard is best managed by immediate shaving. There is a 2–24-hour latent period after vesicating agent exposure before clinical effects are first observed. When the contaminating incident is not noticed, timely decontamination is therefore infeasible.

Progressive ocular irritation with tearing, photophobia, and blepharospasm are noticed first, followed by a dusky skin erythema, productive cough, and hoarseness. Extensive skin blistering, hyperpigmentation, and scarring may follow and delayed healing occurring over many weeks. Skin injuries are more severe in humid and in hot climatic conditions. Vesicating agents are a potent cause of chronic disability; the pulmonary and ocular complications are particularly serious. Severely poisoned individuals may develop a chemical pneumonia that can lead to chronic, fibrotic, bronchiectatic lung disease [30]. Pulmonary involvement is indicated by a persistent, hacking nonproductive cough, shortness of breath, and horseness. Scarred, vascularized corneas and severe dry eyes can be long-term sequelae resulting in bilateral blindness. An ill-understood syndrome of chronic ocular surface inflammation many years after the attack may also occur.

Fluid losses from skin burns are relatively small unlike those experienced in thermal injuries, and fluid overload should be avoided. On the contrary, alimentary absorption causes severe, acute gastrointestinal damage with nausea and vomiting and massive fluid losses. A prolonged leucopenia and pancytopenia is relatively common after severe poisoning and can be a factor in the development of life-threatening infective complications. The bone marrow dyscrasia may require therapy with granulocyte, platelet, and blood transfusions. Two to three percent of military victims die from severe pulmonary disease, death generally occurring a week or two after the attack. The most important affect of these agents is their considerable chronic morbidity requiring long and demanding medical care.

There is no therapy for mustard poisoning other than decontamination, supportive measures, wound care regimens similar to third-degree thermal burn care, and pulmonary management with antibiotics, bronchodilators, intubation, and assisted ventilation. Ocular lubricating ointments and limited topical corticosteroid therapy are used to help ameliorate the ocular surface injuries, sometimes assisted with tectonic surgery and late corneal grafting. Plastic surgery may be required for the late cicatricial skin changes.

Lewisite and phosgene oxime cause lesions similar to the ones caused by mustard agents. However on contact with vapor both cause immediate ocular and skin pain and respiratory symptoms so that detection of exposure and immediate decontamination are much more likely. They produce a similar clinical picture to mustard agents. Eye lesions may be particularly serious. British Anti-Lewisite (BAL: dimercaprol) is an antidote of moderate effectivity in early poisoning by these agents. BAL treatment consists of 3 mg/kg dosage I/M 4-hourly for two days, then 2 mg/kg 12-hourly for the next ten days, varied with body size and disease severity. BAL can also be applied to the eyes and skin if topical preparations are available. Neither agent damages bone marrow nor lymphoid tissue.

Blood Agents (Cyanides)

Hydrogen cyanide and cyanogen chloride are volatile liquids that cause death by interfering with metal-containing enzymes involved in tissue respiration and energy generation, notably the cytochrome oxidases. The most likely route of poisoning is by inhalation. Liquids and aerosols also penetrate skin readily and induce irritation and are absorbed from the gut. The onset of poisoning is rapid.

Nonspecific findings, such as headache, weakness, restlessness, and a feeling of throat constriction characterize sublethal exposures. A high venous PO_2 relative to arterial PO_2 should raise clinical suspicion of the diagnosis, as tissues are unable to utilize oxygen. As severe poisoning develops, there is a brief period of rasping hyperventilation, rapidly followed by convulsions, respiratory failure, apnea, cardiac arrythmias, and death. Cyanosis is notably absent. Prompt diagnosis of symptomatic individuals and therapeutic intervention are critical. Victims who remain asymptomatic several minutes after removal from known cyanide vapor require no oxygen or antidotes. Decontamination of clothing and equipment is unnecessary because of the high volatility of these agents, whose vapor is lighter than air.

Supplemental oxygen at high concentration is given. Hyperbaric oxygen therapy can be useful, if available. The detoxification of cyanide [32,33] can be enhanced by intravenous 25 percent sodium thiosulfate which converts cyanide to thiocyanate. A temporary sequestration of cyanide can also be achieved by using the high binding affinity of ferric ions in methemoglobin for cyanide—intravenous 3 percent sodium nitrate or dimethylaminophenol (DMAP) are used to temporarily produce methemoglobinemia. Intravenous hydroxycobalamin (vitamin B12) can also bind cyanide that is then excreted in the urine.

The effects of cyanogen chloride are similar and its systemic toxicity is due to its conversion to hydrogen cyanide in the body. Cyanogen chloride is particularly irritating to the ocular surface. As these agents are highly volatile, lethal concentrations are difficult to achieve unless released into a confined space.

Choking Agents (Lung Irritants)

Chlorine, phosgene, chloropicrin, and perfluoroisobutylene (a pyrolysis product of Teflon 7) are volatile liquids that cause damage at different levels within the lung. Chlorine principally damages the upper respiratory tract, trachea, and larger bronchi, chloropicrin tends to affect the medium and small bronchi, and phosgene acts directly on the alveolar-capillary membrane barriers in the lung. Exposure to all these agents can lead to acute pulmonary edema. Exertion will worsen the toxic effects. Secondary infective bronchopneumonia is common.

Shortness of breath and a persistent productive cough begin within 4–24 hours of exposure. The ocular and skin surfaces are irritated at concentrations as low as 3 parts per million. After the initial symptomatic period, there may be a variable period in which the symptoms improve or disappear, before the development of pulmonary edema, hypoxia, and hypercarbia. Chest x-rays may show diffuse infiltration of the lung fields. Death can occur as the result of pulmonary failure or from laryngeal spasm. Long exposure to low levels mainly causes pulmonary edema. The effects of exposure can be delayed, and asymptomatic individuals need to be carefully observed for the development of pulmonary edema over 48 hours after exposure.

Decontamination is an urgent necessity. There is no antidote and management is purely supportive with oxygen, bronchodilators, and oral corticosteroid. On occasion, intubation and pulmonary ventilation are required. In most victims, the clinical signs of pulmonary edema, abnormal blood gases, and measures of reduced lung permeability settle within a week. However, chronic lung damage can be a consequence of severe poisoning. Shortness of breath, asthma, and reduced physical activity may persist in some severely poisoned individuals for the remainder of their lives.

Phosgene release is common in building fires as a product of the pyrolysis of chlorinated plastics used in construction materials and furnishings [6]. Chloropicrin is a powerful irritant to the skin and eyes and can result in permanent scarring, especially on contact. Persistent nausea, vomiting, colic, and diarrhea may occur with heavy poisoning.

Psychotomimetic Agents

Chemicals that induce incapacitating psychotic mental changes which are relatively transitory in disabling decision making might have value to a terrorist organization. BZ produces a condition similar to atropine poisoning with dry mouth, bounding palpitations, large mydriatic pupils, impaired near vision, confusion, hallucinations, and coma. Phencyclidine causes disturbed body awareness and vivid dreams. d-Lysergic Acid Diethylamide (LSD) is markedly hallucinogenic. Aerosol inhalation is the most likely route of exposure.

Toxin Agents

By convention, toxins are considered biologically produced substances and their control is incorporated in the Biological and Toxin Weapons Convention (BWTC), even when they are derived synthetically. A few toxins are among the most poisonous substances known and are indeed hazardous chemicals. The most important differences are their poor volatility and lack of skin penetration [34]. Toxins are generally more difficult to produce in large quantities than CW, and many are unstable in aerosols.

Botulinum toxin is the most poisonous substance known and can be weaponized as an aerosol. It is 1500 times more toxic even than VX agent and causes death through paralysis of the respiratory muscles; mechanical ventilation may be required for many weeks or months. Emergency botulinum antiserum and therapy with the diaminopyridines may be helpful.

Other toxins of interest include saxitoxin (paralysis), ricin (cardiac failure), staphylococcal enterotoxin (gastrointestinal and systemic effects), and certain snake venom toxins. There are presently few specific therapeutic interventions for toxin effects. The many classes of toxins and differing mechanisms of action would make identification and management of toxin exposures problematic. The trichothecene mycotoxins and microcystin are unusual in being dermally active. Rifampin protects against microcystin-induced liver damage in animals.

The poor volatility of most toxins means that they do not pose significant environmental threat and neither persist on skin or clothing, making PPE for responders and elaborate decontamination procedures less important. Toxins are also more readily removed from the air by air-conditioning systems. Furthermore, many toxins are immunogenic and potentially neutralizable by appropriate vaccines; this is more applicable to prophylactic military protection. Toxin detection generally requires very sensitive assays as the most potent agents would need to be present in only very small amounts.

There are valuable treatises [5,8,35,36] on the features and management of chemical weapon poisoning that should be consulted whenever a thorough treatment of the subject is desired. A summary of the clinical effects of the major CW agents and appropriate interventions is given in Table 20.2.

Long-Term Consequences of CW Exposure

Long-term sequelae may be caused by several CW agents. Cerebral anoxia and permanent brain damage can result from nerve agents, cyanides, and botulinum toxin. Nerve agent poisoning can also be followed by prolonged muscular weakness and mental disturbances. Chronic pulmonary fibrosis, bronchiectasis, emphysema, or asthma can be produced by vapor and aerosol attack with vesicating and choking agents. Vesicant lung damage may be followed by an increased risk of lung cancer. The destruction of the ocular surface by vesicants can lead to permanent blindness from corneal scarring, dry eyes, and chronic irritation. Plastic surgery may be necessary to ameliorate the cicatricial complications of skin damage. The psychiatric and emotional consequences of chemical attack may be severe. The long-term consequences of poisoning with these highly toxic agents are often poorly appreciated [37]; many individuals are left with chronic ill-health with reduced exercise tolerance, recurrent infections, hepatic, renal, neurologic, psychiatric, and hematotoxic conditions, and an ill-understood premature aging.

Syndromic Medical Management

In view of the potential multiplicity of agents that could be involved in a terrorist attack or accidental chemical release, the specific agent may not be known during the initial phases of patient management. The forensic identification of agents will not be available to aid medical decision making. The emergency management of chemical injuries may depend upon syndromic identification, the general application of supportive therapies, and use of specific therapeutics as a matter of judgment. Table 20.3 illustrates this approach.

Medical Forensic Samples

The first 30 samples from the most contaminated or exposed individuals should rapidly be forwarded to the Emergency Operations Center (EOC) of the Centers for Disease Control and Prevention in Atlanta. Samples should have unique bar-coded labels without personal identifiers.

Table 20.2 Summary of the Clinical Effects of Chemical Weapon Agents and Appropriate Interventions

Agent Type	*Agent Names*	*Unique Characteristics*	*Initial Effects*	*Decontamination*	*Medical Interventions*	*Other Patient Considerations*
Nerve	• Cyclohexyl sarin (GF) • Sarin (GB) • Soman (GD) • Tabun (GA) • VX	• Miosis (pinpoint pupils) • Copious secretions • Muscle twitching/ fasciculations	• Miosis (pinpoint pupils) • Blurred/dim vision • Headache • Nausea, vomiting, diarrhea • Copious secretions/ sweating • Muscle twitching/ fasciculations • Breathing difficulty • Seizures *Note:* the mnemonic "**SLUDGE**": **S**alivation, sweating, **L**acrimation, **U**rination, **D**efecation, drooling, diarrhea, **G**astric upset, and cramps, **E**mesis	• Remove clothing immediately • Gently wash skin with soap and water • Do not abrade skin • For eyes, flush with plenty of water or normal saline • Bleach solutions should NOT be used on people; diluted bleach (one part household bleach to nine parts water) can be used on eyeglasses, equipment, and other hard surfaces	• Atropine • Pralidoxime (2-PAM) chloride • Benzodiazepines should be used for seizures or agitation	• Onset of symptoms from dermal contact with liquid forms may be delayed • Repeated antidote administration may be necessary • In a true nerve agent exposure, pralidoxime therapy should be continued for at least 24 hours
Asphyxiant/ blood	• Arsine • Cyanogen chloride • Hydrogen cyanide	• Possible cherry red skin • Hydrogen cyanide has a bitter almond odor	• Confusion • Nausea • Patients may gasp for air, similar to asphyxiation but	• Remove clothing immediately • Gently wash skin with soap and water	• Rapid treatment with oxygen • For cyanide, use oxygen, sodium bicarbonate, and specific	• Arsine and cyanogen chloride may cause delayed pulmonary edema

			more abrupt onset • Seizures prior to death	• Do not abrade skin • For eyes, flush with plenty of water or normal saline	antidotes (such as nitrites or sodium thiosulfate)	• Arsine causes massive hemolysis
Choking/ pulmonary damaging	• Chlorine • Hydrogen chloride • Nitrogen oxides • Phosgene	• Chlorine is a greenish yellow gas with pungent odor • Phosgene gas smells like newly mown hay or grass	• Eye and skin irritation • Airway irritation • Dyspnea, cough • Sore throat • Chest tightness	• Remove clothing immediately • Gently wash skin with soap and water • Do not abrade skin • For eyes, flush with plenty of water or normal saline	• Fresh air, forced rest • If signs of respiratory distress are present, oxygen with or without positive airway pressure may be needed • Other supportive therapy, as needed	• May cause delayed pulmonary edema, from 12–24 hours, even following a symptom-free period that varies in duration with the amount inhaled
Blistering/ vesicant	• Mustard/ Sulfur mustard (HD, H) • Mustard gas (H) • Nitrogen mustard (HN1,HN2, HN3) • Lewisite (L) • Phosgene oxime (CX)	• Mustard (HD) has an odor like burning garlic or horseradish • Lewisite (L) has an odor like geranium • Phosgene oxime (CX) has a pepperish or pungent odor	• Severe irritation • Redness and blisters of the skin • Tearing, conjunctivitis, corneal damage • Mild respiratory distress to marked airway damage • May cause death	• Immediate decontamination is essential to minimize damage • Remove clothing immediately • Gently wash skin with soap and water • Do not abrade skin • For eyes, flush with plenty of water or normal saline	• Immediately decontaminate skin • Flush eyes with water or normal saline for 10–15 minutes • Give oxygen if there is difficulty breathing • Supportive care	• Possible pulmonary edema • Sulfur mustard has an asymptomatic latent period • There is no antidote or treatment for mustard • Lewisite has immediate burning pain, blisters later

(*continued*)

Table 20.2 (continued) Summary of the Clinical Effects of Chemical Weapon Agents and Appropriate Interventions

Agent Type	*Agent Names*	*Unique Characteristics*	*Initial Effects*	*Decontamination*	*Medical Interventions*	*Other Patient Considerations*
				• Bleach solutions should NOT be used on people; diluted bleach (one part household bleach to nine parts water) can be used on eyeglasses, equipment, and other hard surfaces		• Specific antidote British Anti-Lewisite (BAL) may decrease systemic effects of Lewisite, but its availability is very limited • Phosgene oxime causes immediate pain
Incapacitating/ behavior altering	• Agent 15/BZ	• May appear as mass drug intoxication with erratic behaviors, shared realistic and distinct hallucinations, disrobing and confusion; onset may be delayed (30 to 60 minutes) depending on the agent • Hyperthermia • Mydriasis (dilated pupils)	• Dry mouth and skin • Initial tachycardia • Altered consciousness, delusions, denial of illness, belligerence • Hyperthermia • Ataxia (lack of coordination) • Hallucinations • Mydriasis (dilated pupils)	• Remove clothing immediately • Gently wash skin with water or soap and water • Do not abrade skin	• Remove heavy clothing • Evaluate mental status • Use restraints as needed • Monitor core temperature carefully • Supportive care • Sedation with benzodiazepines may be required	• Hyperthermia and self-injury are largest risks • Hard to detect because it is an odorless and nonirritating substance • Possible serious arrhythmias • Specific antidote (physostigmine) may be considered

Source: Michigan Department of Community Health Revised Recommendations for Medical Providers regarding Chemical Terrorism, November 2004, http://www.michigan.gov/documents/Chemical_mmg_nov_2004_110280_7.pdf.

Table 20.3 Emergency Medical Conditions and Therapeutic Needs Associated with Chemical Exposures

Syndrome and Causative Agents	*Medical Therapeutic Needs*
Burns and trauma	
Corrosives, vesicants, explosives, oxidants, incendiaries, radiologicals	Intravenous fluids and supplies
	Analgesics
	Pulmonary care
	Bandages, splints, and skin care
Respiratory failure	
Corrosives, CW, explosives, oxidants, incendiaries, asphyxiants, irritants, pharmaceuticals, metals	Pulmonary care
	Ventilators and supplies
	Antidotes—if available
	Tranquillizers
Cardiovascular shock	
CW, pesticides, asphyxiants, pharmaceuticals	Intravenous fluids and supplies
	Cardiovascular care
	Antidotes—if available
Neurological toxicity	
CW, pesticides, radiologicals, pharmaceuticals	Antidotes—if available

Source: Centers for Disease Control and Prevention, The Public Health Response to Biological and Chemical Terrorism, Interim Planning Guidance for State Public Health Officials, 2001, www.bt.cdc.gov/Documents/Planning/PlanningGuidance.PDF, Accessed February 11, 2008.

New guidelines were promulgated in November 2006. The following specimens are requested: (1) 25–50 mL + urine samples in screw capped plastic containers identified with the method of collection, stored at −70°C, and transported on dry ice; (2) minimum of 12 mL blood in three 4 mL containers with EDTA (U.S. color-code purple top), inverted—five to six times, and stored at 1°C–10°C; (3) sample in one 5 or 7 mL Na oxalate/NaF anticoagulated tube (U.S. color-code gray top) or one 5 or 7 mL heparinized tube (U.S. color-code green top), inverted—five to six times, and stored at 1°C–10°C; and (4) an empty tube to check as a blank. Chain of evidence documentation must be maintained. Urine specimens should be shipped in a STP741 pack, sealed with evidence tape in the outer Tyvek envelope (STP741) and packed with dry ice in the packaging provided. The blood specimens are to be packed separately in a similar manner, wrapped with foam packaging and laid on a coolant pack [38]. It is recommended that the state laboratories leave investigation of chemical CW releases to federal laboratories. CW specimens are considered

"Biological Substances, Category B" for shipping purposes and shipped overnight. Environmental sampling is the responsibility of the EPA, the Federal Bureau of Investigation (FBI), and private laboratories.

Funds have only been available to members of the Laboratory Response Network (LRN) since 2003 with the purpose of enhancing capabilities and capacities for the detection of chemical agents. Sixty-two state, territorial, and metropolitan public health laboratories are members of the chemical component of the LRN. Developments of the national network continue. Currently, fifteen are level 3 laboratories with competencies in specimen collection and handling; 37 are level 2 laboratories trained to detect exposure to a number of toxic agents in blood and urine including nerve agents and cyanide; and 10 are level 1 laboratories which serve as surge capacity laboratories for CDC with the capability to detect an expanded number of agents [39]. However, a lack of standards and protocols to safely test CW agents and an insufficient capacity across the LRN remain yet-to-be-resolved problems.

Logistics of the Health Services Response to a Civilian Chemical Attack

In the event of most conceivable CW attacks on the homeland, the local and regional capabilities will be decisive in determining the outcome. It is perhaps unlikely that a chemical attack could be mounted in the United States by a nonstatal terrorist group that would lead to more than a few hundred casualties, and might be anticipated to be a much lesser event. Indoor CW attacks in particular need to be incorporated into planning.

An incremental modular system has to be created that provides surge capacities of several magnitudes for the management of contaminated casualties. Considerable planning is being undertaken in the name of homeland defense to provide a system for biological, nuclear, radiological, and chemical terrorist attack on U.S. civilians with "weapons of mass destruction." However, as Aum Shinrikyo discovered in Japan, considerable expertise is necessary for chemical terrorism to create a threat of this magnitude. Local Hazardous Materials (HAZMAT) search and rescue capabilities are well developed in many parts of the United States, and there is therefore cumulative experience in the management of accidental chemical releases. Unlike other types of asymmetric terrorism, appreciable chemical response infrastructure and professional knowledge is already in existence. First-responder (nonmedical) preparedness becomes essentially a matter of degree and complexity. One lesson to be imbued in local law enforcement is that the requirements for crime scene investigation must take second place to the rescue and resuscitation of persons exposed to these highly toxic chemicals. Normal criminal procedures and perhaps some civil rights may require modification in high-level chemical incidents.

Surge capacities are enhanced by collaborative protocols between local and regional health care organizations and by utilizing support from the state public health system. Federal agencies can provide emergency logistic support through the National Response Plan (Chapter 27), under the crisis management of the FBI and the consequence management of FEMA. Much of the federal effort in bolstering terrorism defense has been in the development of state and local infrastructure (see Chapter 28) [38,41,42]. With the first appreciation of a potential chemical event involving numerous casualties, local and regional emergency planning agreements will put all emergency hospitals on alert that are within access by road or medivac helicopter. Regional consortial relationships between health centers will be activated to source needed materiel. Patients will be received at local hospitals from the on-site triage center, after preliminary resuscitation and attempted medical stabilization, and often after extensive decontamination. Disaster plans and their chemical emergency annexes will be activated at each health care facility.

The Crisis Management Team (CMT) at each hospital will be activated to function as the institutional command and control center. This is nowadays likely to be accommodated in a formal well-equipped communications facility ideally located away from major operational aspects of the response site. The average size of a CMT is between five and ten individuals with each member responsible for a particular aspect of the operation, such as command, logistics, operations, legal, information, public relations, safety and security, and finance [43]. Only departmental heads will report to the CMT. The hospital responses will be coordinated with the On-site Incident Command Center.

Bed and intensive care availabilities are collated as the magnitude of the emergency is assessed. The immediate establishment of tight hospital security is a critical element if hospital and staff contamination is to be prevented. Early decisions to transfer in-patients to other facilities may be necessary. The hospital chief pharmacist must be informed of developments to optimize his or her ability to mobilize supplies of the requisite pharmaceuticals and supplies. With some CW agents, there may be considerable surge-demand for emergency respiratory ventilation and intensive care facilities. Consideration may be given to seeking additional ventilatory equipment and supplies through the National Pharmaceutical Stockpile (NPS) that will be delivered within 12 hours from their approval.

The hospital decontamination facilities will need to be greatly enhanced and the engineering and maintenance staff may be required to erect temporary structures and facilities. Triage and patient observation areas may also need to be provided. Contaminated, intermediate, and clean areas must be established with obvious boundary markers, and the sanctity of each area enforced by security officers in PPE. Efficient medical record keeping is required, modified by the demands of the situation. A cadre of officials should be delegated to maintain chain of security and documentation of anything that could be considered evidentiary, including the possessions of victims and of medical specimens. Additional mortuary facilities may be required, as well as provision for the decontamination of the deceased. From the outset, information provided to the public and press must be timely, professional, comprehensive, and honest.

The regional Metropolitan Medical Response System (MMRS) and the National Disaster Medical System (NDMS) will be activated by the FEMA National Emergency Coordinating Center (NECC) and by the Department of Health and Human Services Emergency Operations Center (DHHS EOC) so as to mobilize regional assets into the emergency response. A Disaster Medical Assistance Team (DMAT) may be available from the MMRS for immediate engagement at the incident site. A specialist Chemical DMAT may also be available. The Veterans Administration may be able to deploy an Emergency Medical Response Team (EMRT). The proximity of these assets to the incident site will determine whether they might play a role in the emergency phase of the response or contribute to the mitigation phase. Local National Guard units could be activated by the state governor under title 32 to help with the many logistic tasks that occur during a substantial chemical emergency. As the first responders, the local and state emergency response leadership will set up an emergency operating center to coordinate the HAZMAT search and rescue phase. The FBI will be involved as soon as possible and will ultimately assume the leadership role of the crisis management.

The resources and assets mobilized will depend upon the magnitude and nature of the chemical release, in consultation with the state and FEMA authorities. Small events can be managed in a manner similar to a conventional HAZMAT event, with the addition of considerable FBI and law enforcement activity. Mass casualties will necessitate a full mobilization of the Federal

Response Plan following a declaration of emergency by the U.S. President under Emergency Support Function (ESF) #8, in which the DHHS is the lead agency. These procedures are discussed in detail in Chapter 28.

There are a number of federal specialist chemical response teams that also might play a role in a CW civilian attack [44]. It is only in the case of predeployment at an event such as the Olympic Games or national election that federal assets might influence the outcome of rescue operations. Military chemical response establishments are operated by the Marine Corps, Army (Technical Escort Unit: TEU), Air Force (BEEF Unit), Army Reserve Chemical Companies, National Guard Chemical Units, and Coast Guard Units. Military assets are obtained by state request under the National Response Plan to the Department of Defense Joint Task Force-Civil Support Unit (JTF-CS). The EPA possesses emergency contamination cleanup teams that may be useful to mitigate a contaminated environment.

A major CW attack will generate considerable logistical and personnel problems if operations are to continue at high intensity throughout the medical emergency. But there will be other requirements, such as to maintain essential services and to ameliorate the many consequences of chemical warfare within a community. The greatest need will often be for trained personnel with the skills and the flexibility to take on almost anything. The contaminated area will have to be cordoned off and guarded until the environmental decontamination is completed. There may be considerable need for temporary housing and support structures should a residential area be involved.

The general public must be involved before, during, and following any CW attack. There are considerable misconceptions about the nature of chemicals and about the alleged vulnerability to foreign terrorist attack in the local high street. The resolution of the American people will be a crucial strength, should the civilian population ever be targeted, if people are educated, as a policy matter, about how the public should respond to accidental releases of hazardous materials from, say, a neighborhood chemical plant, and are then taken as full partners into the confidence of local and national leadership should CW terrorism threats arise.

References

1. Convention on the Prohibition of the Development, Production, Stockpiling and Use of Chemical Weapons and on their Destruction, Paris January 13, 1993. ICRC International Humanitarian Law—Treatises & Documents. Internet: http://www.icrc.org/ihl.nsf/FULL/553?OpenDocument (accessed February 10, 2008).
2. National Disaster Education Coalition. Chemical Emergencies. Internet: http://www.disastercenter.com/guide/chemical.html (accessed February 10, 2008).
3. S Binder. Deaths, injuries and evacuations from acute hazardous material releases. *Am J Public Health* 79:1042–1044, 1989.
4. U.S. Department of Health and Human Services. *Managing Hazardous Materials Incidents (MHMI)*, Vols. 1–3. Atlanta, GA: Agency for Toxic Substances and Disease Registry, 2001. Internet: http://www.atsdr.cdc.gov/MHMI/ (accessed December 10, 2008).
5. Chemical Casualty Care Division, U.S. Army Medical Research Institute of Chemical Defense. *Medical Management of Chemical Casualties Handbook*, 3rd ed. Aberdeen Proving Ground, MD: USAMRICD, 2000.
6. Committee on Environmental Health and Committee on Infectious Diseases, American Academy of Pediatrics. Chemical and biological terrorism and its impact on children. *Pediatrics* 105:662–670, 2000. Internet: http://aappolicy.aappublications.org/cgi/reprint/pediatrics;118/3/1267 (accessed February 10, 2008).

7. GL Foltin, DJ Schonfeld, and MW Shannon, eds. Chemical terrorism. In: colon *Pediatric Terrorism and Disaster Preparedness: A Resource for Physicians*. American Academy of Pediatrics. AHRQ Publication No. 06(07)-0056. Rockville, MD: Agency for Healthcare Research and Quality, 2006, pp. 107–141. Internet: www.ahrq.gov/research/pedprep/pedresource.pdf (accessed February 9, 2008).
8. WHO Group of Consultants. *Health Aspects of Biological and Chemical Weapons: WHO Guidance*, 2nd ed 2. Geneva, Switzerland: World Health Organization, 2002. Internet: http://www.who.int/emc/book_2nd_ edition.htm (accessed April 6, 2002).
9. RA Falkenrath, RD Newman, and BA Thayer. America's Achilles heel. *Nuclear, Biological, and Chemical Terrorism and Covert Attack*. Cambridge, MA: MIT Press, 1998.
10. ER Taylor. *Lethal Mists: An Introduction to the Natural and Military Sciences of Chemical, Biological Warfare and Terrorism*. Commack, NY: Nova Science, 1999.
11. DE Kaplan. Aum Shinrikyo. In *Toxic Terror: Assessing Terrorist Use of Chemical and Biological Weapons*. Tucker JB, ed. Cambridge, MA: Belfer Center for Scientific and International Affairs, Harvard University, 2000, pp. 207–226.
12. *Emergency Response to Terrorism Job Aid*, Edition 2.0. Washington, DC: Federal Emergency Management Administration, 2003. Internet: www.usfa.dhs.gov/downloads/pdf/publications/ert-ja.pdf (accessed February 11, 2008).
13. Interagency Intelligence Committee on Terrorism. *Chemical/Biological/Radiological Incident Handbook*. Washington, DC: Central Intelligence Agency, 1998. Internet: http://www.fas.org/irp/threat/cbw/CBR_hdbk.htm (accessed February 11, 2008).
14. Chemical Terrorism Preparedness and Response Card, New York State Department of Health, 2005. Internet: http://www.health.state.ny.us/environmental/emergency/chemical (accessed February 9, 2008).
15. LE Davis T, LaTourrette, DE Mosher, LM Davis, and DR Howell. *Individual Preparedness and Response to Chemical, Radiological, Nuclear, and Biological Terrorist Attacks*. Santa Monica, CA: Rand, 2003, pp. 21–30. Internet: http://www.rand.org/pubs/monograph_reports/MR1731/index.html (accessed February 9, 2008).
16. PA Erickson. *Emergency Response Planning for Corporate and Municipal Managers*. San Diego, CA: Academic Press, 1999.
17. OSHA/NIOSH Interim Guidance, April 1, 2005. Chemical-Biological-Radiological-Nuclear (CBRN) Personal Protective Equipment Selection Matrix for Emergency Responders. Internet: http://www.osha.gov/SLTC/emergencypreparedness/cbrnmatrix/index.html (accessed February 9, 2008).
18. AG Macintyre, GW Christopher, E Eitzen, R Gum, S Weir, C DeAtley, K Tonat, and JA Barbera. Weapons of mass destruction events with contaminated casualties. Effective planning for health care facilities. *JAMA* 283:242–249, 2000. Internet: http://jama.ama-assn.org/cgi/content/full/283/2/242 (accessed February 11, 2008).
19. DC Keyes, JL Burstein, RB Schwartz, and RE Swienton, eds. *Medical Response to Terrorism: Preparedness and Clinical Practice*. Philadelphia, PA: Lippincott Williams & Wilkins, 2004.
20. A Rivkind, P Barach, A Israeli, M Berdugo, and E Richter. Emergency preparedness and response in Israel during the Gulf war. *Annals of Emergency Medicine* 30:513–521, 1997.
21. U.S. Department of Transportation/Transport Canada/Secretariat of Communications and Transportation of Mexico. North America Emergency Response Guidebook, 2004. Internet: http://hazmat.dot.gov/pubs/erg/gydebook.htm (ccessed February 11, 2008).
22. Chemical Manufacturers Association. Chemtrec. Internet: http://www.chemtrec.org/Chemtrec/Resources/ (accessed February 11, 2008).
23. Center for Domestic Preparedness. U.S. Department of Homeland Security. Internet: www.ojp.usdoj.gov/odp/docs/CDP Fact Sheet.pdf (accessed February 10, 2008).
24. Overview of Homeland Defense Program. Edgewood Chemical Biological Center, U.S. Army. Internet: http://www.ecbc.army.mil/hld/ip/fs/hld_overview.htm (accessed February 10, 2008).
25. J Burgess, M Kirk, S Borron, and J Cisek. Emergency department hazardous materials protocol for contaminated patients. *Annals of Emergency Medicine* 34:205–212, 1999.
26. CL Staten. *Emergency Response to Chemical/Biological Terrorist Incidents*. Chicago, IL: Emergency Response and Research Institute, 1997. Internet: http://www.emergency.com/cbwlesn1.htm (accessed February 11, 2008).

27. Organization for the Prohibition of Chemical Weapons. *Chemical Warfare Agents: An Overview of Chemicals Defined as Chemical Weapons*. Geneva, Switzerland: OPCW, Internet: http://www.opcw.org/resp/html/cwagents.html (accessed February 11, 2008).
28. J Sullivan and G Krieger. *Hazardous Materials Technology*. Baltimore, MD: Williams & Wilkins, 1992.
29. M Keim and AF Kaufman. Principles for emergency response to bioterrorism. *Annals of Emergency Medicine* 34:183–190, 1999.
30. JF Waeckerle. Domestic preparedness for events involving weapons of mass destruction. *JAMA* 283:252–254, 2000. Internet: http://jama.ama-assn.org/cgi/content/extract/283/2/252.html (accessed February 11, 2008).
31. Swedish Defense Research Agency. *A FOA Briefing Book on Chemical Weapons: Threats, Effects, and Protection*. Stockholm, Sweden: FOA, 1995.
32. TC Marrs, RL Maynard, and FR Sidell. *Chemical Warfare Agents: Toxicology and Treatment*. Chichester, U.K.: Wiley, 1996.
33. TP Noeller. Biological and chemical terrorism: Recognition and management. *Cleveland Clin J Med* 68:1001–1016, 2001. Internet: www.ccjm.org/pdffiles/BioTerror.pdf (accessed December 11, 2008).
34. DR Franz. *Understanding the Threat. Defense against Toxin Weapons*. Iowa City: Virtual Naval Hospital, University of Iowa, 2002, Chapter 1. Internet: www.usamriid.army.mil/education/defensetox/toxdefbook.pdf (accessed February 11, 2008).
35. North Atlantic Treaty Organization. *Nato Handbook on the Medical Aspects of NBC Defensive Operations*, Part III *Chemical, AmedP-6(B)*. Washington, DC: Departments of the Army, the Navy, and the Air Force, 1996. Internet: www.fas.org/nuke/guide/usa/doctrine/dod/fm8–9/3toc.htm (accessed February 11, 2008).
36. FR Sidwell, ET Takafuji, and DR Franz, eds. Medical aspects of chemical and biological warfare. In: *Textbook of Military Medicine*, R Zajtchuk and RF Bellamy, eds. Series Part 1, *Warfare, Weaponry, and the Casualty*. Washington, DC: TMM8 Publications, Borden Institute, 1997. Internet: http://www.bordeninstitute.army.mil/published_volumes/chemBio/chembio.html (accessed February 11, 2008).
37. K Lohs. Stockholm International Peace Research Institute. *Delayed Toxic Effects of Chemical Warfare Agents*. Stockholm: Almqvist & Wiksell, 1975. Internet: http://books.sipri.org/product_info?c _product_id=302# (accessed February 11, 2008).
38. Centers for Disease Control and Prevention. Emergency Preparedness and Response. Internet: http://www.bt.cdc.gov/chemical/lab.asp (accessed February 10, 2008).
39. Centers for Disease Control and Prevention. Emergency Preparedness and Response. Laboratory Network for Chemical Terrorism. Internet: http://www.bt.cdc.gov/lrn/chemical.asp (accessed February 10, 2008).
40. Centers for Disease Control and Prevention. The Public Health Response to Biological and Chemical Terrorism. Interim Planning Guidance for State Public Health Officials, 2001. Internet: www.bt.cdc.gov/Documents/Planning/PlanningGuidance.PDF (accessed February 11, 2008).
41. General Accounting Office. Chemical and Biological Defense Units Better Equipped, but Training and Readiness Reporting Problems Remain, GAO-01-27. Washington, DC: GAO, 2001. Internet www.gao.gov/new.items/d0127.pdf (accessed February 11, 2008).
42. Centers for Disease Control and Prevention Strategic Planning Group. Biological and Chemical Terrorism: Strategic Plan for Preparedness and Response. *MMWR: Morbidity and Mortality Weekly Report* 49(RR-4):1–14, 2000. Internet: www.cdc.gov/mmwr/preview/mmwrhtml/rr4904a1.htm (accessed February 11, 2008).
43. WM Knapp and LA Knapp. Biological and Chemical Terrorism and the Medical Preparedness Paradigm—A Protective Research Group Perspective. November 1, 2000, 1–23.
44. AE Smithson and L-A Levy. Ataxia: The Clinical and Biological Terrorist Threat and U.S. Response, Stimson Center Report No. 35. Washington, DC: HL Stimson Center, 2002. Internet: http://www.stimson.org/pub.cfm?id=12 (accessed February 11, 2008).

Chapter 21

Chemical Terrorism: Destruction and Decontamination

Dabir S. Viswanath and Tushar K. Ghosh

CONTENTS

Introduction 380
Timeline for Destruction 380
Cost of Destruction 381
Destruction Methods 384
Sea Dumping 386
High-Temperature Destruction Technologies 386
Incineration 388
Pyrolysis 390
Plasma-Based Destruction 390
Molten Metal Systems 392
Hydrogenolysis 393
High-Temperature Destruction of Arsenicals 393
Low-Temperature Destruction Technologies 394
Neutralization 394
Electrochemical Oxidation 400
Solvent Electron Technology 400
Supercritical Water and Wet Air Oxidation 401
Hydrogenation 401

Hydrochlorination....401
Advanced Oxidation Processes....401
Equipment Decontamination....402
References....407

Introduction

A number of countries have stockpiled large amounts of chemical warfare (CW) agents and other toxic chemicals, and are trying to destroy them by safe methods. Factors such as cost, safety, and release of secondary toxic chemicals during destruction, legal and political issues have to be considered before employing any method for the destruction of these chemicals. Although the destruction of toxic chemicals is not new and appears to have started in 1915 after the use of mustard gas by the Germans during World War I, none of the methods as we know today appear to be cost effective, safe, and foolproof. We will outline some methods used at the present time for the destruction of not only chemical weapons but other toxic chemicals. Excellent summary [1] and details [2] of several methods of destruction of toxic chemicals and munitions are available in these two citations. Heyl and McGuire [3] have edited a book entitled *Analytical Chemistry Associated with the Destruction of Chemical Weapons*, which is a collection of papers presented at a NATO Workshop. This book can be an excellent resource for individuals who wish to learn more about the chemistry of destruction.

The 158 countries that have signed the Chemical Weapons Convention have outlined a schedule for the destruction of chemical weapons. Table 21.1 gives an estimate of the amount of chemical weapons and their types stockpiled by some of the countries.

The data shown in Table 21.1 also indicate the urgency of destruction of these chemical agents. The amount of chemical agents possessed by Iraq is pre–Gulf War II estimates based on the findings from the Gulf War I. However, there is no verification on the fate of the chemical agents possessed by Iraq. Following Gulf War II, further inspections found no chemical agents in Iraq and also there are no records of destruction of these chemicals.

Timeline for Destruction

Countries that are signatories to Chemical Weapon Convention (CWC) must also follow the chemical agent destruction timeline set by Organization for Prohibition of Chemical Weapon (OPCW). Each member country of OPCW must adapt to the following:

- Destroy all chemical weapons it owns or possesses.
- Destroy all chemical weapons it may have abandoned in another country.
- Destroy facilities it owns or possesses which were involved in the production of chemical weapons.

The Convention that became effective on April 29, 1997 requires that member countries destroy their chemical weapons within ten years after the CWC entered into force—by 2007. The Convention can grant a request for extension of this destruction deadline by up to five years, until 2012, based on the progress and problems associated with the destruction program. Further extension will require much formal approval processes. The approval of the other OPCW member countries is necessary for this exceptional extension of the destruction timeline.

Table 21.1 Stockpile of Chemicals

Country	*Quantity of Chemical Weapons (tons)*	*Types of Chemical Agents*	*Form of Storage*
Russia	40,000		
United States	32,000		
Iraq[a]	480,000 (CW)		
	1,800,000 (precursors)		
	3,860 (1990)		
North Korea	4,500/year		
Iran	1,000/year		
India	1,044	Sulfur mustard	Stored in bulk containers and about two percent of the agent is in artillery shells.
Albania	16	Mixture of two blister agents	Stored in barrels
Libya[b]	23.62	Mustard agents	Stored in containers
South Korea	-	Sarin gas	Stockpile of 156,000 Sarin artillery shells of binary type
Japan/China[c]	100	-	Chemical shells/munitions

Source: Smithson, A.E., *The Bulletin of Atomic Scientists*, NTI: Country Overview, April 1993; Renner, M., *Bonn International Center for Conversion*, Brief 6, Bonn, Germany, 1996. With permission.

[a] These figures are in liters, and represent the amount of CW and precursors destroyed under the supervision of UNSCOM. Per year figures are production capability.

[b] Libya also possesses 1000 tons of chemical precursors for making nerve agents.

[c] Japan does not possess any chemical weapons or agents; however, Japan abandoned large stocks of chemical munitions in China after World War II. China claims that they are some 2 million shells buried in China, whereas Japan claims that the number is about 70,000.

The timeline set by OPCW is shown in Figure 21.1.

Except Albania, none of the other countries (the United States, Russia, India, South Korea, Libya, and Japan) were able to meet the deadline of 2007. All of them have requested for the extension of the time. The extension requested by these countries and the amount destroyed so far are shown in Table 21.2.

Worldwide destruction of chemical agents and munitions/containers as of June 2008 is given in Table 21.3.

Cost of Destruction

The cost of destruction of CW agents is now a major issue for most of the countries that have stockpiled these agents. It is estimated that the cost of destruction of chemical weapons would be

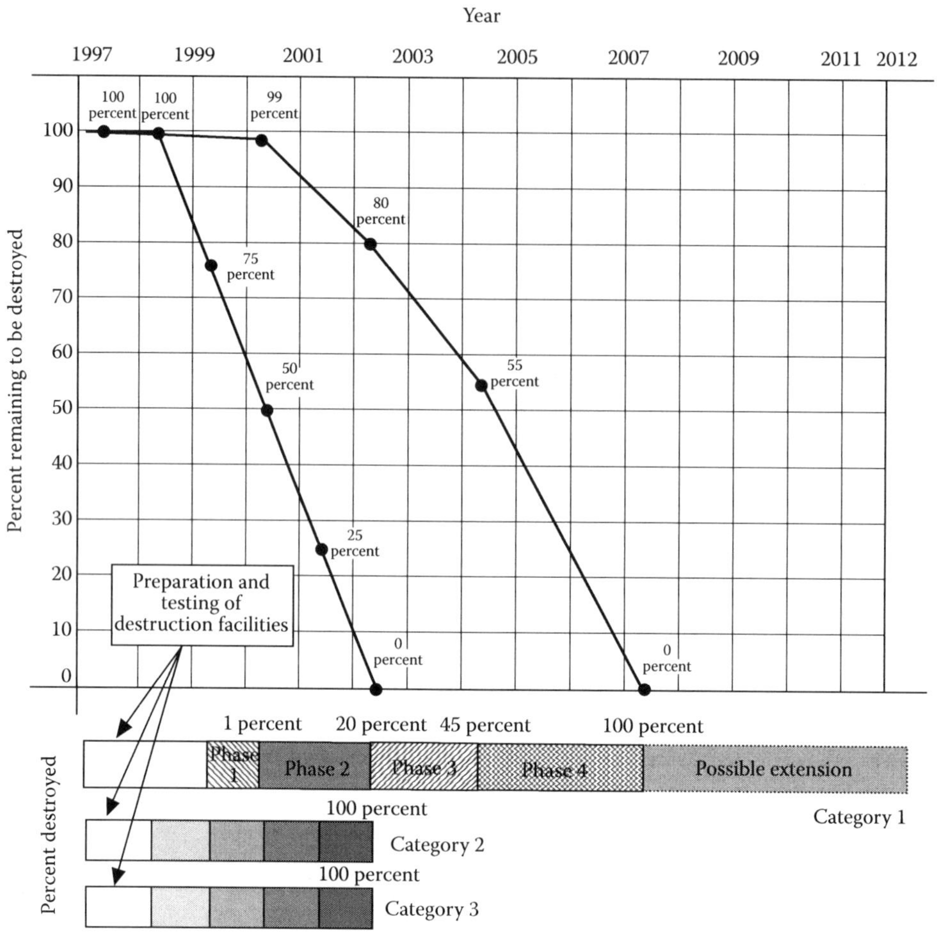

Figure 21.1 Timeline for destruction of chemical agents set by OPCW member countries [6]. Timetable illustrates destruction deadlines for countries that were States Parties on the date of entry into force of the CWC, April 29, 1997.

ten times the cost of production. Renner [6], based on the information available prior to 1995, gives an excellent summary of the cost of disarmament.

In the United States, Congress originally ordered destruction of all U.S. chemical agents by 1996 and thought that the total cost of destruction will be around $1.7 billion. However, as can be seen from Figure 21.2, the cost has escalated significantly and the time line is also changing.

Recently, the U.S. Army projected that the cost can be more than $27.8 billion and it may take at least until 2023 to complete destruction of all chemical agents. To restrict the transportation of the chemical agents, it is preferable to build a destruction unit at or near the storage facilities. As shown in Figure 21.3, the United States stockpiles are stored in several facilities. However, the United States is continuing destruction of its stockpiles and the current status is shown Figure 21.4.

Table 21.2 New Timeline for Destruction of Chemical Weapons for Some Selected Countries

Country	*New Extended Time for Complete Destruction*	*Status*
Albania	—	Completed destruction of all chemical agents. This achievement was confirmed by the OPCW on July 11, 2007.
United States	April 29, 2012	As of December 2007, the United States had destroyed more than 45 percent of its Category 1 stockpile and 100 percent of its Category 3 stockpile.
Russia	April 29, 2012	Destroyed about 22 percent of its Category 1 CW stockpile. Russia has destroyed 100 percent of its Category 2 and Category 3 stockpiles.
Libya	December 31, 2010	Destruction of its Category 1 CW stockpile is not complete. Libya plans to destroy the remaining 63 percent of its Category 2 stockpile by December 31, 2011.
India	April 28, 2009	Destroyed about 80 percent of its Category 1 CW stockpile. India has also destroyed 100 percent of its Category 2 and Category 3 stockpiles.

Source: Organization for the Prohibition of Chemical Weapons, Timeline of Destruction, http://www.opcw.org/our-work/demilitarisation/destruction-timelines/, 11/15/2008.

Table 21.3 Worldwide Declared and Destroyed Amount of Chemical Agents

	Chemical Agent (Metric Ton)	*Munitions/Containers (Million Items)*	*Chemical Weapons Production Facilities (CWPFs)*
Declared	71,315	8.67	65
Destroyed	28,856	3.06	42
Converted for peaceful purposes	n.a.	n.a.	19

Source: Organization for the Prohibition of Chemical Weapons, http://www.opcw.org/.

The estimated cost for eliminating the Russian chemical weapons stockpile is about $5.6 billion. Russia has received significant international assistance for destruction of its stockpile. The United States, Canada, Germany, Italy, the United Kingdom, and other countries have committed almost $2 billion in assistance, with the United States committing the largest amount, about $1.039 billion. A list of the countries and their donations are given in Table 21.4.

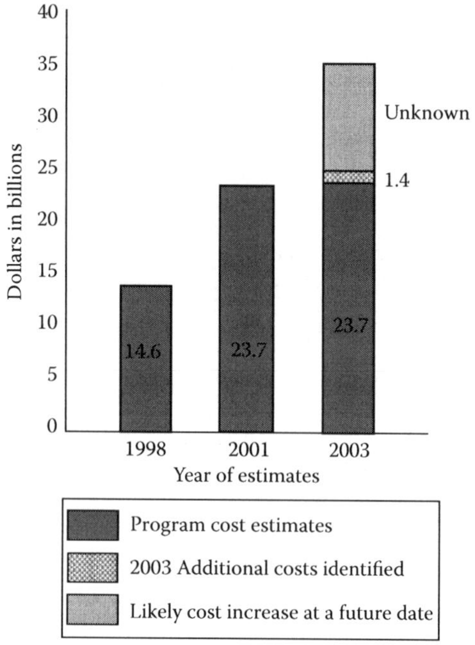

Figure 21.2 Estimated costs for destruction of chemical agents by the United States at different years. (Data from General Accounting Office, Chemical Weapons: Destruction Schedule Delays and Cost Growth Continue to Challenge Program Management, GAO-04-634T, April 1, 2004.)

Over the past six years, Russia has substantially increased its own funding for destruction of chemical weapons. In 2000, the Russian government spent about $16 million for chemical weapons destruction. By 2005, it had spent almost $400 million. For 2006, the Russian government plans to spend more than $640 million.

The United States and a number of other countries continue to assist Albania and Libya to destroy chemical agents. The United States with additional assistance from Greece, Italy, Switzerland, and the European Union has helped Albania to destroy its stockpile. The cost of destruction of Libya's stockpile is estimated at about $100 million, which the United States has agreed to fund with congressional approval.

Destruction Methods

Several technologies [12] are available for destruction of toxic chemicals but most of the technologies are not cost effective. The choice of a particular technology should be based on several criteria including:

1. The effectiveness of the method in completely destroying the chemical.
2. Secondary waste produced.
3. Efficiency.
4. Cost of destruction.
5. Risks involved.
6. Broad class of compounds that can be destroyed.

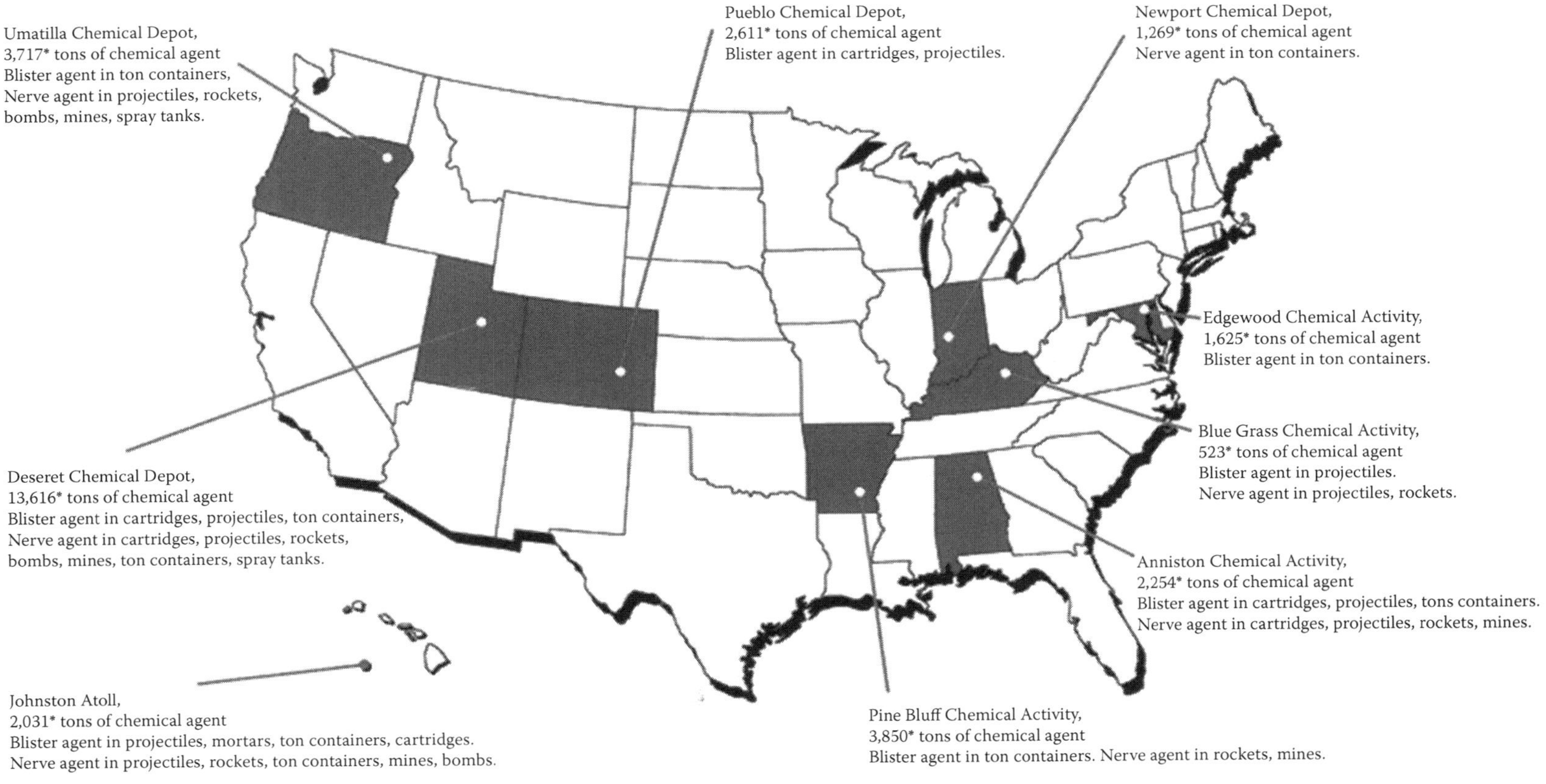

Figure 21.3 Chemical agent storage facilities in the United States. (From Federation of American Scientists, U.S. Chemical Weapons Facility, http://www.fas.org/nuke/guide/usa/cbw/cw.htm, 11/15/2008.) *Note:* *The amount reflects US's original stockpile

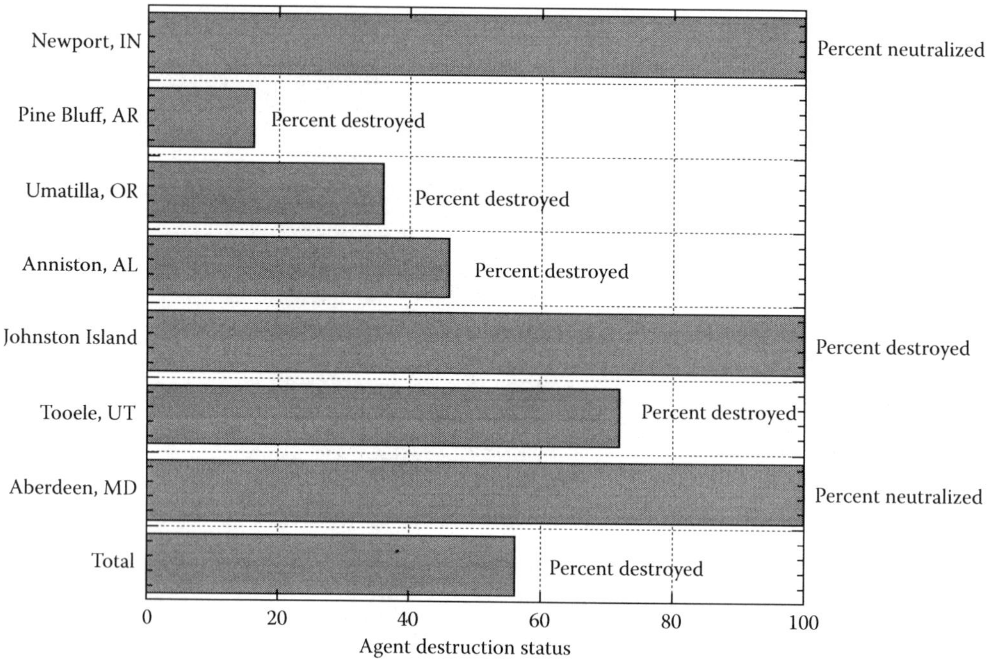

Figure 21.4 Status of destruction of chemical agents at various facilities in the United States as of August 13, 2008. (From U.S. Army Chemical Materials Agency, Creating a Safer Tomorrow, http://www.cma.army.mil/#, 11/15/2008.)

Destruction of CW agents can be broadly classified into the following categories:

1. Sea dumping.
2. High-temperature destruction technologies.
3. Low-temperature destruction technologies.

Sea Dumping

This is a method [13] practiced since World War II. This method will be suitable for chemicals that break down on hydrolysis. One major disadvantage of sea dumping is the effect of these chemicals and the hydrolysis products on marine life. This method is now prohibited by the CWC agreement, but dumping of chemicals in oceans and rivers continues to be a method of disposal of chemicals. It is estimated that after World War II, 46,000 tons of chemical weapons were dumped into the Baltic Sea of which Russia dumped close to 30,000 tons. They were dumped in Baltic Sea areas known as Gotland Deep, Bornholm Deep, and the Little Belt based on the information given to the Helsinki Commission in 1994 [14].

High-Temperature Destruction Technologies

Any chemical can be destroyed completely by applying heat. The complete destruction means that the toxic chemicals are converted to harmless chemicals such as carbon dioxide, water vapor,

Table 21.4 International Assistance for Russian Destruction, as of April 2006

International Donors	*Committed Funding for Russian Destruction (U.S. Dollars)*	*Areas to Receive International Assistance*	*Types of Projects Being Funded*
Belgium	$100,000	Shchuch'ye	To be determined
Canada	89,150,537	Shchuch'ye	Industrial infrastructure, railway, and equipment for Building 101A
Czech Republic	232,458	Shchuch'ye	Industrial infrastructure (electrical substations)
Denmark	117,970	Various locations	Public outreach efforts
European Union	14,156,452	Gorniy, Kambarka, and Shchuch'ye	Equipment at Gorniy and Kambarka, and industrial infrastructure at Shchuch'ye (electrical substation)
Finland	871,771	Gorniy and other locations	Equipment at Gorniy and public outreach efforts
France	7,077,976	Shchuch'ye	Environmental surveys and other projects to be determined
Germany	233,573,198	Gorniy and Kambarka	Equipment for the construction and operation of both facilities
Ireland	94,376	Shchuch'ye	To be determined
Italy	439,660,257	Shchuch'ye and Pochep	Infrastructure (gas pipeline) at Schuch'ye and the construction of the Pochep CWDF
The Netherlands	9,028,325	Shchuch'ye	Equipment for Building 101A

Source: General Accounting Office, Cooperative Threat Reduction: DOD Needs More Reliable Data to Better Estimate the Cost and Schedule of the Shchuch'ye Facility, GAO-06-692, May 2006.

or nitrogen. The extent of destruction depends on the temperature of the process. The processes under this category include:

1. Incineration.
2. Pyrolysis.
3. Plasma pyrolysis.
4. Molten metal technologies.
5. High-temperature destruction of arsenicals.

These processes are energy intensive, require special materials of construction, and the by-products can be more toxic than the precursor depending upon the temperature. Pyrolysis, plasma, and molten metal technologies require smaller vessels compared to incineration. The temperature at which each process operates varies widely from 300 to 10,000 K.

Most of the chemicals used in CW contain heteroatoms of increased molecular complexity, and therefore processes where OH and H radicals attack the parent compound could be useful methods. These chemicals can be broadly classified as nitro- or chloro-compounds, and organophosphates. The chemicals destroyed by these processes are nerve gases, blister agents, and other chemicals.

Incineration

In the United States, incineration by the name of "Baseline Incineration Technology" has been used to destroy CW agents at several facilities [15]. Incineration is a widely used and proven technology with a long history of research and development. The chemistry of the destruction process and conditions for effective operation are well established. This improved understanding has been developed during the past few years and, because of facilities improperly operated in the past, incineration suffers from a poor public image. In the United States, Center for Disease Control's National Center for Environmental Health (NCEH) reviews all Department of Defense (DOD) plans for disposing of chemical weapon stockpiles. DOD incinerators must meet all the local, state, and federal standards for a variety of emissions and must achieve a "destruction and removal efficiency" of 99.9999 percent for the agent being destroyed. This means that no more than 0.0001 percent of the agent being processed can be released from the incinerator stack. Instruments continuously monitor the incinerator stack for the agent at extremely low levels, well below the levels considered safe for the community. If any agent is detected in the incinerator stack, the incinerator automatically shuts down until problems are corrected. Quality control specialists check agent-monitoring instruments in the stacks and elsewhere in the workplace each day. NCEH reviews all agent-monitor quality control reports biweekly to ensure that workers operate the monitors in accordance with standard practices and with site-specific procedures that NCEH helped to develop. A schematic diagram of the baseline incineration system on the United States is shown in Figure 21.5.

The decomposition reactions of various chemical agents during incineration can be written as follows:

Mustard gas:

$$2(ClCH_2CH_2)_2S + 13.5O_2 = 8CO_2 + 6H_2O + 4HCl + 2SO_2$$

GB:

$$2(CH_3)_2CHO(CH_3)POF + 13O_2 = P_2O_5 + 8CO_2 + 9H_2O + 2HF$$

VX:

$$2C_{11}H_{26}NO_2PS + 38.5O_2 = 22CO_2 + 26H_2O + P_2O_5 + 2SO_2 + 2NO$$

Depending on the oxygen content or the amount of air fed during the incineration, NO_2 may be formed instead of NO.

$$2C_{11}H_{26}NO_2PS + 39.5O_2 = 22CO_2 + 26H_2O + P_2O_5 + 2SO_2 + 2NO_2$$

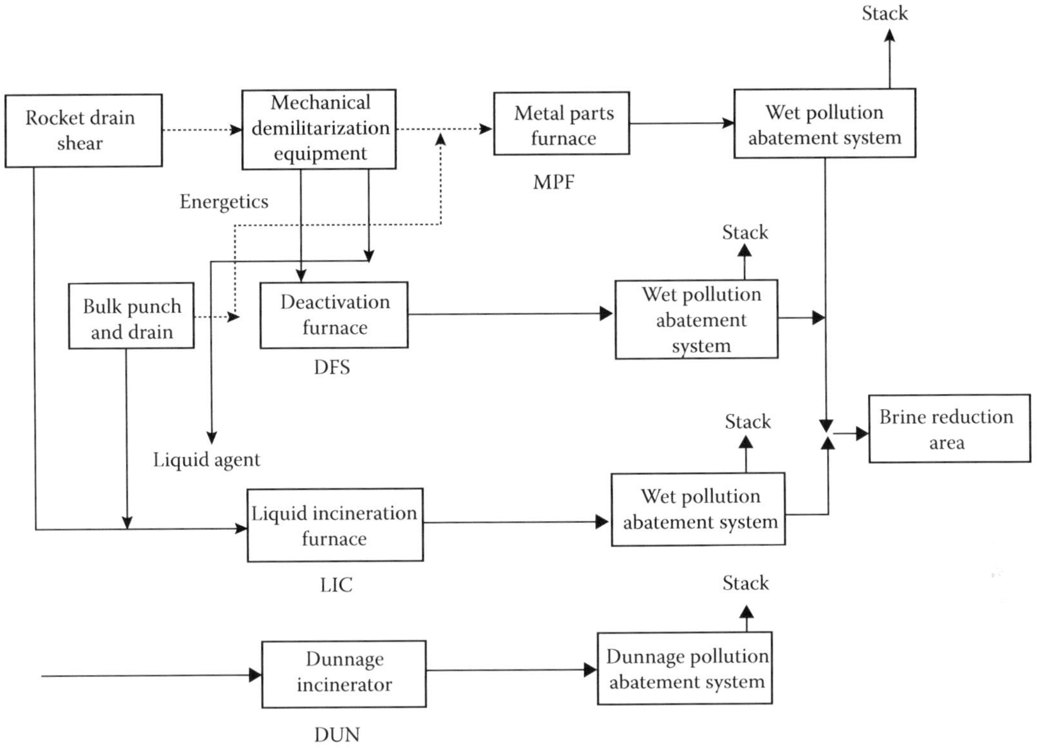

Figure 21.5 U.S. baseline incineration systems. (Modified from National Research Council, Committee on Review and Evaluation of the Army Chemical Stockpile Disposal Program, *Review of Systematization of the Tooele Chemical Agent Disposal Facility,* National Academy Press, Washington, DC, 1996, 92, Appendix B.)

As can be seen from these reactions, various acid gases are released during the incineration process and must be removed before releasing the off-gas to the atmosphere. Generally, sodium hydroxide (NaOH) or sodium bisulfite ($NaHSO_3$) solutions are used for neutralization of these acid gases. The neutralizations reactions are as follows:

$$NaOH + HCl = NaCl + H_2O$$

$$NaOH + HF = NaF + H_2O$$

$$NaOH + SO_2 = NaHSO_3$$

$$NaHSO_3 + NaOH = Na_2SO_3 + H_2O$$

$$O_2 + 2Na_2SO_3 = 2Na_2SO4$$

In the United States, the Tooele Chemical Agent Disposal Facility in Utah has so far destroyed about 1500 tons of sarin gas using baseline incineration technology. The same facility has also destroyed almost 14,000 rockets, bombs, and bulk containers in the process of burning the sarin gas. The incinerator was operated at a temperature of 1750 K, and the products of incineration are sent to a second incinerator or afterburner for complete combustion of even the traces coming out of the first incinerator. The baseline incineration process used at Johnston Atoll destroyed chemical agents in the weapons stored there with an efficiency of 99.9999 percent [15]. Many more incinerators are under construction by the U.S. military so that the CWC treaty's deadline for destruction of CW agents can be accomplished. Several modifications to the original baseline incineration technology were proposed. A Committee on Review and Evaluation of the Army Chemical Stockpile Disposal Program, Board on Army Science and Technology by National Research Council has reviewed these modifications [15]. The baseline incineration system is so named because it was initially the Army's preferred method for destroying chemical agents and assembled chemical munitions. The modified baseline process is distinguished from the baseline incineration system in that both the mustard agent and munitions body are fed to one furnace instead of being separated and sent to different furnaces. This modification is intended to solve the problem of gelled agent that has formed in the aging munitions and cannot be drained from the munitions body. Preliminary testing has shown that the chemical agents in the weapons stored can be destroyed with an efficiency of 99.9999 percent.

The incineration method is most widely used for destruction of chemical agents. More than 65 percent of the agents worldwide are destroyed by this method. Various facilities around the world that used the incineration method are listed in Table 21.5.

Pyrolysis

Chemical agents like nerve agents and, possibly, mustard compounds can be destroyed by the pyrolysis (thermal treatment without oxygen) process. A number of other toxic organic compounds can be also destroyed. The advantage of the pyrolysis process compared to incineration is that for the same amount of materials, pyrolysis requires smaller reactors, no mixing, and lower temperatures. However, pyrolysis may produce toxic by-products which still have to be destroyed by some other processes. If incineration is used, pyrolysis is often the first step in the multistep destruction process.

Plasma-Based Destruction

In this process, a plasma arc generates temperatures around 3,000–15,000 K. At this temperature chemicals break down into atoms or fragments containing few atoms. The reactions proceed very fast at very short residence times. Although a commercial scale unit using plasma-based thermal destruction system for chemical agents is not available, the process has been tested in pilot scale by several companies for destroying other wastes. A schematic diagram of the process is shown in Figure 21.6 and the design of the plasma torch is shown in Figure 21.7. Westinghouse has tested plasma vitrification technology for high and low-level nuclear waste. In this process calcination and vitrification are integrated into a single process. Bruce et al. [18] reported development of a plasma-based thermal treatment process for destroying polychlorinated biphenyls (PCBs) and CW agents. Testing was conducted using simulants for chemical and nerve agents and other energetics. Destruction and removal efficiencies in the range of >99.9999 percent were reported.

In the United States, the plasma pyrolysis method has been tested only with the simulants. However, the National Research Council raised several questions regarding its practicality

Table 21.5 Facilities around the World Designed Based on Incineration for Destruction of Chemical Agents

Facilities	*Agents*	*Method*
Rocky Mountain Arsenal, USA	H	Incineration
Tooele (CAMDS),[a] USA	GB, L, GA, GB, and VX containers	Incineration
JACADS[b]Johnston Atoll, USA, OVT (operational verification test) data	GB, HD, and VX munitions	Incineration
Tooele (CAMDS), USA	VX	Incineration
JACADS Johnston Atoll, USA, OVT data	VX	Incineration
JACADS Johnston Atoll, USA, OVT data	HD	Incineration
Pine Bluff Arsenal, USA	HD, HT containers, GB, and VX munitions	Incineration
Umatilla Chemical Depot., USA	HD containers, GB, and VX munitions	Incineration
Anniston Army Depot., USA	HD, HT, GB, and VX munitions	
DRES Canada	H	Neutralization/incineration
DRES Canada	H	Incineration
DRES Canada	VX, GA, and GB	Neutralization/incineration
Munster, Germany	H, etc.	Incineration
Shikhany, Russia	GB, GD	Neutralization/incineration
Shikhany, Russia (Russian VX)	VR	Neutralization/incineration
Porton Down, U.K.	H	Incineration
Runcorn, U.K.	H	Incineration
Iraq (UNSCOM supervised)	H	Incineration

Source: Pearson, G.S. and Magee, R.S., *IUPAC Tech. Rep. Pure Appl Chem.*, 74(2), 187, 2002. With permission.

[a] CAMDS was a Chemical Agent Munitions Disposal System experimental facility at the Tooele Army Depot, Utah.

[b] This JACADS data is OVT (operation verification test) data obtained prior to the full-scale operation of the Johnston Atoll Chemical Agent Disposal System.

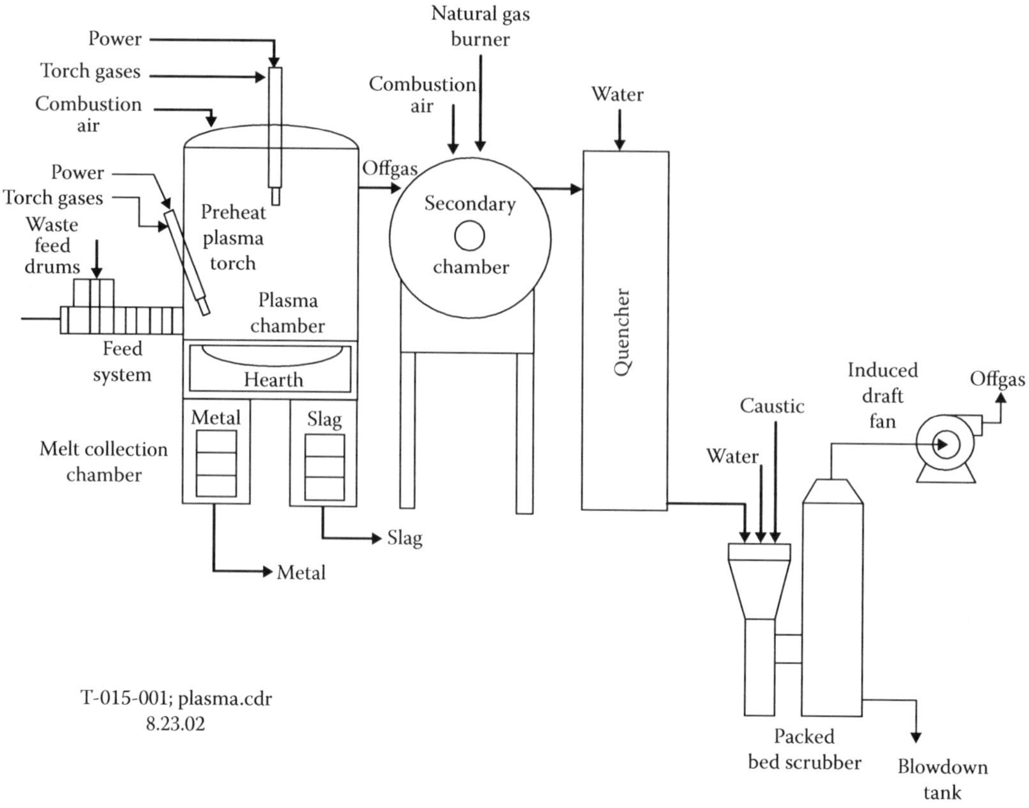

Figure 21.6 A schematic diagram of the plasma-based chemical agent destruction facility. (From Science Applications International Corporation, Assessment of Plasma Arc Technology of Processing of Chemical Demilitarization Wastes, DAAD13-01-D-0007, Task T-02-AT-003, October 2002.)

and commercial use. In Europe, Switzerland and Germany have used plasma pyrolysis plants using the PLASMOX process to destroy chemical agents that also included lewisite at rates of 50 kg/hour.

Molten Metal Systems

Molten metal systems use a heated bath, typically of Fe or Ni, to destroy chemicals. However, such systems require an off-gas treatment facility. Carryover of particulates with the off-gas and the life of the refractory materials used to line the vessel are of great concern. Treatment of wastes using an enclosed molten metal system includes the possibility for the production of useful chemicals, such as syngas ($CO + H_2$), from the decomposition chemistry in the bath. This technology may also find use for treatment of wastes containing metals; for example, arsenic may be captured. The Battelle/Columbus Laboratory in the United States evaluated destruction of HD and VX in a bench scale unit and reported destruction removal efficiency (DRE) of 99.9999 percent. The bath compositions for these two tests are given in Table 21.6.

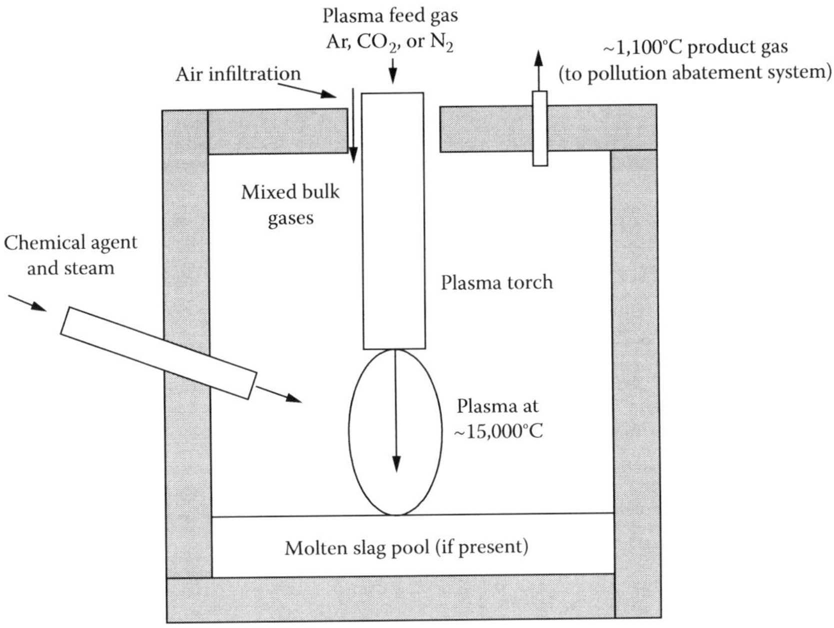

Figure 21.7 The arrangement of the plasma torch. (From Pearson, G.S. and Magee, R.S., *IUPAC Tech. Rep. Pure Appl. Chem.*, 74(2), 187, 2002. With permission.)

Table 21.6 Bath Compositions of the Molten Metal System for Destruction of HD and VX

Agent Tested	*Bath Composition*	*Agent Processing Rate (kg Agent/hour/1000 kg Bath Metal)*
HD	Ni + 2 percent C	7
VX	Fe + 7 percent P + 7 percent S + C	8

Source: Pearson, G.S. and Magee, R.S., *IUPAC Tech. Rep. Pure Appl Chem.*, 74(2), 187, 2002. With permission.

Hydrogenolysis

In this process, hydrogen and steam at about 850°C and atmospheric pressure are used to react with various organic compounds to transform them to less harmful chemicals. Although the process has been used to destroy polychlorinated biphenyls (PCBs) and other organics, it has not been tested with chemical agents.

High-Temperature Destruction of Arsenicals

Although a number of methods have been suggested for destruction of arsenicals, and in particular lewisite, the incineration method appeared to be the best option. Munster plant at Germany is continuing destruction of several arsenicals including Clark agent and mustard-containing various arsenical compounds by incineration. The chemical agent is first subjected to partial pyrolysis at 300°C for up to 12 hours, which is followed by combustion at temperatures of 1000°C–1200°C with a residence time of 2 s. The product gas is further cleaned to remove acid gases and arsenic oxide (As_2O_3).

Low-Temperature Destruction Technologies

The public concern about incineration has led to the development of various nonincineration processes or low-temperature destruction processes. However, all these low-temperature processes must meet the criteria of "base-line" incineration technology. The low-temperature processes explored by various researchers and U.S. military are as follows:

1. Neutralization
2. Electrochemical oxidation
3. Solvent electron technology
4. Supercritical water and wet air oxidation
5. Hydrogenation
6. Hydrochlorination
7. Advanced oxidation process

Among these processes, neutralization method is most widely used for destruction of chemical agents. However, often, following neutralization, the by-products are further destroyed by incineration. The capability and status of these processes are summarized in Table 21.7.

Neutralization

A neutralization process for destroying chemical agents depends on the specific agent or class of agents that are to be destroyed. Moreover, the process may have to be modified even when treating different types of the same agent such as H, HD, and HT. The neutralization process is particularly suitable for mustard gas (HD), because it can be detoxified rapidly at low temperature and pressure. The chemical reaction involved during neutralization process is basically the hydrolysis of chemical agent. The hydrolysis process can be carried out by various ways and are described in the following text.

Neutralization by Hydrolysis

The neutralization of HD takes place according to the following reaction. As can be seen from the reaction, it is a basic hydrolysis reaction forming thiodiglycol [bis(2-hydroxyethyl)sulfide] and hydrochloric acid:

$$S(CH_2CH_2Cl)_2 + 2H_2O = S(CH_2CH_2OH)_2 + 2HCl$$

The reaction is carried out in hot water and produces a number of by-products that need further treatment. The Aberdeen Chemical Disposal Facility at the United States employed the neutralization to destroy mustard gas stockpile. The by-products of the hydrolysis reaction are further treated on site by a biotreatment facility. The schematic flow diagram of the facility is shown in Figure 21.8.

Table 21.7 Summary of Process Capabilities and Status

Process	Stream Treated					Afterburner Needed	Next Step	Comments
	Agent			Metal and Energetics				
	Initial Agent Detox	Complete Organic Oxidation	Need Gas Afterburner	Energetics	Metal			
Low-temperature, low-pressure detoxification								
Base hydrolysis	GB	No	?	No	No	N.A.	PP	Has been used in field for HD, limited by contacting problems
NaOH + H_2O_2	VX	No	Yes	No	No	N.A.	Lab	New finding
$Ca(OH)_2$ at 100°C	HD	No	?	No	No	N.A.	Lab/PP	Limited use in England
KOH + ethanol	HD, GB, and VX	No	?	No	No	N.A.	Lab	
Hypochlorite ion	HD	No	Yes	No	No	N.A.	Lab	Difficult contacting problem with HD
Organic base (ethanolamine)	GB, HD, Possibly VX	No	?	No	No	N.A.	Lab/PP	Limited use in Russia; increase in organic use
Acidic systems								
HCl hydrolysis	GB	No	?	No	No	N.A.	Lab/PP	
Peracid salts (OXONE, others)	VX, perhaps GB and HD	No	Yes	No	No	N.A.	Lab/PP	Increased waste

(continued)

Table 21.7 (continued) Summary of Process Capabilities and Status

	Stream Treated							
	Agent			*Metal and Energetics*				
Process	*Initial Agent Detox*	*Complete Organic Oxidation*	*Need Gas Afterburner*	*Energetics*	*Metal*	*Afterburner Needed*	*Next Step*	*Comments*
Chlorine	VX, perhaps HD and GB	No	Yes	No	No	N.A.	Lab/PP	Increased inorganic waste
Ionizing radiation	All	No	?	Yes?	Yes?	?	Lab	High conversion not yet established
Low-temperature, low-pressure oxidation								
Peroxydisulfate, ClO_3, H_2O_2, and O_3	All	Yes	Yes	No	No	N.A.	Lab	Catalysts generally needed for complete conversion; spent peroxydisulfate can be electrochemically regenerated
UV light with O_3 and H_2O_2	N.A.	Yes	Yes	No	No	N.A.	PP	Very large power requirement, applications have been for very dilute solutions
Electrochemical oxidation	All	Yes	Yes	No	No	N.A.	Lab	
Biological oxidation	N.A.	Yes	Yes	No	No	N.A.	Lab	

Moderate-temperature, low-pressure oxidation								
Wet air and supercritical water oxidation	All	Partially	Yes	Yes?	No	Yes	PP	Residual organic components can be low for supercritical, residual materials are believed suitable for biodegradation
High-temperature, low-pressure pyrolysis								
Kiln (external heat)	All	Partially	Yes	Yes	Yes	Yes	Demo	May need more than one unit to deal with all streams
Molten metal	All	No	Yes	Yes?	Yes	Yes	PP	
Plasma arc	All	No	Yes	Yes?	Yes	Yes	Lab/PP	
Steam reforming	All	Yes	Yes	No?	No	Yes	Lab/PP	
High-temperature, low-pressure oxidation								
Catalytic, fixed bed	N.A.	N.A.	N.A.	No	No	No	Lab/PP	Useful for afterburner
Catalytic, fluidized bed	All	Yes	Yes	Yes	No	Yes	PP	
Molten salt	All	Yes	Yes	Yes?	No	Yes	Pp	Possible use for afterburner and acid gas removal
Combustion	All	Yes	Yes	Yes	Yes	Yes	—	Baseline technology

(continued)

Table 21.7 (continued) Summary of Process Capabilities and Status

	Stream Treated							
	Agent			*Metal and Energetics*				
Process	*Initial Agent Detox*	*Complete Organic Oxidation*	*Need Gas Afterburner*	*Energetics*	*Metal*	*Afterburner Needed*	*Next Step*	*Comments*
Other technologies								
Hydrogenation	All	No	Yes	No	No	No	Lab	
Reaction with sulfur	All	Yes	Yes	No	No	No	Lab	

Source: National Research Council, *Alternative Technologies for the Destruction of Chemical Agents and Munitions, NRC*, National Academy Press, Washington, DC, 1993.

Notes: Question mark (?) indicates uncertainty about the noted application. N.A.: Not applicable; PP: pilot plant; Demo: demonstration; Lab: laboratory.

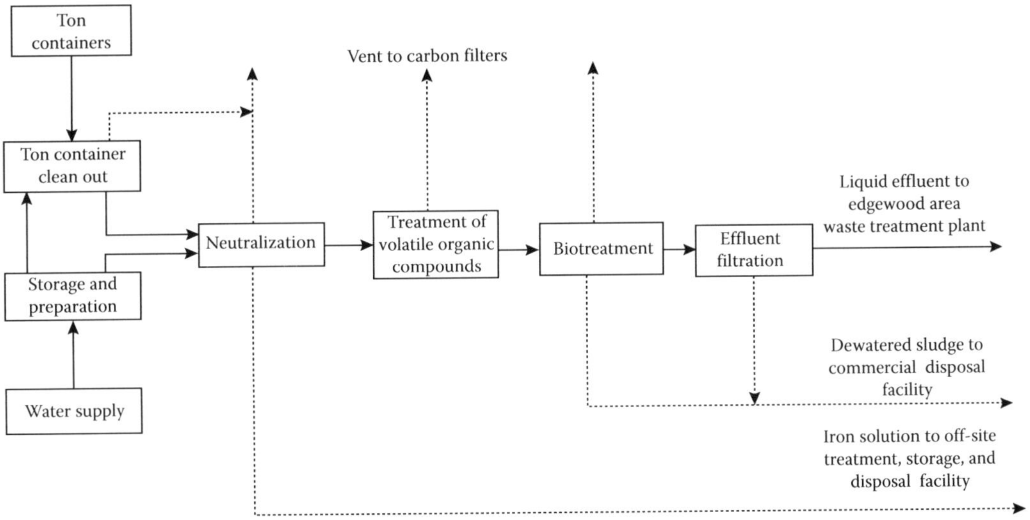

Figure 21.8 A schematic flow diagram of the neutralization process. (From Pearson, G.S. and Magee, R.S., *IUPAC Tech. Rep. Pure Appl. Chem.*, 74(2), 187, 2002. With permission.)

Neutralization by NaOH

Nerve agents (GB, VX) and mustard (H, HD, and HT) can be neutralized using alkaline solution such as aqueous NaOH under mild conditions. The toxicity of the reactions products are much lower compared to original chemical agents. This method of neutralization has been employed for destroying VX by the U.S. Army. A 20 percent aqueous sodium hydroxide solution at 90°C (20.6 mass %) has been used by the U.S. Army to destroy VX in about six hours. Both the VX and other reaction by-products are neutralized by NaOH according to the reactions shown in the following text.

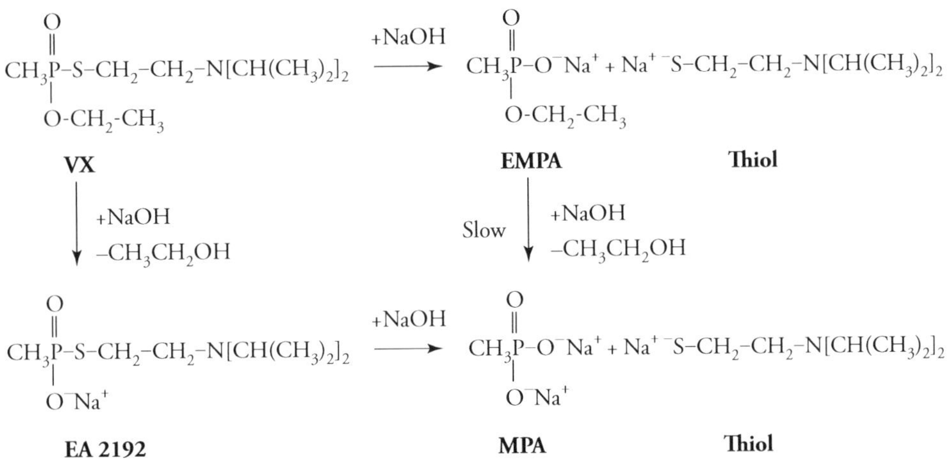

Neutralization Using Amines and Other Chemicals

Mustard and nerve agents can be reacted with monoethanolamine, and VX with potassium isobutylate (potassium 2-methyl-1-propoxide) at 100°C under atmospheric pressure for about an hour to convert these agents to less toxic chemicals. The resulting reaction products can be either incinerated or again react with bitumen to form solid blocks for burial. The reactions with amines are as follows:

Mustard gas neutralization:

$$S(CH_2CH_2Cl)_2 + 3H_2NCH_2CH_2OH = S(CH_2CH_2)_2NCH_2CH_2OH + 2H_2NCH_2CH_2OH \cdot HCl$$

GB or GD neutralization:

$$i\text{-PrO-}\overset{\overset{\displaystyle O}{\|}}{\underset{\underset{\displaystyle CH_3}{|}}{P}}\text{-F} + H_2NCH_2CH_2OH = i\text{-PrO-}\overset{\overset{\displaystyle O}{\|}}{\underset{\underset{\displaystyle CH_3}{|}}{P}}\text{-}OCH_2CH_2NH_2 + H_2NCH_2CH_2OH\cdot HF$$

Nerve agent VR (Russian VX):

$$i\text{-BuO-}\overset{\overset{\displaystyle O}{\|}}{\underset{\underset{\displaystyle CH_3}{|}}{P}}\text{-}SCH_2CH_2NEt_2 + KO\text{-}i\text{-Bu} + i\text{-BuOH} = i\text{-BuO-}\overset{\overset{\displaystyle O}{\|}}{\underset{\underset{\displaystyle CH_3}{|}}{P}}\text{-O-}i\text{-Bu} + KSCH_2CH_2NEt_2$$

Electrochemical Oxidation

In this process, the high reactivity of Ag(II) is utilized in destroying the chemical agents. Two separate 180 kW electrochemical cells, which are connected in parallel through a 360 kW power cell, are used in this system. The anode side of the cell contains an aqueous solution containing 8 M nitric acid and 0.5 M in silver nitrate. Such a cell can treat 0.02–0.03 M agent. Two cells are separated by a membrane. The cathodic compartment contains an aqueous solution of 4 M nitric acid.

The basic cell reactions for the silver II process are as follows:

Anode: $2Ag^+ \Leftrightarrow 2Ag^{++} + 2e$
Cathode: $HNO_3 + 2H^+ + 2e \Leftrightarrow HNO_2 + H_2O$

The National Research Council (NRC) reviewed the results of a test conducted at Porton Down on 14.62 kg of as supplied VX, which contained 12.7 kg of agent. The test was conducted continuously for 6.5 days. The destruction efficiency of VX was greater than 99.99998 percent. The destruction efficiency for conversion of organic carbon to CO_2 and CO was 88.7 percent.

Solvent Electron Technology

Solvent electron technology (SET) developed by Teledyne–Commodore has been tested for destruction of HD, HT, VX, and GB. An SET solution is a mixture of liquid sodium and liquid ammonia that contains about 4 percent solution of sodium. The reaction is carried out at temperatures of 19°C–23°C and pressures of 8.5–12.4 atm. The SET process, followed by hydration, can destroy chemical agents to a destruction efficiency of at least 99.9999 percent. However, considerably more testing and analysis will be required to determine the exact molecular composition, phase distribution, and quantity of reaction products.

Supercritical Water and Wet Air Oxidation

Supercritical water oxidation and wet air oxidation processes operate at temperatures above 700 K and high pressures up to 250–300 bar. Water is used as the supercritical fluid. Although this method requires high pressure and special materials of construction, it has an added advantage that other oxidants such as oxygen, hydrogen peroxide, or any other compound can be used to increase the efficiency of destruction and to reduce the production of other toxic wastes. Los Alamos National Laboratory has designed and built a high-pressure system for the destruction of explosives. It has a capacity of 400 L/day and is made out of inconel and titanium.

The feed stream is generally in the liquid form. Insoluble liquids and solids have to be processed in the form of slurries. Although pure oxygen is the best source of oxidant, compressed air can also be used. Hydrogen peroxide is another oxidant, but is more expensive.

General Atomics Corporation is building a 4000 L/day Super Critical Water Oxidation (SCWO) mobile reactor for propellants and chemical weapon agents. They report having successfully treated GB, VX, and mustard on the laboratory scale. The cost to build a unit running 20 L/minute is $2,000,000.

Hydrogenation

A second chemical method of destruction of chemical agents is by hydrogenation. This process can be used for chemicals like mustard gas but may not be suitable for nerve agents. However, Eco Logic Solutions [20] reports that their gas-phase chemical reduction process is capable of destroying in excess of 99.99 percent of VX and sulfur mustard. This process needs proper catalysts and produces hydrogen sulfide and hydrochloric acid gas as products. Although several methods have been tested for the destruction of explosives, very few methods have been tested for toxic chemicals such as nerve gases. A hydrogenation reactor under standard conditions runs at about 1 bar with threefold excess hydrogen and needs about 1–10 s of reaction time. The reactor temperature for halogenated hydrocarbons is about 850°C.

Hydrochlorination

Yet another chemical destruction method is hydrochlorination wherein dry hydrochloric acid gas is used to react with nerve agents. This method is not expected to produce toxic products, and could be carried out at temperatures between 147 and 247°C.

Advanced Oxidation Processes

Advanced oxidation processes are other alternative methods, and several variations can be researched based on the method of free radical formation. Some of the processes in this category are ozonation, Fenton's reagent, TiO_2 catalysis, and electrochemical peroxidation.

Electrochemical processes depend on Fenton's reaction that creates free radicals. The mechanism is complex but one scheme is:

$$H_2O_2 + Fe^{2+} \rightarrow Fe^{3+} + HO^- + HO^*$$

$$RH + OH^* \rightarrow R^* + H_2O$$

$$R^* + Fe^{3+} \rightarrow R^+ + Fe^{2+}$$

RH is the organic molecule, and if the reaction is carried to completion, it is expected that the organic molecule breaks down into CO_2 and water. The current status of these technologies is summarized in Table 21.8.

Equipment Decontamination

The objective of decontamination is to rapidly and effectively remove poisonous chemical agents both from personnel and equipment to avoid secondary contamination. Decontamination of personnel of chemical agents has been discussed in Chapter 20. In this section, only decontamination of equipment and other exposed surfaces are discussed. Decontamination is time consuming and requires resources; therefore, contamination should be avoided to the extent possible. Some simple measures may be taken to avoid heavy contamination. Equipment can be covered, for example, or easily decontaminated equipment can be chosen by means of suitable design and resistant surface cover.

However, it may be noted that some chemical agents such as nerve agents are highly soluble in paint, plastics, and rubber, making their surface decontamination a difficult task. Similarly, chemical agents can penetrate various materials and remain there undecomposed for a long period of time. The slow decomposition will result in a release of toxic gases for a long period of time. The level of clean up will depend on the regulatory requirement or health concern. As noted by Raber et al. [21] dose information for a number of potential chemical agents is not available or controversial. Environmental regulatory limits or health guidelines are necessary to establish cleanup concentration level. Therefore, the key issues prior to decontamination of a site or equipment are to determine exactly what constitutes a safety hazard and whether decontamination is necessary for a particular scenario. In addition, it should be kept in mind that the need and extent of decontamination can be established only by means of detection. If detection is not possible, then decontamination must be done solely on suspicion of contamination, e.g., if the unit has passed on the fringe of a contaminated area. Moreover, the detection limit of the instrument should be taken into consideration when calculating or assessing health risks.

All decontamination is based on one or more of the following principles [22]:

- To destroy CW agents by chemically modifying them (destruction)
- To physically remove CW agents by absorption, washing, or evaporation
- To physically screen-off the CW agent so that it causes no damage

Most chemical agents can be destroyed using other chemicals. However, a single chemical or a chemical mixture is not available that is effective against all types of agents. The decontaminating chemicals can be corrosive to surface or may remain in the environment creating a secondary problem.

Equipment can be decontaminated by washing and rinsing them with water containing additives such as detergents, soap, paraffin, and carburetor spirit. Emulsified solvents in water can

Table 21.8 A Summary of Emerging Processes for Destruction of Chemical Agents

Process	Hydrolysis of mustard	Hydrolysis of mustard and nerve agents using aqueous NaOH	Reaction of mustard and nerve agents using amines and other reagents	Electrochemical oxidation	Solvated electron technology
Process description	Hydrolysis with hot water	Hydrolysis with aqueous sodium hydroxide	Hydrolysis with monethanolamine followed by bitumenization of reaction products (or incineration)	Ag(II)/Ag(I) electrochemical cell	Reduction by solution of metallic sodium in anhydrous liquid ammonia
Scientific principles	Reaction of mustard with water to produce thiodiglycol and hydrochloric acid	Hydrolysis reaction products dependent on agent and neutralizing reagent concentrations	Hydrolysis reaction products dependent on agent and neutralizing reagent	Ag(II) in acidic medium is one of the most powerful oxidizing agents known	Reduction of mustard to sodium chloride and of GB to sodium fluoride. VX uncertain
Technology status	Used to detoxify mustard agent	Extensively used to detoxify mustard and GB agent	Kuasi mobile system used in Russia to destroy H, GB, and GD munitions	Yet to be operated on a commercial scale	Yet to be operated on a commercial scale
Quantity of agent destroyed	>150 kg H	>700 tons H >3800 tons GB	>300 tons H, GB, GD in Kuasi system with incineration of products	Pilot plant scale (~10 kg quantities) with HD, GB, and VX	0.64 kg HD, 0.59 kg GB, and 0.45 kg VX

(continued)

Table 21.8 (continued) A Summary of Emerging Processes for Destruction of Chemical Agents

Safety considerations	Semibatch process with nonflammable low-temperature (90°C) aqueous streams	Semibatch process with nonflammable low-temperature (90°C) aqueous streams at atmospheric pressure	Batch process with low-temperature (100°C) aqueous monoethanol-amine/RD-4 streams at. atmospheric pressure. Bitumenization at 180°C–200°C	Highly corrosive or reactive materials—aqueous concentrated nitric acid—at 90°C and atmospheric pressure	Liquid sodium and liquid ammonia are highly reactive; sodium persulfate and hydrogen peroxide solutions are reactive oxidizers
Environmental impact	Test prior to release waste salts to landfill water recycle or dilute aqueous discharge to treatment plant	Test prior to release waste salts to landfill water recycle or dilute aqueous discharge to treatment plant	Ability of bitumenized blocks to withstand leaching needs to be determined	Test prior to release aqueous waste salts with low silver concentrations	Effluents not sufficiently characterized

Source: Pearson, G.S. and Magee, R.S., *IUPAC Tech. Rep. Pure Appl. Chem.*, 74(2), 187, 2002. With permission.

be used to dissolve and wash off the agents from equipment. Heat treatment is another option for removing or evaporating agents from equipment surface; however, it may not be convenient, particularly, if the size is too large. The hot water or steam may be used as a heat source if heat treatment is deemed necessary.

Chemical agents can easily penetrate various materials and into crevasses. Water rinsing alone cannot remove the agents from the equipment. When an agent has penetrated into the surface, it is necessary to use a deep-penetrating solution. If such a method cannot be used, the equipment cannot be used for a long period. In those scenarios, the equipment should be left alone for "self-decontamination." The time necessary for self-decontamination is shown in Table 21.9. This may take many days or even weeks. The absorption into the surface and natural chemical degradation are important factors influencing the self-decontamination period. The penetration ability of a CW agent can be enhanced when it is mixed with a solvent. Chemical warfare agent resistant paints and materials may be used to protect the equipment, which implies that water-based methods will become more effective. However, such types of paints or materials are still in the development stage. A modern decontaminant is the German Münster

Table 21.9 Self-Decontamination Times for Contamination on Metal Surfaces and on a Typical (Nonresistant) Paint at +15°C, 4 m/s, and 2 mm Large Droplets

	No Contact Risk	
Substances	Liquid	Gas
Untreated metal surface		
Soman	<5 hour	<5 hour
Mustard agent	<20 hour	< 20 hour
VX	6–8 days	6–8 days
Painted metal surface		
Soman	3–4 hour	1.5 days
Mustard agent	1 day	3 days
VX	6 days	12–15 days

Source: Organization for the Prohibition of Chemical Weapons, http://www.opcw.org/our-work/assistance-and-protection/protection-against-chemical-weapons/protection/decontamination/.

Note: The times for "liquid" only indicate when the surface is free of liquid, e.g., no liquid is transferred when touched. There is still a risk involved in contact and inhalation through release of gas from surfaces where the CW agent has penetrated deeply.

emulsion which consists of calcium hypochlorite, tetrachlorethylene, emulsifier ("phase transfer" catalyst), and water. Instead of tetrachlorethylene, the more environmentally harmless xylene is sometimes used.

When decontaminating by washing, the subsequent treatment of contaminated liquid must be considered. The solution will contain trace amounts of these chemical agents and therefore need further treatment before discharging to the environment. However, often the additives present in the rinse liquid can destroy some agents making discharge of the washing liquid easier. When washing with hot water and detergent, the CW agent will often be decomposed to some extent through hydrolysis. Detergents containing perborates are particularly effective in destroying nerve agents. Without an addition of perborates in the detergent, the hydrolysis products of V-agents may still remain toxic unless the pH is sufficiently high. Mustard agent is encapsulated by the detergent and, consequently, the hydrolysis rate decreases in comparison with clean water. However, the low solubility of mustard agent makes it difficult to remove without the addition of detergent, but the water used will still contain undestroyed mustard agent.

Small areas of terrain or a contaminated site may be decontaminated by removal of the top-soil followed by incineration of the soil or through self decontamination. In the case of self-decontamination, the soil should be isolated and care must be taken to prevent leaching out due to rain. Another alternative is to cover the soil with chlorinated lime powder (sludge), which releases active chlorine slowly over a long period of time. The released chlorine vapor can react with the CW into the soil and eventually destroy them.

A contaminated site can be also covered with a layer of soil or gravel preventing direct contact with the chemical agents. However, this can only be considered a temporary solution. The chemical agent will break down or decompose over time and release toxic vapor that can diffuse through the top layer into the atmosphere and recontaminate equipment. The effect will be improved if bleaching powder is mixed into the covering material. However, this can create a corrosive environment.

Various techniques have been experimented for rapid decontamination of equipment. The Safety Equipment Development AB of Sweden has developed a decontamination tent for decontamination of personal equipment and lighter articles. The tent is heated with a mixture of hot exhaust gases and air from a small jet-pulse engine. The temperature in the tent is kept at about 130°C and in the container at 80°C–130°C, depending on the type of material to be decontaminated. Decontamination time varies between two and five hours depending on the temperature.

Decontamination of vehicles and other large objects, sometimes, is done with steam and suspension or emulsion systems. Alfred Karcher GmbH & Co./VPS of Germany has developed a special equipment, C8-DADS (Direct Application Decontamination System), in which the emulsion is prepared and then dispersed onto the vehicle or the terrain.

Sandia National Laboratory (SNL) in the United States is developing decontaminating foam for destroying chemical agents. Several tests were conducted with chemical agent simulants. The chemical agent simulants used were diphenyl chlorophosphate (simulant for G-agents), 2-chlorethyl phenylsulfide (simulant for H-agents), and *O*-ethyl-*S*-ethyl phenylphosphonothioate (simulant for VX). Testing was done via solution tests where the agent was added to the decontamination foam and surface tests in which the agent was placed on a surface which was then exposed to the foam. The decontamination foam did not generate any toxic or hazardous by-products.

Tests were also conducted using actual agents. The test results for foam decontamination of paper with GD, VX, and HD are given in Figure 21.9. The half-lives for the decontamination of these CW agents by the foam are on the order of 2–15 minutes.

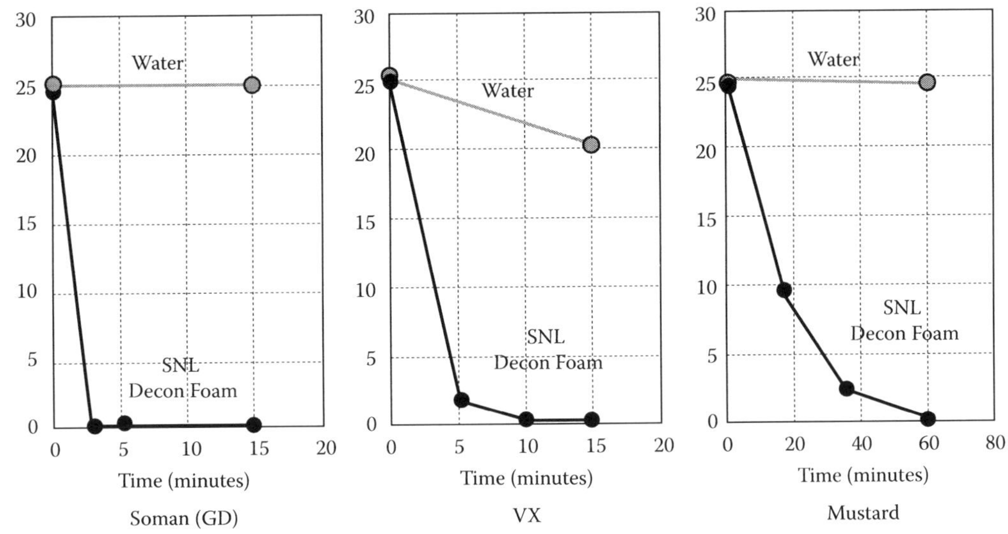

Figure 21.9 Decontamination of paper treated with chemical agent at 25 mg/25 cm^2. Foam was applied on contaminated paper for a given duration. Residual simulant on the paper and in the foam were determined by Gas Chromatography (GC) and added to determine total unreacted agent. (From Sandia National Laboratory, SNL Decon Formulation for Mitigation and Decontamination of CBW Agents, Decontamination Performance for Chemical Agent Simulants, www.nwmp.sandia.gov/SNLdecon/democ/demo1.htm.)

References

1. RW Shaw and MJ Cullinane. Destruction of military toxic materials. In *The Encyclopedia of Environmental Analysis and Remediation*, Vol. 8, R.A. Meyers, Ed., Wiley, New York, 1998. http://www.aro.army.mil/chemb/people/milremed.html
2. National Research Council. *Alternative Technologies for the Destruction of Chemical Agents and Munitions, NRC*, National Academy Press, Washington, DC, 1993.
3. M Heyl and R McGuire, Eds. *Analytical Chemistry Associated with the Destruction of Chemical Weapons*, Kluwer Academic Publishers, Hingham, MA, 1997.
4. AE Smithson. *The Bulletin of Atomic Scientists*. NTI: Country Overview, April 1993.
5. M Renner. *Bonn International Center for Conversion*, Brief 6, Bonn, Germany, 1996.
6. Organisation for the Prohibition of Chemical Weapon. Timeline of Destruction. http://www.opcw.org/our-work/demilitarisation/destruction-timelines/, 11/15/2008.
7. Organisation for the Prohibition of Chemical Weapon. http://www.opcw.org/
8. General Accounting Office. Chemical Weapons: Destruction Schedule Delays and Cost Growth Continue to Challenge Program Management, GAO-04-634T, April 1, 2004.
9. Federation of American Scientists. U.S. Chemical Weapons Facility. http://www.fas.org/nuke/guide/usa/cbw/cw.htm, 11/15/2008.
10. U.S. Army Chemical Materials Agency. Creating a Safer Tomorrow. http://www.cma.army.mil/#, 11/15/2008.
11. General Accounting Office. Cooperative Threat Reduction: DOD Needs More Reliable Data to Better Estimate the Cost and Schedule of the Shchuch'ye Facility, GAO-06-692, May 2006.
12. Disposal of Chemical Weapons: Alternate Technologies, Congress of the United States, Office of Technology Assessment, 1992.

13. M Bowers. The disposal of surplus chemical weapons. In *Coping with Surplus Weapons: A Priority for Conversion Research and Policy*. EJ Laurence and H Wulf, Eds., Chapter 3. Bonn International Center for Conversion, Bonn, Germany, 1995.
14. Report of the NATO Advanced Research Workshop on Destruction of Military Toxic Waste, Naaldwijk, the Netherlands, May 22–27, 1994.
15. National Research Council. Committee on Review and Evaluation of the Army Chemical Stockpile Disposal Program, *A Modified Baseline Incineration Process for Mustard Projectiles at Pueblo Chemical Depot*, Board on Army Science and Technology, National Academy Press, Washington, DC, 2001.
16. National Research Council. Committee on Review and Evaluation of the Army Chemical Stockpile Disposal Program, *Review of Systematization of the Tooele Chemical Agent Disposal Facility*, Appendix B, p. 92, National Academy Press, Washington, DC, 1996. As reported in Ref. 17.
17. GS Pearson and RS Magee. Critical evaluation of proven chemical weapon destruction technologies, *IUPAC Tech Rep Pure Appl Chem* 74(2): 187–316, 2002.
18. KR Bruce, J Lee, D Freed, and L Herdey. Evaluation of plasma based thermal treatment system for destruction of difficult to remediate wastes. *Proceedings of International Conference on Incineration and Thermal Treatment Technologies*, Salt Lake City, UT, May 11–15, 1998.
19. Science Applications International Corporation. Assessment of Plasma Arc Technology of Processing of Chemical Demilitarization Wastes, DAAD13-01-D-0007, Task T-02-AT-003, October 2002.
20. Eco Logic's Gas Phase Chemical Reduction Process. http://www.eco-logic intl.com, 11/15/2008.
21. E Raber, A Jin, K Noonan, R McGuire, and RD Kirvel. Decontamination issues for chemical and biological warfare agents: How clean is clean enough? *Int J Environ Health Res*, 11(2): 128–148, 2001.
22. Organization for the Prohibition of Chemical Weapons. Decontamination of Chemical Warfare Agents. An Introduction to Methods and Chemical for Decontamination. www.opcw.nl/chemhaz/decon.htm
23. Organization for the Prohibition of Chemical Weapons. http://www.opcw.org/our-work/assistance-and-protection/protection-against-chemical-weapons/protection/decontamination/
24. Sandia National Laboratory. SNL Decon Formulation for Mitigation and Decontamination of CBW Agents. Decontamination Performance for Chemical Agent Simulants. www.nwmp.sandia.gov/SNLdecon/democ/demo1.htm

Chapter 22

Chemical Terrorism: Sensors and Detection Systems

Mark A. Prelas and Tushar K. Ghosh

CONTENTS

Introduction 411
Standoff Detection Systems for Chemical Agents 412
Point Detection Methods 415
Techniques for Chemical Vapor Detection 417
Canine 418
Analysis of Canine 418
Gas Chromatograph 419
Analysis of GC 419
Detection Tickets (Colorimetric Method) 420
Ionization-Based Sensors 421
Electron Capture Detector 421
Analysis of ECD 422
Analysis of ECD Combined with GC (ECD/GC) 423
Ion Mobility Spectrometry 423
Analysis of IMS 424
Field Ion Spectrometry 424
Analysis of FIS 425
Mass Spectroscopy 425
Tandem Mass Spectrometer 425
Analysis of TMS 425

UV-IR-Photons Spectroscopy 426
Chemiluminescence 426
Analysis of Chemiluminescence 426
Analysis of Chemiluminescence Combined with GC 427
Raman Scattering 427
Analysis of Raman Scattering 427
Absorption Spectroscopy 428
Analysis of AS 429
Optical Fiber Sensors 429
Analysis of OFS 429
Acoustic-to-Optic Tunable Filters 430
Analysis of ATOFs 430
Laser Induced Breakdown Spectroscopy 430
Terahertz Spectroscopy 430
Sensors Based on Electromagnetic Wavelengths of Millimeter and Beyond 431
Nuclear Magnetic Resonance 431
Analysis of NMR 431
Millimeter Electromagnetic Wave 432
Analysis of MEW 432
Methods That Use Piezoelectric Effects 432
Gas Chromatograph/Surface Acoustic Wave 432
Analysis of GC/SAW 432
Quartz Crystal Microbalance 432
Analysis of QCM 433
Thermal Techniques 433
Thermo-Redox 433
Analysis of TR 434
Surface Effect 434
Charge-Deep Level Transient Spectroscopy 434
Analysis of Q-DLTS 435
Conductivity-Based Sensors 435
Analysis of CBS 435
Metal-Oxide-Silicon Field-Effect Transistor 435
Analysis of MOSFET 436
Radiation-Based Sensors 436
X-Rays 436
Analysis of X-Ray Detection 436
Neutron-Based Detection Systems 437
Thermal Neutron Activation 437
Analysis of TNA 438
Portable Isotopic Neutron Spectroscopy 438
Analysis of PINS 439
Pulsed Fast Neutron Analysis 439
Analysis of PFNA 439
Methods Based on Surface Wipes 439
Analysis of Surface Wipes 440

Antibody-Based Biosensors 440
Analysis of ABBs 440
Antibody-Coated Oscillator 441
Analysis of Antibody-Coated Sensor 441
Conclusions 442
References 443
Bibliography 444

Introduction

The detection of chemical agents is important. One of the worst scenarios is to identify an attack with chemical agents by observation: (1) visible cloud drifts toward the observer, (2) people fall ill and show symptoms of poisoning, and (3) observations are made on dead animals. Trace chemical sensors are a preferable means of detection. The wide deployment of trace chemical sensors is still years away, but great strides in trace chemical detection technology are being made. When these technologies come to fruition, it may be feasible to set up early warning networks in strategic areas or to identify an agent or its precursors prior to release to foil potential attacks.

The detection of chemical agents is needed to address the following basic questions:

- Is there an agent present?
- What is the agent?
- Is a mask required?
- Is body protection necessary?
- Should normal behavior be modified in any special way?
- Will the emergency response equipment require decontamination?

Detection is needed for different purposes. Ideally, a chemical detector should serve multiple purposes. One purpose is for an alarm system. Such a system would continuously monitor the environment with a sensor array for the presence of chemical agents. Such sensor arrays could serve as an advanced warning system for attack with chemical agents provided that it is easy to use, requires minimal personnel training, and is capable of triggering an alarm if a defined minimal level of chemical agent is detected. It is also important that the sensor indicates when the contaminated area is safe because it is very difficult to work in protective clothing and it is desirable to minimize personnel time in the clothing. The sensor should be useful in the verification and identification of agents. Decisions on how to respond to a chemical attack require that you know the type of agent and its concentration. Different types of detection require different types of equipment and methods. (For example, is the gas concentration in the air at a dangerous level, is the soil or equipment contaminated with liquid agent, is it dangerous to handle?) Sensors for mapping of the ground contamination would be valuable to indicate the bounds of the contamination.

Unfortunately, the state-of-the-art technology does not meet all of the requirements of an ideal chemical detector. Technologies which exist or are being developed show great promise in achieving the goals of an ideal detections system. The detection systems for chemical agents can also be divided into two categories:

1. Standoff detection systems
2. Point detection methods

Standoff Detection Systems for Chemical Agents

As described in Chapter 8, a standoff detection system is also necessary for chemical agents. Most of the systems described in Chapter 8 can be used for detection of chemicals with some modifications. The detection of chemicals from a distance is relatively easier compared to biological agents. The Light Detection and Ranging (LIDAR) system used for detection of biological agents can be modified by incorporating a Raman spectrometer to analyze chemical compounds. Raman spectrometer analyzes the Raman shift of the scattered light to identify chemical species. This technique is usually called Raman LIDAR. If the LIDAR technique employs two mid- or near-infrared pulsed lasers and determines the identity of chemical species by measuring the differential absorption between two pulses with similar transit times, the technique is usually called differential absorption LIDAR, or Differential Absorption Lidar (DIAL). The basic arrangements of a Raman LIDAR system is shown in Figure 22.1 [1]. It has been used by Sharma et al. [2] to detect TATB and HMX from 10 m. The Raman spectra of these two explosives are shown in Figure 22.2.

The standoff distance has been extended to 100 m using a directly coupled *f*/2.2 spectrograph with a small (125 mm diameter) telescope and a frequency-doubled Nd:YAG pulsed laser (20 Hz, 532 nm, 25 mJ/pulse) used as the excitation source in a coaxial geometry and to 500 m by the Brookhaven National Laboratory (BNL) using a ultraviolet (UV) laser with large collection optics [3]. Both the systems have been tested with organic compounds. The schematic diagram of the system developed by BNL, called Mobile Raman Lidar Van (MRLV), is shown in Figure 22.3.

Several researchers deployed laser-induced breakdown spectroscopy (LIBS) for the development of standoff detection systems [4]. LIBS can be used for real-time, nondestructive determination of elemental composition of the sample that requires no sample preparation. A focused Nd:YAG laser is used to produce a pulse width of a few nanoseconds. The laser pulse focused on the sample surface dissociates molecules and particulates by creating a microplasma within the sample volume. The emissions from the atomic, ionic, and molecular fragments are captured by a detector to generate the spectrum. The basic components of a LIBS experimental setup is shown in Figure 22.4. The RDX spectrum collected by an Army Research Laboratory's (ARL's) LIBS system is shown in Figure 22.5.

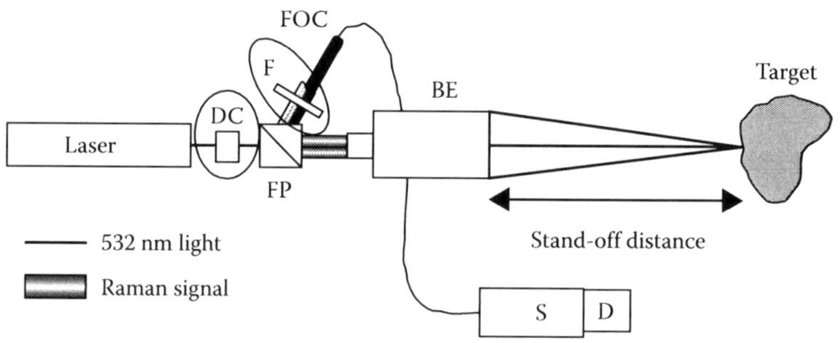

Figure 22.1 A remote Raman spectroscopy system. The system uses a Nd:YAG laser, which is frequency doubled for the Raman system. FOC, fiber optic cable; FP, beam-splitting prism; BE, beam expander; P, plasma; S, spectrograph; D, detector; DC, doubling crystal; F, notch filter for removing 532 nm photons. (From Wiens, R.C. et al., *Spectrochim. Acta Part A* 61, 2324, 2005. With permission.)

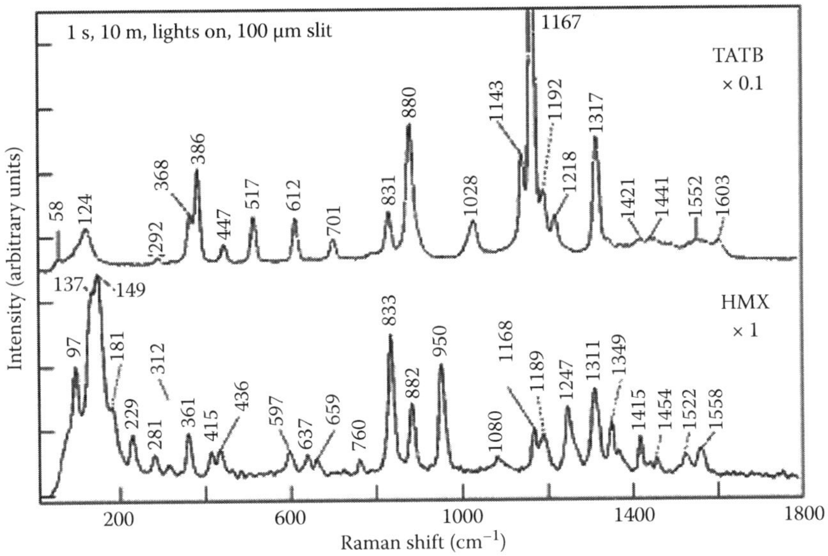

Figure 22.2 Portions of remote Raman spectra of TATB and HMX explosives at 10 m (integration time 1 s, directly coupled system). (From Sharma, S.K. et al., *Spectrochim. Acta Part A,* 61, 2404, 2005. With permission.)

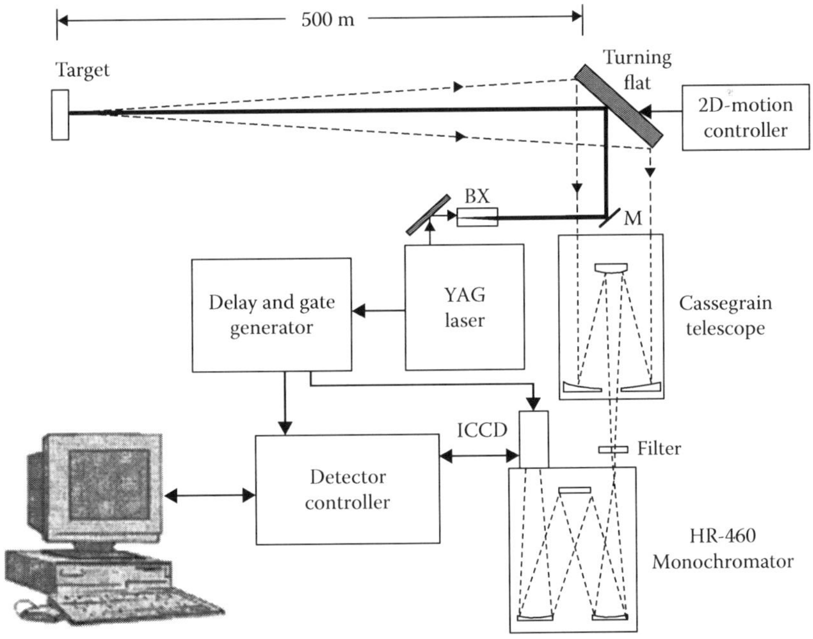

Figure 22.3 Schematic showing the components of the Brookhaven MLRV used to collect Raman returns shown in this paper. Solid or liquid targets were placed 533 m from the MLRV. (From Wu, M. et al., *Appl. Spectroscopy,* 54(6), 800, 2000. With permission.)

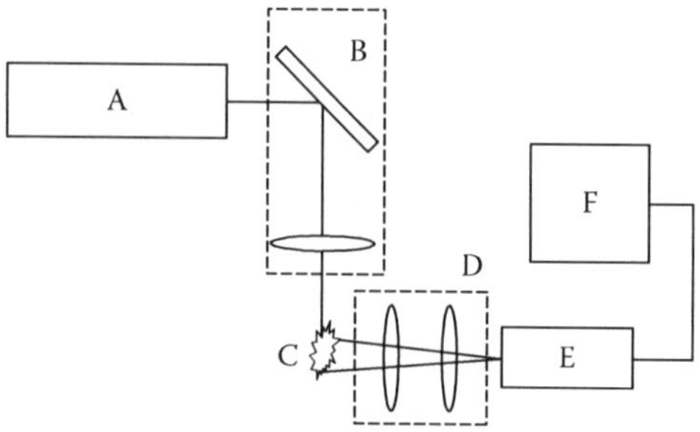

Figure 22.4 Block diagram of LIBS experimental setup (A) pulsed laser, (B) focusing optics, (C) microplasma, (D) collection optics, (E) spectrometer, and (F) data analyzer. (From Munson, C.A. et al., Laser-based detection methods for explosives, ARL-TR-4279, Army Research Laboratory, Aberdeen Proving Ground, MD, September 2007.)

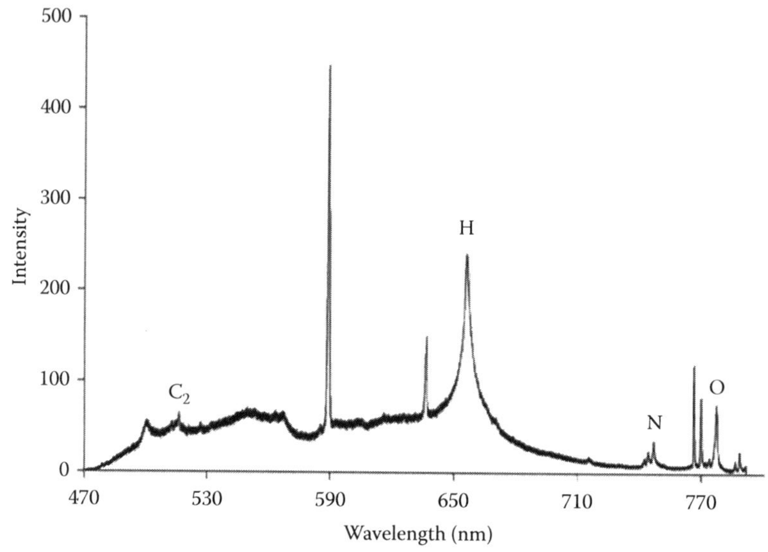

Figure 22.5 LIBS spectrum of RDX collected at 20 m with the ARL standoff LIBS system. The elements present due to RDX are labeled. (From Munson, C.A. et al., Laser-based detection methods for explosives, ARL-TR-4279, Army Research Laboratory, Aberdeen Proving Ground, MD, September 2007.)

Effort is also underway to develop terahertz (THz) spectroscopy for standoff detection [4]. Figure 22.6 shows the components of a typical terahertz spectroscopy system. It contains an ultrafast laser, emission and detection photoconductive antennas, an optical delay line, and various optics to guide and focus the laser and THz emission.

Although the THz spectrometer is capable of penetrating various materials and identify explosives, its standoff detection distance is around 1 m. Zhong [5] explored various methods to extend

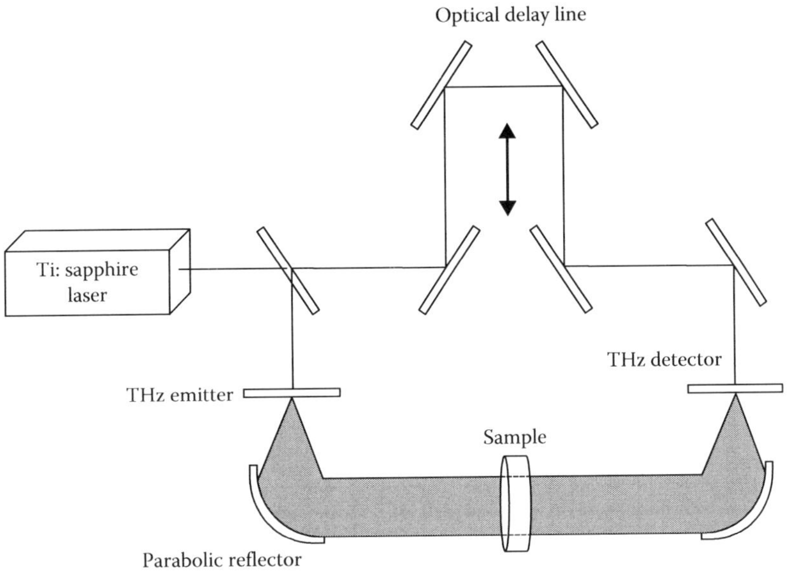

Figure 22.6 Instrument diagram of a typical THz-TDS system. In this configuration, sample transmission is being measured. (From Munson, C.A. et al., Laser-based detection methods for explosives, ARL-TR-4279, Army Research Laboratory, Aberdeen Proving Ground, MD, September 2007.)

the standoff distance. They collected absorption spectra by reflectance at distances of 2.5, 10, 20, and 30 m from the sample. The RDX absorption peak at 0.82 THz was still visible (but broadened) at 30 m.

Point Detection Methods

As described in Chapter 8, the point detection of chemicals is extremely important in combating terrorism. This type of detection system can help first responders in several ways. Point detectors can be used (1) as warning devices to alert personnel to the presence of a toxic vapor cloud, (2) to monitor the vapor contamination originating from a decontamination site, and (3) during postrelease triage to determine the contamination level. Although we are most concerned about the detection of chemical agents or chemical weapons, there are a number of chemicals that can be highly toxic, if the concentration is high. These chemical are knows as toxic industrial chemicals (TICs) or toxic industrial materials (TIMs). A TIC is a specific type of industrial chemical, that is, one that has a LCt_{50} value (lethal concentration for 50 percent of the population multiplied by exposure time) less than 100,000 mg-min/m^3 in any mammalian species and is produced in quantities exceeding 30 tons per year at one production facility. Although they are not as lethal as the highly toxic nerve agents, their ability to make a significant impact on the populace is assumed to be more related to the amount of chemical a terrorist can employ on the target(s) and less related to their lethality [6]. A list of these chemicals is given in Table 22.1.

Table 22.1 TICs Listed by Hazard Index

High	*Medium*	*Low*
Ammonia[a]	Acetone cyanohydrin	Allyl isothiocyanate
Arsine[b]	Acrolein	Arsenic trichloride
Boron trichloride	Acrylonitrile	Bromine[a]
Boron trifluoride	Allyl alcohol	Bromine chloride
Carbon disulfide	Allylamine	Bromine pentafluoride
Chlorine[a]	Allyl chlorocarbonate	Bromine trifluoride
Diborane	Boron tribromide	Carbonyl fluoride
Ethylene oxide	Carbon monoxide[b]	Chlorine pentafluoride
Fluorine	Carbonyl sulfide	Chlorine trifluoride
Formaldehyde	Chloroacetone	Chloroacetaldehyde
Hydrogen bromide	Chloroacetonitrile	Chloroacetyl chloride
Hydrogen chloride[a]	Chlorosulfonic acid	Crotonaldehyde
Hydrogen cyanide[b]	Diketene	Cyanogen chloride[b]
Hydrogen fluoride	1,2-Dimethylhydrazine	Dimethyl sulfate
Hydrogen sulfide	Ethylene dibromide	Diphenylmethane-4,4′-diisocyanate
Nitric acid, fuming	Hydrogen selenide	Ethyl chloroformate
Phosgene[a]	Methanesulfonyl chloride	Ethyl chlorothioformate
Phosphorus trichloride	Methyl bromide[a]	Ethyl phosphonothioic dichloride
Sulfur dioxide	Methyl chloroformate	Ethyl phosphonic dichloride
Sulfuric acid	Methyl chlorosilane	Ethyleneimine
Tungsten hexafluoride	Methyl hydrazine	Hexachlorocyclopentadiene
	Methyl isocyanate[a]	Hydrogen iodide
	Methyl mercaptan	Iron pentacarbonyl
	Nitrogen dioxide	Isobutyl chloroformate
	Phosphine[a]	Isopropyl chloroformate
	Phosphorus oxychloride	Isopropyl isocyanate
	Phosphorus pentafluoride	*n*-Butyl chloroformate
	Selenium hexafluoride	*n*-Butyl isocyanate
	Silicon tetrafluoride	Nitric oxide
	Stibine	*n*-Propyl chloroformate

Table 22.1 (continued) TICs Listed by Hazard Index

High	*Medium*	*Low*
	Sulfur trioxide	Parathion
	Sulfuryl chloride	Perchloromethyl mercaptan
	Sulfuryl fluoride[a]	*sec*-Butyl chloroformate
	Tellurium hexafluoride	*tert*-Butyl isocyanate
	n-Octyl mercaptan	Tetraethyl lead
	Titanium tetrachloride	Tetraethyl pyrophosphate
	Trichloroacetyl chloride	Tetramethyl lead
	Trifluoroacetyl chloride	Toluene 2,4-diisocyanate
		Toluene 2,6-diisocyanate

Source: U.S. Department of Homeland Security, *Guide for the Selection of Personal Protective Equipment for Emergency First Responders*, 2nd edn., Guide 102-06, January 2007.

[a] Choking agent.

[b] Blood agent.

TIC rankings: TICs are ranked into one of the three categories based on their hazards: high, medium, or low hazard. In addition, blood and choking agents are also identified.

High hazard: High hazard indicates a widely produced, stored, or transported TIC that has high toxicity and is easily vaporized.

Medium hazard: Medium hazard indicates a TIC that may rank high in some categories but lower in others, such as number of producers, physical state, or toxicity.

Low hazard: Low hazard indicates that this TIC is not likely to be a hazard unless specific operational factors indicate otherwise.

Blood agents: A blood agent is a TIC, which typically includes the cyanide group, affecting bodily functions by preventing the normal utilization of oxygen by body tissues. The term "blood agent" is a misnomer, however, because these agents do not actually affect the blood in any way. Rather, they exert their toxic effect at the cellular level by interrupting the electron transport chain in the inner membrane of mitochondria.

Choking agents: A choking agent (or pulmonary agent) is a TIC designed to impede a victim's ability to breathe, resulting in suffocation. Choking agents were preferred in WWI but have lost much of their tactical destructive utility since the invention of nerve agents. Choking agents are lethal and are very easily obtained.

Techniques for Chemical Vapor Detection

It is important to note that technology is available for the detection of trace chemicals. A number of technologies are being used in the field, are well along in development or potentially could be developed. These methods can be used solely for explosives or for a variety of chemical agents. Here a number of methods for detecting chemical vapors are discussed along with their potential uses.

These methods are divisible into several categories each with strengths and weaknesses. A discussion of each category of trace chemical detector is described. One should pay attention to the detection time, sensitivity, portability, cost, data gathering, and ability to differentiate different chemical agents. A definition of each of these categories is given below:

- The detection time is defined as the time that it takes the detector to respond to the presence of vapors from a chemical agent or a high explosive.
- The sensitivity of the detector is defined as the minimum amount of chemical vapor or high explosive material that the detector will respond to. This may be defined in parts per billion in air or in nanograms. Some sensors respond in real time to the vapor being flowed through its active region. In this case, parts per billion in air is a direct correlation of the sensor's ability to distinguish vapors in air. Some sensors can accumulate molecules on a detector surface over a long sampling time. In this case, the use of nanograms provides the most accurate information on sensitivity.
- The portability of the detector system is comprised of the size, volume, and mass of the system.
- The cost of the detector system is the combination of purchase price, operational costs, and maintenance costs of the system.
- Data gathering is the ability to detect multiple chemical agents with a single sensor system.
- Differentiation is defined as the ability of the detector to differentiate between chemical agents.
- Field deployed indicates if the unit has been deployed in the field and field-tested.
- Suitability indicates the technology's potential for use in the field as a general chemical sensor.

Before discussing various detection technologies, it is worth mentioning the role of canines in detection of chemicals and drugs. So far, there are no systems available that can match the sensitivity of a well-trained canine in detecting chemicals.

Canine

Canine explosive detection is a unique category. Trained dogs have been used in the field successfully for a very long time. Dogs are able to detect small amounts of drugs or explosive material and are able to distinguish types of explosive if properly trained. No chemical sensor has been able to match a "dog's nose" for sensitivity. For example, dogs are a key component for the South African Mechem Explosive and Drug Detection System (MEDDS) [7,8]. In the MEDDS, a chemical concentrator system is used to collect vapors and this collected material is passed by the dog's nose. Dogs should be able to detect other types of chemical agents or their precursors, if properly trained.

There are problems however; dogs are only able to work for about two hours at a time and not always able to perform at peak condition. In addition, dogs have a 95 percent success rate.

Analysis of Canine

Dogs have been field deployed. They do not appear to be a practical alternative for a portable field unit. The portability of the canine is of concern. A working period of two hours per canine requires that a large pool of canines must be available for continuous monitoring. Additionally, each animal is unique; thus the operation and result from animal to animal would be slightly different. Finally, a success rate of 95 percent is good.

- Detection time: seconds
- Sensitivity: excellent (better than man-made chemical detectors)
- Portability: poor
- Cost: moderate
- Data gathering: low
- Differentiation: potentially excellent depending on the training
- Field deployed: yes

Most of the analytical instruments used for detection of chemical compounds consist of two sections: (1) separation of chemical species from the mixture and (2) detectors. Even when the sample is taken from air, it should be noted that the bulk of the constituents of the sample is still nitrogen and oxygen. Therefore, the targeted chemicals either need to be concentrated in the sample or isolated from the gas mixture before sending to the detector. A number of analytical instruments couple a gas chromatograph (GC) with a detector for identification and quantification (the instrument needs to be calibrated with known concentrations of the targeted chemical compound).

Gas Chromatograph

A GC uses a column of material(s) in which gases of different mass diffuse at different rates, which is the mechanism for differentiation. Depending on the gases to be analyzed, the column materials, its length, and diameter will differ. Lighter gases will have a higher rate of diffusion than a heavier gas. Thus, the time it takes for gas molecules to move through the column is directly related to the mass of the gas molecule. The time it takes from the sample introduction into the column to its exit from the column is the parameter used to distinguish between gas molecules. GCs are typically combined with other sensor technology.

Analysis of GC

As a stand-alone unit, a GC has been field deployed. It has very little utility in field use. However, combined with other sensors, as will be described, it is a very useful technology.

- Detection time: 10–15 s
- Sensitivity: good to excellent (depending on sensor technology)
- Portability: excellent
- Cost: low
- Data gathering: high
- Differentiation: excellent
- Field deployed: yes

Based on the working principle, the point detection technologies may be divided into the following categories:

- Detection tickets (colorimetric method)
- Ionization-based sensors

- UV-IR-photon spectroscopy
- Sensors based on electromagnetic wavelengths of millimeter and beyond
- Methods that use piezoelectric effects
- Thermal techniques
- Surface effect-based sensor
- Radiation-based sensors
- Methods based on surface wipes (SW)
- Antibody-based biosensors (ABBs)

Detection Tickets (Colorimetric Method)

Current detection methods include detection (enzyme) tickets and detection tubes which can be used for nerve agents and mustard agent under field conditions. A manual suction pump is used to draw air through the detection tube or against the ticket. There is a development process to determine the agent.

Detection (enzyme) tickets consist of two parts, one with enzyme-impregnated paper and the other with substrate-impregnated paper. When the package is broken and the enzyme paper wetted, the substrate part is exposed to the agent by means of a pump. The two parts are put together. If the enzyme part of the ticket has turned it to a light blue color, the nerve agent is present in the air. The detection limit is about 0.02–0.05 mg/m^3. The active enzyme, some form of cholinesterase is used, changes to a blue color in the presence of nerve agents:

$$\text{2,6-Dichloroindophenylacetate (red)} + \text{cholinesterase produces 2,6-dichloroindophenol (blue)}$$

The detection tube for mustard agent is a glass tube containing silica gel impregnated with a substrate (DB-3). Sample air is sucked through the tube using a special pump. Using heat, a reaction occurs between the mustard agent and the substrate. A developer is then added. If the silica gel in the tube turns blue, then the sample contains mustard agent.

Substrate reaction with mustard:

$$Cl(CH_2)_2S(CH_2)_2Cl \text{ (mustard agent)} + \text{pyridine-}CH_2\text{-}p\text{-phenylidene-}NO_2 \\ \text{(4-(4-nitrobenzyl)pyridine, colorless)}$$

Reacts at 110°C, in the presence of NaOH to provide

$$Cl(CH_2)_2S(CH_2)_2N = CH\text{-pyridine-}NO_2 \text{ (1-[1-[2-(2-chloroethylthio)etyl]-1,} \\ \text{4-dihydro-4-pyridylidenmethyl]-4-nitrobenzene, blue)}$$

In mapping of ground contamination, it is necessary to map which parts of an area are contaminated with CW agents in liquid form. In this case, detection paper has been the method of choice. Detection paper (e.g., M9 and M8 chemical agent detector papers) is based on certain dyes that are soluble in CW agents. Two dyes and one pH indicator are used, which are mixed with cellulose fibers in a paper without coloring. The chemical agent is absorbed by the paper, and it dissolves one of the pigments. Mustard agent dissolves a red dye and nerve agent a yellow dye. This means that colorless paper will turn red for mustard agent, and similarly it will turn yellow for nerve agent. In addition, VX causes the indicator to turn to blue which, together with the yellow, will become green/green–black. There is a disadvantage in that many other substances can also dissolve the pigments. Consequently, detection paper should not be located in places where drops of solvent, fat, oil, or fuel can fall on them. Drops of water give no reaction. A droplet of 0.5 mm diameter creates a spot sized about 3 mm on the paper. This size droplet corresponds to a ground contamination of about 0.5 g/m^2. The detection limit in favorable cases is 0.005 g/m^2.

Trends in detectors are very promising and are fully discussed in the next section. Some of the important developments are:

- Ion-mobility detector IMS (ion mobility spectroscopy), the chemical agent monitor (CAM), (e.g., the Finnish M86 and the more recent M90).
- Flame photometry FPD (flame photometric detector—uses a hydrogen flame that burns the sample of air, the color of the flame is examined by a photometer. The presence of phosphorus and sulfur can be seen).
- French monitor AP2C and Israeli combined detector and monitor CHASE.
- Enzymes are being developed in the United Kingdom, the Netherlands, and former Soviet Union.
- Optical methods (infrared [IR]) are being developed in the United States and France.
- Biologically active molecules as sensors-same mechanisms that influence the human body when exposed to poisoning. A simple type of biosensor is the enzyme ticket.

Ionization-Based Sensors

Ionization-based sensors use either an electrical field or a source of electrons to ionize the gas sample. A number of ionization-based sensors are described.

Electron Capture Detector

A tritium or Ni^{63} radioisotope, beta emitter, is placed opposite to a positively based electron collector (as shown in Figure 22.7). Helium or argon gas flows between the radioisotope and the collector plate.

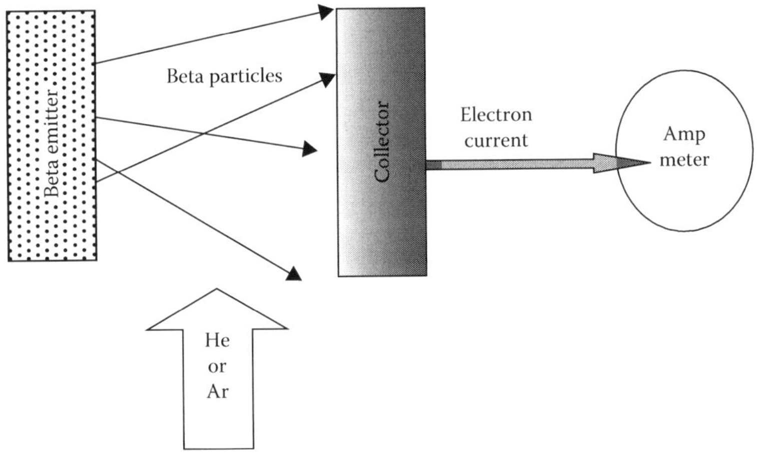

Figure 22.7 Diagram of ECD.

Interactions between helium and argon with energetic electrons are well understood. The electron current collected by the plate comes into equilibrium with its environment. If a vapor of a molecule that can form a negative ion by electron capture is introduced into the gas flow, the electron current from the collector plate is reduced. This reduction in current is related to the molecule type and its concentration. The electron capture rate is proportional to the density of the molecule.

The device is primarily used for explosives but is not able to distinguish between explosives. Also, any molecule that has a high electron capture cross section such as oxygen, carbon halides, carbon dioxide, carbon monoxide, halides, etc. will cause a false trigger.

Analysis of ECD

The stand-alone electron-capture detector (ECD) has been field deployed. It is not very useful for field use.

- Detection time: sub second
- Sensitivity: good (1 part per billion)
- Portability: excellent
- Cost: low
- Data gathering: low
- Differentiation: none
- Field deployed: yes

If the ECD is placed on the top of a GC, then the combined instrument does have the capability of differentiating explosive materials (Figure 22.8). In this case, the collector current is measured as a function of time. The time is matched to the diffusion rate of the molecule in the GC column (Figure 22.9).

Combined GC and ECD units are sold commercially like the SRIEC made by SRI Instrument, Menlo Park, CA.

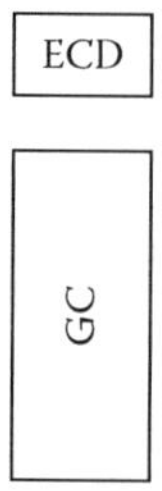

Figure 22.8 A GC combined with ECD.

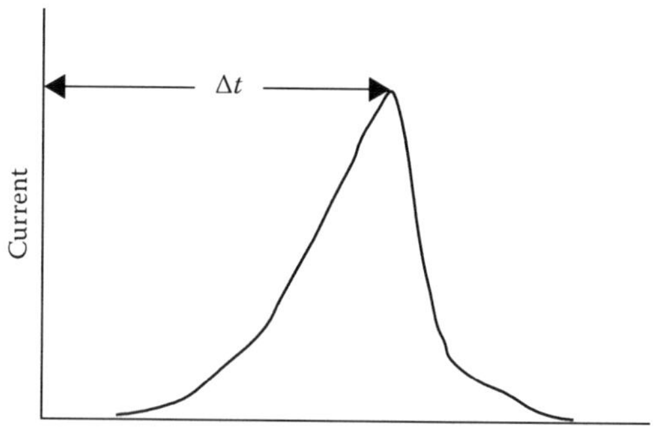

Figure 22.9 The current is measured as a function of time. The time delay, *Δt*, is related to the diffusion time of the molecule in the GC.

Analysis of ECD Combined with GC (ECD/GC)

The ECD combined with a GC has been field deployed. It is able to differentiate explosives in about 18 s with a sensitivity of 1 part per billion. The sensitivity may be adequate for TNT depending on the sealing method that is used, but not for plastic explosives (e.g., RDX). A great deal of data can be gathered with the combined ECD and GC.

- Detection time: about 18 s
- Sensitivity: good (1 part per billion)
- Portability: excellent
- Cost: low
- Data gathering: high
- Differentiation: excellent
- Field deployed: yes

Ion Mobility Spectrometry

The principle of ion mobility spectrometry (IMS) is that in an electric field the drift velocity of an ion is mass dependent. The drift velocity, **u**, of an ion in an electric field is proportional to the electric field with the ion mobility being the proportionality constant.

$$\mathbf{u} = \mu \mathbf{E} \qquad (22.1)$$

where
u is the drift velocity of the ion,
μ is the ion mobility, and
E is the electric field vector (bold symbol represents a vector quantity).

Based on the length of time that it takes for an ion to travel a fixed distance, the ion mass can be determined. The IMS is constructed to first create ions with an ionization source. The ions enter a region of known electric field through a grid electrode and then drift toward an ion collector (see Figure 22.10).

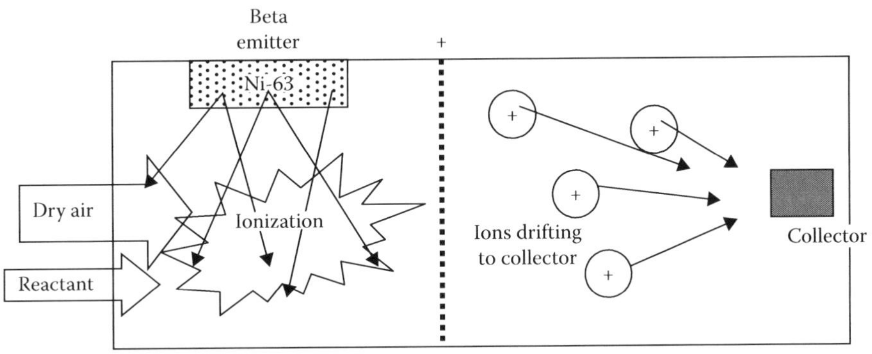

Figure 22.10 Diagram of the IMS.

A number of commercial units based on IMS are available. For example, the Itemiser E and Exfinder 152 are both manufactured by AI Cambridge Ltd. Another unit, which is manufactured in Russia, is the MO_2 portable high-sensitivity explosives vapor detector produced by the Institute of Applied Physics.

Analysis of IMS

IMS technology has been field deployed. It is a viable technology for use in the field. It is sensitive, can differentiate, is portable, and is of low cost. IMS can generate a large amount of data on multiple chemicals. IMS is very adaptable.

- Detection time: about 5–8 s
- Sensitivity: good (sub-nanogram)
- Portability: excellent
- Cost: low
- Data gathering: high
- Differentiation: excellent
- Field deployed: yes

Field Ion Spectrometry

Field ion spectrometry (FIS) is similar to IMS. In FIS, a transverse electric field (meaning perpendicular to the path between the grid and the collector) with both an AC (alternating current) and DC (direct current) component is added (see Figure 22.11). Based on the ion mass, the rate at which the ion moves transverse to the collection path is dependent upon the mass of the ion. When the DC component of the transverse field is varied, a spectrum of ion current is collected. The data collected will be a curve in which DC voltage is plotted on the x-axis and the ion current on the y-axis. The FIS data is manipulated mathematically and is converted into a plot of mass versus dc voltage. In the IMS, time is plotted on the x-axis and ion current on the y-axis.

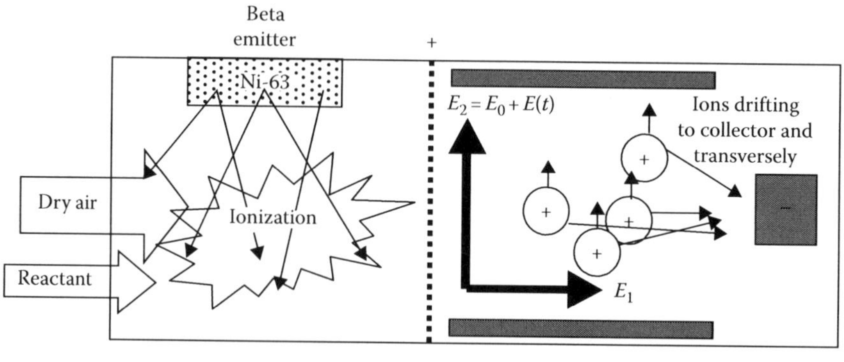

Figure 22.11 Diagram of FIS. The collector path electric field is E_1 while the transverse electric field is E_2, which is made up of a DC component E_0 and a time-dependent component $E(t)$. The field E_0 is varied to obtain data.

The IMS data is manipulated mathematically and is converted into a plot of mass versus time. The advantage of the FIS is that the sample can be continuously introduced into the spectrometer while the IMS requires the grid field and sample introduction to be timed with a pulsing mechanism.

Analysis of FIS

FIS has been field deployed. It is a viable technology for use in the field. It is sensitive, and can differentiate, is portable and cheap. FIS can be used for multiple chemical agents and thus can provide a large amount of data.

- Detection time: about 2 s
- Sensitivity: excellent (picogram)
- Portability: excellent (size about 0.8 ft^3)
- Cost: low
- Data gathering: high
- Differentiation: excellent
- Field deployed: yes

Mass Spectroscopy

Mass spectroscopy (MS) in general uses an ionization region to break the molecule into fragments of different masses followed by some combination of electromagnetic fields to separate ions of different masses. MS is very sensitive, reliable, and viable for use in the field. Many system configurations are possible beyond those described here. A major consideration for a specific MS configuration is its level of development. Some MS configurations are well developed but are not suitable for field use. For example, a number of systems such as the time-of-flight mass spectrometer are not portable.

Tandem Mass Spectrometer

Oak Ridge National Laboratory is developing a tandem mass spectrometer (TMS). The TMS has a high efficiency ion source. The system is in the testing phase but is not field deployable, yet. This system is mentioned because of its high sensitivity that may be of interest for future considerations.

Analysis of TMS

At this point TMS has not been field deployed. It is, however, a promising technology.

- Detection time: several minutes
- Sensitivity: excellent (sub-picogram)
- Portability: unknown
- Cost: unknown
- Data gathering: high
- Differentiation: excellent
- Field deployed: no

UV-IR-Photons Spectroscopy

A number of chemical sensing methods depend on the absorption, scattering, or emission of UV and IR.

Chemiluminescence

When a chemical vapor of certain nitrogen-rich explosives is heated, the gas NO is created. Using this principle, it is possible to build a chemiluminescence (ChL) sensor. The sensor works by interacting the NO with a stream of ozone (O_3) to form NO_2^* (see Figure 22.12). The superscript "*" indicates an excited vibrational state in NO_2. This excited vibrational state in NO_2^* emits an IR sensitive to photomultiplier (PM) tube. The signal from the PM tube is directly proportional to the NO or NO_2 concentration. A density of the chemical vapor from the explosive sample can be related to the amount of NO produced by heating.

The ChL detector is not explosive specific because most nitrogen-rich explosives will produce NO by this method.

Analysis of Chemiluminescence

As a stand-alone high explosive chemical vapor sensor, ChL is able to give a positive or negative result. It is not able to distinguish between explosive materials.

- Detection time: 10 s
- Portability: good
- Cost: good
- Data gathering: low
- Differentiation: none
- Field deployed: yes

Combining a ChL detector with a GC does provide a system that can differentiate between explosives.

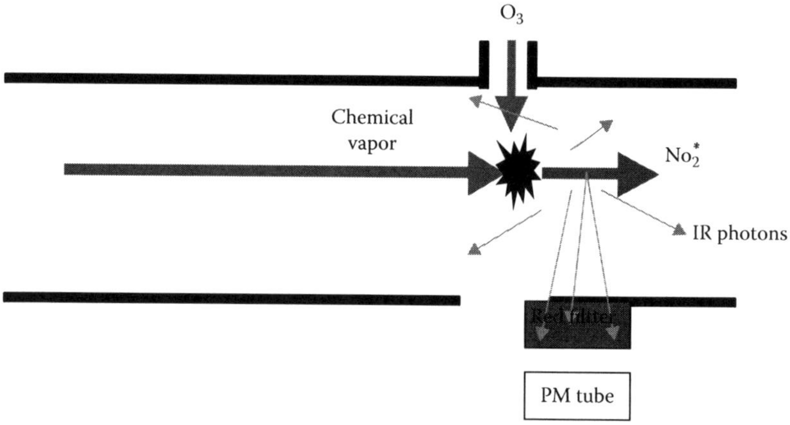

Figure 22.12 A diagram of the ChL detector.

Analysis of Chemiluminescence Combined with GC

A ChL/GC detector has been field deployed for high explosives. A combined ChL with a GC is able to distinguish between explosive materials. The sensor is not capable of being used to sense anything other than an explosive because only chemical vapors from nitrogen-rich compounds can form NO. Thus it has a low data-gathering potential. Chemical vapors from other agents are not detectable.

- Detection time: 18 s
- Sensitivity: excellent (sub-picogram)
- Portability: good
- Cost: moderate
- Data gathering: moderate to high
- Differentiation: excellent
- Field deployed: yes

Raman Scattering

"When a beam of light passes through a solid, liquid, or gas a small part of the scattered radiation has the wavelength shifted by a constant amount. The constant change in wavelength or frequency is characteristic of the material which is scattering the light, and corresponds to the frequency of vibration or the frequency of rotation of the molecules of the material. This particular type of scattering is Raman scattering [9]." Even though commercial chemical vapor sensors using Raman scattering (RS) are not common, RS is nonetheless very powerful. The system is relatively simple to construct (see Figure 22.13).

Analysis of Raman Scattering

RS is an effective chemical sensing system that has not been field deployed so far in this application. It can be made portable, sensitive, and can differentiate between chemical vapors. The question is how sensitive it will be to chemical vapors from the scattering by specific agents. For example, graphite scatters 50 times more light than diamond despite the fact that both materials are made of carbon.

- Detection time: sub-second
- Sensitivity: unknown (material-dependent)
- Portability: good

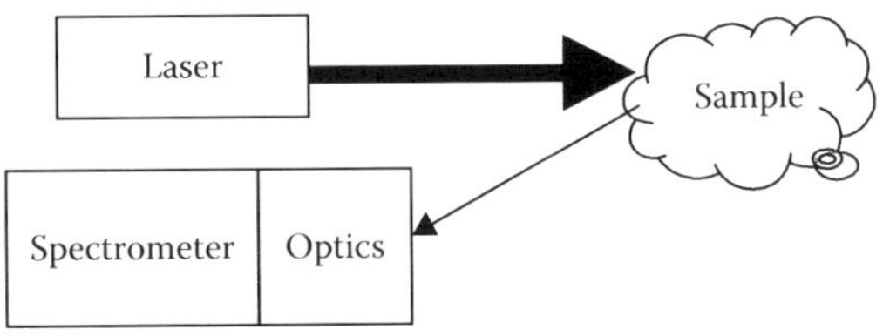

Figure 22.13 Illustration of a RS system.

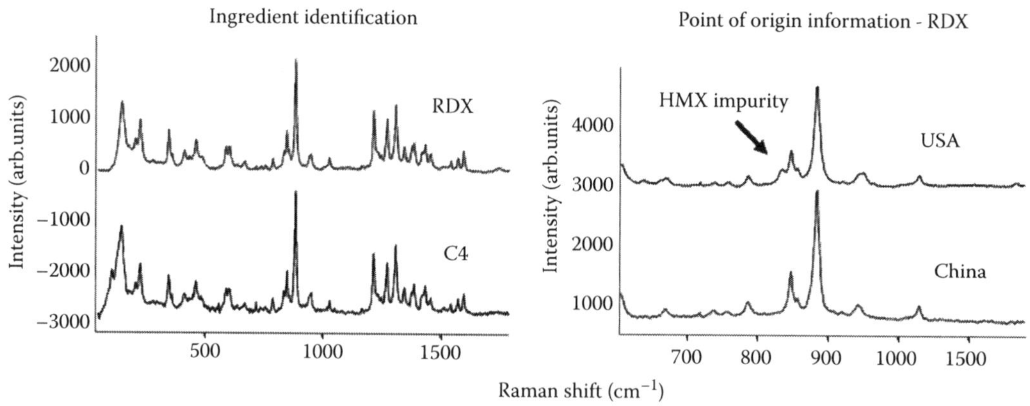

Figure 22.14 FT-Raman spectra of the explosive formulation C-4, its main ingredient RDX, and samples of RDX of different origins. The exciting laser wavelength was 1064 nm.

- Cost: moderate
- Data gathering: high
- Differentiation: excellent
- Field deployed: no

Raman spectrometer is becoming a powerful tool for analyzing explosives. It is possible to detect various trace impurities that are present in the explosives, which can provide a means for identifying its origin. In Figure 22.14 is shown the analysis of C-4 explosives and its main component RDX by Raman spectroscopy. The point of origin of the explosives can be identified using the trace impurities present in them. As shown in the figure, the United States made RDX can be differentiated from the China made RDX by looking at the impurities present in these two samples.

Absorption Spectroscopy

Molecules will absorb light. The exact wavelengths and absorption cross section are dependent on the molecule's quantum structure. Absorption spectroscopy (AS) is a well-known technique. However, specific AS systems for the detection of vapors from chemical agents and explosives are not available. An AS system is relatively simple to construct (Figure 22.15).

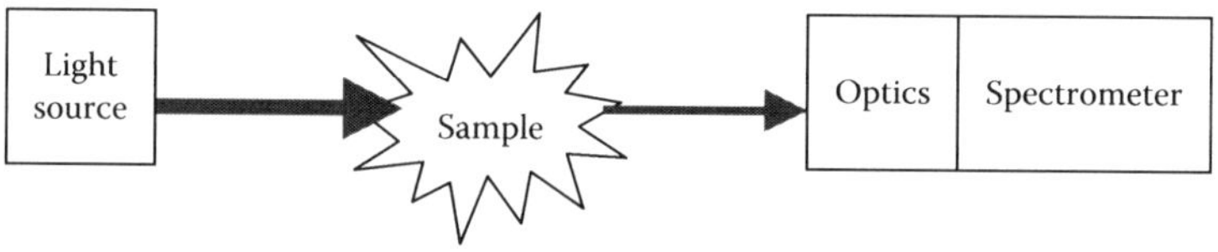

Figure 22.15 A diagram of an absorption spectroscopy system.

Analysis of AS

AS is an effective chemical sensing system that has not been field deployed for this application. It can be made portable, sensitive, and can differentiate between chemical vapors. The question is how sensitive it will be to chemical vapors from specific agents. Various materials behave differently with AS. The sensitivity is dependent on the absorption cross section at various wavelengths, the availability of optics at the absorption wavelengths, the availability of a spectrometer for the absorption wavelengths, and the availability of a sensitive photon detector at the absorption wavelengths.

- Detection time: sub-second
- Sensitivity: unknown (material-dependent)
- Portability: good
- Cost: unknown (depending on frequency)
- Data gathering: low (frequency-specific)
- Differentiation: excellent
- Field deployed: no

Optical Fiber Sensors

Glass fibers with a thin chemically active coating on the sides or ends can respond to the presence of a volatile organic compound [10]. A single frequency or narrowband frequency light source enters the fiber. The chemically active material containing fluorescent dyes immobilized in an organic polymer matrix is used. The volatile organic compound reacts with the thin active coating and the light source by altering the polarity of the dyes. This interaction shifts the fluorescent spectrum (Figure 22.16).

Analysis of OFS

Optical fiber sensors (OFS) is an effective chemical sensing system that has not been field deployed for this application. It can be made portable, sensitive, and can differentiate between chemical vapors but is dependent on the active material. The question of sensitivity has yet to be answered.

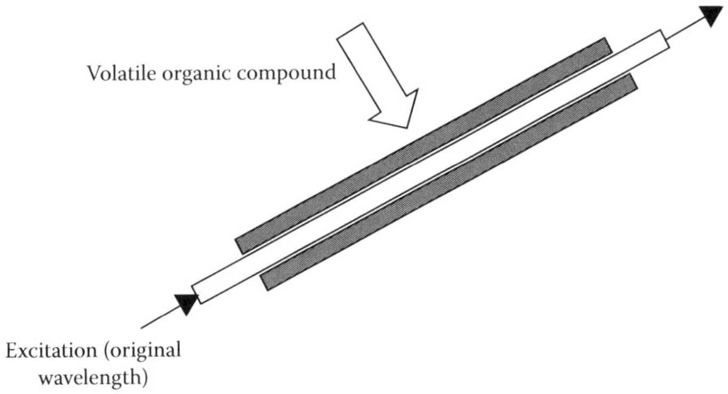

Figure 22.16 Optical-fiber sensor that employs a glass fiber and a chemically active coating. This coating interacts with an excitation light source by shifting its response frequency.

- Detection time: sub-second
- Sensitivity: unknown (material-dependent)
- Portability: good
- Cost: unknown (depending on frequency)
- Data gathering: low (frequency and active chemical specific)
- Differentiation: excellent
- Field deployed: no

Acoustic-to-Optic Tunable Filters

The acoustic-to-optic tunable filters (ATOFs) alter the light filtering properties of a material in response to the change in voltage across the materials' light transmission path.

Analysis of ATOFs

ATOFs are in the research phase. Little can be reported at this time about the potential of the approach.

- Detection time: sub-second
- Sensitivity: unknown (material-dependent)
- Portability: good
- Cost: unknown (depending on frequency and material)
- Data gathering: low (frequency and material specific)
- Differentiation: excellent
- Field deployed: no

Laser Induced Breakdown Spectroscopy

Laser Induced Breakdown Spectroscopy (LIBS) is becoming a powerful tool for analyzing chemical compounds, and particularly explosives. The basic operating and working principles are discussed earlier in this chapter under standoff detection. The success of LIBS for identifying organic compounds based on atomic emission intensity ratios led researchers at The U.S. Army Research Laboratory (ARL) used LIBS to identify organic compounds and now extend its capability to explosive compounds. LIBS spectra were collected from a variety of explosive materials, including highly purified RDX, HMX, TNT, PETN, and NC as well as operational explosives and propellants C-4, A-5, M-43, LX-14, and JA2 [4]. All of the expected atomic lines—carbon, hydrogen, nitrogen, and oxygen—are present.

Terahertz Spectroscopy

The terahertz band, 0.1–10 THz, that falls between the IR and microwave region of the electromagnetic spectrum has been deployed by a number of researchers to detect and identify hidden objects including explosives. Table 22.2 provides the transmission rates of THz energy in various materials that can be used to shield an unwanted object. The signals/peaks of various chemicals and explosives in the THz band is given in Table 22.2.

Table 22.2 THz Transmissive Properties of Common Materials Encountered during Security Screenings

Material	*Trans (%)*	*N (Layers)*	*Trans. % at 1.0 THz*	*Trans. % at 0.5 THz*
Leather glove[a]	4	3	2.8	3.2
Coat	14.7	6	3.8	22.8
T-shirt	87.5	86	70.6	87.4
Sweater	21.6	7	1.9	40.8
Sock[a]	26.7	8	13.2	35.5
Wallet	9	4	0.6	18.3
Laptop bag[a]	3	3	0.8	4.1
Cardboard	62.5	24	9.2	53.7
Carpet	56.7	20	0.3	35.5
Bubble plastic	91.1	128	84.0	95.1

Source: Xu, J. et al., *Proc. SPIE-Int. Soc. Opt. Eng.*, 5070, 17, 2003. With permission.

Note: N indicates the number of layers that result in a signal-to-noise ratio of 1.

[a] The entire item was measured instead of just one layer.

Sensors Based on Electromagnetic Wavelengths of Millimeter and Beyond

The use of electromagnetic waves from the millimeter and beyond is considered. One of the key issues in this wavelength range is the inability of these frequencies to penetrate conducting materials. This deficiency makes this category of detector unsuitable for field use.

Nuclear Magnetic Resonance

Nuclear magnetic resonance (NMR) uses low energy photons, radio frequency (RF), to shift the magnetic moment of nucleons from one quantum state to another. The shift of the quantum sate is dependent on the nuclear structure of the atom. For example, in medical imaging, the magnetic moment of protons is targeted. Two methods have been used for explosive detection:

1. Classical NMR uses a combination of RF and magnetic fields.
2. Quadrapole resonance (QR) uses RF alone.

Analysis of NMR

RF must be able to penetrate the material of interest. If a conductive shield such as a metal casing is present, then the RF will not penetrate. This method is not suitable for field use.

Millimeter Electromagnetic Wave

High-resolution RADAR systems have been developed using millimeter electromagnetic waves (MEWs). This type of system is useful for detecting bulk amounts of materials such as explosives. However, MEWs will not penetrate conductive materials. The inability to penetrate conductive materials makes the system unsuitable for field use.

Analysis of MEW

Because MEWs do not penetrate conductors, MEW is not suitable for field use.

Methods That Use Piezoelectric Effects

Gas Chromatograph/Surface Acoustic Wave

A surface acoustic wave (SAW) crystal works on the principle that a given mass of material on its surface will change its vibrational frequency. By combining a GC with a SAW crystal, the material flowing from the GC condenses on the cooled surface of a SAW crystal (see Figure 22.17). The crystal is vibrated and the frequency change of the crystal is monitored. The mass of the condensing material changes the vibrational frequency. This condensed mass is proportional to the concentration of chemical present in the atmosphere.

The GC/SAW crystal may also operate in reverse to recalibrate the system. In the reverse mode, the crystal can be heated and the condensed material is boiled off.

Analysis of GC/SAW

The GC/SAW chemical sensor is a very effective method of measuring trace chemicals and has been field deployed [11]. This method has been used in detecting the chemical vapors from high explosives. Like other sensors combined with GC, it is suitable for the detection of a number of chemical vapors. Thus, it is suitable for chemical agent detection.

- Detection time: 10–15 s
- Sensitivity: excellent (picogram)
- Portability: good
- Cost: low
- Data gathering: high
- Differentiation: excellent
- Field deployed: yes

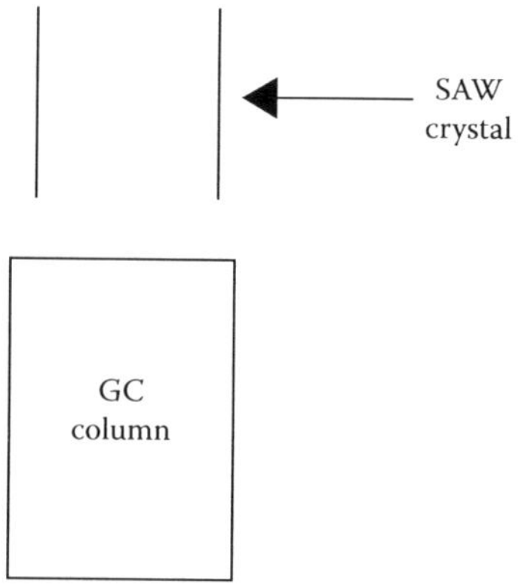

Figure 22.17 Diagram of the GC/SAW crystal.

Quartz Crystal Microbalance

The quartz crystal microbalance (QCM) has a resonating quartz disk with metal electrodes on each side. The device has a characteristic frequency when excited by an oscillating signal. The disk is coated with a polymer that is active with sensing material. When a chemical is absorbed by the polymer, the mass of the disk increases and the resonance frequency is reduced. The QCM can see a mass change of about one picogram. This translates to a concentration of about one part per billion of the chemical agent in air.

Analysis of QCM

QCM is a well-known device and has been used to measure trace amounts of chemicals.

- Detection time: <1 s
- Sensitivity: excellent (picogram)
- Portability: excellent
- Cost: low
- Data gathering: low
- Differentiation: low
- Field deployed: yes

Thermal Techniques

Thermo-Redox

A thermo-redox (TR) detector is similar to the ChL detector. It is basically used for the detection of explosives because it works only with nitrogen-rich materials. Air is flowed into a series of capillary tubes coated with catalytic material. The capillary tubes are heated to a very high temperature. Chemical vapors from explosive materials are chemically broken down. A by-product of this process is NO_2. A group of sensors capable of detecting NO_2 are located at the outlet of the capillary tubes (see Figure 22.18). The signals from the NO_2 sensors are proportional to the amount of chemical vapor from high explosives that are present.

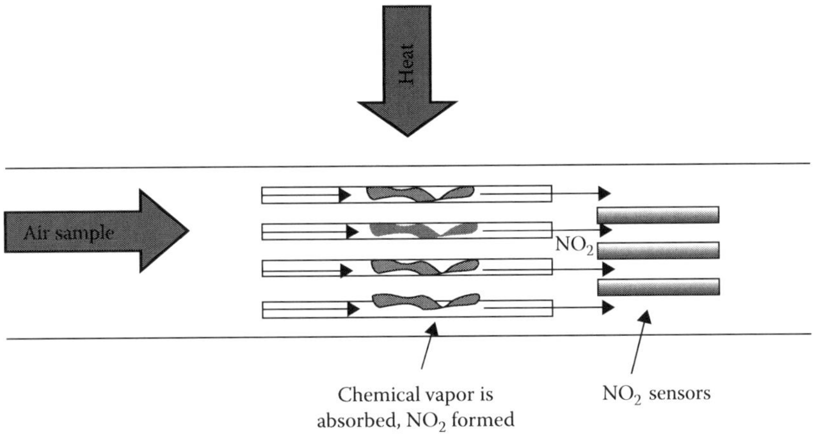

Figure 22.18 Diagram of a thermo-redox detector.

Analysis of TR

TR has been field deployed for high explosives. The TR detector is not able to differentiate the type of explosive. It can detect high vapor pressure explosives like NG and TNT. It will not detect low vapor pressure explosives like RDX and PETN. This limitation makes the TR detector unsuitable for field use.

- Detection time: unknown
- Sensitivity: unknown
- Portability: good
- Cost: low
- Data gathering: low
- Differentiation: none
- Field deployed: yes

Surface Effect

Charge-Deep Level Transient Spectroscopy

Chemical agents have a vapor pressure. Thus molecules from a chemical agent will reach equilibrium with the surrounding air. These molecules will deposit on surfaces. A molecule absorbed by a surface will have a specific differentiable effect on the surface potential of a material. Some materials, such as diamond terminated with hydrogen, have a low surface potential. Charge-deep level transient spectroscopy (*Q*-DLTS) provides information about the effect of molecules on the surface of materials such as diamond. When combined with diamond and diamond-like carbon, the technique is able to measure the quantity and type of molecule absorbed on the surface (see Figure 22.19). The method is in its early stages of research but shows great promise. Initial testing has demonstrated that the method can detect and differentiate parts per billion of water vapor and

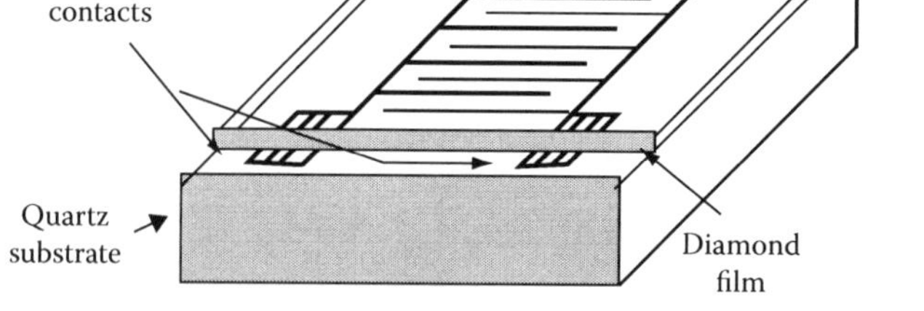

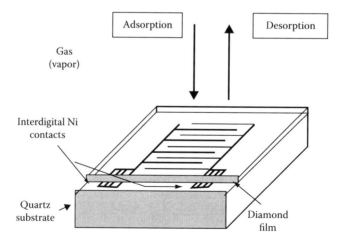

Figure 22.19 Illustration of *Q*-DLTS chip.

ethyl alcohol in air [12]. Theoretically, the method can be orders of magnitude more sensitive than present tests, can differentiate complex molecules, and is potentially hand-sized portable.

Analysis of Q-DLTS

Q-DLTS is in early research stages but has shown impressive results. The technology is promising for field use.

- Detection time: 1–5 s
- Sensitivity: excellent (potentially sub-femtogram)
- Portability: potentially excellent
- Cost: unknown but potentially low
- Data gathering: high
- Differentiation: excellent
- Field deployed: no

Conductivity-Based Sensors

Changes in the resistive properties of materials like metal oxides and conducting polymer when chemicals are present on the surface can be used for conductivity-based sensors (CBSs) [13,14]. Unlike the *Q*-DLTS, in which the transient response is used, CBSs integrate the time response function and look at the real part of the surface impedance.

Analysis of CBS

CBS has been under development by organizations, such as NIST, for chemical detection. The surface resistances of various materials are being examined for specific chemicals. The goal of the program is to develop a database for a number of materials that respond to specific chemicals on their surfaces. These materials can be incorporated on a chip as an array of sensors that would allow the detection of multiple species. Tests have shown that metal oxide CBS sensitivity is in the order of 5–500 parts per million while the conducting polymer CBS sensitivity is in the order of 1–100 parts per million. CBSs will have a baseline drift over their lifetime.

- Detection time: seconds
- Sensitivity: low
- Portability: potentially excellent
- Cost: unknown but potentially low
- Data gathering: low
- Differentiation: moderate
- Field deployed: no

Metal-Oxide-Silicon Field-Effect Transistor

Metal-oxide-silicon field-effect transistor (MOSFET) odor-sensing is based on the principle that chemicals in contact with a catalytic metal produces a reaction in the metal. This reaction can change the electrical properties of the p-type or n-type materials. The sensitivity and selectivity can be varied by changing the type of catalyst, the thickness, and the temperature.

Analysis of MOSFET

MOSFETs are being developed by firms in the United States, France, Germany, the United Kingdom, and Sweden. The sensitivity of these units are in the parts per million range. The units still have batch-to-batch variations. The seal on the chip's electrical connections in a harsh environment is still a problem. Finally, MOSFETs undergo a baseline drift.

- Detection time: seconds
- Sensitivity: low
- Portability: potentially excellent
- Cost: unknown but potentially low
- Data gathering: low
- Differentiation: good
- Field deployed: no

Radiation-Based Sensors

X-Rays

X-rays can penetrate materials. The penetration depth is dependent on the x-ray energy, the material thickness, and the average Z (number of electrons per atom) of the material. As a group, x-ray detection systems rely on the interaction of the x-ray with matter. When an x-ray encounters matter, four things can happen:

1. The x-ray can pass through the matter unaffected.
2. The x-ray can produce the photoelectric effect. An ion pair (electron plus ion) is produced.
3. The x-ray can undergo Compton scattering.
4. The x-ray can undergo pair production, provided the x-ray energy is greater than 1.2 MeV.

From these interactions, it is possible to determine the density of material, the mass absorption coefficient of the material, and the effective Z of the material that the x-rays passed through. Explosives or chemical agents in bulk quantity will have unique interaction characteristics that can differentiate them from surrounding material. However, it is also possible to fool x-ray measurements by very sophisticated countermeasures. A number of x-ray systems are on the market:

- Dual x-ray source:; which uses 75 keV and 150 keV x-rays simultaneously. This allows the detection of low- and high-density explosives.
- Backscatter x-ray:; which is able to see low Z objects.
- Computer tomography: this method will generate a 3D image.

Analysis of X-Ray Detection

X-ray detection has been field deployed for high explosives. The systems trigger on large amounts of explosive material with the ability to resolve shapes, density, and average Z. It is possible to fool x-ray detection systems. X-ray detection systems are not suitable for field use because they work best in resolving large amounts of explosive material but not trace amounts.

- Detection time: seconds
- Sensitivity: poor (needs a substantial amount of explosive: not suitable for a trace analysis system)
- Portability: poor
- Cost: high
- Data gathering: low
- Differentiation: none
- Field deployed: yes

Neutron-Based Detection Systems

Neutrons are much more penetrating than x-rays. Neutrons can interact with matter in the following ways:

1. Pass through the material without interaction
2. Elastic scattering (billiard ball type scatter)
3. Inelastic scattering (soft foam ball type scattering)
4. Neutron capture (results in the release of radiation such as neutrons, beta particles, alpha particles, and gamma rays)

Neutron-based detection systems primarily rely on neutron capture reactions and the subsequent release of radiation. Neutron-based detection systems have a neutron source. This source can be a radioisotope such as californium (Cf) or an accelerator-based source. The neutron source is placed near the object and an array of gamma ray sensors is placed around the object. When neutrons interact with materials, some of the atoms of that material will capture neutrons. The capture reaction results in the release of gamma rays that are characteristic of the atom. The gamma ray energies and intensity are then measured. The data is sent to a computer where it is unfolded to give the density of specific atoms in the material. Additionally, some types of neutron-based detector systems can provide spatial resolution of the material. Chemical agents and high explosives are made up of chemicals. The chemicals are made up of atoms. The specific concentration of various atoms in a chemical can be determined from the gamma rays emitted from the neutron capture reaction. The density of atoms can then be related to the chemical makeup of the material through a database. Thus, chemicals can be identified using neutron capture reactions.

Thermal Neutron Activation

Thermal neutron activation (TNA) uses a thermal neutron source (meaning neutron energies near the average energy of a gas molecule at room temperature, about 0.02 eV). A thermal neutron flux is made by moderating fast neutrons (meaning MeV or greater neutron energies) from an accelerator or californium source with a low Z material such as hydrogen. The thermal neutrons interact with the material of interest, and neutron capture reactions take place. Sodium iodine gamma ray detectors are placed around the object, and the energy and intensity of the gamma rays are measured. The data from the detectors is sent to a computer system for unfolding (see Figure 22.20).

A TNA system is commercially available from SAIC and is field deployed. It is not portable, but could be made portable with a new generation "no shielding" neutron source such as the Daimler–Chrysler Fusion Star neutron source [15].

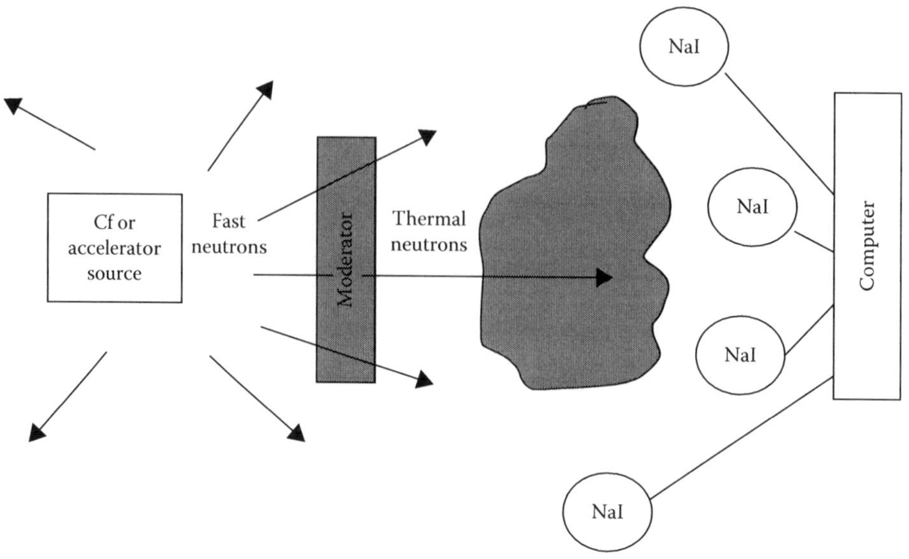

Figure 22.20 Diagram of the TNA system.

Analysis of TNA

The TNA system is capable of probing into metal objects. This capability may be of benefit in examining trace elements inside of a sealed container. Thus, TNA might be useful in the field for sealed units. TNA's sensitivity is highly dependent on the strength of the neutron source. Development of TNA for use in the field is required to sort out sensitivity issues.

- Detection time: minutes
- Sensitivity: ~100 gm of material depending on the strength of neutron source or irradiation time.
- Portability: poor (with Cf or accelerator source) to good (with advanced neutron source)
- Cost: high
- Data gathering: high
- Differentiation: excellent
- Field deployed: yes

Portable Isotopic Neutron Spectroscopy

Portable isotopic neutron spectroscopy (PINS) was developed by EG&G Idaho and the Idaho National Engineering Laboratory as a portable system for chemical assaying. The device uses a Cf neutron source and requires some shielding. The shielding is the main reason for the mass of the system (about 610 lb). The device uses high-purity germanium (HPGe) detectors but otherwise looks very much like the TNA system in Figure 22.15. Because of the HPGe detectors, this system requires a liquid nitrogen refill every 18 hours.

Analysis of PINS

PINS was designed as a portable chemical assay system. This system will be able to do chemical analysis of objects sealed in metal containers. It may be suitable for field use with sealed units. The question of PINS sensitivity for field applications must be addressed.

- Detection time: 100–1000 s
- Sensitivity: ~100 gm of material depending on the strength of neutron source
- Portability: good (for Cf) to excellent (for advanced neutron source).
- Cost: high
- Data gathering: high
- Differentiation: excellent
- Field deployed: yes

Pulsed Fast Neutron Analysis

The pulsed fast neutron analysis (PFNA) system is a commercial unit developed by SAIC for inspecting cargo. This system is not portable. It is large because it uses an accelerator-based neutron source (D [d,n]He^3) for the production of fast neutrons. The system diagram looks similar to the TNA (Figure 22.20), but PFNA has no moderator.

Analysis of PFNA

PFNA was not designed to be portable. The principle of PFNA may be useful for the field. Technology such as the Daimler–Chrysler Fusion Star may have an impact on the portability of the system. This question cannot be answered without further research and development.

- Detection time: sub-second
- Sensitivity: ~100 gm of material depending on the strength of pulsed neutron source
- Portability: poor, but may be improved with advanced neutron source technology
- Cost: high
- Data gathering: high
- Differentiation: excellent
- Field deployed: yes

Methods Based on Surface Wipes

Systems such as the Expray, produced by Genesis Resource, use test paper to wipe a surface. The test paper is then treated with one of the three spays:

1. Expray 1: turns dark brown–violet for TNT; blue–green for DNT; orange for TNB and picric acid
2. Expray 2: turns pink for Semtex H, PETN, NG, smokeless powder, and RDX
3. Expray 3: turns pink with nitrates

Analysis of Surface Wipes

Surface wipes (SW) are useful for identifying trace chemicals on surfaces. This technique may be useful in the field for checking the surface of sealed units.

- Detection time: seconds
- Sensitivity: food (about 20 ng)
- Portability: excellent
- Cost: low
- Data gathering: low
- Differentiation: excellent
- Field deployed: yes

Antibody-Based Biosensors

Immunosensors are immobilized on a solid substrate. The immunosensor is bound to fluorescently labeled signal molecules. When the signal molecules are in the presence of a specific molecule, for example RDX, the system can be designed such that the fluorescently labeled signal molecule is released. Fluorescence is then detected with a photon sensor. The photon intensity is related to the density of fluorescent molecules. The release of fluorescent molecules is then directly proportional to the chemical that is present. The construction of the sensor and reader is shown in Figure 22.21.

Analysis of ABBs

ABBs are under development by the Naval Research Laboratory. The technology is promising, but requires more development for field applications.

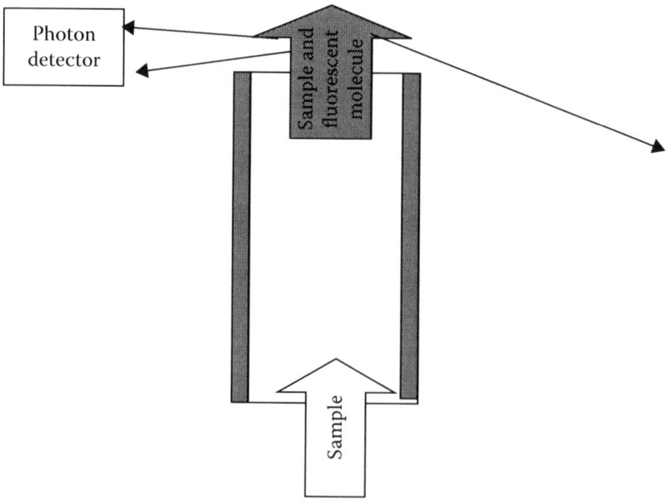

Figure 22.21 ABB diagram.

- Detection time: one minute
- Sensitivity: good (1 ng)
- Portability: excellent
- Cost: unknown
- Data gathering: low
- Differentiation: excellent
- Field deployed: no

Antibody-Coated Oscillator

This device uses an oscillator with a coating of antibody. As the sample flows around the coated oscillator, the chemical deposits on the antibody coating. The added mass changes the effective mass of the oscillator, which changes the frequency. This change in frequency can be measured and correlates with the amount of chemical present.

Analysis of Antibody-Coated Sensor

The antibody-coated sensor (ACS) is very promising, but the technology is still in the research phase.

- Detection time: unknown
- Sensitivity: unknown
- Portability: excellent
- Cost: unknown
- Data gathering: low
- Differentiation: excellent
- Field deployed: no

The rating scale is based upon

- Sensitivity: "poor" indicates more than 1 part per billion or greater than 20 ng; "good" indicates sub parts per billion or below 20 ng; "excellent" indicates less than parts per trillion and less than a picogram.
- Portability: "NP" indicates that it is not portable; "poor" indicates 300–1000 lb; "good" indicates 100–299 lb; "excellent" indicates less than 100 lb.
- Cost: "low" indicates less than \$60,000; "moderate" indicates \$60,00–\$299,000; and "high" indicates \$300,000 and above.
- Data gathering: "low" indicates not intrusive as applied to field use; "moderate" indicates some chemicals can be distinguished as applied to field use; "high" indicates most chemicals can be distinguished as applied to field use.
- Differentiation: "none" indicates that chemicals cannot be differentiated; "poor" indicates that only explosives can be differentiated; "moderate" indicates that explosives and some other chemicals can be differentiated; "excellent" indicates that most chemicals can be differentiated.
- Deployed: "no" indicates that the device has not been field deployed or tested; "yes," indicates that the device has been field deployed and tested.

A comparison of different methods for detection of chemical agents is provided in Table 22.3.

Table 22.3 Evaluation of Chemical Sensor Technology

Method	*Time (s)*	*Sensitivity*	*Portability*	*Cost*	*Deployed*
Canine	<69	Excellent	Poor	Moderate	Yes
GC	10–15	Good	Good	Low	Yes
ECD	<1	Good	Excellent	Low	Yes
ECD/GC	18	Good	Excellent	Low	Yes
IMS	5–8	Good	Excellent	Low	Yes
FIS	2	Excellent	Excellent	Low	Yes
TMS	>100	Excellent	Excellent	Unknown	No
ChL	10	Good	Good	Moderate	Yes
ChL/GC	18	Good	Good	Moderate	Yes
RS	<1	Unknown	Good	Moderate	No
OFS	<1	Unknown	Good	Unknown	No
GC/ SAW	10–15	Excellent	Good	Low	Yes
TR	Unknown	Unknown	Good	Low	Yes
MOSFET	1–5	Excellent	Excellent	Low	No
CBS	1–5	Poor	Excellent	Low	No
Q-DLTS	1–5	Excellent	Excellent	Unknown	No
TNA	>100	Poor	Poor	High	Yes
PINS	>100	Poor	Good	High	Yes
PFNA	<1	Poor	NP	High	Yes
ABB	>60	Good	Excellent	Unknown	No

Conclusions

The ability to measure trace chemicals in the field such as the vapor from high explosives has been demonstrated. It appears that these technologies, which were developed for security and police purposes, can be applied to many other areas including a counterterrorism tool for chemical agents.

In comparing the capabilities of chemical agent sensors with those of sensors for other agents of mass destruction, it is clear that radiation sensors are far more capable and biological sensors are far less capable.

The ultimate goal of counterterrorism is to detect the nuclear, biological, or chemical agents prior to their release. Radiation sensors can detect single gamma rays or can determine the energy spectrum of gamma rays with a small number of photons. It is feasible to use radiation sensors in a prerelease mode in that these sensors can identify the radiation from nuclear materials prior to their release. Biological sensors are in their infancy and there is virtually no capability to detect biological agents prior to their release. Chemical sensors, on the other hand, are getting near the sensitivity required to detect chemical agents or their precursors prior to the release of the agent. Right now chemical sensors are being used to detect explosives at close proximity. Thus, they can be used in situations where people are funneled to a small area such as is currently the practice in airports.

No countermeasure is completely secure. For example, at the time of this writing, Richard Colvin Reid, with his shoes containing plastic explosives, boarded Americans Airlines Flight 63 from Paris to Miami [16]. The only way that the plastic explosive could have been detected at the Charles de Gaulle Airport was if a bomb sniffing dog was used to check passengers, or if Mr. Reid had been asked to place his shoes on the hand luggage x-ray machine or if Mr. Reid had been stopped and his shoes wiped and tested for the residue from the explosive material. None of these were common practices at the time.

The only man-made sensor used in airports today is the residue test, and it requires that the item be physically wiped. This method can detect about a nanogram of explosive material. Other types of chemical sensor technology are available that can detect sub-picograms and thus could be used to detect the vapors from explosives within close proximity. These and more advanced technologies will eventually find their way into airports and high-risk areas.

References

1. RC Wiens, SK Sharma, J Thompson, A Misra, and PG Lucey. Joint analyses by laser-induced breakdown spectroscopy (LIBS) and Raman spectroscopy at stand-off distances. *Spectrochimica Acta Part A* 61: 2324–2334, 2005.
2. SK Sharma, AK Misra, and B Sharma. Portable remote Raman system for monitoring hydrocarbon, gas hydrates and explosives in the environment. *Spectrochimica Acta Part A* 61: 2404–2412, 2005.
3. M Wu, M Ray, K-H Fung, MW Ruckman, D Harder, and AJ Sedlacek. Stand-off detection of chemicals by UV Raman spectroscopy. *Applied Spectroscopy* 54(6): 800–806, 2000.
4. CA Munson, JL Gottfried, FC De Lucia, Jr., KL McNesby, and AW Miziolek. Laser-based detection methods for explosives, ARL-TR-4279. Army Research Laboratory, Aberdeen Proving Ground, MD, September 2007.
5. H Zhong. Terahertz Wave Reflective Sensing and Imaging. Doctoral dissertation, Rensselaer Polytechnic Institute, Troy, NY, 2006.
6. U.S. Department of Homeland Security. *Guide for the Selection of Personal Protective Equipment for Emergency First Responders*, 2nd edn. Guide 102-06, January 2007.
7. Mine detection equipment, South Africa, U.S. Army, NGIC-1142-652A-98.
8. DW Hannum and JE Parmeter. Survey of Commercially Available Explosive Detection Technologies and Equipment, *National Institute of Justice*, NCJ 171133, September 1998.
9. Raman Cells, 24 Hour Battle 037, Janes.
10. HT Nagle, R Gutierrez-Osuna, and SS Schiffman. The how and why of electronic noses, *IEEE Spectrum*, 43(9): 22–35, September, 1998.
11. VI Polyakov, AI Rukovishnikov, AV Khomich, BL Druz, D Kania, A Hayes, MA Prelas, RV Tompson, TK Ghosh, and SK Loyalka. Surface phenomena of the thin diamond-like carbon films. *Proceedings of the Materials Research Society* 555: 345–347, 1999.

12. BA Tuttle, JA Ruffner, WR Olson, WK Schubert, SJ Martin, MA Mitchell, PG Clem, D Dimos, and TJ Garino. Surface micromachined flexural plate wave device integrable on silicon. Electronic Optical Materials Dept., Sandia National Laboratories, Albuquerque, NM. Sandia Natl. Lab. [Tech. Rep.] SAND (1998), (SAND98-2683), pp. 1–31.
13. FAS. Global Proliferation of Weapons of Mass Destruction: A Case Study on the Aum Shinrikyo, Senate Government Affairs Permanent Subcommittee on Investigations, October 31, 1995 (http://fas.org/irp/congress/1995_rpt/aum/part01.htm).
14. BT Cunningham, R Kant, C Daly, MS Weinberg, J Pepper, C Wu, C Clapp, R Bousquet, and B Hugh. Chemical vapor detection using microfabricated flexural plate silicon resonator arrays. *Proceedings of SPIE-International Society for Optical Engineering* 4036: 151–162, 2000.
15. Fusion Star, Daimler-Chrysler, x-ray free neutron source based on Inertial Electrostatic Confinement technology, Daimler-Chrysler Aerospace, Space Infrastructure Center, Trauen, Eugene-Sanger Strabe 52, D-20328, Fassberg, Germany.
16. DG McNeil. French authorities wonder: How could it have happened? *New York Times*, December 24, 2001. (http://www.nytimes.com/2001/12/24/national/24PARI.html).

Bibliography

NS Arnold, JP Dworzanski, HLC Muezelaar, and WH McClennen. Present and future challenges of developing a GC/IMS based personal chemical warfare agent detector. In DA Berg (Ed.), *Proceedings of the ERDEC Science Conference on Chemical and Biological Defense Research*, National Technical Information Service, Springfield, VA, 1996, pp. 653–659.

WA Bryden, RC Benson, HW Ko, M Donlon, and S Milton. Universal agent sensor for counterproliferation applications. *Johns Hopkins APL Technical Digest* 18(2): 302–308, 1997.

JP Carrico. Chemical-biological defense remote sensing: What's happening. *Proceedings of SPIE-International Society for Optical Engineering* 3383: 45–56, 1998.

CM Gittins and WJ Marinelli. AIRIS multispectral imaging chemical sensor. *Proceedings of SPIE-International Society for Optical Engineering* 3383: 65–74, 1998.

N Gopalsami and AC Raptis. Millimeter-wave imaging of thermal and chemical signatures. *Proceedings of SPIE-International Society for Optical Engineering* 3703: 130–138, 1999.

R Haeber and J Hedtmann. Unexploded ordnance devices: Detection, recovery and disposal. *NATO ASI Series, Series* 1(7), 1996, pp. 73–86.

L Halasz. The role of remote sensing equipment in air monitoring system. *NATO ASI Series* 1, 1997, pp. 241–253.

DW Hannum and JE Parmeter. Survey of Commercially Available Explosive Detection Technologies and Equipment, National Institute of Justice, NCJ 171133, September 1998.

PM Holland, RV Mustacich, JF Everson, W Foreman, M Leone, WJ Naumann, EB Overton, and KR Carney. Handheld GC instrumentation for chemical weapons convention treaty verification inspections. *Proceedings of the International Symposium on Field Screening Methods for Hazardous Wastes and Toxic Chemicals*. Air & Waste Management Association, Pittsburgh, PA, 1995, pp. 229–235.

BF Myasoedov. Analytical control for destruction of chemical weapons. Requirements and organization. *NATO ASI Series, Series* 1, 1997, pp. 39–58.

RJ Pollina and J Baker. DOE cooperative monitoring test bed for unattended chemical sensors. *Proceedings of SPIE-International Society for Optical Engineering* 3081: 254–265, 1997.

TH Rider and L Smith. Optoelectronic sensor (Massachusetts Institute of Technology, Cambridge, MA). PCT Int. Appl. 25, 1999.

A Snelson, S Mainer, P Baum, and G Sresty. FTIR fiber-optic evanescent wave spectroscopy (FEWS) for bulk analysis of CWC-related compounds. In DA Berg (Ed.), *Proceedings of the ERDEC Science Conference on Chemical and Biological Defense Research*. National Technical Information Service, Springfield, VA, 1999, pp. 123–129.

CR Swim and JA Fox. Tunable UV and compact 2-12 micron laser development. *Proceedings of SPIE-International Society for Optical Engineering* 3382: 68–77, 1998.

J Xu, H Liu, T Yuan, R Kersting, and X-C Zhang. Advancing terahertz time-domain spectroscopy for remote detection and tracing. *Proceedings of SPIE-International Society for Optical Engineering*, 5070: 17–20, 2003.

A Zardecki and RB Strittmatter. Chemical and isotopic determination from complex spectra, *Nuclear Materials Management* 24: 817–822, 1995.

RW Zywicki. Radiometric calibration of an airborne chemical imager. *Proceedings of SPIE-International Society for Optical Engineering* 3537: 237–248, 1999.

Chapter 23

Chemical Terrorism: Weaponization and Delivery System

Mark A. Prelas and Tushar K. Ghosh

CONTENTS

Introduction 447
Delivery Systems 448
Binary Chemical Weapons 452
Small-Scale Delivery 453
References 455

Introduction

Methods of delivery for chemical weapons have been under development since World War I. The science and technology of dispersion and dissipation of chemical agents range from the sophistication of weapons of war to the simple for the purpose of terrorism. This chapter discusses how chemical agents are dispersed and dissipated. General Accounting Office of the United States analyzed various technical data, and on the basis of their discussion with chemical and biological warfare experts, noted that a number of obstacles must be overcome for effective delivery and dispersion of agents. Figure 23.1 describes these obstacles.

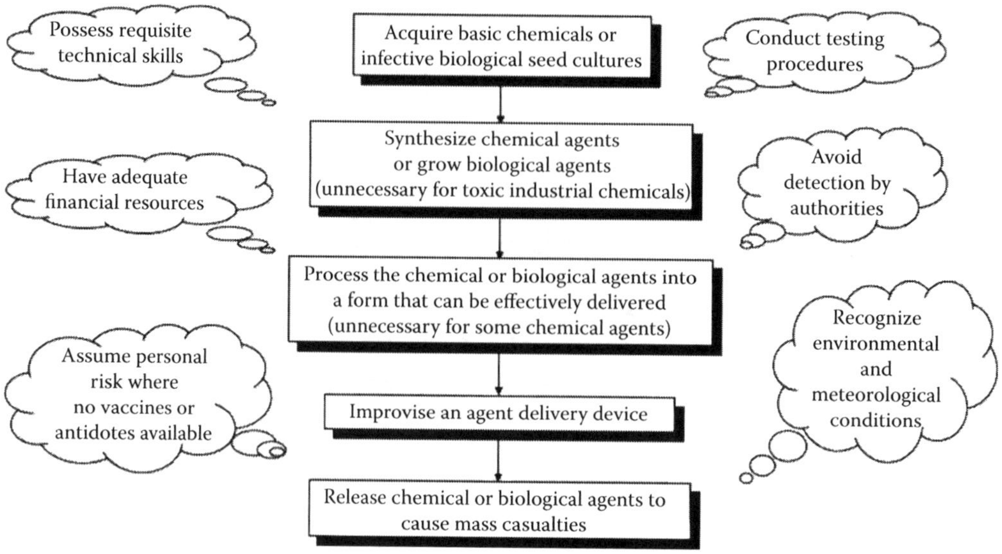

Figure 23.1 Stages and obstacles for chemical and biological terrorism. (Data from General Accounting Office, COMBATING TERRORISM: Observations on the Threat of Chemical and Biological Terrorism, GAO/T-NSIAD-00-50, October 20, 1999.)

Delivery Systems

As discussed in Chapter 6, the key to effective use of either biological agents or chemical agents is the dispersion and dissipation of the agent. The routes for exposure to chemical agents are

- Inhalation from vapor
- Skin contact from vapor or liquid
- Ingestion from liquid

The methods for delivery and dispersion of chemical agents depend on its intent: military use or domestic terrorism. The dispersion methods may be different as the objectives of domestic terrorism are more for creating panic and economic damage rather than for mass casualties or incapacitating the public. For military use, a wide variety of projectiles, mines, bombs, and sprayers were developed. During World War I, chemicals such as chlorine, mustard gas, and phosgene were released in vapor form. More sophisticated weaponization techniques deliver the agent in a fine mist or spray. Many countries have weaponized chemical agents. For example, the United States began developing chemical munitions in 1950. As shown in Figure 23.2, along with the development of chemical agents, the dispersion techniques were also explored. Without proper dispersion techniques, these agents may not be very effective.

Projectiles were developed for direct use of GB or VX. The agent was placed in a shell along with a fuse and a bursting charge. A simplified shell is shown in Figure 23.3.

Examples of shells include a 4.2 in. mortar shell (e.g., M2A1), 105 mm, 155 mm, and 203 mm Howitzer projectiles (e.g., M360 GB, M121A1 GB or VX, and M426 GB or VX). Binary shells were also developed in which the mixture of two relatively benign chemicals

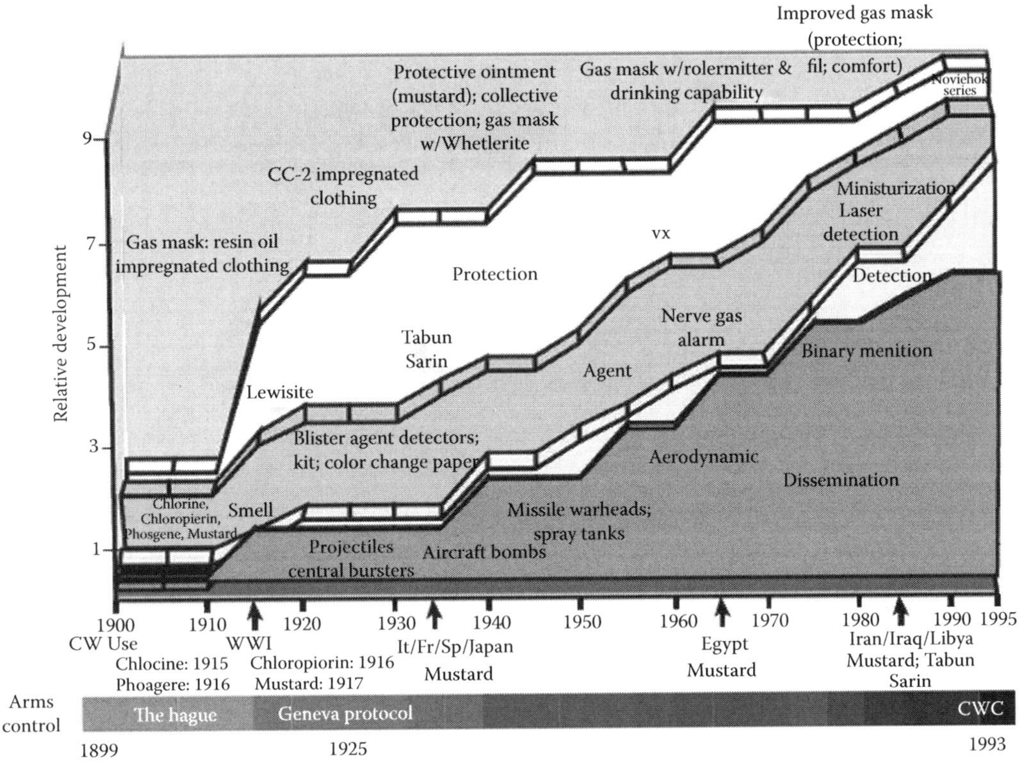

Figure 23.2 Development of various chemical weapon technologies. (From The Militarily Critical Technologies List Part II: Weapons of Mass Destruction Technologies (ADA 330102), Chemical Weapons Technology—U.S. Department of Defense, Office of the Under Secretary of Defense for Acquisition and Technology, February 1998.)

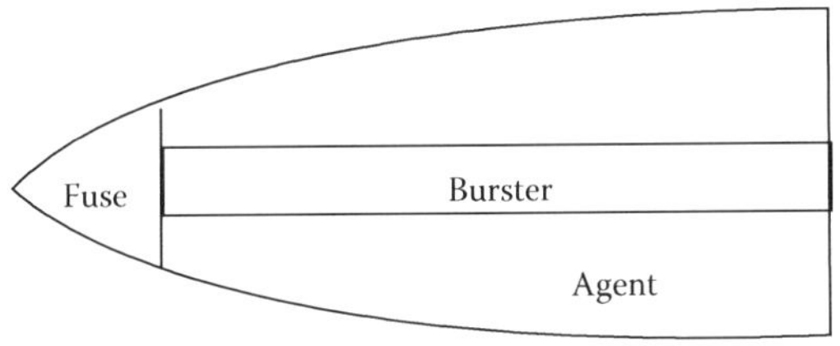

Figure 23.3 Simplified diagram of a shell.

formed GB or VX. These binary shells include the 155 mm M687 GB-2 projectile and the 203 mm XM736 VX-2 projectile.

A number of munitions were developed for air delivery including bombs and spray tanks. The bombs include the M134 GB cluster, the 750 lb MCl, the 500 lb MK116, and the BLU 80/B binary VX. A MC-1 gas bomb developed by the United States is shown in Figure 23.4.

Figure 23.4 MC-1 gas bomb. (From The Militarily Critical Technologies List Part II: Weapons of Mass Destruction Technologies (ADA 330102), Chemical Weapons Technology—U.S. Department of Defense, Office of the Under Secretary of Defense for Acquisition and Technology, February 1998.)

Spray tanks were also developed for air delivery including the Aero 14B and a TMU 28B cruise missile with spray tank. The Aero 14B was very much like a spray tank used in crop dusters.

Chemical agents were also used in missiles. Examples of these include the Little John (M206), the Honest John (M79), the improved Honest John (M190), and the Sergeant (M212). A warhead is more complex than a shell in that it is filled with submunitions or bomblets, such as the M139. The submunitions have a similar design as a shell in that there is a fuse, a burster, and an agent. The submunitions are designed to take disperse flight paths so as to cover the maximum area when they burst. Figure 23.5 shows an Honest John missile. An illustration of the warhead is shown in Figure 23.6.

In military applications, a chemical weapon is detonated to create a cloud containing the chemical agent. The chemical agent is either in the vapor form or as aerosols and drifts with the cloud; ultimately settling in the ground and thereby contaminates it. The ground contamination by the chemical agent has a finite lifetime depending on its persistence time. The persistence of various chemical agents is given in Table 23.1. The agent can injure a person from direct contact, or from contact with a secondary cloud of agent that has evaporated from the ground contamination. The chemical agent will eventually degrade and get diluted below toxic levels by physical action.

The factors that can affect the dispersion of chemical agents in the atmosphere include

- Wind direction
- Wind speed
- Turbulence

Figure 23.5 An Honest John missile with launcher.

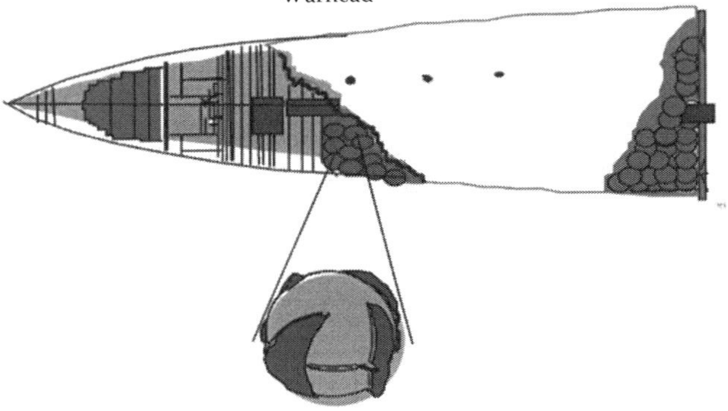

Figure 23.6 Illustration of a warhead filled with submunitions for bomblets.

- Temperature
- Humidity
- Precipitation

The principal method expected of disseminating chemical agents by military has been the use of explosives. However, this method has several inherent problems. Various tests show that much of the agent is lost by incineration and by being forced onto the ground. Flammable aerosols frequently "flash" (ignite) when explosively disseminated. For example, explosively disseminated VX ignited roughly one third of the time it was employed. Also, it is not possible to control the size

Table 23.1 Persistence Time for Various Chemical Agents under Two Atmospheric Conditions

Agent	*Persistence Time*	
	During Winter (−10°C)	*During Summer (15°C)*
VX	Eight days	Three days
GA, Tabun	Four days	One day
Mustards	Four days	One day
GD, Soman	Two days	Five hours
L, Lewisite	One day	One hours
GB, Sarin	Eight hours	30 minutes
Cyanide	Two minutes	Instantaneous

Source: Data from Dispersal and Fate of Chemical Warfare Agents. http://www.noblis.org/DispersalAndFateOfChemicalWarfareAgents.htm.

of aerosols. Often, a bimodal distribution of aerosol particles has been observed; fine and coarse particles. Aerodynamic dissemination and sprays as line sources have been attempted to control the aerosol particle sizes of the released chemical agents. Attempts have also been made for thermal dissemination of chemical agents. The other delivery issues are related to transportation, handling, loading into munitions, and storage of these highly toxic chemicals. To minimize the transportation of these toxic chemical agents, binary chemical weapons were developed.

Binary Chemical Weapons

The U.S. Army developed binary chemical weapons in the early 1980s to modernize its aging chemical weapons stockpile. One of the driving forces for binary chemical weapons was safety and security. Designed to mix two nonlethal chemicals while in flight to a target to form chemical agent, binary chemical weapons development helped prompt the Soviet Union into arms reduction negotiation and the signing of a bilateral agreement in 1990. This agreement led to the Chemical Weapons Convention, the international treaty signed by 153 countries that mandates the elimination of chemical warfare materiel and former chemical weapons production facilities. For example, a liquid precursor (QL) can be mixed with sulfur powder to form the nerve agent VX. A delivery system, called Bigeye, was designed to mix the two agents after release from an aircraft and spray VX over the intended target area. The liquid chemical QL was to be stored in the bomb, and the sulfur powder was to be stored in a cylindrical tube known as the ballonet, which is kept separately from the bomb. Two hundred test weapons were produced prior to termination of the project. The M-687 155 millimeter binary artillery projectile was the only binary weapon to reach the full-scale production. The projectile utilized a liquid precursor (DF) and a nonlethal compound (OPA) to form the nerve agent GB. An M-687 binary chemical projectile is shown in Figure 23.7.

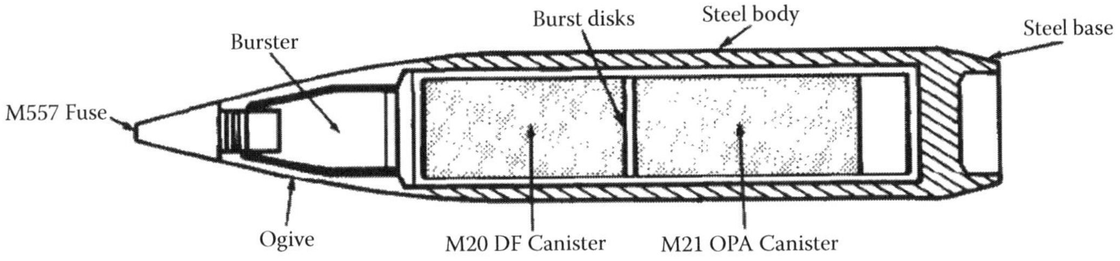

Figure 23.7 M-687 binary chemical projectile. (From Chemical weapons: Status of the army's M687 binary program. GAO/NSIAD-90-295, September 1990.)

Small-Scale Delivery

Munitions are a very effective means of delivering a lethal dose of agent over a large area because they were designed for military use. However, munitions are not the only means of delivery. Chemical agents can be delivered on a small-scale by potential terrorists via:

- Air
- Water supply
- Food supply

On March 20, 1995 the doomsday cult Aum Shinrikyo attacked the subway in Tokyo with sarin [5,6]. A man in a surgical mask sat down in the eighth car of the B711T train on Tokyo's Hibiya line. He pierced a plastic bag containing sarin and left it on the floor and a liquid puddle formed. Soon afterwards passengers around the puddle became ill. All in all, five such bags were placed in subway cars simultaneously, and the attack resulted in 12 deaths and 5000 injuries. Had the sarin been delivered more effectively, there is no telling how high the death total would have been.

To effectively deliver the agent, it must be aerosolized. Aerosolization can be achieved in many ways. For example, a simple garden sprayer is very effective in aerosolizing chemicals. Sprayers have been designed for crop dusters so as to allow the maximum coverage of an area with a chemical.

Generally, it is difficult to contaminate water supply by chemical agents. Not only a large quantity of chemical agents will be necessary to deliver an effective dose, but most of the pipelines used for water transportation are also under higher pressure. Therefore, injecting of chemical agents will be extremely problematic and is unlikely to go unnoticed.

Although the contamination of food supply by injecting poisons has been reported, the major impact was economical. One such incident was reported on March 1989, when two grapes in a crate imported from Chile were found to be laced with cyanide at the Philadelphia port. The U.S. Food and Drug Administration (USFDA) launched the most intensive food safety investigation in Food and Drug Administration history. Fruits in stores were returned or destroyed, and shipments coming into the country from Chile were halted for four days. The estimated loss to Chile was 400 million dollars. However, various studies later raised the question of difficulties of injecting grapes with cyanide, and also it was mentioned that acidic nature of the grape would neutralize or decompose the cyanide fairly quickly.

Table 23.2 Research Program at Various U.S. Agencies for Development of Small-Scale Delivery System

Weapon	*Detail*	*Developer*
Forty millimeters (40 mm) nonlethal crowd dispersal cartridge	M203 grenade launched munition with range of 10–50 m and payload of rubber "sting" balls	ARDEC, U.S. Army
Acoustic bioeffects and acoustic generators	Use of extremely low frequency sound (infrasound) as an acoustic weapon (program ended in 1999 due to lack of demonstrated effects)	ARDEC, U.S. Army, and SARA Inc.
MCCM	Variant of the Claymore mine delivering a payload of rubber "sting" balls	ARDEC, U.S. Army
VMADS	Prototype directed energy millimeter wave weapon mounted on a HMMWV armored vehicle, initially developed for physical security applications (program classified at the time)	AFRL, U.S. Air Force
Sixty–six millimeters vehicle launched grenade	Grenade launched LVOSS with a range of 50–100 m and two different payloads: rubber "sting" balls or flash-bang	ARDEC, U.S. Army
UAV nonlethal payload program	Dispenser developed for UAV's, such as the Dragon Drone to deliver various payloads including: riot control agents, malodorants, electronic noise/siren, rubber "sting" balls, and marker dye	NSWCDD, U.S. Navy, and MCWL, U.S. Marines
BNLM	Variant of the M16A2 antipersonnel mine with various different payloads proposed: rubber "sting" balls, electric-shock net, malodorants, riot control agents, and marker dye (Program ended post-2002)	ARDEC, U.S. Army
CLADS	Adaptation of volcano mine dispenser system, mounted on HMMWV armored vehicle to rapidly deliver 20 mines containing rubber "sting" balls (Program ended post-2002)	ARDEC, U.S. Army
Foam systems	Nonlethal slippery foam to deny access to people and vehicles (also rigid foam but for antimaterial applications only)	ECBC, U.S. Army, and SWRI

Table 23.2 (continued) Research Program at Various U.S. Agencies for Development of Small-Scale Delivery System

Weapon	*Detail*	*Developer*
Vortex ring gun	Investigation into the adaptation of the Mk19-3 grenade launcher to deliver payloads, such as riot control agents, malodorants, or smokes via gas vortices (program ended in 1998 due to unpredictable effects and limited range)	ARL and ARDEC, U.S. Army
Under-barrel tactical payload delivery system	Devices for delivery of various payloads, mounted under M16A2 and M4 rifles. (program ended post-2002)	ARDEC, U.S. Army

Source: Data from Davison, N., The Development of "Non-Lethal" Weapons During the 1990s. Occasional Paper No. 2, Bradford Non-Lethal Weapons Research Project (BNLWRP) Department of Peace Studies, University of Bradford, Bradford, U.K., March 2007.

Note: ARDEC, Army Research, Development and Engineering Center; AFRL, Air Force Research Laboratory; BNLM, bounding nonlethal munition; CLADS, canister launched area denial system; ECBC, Edgewood Chemical and Biological Center; LVOSS, Light Vehicle Obscuration Smoke System; MCCM, modular crowd control munitions; MCWL, Marine Corps Warfighting Laboratory; NSWCDD, Naval Surface Warfare Center, Dahlgren Division; SARA, Scientific Applications & Research Associates; SWRI, Southwest Research Institute; UAV, unmanned aerial vehicle; VMADS, vehicle-mounted active denial system. HMMWV, high mobility multipurpose wheeled vehicle.

Various delivery devices are currently under development by the U.S. Joint Non-Lethal Weapons Program to disperse chemicals for domestic riot control purposes. These include chemical land mines, 81 mm chemical mortar shells with a 1.5 km range, and a 120 mm frangible mortar. Various research projects that are undertaken by various U.S. agencies are listed in Table 23.2.

References

1. General Accounting Office. Combating Terrorism: Observations on the Threat of Chemical and Biological Terrorism, GAO/T-NSIAD-00-50, October 20, 1999.
2. The Militarily Critical Technologies List Part II: Weapons of Mass Destruction Technologies (ADA 330102), Chemical Weapons Technology—U.S. Department of Defense, Office of the Under Secretary of Defense for Acquisition and Technology, February 1998.
3. Dispersal and Fate of Chemical Warfare Agents. http://www.noblis.org/DispersalAndFateOfChemicalWarfareAgents.htm
4. Chemical weapons: Status of the army's M687 binary program. GAO/NSIAD-90-295, September 1990.
5. D Van Biema. Prophet of poison. *Time*, 145(14), April 3, 1995.

6. FAS. Global Proliferation of Weapons of Mass Destruction: A Case Study on the Aum Shinrikyo. Senate Government Affairs Permanent Subcommittee on Investigations, October 31, 1995 (http://fas.org/irp/congress/1995_rpt/aum/part01.htm).
7. N Davison. The Development of "Non-Lethal" Weapons During the 1990s. Occasional Paper No. 2, Bradford Non-Lethal Weapons Research Project (BNLWRP) Department of Peace Studies, University of Bradford, Bradford, U.K., March 2007.

Chapter 24

Chemical Terrorisms: Threats and Countermeasures

L. David Ormerod, Tushar K. Ghosh, and Dabir S. Viswanath

CONTENTS

Introduction 457
Risk Analysis of the Possibility of Chemical Weapon Attacks on U.S. Civilians 460
Industrial Chemicals as Terrorist Agents.......... 463
Countermeasures 464
Indicators of Chemical Agent Proliferation Activities 464
Research and Development Signatures 465
External Production Signatures 465
Internal Production Signatures..........465
Chemical Signatures..........465
Detecting Clandestine Production..........465
Remote Detection of Chemical Agent Release..........465
Summary.......... 466
References.......... 467

Introduction

In the twentieth century, the propagation of chemical warfare agents and the development of technologies for their defense were strategic considerations of most major powers and many secondary ones as well. On January 3, 1915, Germany fired 18,000 shells containing liquid xylyl bromide tear gas on Russian troops during the Battle of Bolimov near Warsaw, but the chemical froze and failed to vaporize. The seminal introduction of mass chemical warfare occurred near Ypres in Belgium on April 22, 1915, when German military forces released 180 tons of chlorine gas upon French, Algerian, and Canadian positions, temporarily creating a 3-mi gap in the Allied lines north of Ypres. Respirator protection was devised as protection against the inhalation of these new chemical weapons (CWs). On December 19, 1915, Germany first used combined phosgene (CG) and chlorine on British troops resulting in more than a 1000 casualties. In 1916, the British Expeditionary Force introduced chloropicrin (PS) and the French developed hydrogen cyanide (AC). In 1917 (again near Ypres), the first use of sulfur mustard (H/HD) by Germany inaugurated a CW with marked cutaneous reactivity and systemic absorption through the skin, thereby increasing the complexity of CW warfare and of its protection. Furthermore, the oily mustard liquids persisted and contaminated the battlefield. Despite the use of 113,000 tons of CW in World War I with 1.3 million CW casualties and 90,000 deaths, their role remained principally tactical rather than as a strategic weapon of mass destruction (WMD).

Subsequently, chemical warfare was utilized in military operations in Morocco (1923–1926), Libya (1930), Sinkiang (1934), Ethiopia (1935–1940), China (1937–1942), Vietnam (1961–1975), Yemen (1963–1967), and in the Iran–Iraq war (1980–1988) [1]. Although extensive stockpiles were assembled by both sides in World War II, CWs were not used during the seven years of global conflict, owing to the combination of the ready availability of high quality defensive measures and because of the risks of massive military retribution.

Changing international concerns, however, have now proscribed the development, production, and the use of CWs. The 1925 Geneva Protocol prohibited the use of chemical and biological weapons, but not their development and accumulation. The 1972 Biological and Toxin Weapons Convention (BTWC) prohibited the development, production, stockpiling, and use of toxins (and biological weapons) and mandated their destruction. The 1993 Chemical Weapons Convention (CWC) finally outlawed the development, production, stockpiling, and use of CWs, and their destruction was enjoined under a phased protocol that was to have been completed by April 27, 2007, with a five-year grace period [2]. The CWC is universally applicable to all nations and contains rigorous provisions on monitoring and verification that routinely and broadly regulate pertinent aspects of the international chemical industry. Both conventions included provision for international assistance in the event or threat of attack.

The Organization for the Prohibition of Chemical Weapons (OPCW) is the (unique) implementing secretariat for the 1993 Convention based at The Hague, and is responsible for overseeing the destruction of CW stockpiles or abandoned weapons under its monitoring provisions. Approximately 70 different CW agents were stockpiled during the twentieth century, although many had failed to stand the test of time. The U.S. stockpile is the second largest, after Russia, and consists mainly of nerve gas (GB and VX) and vesicants (primarily mustard agents: H and HD). Approximately 60 percent of the U.S. stockpile in 2000 was in bulk storage containers, and 40 percent was contained in munitions—of 150,000 gross tonnage. Table 24.1 breaks down the aggregate total of 71,330 metric tons of weaponized chemicals declared to OPCW by its member states as of February, 2008; over one-third had been verifiably destroyed to date [3].

The Convention called for all possessor states to destroy 45 percent of their stockpile, without endangering humans or the environment, by April 2004. The U.S. program has fallen markedly behind schedule, delayed by technical difficulties, local community concerns/legal challenges, and by program management issues [4]. The nature of the weapon system itself determines how it must be destroyed. Some of the stockpile is stored in bulk containers that have to be emptied, their

Table 24.1 Aggregate Quantities of Chemical Weapon Agents Declared to the Organization for the Prohibition of Chemical Weapons (OPCW), December 31, 2000

	Total Tonnage
Category 1 Chemical weapons	
Lewisite (L)	6,745
Mustard/Lewisite mixtures	344
Mustard agent	13,839
Runcol (HT) (mustard 60 percent + Agent T 40 percent)	3,536
Degraded sulfur mustard	1
Tabun (GA)	2
Sarin (GB)	15,048
Soman (GD)	9,175
Medemo	<1
Agent VX	4,032
Agent VR	15,558
Difluor (DF) {binary}	444
OPA {binary}	731
EDMP {binary}	46
Unknown	4
Category 2 Chemical weapons	
Chloroethanol	302
Thiodiglycol	51
Phosgene	5

Source: Organization for the Prohibition of Chemical Weapons. The chemical Weapons Ban; Facts and Figures. Internet: http:/www.opcw.org/factsandfigures/index.html#participation.
Note: American military CW nomenclature is included.

contents neutralized, and the containers destroyed. Other chemical armaments are contained within ballistic and cruise missile warheads and tactical rocketry, artillery shells, mortars, grenades, land mines, aircraft bombs, spray tanks, and binary munitions (in which the precursors are combined on firing). Munitions present a magnitude of increased complexity as the weapons must be robotically dismantled and drained in explosive-proof facilities before the components are variously incinerated [4]. In many of these weapons, explosives are used to distribute the agent.

(Commonly designed to detonate at 200 to 300 ft ground level).* Rocket propellant also presents difficulties. The U.S. CW stockpile is stored at 9 storage/destruction facilities across the nation: Aberdeen Proving Ground, MD; Anniston, AL; Richmond, KY; Newport, IN; Pine Bluff, AK; Pueblo, CO; Tooele, UT; Umatilla, OR; and Johnston Atoll, HA.

The U.S. army's Chemical Materials Agency [5] is the supervising authority. The prime contractors undertaking construction work, plant operations, and decommissioning, include defense giants Batelle, Bechtel, General Dynamics, Honeywell, Parsons, Raytheon, and Westinghouse. Twenty-six percent of the stored chemical agents in the United States and 39 percent of the chemical munitions had been destroyed [4] by February 2004. The 45 percent overall destruction milestone under the CW convention was met in June 2007. With the destruction of the last GB and VX-filled m55 rocket on February 29, 2008, the cumulative storage risk to the public has been reduced by 94 percent. The Johnston Atoll and Aberdeen, MD, facilities have completed their tasks and are decommissioned. The Pueblo, CO, and Richmond, KY, destruction facilities are still under construction. Final destruction of the U.S. CW arsenal is now scheduled for 2017 [5].

The countries that have declared CWs production facilities include Boznia and Herzogovina, China, France, India, Iran, Japan, Libya, Russia, Serbia, Britain, the United States, and one anonymous state. Sixty-one of 65 facilities have been certified as destroyed or converted to peaceful purposes as of February 2008 [3]. Albania is the latest state to announce the complete destruction of its CW stockpile. Russia, the United States, India, Libya, and an unidentified state (South Korea?) retain undestroyed CW.

Risk Analysis of the Possibility of Chemical Weapon Attacks on U.S. Civilians

It is unlikely that a terrorist group would be able to obtain munitions weapons, particularly since the advent of international CW disarmament activities under the CWC (1993). There has been concern that the poor security of stored CW agents in several countries of the former Soviet Union and sales from stockpiles left over from the Iran–Iraq war of 1980–1988 might result in a market for CWs among terrorist groups. This situation has improved with the cooperation of governments and with U.S. employment-subsidization of former Soviet government scientists with chemical (or biological) weapon expertise. There remains some concern that North Korea, Syria, and Somalia may have stockpiles of weaponized chemicals undeclared to the OPCW, and they remain among the six nations yet to sign the convention [3]. Sudan and China are also suspected of incomplete disclosure. Although there is a perceived risk that unaccounted CW could disseminate to terrorist organizations, there is no objective evidence that any illicit acquisition of CW munitions by terrorist groups has occurred [7]. Detection of CW (or BW) proliferation by a nation-state would lead to international opprobrium and the likelihood of massive retaliation.

The question then arises as to the magnitude of the risk that international or parastatal terrorist organizations could manufacture, store, and disperse their own CWs. Extensive U.S. and international laws now exist to monitor access to precursor chemicals and to certain manufacturing equipment. Still, many precursor chemicals and much equipment is dual-use and readily available commercially. There are, moreover, major constraints in the fairly sophisticated scientific skills, in the specialized

* Aerodynamic distribution controls particle size and enhances propagation, but the altitude of dissemination, wind speed, and direction are more critical for CW dispersal [6].

manufacturing equipment necessary to manufacture, and in safety, remains for most of the recognized CW agents. Such constraints are commonly underestimated in political and journalistic commentaries. For a terrorist organization to make the considerable technical and financial investment in developing unconventional CWs, and to undertake the prolonged acquisition process, with the high risks of detection, there will have to be a cogent strategic advantage. The regular tools of the terrorist trade are much easier to acquire and use, and would be expected to serve their purposes at least equally as well. In the open air, for example, it is estimated that approximately 1000 kg of sarin (GB) would be necessary, if expertly deployed, to exceed the potential of conventional explosives. Unless there is direct state or proxy support of CW acquisition or development, the large-scale use of CW by nonstatal protagonists is unlikely. Improved U.S. intelligence capabilities are also a potent disincentive.

However, the manufacture of a variety of CWs by Aum Shinrikyo, the 1994 sarin attacks on the judges' compound in Matsumoto, and on the Tokyo underground in 1995 brought into clear focus that a determined civilian group with extensive financial and scientific resources could actually threaten a sovereign state [8,9]. There were also failed attacks by Aum Shinrikyo using botulinum toxin and biological weapons. The potential for mass civilian casualties was achieved, but the effectiveness of the cult's attacks was undermined by both unresolved technical difficulties and by the vagaries of cult-dominated behavior. Aum Shinrikyo has been the only nonstate organization known to potentially develop a WMD.

Complex toxic chemicals are produced by reacting precursor chemicals through a series of chemical reactions, each of which requires specific conditions of heating or cooling, the containment of toxic substances and gases, the use of catalysts or quenchers, and often a requirement for specialized or corrosive-resistant reaction vessels [10,11]. To obtain high agent purity will almost invariably require specialized equipment. Although some ubiquitous chemical precursors can be ordered in relatively small amounts without undue suspicion, others may require attempts at legitimization afforded by the establishment of elaborate front companies to help allay the suspicions of suppliers.

The "classic" agents and vesicants can be manufactured using existing chemical infrastructure [12]. Chlorine is an almost ubiquitous industrial chemical, and chlorination the most common preparative reaction in the chemical industry. Hydrogen cyanide is produced worldwide as an intermediate in acrylic manufacture. A small-sized phosgene plant could be built without too much difficulty for $10–$14 million. There are several ways to manufacture sulfur mustard without sophisticated technology or special materials: in the Levenstein process, dry ethylene is bubbled through sulfur monochloride; and an alternative technology involves the chlorination of thiodiglycol, an ink ingredient [12]. The preparation of Lewisite is also a fairly unsophisticated chemical process, although it requires large amounts of arsenates. The production of G nerve agents requires considerably more sophisticated chemical processing, and with the exception of tabun (GA), involve both chlorination and fluoridation steps that require expensive corrosive-resistant equipment. There are a number of synthetic methods, but most involve a stable intermediary, methylphosphonic dichloride (DC). Later reactants are highly toxic and corrosive [12] necessitating controlled air handling and filtering, and high nickel alloy or precious metal equipment and piping. The production of VX agent is sophisticated and fraught with technical difficulties.

Small quantities of chemicals are likely to escape detection [13]. The CWC requires reporting of all facilities that use more than 100 g of certain military precursors with no commercial use, more than 1 ton a year of a defined group of high-risk, dual-use precursors, and of 30 tons per annum usage of lesser-risk precursors in common commercial usage [13]. Since 1985, restrictions on the commercial availability of dual-use chemicals and critical equipment has reflected the conventions of the Australia Group [14], an informal forum of countries that seek to control CW proliferation through the harmonization of export controls and by active surveillance.

Controlled dual-use equipment includes P3/P4 containment equipment and specific capacities of fermenters, centrifugal separators, cross-flow filtration equipment, freeze-dryers, protective and containment equipment, and spraying or fogging systems. Risks from fires, explosions, and leaks during production and storage using small-scale facilities would be a constant threat. Equipment for the small-scale synthesis of kilogram quantities of several CWs would probably fall below export thresholds. Indeed, small production lines for a number of CW agents could be set up on the bench using laboratory glassware [8]. Skilled mechanical and electrical engineers might also be capable of building a satisfactory chemical sprayer or explosive buster. Small-scale production is compatible with unconventional dissemination methods—from trucks, boats, from crashing into a building, or using backpacks, canisters, fire extinguishers, or crop dusters.

One critical question is whether specific terrorist groups have sufficient motivation and financing to undertake the technical developments necessary for CW success. The direct release of commercially available hazardous chemicals and the purchase of stolen weaponized chemicals are easier options, should opportunity present itself. Among commercially available poisons that could be used as a small-scale weapon are heavy metals; volatile toxins such as benzene, chloroform, and trihalomethanes; pulmonary agents such as vinyl chloride, persistent and nonpersistent pesticides; and dioxins, furans, and polychlorinated biphenyls (PCBs).

Another option for the terrorist that has much less technical requirement is to sabotage or bomb a critical area of an already existing chemical plant. During favorable weather conditions, a toxic cloud could be released downwind over an adjacent population area. Knowledge of chemical plants would be a prerequisite. An almost entirely indiscriminate attack might result, but in certain circumstances a dangerous weapon could be created. Chlorine, cyanides, nitriles, and corrosive acids and bases are among common, volatile toxic agents used in chemical plants. The most reliable example is the accidental release of methylisocyanate from a Union Carbide insecticide plant in Bhopal, Madhya Pradesh, India, in 1984. In Consequence, 11,000 persons were disabled and up to 3800 individuals died [7]. This accident led to an EPA-enforced Toxics Release Inventory (TRI) for 66,000 industrial facilities across the United States that provides enhanced awareness of the presence of hazardous chemicals within the community, and facilitates disaster management planning. The Offsite Consequence Analysis (OCA) parts of these reports were not released to the public in case this information might encourage terrorism [15].

Although considerable public comment confuses vulnerability with risk in considering the likelihood of chemical attack on civilians it is recognized there remain many variables, including international political considerations and the strategic motivation of terrorist groups [10]. The most likely chemical attack scenario would release a chemical in an enclosed space—in a building, indoor stadium, or convention center [16]. With limited CW availability, indoor dissemination might be expected to be more successful than an open-air attack. For a number of technical reasons, it is doubtful at present that a nonstatal adversary could target effectively a group of people larger than a few hundred individuals [17], although the potential for much more widespread terror remains disproportionate.

It is useful to reflect that there was only one fatality from CW attack within the U.S. homeland during the twentieth century. In 1973, the homegrown Symbionese Liberation Army terrorist group assassinated a Californian school superintendent with a cyanide-tipped bullet [18]. Some perspective is needed, therefore, in assessing the current risk of chemical attack to the United States. If it is decided that, indeed, cogent asymmetric threats exist to the U.S. civilians, the nation must assess the magnitude of the investment necessary to counter that threat. The possibility of a low-probability catastrophic event has to be weighed against the possibility of public health hazards of higher probability but of much smaller magnitude. Preparedness can itself be an element of deterrence.

Industrial Chemicals as Terrorist Agents

Industrial chemicals are ubiquitous in many counties across the United States and could be utilized as CWs, particularly perhaps by indigenous terrorists. To assist local public health and safety officials in preventing and mitigating such hazards, the Agency for Toxic Substances and Disease Registry (ATSDR) has proposed a ten-step procedure [19] to formalize local and regional planning.

- Identify, assess, and prioritize threats
- Identify local sources of chemicals with attendant risks
- Evaluate potential exposure pathways
- Identify potential acute and chronic health impacts
- Estimate potential infrastructure and environmental effects
- Identify health risk communication requirements
- Identify methods to mitigate potential hazards
- Identify preventive methods to reduce access to candidate CW
- Incorporate threat assessment, mitigation, and prevention strategies into emergency response plans
- Training exercises to prevent and mitigate identified hazards

The enhanced political accountability for the presence of hazardous chemicals within the community has brought better security to chemical production and storage facilities. Chemical transportation, however, because of the magnitude and geographic dispersion of the problem remains a vulnerable area in which considerable future improvements must be made. The potential for the illicit importation of dangerous chemicals in freight containers across porous national borders is also unresolved.

One of the major problems in combating chemical terrorism is the presence of dual-use chemicals [20], as shown in Table 24.2. The globalization of the chemical industry has led to large international flows of numerous otherwise innocuous chemicals that can be precursors for a number of chemical warfare agents [19]. Chemicals such as ammonia, ethanol, isopropanol, sodium cyanide, yellow phosphorus, sulfur monochloride, and sulfur are commodity chemicals that are used in commercial industry at the level of millions of tons per year, and hence are impossible to control, and can be precursor chemicals for tabun agent (GA). Hydrogen fluoride is another chemical that can be used in the production of nerve agents, and which is available commercially in large quantities for use in oil refining; it is also easily derived as a by-product from phosphate deposits. Dual-use chemicals manufactured in much smaller volumes are much easier to control internationally, including phosphorus trichloride (with 40 producers worldwide), trimethyl phosphite (21 producers), and—for tabun only—phosphorus oxychloride (40 producers). Even then, some chemicals have widespread uses; for example, phosphorus oxychloride is used extensively in hydraulic fluids, insecticides, flame-retardants, plastics, and silicon. As a further example, di-methyl methylphosphonate (DMMP), an intermediate in nerve-agent production, is produced as a flame retardant by eleven companies in the United States and by three in Europe (Belgium, the United Kingdom, and Switzerland).

Table 24.2 Examples of Dual-Use Chemicals with Potential CW Utility

Dual-Use Chemical	*CW Agent*	*Commercial Product*
Thiodiglycol	Sulfur mustard	Plastics, dyes, inks
Thionyl chloride	Sulfur mustard	Pesticides
Sodium sulfide	Sulfur mustard	Paper
Phosphorus oxychloride	Tabun	Insecticides
Dimethylamine	Tabun	Detergents
Sodium cyanide	Tabun	Dyes, pigments, gold recovery
Dimethyl methylphosphonate	G agents	Fire retardants
Dimethyl hydrochloride	G agents	Pharmaceuticals
Potassium bifluoride	G agents	Ceramics
Diethyl phosphite	G agents	Paint solvent

Source: GA Snidle, United States Effort in Curbing Chemical Weapons Proliferation, U.S. Arms Control and Disarmament Agency, Military Expenditures and Arms Transfers 7939, Washington, DC: U.S. Government Printing Office, October 1990, p. 23.

Countermeasures

Much of the developing countries do not have the technological capabilities to establish a chemical factory for the production of toxic chemical agents without the aid of industrialized countries. Assistance is needed for equipment and plant design, installation, and start-up. In general, specialist equipment must be purchased from Western countries. Recognizing this dependency, Western governments have attempted to slow CW proliferation by establishing the Australia Group to coordinate national export-control regulations and to restrict the sale of key CW precursors to suspected proliferants. Nevertheless, the export controls coordinated by the Australia Group cannot prevent countries that are outside this body from selling precursor chemicals. An overriding difficulty may lie with the terrorist groups themselves, the great majority of whom may not have the capability or resources to develop a plant for producing chemical agents, even if the precursor chemicals could be obtained. The Al Qaeda, network may be a possible exception. There are a number of downstream measures of CW dissemination that can also be monitored.

Indicators of Chemical Agent Proliferation Activities

Verification of the production of chemical agents is a challenging task. It is not necessary for a facility to be large to produce chemicals. A small production facility could manufacture significant quantities of CW agent over several years. Several potential indicators, or "signatures," of CW development, production, and weaponization can be used to detect the production intent of a country or a terrorist group. Each signature taken in isolation is probably inadequate to identify such facility, but a "package" of signatures from various sources may be highly suggestive of a CW capability. Some of these signatures are discussed in the following text.

Research and Development Signatures

A country interested in developing a CW capability may first try to initiate its own laboratory research in chemical agent development. The country may involve a core group of local scientists or chemists, and a terrorist group may try to recruit scientists to set up a small laboratory. Scientists traditionally publish their work in scientific journals and a disappearance of attributions in the scientific literature may be an indication of engagement that does not permit publication.

External Production Signatures

It is difficult to distinguish between illicit and legitimate acquisition of dual-use chemicals. However a country's new or enhanced interest in the production of chemical products utilizing dual-use chemicals should be taken seriously and investigated. Aerial photography and remote sensing may be used to gather external evidence of such activities.

Internal Production Signatures

Under the CWC verification regime, external signatures obtained noncovertly through overhead photography and remote sensing can be supplemented with internal signatures obtained by authorized on-site inspections.

Chemical Signatures

Samples are collected and analyzed during on-site inspections of chemical plants and suspect facilities to detect signatures of illicit CW production.

Detecting Clandestine Production

The detection of clandestine CW agent production in a nondeclared facility requires human intelligence collection or the covert emplacement of sensors or the use of remote sensing. The development of such information could be then used to cue a challenge inspection.

Remote Detection of Chemical Agent Release

There is considerable technological endeavor to develop reliable, specific, and sensitive sensors to detect CW (and BW) releases that can be relayed to central surveillance stations. The technology of remote detection is discussed in detail in Chapter 22. Handheld sensors are deployed with frontline U.S. military forces, and fixed units installed in vehicles and buildings, as an integral part of modern defense. It has also become standard practice to deploy networked CW agent detectors at major events, such as the Olympics and major international conferences, and they are increasingly used at strategic sites in major world capitals including embassies. The specificity and robustness of the present generation of detectors requires further improvement. As the technologies improve (incorporating such techniques as ion mobility spectroscopy and gas chromatography) [21], they will invariably be widely deployed in the United States and elsewhere as a general countermeasure against chemical releases, and an important aid in CW response preparedness.

Summary

Treaties on the prohibition of the use of CWs date back to 1946, the latest being the September 3, 1992 Treaty and opened for signing on January 13, 1993. One hundred and eighty three countries are member states and an additional five nations are signatory states as of February 2008. The United States ratified the agreement on April 25, 1997, Russia in November 1997, and Libya in January 2004. The Treaty has proven to be a highly effective means for controlling the illicit dissemination of many dual-use chemicals and in preventing their falling into the hands of covert violators. Universal acceptance of the elimination of this entire category of WMD is fast approaching.

According to the CWC agreement, countries manufacturing toxic chemicals, precursors, and other chemicals (including those in Table 19.2) must notify OPCW. The OPCW has developed a database of 1500 CW-related compounds. It is necessary for the parties to declare plant sites that produce aggregate quantities of discrete organic chemicals (DOCs) in excess of 200 tons per year as well as plants producing more than 30 tons per year of a DOC containing the elements phosphorus, sulfur, or fluorine. Production data for such materials must be provided to the Agency. A vigorous inspection regime of facilities with the potential to manufacture CW raw materials is carried out. Because many of these chemicals have important commercial uses, the nonsignatories have economic and political incentives to ratify and support the Treaty. In spite of these and other regulations, it may be impossible to prevent the risk of some dual-use chemicals getting into the hands of terrorists or terrorist organizations that have the sufficient motivation and skillbase to manufacture CWs.

However, OPCW is endeavoring to ratchet further supervision over the worldwide production of assigned CW component chemicals and to safeguard them in accordance with the CW Convention and with international law. Table 24.3 is a summary of Reporting and Inspection Requirements under the CWC. The amounts of chemicals noted are based on per annum

Table 24.3 Summary of Reporting and Inspection Requirements under the CWC (OPCW, 2001)

Chemical	*Reporting Threshold*	*Inspection Threshold*	*Affected Organizations*
Schedule 2 A	100 kg	1 ton	Producers, processors, consumers, importers, and exporters
Schedule 2 A	1 kg	10 kg	Producers, processors, consumers, importers, and exporters
Schedule 2 B	1 ton	10 tons	Producers, processors, consumers, importers, and exporters
Schedule	330 tons	200 tons	Producers, importers, and exporters
Unscheduled	200 tons	200 tons	Producers
Discrete Organic chemical			
PSF chemicals	30 tons	200 tons	

production. Production is calculated over an entire industrial site, chemical-by-chemical, and aggregated for all unscheduled DOCs. PSF chemicals (containing phosphorus, sulfur, or fluorine) must be aggregated by individual production facility and identified chemical-by-chemical. Initial reports by ratifying States to the OPCW are due 30 days after the Convention enters into force. Annual reports are required from national Governments with separate declarations of past and anticipated future activities. Governments are also required to report all unscheduled activities at reporting facilities.

References

1. Chemical Casualty Care Division, U.S. Army Medical Research Institute of Chemical defense. *Medical Management of Chemical Casualties Handbook*, 3rd edn. Aberdeen Proving Ground, MD: USAMRICD, 2000. Internet: www.brooksidepress.org/Products/OperationalMedicine/DATA/operational med/ Manuals/Red Handbook /001TitlePage.htm (accessed March 5, 2008).
2. WHO Group of Consultants. *Public Health Response to Biological and Chemical Weapons: WHO Guidance*, 2nd edn. Geneva, Switzerland: World Health Organization, 2004. Internet: whqlibdoc.who.int/publications/2004/9241546158.pdf (accessed March 6, 2008).
3. Organization for the Prohibition of Chemical Weapons. The Chemical Weapons Ban; Facts and Figures. Internet: http://www.opcw.org/factsand figures/index. html#participation (accessed March 4, 2008).
4. C McCarthy and J Fischer. *Inching Away from Armageddon: Destroying the U.S. Chemical Weapons Stockpile*. Washington, DC: Henry L. Stimson Center, 2004. Internet: www.stimson.org/cbw/pdf/chemdemilguide.pdf (accessed March 4, 2008).
5. U.S. Army Chemical materials Agency. Internet: http://www.cma.army.mil/ (accessed March 4, 2008).
6. Anonymous. Dissemination, dispersion, and weapons testing. In *Military Critical Technologies List, Part II: Weapons of Mass Destruction Technologies*, Section 4, Chemical Weapons Technology. Washington, DC: Office of the Under Secretary of Defense for Acquisition and Technology, 1998. Internet: http://www.fas.org/irp/threat/mctl98-2/p2sec04.pdf (accessed March 6, 2008).
7. AH Cordesman. *Defending America: Redefining the Conceptual Borders of Homeland Defense. Terrorism, Asymmetric Warfare and Chemical Weapons*. Washington, DC: Center for Strategic and International Studies, 2001. Internet: http://www.csis.org/burke/sa/reports/ (accessed March 6, 2008).
8. RA Falkenrath, RD Newman, and BA Thayer. *America's Achilles Heel. Nuclear, Biological, and Chemical Terrorism and Covert Attack*. Cambridge, MA: MIT Press, 1998.
9. DE Kaplan. Aum Shinrikyo. In *Toxic Terror: Assessing Terrorist Use of Chemical and Biological Weapons*. JB Tucker, ed. Cambridge, MA: Belfer Center for Scientific and International Affairs, Harvard University, pp. 207–226, 2000.
10. Office of Technology Assessment. Technologies Underlying Weapons of Mass Destruction, OTA-BP-ISC-115. Washington, DC: OTA, 1993. Internet: www.fas.org/spp/starwars/ota/934401.pdf (accessed March 6, 2008).
11. General Accounting Office. Combating Terrorism: Need for Comprehensive Threat and Risk Assessments of Chemical and Biological Attacks, GAO/NSAID-99-163. Washington, DC: GAO, 1999. Internet: www.gao.gov/archive/1999/ ns99163.pdf (accessed March 6, 2008).
12. Chemical Weapon Production and Storage. Federation of American Scientists. Internet: http://www.fas.org/programs/ssp/bio/chemweapons/production.html (accessed March 5, 2008).
13. AE Smithson, D Mahley, and E Harris. *The Chemical Weapons Convention Handbook, Stimson Center Handbook No. 2*. Washington, DC: Henry L. Stimson Center, 2001.
14. The Australia Group. Internet: http://www.australiagroup.net/en/index.html (accessed March 5, 2008).
15. Environmental Protection Agency. Title 40: Chapter 1, Part 370. Hazardous chemical reporting: community right-to-know. Internet: www.epa.gov/earth 1r6/6sf/ pdffiles/ok_epcra_regulation.pdf (accessed March 6, 2008).
16. N Gurr and B Cole. *The New Face of Terrorism. Threats from Weapons of Mass Destruction*. London, U.K.: Tauris, 2000.

17. R Purver. Chemical and Biological Terrorism: the Threat According to the Open Literature. Ottawa, Canadian Security Intelligence Service, 1995. Internet: http://www.csis-scrs.gc.ca/en/publications/other/c_b_terrorism01.asp (accessed March 6, 2008).
18. JB Tucker and A Sands. An unlikely threat. *Bull Atomic Scientists* 55(4):46–52, 1999.
19. JL Hughart and MM Bashor. *Industrial Chemicals and Terrorism: Human Health Threat Analysis, Mitigation and Prevention.* Atlanta, GA: Agency for Toxic Substances and Disease Registry, U.S. Department of Health and Human Services, 1999. Internet: www.mipt.org/pdf/ industrial chemicals and terrorism.pdf (accessed March 6, 2008).
20. GA Snidle. United States Efforts in Curbing Chemical Weapons Proliferation. U.S. Arms Control and Disarmament Agency, World Military Expenditures and Arm Transfers 1989, Washington, DC, October 1990, p. 23.
21. Noblis. Chemical Agent Detection, Verification, and Identification. Internet: http://www.noblis.org/ChemicalAgentDetectionVerificationAndIdentification.htm (accessed March 5, 2008).

Chapter 25

Cyber-Terrorism

Harry W. Tyrer

CONTENTS

The Nature of Cyber-Terrorism 470
Definition of Cyber-Terrorism 470
Distinctions 471
The Stories 471
Terrorism 472
Extortion 473
Internet Use by Terrorists 474
Ubiquitous Computing and Its Vulnerability 475
Embedded Systems 475
Personal Computers 475
Personal Device Assistants 475
Corporate and Enterprise Intranets 476
Supercomputing Clusters 476
Software Threats 476
The Vulnerable Network 478
Components of Computer Networks 479
Operation of a Computer Network 481
TCP/IP 482
Queuing and Network Delays 483
What Can Be Done 488
Individual Computer Protection 488
Malicious Programs 489
Firewalls 489
Security and Encryption 490
Encryption 490

Conclusion....491
References....491
Bibliography....492

The Nature of Cyber-Terrorism

Terrorism elicits terror—not inconveniences, nuisance, or concern—but terror. However, terrorism must have a purpose, one uses terror, violence, and intimidation as means to achieve an end. The system of government may use a system of terror to rule, and they would use fear and subjugation to achieve these aims. Those opposing a government may use terror to coerce public opinion to achieve their aims. A formal definition comes from the U.S. Department of State:

> The term terrorism means pre-meditated, politically motivated violence perpetrated against non-combative targets by sub-national groups or clandestine agents.

Wiener [1], the well-known MIT mathematician who developed the Wiener–Hopf equation for signal filtering, coined the term "cybernetics" and used it for the title of his book. Cybernetics is Greek for steersman, it is the name Wiener and his colleagues gave to the entire field of control and communication, whether in the machine or animal. Wiener justifies his choice of terms based upon a paper by Maxwell on feedback dated 1868, where Maxwell used the term governor, a Latin corruption of the Greek steersman. To Wiener and colleagues an essential aspect of control is the communication required to change the control, in other words feedback. Moreover, cybernetics arose in the context of feedback in control systems. We may presume that cyber is a popular corruption of cybernetics. Incidentally, Wiener was born in Columbia, Missouri, where his father was a professor of linguistics at the University.

On the other hand, cyberspace refers to the vague entity of human communication using computers and their power as a medium. Cyberspace is not merely telephone lines, but the additional intelligence that is available by computational means. Although e-mail is certainly considered a component of cyberspace, e-mail alone is not cyberspace. Cyberspace includes the communication of computing resources directed toward some end, usually requiring and transmitting intelligence. Additional components include the World Wide Web and even such new technologies as agent-directed intelligence [2].

Definition of Cyber-Terrorism

Cyber-terrorism, then, is a coinage that involves both cyberspace and terrorism. Additionally, some believe cyber-terrorism must contain a political component as the end for which cyber-terrorism is the means. Pollitt [3] has proposed that cyber-terrorism is the premeditated, politically motivated attack against information, computer systems, computer programs, and data, which results in violence against noncombative targets by subnational groups or clandestine agents.

However, this definition fails to explicitly take into account the severity of terrorism. Indeed, some have proposed that cyber-terrorism is the use of information technology to disrupt critical infrastructure. This definition expands the scope of cyber-terrorism to include those elements that may be controlled by the information technology resources.

A useful definition comes from Denning [4], who considers cyber-terrorism to the convergence of terrorism and cyberspace. By that, she means the unlawful attacks and threats of attacks against computers, networks, and the information stored therein when done to intimidate or coerce a government, or its people in furtherance of political or social objectives. She believes that to qualify as cyber-terrorism, the attacks should result in violence against persons or property, or at least cause enough harm to generate fear.

For our purposes here, cyber-terrorism involves the use and abuse of information technology to generate violence, damage, and fear. Cyber-terrorism, then, is the use of information technology to effect violence directly on or indirectly on an infrastructure and resources, and to generate fear in people directed toward some political aim.

Interestingly, under British Law, cyber-terrorists, who include hackers, are to be treated the same as any run-of-the-mill terrorist. Measures have been written into the definition of terrorists: anyone who tries to seriously disrupt an electronic system with the intention of threatening or influencing the government or public, and to advance a political, religious, or ideological cause, are considered cyber-terrorists.

Distinctions

Denning also provides an interesting softening of cyber-terrorism in using the term "hack-activism" [5]. Hack-activism combines hacker with activism. Here, the severity of the damage ranges from nuisance to just before generating fear. Most writers up to the spring 2001 indicated that the world has yet to experience an act of cyber-terrorism. The plain fact is that terrorism of the noncyber variety is much more effective than the nuisance value of turning out the lights.

Some apologists have tried to caricature hackers as the good guys, and crackers as the bad guys, the fact is that such distinctions are useless; hackers cannot control the collateral damage that they impose, and usually have little ability to curb the damage that they have initiated. The best examples are the shutting down of a large number of military computers, the "I Love You" e-mail virus, and its variants. Both these acts caused inestimable damage that was beyond the control of the hackers perpetrating such acts, and netted these hackers criminal liability.

The broadness of the definition of cyber-terrorism requires its distinction from hack-activism. That distinction is the threshold of the violence imposed by Denning; it delineates those activities that should correctly be termed cyber-terrorism. Unfortunately, the tools used by the hacker and the cyber-terrorist are the same or similar. It is a matter of degree rather than substance.

The Stories

The simple attacks reported in the late 1990s were true cyber-terrorism; attacks in furtherance of political and social objectives. They included the following:

1. A Massachusetts ISP was disabled, and part of their record keeping damaged by a hacker associated with a white supremacist movement.
2. Spanish protesters bombarded the Institute for Global Communication with thousands of bogus e-mail messages. E-mail was tied up and undeliverable to associated users.
3. Tamil guerillas swamped embassies in Sri Lanka over a two-week period with around 1000 e-mails a day.
4. During the Kosovo conflict of 1999, NATO computers were blasted with e-mail bombs. Denial-of-service attacks with a political message screen Web sites conducted with sit-ins in support of the Mexican uprising in Chiapas. In this technique, thousands of protesters point their browsers to a target site at a given time. The software floods the target with

rapid and repeated download requests. Similar Web incidents occurred against WTO in Seattle.

5. In the Arab–Israeli conflict, there are numerous incidences of hacking, but none has been classified as cyber-terrorism. The primary damage is breaking into and modifying the Web site hacking mail services effecting a distributed denial of service. Furthermore, denials of service in various important Israeli government sites have been affected.

This is a baseline of hacking activity, which is more nuisance than anything else, and some of this actually becomes fraud. The cyber-terrorism described earlier is simple and more hack-activism than cyber-terrorism. Nonetheless, continuing improvements in technology and in the hacker's trade should motivate organizations and governments to protect themselves against future terrorism.

The Naval Post-Graduate School, in Monterey, California, assessed the prospects of terrorists pursing cyber-terrorism. They concluded that the barrier for entry for anything beyond annoying attacks is quite high. They defined three levels of cyber-terrorism capability:

1. Simple, unstructured: Hacking with tools.
2. Advanced, structured: Sophisticated attacks against multiple systems, using elementary target analysis, command and control, and learning capability.
3. Complex, coordinated: The capability for coordinated attacks capable of causing mass disruption against integrated, heterogeneous defenses. They estimate that, starting from the beginning, to reach the complex coordinated level, would require about eight to fourteen years.

If we assume that the popular Internet started with the creation of Netscape in 1994, then the complex coordinated level of cyber-attack can be expected to begin from 2002 to 2008. Hacking has become more than just a simple nuisance, and a prank. Although earlier efforts resulted in surreptitiously access to workstations by different people, current efforts are much more onerous resulting in downtime of resources and criminal extortion. It is not difficult to image that in 20 years the continued emphasis and training in computing will provide more dedicated computer literate cyber-terrorists. The two cases considered in the following text show that complex coordinated attack is increasing in frequency.

Terrorism

Estonia suffered a distributed denial-of-service attacks (DDoS) on April 27, 2007 [6–10]. Sustained attacks included Web sites of government ministries and, the prime minister's Reform Party. The main targets were the Web sites of the Estonian presidency and its parliament, almost all of the country's government ministries, three of the country's six big news organizations, two of the biggest banks, and firms specializing in communications.

A three-week wave of massive cyber-attacks is the first known incidence of such an assault on a state [9,10]. The size is not necessarily groundbreaking; it is about 100 or 200 MBps. In DDoS, Web sites swamped by tens of thousands of visits, jam and disable servers running the sites by overcrowding the bandwidths.

More speculative, while the attacks poured in from all over the world, Estonian officials and computer security experts believed that, particularly in the early phase, some attackers were identified by their Internet addresses—many of which were Russian, and some of which were from Russian state institutions. The cyber-attacks appear prompted by the Estonians' relocation on April 27, of the "Bronze Soldier," a Soviet-era war memorial commemorating an unknown Russian who died fighting the Nazis. More easily verified is that Ethnic Russians staged protests against the removal, during which 1300 people were arrested, 100 people were injured, and one person was killed; there was also the blockading of the Estonian Embassy in Moscow.

Because Estonia is a member of NATO, does this act of aggression trigger a response? At present, NATO does not define cyber-attacks as a clear military action. This means that the provisions of Article V of the North Atlantic Treaty, or, in other words collective self-defense, will not automatically be extended to the attacked country.

Estonia, a country of 1.4 million people, including a large ethnic Russian minority, is one of the most wired societies in Europe and a pioneer in the development of e-government. As it is highly dependent on computers, it is also highly vulnerable to cyber-attack

Extortion

Although the aforementioned episode in Estonia is clearly an example of cyber-terrorism, the motivation for the majority of DDos cases is extortion. In a specific, true example, a gambling Web site was threatened with a DDos attack unless the gambling Web site paid $40,000 within a few days. Because the attack would come at a time of an important event in which gambling occurred, the loss of the Web site for a few days or even hours would result in loss for the gambling site.

As the gambling site resisted, the extortion amount increased and deadlines decreased. Communicating by e-mail the DDos site tried to dictate terms, and the gambling site just played for time as they worked out a fix. The gambling site spent three weeks working with a consultant who provided an alternative ISP that could handle the DDos traffic. In effect, the alternative ISP accepted the traffic at the rate received until the DDos gave up the effort. In the end, the DDos did give up. The gambling site estimates that it lost over a million dollars, but their willingness to fight also allowed them to create a means to prevent such a shakedown in the future [13]. In essence, they helped establish a company called Prolexia. In a true happy enduing, the consultant developed contact with the DDos organization's Web master, who in an unguarded moment allowed his site to be identified, resulting in his arrest.

The infrastructure for DDos attacks requires a sophisticated and dedicated effort. It requires the recruiting of a few servers for e-mail spoofing and many servers for providing the attack. The latter have the name zombies. In summary, malicious code embedded as a Trojan horse, or virus is uploaded on randomly recruited servers that then become zombies. The zombies can be triggered in a variety of ways, including sending e-mail messages. In addition, they can send requests for communication which requires the receiver to respond and so the receiver spends all its time responding to the messages in effect bringing the Web site down. There are varieties of additional targets including the target site's Web service provider. At present, other network devices become the target including routers.

The size of the DDos attack can be given in packets per second. Such a count gives a metric that has meaning but not really a usefully working parameter in terms of resources available to respond. More usefully is the bandwidth metric of bits per second. With such a metric, we are able to evaluate the size of the attack with an ability to assess what needs to be done to remediate such an attack.

Figure 25.1 shows the growth in attack size. It should be noted that the attacks have grown from negligible to 17 Gbps in nearly five years. The latest estimate clocks these attacks at 24 Gbps, nearly a 50 percent increase.

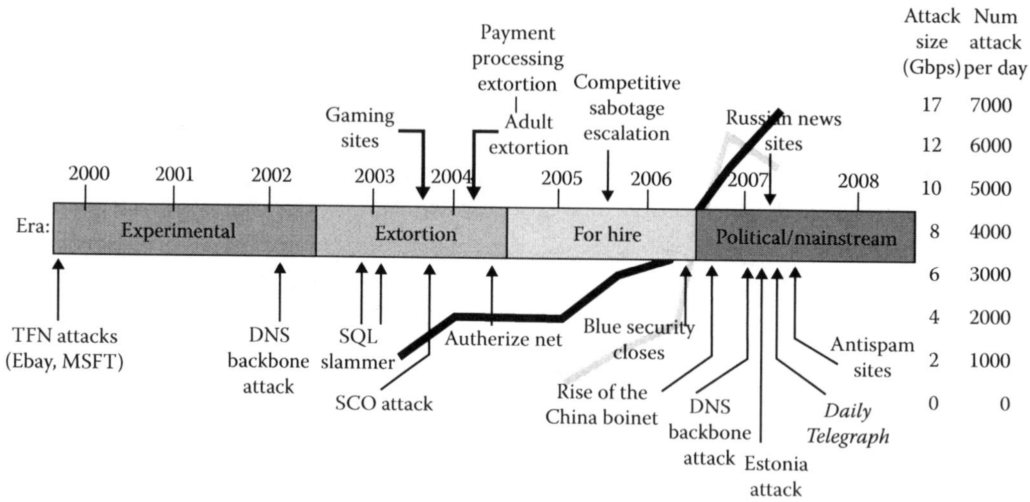

Figure 25.1 Growth in attack size.

Internet Use by Terrorists

Those discussing the combination of terrorism and the Internet, focus on the possibly overrated threat posed by cyber-terrorism, but largely ignore the numerous daily uses that terrorists make of the Internet. In terrorism's usage, the Internet is dynamic: Web sites suddenly emerge, change, disappear, or, change their URL but keep the same content.

Terrorists of different stripes including Islamist, Marxist, nationalist, separatist, and racist have learned the great virtues of the Internet. By its very nature, the Internet is in many ways an ideal arena for activity by terrorist organizations. Most notably, it is ubiquitous, unregulated, and inexpensive; its potential audience is huge, worldwide, and has easy access; communication is anonymous, fast, and robust; the multimedia environment facilitates development, maintenance, and download; finally, it can shape coverage in the traditional mass media. Internet terrorists target their sites to three different audiences:

- Current and potential supporters
- International public opinion
- Citizens of the states against whom the terrorists are fighting (i.e., to stimulate public discussion)

Terrorists use the Internet in eight different ways, which differ little from the ways most use the Internet:

- Psychological warfare to spread disinformation, to deliver threats, disseminate terrifying images of actions, creating the fear of cyber-terrorism, "cyber-fear".
- Publicity and propaganda.
- Data mining the Internet to learn details about putative targets including transportation facilities, nuclear power plants, public buildings, airports, and ports, and even about counter-terrorism measures.

- Fundraising.
- Recruitment and mobilization, not passively but actively in that terrorist organizations go looking for recruits in the Internet using religious decrees, anti-American propaganda, access to training manuals, and finally giving specific operational orders.
- Networking supports loosely interconnected groups because many terrorist groups have undergone a transformation from strictly hierarchical organizations.
- To exchange ideas, suggestions, and practical information by sharing information.
- Planning and coordination of specific attacks.

Ubiquitous Computing and Its Vulnerability

Although the number of installed personal computers in the world numbers in the hundred of millions, it is usually forgotten that this is 2 percent of the installed base of all computers. The other 98 percent are embedded computers, which provide the controlling mechanism to a wide variety of equipment. Let us consider the totality of computer systems in terms of their user classification.

Embedded Systems

A computer is "embedded" into a stand-alone device to control the operation of the device. The software is usually provided by firmware and the operation of the system is in a never-ending loop. The system starts, set to the first instruction, executes all instructions in order, returns to the original first instruction, and executes the instructions in order again. It continues until the device is no longer operating. In more complicated devices, such as an airplane, there may be subloops within the loops. The subloops become effective when the operator actuates a particular sequence of operations. Embedded systems commonly implement real-time systems. Real-time is defined as the execution of a particular process within a given time constraint.

Many of these devices are taking advantage of the Internet and other networking infrastructure to receive remote signals for operation. In particular, the connectivity to embedded computers in automobiles to provide global positioning services is well advertised. Embedded systems also control the rate of gasoline flow and the production of the spark to achieve an optimal operating point, hence reducing gasoline usage. Computers used in controlling airplane wing surfaces have demonstrated substantial improvement in performance of fighter jets. In consumer electronics, computers control VCRs and compact disc systems.

Personal Computers

The wide range of personal computers exists in the home and businesses, small and large. The desktop and laptop units form an infrastructure connected via the Internet, which allows many of these devices to communicate with each other. The Microsoft Windows Operating System on the majority of these machines is very weak in providing security resources.

Personal Device Assistants

These handheld devices are used extensively for note taking and time management systems. Some have wireless networking capability that allows access through the Internet to the larger systems for either upload or download of relevant files. One class of these devices is cell phones with Web access.

Corporate and Enterprise Intranets

Business, universities, and other enterprises may connect some or all of their computers together into a set of local area networks. The topology of choice is usually the client server system with any single workstation able to perform the function of both client and server. Furthermore, the connectivity in the same local area network allows all interconnected devices to communicate. Within the intranet, all networks are allowed to communicate. In addition, all connected workstations may have access to the single server connected to the Internet.

Supercomputing Clusters

Reminiscent of the typical technology of the 1970s where a single large computer served the needs of all the users, very powerful machines exist within organizations to support the high performance computing required for advanced applications. The best-known examples are the San Diego Super Computer Center, and the National Center for Super Computer Applications at the University of Illinois. These facilities have machines capable of operating at teraflops per second (10^{12} floating point operations per second). These types of machines are available typically at a single location within a business or military installation. Thus, it is imperative that such machines facilitate remote communication because putative users will typically exchange data with their local machines and the super computer electronically.

Therefore, there are a lot of computers, and they are connected together. Let us focus now on issues devoted to the individual processor, and later deal with issues devoted to the network.

Software Threats

Malicious programs are in the class of software whose execution inflicts damage to the data or the computer system. They have had a multidecade existence, and were common nuisances. What has changed is the ubiquity of computing; making software threats remain a common problem. Further, the pervasive intercommunication between computers allows loading computers with these malicious programs to effect whatever damage is desired.

There are six recognized classifications of this threatening software (Table 25.1). They are as follows.

Trapdoor: This is a bypass of the security framework of a program. Typically, developers place trapdoors in programs under development to more rapidly get into the program's operation.

Table 25.1 Software Threats and Their Properties

	Penetration	*Hosting by*	*Infection*	*Infection Means*
Trap doors	Inside	Program	None	None
Logic bombs	Inside	Program	None	None
Trojan horse	Inside/ communication	Program/none	Yes	None
Worms	Communication	None	Yes	Communication
Bacteria	Communication	None	Yes	Comm/disk
Virus	Communication	Program/data	Yes	Comm/disk

They intend to remove these aids once the development is complete. Occasionally, the developer may leave such security holes available for future use, and only the developer knows about their existence.

Logic bomb: This is an internal piece of code, which activates upon a condition or an event, such as date and time. An interesting logic bomb used the absence of two sequential paychecks to the developer, in which case the program would self-destruct.

Trojan horse: As the name implies, the malicious program masquerades as a beneficial program. It may then spawn a logic bomb or another form of maliciousness. The Trojan horse may be embedded into a program, or it may be communicated similar to a worm.

Worm: An agent traveling from computer to computer to implement the malicious program. It may then spawn a further malicious program.

Bacteria: These are programs that primarily replicate themselves, and contain no damaging code. The damage from the bacteria comes from the exponential growth of the replication, which will eventually overload resources including memory and disk storage.

Viruses: Certainly the most common of the malicious programs, and the generic name given incorrectly to most forms of software threats. A fundamental property of the virus is that it must attach itself to a program so that it can spawn further. A virus goes through a dormant phase, where it is idle. It then enters a propagation phase, where an identical copy of the virus is placed into other programs or certain system areas, such as the disk boot block. In the triggering phase, the virus is activated to perform its intended function, and finally, during the execution phase, the function is performed. A virus attaches itself to another program, and executes when the host program is run. The viruses may attach to data, or programs, but must have an execution portion. This damage ranges from a benign message to the screen, to the destruction of files or the system.

Table 25.1 shows each of the software threats and some of their properties. The perpetrator of a software threat may be an insider, that is, a developer or someone who has access to the source code. In contrast, malicious programs or software threats that communicate can attach onto other programs. The hosting requirements of these malicious programs may be data, programs, or they may be independent. Typically, a malicious program requires some means of execution; and the easiest way to ensure execution is to attach it onto a program. On the other hand, macroviruses common in Microsoft Word systems attach to data (i.e., a word file or .doc file). However, the virus is a macro, which executes with the document, usually when the document opens. Finally, there are a number of independent entities, and reside as self-contained programs on the system without attachment to either program or data.

Most software threats have an infection capability. That is, they exist on a system or some medium and then proceed to propagate themselves through the same medium, or through the network connectivity. The exceptions are trap door and logic bombs, which inherently require a host program for implementation, and have no inherent replication capability. Trojan horses and worms typically infect by network communication, whereas viruses and bacteria can pass their infection by disks, or attachment to programs.

Pathologies in computer system usually become apparent by reduced performance. This translates to the system slowing down. Slowdown can be effected by overloading memory, and storage such as a disk. Additionally, the processor may be given too many programs to execute, having the effect of slowing the system. However, it is the surreptitious malicious program that may do the most damage. After all, the computer needs to execute to invoke the effect of a program. These can be used to alter the operating system's data structures and changing its effect by producing unpredictable results. It should be clear that there is very little that can be done to physically damage a computer workstation. However, one can do substantial damage to the operating system and software in the system.

Worse, the sophisticated cyber-terrorist can surreptitiously enter a computer and can use the computer as a weapon to wreak havoc in a major way. This requires Internet working such as that available in the Internet.

The ubiquity of the Internet and access to connected computers has made advertisement and assessment individual behavior an important economic commodity. This has resulted in malicious programs or malware that manifests itself as spyware or adware.

Spyware is used to collect demographic and usage information from a computer, usually for advertising purposes. It may also perform activities hidden to the user.

Adware includes pop-up windows or hotlinks that are not part of a page's code, typically they give users little to no notice or control, and generates advertisements.

These are actually Trojan horses with a virus. Typically the infection route is through visiting a desired Web site and the malware is installed onto the machine. One form is to store a cookie. Cookies are used by browsers to inform a Web site that it has had a prior visit. For example, a cookie remembers the ID and password saving the user that concern.

So these have become malicious programs or malware because the user may not have explicitly granted the spyware or adware permission. Although spyware has the potential to store keystrokes and hence data on the individual, adware is more passive but can cause instabilities on the machine and make it function slowly or not at all.

Their removal range from the simply removing the offending file to reinstalling the entire system, and that may not do it. A number of programs are available to remove this malware. In an interesting turn, some free malware removal systems actually install their own harmful code. For the terrorist this is yet another tool to recruit computers for their efforts.

The Vulnerable Network

How does the network facilitate the opportunity for cyber-terrorism? That is, how does a cyber-terrorist inflict damage on the networking system? To do this, we must evaluate networks and their performance from a fairly high level.

A network protocol is the agreement—or standard—defining how two or more computers will communicate. It is assumed that the function "to send" begins with data in a user application. The data is formatted into an integer number of units, and converted to a signal that traverses by either cable or wireless means. The receive function requires the inverse of the sender's operation be performed. That is, signal converted to data, data appropriately formatted to form the message, and finally, acceptance by the user application. The user application can be the user communicating through the operating system.

The network protocol is enshrined in a standard, and there is a bewildering array of standards depending upon the type of data transfer, whether voice, video, or data communications. Each has its own set of requirements.

Data communication requires only that data be sent and restored at the destination. Typically, a single interaction is called a message, and the message is broken up into variable length packets, which are the units of data transmitted throughout the network.

In audio communication, the fixed-length packets must be transmitted in order, received in order, and made available to the user at a fixed rate; otherwise, audio distortions will occur.

Although a single packet loss may be tolerable, neither out of order packets nor variable delays can be tolerated.

Video suffers from the same constraints as audio, namely, fixed-length packets must be transmitted in order and they must be played back to the user within a certain delay time. Video, because it has more information than audio, requires substantially greater bandwidth and tighter specifications. Although the loss of one or two packets spaced far apart is tolerable, variations in packet order and jitter in arrival time are not tolerable. The quality of service (QoS) of a network provides a mechanism for handling these difficulties.

Components of Computer Networks

As in all computing applications, software and hardware intimately interact to produce an effect. We will show the relationship between the Seven-Layer Reference (ISO/OSI, see Figures 25.2 and 25.3) Model and a much simpler Three-Layer Architecture. We describe the memory and hardware layout of a typical networked computer so the relationship between memory and network adapter becomes clear. We will then show the contents of the packet, and the code that allows two connected computers to communicate.

Three-layer model	ISO/OSI 7 Layer model	Internet
Local	Application Presentation Session	
Network	Transport Network	TCP IP
Communication	Data link Physical	

Figure 25.2 Three-layer ISO/OSI standard.

Three-layer model		Computer hardware	
Local		User program User space Operating sytem System data	Memory
Network		Network program	
Communication		Adapter Signal	Network connection

Figure 25.3 Computer hardware for three-layer model.

It is useful to compare the International Standards Organization/Open Systems Interconnect (ISO/OSI) seven-layer standard to a much more simplified three-layer standard. We will use this three-layer standard throughout our discussion here.

Figure 25.2 shows the seven-layer ISO/OSI standard, and the corresponding three-layer standard. It also shows the layered architecture reference model for Transmission Control Protocol/Internet Protocol (TCP/IP). The three-layer models are defined as follows.

In the local layer, the system accesses users' tasks and the operating system. It is here that the initial standardization of say a video strain takes place. This is passed to the network layer.

The network layer provides the end-to-end communication, routing, and congestion control in an end-to-end sense. Typically, the local layer organizes the data to be transmitted in such a way that the network layer may gain access to it to provide for the resources that it needs.

The communication layer takes the packet from the network layer and converts it into a signal so that the physical electrical data connection can be made.

In terms of the operation of the computer, Figure 25.3 shows the relationship between the operation of the computer, and the Three-Layer Model.

The local layer interfaces to the user space, local programs, and the operating system. Typically, through the operating system, connection is made to the network program, in which the network layer resides. At this point, the data then physically passes to the communication layer by going through the network adapter (variously called network interface card [NIC], or controller). This physically converts the data to a signal.

In a more abstract sense, Figure 25.4 shows hierarchical relationship between the three layers and the transformation that the data packet undergoes in each layer. If we begin with the sending function, the local layer identifies the data to be transmitted and formats it into a unit that contains data only. The local layer may perform operations such as encryption of the data, or transformation of the data into a way that is known by the receiver so that it can be applied to its appropriate use. The network layer appends part of the header of the packet. The information contained therein may be the length of the data, the destination address, and the sender's address.

The data and network header then physically transfers to the communication layer. This layer appends still another header (the link header), which contains synchronizing patterns, source and destination addresses, and packet length. This layer also provides error-correcting information, which is usually appended as a trailer to the packet (Figure 25.4).

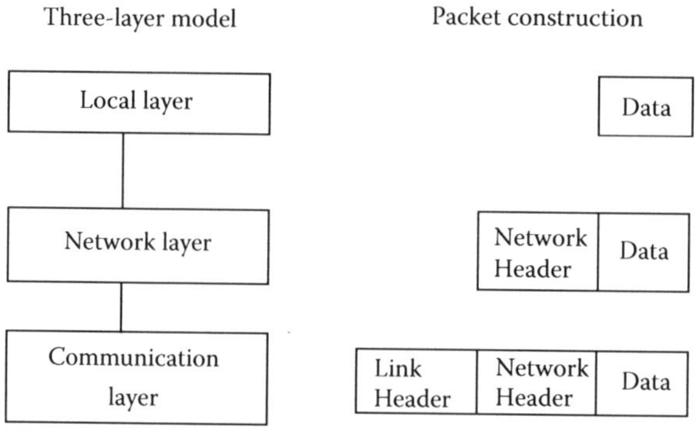

Figure 25.4 Packet construction of three-layer model.

Packet data communication requires the distinction between the source and destination, and the intermediate destinations in routing the packet to its destination. An important assumption is that the communications layer performs the routing, and it is done between two adjacent workstations. The network layer performs the end-to-end communication, and it is between the sender and receiver. Data is left intact until the packet reaches its destination.

Operation of a Computer Network

To get down to the level of operation of computer networking, we can idealize the computer as shown in Figure 25.5. The computer consists of the central processing unit (CPU), memory unit, and peripheral controller to provide keyboard and other access to the outside world, and finally, storage to represent archival storage within the system. Also shown, is the NIC, which we have labeled adapter.

The adapter transforms the data arriving from the system bus into the physical format required by the connection between the controllers. This connection may implement Ethernet, token-ring, or even optical systems.

Code to perform the send and the receive function follows this form:

```
Sender {
Send data
Set time out
Wait for acknowledgment
}
Receiver {
Wait for data
If (data is in error)
Send negative acknowledgment
Else
Send acknowledgment
}
```

Because each of the two workstations has a sender and receiver, the interaction between them takes place to transfer data. This example is a little misleading because there is no address requirement. As long as two machines are connected together, they can interact whenever they choose. However, the addition of three or more machines requires that each machine have a unique address. In this way the controller can examine the destination of each packet and accept those packets intended for its workstation.

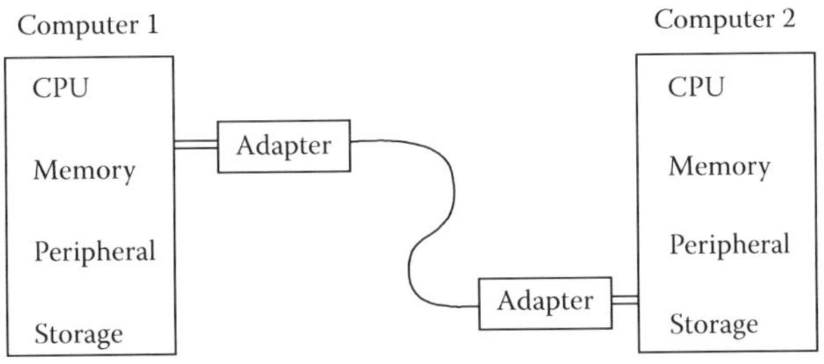

Figure 25.5 Network connection protocol.

TCP/IP

The Internet Protocol (IP) is the commonly used Internet protocol to assure the transfer of a packet from router to router. The best way to understand the capabilities available in IP is to look at its packet header. The structure follows that similar to C programming language.

```
IP Packet Header [
Nibble        IP version #, header length
Byte          type of service (no longer in use)
Word          packet length note that the length of the packet
               is limited to 64K
Word          fragmentation identifier
Nibble        flags the number of fragments to follow
Offset        the offset of this specific fragment in the message
Byte          time to live
Byte          protocol whether TCP or UDP or other protocols
Check sum     check sum calculated from the IP header
Double word   source address
Double word   destination address
Double word   options (and padding)
Data]
```

Very quickly, we see the source and destination addresses. The fragmentation and reassembly word that allows the packet to traverse different networks whose packet length may differ. Thus, the packet may start out as a 64K byte packet, but an Ethernet network will truncate it to less than 1500 bytes. These smaller packets, then, must be reassembled at the destination to form the appropriate full-length packets.

The end-to-end message sending in an Internet system is handled by TCP, the transport control protocol. This has two issues, one the way that the packet is sent, and two, the reconstruction of the message.

TCP is a connection-oriented datagram transmission system, so it must establish the communication path before transmitting. Establishing that path uses the TCP three-way handshake as follows. The sender requests a connection, the receiver grants the connection, and the sender acknowledges the grant. Thus, the connection is established.

In operation, TCP begins data transmission using the slow start: TCP sends exponentially increasing numbers of packets, beginning with one until it reaches the windows size. Each exponentially growing set is allowed to continue as long as it receives the acknowledgment from the sender. Once the acceptable window size has been received, the receiver maintains the window size.

TCP provides what is referred to congestion control. It does so by granting permission by means of the window protocol. In its simplest form, the window protocol allows the sender to send the number of packets up to the size of the window. Suppose window size is eight, we allow the sender to send eight packets. The sender cannot send any more packets until it receives an acknowledgment for all eight packets. Now we introduce an interesting problem. That is, how do we count the next set of packets? Although in practice, the maximum size of the window can be substantial. In this example, we will assume it is eight. Thus, the next packet to be sent would be zero. How do we know that it is not the original zero packet? Because, acknowledgment for the first zeroed packet has been received by the sender, and need not be considered further.

When a sender error occurs it times out, the receiver senses such a timeout because the sender retransmits the same packets. At this point, the receiver shuts down and requires the sender to retransmit beginning again with the slow start and going up to one-half the size of the previous maximum window size, thus effecting congestion control.

Quite clearly, a determined offender can defeat the TCP/IP system by requiring the receiver to continuously shut down its window forcing congestion on the system. In addition, changing the default settings on the packet header fields can cause substantial changes in the operation of the networking system. Address spoofing is a typical example.

Future revisions of IP promise to have multicasting, the ability to broadcast to a defined group of workstations. This will make life easier for the determined intruder. Mitigating this is the promise that a more secure standard will be forthcoming. As the technology changes, the need to maintain security will unfortunately mitigate improvements in addressability and connectivity.

Queuing and Network Delays

Here we develop the queuing delay equations and show how delays arise from propagation, transmission, and waiting in the workstation (largely due to queuing). Excessive queuing can lead to buffer overloading and possible loss of packets.

Because the derivation is based on an infinite queue, delay increases without bounds. However, in the finite queue, we note that packets get lost and more realistically mimic the true case. Unfortunately, network traffic is statistically self-similar, so the problem is worse because the standard deviation cannot be counted upon to decrease, as in the Markovian only case.

In Communicating between two machines, as described earlier, transmission of the data takes place in unknown ways. What is important is the sending and receiving machine. In this way, the delay of transmission between the two machines, t_d, is shown in

$$t_d = t_p + t_t + t_w$$

The time delay of propagation, t_p, is given by the speed of light in the transmission medium. The delay due to transmission, t_t, is the time that the controller takes up in placing the data in the transmission medium. Typically, this is the data length divided by the data transmission rate.

The workstation delay, t_w, is many cases an ignored, but fundamentally important component of the delay in the system. The components of the workstation delay are shown in

$$t_w = t_i + t_o + t_q$$

The instruction delay, t_i, consists of the time required to complete the currently executing instruction, plus the time required to access the interrupt service routine, and the time required to return from the interrupt service routine. Typically, at this point, control is transferred to the operating system to respond appropriately to the data available at the computer. This operating system time, t_o, can be substantial, on the order of hundreds of microseconds.

Finally, there is the queuing delay, t_q. This is the time required to wait in the NIC queue until something useful can be done with the arrival packet. An opportunity for mischief comes in because of increasing transmission delay due to inadequate bandwidth, increasing queuing delay due to an overloading of traffic, and deadlocking the buffers.

A "queue" is a collection of objects in which each object enters, stays for a while, and leaves. The "arrival rate" is the rate at which the object arrives in the queue. The time of arrival is randomly distributed. We usually deal with the mean arrival rate λ in objects (or elements) per second (Figure 25.6).

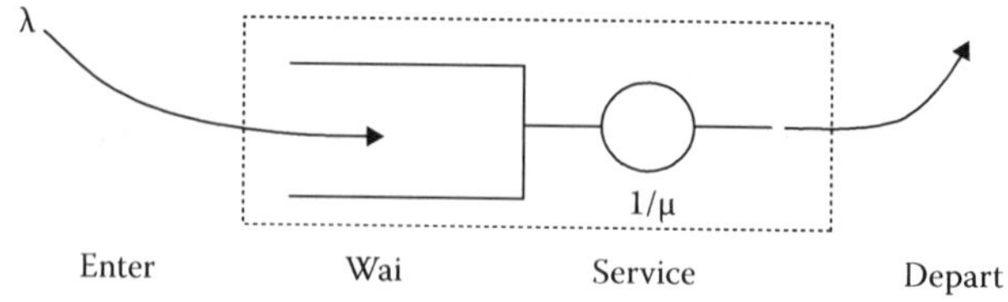

Figure 25.6 The queuing system of an object.

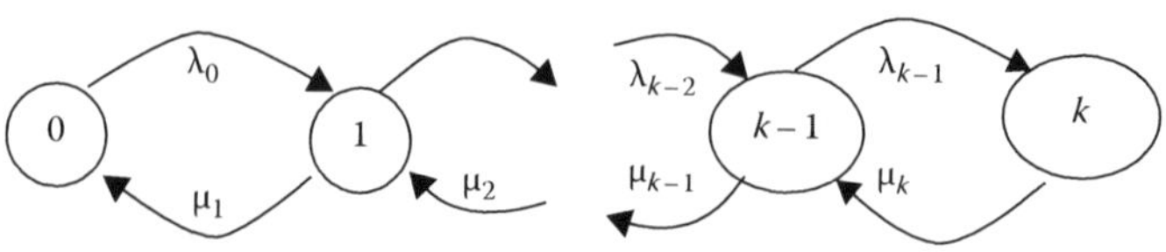

Figure 25.7 A Markoff chain for the queuing system.

The duration of stay in the queue depends upon the "service time" of the server. Each object in the queue waits as long as it needs, until it gets service. It waits until all objects in front of it are served, then it is allocated a specific service time. Mostly we deal with the average service time $1/\mu$ in seconds per object. After the object gets service, it departs the queue.

The traditional way to model, the queue makes use of Markov chains in which each state of the chain is equivalent to the number of people in the queue. The figure shows such a chain (Figure 25.7).

Initially, in state 0, there are 0 people in the queue, and the probability with which the system goes to state 1 is $p_0\lambda_0$. This is called the probability flow and is the probability of being in state 0 times the arrival rate from state 0 to state 1. Similarly, the probability flow that returns to state 0 from state 1 is $p_1\mu_1$ and is the probability of being in state 1 multiplied by service rate of the queue. That is, the arrival rate increases the number of customers in the queue while the service rate of the queue decreases the number of customers in the queue. The queue increases by one customer at a time until it gets to state *k*. Thus, one of the important assumptions is that one, and only one, customer enters the queue at a time. Moreover, one, and only one, customer is serviced and departs the queue at a time.

In the steady state, that is after the queue has passed through its transient phases, the queue remains stationary and it is said to be stationary in the steady state. At this point, we can solve for the probability of being in the *k*th state, and we can solve for that in terms of all of the previous succeeding states. Let us show how this is done.

First, we cut through the probability flows between state 0 and state 1, then the probability of flow from state 0 to state 1 is equal to the probability of the flow from state 1 to state 0. This follows because the chain is in equilibrium. Furthermore, we solve for the p_1, the probability of being in state 1

$$p_0\lambda_0 = p_1\mu_1$$

$$p_1 = \frac{\lambda_0}{\mu_1} p_0$$

Similarly, the cut between state 1 and state 2 and equilibrium allows us to equate the probability of flows from state 1 to state 2 and the return

$$p_1\lambda_1 = p_2\mu_2$$

$$p_2 = \frac{\lambda_1}{\mu_2} p_1$$

$$= \frac{\lambda_0}{\mu_1}\frac{\lambda_1}{\mu_2} p_0$$

We have also used the previously solved value of p_1, so that the only unknown that remains is the probability of being in state 0, p_0, the empty state. We assume that we know the arrival and departure rates of each state.

We repeat this up to state k, cut between state k–1 and k, and equate the flows. We make a further simplifying assumption, and that is to make all arrivals and departures independent of state. This has the effect of removing the subscripts on λ and μ.

We solve for each p_k and substitute the previous values of λ and μ and arrive at an expression of products of λ and μ with again the only unknown being p_0.

$$p_{k-1}\lambda = p_k\mu$$

$$p_k = \frac{\lambda}{\mu} p_{k-1}$$

$$p_k = \frac{\lambda}{\mu}\frac{\lambda}{\mu}\cdots\frac{\lambda}{\mu} p_0 = \left(\frac{\lambda}{\mu}\right)^k p_0$$

This gives us the probability of k customers in a queue. It remains to find the value of p_0.

But first another simplification and that is to redefine the ratio of λ/μ to be equal to ρ, which becomes the efficiency of the queue. This is called the utilization of the queue and it is also a measure of the traffic. We will see that a theoretical and important condition for queue performance is $\rho < 1$. Therefore, we have

$$p_k = \rho^k p_0$$

The constitutional equation of probability is that the sum all of the probabilities is equal to 1, and we can therefore obtain an explicit expression for p_0

$$\sum_{k=0}^{\infty} p_k = 1 = \sum_k \rho^k p_0 = \frac{1}{1-\rho} p_0$$

$$p_0 = 1 - \rho$$

So that the final value of the probability of a queue in state k is

$$p_k = (1-\rho)\rho^k$$

We again see the important role that $\rho = \lambda/\mu$ plays. It is a ratio of input rate to service rate, clearly, the service rate must always be less than 1 or the queue grows without bounds. It should be noted that the mathematical difficulties we get into if ρ is the same as or exceeds 1. The important result here is that physically the arrivals can overwhelm the service times, resulting in pathological queue behavior.

So how do we use this information? We can obtain the average number of customers in the queue N and the average transit time T through the queue system. We find N by taking the mean of the elements in the queue. For convenience, we have substituted n for k.

$$N = \sum_{n=0}^{\infty} n \cdot p_n$$

$$= \sum_{n=0}^{\infty} n \cdot \rho^n p_0$$

$$= (1-\rho)\sum_{n=0}^{\infty} n \cdot \rho^n \qquad \text{Aside}: \sum_{i=0}^{\infty} i \cdot a^i = \frac{a}{(1-a)^2} \qquad \text{Geometric Series}$$

$$= (1-\rho)\frac{\rho}{(1-\rho)^2}$$

$$= \frac{\rho}{(1-\rho)}$$

This result shows that N depends only on the traffic ρ. For a fixed service time, we can vary the arrival rate. Thus, ρ appears as arrival normalized by the service time. We can plot this and see the effect of the denominator: N increases without bounds as the traffic increases (Figure 25.8).

Now to find the average time a customer requires to wait in the queue and get service, that is, the time required to traverse the queue system, T, requires an important relationship called Little's Law. Little's Law relates the number of elements in the system (N) to the average total wait time (T) in the system.

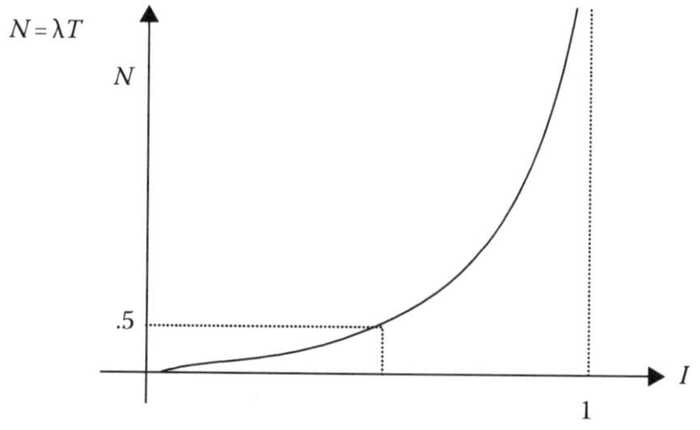

Figure 25.8 A plot number of elements of the system (*N*) versus the traffic (*I*).

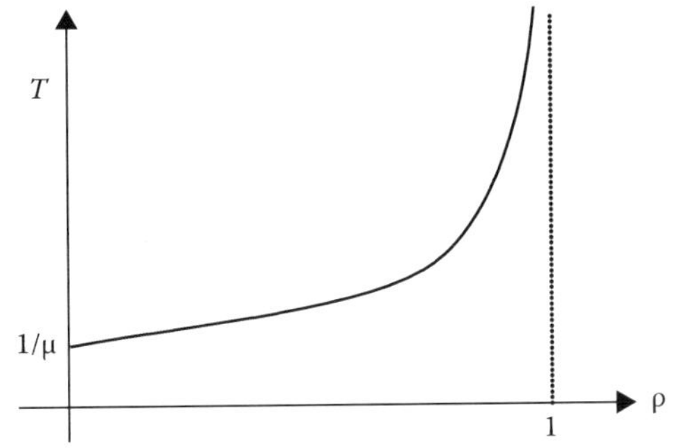

Figure 25.9 A plot of number of elements of the system (*N*) versus the traffic (ρ).

To find *T*, substitute *N* into Little's law and carry out the algebra. It should be noted that we have also substituted for ρ. Therefore, the average wait time in the queue is the following:

$$T = \frac{N}{\lambda} = \frac{\lambda/\mu}{\left(1-\lambda/\mu\right)} \cdot \frac{1}{\lambda} = \frac{1}{\mu\left(1-\lambda/\mu\right)} = \frac{1}{\mu-\lambda}$$

We plot *T* again as a function of ρ, which we can do easily because (See Figure 25.9)

$$T = \frac{1}{\mu-\lambda} = \frac{1/\mu}{1-\rho}$$

It should be noted that the plot again has increasing wait time with increasing traffic. There are some interesting insights that the plot will give. At a very small traffic rate, the wait time is due only to the service of the queue. That is consistent with Little's law. With no customers, waiting service occurs immediately and the only delay is due to that of obtaining service. Further, as the traffic rate increases, the effect of waiting in the queue for service comes in. It is instructive to observe that for $\rho < 0.5$ the average number of customers is always less than 1. However as ρ increases above 0.5 the number of customers in the queue increases and continues without bound up to $\rho = 1$, for an indeterminately large wait time.

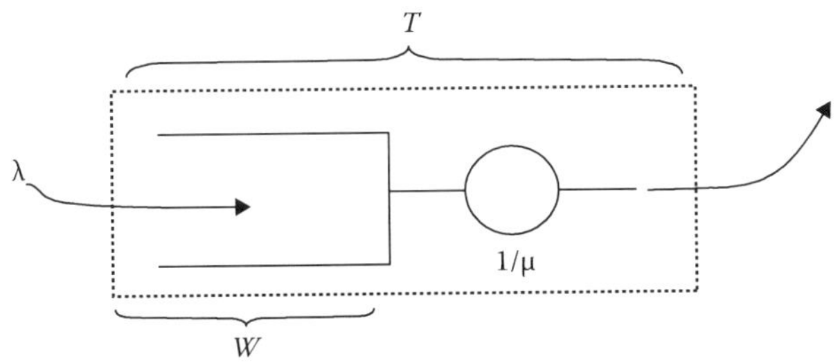

Figure 25.10 Relationship between *T* and *W*.

Now we can find other parameters describing the queue such as the wait within the queue itself, *W*. The diagram shows the relationship between *T* and *W* (See Figure 25.10).

To find the value of *W* we observe that the total system wait time or the average time that a customer takes to traverse the system, is the sum of the service time and the wait in the queue as follows:

$$T = \frac{1}{\mu} + W$$

$$W = T - \frac{1}{\mu} = \frac{1}{\mu}\left(\frac{1}{1-\rho} - 1\right) = \frac{1}{\mu}\left(\frac{\rho}{1-\rho}\right)$$

$$W = \frac{\rho}{\mu - \lambda}$$

Similarly, we can find the number of customers getting service and the number of customers in the queue either by using Little's law or by observing that the number of customers in the queue system is due to those waiting and that in service.

As the traffic increases, so do the number of customers in the queue and the time to traverse the queue. This gives rise to a common technique used by cyber-terrorists—denial of service. By increasing the number of arrivals, the queue size increases and the service provided to a particular customer decreases. The same effect can be gained by decreasing the service time. However, in practice queues are finite. So the effect is worse, packets get lost and messages cannot be reconstructed.

A common pathology of queues is that it fills with incomplete messages, so that the queue cannot empty. A deadlock occurs in which the system cannot remove completed messages from the queue, so resent packets have no place in the queue and are discarded, the messages cannot be reconstructed because the packets are lost, and the queue cannot empty. In large measure, the solution to this problem is obvious, empty the queue. This will be much easier when system designers provide a "queue full" error message.

A case in point is that e-mail queues get full when their owners do not (or cannot) empty them. One finds out that the intended recipient has a full queue when "e-mail undeliverable" error messages return. The recipient in each case is unaware of the problem, but the sender knows well that the buffer is full.

What Can Be Done?

Individual Computer Protection

The most common means for protection is password access. The password is intended to be a secret from all those except authorized individuals who need to use the password to gain access to the resources. The password system has been in use with computing as it was realized that it was not a good idea to give everyone access to a particular computer system.

The password system is enhanced by requiring a user ID, thus, the intruder must know both the user ID as well as the password to gain access to the system.

Let us consider the number of distinct attempts that must be tried to use all possible combinations of a particular password. If a password uses only one letter of the alphabet, an exhaustive attempt by an intruder to try all the possible passwords would simply be 26, the number of letters in the alphabet. However, for two letters in the alphabet, the number of attempts is 26 × 26, or the number of characters squared. Continuing on with increasing characters in the password, the general rule is that the alphabet size taken to the power of the size of the password is the number of times that is required in order for the exhaustive search of the password to be found. For example, if we allow ourselves to consider all ASCII characters (an alphabet with size 128 characters), and the password to have a width of 6, as required in many systems, the possible number of distinct passwords is 128^6 which is approximately equal to 10^{13}

Thus, we see that approximately 10 trillion attempts exhaustibly try all possible passwords. It is entirely possible that a determined intruder can gain access on the first try, or may need to wait for the last try. Thus, password searches usually attempt to use information about the user whose account is being surreptitiously accessed to reduce the number of tries.

Although password access is not perfect, it is certainly useful and discouraging to most but no to the most determined intruders. However, associated with the password is the access privilege within the system, which means the privilege of accessing particular files or directories. It is well known in the UNIX systems that privilege is granted on read, write, and execute basis. Read means that the file can be opened and read; write allows modification of the file; and, finally the permission to execute the files. Each of these permissions can be granted to a file owner, who along with the super-user may change the file permissions. Permissions may be also granted to the system defined group, and to the world, which is everybody else.

Malicious Programs

The most common way to prevent malicious programs from entering the system is to use one of the many surveillance programs available to identify viruses, and other software threats in the system. Typically, the surveillance programs can be run by the user to test suspicious files, or by the system when entering new media, such as a disk, into the system. These programs require continuous updates to keep up with the variety of software threats that continue to grow.

Firewalls

With the rise of the Internet, and the implied promise of public access to a wide variety of networks, it became clear that organizations need to distinguish between private data and public data.

Furthermore, in the early days of the Internet, security precautions were seen not as a necessary safety feature, but as nonsense. After all, visitors were encouraged to visit the sites that were available, and were assumed well behaved.

The issues, then of privacy and control security, gave rise to firewalls to protect local networks. In essence, a firewall is a server that exists between the local site and the rest of the Internet.

An essential feature of firewall protection is that the local site can have one, and only one, entrance from the outside, and that is through the firewall. Access to any other source, whether it be telephone or a local area network, is not allowed. Although there are many ways to classify firewalls, we consider only two—filter based and proxy based.

The filter-based firewalls are the most widely deployed type. A particularly useful filtering uses IP addresses and TCP ports. Originating and destination addresses and ports can be filtered out, and not forwarded to their destination location.

Of course, spoofing techniques can defeat filter-based firewalls. This requires more sophisticated effort such as identifying inconsistencies in the IP address, e.g., an internal source address entering from the outside. However, the primary advantage is that any data allowed into the network must first go through the firewall. Logs of activity can be maintained for an audit trail of suspicious activity.

Proxy-based firewalls provide a separation from the external client to the local server. The firewall itself acts as a server, which caches the incoming packets. The server can analyze the message for suitability. For example, a request authorized to access a private area may have a different URL from a request that has no such authority. Such information is not available from a simple examination of IP addresses.

Security and Encryption

With economically valuable information traversing the networking wires of the world, some means to protect that information must be implemented. There are substantial efforts to provide security measures to protect such data based on encryption techniques. The purpose of encryption is to provide several levels of protection, and assurance concerning the data. These are authorization, privacy, integrity, and authentication.

Authorization is the granting of access to resources. It is the ability to receive permission to use protected resources. Password protection provides authorization to machines. Furthermore, encryption techniques may be also used to establish that authorization has been granted to use a set of resources.

Privacy is the guarantee that only the sender and the receiver have access to the information. In some cases, of course, it is possible that only the sender knows the extent of the message, and the receivers only receive portions, and vice versa. Privacy is maintained by encryption.

Integrity is the assurance that the security of the message has not been compromised, and that the message itself has not been compromised. The integrity of security can be maintained primarily by the trust in the encryption system. The integrity of the message may also require more error dictation systems as well as the trustworthiness of the encryption systems.

Authentication is the assurance that the message as sent to the intended recipient, or that the message was sent from the authorized sender. Authentication assures that the sender and receiver are true, and that the message can be trusted as being indeed sent by the sender, or received by the recipient. Authentication techniques are required to publish digital signatures, or watermarks.

Encryption

Encryption is a large area of mathematics that studies the means to transform a message into a nonreadable form to all but the receiver. That is, to encrypt the message, and to allow the receiver to convert the message back to its original state. In terms of encryption vocabulary, the original message is referred to as plain text, which is converted to encrypted text, which in turn is decrypted back to the plain text. Of the many systems that are in use today, we will discuss two systems. The first is called data encryption standard (DES), and the second one is referred to as RSA, after the authors of the technique.

DES reorders the characters in the message, and substitutes new characters for the original characters. The algorithm for reordering and substitution is maintained in what is referred to as a key. Because the key expresses the algorithm, the key must be kept secret. This technique is referred to as private key encryption, and requires the same key for encryption and decryption. Thus, a fundamental weakness of this encryption standard is the need for maintaining private keys. In operation, DES has a 64-bit plain text block, and uses a 64-bit encryption key to produce the encrypted text. Within the encryption key, there are 3 transpositions and 16 substitutions. Operation of the system requires the encryption algorithm, the decryption algorithm, and the key. The trustworthiness of such systems can be brought into serious question. In the early part of World War II the German encoding system, which was primarily a reorder and substitution system, was broken by the British, and used throughout the war to decode German messages.

In contrast, the RSA system is a public key system. The public key is provided to all who need to have access. That is, it is made public for the purposes of encrypting a message. It cannot be used to decrypt the message. The decryption key is not derivable from the encryption key and is kept in private. It is also referred to as the secret key. Thus, only the recipient can decrypt the message. Not even the sender can decrypt the encrypted message.

The RSA technique uses the computational cost of factoring large prime numbers to create the encrypted message. Factoring large numbers is computationally expensive and factoring the message without the key is exponentially more expensive than with the key. The decryption requires a substantial algorithm and is two to three times slower than DES.

Conclusion

The basics of cyber-terrorism remain: the ubiquity of connected computing and the commoditization of computing gives rise to the notion that important infrastructure can be compromised for political gains. Moreover, in the last few years the banks and infrastructure of a highly wired country, Estonia, did suffer three weeks of cyber-warfare. However, the main use of the Internet by terrorists is its normal use for communications, data dissemination, and product distribution. Nevertheless, commercial uses of important technologies have been subverted to spyware and adware. Furthermore, as speeds have increased, so have the abilities of extortionists to unethically shut down legitimate commercial sites, demonstrating the power of the complex coordinated attack. Between this second edition and the first edition of this book, much practice has been demonstrated. The future will surely show additional such capability.

References

1. N Wiener. *Cybernetics*, 2nd edn., MIT Press, New York, 1961.
2. Stock broker, *People*, November 9, 2000, p. 158.
3. MM Pollitt. Cyber-Terrorism-Fact or Fancy? http://www.cs.georgetown.edu/~denning/infosec/pollitt.html, accessed on 07/12/09
4. DE Denning. Cyber-Terrorism. http://www.cs.georgetown.edu/~denning/infosec/cyberterror-GD.doc
5. DE Denning. Activism, Hackactivism, and Cyber-terrorism: The Internet as a Tool for Influencing Foreign Policy. http://www.nautilus.org/info-policy/workshop/papers/denning.html
6. I Traynor. Russia accused of unleashing cyber-war to disable Estonia, *The Guardian*, May 17, 2007. http://www.guardian.co.uk/world/2007/may/17/topstories3.russia
7. R Vamosi. Cyberattack in Estonia—What it really means, *CNET News.com* Published: May 29, 2007 4:00 AM PDT. http://www.news.com/Cyberattack-in-Estonia-what-it-really-means/2008-7349_3-6186751.html?tag=sas.email
8. J Davis. Hackers take down the most wired country in Europe, *Wired*, issue 15.09, September 2007.
9. G Weimann. Cyberterrorism: How Real Is the Threat? http://www.usip.org/pubs/specialreports/sr116.pdf
10. M Myers, Gambling sites hedge bets, *Wired Magazine* 1, 24, 05, January 2005. http://www.wired.com/techbiz/it/news/2005/01/66358

Bibliography

Networking

JF Kurose and KW Ross. *Computer Networking* Addison Wesley, Boston, MA, 2001.

LL Peterson and BS Davie. *Computer Networks, A Systems Approach*, 2nd edn, Morgan Kaufmann Publishers, San Francisco, CA, 2000.

Queueing Theory

G Bolch, S Greiner, H de Meer, and KS Trivedi. *Queueing Networks and Markov Chains*, John Wiley & Sons, New York, 1998.

L. Kleinrock. *Queueing Theory*, Vol 1, John Wiley & Sons, New York, 1975, Chap. 6.

Security

Scientific American 279(4): 95–117, October 1998.

W Stallings. *Cryptography and Network Security*, 2nd edn, Prentice Hall, Englewood Cliffs, NJ, 1998.

Chapter 26

Personal Protective Equipment

Glenn P. Jirka and Wade Thompson

CONTENTS

Introduction 493
Selecting Personal Protective Equipment 494
Risk Assessment..... 494
Doctrine 495
Available Technologies..... 496
Respiratory Protection 497
Air-Purifying Respirators..... 497
Atmosphere-Supplying Respirators.....498
Respirator Design 499
Dermal Protection 501
Chemical Protection 501
Biological Protection..... 504
Radiological Protection..... 505
Thermal Protection 505
Blast Protection 505
Emerging Technologies..... 506
Conclusions 507
Bibliography 507

Introduction

Personal protective equipment (PPE) is the clothing and other protective gear that workers wear to protect themselves from the environmental hazards associated with a task or job. The "worker" in the case of terrorism response is most often either a warrior (military troop) or a first responder (firefighter, emergency medical worker, and law enforcement officer). Although these two types of responders have markedly different jobs, they face similar environmental hazards while responding to terrorist or potential terrorist activities. Because these environmental hazards are similar, the technologies most often utilized to protect the responder are also very similar.

Selecting Personal Protective Equipment

There is a wide array of protective clothing and equipment being marketed to both the military and public sector first responder communities. To select the best personal protection for a given task, the users must perform a risk assessment. In other words, the user must assess the potential hazards, hazard level, and the probability of being exposed to that hazard. Additionally, the user must have a firm grasp of the doctrine by which their organization does business in a hazardous environment. The responder must combine the results of their risk assessment, knowledge of their organizational doctrine, and a basic knowledge of PPE technologies to select the protective equipment available in the marketplace that is best suited for the task. This chapter addresses the basic principles of risk assessment as it relates to PPE selection, the concept of doctrine as it relates to weapons of mass destruction (WMD) PPE selection, and the basic technologies that are available in the marketplace to protect responders.

Risk Assessment

The use of risk assessment techniques to aid in the selection of PPE is common practice in the manufacturing and environmental response sectors. In fact, the U.S. Occupational Health and Safety Administration (OSHA) has codified basic hazard assessment and PPE selection guidance in 29 CFR 1910 (Code of Federal Regulations), Subpart I, Appendix B. One method for performing a PPE risk assessment utilizes the following five-step process.

- Step 1—Define the mission/tasks. The first step to any assessment is determining the type of mission to be performed while wearing the PPE. The type of mission will subsequently dictate the tasks to be accomplished. A member entering a chemical hazard area to draw an air sample will face different hazards than a member entering the same environment to apprehend suspects who may be armed and protected from the chemical hazard.
- Step 2—Assess the hazards. With the mission and tasks in mind, the next step of the assessment process is to identify the hazards and potential hazards to the greatest extent possible. The obvious WMD hazards include biological agents and toxins, nuclear devices and radioactive materials, incendiary devices, chemical agents, and explosive devices (termed "b-nice" hazards). In addition to the b-nice hazards, responders must also concern themselves with slip, trip, and fall hazards; heat and cold temperature conditions; sharp objects; and sources of electromagnetic radiation.
- Step 3—Determine the risk. Once all the tasks and possible hazards have been identified, the user should identify the areas or systems of the body vulnerable during the given tasks. In addition to the areas of the body that are vulnerable, the user needs to assess the likelihood that the exposure will occur and the consequence of such an exposure. When estimating the likelihood and consequences of exposure, it is advisable to assign numeric values so that priorities can be identified.

Table 26.1 Possible System for Assigning Numeric Value to Potential Exposures When Performing Risk Assessments

Value	*Likelihood of Exposure*	*Consequence of Exposure*
0	Extremely unlikely	No health effect
2	Very unlikely	Temporary health effect
4	Unlikely	Minor/treatable injury
6	Likely	Serious injury
8	Multiple exposure likely	Debilitating injury
10	Continuous exposure likely	Probable death

Table 26.1 offers one possible system for assigning numeric values to risk. The system results in risk values from 0 to 100 with 100 indicating the greatest risk and 0 indicating minimal risk. Such a system can be used to quantify risks from all hazards including chemical, biological, radiological, and physical hazards such as slip, trip, and fall hazards. Numeric values will help a user to determine priorities when selecting PPE. For example, if one possible exposure is to a chemical that is skin absorptive and extremely toxic (causing possible death) through skin absorption and the likelihood of exposure to that chemical is very unlikely, then the estimated risk value would be 20 (10 × 2). Another chemical may produce minor treatable injuries on contact but exposure is likely to be continuous. In this case, the estimated risk value would be 40 (4 × 10).

- Step 4—Compare need and available PPE. Once likelihood and consequence of exposure (risk value) has been assessed, the responder must compare the risk values, available PPE, and the capabilities of the PPE to protect from the various risks. Although at first glance this may appear a simple exercise, many responders find this process an extremely frustrating exercise once they begin it. Responders quickly realize that the PPE required to protect them from all the identified risks often does not exist.
- Step 5—Select the most appropriate PPE. With the comparison of need and requisite PPE capabilities in hand, the responder must choose the most appropriate PPE for the mission. In other words, the responder needs to select the PPE that minimizes risk. In some instances, the responder may find that the possible benefit associated with a mission does not warrant exposing responders to the residual risk and choose to abort the mission. Alternately, responders may find that they can institute environmental or procedural controls that will minimize risks previously identified and allow for safe use of some of the identified PPE.

Doctrine

Each response organization has a set of formal and informal beliefs that compose its organizational doctrine. This compilation of core beliefs dictates what the organization and its leaders view as an acceptable level of risk during a given mission. The level of acceptable risk will subsequently affect PPE selection for the particular mission or task. As an example, consider a response into an indoor environment in which there has already been a dispersal of a chemical agent. Additionally, assume there is potential for the additional dispersion of mist/droplets in the area.

One possible doctrinal point of view is the no allowable exposure view. In other words, when dealing with hazardous chemicals (or any hazard), no exposure of a user to the chemical is acceptable. This doctrine is based on the belief that all exposure carries with it risk, and that risk to the responder should be minimized regardless of economic or social factors. It places the welfare of the responder above all other considerations. Organizations that prescribe to this doctrine would need to select PPE that totally protects the user from chemical exposure for the entire duration of the mission in the environment given as an example.

An alternate viewpoint is the as low as reasonably achievable (ALARA) view. This doctrinal position holds that users should be protected to levels that are "reasonable" taking economic and social factors into account. This viewpoint includes the belief that all exposures carry some risk, and subsequently that as exposure increases so does the likelihood of harm. This doctrine is the guiding principle of radioactive material safety. Protection from radioactive materials is considered optimized when the level of protection needed to further decrease exposure is not achievable without an unreasonable social or economic cost. In our example, this ALARA principle would indicate that exposure should be limited to levels not likely to cause injury or illness where reasonable and while considering social and economic factors. In other words, PPE would be selected that would maintain the exposure over a mission period at or below a permissible level.

An alternate doctrine is that of conditional exposure. Those responders who operate under this doctrine hold that exposure to some identified level of a chemical (or other hazard) is acceptable for a particular benefit. For example, an organization may hold that it is reasonable to risk exposure to levels of a chemical that can cause nonpermanent injury to gain control of a situation. They may believe that allowing exposure to a chemical at levels that may cause serious injury is acceptable if that exposure is likely to facilitate the rescue of viable victims. At the extreme of the conditional exposure spectrum of beliefs is the belief that exposure to levels of a chemical that will likely cause serious health effects or death may be warranted to achieve an identified tactical objective. This view is known as the acceptable losses viewpoint. In our example, PPE would be selected that allowed for completion of the mission with less regard for the health and welfare of the responder.

Regardless of the specific doctrine that an organization subscribes to, that doctrine will affect the specific PPE selected by the organization. Therefore, in addition to a risk assessment, the individual responsible for selecting PPE for use in various WMD events must have a thorough understanding of their organization's doctrine. Finally, the responder must have knowledge of the different technologies available to provide protection from the various hazards.

Available Technologies

The hazards faced by the terrorism responder fall into five basic categories: biological agents and toxins, nuclear/radioactive materials, incendiary devices, chemical agents, and explosive devices. Each of these hazards acts on the body in one or more ways to inflict its harm. The role of PPE is to prevent or minimize those interactions. The PPE utilized in WMD response can be generally examined in two broad categories: respiratory protection and dermal protection. Within each of these broad categories there are a few basic types of technology that provide responders with protection from the wide array of materials and situations they may face.

Respiratory Protection

The respiratory tract is designed to allow for the rapid exchange of material between our circulatory system and the surrounding environment. Unfortunately, the same features that make the system so efficient at supporting our respiration also make it sensitive to many of the environmental hazards responders face in WMD incidents. The moist, sensitive, and relatively permeable tissues of the respiratory tract may be easily damaged or allow the permeation of unwanted materials and organisms into the body. In fact, many early chemical warfare agents were designed to target the cavalry soldier by inflicting harm via the respiratory tract. Consequently, early PPE was designed to protect the respiratory tract of the cavalry soldier and his horse as shown in Figure 26.1.

Respiratory protection equipment currently utilized for WMD response can be classified as either atmosphere-supplying or air-purifying equipment. The primary difference between the two types of respirator lies in the source of the air the user inhales. In an air-purifying respirator, the air comes from the immediate surroundings of the user. Atmosphere-supplying respirators utilize a controlled air source known to be safe for respiration and free of contaminants.

Air-Purifying Respirators

The air-purifying respirator, referred to as an APR, filters or chemically scrubs the user's air prior to inhalation. APRs are relatively lightweight, easily transportable, offer relatively long mission durations, and can be effective for specified atmospheres. To ensure effectiveness, the APR must be fitted with a cartridge(s) that is appropriate for the atmosphere that is entered. For example, high-efficiency particulate air (HEPA) filters are used to filter particulate matters such as asbestos, radioactive particles, and biological agents such as anthrax spores. Alternately, organic vapor cartridges

Figure 26.1 Cavalry soldier and horse each utilizing an air-purifying respirator to protect the respiratory tract.

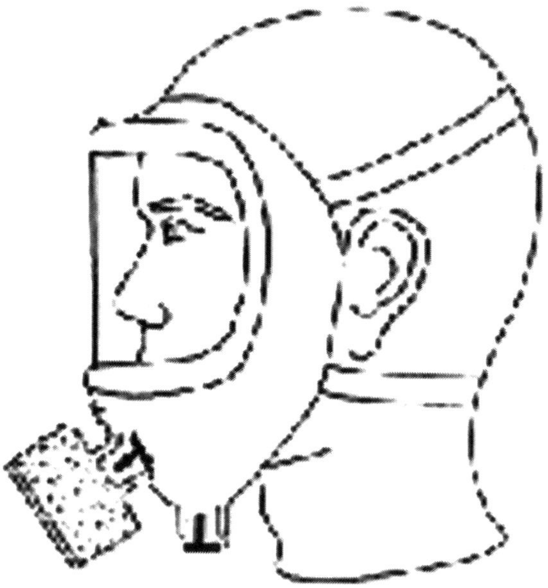

Figure 26.2 Schematic representation of an APR.

are utilized for filtering many of the organic-based chemical agents. Figure 26.2 shows a schematic view of a full-face APR.

APR cartridges and filters have several limitations. The functional life of a cartridge is limited and requires replacement at designated intervals after opening the sealed container in which it is packaged. The cartridges and filters also have shelf lives and must be discarded upon expiration to avoid degraded performance.

Additionally, although cartridges are effective at purifying air passing through them, they do not produce oxygen and therefore cannot be used in oxygen-deficient atmospheres. Finally, the APR user has the added respiratory burden caused by pulling the inhaled air through the cartridges.

To reduce the stress placed on the user using an APR, APRs equipped with powered fans have been introduced in the marketplace. These fan-powered APRs are known as powered air-purifying respirators or PAPRs. Figure 26.3 shows a typical PAPR composed of a hooded loose-fitting facepiece that is connected to a fan unit by a breathing hose. The belt mounted fan unit draws air through the filters and forces air through the breathing tube to the facepiece of the respirator. PAPRs are powered by either disposable or rechargeable batteries and typically can operate for approximately six hours before replacement.

Atmosphere-Supplying Respirators

Atmosphere-supplying respirators are those that supply air from a fixed source directly to the user. The atmosphere is typically supplied from a cylinder of pressurized air either carried by the user or maintained within 300 ft. Air is allowed to flow to the user through a pressurized hose from the cylinder. Although not commonly used by responders, the air supply may also be a breathing air compressor located near the use site.

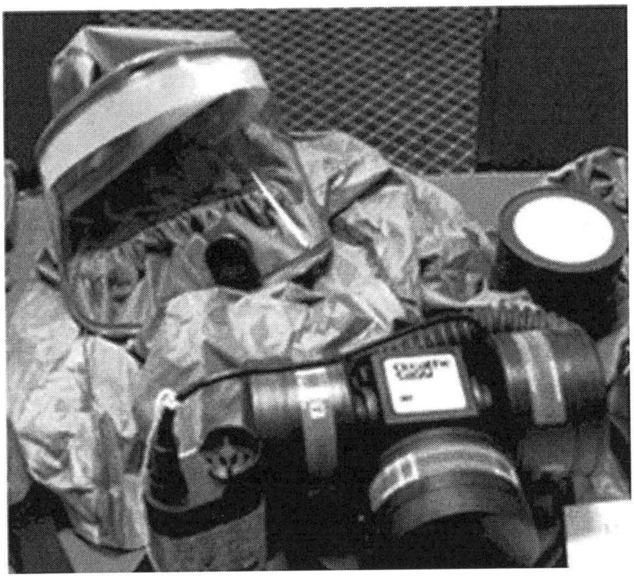

Figure 26.3 A hooded loose-fitting facepiece powered APR. Note the fan/filter unit in the foreground with the battery.

Atmosphere-supplying respirators are considered as the highest level of respiratory protection available. They provide the highest level of protection because they supply a known-safe air supply to the user. However, this characteristic leads to many disadvantages in using this type of device during WMD response. The user must carry their air supply in a cylinder or be tethered to the air supply. Compressed breathing air is carried in metal or composite cylinders on the back or waist of the user. These cylinders are relatively heavy and must be refilled after 20–60 minutes of operation in the most commonly used configuration. This configuration of the supplied-atmosphere respirator is known as a self-contained breathing apparatus (SCBA). The SCBA shown in Figure 26.4 is commonly used by responders to WMD events and operates in an open circuit mode. Open circuit SCBA users exhale their respirations out of the system and to the atmosphere. Closed circuit SCBA recycle or scrub exhaled air in an attempt to maximize use of the air supply. Closed circuit SCBA have seen limited use in the WMD arena because they can increase mission duration up to approximately two to four hours, but are more bulky than open circuit SCBA and may hamper operations.

Respirator Design

Respirator designs vary widely and can markedly affect the way a respirator protects a user from a given hazard. Respirators may be either tight fitting or loose fitting. Tight-fitting respirators are those that press tightly against the user's face and seal the surrounding atmosphere out. Tight-fitting respirators require that users be properly fit, and require that nothing pass between the seal of the respirator and the face. This requirement precludes users with facial hair or eyewear that breaks the seal of the mask from utilizing the respirator. Tight-fitting respirators are available in either full-face or half-face construction. Half-face tight-fitting respirators encapsulate the nose and mouth but

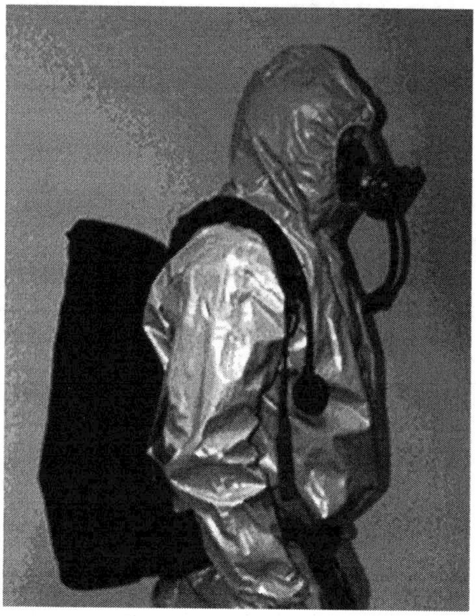

Figure 26.4 Responder wearing a level B ensemble consisting of a self-contained breathing apparatus and a splash-protective nonwoven polymer coverall. (Photo courtesy of the University of Missouri Fire and Rescue Training Institute.)

leave the eyes exposed. Full-face tight-fitting respirators encapsulate the eyes, nose, and mouth and are preferred because they provide additional protection to the eyes that are focal points of chemical absorption.

Loose-fitting respirators are constructed as hoods that enclose the user's head and secure around the upper torso or neck. Airflow into the hood prevents contaminated air from entering the user's air supply. This configuration allows users with facial hair and eyewear to utilize a respirator without altering the eyewear or facial hair. They do, however, use more air because of the air required to maintain the airflow out of the hood. This added airflow keeps contaminants from entering the hood. Hooded respirators are either supplied-atmosphere or PAPR style respirators.

Construction materials can also be vitally important to the user of a respirator. Construction materials that allow permeation of chemicals to which the respirator will be exposed are unacceptable. There are several different seal materials used in respirator facepieces, some of which are not as resistive to chemical agents as a user would need to offer protection. Additionally, many respirators designed for use in WMD environments are equipped with shrouds to protect the head from contact with harmful chemicals as shown in Figure 26.5. In addition to a Nomex protective hood, the Swat-Pak™ SCBA shown in Figure 26.4 incorporates black materials to reduce visibility of the wearer in tactical situations.

The National Institute of Occupational Safety and Health (NIOSH) has authority for approving all nonmilitary respiratory protective equipment utilized in the United States. NIOSH requires that respirators be approved for use in the intended environment. This approval requires tests that are designed to ensure that the respirator indeed provides the user with protection. Unfortunately, until recently, there was no NIOSH program in place to evaluate SCBA for use in

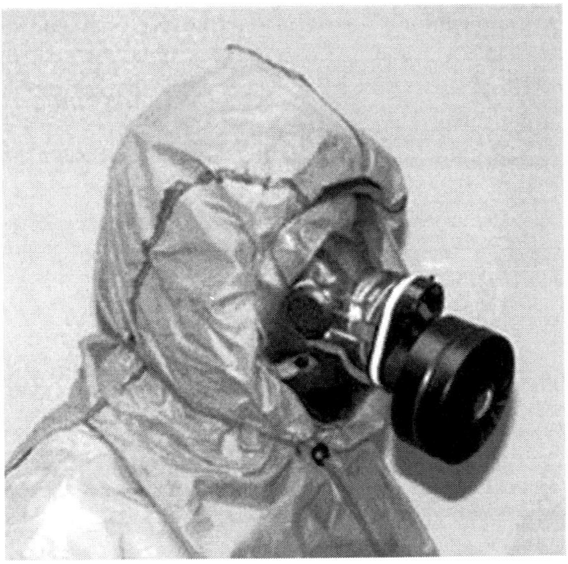

Figure 26.5 Self-contained breathing apparatus. (Photo courtesy of Boone County [MO] Fire Protection District Hazardous Incident Response Team and Missouri Urban Search and Rescue Task Force One WMD Response Unit.)

chemical warfare agent environments and thus no SCBAs approved for public safety use in these environments. NIOSH, in January 2002, instituted a program to test and certify SCBA for use in these environments.

Dermal Protection

Dermal protection from chemicals, biological materials, radioactive materials, thermal hazards, and blast effects is necessary for responders to WMD-type incidents. There is no one garment or suit that provides protection from all these hazards simultaneously, thus the responder to terrorist activities must choose from garments based on a variety of technologies and designed for a variety of uses. One convenient manner to examine these technologies is by the hazard that they are used to protect from.

Chemical Protection

Chemically protective garments utilized for protection during WMD-type events are constructed of materials based either on adsorptive technologies or on nonwoven polymer barrier technologies. Adsorptive technologies are the basis for the battle dress overgarments (BDOs) utilized by military agencies in mission-oriented protective posture (MOPP), while nonwoven polymer fabrics are commonly associated with industrial chemical protective garments.

Chemical protective garments based on adsorptive technology are constructed in a straightforward manner and are often referred to as "permeables." These garments are based on a carbon-based sorbent core that provides the bulk of the chemical protection. The BDO core consists of an activated charcoal impregnated foam. In chemically protective undergarments (CPUs) used in Joint Services Light Integrated Suit Technology (JSLIST), a polymerically encapsulated activated carbon is utilized to provide the sorptive protection from agents. Civilian first responders are also using the CPU-type garments for their response to WMD events.

The sorbent core of these garments is surrounded with an outer and inner shell. These shells are made up of fabrics designed to promote air permeability and evaporative cooling. This airflow increases user comfort and decreases heat stress. The outer shell (between the sorbent layer and the environment) is designed to limit liquid penetration or redistribute liquid to decrease concentration. The inner shell (the fabric between the core and the user) is designed to wick away perspiration and provide a comfortable interface for the user.

Activated charcoal looses its ability to adsorb contaminants as it is exposed to ambient air, moisture, and contaminants. Therefore, garments based on activated charcoal have limited lifetimes ranging from a few days up to a few months. Users of these garments store them in clean or sealed environments. Additionally, the garments are used only for limited time frames once they have been placed into service. In some instances, these sorbent garments may be laundered and reused a limited number of times.

Nonwoven polymer-based garments are composed of a polymer support with one or more barrier film layers laminated to the support. The chemical resistance and physical properties of these multilayered fabrics varies widely depending on the composition of each layer and the number of layers. For example, some polymer films are excellent at resisting corrosive chemicals yet rapidly degrade when exposed to organic solvents.

Nonwoven chemically protective clothing is available in different styles with different construction features. Typically, this clothing is broadly defined as either splash protective or vapor protective. Vapor-protective clothing is designed to fully encapsulate the user and their respiratory protection within a vapor-resistant envelope that provides vapor, liquid splash, and particulate protection from the hazardous chemicals that pose the risk. Vapor-protective garments resist both vapor and liquid penetration and permeation. Penetration is the process by which chemicals pass through the garment via the openings in the garment such as seams, closures, and imperfections in the material. Permeation is the diffusion of a chemical through the molecular structure of the material. Liquid splash-protective garments protect from liquid penetration or permeation and particulate permeation, but provide little or no protection from vapor hazards.

Selecting a liquid splash-protective garment or a vapor-protective garment can be difficult considering the vast options in the marketplace. Selection needs to be based on the risk assessment performed, the organizational doctrine, and a knowledge of the performance of the garment or ensemble considered for use. Unfortunately, the performance of garments available in the marketplace varies widely. Therefore, responders often turn to consensus standards to assist them in choosing well-constructed general purpose chemically resistant clothing. The most widely utilized consensus documents for chemically protective clothing are those produced by the National Fire Protection Association (NFPA).

The NFPA issues a number of standards that define minimum performance requirements for PPE utilized during emergency response. These personal protective clothing and equipment standards include the three standards listed in Table 26.2 that define minimum levels of performance for chemical and biological protective ensembles and clothing. The NFPA technical committees responsible for these standards have emphasized an ensemble concept that ensures that a PPE is designed and tested in such a way as to ensure protection at the interfaces between components. In other words, for a splash protective ensemble, its performance against liquid splash is defined

Table 26.2 NFPA Consensus Standards That Set Minimum Performance Criteria for Chemically Protective Clothing

NFPA Standard No.	*Current Edition*	*Title*
1991	2000	Standard on Vapor-Protective Ensembles for Hazardous Materials Emergencies
1992	2000	Standard on Liquid Splash-Protective Ensembles and Clothing for Hazardous Materials Emergencies
1994	2001	Standard on Protective Ensembles for Chemical/ Biological Terrorism Incidents

as an ensemble including gloves, clothing, boots, and all the interfaces between the components of the ensemble rather than as individual items that leave the user to guess at proper interfacing techniques and protection levels.

Specifically, NFPA 1994 (2001 ed.) defines minimum performance standards for three classes of ensembles designed to provide protection to responders responding to chemical or biological terrorism incidents.

- Class 1 Ensembles. Class 1 ensembles are vapor-protective (EPA level A) ensembles similar to NFPA 1991 compliant garments with reduced abrasion and flame-resistance characteristics. Class 1 ensembles would likely be used in environments where droplet or particulate exposure is extremely likely and concentrations of agent are high (at or above the immediately dangerous to life and health [IDLH]).
- Class 2 Ensembles. Class 2 ensembles are splash-protective (EPA level B/C) garments that provide a minimal level of vapor protection in addition to the splash protection. Concentration of the hazards in the environment where this ensemble is used will be below the IDLH. A hooded coverall with taped sleeves does not meet the performance requirements of this class. A class 2 ensemble will likely include attached gloves and visor hoods or shrouds to prevent liquid penetration around the neck of the user.
- Class 3 Ensembles. Class 3 ensembles are splash-protective garments (level B/C) that provide no vapor protection. They are likely to be used in areas where there is little threat of direct contamination. Such an environment might include securing a perimeter where exposure levels will be below the short-term exposure limit (STEL).

All three classes require penetration and permeation testing against particular levels of "live" chemical warfare agents such as VX, Sarin (GB), Mustard (HD), and Lewisite (L). The challenge level is greater for class 1 ensembles than for the class 2 and class 3 ensembles. All ensembles are additionally required to resist permeation and penetration from representative toxic industrial chemicals (TICs) or as they are alternately known, toxic industrial materials (TIMs). Finally, the ensembles are required to resist penetration by viral agents as well as provide minimum levels of rip and puncture resistances.

Unlike the permeable garments discussed earlier, the nonwoven polymer-based clothing does not allow for airflow or evaporative cooling to any great extent. This characteristic increases the heat stress experienced by the user and often limits the duration of missions that may be performed in this type of garment. However, the overall chemical resistance of the nonwoven barrier is typically superior to the permeable technologies. Consequently, gloves, boots, and respirator facepieces are constructed out of polymeric materials.

Although chemically protective clothing is classed as either splash-protective or vapor-protective, it is not worn without associated respiratory protection. The U.S. Environmental Protection Agency utilizes a four tier system to classify the respiratory protection/chemical protection combinations used by responders. This classification system, summarized in Table 26.3, is based on four levels of protection commonly used in response and normal chemical handling.

Finally, users must carefully consider the construction features of nonwoven chemically protective clothing. Garments that look identical in construction may actually differ greatly. For example, consider two garments constructed out of the same nonwoven polymer chemically protective material. Although the portion of the garment that is protecting the majority of the body is made of the same material, the visor materials may be different, the glove materials may be different, or the seams may be closed and sealed differently. In this case, the permeation resistance for the main fabric would be identical but the actual ability of the PPE to resist chemical permeation and penetration may be significantly different.

Biological Protection

Protective clothing designed to protect users from biological agents is commonly produced from the same impermeable polymer membrane films utilized for the nonwoven chemical protection described previously. Garments certified resistant to biopenetration are done so in accordance with standardized test procedures such as the American Society for Testing of Materials (ASTM) Standard F 1671. This test utilizes the surrogate biological agent *Phi-X174 Bacteriophage* to assess resistance to biopenetration. In addition to the protective clothing, respiratory protection including atmosphere-supplying respirators and air-purifying respirators are used to protect the respiratory tract of the responder from inhalation of biological agents.

Table 26.3 NFPA Consensus Standards That Cover Chemically Protective Clothing

Level	*Skin Protection*	*Respiratory Protection*	*Use*
A	Vapor-protective Liquid splash-protective Particulate-protective	Supplied-atmosphere respirator	High splash or immersion environments, vapors skin toxic, or corrosive
B	Liquid splash-protective Particulate-protective	Supplied-atmosphere respirator	Incidental splash, limited chemical exposure, hazardous vapors not corrosive to skin or skin toxic
C	Liquid splash-protective Particulate-protective	Air-purifying respirator	Incidental splash, limited chemical exposure, vapors below permissible exposure limits
D	Minimum to no chemical protection	N/A	No chemical exposure

Radiological Protection

Protective clothing designed to provide protection from radioactive material is generally designed to meet the requirements set forth for chemical particulate matter or liquid splashes. If an ensemble is capable of protecting from these other hazards, it will also provide protection from radioactive particulate. Radioactive protective equipment typically consists of respiratory protection such as an APR or PAPR with HEPA filtration and a nonwoven polymer film splash-protective garment. This type of ensemble limits the likelihood of radioactive particulate entering the respiratory tract and the digestive tract and provides dermal protection as well. However, radiation in the form of waves, such as gamma- or x-rays will easily penetrate this ensemble.

Thermal Protection

Responders to terrorism incidents may wear thermal protective gear during initial response to the incident. Responders wear this type of gear for one of two reasons, either because the event has resulted in or poses a threat of fire or because they are firefighters and are utilizing the gear to minimize exposure to chemical or biological agents. Thermal protective gear includes the standard firefighter's gear, proximity gear, and entry gear. Entry gear is designed to allow users to make brief entries in areas where there will be direct flame contact with the PPE. Proximity gear is designed for working close to large open flame fires such as those caused by aviation fuel released during plane crashes. Structural firefighting gear is the most commonly utilized thermal protective gear and is utilized by firefighters to make entry into burning buildings. It is designed to provide limited thermal protection and a moderate level of physical hazard protection.

Thermal protective gear is constructed of an outer shell, a moisture barrier, and a thermal protective layer. The outer shells of these garments are made from fabric woven from durable polymers such as Nomex and Kevlar. In some instances, the outer shell is aluminized to increase its ability to reflect heat from the wearer. The vapor barrier limits the ability of superheated vapors to penetrate the garment, and the thermal protective layer consists of one or more layers of thermally insulating material.

In addition to providing thermal protection, structural firefighting gear has been shown to provide some limited protection from chemical agents when utilized with SCBA. The U.S. Army Soldier Biological Chemical Command (SBCCOM) has tested structural firefighter's gear and issued guidelines for the use of such gear in WMD environments. Although not designed for this use, the gear has been shown under some conditions to allow for the entry into a contaminated area for very brief periods to rescue a victim. It is, however, important to emphasize that structural firefighter's gear is not designed to provide this type of protection and users wearing it in certain environments are at danger of serious health effects and possible death if durations or limiting conditions are exceeded.

Blast Protection

The primary concern of Explosive Ordnance Disposal (EOD)/bomb response unit personnel is achieving blast protection. Blast protection is provided by basic ballistic protective fabrics and vest-type technologies commonly in use in the law enforcement community. Additionally, responders need to concern themselves with basic chemical, biological, and radioactive protection

Figure 26.6 A bomb technician wearing a SRS-5 blast resistant garment with SCBA and chemically protective undergarment. (Photo courtesy of Missouri State Highway Patrol Bomb Squad.)

because of the potential use of improvised explosive devices (IED) containing contaminants. These "dirty bombs" pose a greater risk to the bomb technician than a standard explosive device. The current state-of-the-art protection available to the EOD/bomb response team member for this type of event utilizes chemical protective clothing beneath blast protective clothing. Although the integration of chemical protection with blast protection seems initially trivial, the ability of a garment to withstand a blast and chemical penetration at the time of a blast is quite a rigorous task. Figure 26.6 shows a blast protective garment specifically designed to accommodate SCBA and chemically protective clothing. Typically, a nonwoven polymer garment will be utilized under this garment to provide chemical protection.

Emerging Technologies

There are ongoing efforts to develop better protective materials and garments for responders to WMD incidents. Many of the efforts utilize technologies currently being utilized in either the high-tech or the military sector. In some instances, these technologies are being simultaneously developed for use in all the sectors. For example, selectively permeable membrane materials like those shown in Figure 26.7 are currently under investigation by both private and public agencies. The technology is currently being utilized by the military under a Joint Service Defense Technology Objective. Under this program a selectively permeable membrane is being used to replace the carbon-based sorptive materials normally used in sorptive garments. Replacing the carbon-based materials with a selectively permeable membrane reduces the garment weight by as much as 50 percent while maintaining chemical resistance and airflow through the garment. Currently, researchers are focusing efforts on a cellulose-based membrane and an amine-based membrane.

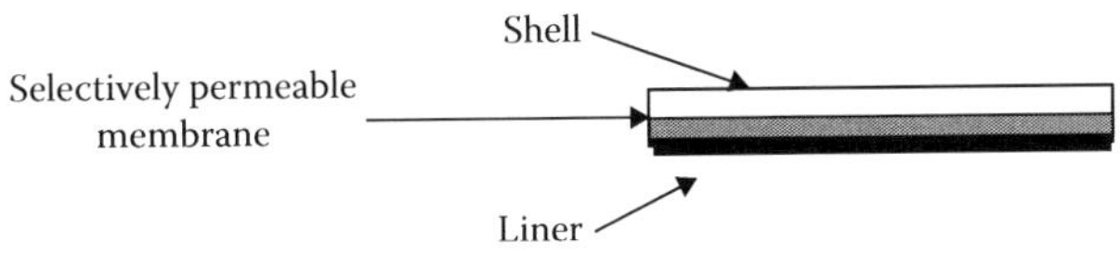

Figure 26.7 Construction schematic of selectively permeable membrane fabrics currently being developed for WMD use.

In addition to the development of improved fabrics, many organizations are working to increase work/mission durations of the user by increasing comfort and limiting physiological stress to the user of the WMD PPE. Lightweight microclimate conditioning systems designed to regulate the user's physiologic environment and increase work times are being tested by the military. Breathing apparatus designed to regulate the temperature of inhaled air and subsequently provide additional physiological control and comfort are also under investigation in both the public and private sectors.

Conclusions

Protective clothing utilized by both civilian and military responders to terrorist and WMD-type events is diverse and based upon a limited number of technologies. Responders need to have a clear understanding of the risks they face, hazard and risk assessment techniques, their organizational doctrine, and the available technologies to select appropriate PPE for use at WMD incidents. PPE for use at terrorism incidents is currently evolving to provide greater protection to the user, greater comfort, and decreased physiological stress on the user.

Bibliography

NJ Bollinger and RH Schultz, NIOSH Guide to Industrial Respiratory Protection, U.S. Health and Human Services, Public Health Service Centers for Disease Control National Institutes for Occupational Safety and Health, Division of Safety Research, September 1987.

J Dunbar and JP Zeigler, Change of clothing, *Fire Chief*, pp. 30–32, July, 2000.

GP Jirka, WMD protective clothing for the first responder, *Advanced Rescue Technology*, August/September 2001.

R Masadi, Dismounted warrior lightweight-low power microclimate cooling, presentation at U.S. Army Soldier Biological Chemical Command Fire and Emergency Services Technology Innovation Conference, March 2001.

OSHA 29 CFR 1910 Subpart I, Appendix B.

Q Truong and E Wilusz, Advanced lightweight CB protection, *Presentation at U.S. Army Soldier Biological Chemical Command Fire and Emergency Services Technology Innovation Conference,* San Diego, CA, March 2001.

JP Zeigler, FAQs & fables about protective clothing, *Occupational Health and Safety*, 69(7): 42–54, July 2000.

M Ziskin and D Han, Personal protective clothing, *Hazardous Materials Desk Reference*, New York, NY, McGraw Hill, 2000, Chapter 9, p. 119.

Chapter 27

National Response Plan and Preparedness

Tushar K. Ghosh

CONTENTS

Introduction 509
National Response Framework 512
Local and State Response Plan 513
Response to Terrorist Attack 515
Role of First Responders—Terrorist Incident 520
WMD Awareness Capability Level 521
WMD Defensive or Operator Capability Level 522
WMD Performance (Offensive) Level B (Technician Level) 522
WMD Advanced Operations and Technician Capability Level—Specialized Training 523
National Preparedness Guidelines 524
National Planning Scenario 524
References 527

Introduction

The "National Strategy for Homeland Security" and the Homeland Security Act of 2002 (Public Law 107-296, November 25, 2002) established the Department of Homeland Security (DHS) to mobilize our nation to secure the homeland from terrorist attacks. The DHS united 22 agencies on March 1, 2003, putting the strategy into action. The original 22 agencies that were incorporated in the DHS are given in Table 27.1.

Table 27.1 The Initial 22 Agencies That Became Part of the Department of Homeland Security

The U.S. customs service (treasury)
The immigration and naturalization service (justice)
The federal protective service
The transportation security administration (transportation)
Federal law enforcement training center (treasury)
Animal and plant health inspection service (part)(agriculture)
Office for domestic preparedness (justice)
The federal emergency management agency (FEMA)
Strategic national stockpile and the national disaster medical system (HHS)
Nuclear incident response team (energy)
Domestic emergency support teams (justice)
National domestic preparedness office (FBI)
CBRN countermeasures programs (energy)
Environmental measurements laboratory (energy)
National BW defense analysis center (defense)
Plum island animal disease center (agriculture)
Federal computer incident response center (GSA)
National communications system (defense)
National infrastructure protection center (FBI)
Energy security and assurance program (energy)
U.S. coast guard
U.S. secret service

Note: The original home of these department or agencies is shown in bracket.

In July 2005, the DHS had further reorganized its organizational structure, when three directorates: Border and Transportation Security, Emergency Preparedness and Response, and Information Analysis and Infrastructure Protection that were created by the Homeland Security Act of 2002, were abolished. Their responsibilities were transferred to other departments. The current organizational chart of the DHS is shown in Figure 27.1. During the reorganization of the department, the following six goals were set:

1. Increase overall preparedness, particularly for catastrophic events
2. Create better transportation security systems to move people and cargo more securely and efficiently

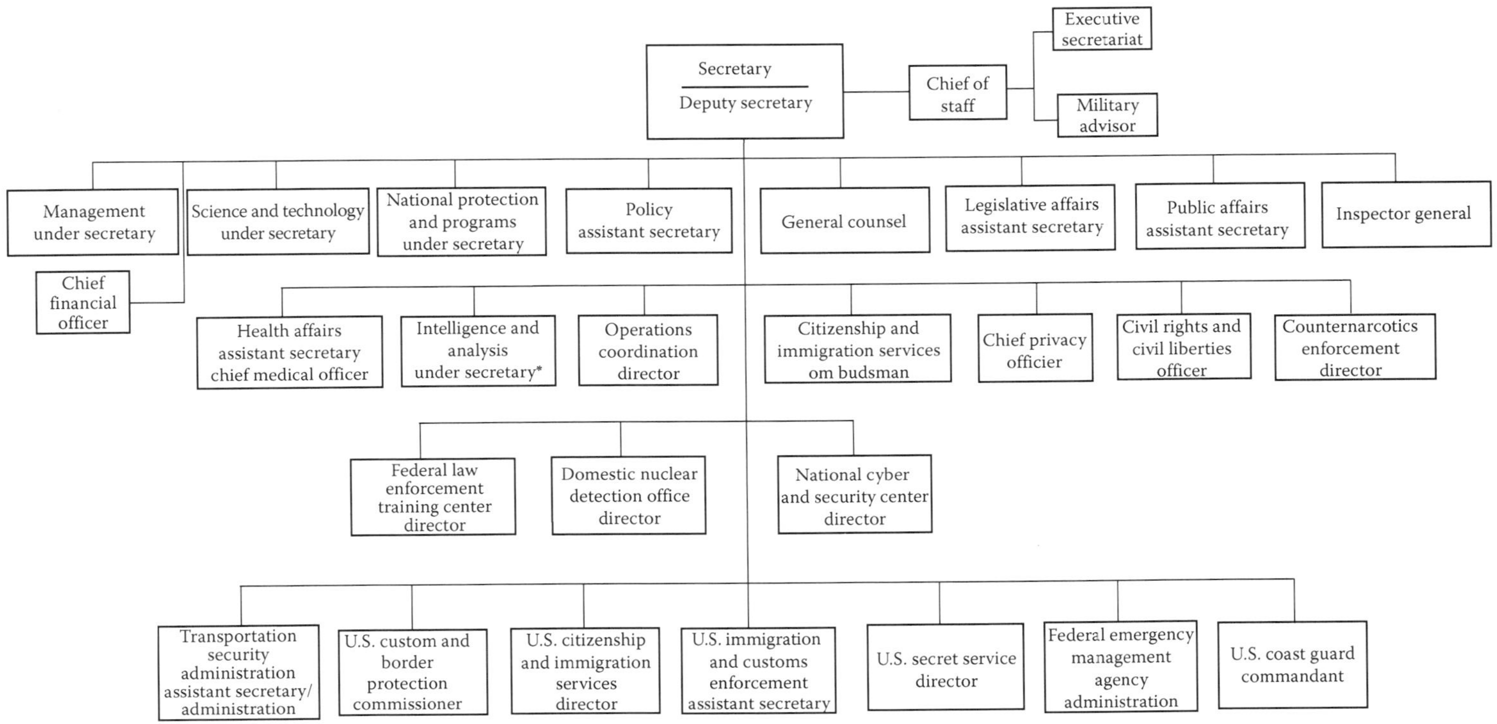

* Under secretary for intelligence & analysis title created by public law 110-53, August 3, 2007. Approved 3/20/2008.

Figure 27.1 The organizational chart of the Department of Homeland Security. (Data from Department of Homeland Security, Department Structure, http://www.dhs.gov/xabout/structure/)

3. Strengthen border security and interior enforcement and reform immigration processes
4. Enhance information sharing with our partners
5. Improve DHS financial management, human resource development, procurement, and information technology
6. Realign the DHS organization to maximize mission performance.

The DHS undertook two major initiatives to counter terrorism and terrorist incidents under Homeland Security Presidential Directive-5 (HSPD-5) that was initiated on February 2003, and Homeland Security Presidential Directive-7 (HSPD-7) that was initiated on December 2003. Under HSPD-5, the National Incident Management System (NIMS) was created on March 1, 2004 to provide a consistent incident management approach for federal, state, local, and tribal governments. All federal departments were required to adopt the NIMS under this directive and to use it in their individual domestic incident management and emergency prevention, preparedness, response, recovery, and mitigation programs and activities. HSPD-7 relates to Critical Infrastructure Identification, Prioritization, and Protection. This directive establishes a national policy for federal departments and agencies to identify and prioritize U.S. critical infrastructure and key resources and to protect them from terrorist attacks.

Another major initiative by the DHS was the creation of the National Response Plan (NRP). The initial plan was presented in December 2004, whose objective was to align federal coordination structures, capabilities, and resources into a unified, all-discipline, and all-hazards approach to domestic incident management. The NRP was built on the template of the NIMS. On January 22, 2008, the National Response Framework (NRF) was introduced as an updated version of the NRP. The NRF became effective on March 22, 2008. This NRF document states that it "is a guide to how the Nation conducts all-hazards response. It is built upon scalable, flexible, and adaptable coordinating structures to align key roles and responsibilities across the Nation, linking all levels of government, nongovernmental organizations, and the private sector. It is intended to capture specific authorities and best practices for managing incidents that range from the serious but purely local, to large-scale terrorist attacks or catastrophic natural disasters. The NRF core document, along with the Emergency Support Function Annexes and Support Annexes [2] supersedes the corresponding sections of the NRP (2004, with 2006 revisions). The Incident Annexes remain in effect until superseded at a later date."

It should be also noted that the NRF "document is an outgrowth of previous iterations of Federal planning documents. A brief discussion of its history underscores important elements of the Framework and highlights improvements to the previous NRP. This Framework was preceded 15 years earlier by a Federal Response Plan (1992) that focused largely on Federal roles and responsibilities."

To provide effective response to an incident; natural disasters, terrorist attacks, or any type of emergencies, responders and emergency managers—doers and planners—must be prepared (i.e., plan, organize, equip, train, exercise, and continuously evaluate actual performance). There are six essential activities for responding to an incident: plan, organize, train, equip, exercise, and evaluate and improve. This is also called preparedness cycle (Figure 27.2) that must be exercised and evaluated periodically.

National Response Framework

The objective of the NRF is to response effectively to a large-scale terrorist attacks or catastrophic natural disasters. The Framework includes immediate actions to save lives, protect property and the environment, and meet basic human needs. The NRF defines the principles, roles, and structures that organize how we respond as a nation. The NRF

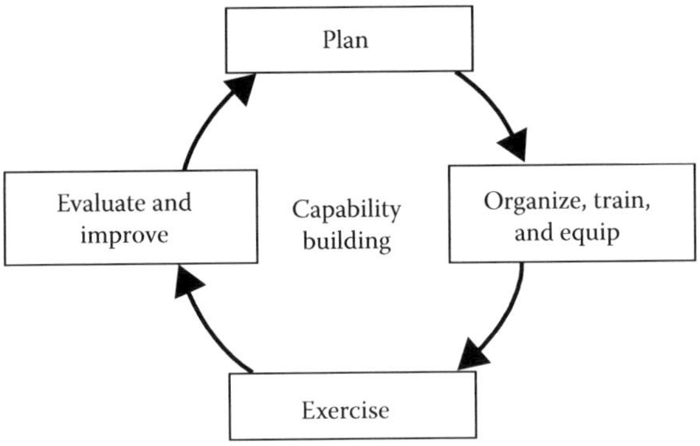

Figure 27.2 The preparedness cycle. (Data from National Response Framework, Department of Homeland Security, January 2008.)

- Describes how communities, tribes, states, the federal government, private sectors, and nongovernmental partners work together to coordinate national response.
- Describes specific authorities and best practices for managing incidents.
- Builds upon the NIMS, which provides a consistent template for managing incidents.

There are 15 Emergency Support Functions (ESF) to carry out the aforementioned mission of saving life, limiting the damages, and recovery efforts. The document does not appear to be a very cohesive document and there is some disconnect between the Executive Branch and the Congress. This document places less emphasis on the Federal Emergency Management Agency (FEMA) whereas the 2006 Act of Congress enacted after the Katrina incident strengthens the FEMA. It is not clear why an agency such as FEMA is left out. Of these 15 functions, 12 refers to in one way or other to terrorism, although the major disasters that need response are hurricanes, forest fires, tornadoes, floods, oil spills, and other disasters—natural and man-made—which occur every year. These emergencies require a great deal of cooperation, flexibility, and quick improvisation to provide relief to the affected population and handling emergency management. There have been several documents released during the past five years and remains to be seen what the new administration will do.

The NRP consists of four elements: Appendixes, Emergency Support Functions Annexes, Support Annexes, and Incident Annexes. These are given in Table 27.2. The role of these elements is discussed in detail in the document. However, in Table 27.3, the scope of various emergency support functions are described.

Local and State Response Plan

In the case of a disastrous event—natural or terrorist attacks—the local and state police, fire, public health and medical, emergency management, public works, environmental response, and other personnel are often the first to arrive and the last to leave an incident site. In some instances, a federal agency in the local area may act as a first responder, and the local assets of federal agencies may be used to advise or assist State or local officials in accordance with agency authorities and procedures.

Table 27.2 The Elements of Basic National Response Plan

Base Plan	
Appendixes	• Glossary of key terms
	• List of acronyms
	• Authorities and references
	• Compendium of national/international interagency plans
	• Overview of initial federal involvement under the Stafford act
	• Overview of federal-to-federal support in non-Stafford act Situations
Emergency support function annexes	• ESF # 1 transportation
	• ESF # 2 communication
	• ESF # 3 public works and engineering
	• ESF # 4 firefighting
	• ESF # 5 emergency and management
	• ESF # 6 mass care, housing, and human
	• Services
	• ESF # 7 resource support
	• ESF # 8 public health and medical services
	• ESF # 9 urban search and rescue
	• ESF # 10 oil and hazardous materials response
	• ESF # 11 agriculture and natural resources
	• ESF # 12 energy
	• ESF # 13 public safety and security
	• ESF # 14 long-term community recovery and mitigation
	• ESF # 15 external affairs
Support annexes	• Financial management
	• International coordination
	• Logistics management
	• Private sector coordination

Table 27.2 (continued) The Elements of Basic National Response Plan

Base Plan	
	• Public affairs
	• Science and technology
	• Tribal relations
	• Volunteer and donations management
	• Worker safety and health
Incident annexes	• Biological incident
	• Catastrophic incident
	• Cyber incident
	• Food and agriculture incident (to be published in a subsequent version of this plan)
	• Nuclear/radiological incident
	• Oil and hazardous materials incident
	• Terrorism incident law enforcement and investigation

Source: National Response Plan, Department of Homeland Security, December 2004.

When State resources and capabilities are overwhelmed, Governors may request federal assistance under a Presidential disaster or emergency declaration. The responsibilities of the Governor, Local Chief Executive Officer, and Tribal Chief Executive Officer are summarized in the following text. All the states have developed their own response plans. The basic concept of such a plan remains the same—drawn from various plans to develop an overall state or local plan. The basic approach of developing such a plan is given in Figure 27.3. States, along with their local jurisdictions, have their own emergency operations plans describing who will do what, when, and with what resources. In addition, many voluntary, private, and international organizations have emergency or contingency plans. The NRP approach for federal involvement is shown in Figure 27.4.

Response to Terrorist Attack

Terrorism in any form is a criminal act. In the event of a terrorist attack, not only all the emergency support functions need to be carried out, but also various criminal investigations must be carried out. The response structure for a terrorist incident is shown in Figure 27.5.

> The NRF states that:
> "The law enforcement and investigative response to a terrorist threat or incident within the United States is a highly coordinated, multiagency State, local, tribal, and Federal responsibility. In support of this mission, the following Federal agencies have primary responsibility for certain aspects of the overall law enforcement and investigative response:

Table 27.3 Scope of Emergency Support Functions

ESF	*Scope*
ESF # 1 Transportation	• Federal and civil transportation support
	• Transportation safety
	• Restoration/recovery of transportation infrastructure
	• Movement restriction
	• Damage and impact assessment
ESF # 2 Communication	• Coordination with telecommunication industry
	• Restoration/repair of telecommunications infrastructure
	• Protection, restoration, and sustainment of national cyber and information technology resources
ESF # 3 Public works and engineering	• Infrastructure protection and emergency repair
	• Infrastructure restoration
	• Engineering services, construction management
	• Critical infrastructure liaison
ESF # 4 Firefighting	• Firefighting activities on federal lands
	• Resource support to rural and urban firefighting operations
ESF # 5 Emergency and management	• Coordination of incident management efforts
	• Issuance of mission assignments
	• Resource and human capital
	• Incident action planning
	• Financial management
ESF # 6 Mass care, housing, and human services	• Mass care
	• Disaster housing
	• Human services
ESF # 7 Resource support	• Resource support (faculty space, office equipment and supplies, contracting services, etc.)
ESF # 8 Public health and medical services	• Public health
	• Medical

Table 27.3 (continued) Scope of Emergency Support Functions

ESF	*Scope*
	• Mental health services
	• Mortuary services
ESF # 9 Urban search and rescue	• Life-saving assistance
	• Urban search and rescue
ESF # 10 Oil and hazardous materials response	• Oil and hazardous materials (chemical, biological, radiological, etc.) response
	• Environmental safety and short-term and long-term cleanup
ESF # 11 Agriculture and natural resources	• Nutrition assistance
	• Animal and plant disease/pest response
	• Food safety and security
	• Natural and cultural resources and historic properties protection and restoration
	• Mitigation analysis and program implementation
ESF # 12 Energy	• Energy infrastructure assessment, repair, and restoration
	• Energy industry utilities coordination
	• Energy forecast
ESF # 13 Public safety and security	• Facility and resource security
	• Security planning and technical and resource assistance
	• Public safety/security support
	• Support to access, traffic, crowd control
ESF # 14 Long-Term community recovery and mitigation	• Social and economic community impact assessment
	• Long-term community recovery assistance to states, local government, and other private sectors
ESF # 15 External affairs	• Emergency public information and protective action guidance
	• Media and community relations
	• Congressional and international affairs
	• Tribal and insular affairs

Source: National Response Plan, Department of Homeland Security, December 2004.

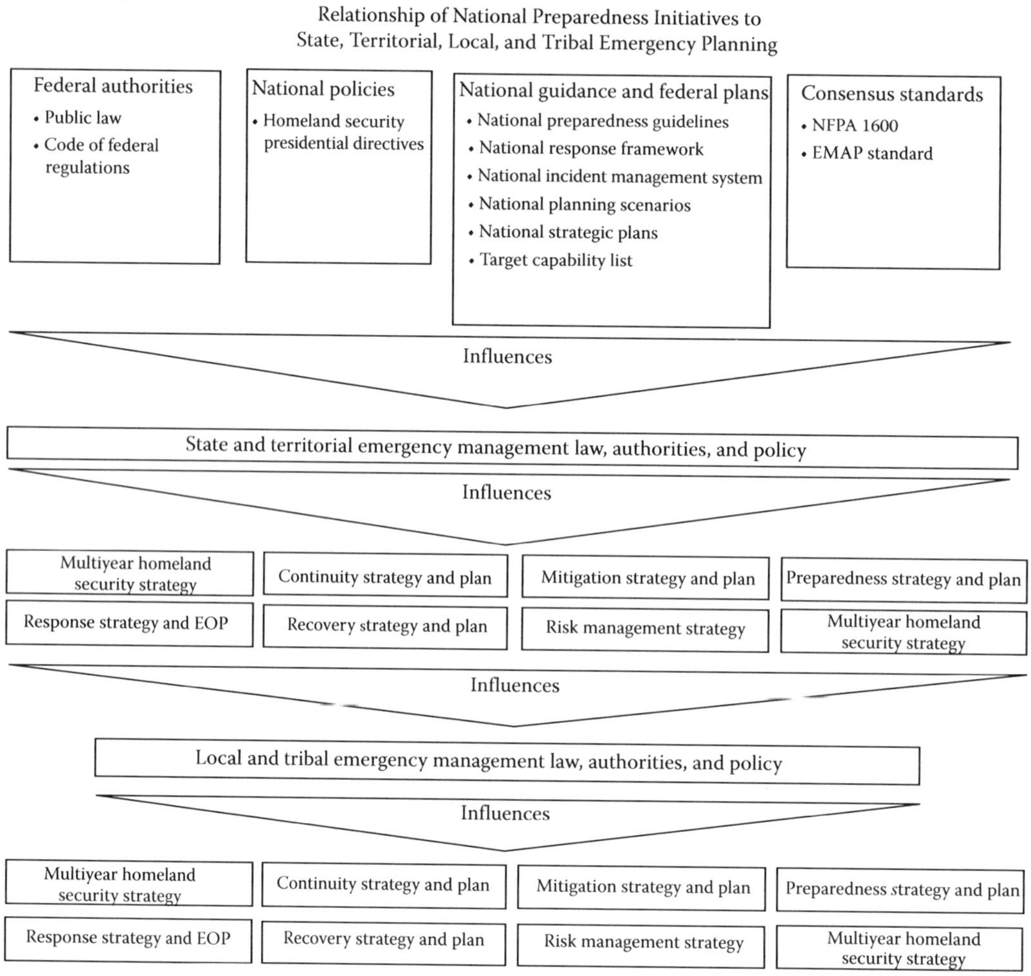

Figure 27.3 Emergency planning relationship between various local, state, federal, and private group's plans. (Data from Comprehensive Preparedness Guide [CPG] 101, Producing Emergency Plans: A Guide for All-Hazard Emergency Operations Planning for State, Territorial, Local, and Tribal Governments, *INTERIM Version 1*, August 2008, FEMA, Department of Homeland Security, January 2003.)

Department of Defense (DOD)
Department of Energy (DOE)
Department of Health and Human Services (HHS)
Department of Homeland Security (DHS)
Department of Justice/Federal Bureau of Investigation (FBI)
Environmental Protection Agency (EPA)

According to HSPD-5,

The Attorney General has lead responsibility for criminal investigations of terrorist acts or terrorist threats by individuals or groups inside the United States, or directed at U.S. citizens or

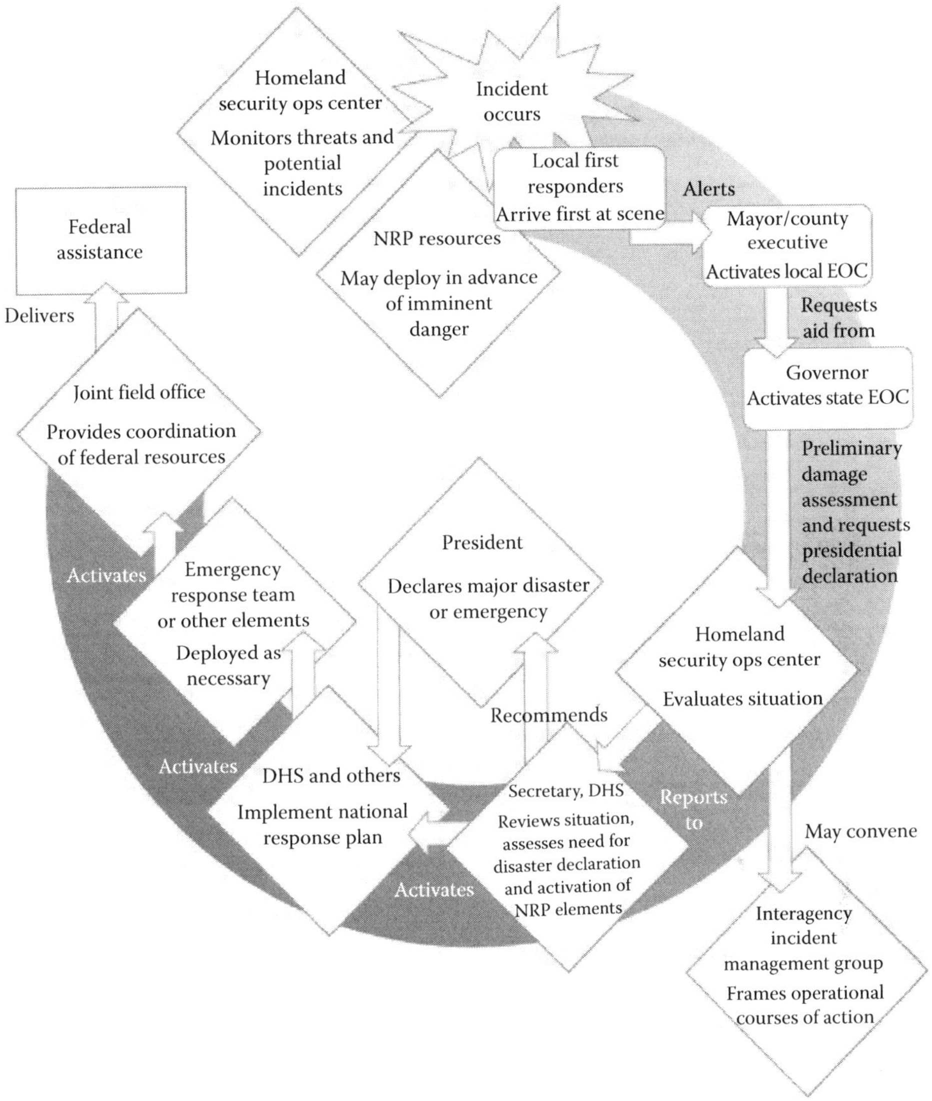

Figure 27.4 Overview of initial federal involvement under the Stafford Act. (From National Response Plan, Department of Homeland Security, December 2004.)

institutions abroad, where such acts are within the federal criminal jurisdiction of the United States, as well as for related intelligence collection activities within the United States, subject to the National Security Act of 1947 and other applicable law, Executive Order 12333, and Attorney General approved procedures pursuant to that Executive order. Generally acting through the Federal Bureau of Investigation, the Attorney General, in cooperation with other federal departments and agencies engaged in activities to protect our national security, shall also coordinate the activities of the other members of the law enforcement community to detect, prevent, preempt, and disrupt terrorist attacks against the United States. Following a terrorist threat or an actual

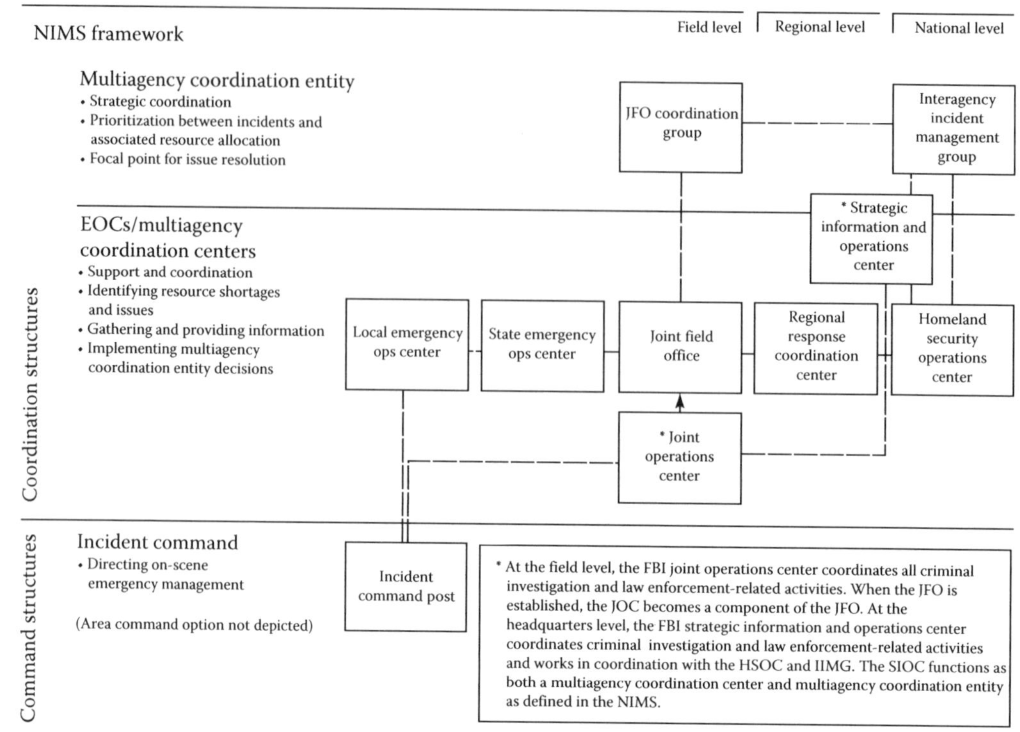

Figure 27.5 Structure for NRP coordination for a terrorist incident. (From National Response Plan, Department of Homeland Security, December 2004.)

incident that falls within the criminal jurisdiction of the United States, the full capabilities of the United States shall be dedicated, consistent with U.S. law and with activities of other federal departments and agencies to protect our national security, to assisting the Attorney General to identify the perpetrators and bring them to justice. The Attorney General and the Secretary shall establish appropriate relationships and mechanisms for cooperation and coordination between their two departments.

As noted earlier, the FBI is the lead agency for criminal investigations of terrorist acts or terrorist threats and intelligence collection activities within the United States. The FBI sets up a command post or Joint Operations Center (JOC) to coordinate between State, local, and tribal law enforcement agencies. The command post structure in shown in Figure 27.6.

Role of First Responders—Terrorist Incident

A chemical, biological, radiological/nuclear, or explosive/incendiary attack would pose unprecedented challenges to the first responders. The following groups are generally considered first responders: Law enforcement (Police), Fire service, Hazmat team, Emergency medical service, Public works, Public health, and Emergency management personnel. A basic understanding of the WMD incident is necessary to respond Effectively and safely. The first responders should have the awareness of the situation, be capable of performance evaluation, and have the knowledge of planning and management of the situation. There are many commonalities among each subsection.

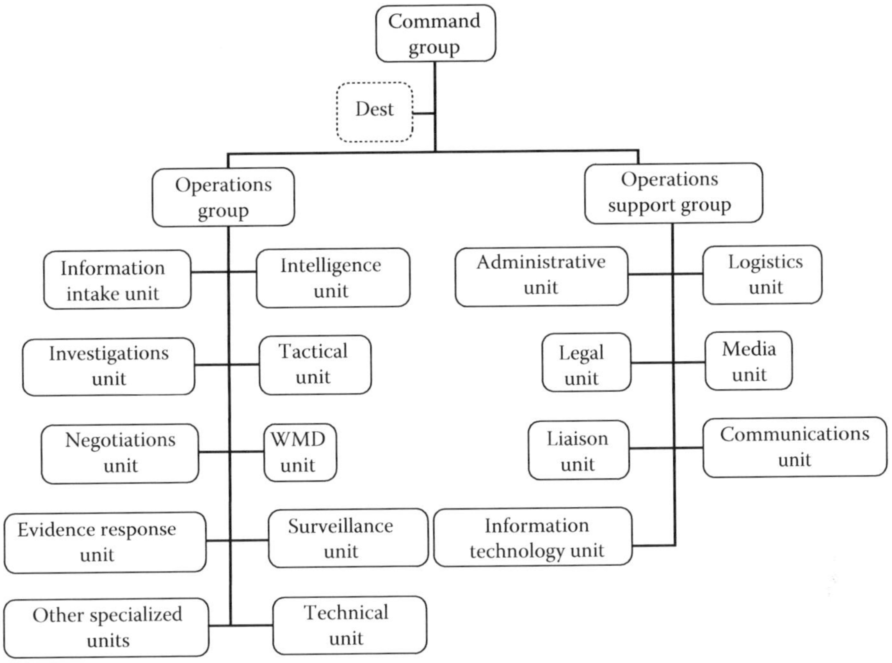

Figure 27.6 FBI command post.

These commonalities reflect the reality that effective WMD response strategies must be built on the interoperability and an understanding of how all the pieces of the response fit together. The training and preparedness of first responders depend on the WMD response level. Generally, four training and response levels are suggested [6].

WMD Awareness Capability Level

The objective of training at this level is to have "a capability to recognize a WMD incident." Emergency responders may be required to respond to or support an emergency involving a WMD incident. The guidelines for training at this level are as follows:

I. Recognize hazardous materials incidents.
II. Know the protocols used to detect the potential presence of weapons of mass destruction (WMD) agents or materials.
III. Know and follow self-protection measures for WMD events and hazardous materials events.
IV. Know procedures for protecting a potential crime scene.
V. Know and follow agency/organization's scene security and control procedures for WMD and hazardous material events.
VI. Possess and know how to properly use equipment to contact dispatcher or higher authorities to report information collected at the scene and to request for additional assistance or emergency response personnel.

Competency at this level is evidenced by compliance with National Preparedness Guidelines standards, National Fire Protection Association training standards associated with competencies for emergency responders at the Awareness Level (NFPA 472, Chapter 2) and applicable U.S. Department of Transportation (DOT), Environmental Protection Agency (EPA), Occupational Safety and Health Administration (OSHA), and other appropriate state and local requirements.

WMD Defensive or Operator Capability Level

Responders at this level should have all the training and skill of WMD Awareness Capability Level training and a modest increase in capability to respond to a WMD incident. Emergency responders at this level are expected to respond in a defensive fashion to control the incident from a safe distance and keep it from spreading. This is also called Performance Level A (Operation Level) skill or training. "These individuals will conduct on-scene operations within the warm zone or the hot zone (if properly trained and equipped) that has been set up on the scene of a potential WMD or hazardous materials event to control and close out the incident. It is expected that those officers trained for Performance Level A will work in the warm zone and cold zone and support those officers working in the hot zone. The guidelines for training at this level include:

- Have successfully completed adequate and proper training at the awareness level for events involving hazardous materials, and for WMD and other specialized training.
- Know the Incident Command System and be able to follow Unified Command System procedures for the integration and implementation of each system. Know how the systems integrate and support the incident. Be familiar with the overall operation of the two command systems and be able to assist in implementation of the Unified Command System if needed.
- Know and follow self-protection measures and rescue and evacuation procedures for WMD events.
- Know and follow procedures for working at the scene of a potential WMD event.

First responders with training at this level should be able to demonstrate by performance of required skills and for meeting all requirement for previous level and possessing general knowledge of biological, nuclear/radiological, and chemical agents; personal protective equipment, emergency decontamination, as well as compliance with Office for Domestic Preparedness Performance (Level A) Level training standards, National Fire Protection Association training standards associated with competencies for the emergency responder at the Operations Level (NFPA 472, Chapter 3) and applicable U.S. Department for Transportation (DOT), Environmental Protection Agency (EPA), Occupational Safety and Health Administration (OSHA), and other appropriate state and local requirements.

WMD Performance (Offensive) Level B (Technician Level)

Emergency responders at this level respond to releases or potential releases of WMD materials as part of the initial response to the incident or provide support for reducing or eliminating the source or effects of the WMD materials. Responders at this level should be certified technicians, trained and equipped to operate in a fully encapsulated environment in the hot zone to detect and neutralize a hazardous material. This level can only be achieved if the jurisdiction has a technician-level certified HazMat Team. The guidelines for training at this level are the following ones in addition to those mentioned in WMD Defensive or Operator Capability Level A:

- Have successfully completed training at the Awareness Level and Performance Level A for events involving hazardous materials and for WMD and other specialized training.
- Know and follow self-protection measures and rescue and evacuation procedures for WMD events.
- Know and follow procedures for performing specialized work at the scene of a potential WMD event.
- Know and follow Incident Command System and Unified Command System procedures and steps required for implementation of each system. Understand how these two systems are to work together.

Successful completion of this level includes demonstration by performance of required skills for previous two Levels and possessing advanced capabilities to work in the affected area of a WMD material release, as well as compliance with National Fire Protection Association training standards associated with competencies for the emergency responder at the Operations Level (NFPA 472, Chapter 4) and applicable U.S. Department for Transportation (DOT), Environmental Protection Agency (EPA), Occupational Safety and Health Administration (OSHA), and other appropriate state and local requirements.

WMD Advanced Operations and Technician Capability Level—Specialized Training

This level can generally be defined as having an "advanced WMD operations and equipment capability to respond to a WMD incident." Emergency responders at this level have met or exceed all emergency response operational, training, and equipment requirements for their jurisdiction to respond to or support the response to a WMD incident. "These personnel are expected to manage on-site law enforcement resources and assist the incident commander in bringing the event to a successful conclusion. Generally, all of the actions to be taken by these law enforcement managers should be conducted from within the cold zone." The guidelines for training at this level are:

- Have successfully completed training in awareness, performance, and management levels for events involving hazardous materials and for WMD.
- Know Incident Command System and the Unified Command System's procedures and the steps required for implementation of each system. Understand how the systems are integrated and implemented to work together and what information the on-scene manager needs from the law enforcement manager. Be familiar with the full range of incident command functions, and be able to fulfill any functions related to law enforcement operations.
- Know protocols to secure and retain control of the emergency scene and to allow only authorized persons involved with the emergency incident to gain access to the scene of WMD agents or hazardous materials.
- Know and follow self-protection measures and protective measures for personnel on the scene of WMD events and hazardous materials events.
- Know and follow procedures for protecting a potential crime scene.
- Know plans and assets available for the crime scene investigation and control of WMD and hazardous materials events to secure and retain evidence removed from the scene.

National Preparedness Guidelines [7]

On September 13, 2007, the DHS released the National Preparedness Guidelines as part of the directives of Homeland Security Presidential Directive-8. There are four critical elements to the National Preparedness Guidelines:

1. The national preparedness vision, which provides a concise statement of the core preparedness goal for the nation.
2. The 15 National Planning Scenarios, which collectively depict the broad range of natural and man-made threats facing our nation and guide overall homeland security planning efforts at all levels of government and with the private sector. They form the basis for national planning, training, investments, and exercises needed to prepare for emergencies of all types.
3. Universal Task List (UTL), which is a menu of some 1600 unique tasks that can facilitate efforts to prevent, protect against, respond to, and recover from the major events that are represented by the National Planning Scenarios. Although no single entity will perform every task, the UTL presents a common language and vocabulary that supports all efforts to coordinate national preparedness activities.
4. Target Capabilities List (TCL), which defines 37 specific capabilities that states and communities and the private sector should collectively develop to respond effectively to disasters.

These elements are discussed in detail in the guidelines. However, a brief discussion of 15 national planning scenarios is provided in the following text.

National Planning Scenario [8]

The objective of developing 15 scenarios based on natural disasters and terrorist attacks is to establish the range of response requirements to facilitate preparedness planning. The scenarios are planning tools for use in national, federal, state, and local homeland security preparedness activities. These 15 national planning scenarios are:

Scenario 1: Nuclear Detonation—10-kiloton Improvised Nuclear Device
Scenario 2: Biological Attack—Aerosol Anthrax
Scenario 3: Biological Disease Outbreak—Pandemic Influenza
Scenario 4: Biological Attack—Plague
Scenario 5: Chemical Attack—Blister Agent
Scenario 6: Chemical Attack—Toxic Industrial Chemicals
Scenario 7: Chemical Attack—Nerve Agent
Scenario 8: Chemical Attack—Chlorine Tank Explosion
Scenario 10: Natural Disaster—Major Hurricane
Scenario 11: Radiological Attack—Radiological Dispersal Devices
Scenario 12: Explosives Attack—Bombing Using Improvised Explosive Devices
Scenario 13: Biological Attack—Food Contamination
Scenario 14: Biological Attack—Foreign Animal Disease (Foot-and-Mouth Disease)
Scenario 15: Cyber-Attack

These planning scenarios are designed to serve the response required for the mission areas shown in Table 27.4.

Table 27.4 Response Requirements Generated by the Scenarios

Mission Areas	*Requirements*
Prevention/deterrence	The ability to detect, prevent, preempt, and deter terrorist attacks and other man-made emergencies
Infrastructure protection	The ability to protect critical infrastructure from all threats and hazards
Preparedness	The ability to plan, organize, equip, train, and exercise homeland security personnel to perform their assigned missions to nationally accepted standards—this mission area includes public education and awareness
Emergency assessment/ diagnosis	The ability to achieve and maintain a common operating picture, including the ability to detect an incident, determine its impact, determine its likely evolution and course, classify the incident, and make government notifications
Emergency management/ response	The ability to direct, control, and coordinate a response; manage resources; and provide emergency public information—this outcome includes direction and control through the Incident Command System, Multiagency Coordination Systems, and Public Information Systems
Hazard mitigation	The ability to control, collect, and contain a hazard; lesson its effects; and conduct environmental monitoring—mitigation efforts may be implemented before, during, or after an incident
Evacuation/shelter	The ability to provide initial warnings to the population at large and at risk; notify people to shelter-in-place or evacuate; provide evacuation and shelter support; and manage traffic flow and ingress and egress to and from the affected area
Victim care	The ability to treat victims at the scene; transport patients; treat patients at a medical treatment facility; track patients; handle, track, and secure human remains; provide tracking and security of patients' possessions and evidence; and manage the worried well
Investigation/apprehension	The ability to investigate the cause and source of the incident and identify, apprehend, and prosecute those responsible for terrorist attacks and other man-made emergencies
Recovery/remediation	The ability to restore essential services, businesses, and commerce; cleanup the environment and render the affected area safe; compensate victims; provide long-term mental health and other services to victims and the public; and restore a sense of well-being in the community

Source: National planning scenarios, created for use in national, federal, state, and local homeland security preparedness activities, version 21.3 final draft, March 2006.

In the NRF document, several criteria have been developed to assess the impact of these planning scenarios and their usefulness in the preparedness exercise. It was also noted that although there are fifteen planning scenarios, but there are commonalities among them and may be grouped into seven key areas (See Table 27.5).

This chapter presents some salient features of the NRF man-made and natural disasters. As noted at the beginning of this chapter, these plans have evolved over time and experience. We anticipate that the NRF in its present form will be revised to take into consideration some of the lacunae in this plan.

Table 27.5 Relationship of Scenario Sets to Planning Scenarios

Key Scenario Sets	*National Planning Scenarios*
1. Explosives attack—bombing using improvised explosive device	Scenario 12: Explosives attack—bombing using improvised explosive device
2. Nuclear attack	Scenario 1: Nuclear detonation—improvised nuclear device
3. Radiological attack—radiological dispersal device	Scenario 11: Radiological attack—radiological dispersal device
4. Biological attack—with annexes for different pathogens	Scenario 2: Biological attack—aerosol anthrax
	Scenario 4: Biological attack—plague
	Scenario 13: Biological attack—food contamination
	Scenario 14: Biological attack—foreign animal disease
5. Chemical attack—with annexes for different agents	Scenario 5: Chemical attack—blister agent
	Scenario 6: Chemical attack—toxic industrial chemicals
	Scenario 7: Chemical attack—nerve agent
	Scenario 8: Chemical attack—chlorine tank explosion
6. Natural disaster—with annexes for different disasters	Scenario 9: Natural disaster—major earthquake
	Scenario 10: Natural disaster—major hurricane
7. Cyber-attack	Scenario 15: Cyber-attack
8. Pandemic influenza	Scenario 3: Biological disease outbreak—pandemic influenza

Source: National response framework, Department of Homeland Security, January 2008.

References

1. Department of Homeland Security, Department Structure, http://www.dhs.gov/xabout/structure/
2. NRF Resource Center, http://www.fema.gov/NRF.
3. National Response Framework, Department of Homeland Security, January 2008.
4. National Response Plan, Department of Homeland Security, December 2004.
5. Comprehensive Preparedness Guide (CPG) 101, Producing Emergency Plans: A Guide for All-Hazard Emergency Operations Planning for State, Territorial, Local, and Tribal Governments, *INTERIM Version 1., August 2008, FEMA,* Department of Homeland Security, January 2003.
6. Certification of Tier Level, www.nd.gov/des/homeland/docs/brief08/FY%2008%20Certification%20of%20**Tier**%20Level.doc
7. National Preparedness Guidelines, Department of Homeland Security, http://www.dhs.gov/xlibrary/assets/National_Preparedness_Guidelines.pdf, September 2007.
8. National Planning Scenarios, Created for Use in National, Federal, State, and Local Homeland Security Preparedness Activities, Version 21.3 Final Draft, March 2006.

Chapter 28

Government and Voluntary Agencies

Julie A. Bentz and Theresa M. Crocker

CONTENTS

Introduction 530
Lead Federal Agencies....532
Department of Justice, Federal Bureau of Investigation....533
Federal Emergency Management Agency 539
Department of Defense....539
Department of Energy....542
Environmental Protection Agency 543
Department of Health and Human Services....544
Planning Assumptions....548
Concept of Operations....549
Integration of Response, Recovery, and Mitigation Actions....550
Military Support....550
Federal Law Enforcement Assistance 551
Response and Recovery Actions....552
Initial Actions....552
Continuing Actions 554
Bibliography 555

Introduction

Communities, tribes, states, the federal government, nongovernment organizations (NGOs), and the private sector play a prominent role in developing capabilities needed to respond to all types of incidents. Although, all incidents begin and end at the local level, there are unique response obligations that are coordinated with state, federal, and private sector support teams. Emergency management is the coordination and integration of all activities necessary to build, sustain, and improve the capability to prepare for, protect against, respond to, recover from, or mitigate against threatened or actual natural disasters, acts of terrorism, or other man-made disasters.

The combined emergency management authorities, policies, procedures, and resources of local, state, and federal governments as well as voluntary disaster relief organizations, the private sector, and international sources constitute a national disaster response framework for providing assistance following a major disaster or emergency. Within this framework, the federal government can provide personnel, equipment, supplies, facilities; and managerial, technical, and advisory services in support of state and local disaster assistance efforts.

Communities depend on the leadership and engagement of local government, NGO, and the private sector. Local police, fire, emergency medical services, public health and medical providers, emergency management, public works, environmental response professionals, and others in the community are often the first to detect a threat or hazard, or respond to an incident. They are also often the last to leave an incident site or otherwise to cope with the effects of an incident. The local elected or appointed official (the mayor, city manager, or county manager) is responsible for ensuring the public safety and welfare of its residents. They organize and integrate their capabilities and resources with neighboring jurisdictions, the state, NGOs, and the private sector. Businesses are also vital partners within communities wherever retail locations, service sites, manufacturing facilities, or management offices are located. NGOs and not-for-profit organizations also play a key role in strengthening communities' response efforts through their knowledge of hard-to-reach populations, outreach, and services.

States, territories, and tribal governments are responsible for the public health and welfare of the people in their jurisdiction. State and local governments have always had the lead role in response and recovery. During response, states play a key role in coordinating resources and capabilities throughout the state and obtaining resources and capabilities from other states. States are sovereign entities, and the governor is responsible for public safety and welfare. The role of the state government in response is to supplement local efforts before, during, and after incidents. If a state anticipates that its resources may be exceeded, the governor can request assistance from the federal government or from other states through mutual aid and assistance agreements such as the Emergency Management Assistance Compact (EMAC).

The federal government maintains a wide array of capabilities and resources that can be made available upon the request of the governor. When an incident occurs that exceeds or is anticipated to exceed state, tribal, or local resources, the federal government may provide resources and capabilities to support the state response. For incidents involving primary federal jurisdiction or authorities (e.g., on a military base or a federal facility or lands), federal departments or agencies may be the first responders and the first line of defense, coordinating activities with state, territorial, tribal, and local partners. The federal government also maintains working relationships with the private sector and NGOs.

The private sector and NGOs contribute to response efforts through engaged partnerships with each level of the government. Private-sector organizations play an essential role in protecting critical infrastructure systems and implementing plans for the rapid restoration of normal commercial activities and critical infrastructure operations in the event of disruption. The protection of critical infrastructure and the ability to rapidly restore normal commercial activities can mitigate the impact of an incident, improve the quality of life of individuals, and accelerate the pace of recovery for communities and the nation. There are not-for-profit owners/operators of critical infrastructure and key resources (CIKR) facilities, notably in healthcare and power generation. NGOs also serve a vital role at the local, state, and national levels by performing essential service missions in times of need. They provide sheltering, emergency food supplies, and other vital support services. NGOs bolster and support government efforts at all levels.

The National Response Framework (*Framework*) is a guide to how the nation conducts all-hazards response. The core document, along with the Emergency Support Function (ESF) Annexes and Support Annexes (available at the NRF Resource Center, http://www.fema.gov/NRF), supersedes the corresponding sections of the National Response Plan (NRP) (2004, with 2006 revisions). This document is an outgrowth of previous iterations of federal planning documents. A brief discussion of its history underscores important elements of the *Framework* and highlights improvements to the previous *NRP*. This *Framework* was preceded 15 years earlier by a *Federal Response Plan* (1992) that focused largely on federal roles and responsibilities. Following the 9/11 terrorist attacks, more urgent efforts were made to understand and implement common incident management and response principles and to develop common planning frameworks. The 2004 *NRP* was an early outgrowth of those discussions, replacing the *Federal Response Plan*. It was published one year after the creation of the Department of Homeland Security (DHS). The *NRP* broke new ground in integrating all levels of government in a common incident-management framework. It incorporated incident coordination roles for federal agencies as defined by several new laws and Presidential Directives. Nine months after Hurricane Katrina's landfall in 2005, a notice of change to the *NRP* was released, incorporating preliminary lessons learned from the 2005 hurricane season. Stakeholders suggested changes to the *NRP*—both structural and substantive. Stakeholders advised that both the initial *NRP* and its 2006 iteration were bureaucratic and internally repetitive. It was evident that the *NRP* and its supporting documents did not constitute a true operational plan in the sense understood by emergency managers. Its content was inconsistent with the promise of its title.

The *Framework* is built upon scalable, flexible, and adaptable coordinating structures to align key roles and responsibilities across the nation, linking all levels of government, NGOs, and the private sector. It is intended to capture specific authorities and best practices for managing incidents that range from the serious but purely local, to large-scale terrorist attacks, or catastrophic natural disasters. The term "response" as used in this *Framework* includes immediate actions to save lives, protect property and the environment, and meet basic human needs. Response also includes the execution of emergency plans and actions to support short-term recovery. The *Framework* is always in effect, and elements can be implemented as needed on a flexible, scalable basis to improve response.

The *National Incident Management System* (*NIMS*) is a companion document to the *Framework* that provides standard command and management structures that apply to response activities. This system provides a consistent, nationwide template to enable federal, state, tribal, and local governments, the private sector, and NGOs to work together to prepare for, prevent, respond to, recover from, and mitigate the effects of incidents regardless of cause, size, location, or complexity. This consistency provides the foundation for utilization of the *NIMS* for all incidents, ranging from daily occurrences to incidents requiring a coordinated federal response.

Lead Federal Agencies

When an incident occurs that exceeds or is anticipated to exceed local or state resources—or when an incident is managed by federal departments or agencies acting under their own authorities—the federal government involves all necessary department and agency capabilities, organizes the federal response, and ensures coordination with response partners.

The President leads the federal response to ensure that the structures, leadership, and resources are applied quickly and efficiently to large-scale and catastrophic incidents. The President's Homeland Security Council and National Security Council, which bring together Cabinet officers and other department or agency heads as necessary, provide national strategic and policy advice to the President during large-scale incidents that affect the nation. When the overall coordination of federal response activities is required, it is implemented through the Secretary of Homeland Security consistent with Homeland Security Presidential Directive (HSPD) 5. Other federal departments and agencies carry out their response authorities and responsibilities within this overarching construct. The Secretary of Homeland Security is the principal federal official for domestic incident management. By presidential directive and statute, the secretary is responsible for coordination of federal resources utilized in the prevention of, preparation for, response to, or recovery from terrorist attacks, major disasters, or other emergencies. The FEMA administrator, is the principal advisor to the president, the secretary, and the Homeland Security Council on all matters regarding emergency management. The attorney general is the chief law enforcement officer of the United States. Generally acting through the Federal Bureau of Investigation (FBI), the attorney general has the lead responsibility for criminal investigations of terrorist acts or terrorist threats by individuals or groups inside the United States or directed at U.S. citizens or institutions abroad, as well as for coordinating activities of the other members of the law enforcement community to detect, prevent, and disrupt terrorist attacks against the United States. The primary mission of the Department of Defense (DOD) and its components is national defense. DOD elements in the National Guard forces under the command of a governor will coordinate closely with response organizations at all levels. The Secretary of State is responsible for managing international preparedness, response, and recovery activities relating to domestic incidents and the protection of U.S. citizens and U.S. interests overseas. The Director of National Intelligence leads the Intelligence Community, serves as the President's principal intelligence advisor, and oversees and directs the implementation of the National Intelligence Program.

Federal departments or agencies may play primary, coordinating, or support roles based on their authorities and resources and the nature of the threat or incident. In situations where a federal department or agency is responsible for directing or managing a major aspect of a response being coordinated by DHS, that organization is part of the national leadership for the incident and is represented in the field at the Joint Field Office (JFO) in the Unified Coordination Group (UCG), and at headquarters through the National Operations Center (NOC) and the National Response Coordination Center (NRCC), which is part of the NOC. In addition, several federal departments and agencies have their own authorities to declare disasters or emergencies. For example, the Secretary of Health and Human Services (HHS) can declare a public health emergency. These declarations may be made independently or as part of a coordinated federal response.

The JFO is the primary federal incident-management field structure (Figure 28.1). The JFO is a temporary federal facility that provides a central location for the coordination of federal, state, tribal, and local governments, private sector, and NGOs with primary responsibility for response and recovery. As the primary field structure, the JFO provides the organizing structure to integrate diverse federal authorities and capabilities and coordinate federal response and recovery operations.

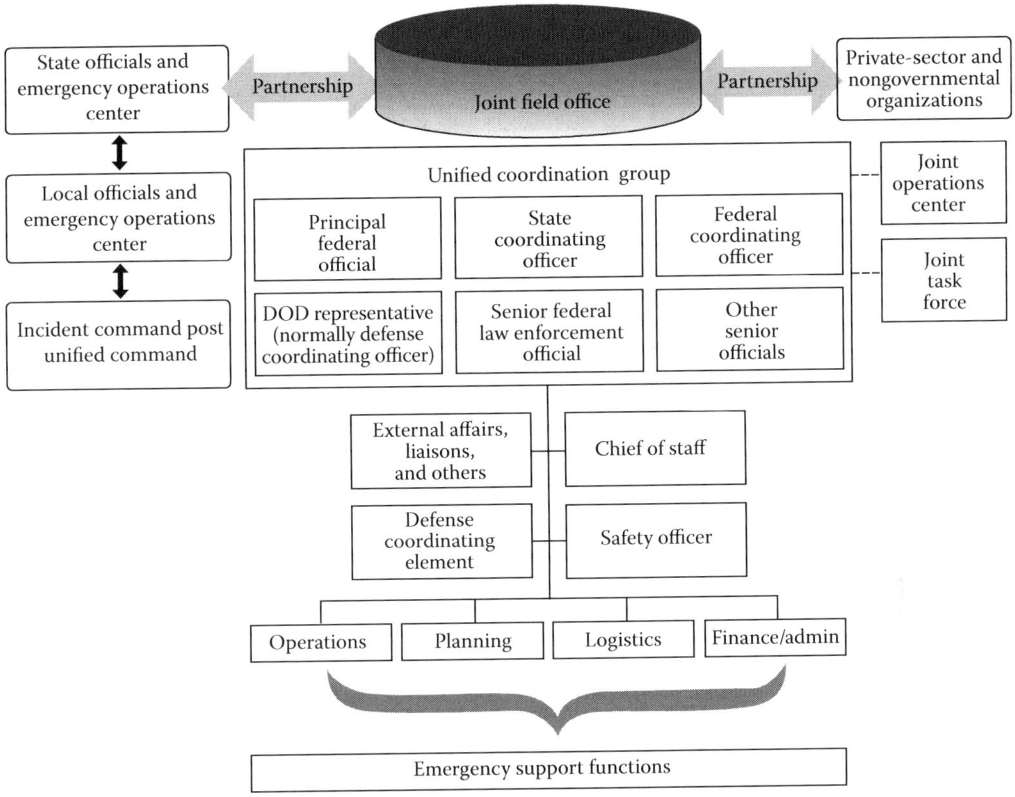

Figure 28.1 An overview of the JFO and its key components.

The ESFs provide the structure for coordinating federal interagency support for a federal response to an incident. They are mechanisms for grouping functions most frequently used to provide federal support to states and federal-to-federal support, both for declared disasters and for emergencies under the Stafford Act and for non-Stafford Act incidents (see Table 28.1).

The Incident Command System provides for the flexibility to assign ESF resources according to their capabilities, taskings, and requirements to augment and support the other sections of the JFO/Regional Response Coordination Center (RRCC) or NRCC.

Although ESFs are typically assigned to a specific section at the NRCC or in the JFO/RRCC for management purposes, resources may be assigned anywhere within the Unified Coordination structure. Regardless of the section in which an ESF may reside, that entity works in conjunction with other JFO sections to ensure that appropriate planning and execution of missions occur.

Department of Justice, Federal Bureau of Investigation

As attention increasingly focused on weapons of mass destruction (WMD) and their potential allure for terrorists, President Bush signed Homeland Security Presidential Directive 5 (HSPD 5): Management of Domestic Incidents, on February 28, 2003, assigning specific responsibilities to the attorney general. These are discussed in Chapter 27.

Table 28.1 Table of Roles and Responsibilities of the ESFs

ESF	*Scope*
ESF #1 Transportation	Aviation/airspace management and control
	Transportation safety
	Restoration/recovery of transportation infrastructure
	Movement restrictions
	Damage and impact assessment
ESF #2 Communications	Coordination with telecommunications and information technology industries
	Restoration and repair of telecommunications infrastructure
	Protection, restoration, and sustainment of national cyber and information technology resources
	Oversight of communications within the federal incident management and response structures
ESF #3 Public works and engineering	Infrastructure protection and emergency repair
	Infrastructure restoration
	Engineering services and construction management
	Emergency contracting support for life-saving and life-sustaining services
ESF #4 Firefighting	Coordination of federal firefighting activities
	Support to wildland, rural, and urban firefighting operations
ESF #5 Emergency management	Coordination of incident management and response efforts
	Issuance of mission assignments
	Resource and human capital
	Incident action planning
	Financial management
ESF #6 Mass care, emergency assistance, housing, and human services	Mass care
	Emergency assistance
	Disaster housing
	Human services

Table 28.1 (continued) Table of Roles and Responsibilities of the ESFs

ESF	*Scope*
ESF #7 Logistics management and resource support	Comprehensive, national incident logistics planning, management, and sustainment capability
	Resource support (facility space, office equipment and supplies, contracting services, etc.)
ESF #8 Public health and medical services	Public health
	Medical
	Mental health services
	Mass fatality management
ESF #9 Search and rescue	Life-saving assistance
	Search and rescue operations
ESF #10 Oil and hazardous materials response	Oil and hazardous materials (chemical, biological, radiological, etc.) response
	Environmental short- and long-term cleanup
ESF #11 Agriculture and natural resources	Nutrition assistance
	Animal and plant disease and pest response
	Food safety and security
	Natural and cultural resources and historic properties protection and restoration
	Safety and well-being of household pets
ESF #12 Energy	Energy infrastructure assessment, repair, and restoration
	Energy industry utilities coordination
	Energy forecast
ESF #13 Public safety and security	Facility and resource security
	Security planning and technical resource assistance
	Public safety and security support
	Support to access, traffic, and crowd control
ESF #14 Long-term community recovery	Social and economic community impact assessment
	Long-term community recovery assistance to states, local governments, and the private sector
	Analysis and review of mitigation program implementation

(continued)

Table 28.1 (continued) Table of Roles and Responsibilities of the ESFs

ESF	*Scope*
ESF #15 External affairs	Emergency public information and protective action guidance
	Media and community relations
	Congressional and international affairs
	Tribal and insular affairs

The FBI is the lead agency for criminal investigations of terrorist acts or terrorist threats and intelligence collection activities within the United States. Investigative and intelligence activities are managed by the FBI from an FBI command post or Joint Operations Center (JOC). The command post or JOC coordinates the necessary federal law enforcement assets required to respond to and resolve the threat or incident with state, local, and tribal law enforcement agencies. The FBI Special Agent in Charge (SAC) of the local Field Office establishes a command post to manage the threat based upon a graduated and flexible response. This command post structure generally consists of three functional groups: Command, Operations, and Operations Support, and is designed to accommodate participation of other agencies.

When the threat or incident exceeds the capabilities and resources of the local FBI Field Office, the SAC can request additional assistance from regional and national assets to augment existing capabilities. In a terrorist threat or incident that may involve a WMD or CBRNE material, the traditional FBI command post will transition to a JOC, which may temporarily incorporate a fourth functional entity, the Consequence Management Group in the absence of an activated JFO. When, in the determination of the Secretary of Homeland Security, in coordination with the attorney general, the incident becomes an Incident of National Significance and a JFO is established, the JOC becomes a section of the JFO and the FBI SAC becomes the Senior Federal Law Enforcement Official (SFLEO) in the JFO Coordination Group. In this situation, the JOC Consequence Management Group is incorporated into the appropriate components of the JFO.

The JOC structure may also be used to coordinate law enforcement, investigative, and intelligence activities for the numerous threats or incidents that occur each year that do not escalate to Incidents of National Significance.

A threat assessment is conducted to determine whether the potential threat is credible, and confirm whether WMD or CBRNE materials are involved in the developing terrorist incident. Intelligence varies with each threat and impacts the level of the federal response. If the threat is credible, the situation requires the tailoring of response actions to use federal resources needed to anticipate, prevent, or resolve the situation. The federal response focuses on law enforcement/investigative actions taken in the interest of public safety and welfare, and is predominantly concerned with preventing and resolving the threat. In addition, contingency planning focuses on the response to potential consequences and the prepositioning of tailored resources, as required. The threat increases in significance when the presence of a CBRNE device or WMD capable of causing a significant destructive event, prior to actual injury or loss, is confirmed or when intelligence and circumstances indicate a high probability that a device exists. In this case, the threat has developed into a WMD or CBRNE terrorist situation requiring an immediate process to identify, acquire, and plan the use of federal resources to augment state, local, and tribal authorities in lessening or averting the potential consequence of terrorist use or employment of WMD or CBRNE material. It should be noted that a threat assessment would also be conducted if an incident occurs without warning. In this case, the assessment is focused on criminal intent, the extent of the threat, and the likelihood of secondary devices or locations.

The FBI manages a Terrorist Threat Warning System to ensure that vital information regarding terrorism reaches those in the U.S. counterterrorism and law enforcement community responsible for countering terrorist threats. This information is coordinated with DHS and the NCTC, and is transmitted via secure teletype. Each message transmitted under this system is an alert, an advisory, or an assessment—an alert if the terrorist threat is credible and specific, an advisory if the threat is credible but common in both timing and target, or an assessment to impart facts or threat analysis concerning terrorism.

Upon determination of a credible threat, FBI headquarters activates its SIOC to coordinate and manage the national-level support to a terrorism incident. At this level, the SIOC generally mirrors the JOC structure operating in the field. The SIOC is staffed by liaison officers from other federal agencies who coordinate with and assist the FBI. The SIOC serves as the focal point for law enforcement operations and maintains direct connectivity with the HSOC. The HSOC is notified immediately by the SIOC once a threat has been determined to be credible. In turn, this notification may result in activation of NRP components in coordination with the FBI.

The JOC is established by the FBI under the operational control of the FBI SAC, and acts as the focal point for the field coordination of criminal investigation, law enforcement, and intelligence activities related to the threat or incident. When a PFO is designated for a terrorism incident, the FBI SAC provides full and prompt cooperation, resources, and support to the PFO, as appropriate and consistent with applicable authorities. The PFO (or an initial PFO designated by the Secretary of Homeland Security) may elect to use the JOC as an initial operating facility for strategic management and identification of state, local, and tribal requirements and priorities, and coordination of the federal response. The FBI SAC coordinates with the PFO, in providing incident information to the PFO as requested, coordinating the public communications strategy with the PFO, and approving federal interagency communications for release to the public through the PFO. It is recognized, however, that in some cases it may be necessary for the FBI SAC to respond directly to media/public inquiries on investigative operations and matters affecting law enforcement operations, particularly during the early stages of the emergency response.

The local FBI Field Office activates a Crisis Management Team to establish the JOC in the affected area, possibly collocated with an existing emergency operations facility. In locating the JOC, consideration is given to the possibility that the facility may have to accommodate other federal incident-management field activities including the JFO, the JIC, and other supporting teams. Additionally, the JOC is augmented by outside agencies, including representatives from the DEST (if deployed), who provide interagency technical expertise as well as interagency continuity during the transition from an FBI command post structure to the JOC structure.

The Domestic Emergency Support Team (DEST) is a specialized interagency team composed of subject-matter experts from the FBI, the DHS/Emergency Preparedness and Response/Federal Emergency Management Agency (DHS/EPR/FEMA), DOD, DOE, HHS, and EPA. It provides guidance to the FBI SAC concerning WMD threats and actual incidents.

Based upon a credible threat assessment and a request by the SAC, the FBI director and DHS Under Secretary for Emergency Preparedness and Response, in consultation with the attorney general and Secretary of Homeland Security, may request authorization through the National Security Council to deploy the DEST to assist the SAC in mitigating the crisis situation. The DEST is a rapidly deployable, interagency team responsible for providing expert advice and support concerning the federal government's capabilities in resolving the terrorist threat or incident. This includes law enforcement, criminal investigation, and emergency management assistance, technical and scientific advice, and contingency planning guidance tailored to situations involving chemical, biological, or nuclear/radiological weapons.

Upon arrival at the FBI command post or JOC, the DEST may act as a stand-alone advisory team to the SAC providing recommended courses of action. Although it would be unusual, the DEST may be tasked to deploy before a JOC is established. The DEST may handle some of the specialized interagency functions of the JOC until the JOC is fully staffed. The DEST emergency management component merges into the Consequence Management Group in the JOC structure (see Figure 28.2).

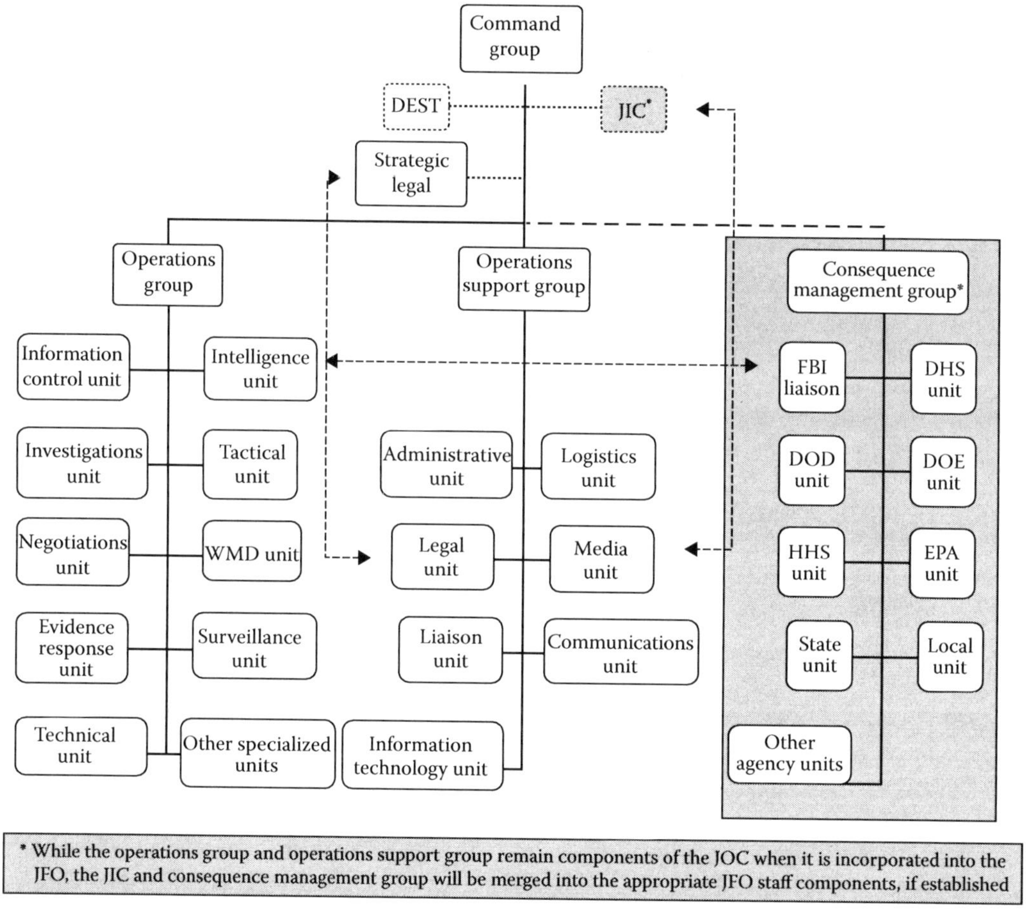

Figure 28.2 Joint operations center.

Federal Emergency Management Agency

On March 1, 2003, the Federal Emergency Management Agency (FEMA) became part of the U.S. DHS. The primary mission of the DHS/FEMA is to reduce the loss of life and property and protect the nation from all hazards, including natural disasters, acts of terrorism, and other man-made disasters, by leading and supporting the nation in a risk-based, comprehensive emergency management system of preparedness, protection, response, recovery, and mitigation.

On October 4, 2006, President George W. Bush signed into law the Post-Katrina Emergency Reform Act (PKEMRA), which is Title VI of the DHS Appropriations Act, 2007, Pub. L. 109-295, 120 Stat. 1355 (2006). The act significantly reorganized the Homeland Security Act and DHS/FEMA, provided it substantial new authority to remedy gaps that became apparent in the response to Hurricane Katrina in August 2005, with respect to the organizational structure, authorities, and responsibilities of FEMA and the FEMA Administrator. The DHS/FEMA Administrator is assigned responsibility to lead the nation's efforts to prepare for, protect against, respond to, recover from, and mitigate against the risk of natural disasters, acts of terrorism, and other man-made disasters, including catastrophic incidents. DHS/FEMA will now partner with state, local, and tribal governments and emergency response providers, other federal agencies, the private sector, and NGOs to build a national system of emergency management that can effectively and efficiently utilize the full measure of the nation's resources to respond to natural disasters, acts of terrorism, and other man-made disasters, including catastrophic incidents. Another role of the Administrator is to develop a federal response capability that, when necessary and appropriate, can act effectively and rapidly deliver assistance essential to saving lives or protecting or preserving property or public health and safety in a natural disaster, act of terrorism, or other man-made disasters.

DHS/FEMA, under the leadership of the secretary, coordinates with the Commandant of the Coast Guard, the Commissioner of Customs and Border Protection, the Assistant Secretary of Immigration and Customs Enforcement, the NOC, and other agencies and offices in the department to take full advantage of the substantial range of resources in the department.

Among other duties, the Homeland Security Act also assigns certain responsibilities to the DHS/FEMA Administrator specific to the *NRP*, now the *NRF*, and the *NIMS*, including: building a comprehensive national incident-management system with federal, state, and local government personnel, agencies, and authorities to respond to attacks and disasters; consolidating existing federal emergency response plans into a single, coordinated national response plan; and administering and ensuring the implementation of the *NRF*, including coordinating and ensuring the readiness of each ESF under the *NRF*.

Department of Defense

The primary mission of the DOD and its components is national defense. In some instances, national defense assets may be available to support civil authorities for routine and catastrophic incidents. Defense Support of Civil Authorities (DSCA) refers to support provided by U.S. military forces (Federal military, Reserve, and National Guard), DOD civilians, DOD contract personnel, DOD agency, and DOD component assets.

DOD normally provides DSCA in response to requests for assistance (RFAs) from other federal departments or agencies, or in some cases, local, tribal, or state governments. Support provided in response to such RFAs may help civil authorities prepare for, prevent, protect against, respond to, and recover from domestic incidents including terrorist attacks, and major disasters. Such assistance may also be used to support domestic special events of national importance, such as the national political conventions. DOD assets are usually requested if local, tribal, state, and other federal assets are not available. However, DOD resources are not typically required to mitigate every domestic incident. For example, of the 65 disasters presidentially declared as major disasters or emergencies in 2005, DOD responded to only three.

DOD is a full partner in the federal response to domestic incidents and the DOD response is fully coordinated through the mechanisms outlined in the *NRF*. In providing DSCA, the Secretary of Defense will always retain command of DOD personnel, with the exception of National Guard forces under the command and control of the governors. Nothing in the NRF impedes the Secretary of Defense's statutory authority pertaining to DOD personnel and resources.

During the immediate aftermath of an incident that may ultimately qualify for assistance under the Stafford Act, the governor of the state in which an incident occurred may request the President to direct the Secretary of Defense to utilize DOD resources to perform emergency work that is essential for the preservation of life and property. The President may direct this emergency work for a period not exceeding ten days.

As directed in PDD-39, the DOD will activate technical operations capabilities to support the federal response to threats or acts of WMD terrorism. DOD will coordinate military operations within the United States with the appropriate civilian lead agency(ies) for technical operations. Nuclear, biological, and chemical weapons defense has long been part of the military's portfolio. The U.S. Army Institute for Infectious Disease, the U.S. Army Institute for Chemical Defense, the Army's Technical Escort Unit, the National Guard Civil Support Teams, and the Naval Medical Research Center are prime examples of preexisting pockets of military, nuclear, biological, and chemical defense expertise. Due to its expertise, the U.S. Army was tasked with building a series of training courses for first responders, in coordination with other relevant agencies. In turn, the Army established the Domestic Preparedness Program at Soldier and Biological Chemical Command to develop and execute the training. This Army command also housed another entity that the legislation requested to assist local personnel in chemical and biological weapons incidents, the Chemical and Biological Rapid Response Team.

Nunn-Lugar-Domenici tapped the Pentagon and its chemical and biological weapons expertise from the beginning, reasoning that no one is better prepared to teach the fundamentals of an unfamiliar threat to a lay audience than the experts who know how to defend against it. In restructuring its consequence management architecture, the Pentagon created a unit specifically dedicated to coordinating the military's response to an unconventional attack at home. The Joint Task Force (JTF)–Civil Support Team integrates domestic unconventional terrorism responses from all the services. Based out of Norfolk, Virginia, at U.S. Joint Forces Command, the new task force is envisioned as the funnel through which all military assistance to first responders would flow in a crisis. The Chemical and Biological Rapid Response Team is a joint asset based at Soldier and Biological Chemical Command at Aberdeen, Maryland, which coordinates existing operational specialized military teams capable of addressing particular elements of a chemical and biological weapons crisis. The Army's Technical Escort Unit combines chemical and biological weapons expertise with explosive ordnance disposal capabilities and has more than five decades of varied mission experience. The Technical Escort Unit can bring capabilities in advanced detection, explosive ordnance disposal, decontamination, sampling, and personnel protection. For years, the Technical Escort Unit was virtually the only military unit capable of filling this sort of role—that is, until 1995 when the Marines began to assemble the Chemical and Biological Incident Response Force. The Marines have trained nearly 400 people for chemical and biological terrorism missions, with expertise in reconnaissance, agent detection and identification, decontamination, security, victim recovery, and casualty treatment. The unit's mission includes force protection as well as consequence management duties. The U.S. Army Medical Research Institute for Infectious Disease (USAMRIID) and the U.S. Army Medical Research Institute for Chemical Defense (USAMRICD) each have biological and chemical technical assets. Based at Fort Detrick in Frederick, Maryland, USAMRIID is the cornerstone of the military's biological defense community, housing expertise in diagnosis, pathology, delivery means, and countermeasures for biological weapons agents. Along with a pool of relevant technical advice, USAMRIID also has an Aeromedical Isolation Team, capable of deploying within 12 hours and transporting two patients in high containment. USAMRICD is located at Aberdeen Proving Ground, Maryland, and represents a parallel center of knowledge about chemical warfare agents, available antidotes, and treatment guidelines. USAMRICD also has a Chemical Casualty Site Team, made up of physicians, nurses, toxicologists, and laboratory specialists, that is rapidly deployable to give advice on sampling, treatment, and agent identification. Experts from USAMRIID and USAMRICD make up the National Medical Chemical and Biological Advisory Team, a small cell of experts that can deploy within four hours to give first responders specific treatment guidance and decontamination strategies for victims of chemical or biological warfare agents. Given its size, however, this team is an advisory asset, rather than a mass casualty treatment unit. Much like the national team, other short-notice advisory teams are available through Specialized Medical Augmentation Response Teams via the Army's regional medical commands. Focus areas include chemical and biological concerns and preventive medicine, the latter coming from the Center for Health Promotion and Preventive Medicine, also located at Aberdeen Proving Ground. In addition to Army units, there are Chemical, Biological, Radiological, Environmental Defense Response Teams from the Naval Environmental and Preventive Medicine Units in Hawaii, California, and Virginia. The Navy teams are best suited to assist in the remediation process, identifying the lingering environmental hazards after a chemical or biological attack, and advising on long-term ways to address any remaining contamination. The Army's 52nd Explosive Ordnance Group has capabilities to render safe a range of sophisticated and improvised explosive devices.

Imminently, serious conditions resulting from any civil emergency may require immediate action to save lives, prevent human suffering, or mitigate property damage. When such conditions exist and time does not permit approval from higher authorities, local military commanders and responsible officials from DOD components and agencies are authorized to take necessary action to respond to the requests from civil authorities. This response must be consistent with the Posse Comitatus Act (18 U.S.C. § 1385), which generally prohibits federal military personnel and Federalized National Guard personnel from acting in a law enforcement capacity (e.g., search, seizures, and arrests) within the United States, except where expressly authorized by the Constitution or Congress.

Federal military support to law enforcement is provided in accordance with appropriate statutes, when directed by the President. The attorney general and the Secretary of Defense are key advisors to the President during the decision-making process for certain types of assistance, e.g., assistance provided under Chapter 15 of Title 10, U.S. Code, "Enforcement of the Laws to Restore Public Order." Provision of law enforcement support does not have to be initiated by a request for assistance.

Based on the magnitude, type of incident and anticipated level of resource involvement, the combatant commander may utilize a JTF to command federal military forces (excluding U.S. Army Corps of Engineers resources) in support of the incident response. If a JTF is established, consistent with operational requirements, its command and control element will be colocated with the senior on-scene leadership at the JFO to ensure coordination and unity of effort.

Defense Reform Initiative Directive #25, Presidential Decision Directive 62, and the National Security Strategy of October 1998 directed that the military maintain augmentation forces for WMD consequence management, and cited the National Guard as having an important role in this mission area. The National Command Authority has implemented a strategy, which leverages the National Guard's ties to the communities throughout the nation, and long-standing tradition of responding to national emergencies, to provide the essential elements and support, which the emergency manager requires to manage the potentially catastrophic effects of a WMD emergency. The National Guard's geographic dispersion across the nation reduces the response time, and provides coverage for the major part of the country. The National Guard becomes the lead military element and employs as a state response asset, when called upon by the governor, to answer the call for assistance. As demonstrated during the many floods, droughts, hurricanes, fires, and the several WMD attacks in the United States, the civil emergency management structure is highly capable of managing large-scale catastrophic events. The local and state response forces generally provide a highly capable immediate response, and duration disaster relief. In some cases, however, available resources at the local and state levels will require military support, determined by the local and state emergency managers and validated by the governor of the state or the designated executive agent. When military support is required, the majority of the requests for assistance are performed by the National Guard as a state response asset, under the command and control of the Adjutant General. As a means of assisting the Incident Commander on the ground with the management of a WMD emergency, National Guard Civil Support Teams (CSTs) were fielded to provide the vital bridge between crisis and consequence management, local and state tiers to federal support, and civil to military operations. The CST mission is to support civil authorities at a domestic CBRNE incident site by identifying CBRNE agents/substances, assessing current and projected consequences, advising on response measures, and assisting with appropriate requests for state support. The Civil Support Teams provide a full military capability for terrorism response, the ability to determine if a WMD emergency exists, and if so, consult with the Incident Commander (IC) to undertake immediate actions to attempt to control or limit the attack, and subsequently shape the follow-on support.

Department of Energy

The Department of Energy (DOE) has extensive capabilities for radiological accidents/incidents, WMD, and terrorism incidents. DOE gathers, assesses, and shares information on energy system damage and estimations on the impact of energy system outages within affected areas. The suddenness and devastation of a disaster may sever key energy lifelines, constraining supply in affected areas and adversely impacting adjacent areas that have supply links to the directly affected areas. Such an event also could affect transportation, communications, and other lifelines needed for public health and safety. DOE serves as the focal point within the federal government for receipt of reports on damage to energy supply and distribution systems and requirements for system restoration. DOE advises federal, state, and local authorities on priorities for energy restoration, assistance, and supply. DOE assists industry, state, and local emergency response actions and assists federal departments and agencies by locating fuel for transportation, communications, emergency operations, and national defense. DOE has fixed and rotary wing aircraft for aerial radiological surveys and can provide health professionals, monitoring and other expertise. DOE's Nuclear

Emergency Search Team (NEST) can locate and render safe nuclear or radiological devices. Upon activation, DOE headquarters will establish the Headquarters Emergency Management Team (EMT). DOE headquarters will assign personnel to temporary duty at the JFO, NRCC, or RRCC as needed. The priority will be to save lives, protect property, and assist in the restoration of damaged energy systems. As directed in PDD-39, DOE will activate technical operations capabilities to support the federal response to threats or acts of WMD terrorism.

Environmental Protection Agency

As directed in PDD-39, the Environmental Protection Agency (EPA) will activate technical operations capabilities to support the federal response to acts of WMD terrorism.

The response to oil and hazardous materials incidents is generally carried out in accordance with the National Oil and Hazardous Substances Pollution Contingency Plan (NCP), 40 CFR Part 300. Hazardous materials include chemical, biological, and radiological substances, whether accidentally or intentionally released. The NCP is authorized by the Comprehensive Environmental Response, Compensation, and Liability Act (CERCLA) and the Federal Water Pollution Control Act (FWPCA) as amended by Section 311 of the Clean Water Act and the Oil Pollution Act of 1990 (OPA 90).

As described in the *Framework* core document, some federal responses do not require coordination by the DHS and are undertaken by other federal departments and agencies consistent with their authorities. Federal responses to oil and hazardous materials incidents under the authorities of CERCLA and the FWPCA that do not warrant DHS coordination are conducted under the NCP. The Environmental Protection Agency (EPA) or DHS/U.S. Coast Guard (USCG) may also request DHS to activate other *NRF* elements for such incidents, if needed, while still retaining overall leadership for the federal response.

The NCP describes the National Response System (NRS), which is an organized network of agencies, programs, and resources with authorities and responsibilities in oil and hazardous materials response. Key components of the NRS include the National Response Center, National Response Team (NRT), Regional Response Teams (RRTs), Federal On-Scene Coordinators (OSCs), Regional and Area Contingency Plans, and State and local plans. States and tribes participate in the NRS at the regional and local levels.

The NCP requires that oil and hazardous materials releases be reported to the National Response Center (see 40 CFR 300.125.). The National Response Center provides notifications of such reports to the NOC to promote situational awareness.

The NRT is the national-level organization for coordinating federal interagency activities under the NCP. On a day-to-day basis, EPA serves as Chair and DHS/USCG as Vice Chair of the NRT. For an incident-specific NRT activation, the NRT Chair would be the agency providing the federal OSC. The NRT provides support, assistance, and advice to the federal OSC and RRT as requested (Precise jurisdictional boundaries between EPA and DHS/USCG have been determined by EPA-DHS/USCG agreements and are described in the NCP and in greater detail in Regional and Area Contingency Plans. In general, EPA is the lead for incidents in the inland zone and DHS/USCG is the lead for incidents in the coastal zone). Thirteen RRTs coordinate NCP interagency activities at the federal regional level. The RRTs are cochaired by EPA and DHS/USCG on a day-to-day basis. The RRTs serve as planning and preparedness bodies before a response. For an incident-specific RRT activation, the RRT Chair would be the agency providing the federal OSC. The RRTs are coordinating bodies. As needed during a response, RRTs convene to address interagency response issues and provide assistance and advice to the federal OSC(s), including resource acquisition support as requested.

At the tactical, on-scene Incident Command Post (ICP) level, the federal OSC carries out his or her responsibilities under the NCP to coordinate, integrate, and manage overall oil and hazardous materials response efforts in accordance with existing delegations of authority. For oil discharges, depending on the location, the agency providing the federal OSC is either EPA or DHS/USCG. For hazardous substance emergencies, the agency providing the OSC may be EPA, DHS/USCG, the DOE, or the DOD, depending on the location and source of the release. DOE and DOD are generally responsible for hazardous substance emergencies involving their facilities, vessels, materials, and weapons, including transportation-related incidents. Under 40 CFR 300.120, for those hazardous substance emergencies for which DOE or DOD provides the OSC, the OSC is responsible for taking all response actions (both onsite and offsite). Other federal agencies provide OSCs for hazardous substance removal actions that are not emergencies. Federal OSCs have an independent authority under the NCP to respond to an oil or hazardous materials incident. The NCP provides that EPA or DHS/USCG may classify an oil discharge as a Spill of National Significance (SONS) (See 40 CFR 300.323 for a description of a SONS.). For a SONS, EPA or DHS/USCG may name a "senior Agency official" (EPA) or National Incident Commander (DHS/USCG) who assists the OSC, or assumes certain functions of the OSC, respectively (e.g., communicating with the affected parties and public, coordinating resources at the national level). Under the *NRF*, EPA and DHS/USCG maintain authority for classifying a discharge as a SONS for purposes of the NCP. DHS may or may not decide that it should coordinate the federal response to a SONS. If not, EPA or DHS/USCG lead the federal response in accordance with the NCP. For a SONS for which DHS coordinates the overall federal response, the EPA senior agency official or DHS/USCG National Incident Commander may also assume a role within the JFO UCG.

Department of Health and Human Services

As directed in PDD-39, the Department of HHS will activate technical operations capabilities to support the federal response to threats or acts of WMD terrorism.

The Secretary of HHS leads all federal public health and medical response to public health emergencies and incidents covered by the *Framework*. The response addresses medical and other functional needs of those in need of medical care, including assistance or support in maintaining independence, communicating, using transportation, or requiring supervision.

The Secretary of HHS shall assume operational control of federal emergency public health and medical response assets, as necessary, in the event of a public health emergency, except for members of the Armed Forces, who remain under the authority and control of the Secretary of Defense.

The Secretary of HHS, through the Office of the Assistant Secretary for Preparedness and Response (ASPR), coordinates national public health and medical services preparedness, response, and recovery actions. These actions do not alter or impede the existing authorities of any department or agency supporting health and medical response.

HHS coordinates all response actions consistent with HHS internal policies and procedures (e.g., HHS Concept of Operations Plan for Public Health and Medical Emergencies, and the National Disaster Medical System [NDMS] Four Partner Memorandum of Agreement). State, local, and tribal public health and medical support agencies are responsible for maintaining administrative control over their respective response resources after receiving coordinating instructions from HHS. The Emergency Management Group (EMG), operating from the HHS Secretary's Operations Center (SOC), coordinates the overall national health and medical response for the ASPR and maintains constant communications with the SOC. All headquarters and regional organizations participating in response operations report public health and medical requirements to the appropriate representative operating in the NRCC, the RRCC, or the JFO when activated.

The Joint Information Center (JIC) will be established to coordinate incident-related public information, and is authorized to release general medical and public health response information to the public. When possible, a recognized spokesperson from the public health and medical community (state, tribal, or local) delivers relevant community messages. After consultation with HHS, the lead Public Affairs Officer from other JICs may also release general medical and public health response information.

In the event of a zoonotic disease outbreak and in coordination with Agriculture and Natural Resources, public information may be released after consultation with the Department of Agriculture (USDA). In the event of an oil, chemical, biological, or radiological environmental contamination incident, HHS coordinates with EPA on the release of public health information.

As the lead agency for public health and medical response, HHS determines the appropriateness of all requests for release of public health and medical information and is responsible for consulting with and organizing federal public health and medical subject-matter experts, as needed.

In the early stages of an incident, it may not be possible to fully assess the situation and verify the level of assistance required. In such circumstances, HHS may provide assistance under its own statutory authorities. In these cases, every reasonable attempt is made to verify the need before providing assistance.

During the response period, HHS has a primary responsibility for the analysis of public health and medical assistance, determining the appropriate level of response capability based on the requirement contained in the action request form as well as developing updates and assessments of public health status.

HHS has beefed up front-line preparedness by developing local medical response teams geared to offer medical services in the wake of a poison gas or germ attack. A Lab Response Network (LRN) has been institutionalized throughout the nation, and has increased lab capacity to the local levels. The growing involvement of HHS in terrorism preparedness is logical given the agency's established role in the *Framework* for public health issues and its long-time involvement in the National Disaster Medical System (NDMS). In June 1996, HHS issued a plan on how best to grapple with the unique health and medical consequences of a chemical or biological terrorist incident, including the increased demand for pharmaceuticals, antidotes, and specialized equipment, as well as the narrow window of opportunity to treat victims and counteract the adverse effects of the agents to which they were exposed. Working within the existing crisis and consequence management architecture, the HHS plan committed various agencies to handle key elements of the immediate medical response. Biological agent identification would fall to the Centers for Disease Control and Prevention, as would the epidemiological investigation; pharmaceutical support would come from the Food and Drug Administration; and coordination of mortuary services, transportation and supplies, pathology, and public affairs would fall to the NDMS throughout the HHS Office of Emergency Preparedness.

HHS has articulated its strategy for bioterrorism preparedness centering on five key programming areas: (1) deter or prevent bioterror attacks through tightened shipping controls; (2) upgrade state and local surveillance capabilities; (3) develop better local and national medical and public health responses to bioterrorism; (4) build a national pharmaceutical stockpile; and (5) research additional vaccines and rapid screens for toxic agents. HHS has tried to build local capacity that could manage without federal help during the immediate hours after an attack before meaningful federal help could arrive. The LRN is one of these examples. HHS terrorism preparedness programs, both federally and locally, are directed primarily by the HHS Office for Emergency Preparedness and the CDC.

The Office of Public Health Emergency Preparedness (OPHEP) was established on June 12, 2002. On behalf of the HHS secretary, OPHEP directs and coordinates HHS-wide efforts with respect to preparedness for and response to bioterrorism and other public health and medical emergencies. OPHEP is an office of the Public Health Service (PHS) and is responsible for developing preparedness and response capabilities, as well as directing and coordinating the relevant activities of the HHS Operating Divisions (OPDIV). OPHEP is headed by the Assistant Secretary for Public Health Emergency Preparedness (ASPHEP), who reports directly to the secretary. OPHEP's areas of program emphasis are (1) enhancement of state and local medical and public health preparedness—primarily health departments and hospitals; (2) development and use of National and Departmental policies and plans relating to the response to public health and medical threats and emergencies, e.g., ESF #8 of the National Response Framework, Homeland Security Presidential Directives (HSPD) #5 and #10, HHS's Concept of Operations Plan for Public Health and Medical Emergencies (CONOPS) and the Incident Response Coordination Team (IRCT); (3) coordination with relevant entities inside and outside HHS such as state, local, and tribal public health and medical officials, the Departments of Homeland Security (DHS), Defense (DOD), Veterans Affairs (VA), Justice (DOJ), the Homeland Security Council (HSC), other partner organizations, and others within the National security community; (4) rapid public health and medical support to federal, state, local, and tribal governments who may be responding to Incidents of National Significance or public health and medical emergencies; (5) coordination of and participation in research, development, and procurement activities related to public health emergency medical countermeasures destined for the Strategic National Stockpile (SNS); (6) leadership in international programs, initiatives, and policies that deal with public health emergency preparedness and response related to naturally occurring threats such as infectious diseases and deliberate threats from biological, and chemical and radiation sources; and (7) leadership and oversight on medical, science, and public health policies, issues, and programs.

HHS had assigned the Department of Veterans Affairs the task of maintaining the pharmaceutical stock caches, a selection that made sense in light of its experience with managing pharmaceuticals for the Veterans Affairs hospital network. The Centers for Disease Control and Prevention (CDC) has also focused on building capacities at the local, state, and federal levels. Rooted in the U.S. antimalaria program in World War II, the CDC began in 1946 as the Communicable Disease Center. Since that time, it has served as the primary U.S. brain trust on disease origins, recognition, control, and prevention.

The dozen-odd research centers and offices that fall under the CDC's umbrella cover everything from occupational health to disease research, with several playing an integral role in U.S. preparedness for bioterrorism. The particular advantage of CDC's bioterrorism programs lies in their multiple utility: improvements to the public health infrastructure bring day-to-day benefits regardless of the specific disease or its source and are useful well beyond the worst case bioterrorist scenarios. Although CDC carved out an office in the National Center for Infectious Diseases dedicated to bioterrorism preparedness in December 1998, it also set about making widespread improvements to its approach in managing infectious disease. The CDC also began working through state public health agencies to rejuvenate *local* public health infrastructure, creating a layered system of consultation and information sharing among laboratories of varying capacity and specialization. The Laboratory Response Network for Bioterrorism includes four functional levels of laboratories:

- Level A: public health and hospital laboratories with minimal biosafety facilities
- Level B: state and county public health agency facilities capable of testing for specific agents and forwarding specimens to higher containment facilities
- Level C: state agencies, academic research or federal laboratories equipped for toxicity testing and advanced diagnostics
- Level D: federal laboratories with highest level of containment and technological sophistication (e.g., CDC, U.S. Army Medical Research Institute for Infectious Diseases)

To prevent inundation at the top of the laboratory pyramid, CDC began spreading diagnostic technology down the line to Level B and C laboratories so that they can conduct sample testing. Nevertheless, CDC's rapid response laboratory remains on standby, 24 hours a day, seven days a week, to confirm local laboratory findings and serve as a reference for questions that pop up in the course of an investigation.

A release of selected biological or chemical agents targeting the U.S. civilian population will require rapid access to large quantities of pharmaceuticals and medical supplies. Such quantities may not be readily available unless special stockpiles are created. No one can anticipate exactly where a terrorist will strike and few state or local governments have the resources to create sufficient stockpiles on their own. Therefore, a national stockpile has been created as a resource for all. As part of the Department of HHS 1999 Bioterrorism Initiative, CDC was designated to lead an effort working with governmental and nongovernmental partners to upgrade the nations' public health capacity to respond to biological and chemical terrorism and establish a Bioterrorism Preparedness and Response Program. Critical to success of this initiative is to ensure that capacity is developed at federal, state, and local levels. The SNS Program is an essential response component of CDC's larger Bioterrorism Preparedness and Response Initiative.

The mission of CDC's SNS Program is to ensure the availability of life-saving pharmaceuticals, antidotes, and other medical supplies and equipment necessary to counter the effects of nerve agents, biological pathogens, and chemical agents. The SNS Program stands ready for immediate deployment to any U.S. location in the event of a terrorist attack using a biological, toxin, or chemical agent directed against a civilian population. The SNS is comprised of pharmaceuticals, vaccines, medical supplies, and medical equipment that exist to augment depleted state and local resources for responding to terrorist attacks and other emergencies. These packages are stored in strategic locations around the United States to ensure rapid delivery anywhere in the country.

Following the federal decision to deploy, the SNS will typically arrive by air or ground in two phases. The first phase shipment is called a 12-hour Push Package. "12" because it will arrive in 12 hours or less, "push" because a state need only ask for help-not for specific items, and "package" because the Program will ship a complete package of medical materiel—to include nearly everything a state will need to respond to a broad range of threats. Inventory supplies known as Vendor Managed Inventory, or VMI packages are also available. VMI packages can be tailored to provide pharmaceuticals, vaccines, medical supplies, or medical products specific to the suspected or confirmed agent or combination of agents.

A CDC team of five or six technical advisors will also deploy at the same time as the first shipment. Known as a Technical Advisory Response Unit (TARU), this team is comprised of pharmacists, emergency responders, and logistics experts that will advise local authorities on receiving, distributing, dispensing, replenishing, and recovering SNS materiel. The SNS Program was tested in a real-life terrorist attack in response to the tragic events of September 11th when New York state and local officials requested large quantities of medical materiel and logistical assistance. With the support of local and state public health and emergency response officials, all facets of the New York operation performed exactly as intended. The SNS Program has also assisted many states and cities by providing pharmaceutical and logistical support to areas affected by the anthrax attacks in October and November 2001.

The CDC, in consultation with other partners in chemical/biological preparedness, have developed a stockpile to respond to biological or chemical terrorism emergencies. To determine and review the composition of the SNS, CDC considers many factors, such as current biological or chemical threats, the availability of medical materiel, and the ease of dissemination of pharmaceuticals. One of the most significant factors in determining SNS composition, however, is the medical vulnerability of the U.S. civilian population. SNS assets are stored at strategic locations throughout the United States to assure the most rapid response possible. CDC ensures that the medical materiel in these SNS storage facilities is rotated and kept within potency shelf life limits.

In a biological or chemical terrorism event, state, local, and private stocks of medical materiel will deplete quickly. The SNS can support local first response efforts with a Push Package followed by quantities of materiel specific to the terrorist agent used (utilizing VMI). The SNS is not a first response tool. State and local first responders and health officials can use the SNS to bolster their response to a biological or chemical terrorism attack—thereby increasing their capacity to more rapidly mitigate the results of this type of terrorism.

As part of CDC's Bioterrorism Response, CDC will transfer authority for the SNS materiel to the state or local authorities once it arrives at the airfield. State or local authorities will then repackage and label bulk medicines and other SNS materiel according to their state terrorism contingency plan. CDC's technical advisors will accompany the SNS to assist and advise state/local officials in putting the SNS assets to prompt, effective use.

The decision to deploy SNS assets may be based on evidence showing the overt release of an agent that might adversely affect public health. It is more likely, however, that subtle indicators, such as unusual morbidity or mortality identified through the nation's disease outbreak surveillance and epidemiology network, will alert health officials to the possibility (and confirmation) of a biological or chemical terrorism incident. To receive SNS assets, the affected state can directly request the deployment of the SNS from the Director of CDC. Once requested, the Director of CDC has the authority, in consultation with the Surgeon General, and the Secretary of HHS, to order the deployment of the SNS.

Planning Assumptions

A major disaster or emergency will cause numerous fatalities and injuries, property loss, and disruption of normal life-support systems, and will have an impact on the regional economic, physical, and social infrastructures. The extent of casualties and damage will reflect factors such as the time of occurrence, severity of impact, weather conditions, population density, building construction, and the possible triggering of secondary events such as fires and floods. The large number of casualties, heavy damage to buildings and basic infrastructure, and disruption of essential public services will overwhelm the capabilities of the state and its local governments to meet the needs of the situation, and the President will declare a major disaster or emergency. Federal agencies will need to respond on short notice to provide timely and effective assistance. The degree of federal involvement will be related to the severity and magnitude of the event as well as the state and local need for external support. The most devastating disasters may require the full range of federal response and recovery assistance. Less damaging disasters may require only partial federal response and recovery assistance. Some disasters may require only federal recovery assistance.

The President leads the nation in responding effectively and ensuring the necessary resources are applied quickly and efficiently to all Incidents of National Significance. As necessary, the Assistant to the President for Homeland Security convenes interagency meetings to coordinate policy issues. During actual or potential Incidents of National Significance, the overall coordination of federal incident-management activities is executed through the Secretary of Homeland Security. Other federal departments and agencies carry out their incident management and emergency response authorities and responsibilities within this overarching coordinating framework. The Secretary of Homeland Security utilizes multiagency structures at the headquarters, regional, and field levels to coordinate efforts and provide appropriate support to the incident command structure. At the federal headquarters level, incident information sharing, operational planning, and deployment of federal resources are coordinated by the Homeland Security Operations Center (HSOC), and its component element, the NRCC. Issues beyond the secretary's authority to resolve are referred to the appropriate White House entity for resolution.

At the regional level, interagency resource coordination and multiagency incident support are provided by the RRCC. In the field, the Secretary of Homeland Security is represented by the Principal Federal Official (PFO) (or the Federal Coordinating Officer [FCO]/Federal Resource Coordinator [FRC] as appropriate). Overall Federal support to the incident command structure, on-scene, is coordinated through the JFO. For terrorist incidents, the primary responsibilities for coordinating and conducting all federal law enforcement and criminal investigation activities are executed by the attorney general acting through the FBI. During a terrorist incident, the local FBI special agent-in-charge (SAC) coordinates these activities with other members of the law enforcement community, and works in conjunction with the PFO, who coordinates overall federal incident-management activities. When a terrorist threat or actual incident falls within the criminal jurisdiction of the United States, any incident-management activity by any other federal department or agency that could adversely affect the attorney general's ability to prevent, preempt, disrupt, and respond to such a threat or incident must be coordinated with the attorney general through the Senior Federal Law Enforcement Officer (SFLEO) (i.e., the FBI SAC). The framework created by these coordinating structures is designed to accommodate the various roles the federal government plays during an incident, whether it is federal support to (and in coordination with) state, local, or tribal authorities; federal-to-federal support; or direct implementation of federal incident-management authorities and responsibilities when appropriate under federal law. This structure also encompasses the dual roles and responsibilities of the Secretary of Homeland Security for operational and resource coordination in the context of domestic incident management.

Concept of Operations

The majority of disasters and emergencies are handled by local and state responders. The federal government is called upon to provide supplemental assistance when the consequences of a disaster exceed local and state capabilities. If needed, the federal government can mobilize an array of resources to support state and local efforts. Various emergency teams, support personnel, specialized equipment, operating facilities, assistance programs, and access to private-sector resources constitute the overall federal disaster operations system.

Various federal statutory authorities and policies provide the basis for federal actions and activities in the context of domestic incident management. The *Framework* uses the foundation provided by the Homeland Security Act, HSPD-5, and the Robert T. Stafford Disaster Relief and Emergency Assistance Act (Stafford Act) to provide a comprehensive, all-hazards approach to domestic incident management. Nothing in the *Framework* alters the existing authorities of individual federal departments and agencies. The *Framework* does not convey new authorities upon the Secretary of Homeland Security or any other federal official. Rather, this plan establishes the coordinating structures, processes, and protocols required to integrate the specific statutory and policy authorities of various federal departments and agencies in a collective framework for action to include prevention, preparedness, response, and recovery activities. The *Framework* may be used in conjunction with other federal incident management and emergency operations plans developed under these and other authorities as well as memorandums of understanding (MOUs) among various federal agencies.

The *Framework* employs a multiagency operational structure that uses the principles of the Incident Command System (ICS), based on a model adopted by the fire and rescue community. ICS can be used in any magnitude or type of disaster to control response personnel, facilities, and equipment. ICS principles include use of common terminology, modular organization, integrated communications, unified command structure, action planning, manageable span-of-control, predesignated facilities, and comprehensive resource management. The basic functional modules of ICS (e.g., operations and logistics) can be expanded or contracted to meet requirements as an event progresses. *NIMS* is a system mandated by HSPD-5 that provides a consistent, nationwide approach for federal, state, local, and tribal governments; the private sector; and NGOs to work effectively and efficiently together to prepare for, respond to, and recover from domestic incidents, regardless of cause, size, or complexity. To provide for interoperability and compatibility among federal, state, local, and tribal capabilities, the NIMS includes a core set of concepts, principles, and terminology. HSPD-5 identifies these as the ICS; multiagency coordination systems; training; identification and management of resources (including systems for classifying types of resources); qualification and certification; and the collection, tracking, and reporting of incident information and incident resources.

Integration of Response, Recovery, and Mitigation Actions

Subsequent to a disaster, immediate response operations to save lives, protect property, and meet basic human needs have precedence over recovery and mitigation. However, initial recovery planning should commence at once in tandem with response operations. Actual recovery operations will be initiated commensurate with state priorities and based on availability of resources immediately required for response operations. In recognition that certain response and recovery activities may be conducted concurrently, coordination at all levels is essential to ensure consistent federal actions throughout the disaster. Mitigation opportunities should be actively considered throughout disaster operations. Decisions made during response and recovery operations can either enhance or hinder subsequent mitigation activities. The urgency to rebuild as soon as possible must be weighed against the longer term goal of reducing future risk and lessening possible impacts should another disaster occur.

Military Support

DOD maintains significant resources (personnel, equipment, and supplies) that may be available to support the federal response to a major disaster or emergency. DOD will normally provide support only when other resources are unavailable, and only if such support does not interfere with its primary mission or ability to respond to operational contingencies.

DOD provides Defense Security Cooperation Agency (DSCA) in response to requests for assistance during domestic incidents to include terrorist attacks, major disasters, and other emergencies. DSCA refers to DOD supports provided by federal military forces, DOD civilians and contract personnel, and DOD agencies and components, in response to requests for assistance. Continuous coordination with federal, state, local, and tribal elements before, during, and after an event is essential for efficient and effective utilization of DOD's DSCA efforts. In most instances, DOD provides DSCA in response to requests for assistance from a lead or primary agency. However, support provided under Immediate Response Authority (described in the following text) is authorized by the DOD directive and prior approval of the Secretary of Defense. DSCA normally is provided when local, state, and federal resources are overwhelmed, provided that it does not interfere with the Department's military readiness or operations. DOD typically provides DSCA on a reimbursable basis as authorized by the law.

Initial requests for assistance are made to the Office of the Secretary of Defense, Executive Secretariat. If approved by the Secretary of Defense, DOD designates a supported combatant commander for the response. The supported combatant commander determines the appropriate level of command and control for each response and usually directs a senior military officer to deploy to the incident site. Under most circumstances, the senior military officer at the incident site is the DOD Coordinating Officer (DCO). The DCO serves as DOD's single point of contact in the JFO. Requests for DSCA originating at the JFO will be coordinated and processed through the DCO with the exception of requests for United States Army Corps of Engineers (USACE) support, National Guard forces operating in State Active Duty or Title 32 status (i.e., not in federal service), or, in some circumstances, DOD forces in support of the FBI. These exceptions are elaborated later in this section. Specific responsibilities of the DCO are subject to modification by the supported combatant commander based on the situation. Based on the magnitude, type of disaster, and anticipated level of resource involvement, the supported combatant commander may utilize a JTF to consolidate and manage supporting military activities. A JTF commander exercises operational control of all allocated DOD resources (excluding USACE resources, National Guard forces operating in State Active Duty or Title 32 status, and, in some circumstances, DOD forces in support of the FBI). In the event that a JTF is utilized, the DCO may continue to perform all duties set forth earlier.

Requests for DSCA originating at the JFO will be coordinated and processed through the DCO with the exception of requests for DOD/USACE support, National Guard forces operating in State Active Duty or Title 32 status, and, in some cases, DOD forces in support of the FBI.

Federal Law Enforcement Assistance

In a disaster or emergency, each state has a primary responsibility for law enforcement, using state and local resources, including the National Guard (to the extent that the National Guard remains under state authority and has not been called into federal service or ordered to active duty). If a state government should experience a law enforcement emergency (including one in connection with a disaster or emergency) in which it could not provide an adequate response to protect the lives and property of citizens, the state (on behalf of itself or a local unit of government) might submit an application in writing from the governor to the attorney general of the United States to request emergency federal law enforcement assistance under the Justice Assistance Act of 1984 (42 U.S.C. 10501-10513) as prescribed in 28 CFR 65. The attorney general will approve or disapprove the application no later than ten days after receipt. If the application is approved, federal law enforcement assistance may be provided to include equipment, training, intelligence, and personnel.

In the event that state and local police forces (including the National Guard operating under state control) are unable to adequately respond to a civil disturbance or other serious law enforcement emergency, a governor may request, through the attorney general, federal military assistance under 10 U.S.C. 15. Pursuant to 10 U.S.C. 331-333, the President will ultimately determine whether to use the Armed Forces to respond to a law enforcement emergency. Under Title 10 authority, the President may federalize and deploy all or part of any state's National Guard.

Response and Recovery Actions

Federal agencies are prepared to take a variety of actions to assist state and local governments in responding to and recovering from a major disaster. These actions range from initial notification of a disaster to preparation of a final disaster after-action report. They are not necessarily in sequential order; some may be undertaken concurrently. An overview of an entire disaster operation, indicating key operational components and the typical sequence of actions, appears in Chapter 27.

Recovery involves actions needed to help individuals and communities return to normalcy when feasible. The JFO is the central coordination point among federal, state, local, and tribal agencies and voluntary organizations for delivering recovery assistance programs. The JFO Operations Section includes the Human Services Branch, the Infrastructure Support Branch, and the Community Recovery and Mitigation Branch. The Human Services and Infrastructure Support Branches of the JFO Operations Section assess state and local recovery needs at the outset of an incident and develop relevant timeframes for program delivery. These branches ensure federal agencies that have relevant recovery assistance programs are notified of an incident and share relevant applicant and damage information with all involved agencies as appropriate, ensuring that the privacy of individuals is protected.

Initial Actions

The Homeland Security Operations Center (HSOC) receives threat and operational information regarding incidents or potential incidents and makes an initial determination to initiate the coordination of federal information-sharing and incident-management activities. Suspicious activity, terrorist threats, and actual incidents with a potential or actual terrorist nexus are reported immediately to a local or regional Joint Terrorism Task Force (JTTF) (or the National Joint Terrorism Task Force [NJTTF], in the case of federal departments/agencies). Subsequently, the FBI Strategic Information and Operations Center (SIOC) immediately reports the terrorist threat, if the FBI deems the threat to be credible, or the actual incident to the HSOC and the National Counter Terrorism Center (NCTC). Additionally, actual incidents, regardless of whether or not there is a terrorist nexus, are reported immediately to the HSOC by appropriate governmental and nongovernmental entities. Federal departments and agencies are required to report information relating to actual or potential Incidents of National Significance to the HSOC. State and tribal governments and emergency management agencies use established reporting mechanisms and are encouraged to report information relating to actual or potential Incidents of National Significance to the HSOC, using procedures established by DHS. (Information regarding potential terrorist threats should be reported through the local or regional JTTF.) Local governments communicate information regarding actual or potential Incidents of National Significance to the HSOC through established reporting mechanisms in coordination with state government officials and Emergency Operations Centers (EOCs). Private sector and NGOs are encouraged to communicate information regarding actual or potential Incidents of National Significance to the HSOC through existing jurisdictional reporting mechanisms, as well as established information-sharing and analysis organizations (ISAOs).

The HSOC maintains daily situational awareness to identify and monitor threats or potential threats inside, on, or approaching the borders of the United States. Upon receipt, the HSOC passes such information to the appropriate federal, state, local, and tribal intelligence and law enforcement agencies as expeditiously as possible, according to established security protocols and in coordination with the FBI and NCTC. The HSOC coordinates with other departments and agencies regarding further field investigation, as required. The FBI, NCTC, and DHS/Information Analysis and Infrastructure Protection (IAIP) evaluate intelligence relating to terrorist threats and other potential incidents. All federal, state, local, and tribal departments and agencies must notify their local or regional FBI JTTF regarding information associated with a threat of terrorism or an actual terrorist incident. Additionally, the HSOC is notified immediately in the case of an actual incident, regardless of whether or not there is a terrorist nexus. In the case of a threat, the local FBI JTTF notifies the NJTTF. Federal department and agency headquarters should notify the NJTTF or FBI SIOC with similar information. Upon receipt of a threat of terrorism, the FBI conducts a formal threat credibility assessment, which may include assistance from select interagency experts. If a threat is deemed credible, the FBI SIOC notifies the HSOC immediately. Watches, warnings, and other emergency bulletins are issued by various agencies based on their statutory missions and authorities. The HSOC coordinates with the NCTC, Terrorist Screening Center (TSC), FBI, Department of HHS, and similar programs for terrorism-related threat analysis and warning, and disseminates homeland security threat warnings and advisory bulletins. The ongoing fusion of intelligence at the national level may result in the detection of a potential terrorist threat of a specific and credible nature. Unlike incidents reported from the field, this process results in the initiation of initial incident-management actions at the headquarters level and generates a "top-down" response to deter, prevent, and otherwise respond to the terrorist threat. The HSOC, NCTC, and FBI SIOC coordinate information regarding terrorist threats. When the FBI or DHS/IAIP determines that a credible threat exists, it notifies and coordinates with the HSOC, which immediately notifies the FBI SIOC, if it has not been already informed. The HSOC then notifies the Secretary of Homeland Security, who may elect to activate any or all of the NRP organizational elements, as well as initiate the coordination of interagency policy issues and operational courses of action through the White House, as appropriate. The secretary may also elect to activate and prepare to deploy various special teams to conduct prevention, preparedness, response, and recovery activities.

For actual or potential Incidents of National Significance, the HSOC reports the situation to the Secretary of Homeland Security or senior staff as delegated by the secretary, who then determines the need to activate components of the *Framework* to conduct further assessment of the situation, initiate interagency coordination, share information with affected jurisdictions and the private sector, or initiate deployment of resources. When the secretary declares an Incident of National Significance, federal departments and agencies are notified by the HSOC (as operational security considerations permit), and may be called upon to staff the Interagency Incident Management Group (IIMG) and NRCC. The affected state(s) and tribes are also notified by the HSOC using appropriate operational security protocols. For acts of terrorism, information sharing, deployment of resources, and incident-management actions during actual or potential terrorist incidents are coordinated with DOJ. The NRCC and the Regional Response Coordination Center (RRCC) deploy, track, and provide incident-related information until the JFO is established.

Regional resources may be activated to monitor and assess the need for federal incident-management support. The DHS/EPR/FEMA Regional Director deploys a liaison to the state EOC to provide technical assistance including advice on the Stafford Act declaration process and available federal assistance, and also partially or fully activates the RRCC including, where appropriate, regional representatives of federal departments and agencies. The RRCC and the NRCC Logistics Sections support the establishment of a JFO and mobilization center(s). The RRCC coordinates federal support of state requirements until the FCO or the Fast Response Cutter (FRC) assumes those responsibilities. A Joint Information Center (JIC) may be established, as required, to provide a central point for coordinating emergency public information activities.

Continuing Actions

Once an incident occurs, the priorities shift from prevention, preparedness, and incident mitigation to immediate and short-term response activities to preserve life; property; the environment; and the social, economic, and political structure of the community. In the context of a terrorist threat, simultaneous activities are initiated to assess regional and national-level impacts, as well as to assess and take appropriate action to prevent and protect against other potential threats. Reinforcing the initial response to an incident, some federal agencies may operate in the ICP as federal first responders and participate in the Unified Command structure. Once the JFO is established, the JFO Coordination Group sets federal operational priorities. The JFO provides resources in support of the Unified Command and incident-management teams conducting on-scene operations through the state and local EOCs. Depending upon the scope and magnitude of the incident, the NRCC or the RRCCs activate the appropriate ESFs, as needed, to mobilize assets and the deployment of resources to support the incident. The NRCC or the RRCCs facilitate the deployment and transportation of the ERT and other teams and specialized capabilities such as, but not limited to, teams under the NDMS, the HHS Secretary's Emergency Response Team, the Epidemic Intelligence Service, HHS behavioral health response teams, the U.S. Public Health Service Commissioned Corps, and Urban Search and Rescue teams. Other response actions include the establishment of the JFO and other field facilities and providing a wide range of support for incident management, public health, and other community needs. Response actions also include immediate law enforcement, fire, ambulance, and emergency medical service actions; emergency flood fighting; evacuations; transportation system detours; emergency public information; actions taken to minimize additional damage; urban search and rescue; the establishment of facilities for mass care; the provision of public health and medical services, food, ice, water, and other emergency essentials; debris clearance; the emergency restoration of critical infrastructure; control, containment, and removal of environmental contamination; and protection of responder health and safety. During the response to a terrorist event, law enforcement actions to collect and preserve evidence and to apprehend perpetrators are critical. These actions take place simultaneously with response operations necessary to save lives and protect property, and are closely coordinated with the law enforcement effort to facilitate the collection of evidence without impacting ongoing life-saving operations. In the context of a single incident, once immediate response missions and life-saving activities conclude, the emphasis shifts from response to recovery operations and, if applicable, hazard mitigation.

Bibliography

The Defense Production Act of 1950 (DPA), 64 Stat. 798 (1950) (codified at 50 U.S.C. App. §§ 2061, et seq. (2007)) is the primary authority to ensure the timely availability of resources for national defense and civil emergency preparedness and response.

The Emergency Federal Law Enforcement Assistance Act, 42 U.S.C. § 10501 (2007), authorizes the Attorney General, in a law enforcement emergency and upon written request by a Governor, to coordinate and deploy emergency federal law enforcement assistance to state and local law enforcement authorities.

FBI WMD Incident Contingency Plan, http://www.fbi.gov.

Federal Emergency Management Agency in the Department of Homeland Security Appropriations Act of 2007, Pub. L. 109-295, 120 Stat. 1355 (2006) established a Department of Homeland Security (DHS) as an executive department of the United States.

Federal Radiological Emergency Response Plan, http://www.fema.gov/pte/rep/350-5.htm, accessed 5/2002.

Federal Response Plan, http://www.fema.gov/r-n-r/frp/, accessed 5/2002.

HHS Health and Medical Services Support Plan for the Federal Response to Acts of Chemical/Biological Terrorism.

The Homeland Security Act of 2002, Pub. L. 107-296, 116 Stat. 2135 (2002) (codified predominantly at 6 U.S.C. §§ 101–557).

Homeland Security Presidential Directive 5: Management of Domestic Incidents, February 28, 2003, requires the Secretary of Homeland Security to develop, submit, and administer a *National Incident Management System (NIMS)* that will provide a consistent nationwide approach for federal, state, and local governments to work effectively and efficiently together to prepare for, respond to, and recover from domestic incidents, regardless of cause, size, or complexity.

Homeland Security Presidential Directive 10: Biodefense for the 21st Century (April 28, 2004), establishes strategies for preventing, protecting against, and mitigating biological weapons attacks perpetrated against homeland and global interests.

Homeland Security Presidential Directive 21: Public Health and Medical Preparedness (October 18, 2007), establishes a national strategy that will enable a level of public health and medical preparedness sufficient to address a range of possible disasters.

Military Support for Civilian Law Enforcement Agencies, 10 U.S.C. §§ 371–382 (2007), authorizes the United States military to assist state and local law enforcement agencies without engaging in the execution of the law by sharing information and expertise; furnishing equipment, supplies, and services; and helping to operate equipment.

National Contingency Plan, http://www.fema.gov/r-n-r/frp/frpintro.htm, accessed 5/2002.

The National Emergencies Act, 50 U.S.C. §§ 1601-1651 (2007), establishes procedures for Presidential declaration of a national emergency and the termination of national emergencies by the President or Congress.

National Guard Authority. Under Title 10, U.S.C., the federal government calls up and funds the National Guard for active duty for national service. Under Title 32, U.S.C., State Governors can activate and command Guard units for missions. Additionally, under 32 U.S.C. § 502(f), the National Guard may be called up for federal service while remaining under the control of the Governor. National Guard forces operating in a State Active Duty or Title 32 status are not subject to the Posse Comitatus Act.

National Incident Management System, http://www.fema.gov/emergency/nims/AboutNIMS.shtm

National Infrastructure Protection Plan, http://www.dhs.gov/xprevprot/programs/editorial_0827.shtm

The National Oil and Hazardous Substances Pollution Contingency Plan (NCP), 40 CFR § 300 (2006), provides for the coordinated and integrated response by the federal government, as well as state and local governments, to prevent, minimize, or mitigate a threat to public health or welfare posed by discharges of oil and releases of hazardous substances, pollutants, and contaminants.

National Response Framework, http://www.fema.gov/emergency/nrf/.

National Response Plan, http://www.dhs.gov/xnews/releases/press_release_0581.shtm

The Occupational Safety and Health Act, 29 U.S.C. §§ 651-678 (2007), establishes and enforces standards to assure safe and healthful working conditions for working men and women, and provides mechanisms to assist the states in their efforts to assure safe and healthful working conditions.

PDD-39, Domestic Deployment Guidelines (classified).

PDD-62, Protection against Unconventional Threats to the Homeland and Americans Overseas (classified).

The Posse Comitatus Act, 18 U.S.C. § 1385 (2007), prohibits the use of the Army or the Air Force for law enforcement purposes, except as otherwise authorized by the Constitution or statute.

The Post-Katrina Emergency Management Reform Act (PKEMRA), which is Title VI of the Department of Homeland Security Appropriations Act, 2007, Pub. L. 109-295, 120 Stat. 1355 (2006), clarified and modified the Homeland Security Act with respect to the organizational structure, authorities, and responsibilities of FEMA and the FEMA Administrator.

Presidential Decision Directive 39, U.S. Policy on Counterterrorism (classified). An unclassified extract may be obtained from FEMA.

The Public Health Service Act, 42 U.S.C. § 201, et seq. (2007), as amended, provides authority for the Secretary of the Department of Health and Human Services to take actions to protect the public health and welfare, including, among other things: Declaring a public health emergency, imposing quarantine and isolation; awarding grants, contracts and cooperative agreements; deploying the commissioned corps the National Disaster Medical System and the Medical Reserve Corps; and maintaining the Strategic National Stockpile.

The Robert T. Stafford Disaster Relief and Emergency Assistance Act, Pub. L. 93-288, 88 Stat. 143 (1974), codified in 42 U.S.C. §§ 5121-5206 (2007), describes the programs and processes by which the federal government provides disaster and emergency assistance to state and local governments, tribal nations, eligible private nonprofit organizations, and individuals affected by a declared major disaster or emergency.

Section.085 of Title 28, Code of Federal Regulations, designates the Federal Bureau of Investigation as the agency with primary responsibility for investigating all crimes for which it has primary or concurrent jurisdiction and which involve terrorist activities or acts in preparation of terrorist activities within the statutory jurisdiction of the United States.

Section 382 of Title 10, United States Code (2007), authorizes the Attorney General to request assistance from the Secretary of Defense when both the Attorney General and the Secretary of Defense agree that an "emergency situation" involving biological or chemical weapons of mass destruction exists and the Secretary of Defense determines that the requested assistance will not impede military readiness.

Section 2567 of Title 10, United States Code (2007), authorizes the Secretary of Defense (following a determination by the President to invoke 10 U.S.C. § 333(a)(1)(A) of the Restoration Act) to provide supplies, services, and equipment to persons affected by a public emergency.

Chapter 29

The National Infrastructure Protection Plan

Allen Krotman, Janice R. Ballo, and Marion C. Warwick

CONTENTS

Introduction 558
Background History of the National Infrastructure Protection Plan 560
National Infrastructure Protection Plan Sector Partnership Model 562
History of the Partnership Model 562
Sector-Level Partnerships 563
Cross-Sector Coordination 564
Critical Infrastructure Partnership Advisory Council 564
The Value Proposition for the Sector Partnership 566
The NIPP Risk Management Framework 566
Set Security Goals 567
Identify Assets, Systems, Networks, and Functions 567
Assess Risks (Consequences, Vulnerabilities, and Threats) 567
Prioritize Infrastructure 568
Develop and Implement Protective Programs 568
Measure Progress and Effectiveness 568
Support for the Risk Management Framework 569
CIKR Protection Research and Development 569
Sources for More Information on the NIPP 569
References 569

Introduction

The overarching goal of the National Infrastructure Protection Plan (NIPP) [1] is to:

> Build a safer, more secure, and more resilient America by enhancing protection of the Nation's CIKR to prevent, deter, neutralize, or mitigate the effects of deliberate efforts by terrorists to destroy, incapacitate, or exploit them; and to strengthen national preparedness, timely response, and rapid recovery in the event of an attack, natural disaster, or other emergency.

The structure of the NIPP with its Risk Management Framework provides for the integration of existing and future critical infrastructure/key resources (CIKR) efforts into a national program. The NIPP complements the National Response Plan (NRP) and the newly established National Response Framework, so that, together these documents provide a comprehensive and collaborative approach across the spectrum of homeland security—Prevention, Protection, Preparedness, and Response.

The NIPP was originally published in June 2006. A revised version of the NIPP will be published in 2009. In draft form, the 2009 NIPP captures the evolution and maturation of the processes and programs that were initially established via the original NIPP. The NIPP continues to describe national priorities, goals, and requirements that ultimately allow funding and resources to be distributed effectively so that the nation continues to function effectively during incidents of national significance.

To achieve the NIPP's goal for "building a safer, more secure, and resilient America," the following objectives are put forth [1]:

- Understanding and sharing information about terrorist threats and other hazards
- Building partnerships to share information and implement CIKR protection programs
- Implementing a long-term risk management program
- Maximizing efficient use of resources for CIKR protection

Infrastructure resilience has been defined in various ways. For this study, we have adopted the definition provided by Stephen Flynn (2008) [2]. Resilience includes four factors: (1) robustness—the ability to keep operating or stay standing in the face of disaster, (2) resourcefulness—skillfully managing a disaster once it unfolds, (3) rapid recovery—the capacity to get things back to normal as quickly as possible after a disaster, and (4) learning—the ability to absorb new lessons that can be drawn from a catastrophe.

The 2009 NIPP will define 18 national critical infrastructure and key resource sectors. Each of these sectors has the responsibility to begin addressing the protection efforts for their CIKR across physical, cyber, and human aspects. Throughout this chapter, the word *sectors* will be used to refer to both sectors and key resources.

The 18 national CIKR are currently defined as shown in Table 29.1.

Each Sector has the responsibility for developing a Sector-Specific Plan (SSP), which together provide the way the NIPP is implemented across all sectors [1]. To support this, each sector also prepares an Annual Report to the Department of Homeland Security, describing progress toward required goals, and plans for the coming year. Each sector is also required to conduct education, outreach, awareness activities, and to develop plans for sharing information within and between other sectors.

Table 29.1 Sector-Specific Agencies

Sector	*Sector-Specific Agency (SSA)*
Agriculture and food	Departments of Agriculture, Health and Human Services and the Food and Drug Administration
Banking and finance	Department of the Treasury
Chemical	Department of Homeland Security, Infrastructure Protection
Commercial facilities	Department of Homeland Security, Infrastructure Protection
Communications	Department of Homeland Security, Cyber Security, and Communications
Critical manufacturing	Department of Homeland Security, Infrastructure Protection
Dams	Department of Homeland Security, Infrastructure Protection
Defense industrial base	Department of Defense
Drinking water and water treatment systems	Environmental Protection Agency
Energy	Department of Energy
Emergency services	Department of Homeland Security, Infrastructure Protection
Government facilities	Department of Homeland Security, Immigration and Customs Enforcement, and the Federal Protective Service
Information technology	Department of Homeland Security, Cyber Security, and Communications
National monuments and icons	Department of the Interior
Nuclear reactors, materials, and waste	Department of Homeland Security, Infrastructure Protection
Postal and shipping	Department of Homeland Security, Transportation Security Administration
Public health and healthcare	Department of Health and Human Services
Transportation systems	Department of Homeland Security, Transportation Security Administration and the U.S. Coast Guard

Source: National infrastructure advisory council report to xx, critical infrastructure partnership strategic assessment final report and recommendations, http://www.dhs.gov/xlibrary/assets/niac/niac_critical_infrastructure_protection_assessment_final_report.pdf (accessed November 2008).

Partnership is the key to success in this inherently complex mission area. According to this document [1] "Building this partnership under the NIPP has been its major accomplishment to date and has facilitated closer cooperation and a trusted relationship in the 18 CIKR sectors."

The two elements of the NIPP that are the core components for achieving its goals and objectives are (1) the NIPP Sector Partnership Model and (2) the NIPP Risk Management Framework. The NIPP Partnership Model describes what entities are intended to be involved with the NIPP process along with the organizational constructs. The NIPP Risk Management Framework provides for a consistent process for which the sectors can follow in executing their sector plans.

The following sections are intended to

- Provide a brief history of the NIPP
- Describe the NIPP Sector Partnership Model and
- NIPP Risk Management Framework

Background History of the National Infrastructure Protection Plan

Although the foundation for the NIPP was laid in previous decades, concern for protecting key resources in the United States was uneven throughout most of the country's history and largely centered upon national crises [3]. The rise of terrorism on the world stage in the 1990s provided the impetus toward more proactive infrastructure protection plan culminating in a series of Presidential Orders and Directives aimed at addressing the nation's "Critical Infrastructures".

Presidential Directive 39 (PDD-39), "U.S. Policy on Counterterrorism," signed January 21, 1995, defines policies regarding the federal response to threats or acts of terrorism involving nuclear, chemical, biological, or weapons of mass destruction (WMD). Under PDD-39, departments and agencies are directed to perform specific responsibilities that may affect the performance of their responsibilities under the Federal Response Plan. In this directive, the attorney general is responsible for chairing a Cabinet Committee to "review the vulnerability to terrorism of government facilities in the United States and critical national infrastructure" [4].

Executive Order (EO) 13010 follows in 1996 and establishes a formal definition for "critical infrastructures" as entities "so vital that their capacity or destruction would have a debilitating impact on the defense or economic security of the United States." EO13010 also established the President's Commission on Critical Infrastructure Protection (PCCIP) to evaluate infrastructure threats and vulnerabilities. The commission's report, released in 1997, defined critical infrastructures areas for energy, finance, banking, transportation, vital human services, and communications [5].

Presidential Directives 62 and 63 in 1998 create more organization and structure in the federal system for dealing with the challenges of critical infrastructure protection. Presidential Directive 62 (PDD-62), "Protection against Unconventional Threats to the Homeland and Americans Overseas," establishes the Office of the National Coordinator for Security, Infrastructure Protection and Counter-Terrorism and makes it responsible for the protection of critical infrastructure [6]. Presidential Directive 63 (PDD-63), "Protecting America's Critical Infrastructures," establishes the initial national strategy for cooperative efforts by the government and the private sector. The directive responds to the PCCIP and is the culmination of an interagency effort to evaluate the commission's recommendations and produce a framework for critical infrastructure protection in the United States. PDD-63 "sets up a new structure," which includes a National

Infrastructure Protection Center (NIPC), Information Sharing and Analysis Centers (ISACS), a National Infrastructure Assurance Council, and a Critical Infrastructure Assurance Office (CIAO). The CIAO is to provide support to the National Coordinator's work with government agencies and the private sector in developing a "national plan" [7]. PDD-63 also established critical infrastructure protection as a national goal and set timelines for when the United States was to have achieved the operating capabilities to achieve that goal [8].

In an attempt to bring the industry and the government closer together, President Clinton issued EO-13130 in 1999. EO-13130 orders the establishment of the National Infrastructure Assurance Council (NIAC). The 30 Council members, appointed by the president and selected from the private sector, are to represent the critical infrastructures identified in EO-13010. Two important functions of the NIAC as defined in the EO are to enhance the partnership of the public and private sectors in protecting the nation's critical infrastructure and encourage private industry to perform periodic risk assessments of critical processes [9]. EO-13130 was revoked in 2001 when President George W. Bush issued EO 13231 "Critical Infrastructure in the Information Age" on October 16, 2001. EO-13231 established the President's Critical Infrastructure Protection Board, and the NIAC was replaced with the National Infrastructure Advisory Council [10].

The terrorist attacks on September 11, 2001 created more urgency to define and protect the nation's critical infrastructure sectors. Following EO-13231, the Homeland Security Act of 2002 created the Department of Homeland Security (DHS). The new agency was assigned primary responsibility for protecting the Nation's Critical Infrastructure and Key Resources (CIKR) and developing a comprehensive national plan for the security and protection of those resources in coordination with other federal agencies, and in cooperation with state and local governments and the private sector ([1], NIPP, p. 2). In February 2003, President Bush released "The National Strategy for the Physical Protection of Critical Infrastructures and Key Assets," which builds on the sector approach. Under this strategy, the DHS is responsible for providing cross-sector coordination and serves as the primary liaison between federal, state, and local governments [11].

In December 2003, Homeland Security Presidential Directive-7 (HSPD-7) "Critical Infrastructure Identification, Prioritization, and Protection" was issued by President Bush. Created a framework for a national approach to infrastructure protection HSPD-7 and called for "a national policy for federal departments and agencies to identify and prioritize United States critical infrastructure and key resources and to protect them from terrorist attacks." The Secretary of the Department of Homeland Security was designated to lead those efforts [12]. In June 2006, the Department of Homeland Security (DHS) published the "National Infrastructure Protection Plan." DHS will publish the revised NIPP early in 2009.

A number of other statutes provide authorities both for cross-sector and sector-specific CIKR protection efforts. Some examples of other CIKR protection-related legislation include: The Public Health Security and Bioterrorism Preparedness and Response Act of 2002, which was intended to improve the ability of the United States to prevent, prepare for, and respond to acts of bioterrorism and other public health emergencies; the Maritime Transportation Security Act; the Energy Policy and Conservation Act; the Critical Infrastructure Information Act; the Federal Information Security Management Act; Implementing Recommendations of the 9/11 Commission Act of 2007; and various others.

Many different HSPDs are also relevant to CIKR protection, including

- HSPD-3, Homeland Security Advisory System
- HSPD-5, Management of Domestic Incidents: addresses the national approach to domestic incident management

- HSPD-8, National Preparedness
- HSPD-9, Defense of the U.S. Agriculture and Food
- HSPD-10, Biodefense for the Twenty-First Century
- HSPD-19, Combating Terrorist Use of Explosives in the United States
- HSPD-20, National Continuity Policy

National Infrastructure Protection Plan Sector Partnership Model

This NIPP Partnership Model provides for collaboration, interaction between Federal, State, Local, Tribal and Territorial agencies, CIKR owners/operators, and other sector-based entities. The partnership model establishes parallel councils for a voluntary industry owner and operator Sector Coordinating Council (SCC) and the Government (Federal, State, Local, Tribal and Territorial) Coordinating Councils (GCCs).

The SCCs are supported by a Private Sector Cross-Sector Council while the GCCs are supported by both a Government Cross-Sector Council and a Cross-Sector State, Local, Tribal, and Territorial Council. These entities are contained within these cross-sector councils: (1) the Partnership for Critical Infrastructure Security (PCIS), which coordinates private sector interests; (2) the Federal Senior Leadership Council (FSLC), which coordinates federal government interests; and (3) the State, Local, Tribal, and Territorial Government Coordinating Council (SLTTGCC), which coordinates the interests of all other government entities. This partnership model fosters an integrated national framework for CIKR preparedness, protection, response, and recovery across sectors.

The Sector Partnership Model is one of the most comprehensive public–private collaborations ever undertaken by the federal government. As described in the NIPP, this partnership model is intended to engage every major sector of the economy and every level of government to ensure safe, secure, and resilient infrastructures. From 2006, when the NIPP was first published, progress has been made via the partnership model in building trusted relationships among partners, creating information-sharing mechanisms, and implementing government and industry programs designed to mitigate infrastructure risks.

Each sector now has a tailored SSP that outlines goals and strategies for protecting their infrastructure, and reports annual progress toward these goals via a sector annual report (SAR).

History of the Partnership Model

The sector partnership model envisioned in HSPD-7, was a role that would act much like the designated "sector coordinator" named in the 1998 Presidential Directive-63 [4] "Critical Infrastructure Protection."

During the summer of 2005, the National Infrastructure Advisory Council (NIAC) established a Sector Partnership Model Working Group as the outcome of a study conducted at the request of DHS, and provided recommendations on its structure, function, and implementation. In October 2005, this Working Group presented its Initial Report and Findings to the NIAC [2], supporting the structure of the partnership model and recommending key operating principles, including that the partnership be considered a collaboration of equals between the government and the private sector.

Sector-Level Partnerships

For effectiveness, the NIPP provides organizational structures and partnerships that enable the collaboration required to accomplish the goals and objectives of the NIPP. The key organizational structures and partnerships cover each of the 18 sectors and span the Federal, State, Local, Tribal, Territorial, and Private sector communities. For National-level coordination, the DHS Office of Infrastructure Protection in partnership with the Sector-Specific Agencies (SSAs) is responsible for the NIPP Partnership organization and information sharing across the specific sectors.

Figure 29.1 graphically depicts and reflects the framework for collaboration and partnerships. For each of the 18 sectors identified in the NIPP, the structure in Figure 29.1 creates the structure that enables collaboration and participation across the Federal, State, Local, Tribal, Territorial, and Private sector partners.

The entities supporting sector partnerships include:

Sector-Specific Agency (SSA)—The SSA provides the coordinating mechanism, a role envisioned in HSPD-7 [3], will act much like the designated "sector coordinator" named in 1998 in PDD-63 [4] "Critical Infrastructure Protection." Each of the sectors has an assigned SSA. The SSA has the following responsibilities:

- To identify, prioritize, and coordinate the protection of CIKR.
- To facilitate sharing of information about physical and cyber threats, vulnerabilities, incidents, potential protective measures, and best practices.

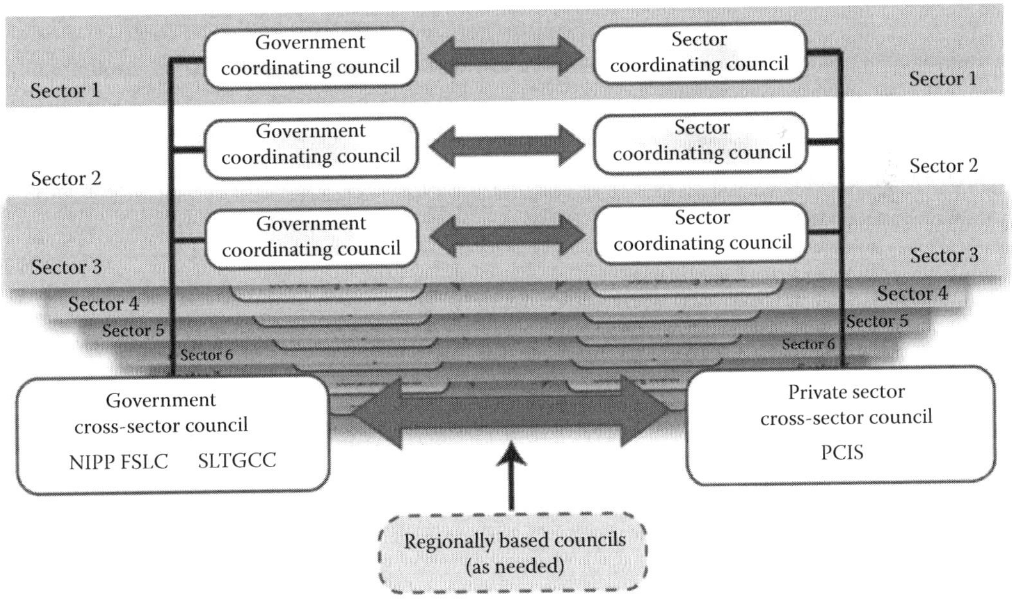

Figure 29.1 Sector partnership model. (Adapted from U.S. Department of Homeland Security, National Infrastructure Protection Plan (2006), 2006, U.S. Department of Homeland Security, Washington, DC.)

Sector Coordinating Councils (SCC)—The sector partnership model encourages CIKR owners and operators to create or identify an SCC as the principal entity for coordinating with the government on a wide range of CIKR protection activities and issues. Specific membership varies by sector, reflecting the unique composition of each sector, however, membership is intended to be representative of a broad base of owners, operators, associations, and other entities—large and small—within a sector. Cross-sector issues and interdependencies between the SCCs are addressed through a Private Sector Cross-Sector Council, the PCIS. The PCIS provides senior-level, cross-sector strategic coordination through partnership with DHS and the SSAs.

Government Coordinating Councils (GCCs)—The GCC is the government counterpart for the SCC to enable interagency and cross-jurisdictional coordination. The GCC is comprised of representatives across various levels of government (Federal, State, local, or tribal) as appropriate to the security landscape of each sector.

Federal Senior Leadership Council (FSLC)—The FSLC enables communications and coordination between and among federal departments and agencies with a role in implementing the NIPP and HSPD-7.

State, Local, Tribal, and Territorial GCC (SLTTGCC)—The SLTGCC provides an organizational structure to coordinate across jurisdictions on State- and local-level CIKR protection, guidance, strategies, and programs.

Private Sector Cross-Sector Council (PCIS)—The Private Sector Cross-Sector Council (i.e., the Partnership for Critical Infrastructure Security [PCIS]), the Government Cross-Sector Council (made up of two subcouncils: the NIPP Federal Senior Leadership Council [FSLC] and the State, Local, and Tribal Government Coordinating Council [SLTGCC]) and individual Sector Coordinating Councils and Government Coordinating Councils create a structure through which representative groups from Federal, State, local, and tribal governments and the private sector can collaborate and develop consensus approaches to CIKR protection.

Cross-Sector Coordination

The cross-sector coordinating council was established to address common and cross-sector concerns of the private sector as well as being the key private sector group providing input into the NIPP development. The PCIS formed in 2000 and was comprised of the designated Sector Coordinators, a role identified in 1998 in Presidential Decision Directive-63 "Critical Infrastructure Protection." Subsequently, PCIS has reorganized to align itself with the new roles of sector coordinating mechanism envisioned in HSPD-7, and has been serving as the unofficial cross-sector coordinating council. The Sector Coordinating Councils are the members of the cross sector group and are represented on the PCIS by the chair. Related to NIPP implementation, the cross-sector group is providing input to DHS on a number of issues that affect many sectors, including information sharing, physical and cyber security, and research and development.

Critical Infrastructure Partnership Advisory Council

The Critical Infrastructure Partnership Advisory Council (CIPAC) directly supports the sector partnership model by providing a legal framework for members of the SCCs and GCCs to engage in joint CIKR protection-related activities. The CIPAC serves as a forum for government and private sector security partners to engage in a broad spectrum of activities that includes planning, coordination, implementation, and operational issues; implementation of security programs; operational activities related to CIKR protection including incident response, recovery, and reconstitution; and development and support of national plans, including the NIPP and SSPs.

The coordination mechanisms described in the following text establish linkages among CIKR protection efforts at the Federal, State, regional, local, tribal, and international levels as well as between public and private sector security partners. In addition to direct coordination between security partners, the structures described in the following text provide a national framework that fosters relationships and facilitates coordination within and across CIKR sectors:

- *Federal*: According to HSPD-7, DHS is responsible for leading, integrating, and coordinating the overall effort to enhance CIKR protection. SSAs work with DHS to implement the NIPP Sector Partnership Model, develop protective programs and related requirements, provide sector-level CIKR protection guidance, and encourage sharing of security-related information, when appropriate, among private entities within the sector and between the public and private sectors. Additionally, SSAs collaborate with security partners to develop SSPs.
- *Regional coordination*: Regional partnerships, groupings, and governance bodies enable CIKR protection coordination among security partners within and across geographical areas and sectors. Regional security partnerships include a variety of public–private sector initiatives that cross-jurisdictional or sector boundaries and focus on homeland security preparedness, protection, response, and recovery within or serving the population of a defined geographical area. Regional partners collaborate to implement NIPP-related CIKR risk assessment and protection activities, promote education and awareness of CIKR protection efforts occurring within their region, and coordinate regional exercise and training programs.
- *Local*: Local entities provide critical public services in conjunction with private sector owners and operators, and thus they drive emergency preparedness and local participation in NIPP and SSP implementation. As a NIPP partner, local governments (a) facilitate the exchange of information among and between public and private entities; (b) apply documented lessons learned from predisaster mitigation efforts, exercises, and actual incidents to CIKR protection; and (c) act as a focal point for protective and emergency response activities, preparedness programs, and resource support among local agencies, businesses, and citizens.
- *State*: As outlined in the NIPP, states are primarily responsible for developing and implementing statewide/regional CIKR protection programs. To effectively implement these programs, states should establish security partnerships, facilitate coordinated information sharing, coordinate regional and local efforts with the private sector, and cut across all sectors present within the state to support national, state, and local priorities.
- *Private sector*: Private sector owners and operators are responsible for supporting risk-management planning and investments in security as a necessary component of prudent business planning and operations. The CIKR protection responsibilities of specific owners and operators vary widely within and across sectors. Some sectors have regulatory or statutory frameworks that govern private sector security operations within the sector; however, most sectors are guided by voluntary security regimes or adherence to industry-promoted best practices. Fortifying CIKR security within this diverse sector requires implementing protective actions and programs to reduce identified vulnerabilities appropriate to the level of risk presented.
- *International coordination*: The United States–Canada–Mexico Security and Prosperity Partnership, the North Atlantic Treaty Organization's Senior Civil Emergency Planning

Committee, certain government councils such as the Committee on Foreign Investment in the United States, and consensus-based nongovernmental or public–private organizations enable a range of CIKR protection coordination activities associated with established international agreements.

The Value Proposition for the Sector Partnership

One of the most important and elusive challenges of the sector partnership is defining a compelling value proposition for businesses to engage in the sector partnership for a sustained period. Different sector characteristics and circumstances influence each sector's motivation and interest in collaborating with the government on infrastructure protection issues. Even within a given sector or company, the value proposition can vary widely. The Partnership model attempts to engage the owners and operators on a continual basis because their interest may vary from time to time. During an incident, there is typically a higher interest as owners and operators are motivated by a direct concern to protect assets, customers, and people while in steady state, owners and operators interests may shift to an interest in shaping national policy and minimizing regulatory influences.

The NIPP Risk Management Framework

As described, the NIPP partnership model allows for experts from all aspects of each sector to participate in discussions about protection, whether about threats, risks, vulnerabilities, preparedness, response, or recovery. The NIPP Risk Management Framework consists of processes supported and directed by the Sector Partnership that include roles and responsibilities for DHS, SSAs, and other Federal, State, local, tribal, territorial, and private sector security partners. Taking into account physical, cyber, and human considerations, the NIPP Risk Management Framework allows the sector security partners to develop risk and consequence mitigation strategies for protecting the sector's most CIKR.

By managing risk and consequence, the goal of the NIPP Risk Management Framework is to make our nation and each sector more resilient by deterring terrorist threats, mitigating vulnerabilities, and minimizing consequences of disasters. The NIPP Risk Management Framework, as depicted in Figure 29.2, is not a once and done set of activities. The Framework provides a model

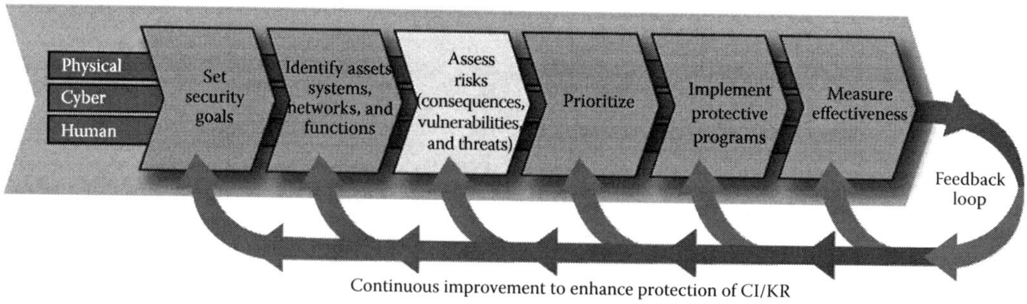

Figure 29.2 NIPP risk management framework. (Adapted from U.S. Department of Homeland Security, National Infrastructure Protection Plan (2006), 2006, U.S. Department of Homeland Security, Washington, DC.)

for the ongoing and continuous process to enhance the protection of the nation's and the specific sector's CIKR. These activities are focused on (NIPP p. 75)

1. Set security goals
2. Identify assets, systems, networks, and functions (goods and services)
3. Assess risks (consequences, vulnerabilities, and threats)
4. Prioritize (infrastructure)
5. (Develop and) implement protective programs
6. Measure effectiveness

Set Security Goals

The security partnership for each sector identifies and develops goals and objectives for protection. The sector goals and objectives should be outcome based, as this will ease the measurement of how a given sector is making progress. In addition, the goals and objectives should take an "all hazards" approach (events occurring naturally, man-made, or terrorist).

Identify Assets, Systems, Networks, and Functions

Each sector must then develop an approach for defining the sector's most critical Assets, Systems, Networks, and Functions. Each sector is unique—some sectors are more traditional and are asset based while other sectors, like Emergency Services, Food and Agriculture, and Healthcare and Public Health, are oriented toward the goods and services the sector delivers. Sector interdependencies and intradependencies also need to be examined, as these relationships will often highlight specific sector CIKR.

The process of each sector for identifying and creating an inventory of its CIKR should be objective and repeatable. The inventory should also consider CIKR (or the materials use for that CIKR) are located outside the United States (e.g., key components or ingredients are imported to produce the end product).

DHS is defining a taxonomy that will represent standard terms that will help to increase consistency among the disparate sources.

Assess Risks (Consequences, Vulnerabilities, and Threats)

As the sector's CIKR are identified, each sector has the responsibility for assessing risk. Risk is identified in the context of (1) how severe are the consequences if the asset is damaged or becomes unavailable, (2) how vulnerable the asset is, and (3) how likely it is that a particular threat might occur.

As defined by the NIPP, Risk is the product of consequences, vulnerability, and threat (NIPP, p. 35).

$$\text{Risk} = \text{function of (consequences} \times \text{vulnerability} \times \text{threat)}$$

$$R = f(C,V,T)$$

Although a wide variety of risk assessment tools are in use and many assessments have already been completed with differing tools, an overall assessment of a sector will be most efficient if some method of comparing these tools is devised. This would enable faster completion according to the criteria established by DHS. To help to integrate these assessments, the DHS is requiring all sectors to use a common tool for assessing consequences, called the Strategic Homeland Infrastructure Risk Assessment (SHIRA), which considers not only risk to the asset for the sector in isolation, but also the cascading consequences of its failure for other sectors.

Vulnerabilities considered for each asset include cyber, physical, insider threats, natural disasters; other threats such as chemical, biological, radiological, nuclear, and explosive; how easy the asset is to identify; and the likelihood that protective measures being put in place will be successful.

Prioritize Infrastructure

Prioritization is based on criteria such as whether the asset performs a unique function, how difficult it might be to replace it, how catastrophic its absence would be, how many people or how large an area are depending on it, whether it is critical to other sectors, and so forth. Prioritization is anticipated to be an iterative process, performed annually in each sector with an accompanying review and update of the criteria used to assess risk and its components of consequences, vulnerabilities, and threats.

Develop and Implement Protective Programs

Many government agencies already administer protective programs to bolster the security of assets within their scope. Almost all critical infrastructure assets in the private sector have at least some security measures in place. Ideally, security programs should address the three components of risk—threats, vulnerabilities, and consequences; coordinate with security plans in other institutions, such as business partners, local law enforcement, and providers of essential supplies or services; and have a policy of ongoing review and improvement. Goals of these programs are to prevent incidents, detect incidents, mitigate and respond to incidents, recover from incidents, and foster cooperation.

Measure Progress and Effectiveness

Developing criteria, or metrics, to evaluate the performance of protective programs is important to allow for comparison between sectors. Metrics have three categories: (1) descriptive: those that measure the cataloging of sector resources and activities, (2) process: those that measure the processes or progress toward particular tasks, and (3) outcome: those that measure progress toward achievement of strategic CIKR protection goals. Examples of descriptive metrics are the percentage of assets characterized by class, or the number of assets with potential for high consequences if damaged. Examples of outcome metrics are the percentage of high-consequence assets with audited plans or with risk and vulnerability assessments completed. Each metric, or criteria to measure effectiveness, must include what kind of metric it is, a description, and state what authority is responsible for assessing it and how it will be assessed. Performance is measured across Sectors using both standard metrics developed by DHS and additional metrics developed by each Sector.

Identifying sector resources and activities is especially challenging for those sectors whose assets are widely distributed and exist mostly in the private sector. Whether assets are identified by survey, research, or some other method, verification is necessary to determine that the information collected is accurate. Information should be capable of being aggregated and disaggregated, should protect proprietary information (if collected), and address a plan for continuous updating. Each SSA is required to report annually to the Secretary of Homeland Security on their progress in implementing protection programs.

Support for the Risk Management Framework

CIKR Protection Research and Development

Each sector is also required to develop plans for a Research and Development (R&D) agenda, to develop requirements for Sector-related research, and to communicate them to DHS for use in national R&D planning. The DHS and the Office of Science and Technology Policy (OSTP) have been designated to coordinate interagency R&D to enhance protection of CIKR, and have established nine research theme areas: Detection and Sensor Systems; Protection; Entry portals; Insider Threats; Analysis and Decision Support Methods; Response, Recovery, and Reconstitution; New and Emerging Threats and Vulnerabilities; Advanced infrastructure Architectures and System Designs; and Human/Social Issues.

Sources for More Information on the NIPP

The NIPP was established under the authorities of "The National Strategy for Homeland Security," the "Homeland Security Act of 2002," the "National Strategy to Secure Cyberspace," the "National Strategy for Physical Protection of Critical Infrastructure and Key Assets," and "Homeland Security Presidential Directive 7." An FEMA Independent Study Course is available for an introduction to the NIPP.

References

1. U.S. Department of Homeland Security. 2006. National Infrastructure Protection Plan (2006). Washington, DC: U.S. Department of Homeland Security. http://www.dhs.gov/xlibrary/assets/NIPP_Plan.pdf (last accessed on 7/27/2009).
2. National Infrastructure Advisory Council report to DHS. Critical Infrastructure Partnership Strategic Assessment Final Report and Recommendations. http://www.dhs.gov/xlibrary/assets/niac/niac_critical_infrastructure_protection_assessment_final_report.pdf (last accessed on 7/27/2009).
3. Brown, Kathi A. 2006. *Critical Path: A Brief History of Critical Infrastructure Protection in the United States*, Spectrum Publishing, Fairfax, VA.
4. Presidential Directive 39. U.S. Policy on Counterterrorism, June 21, 1995 [Portions redacted and as declassified, 1/24/97.], http://www.fas.org/irp/offdocs/pdd39.htm (last accessed on 7/27/2009).
5. President's Commission on Critical Infrastructure Protection. Critical Foundations: Protecting America's Infrastructure, October 1997.
6. White House Fact Sheet. Presidential Directive 62.
7. White House Fact Sheet. Protecting America's Critical Infrastructures: PPD 63, Presidential Directive 63, May 22, 1998, http://www.fas.org/irp/offdocs/pdd-63.htm (last accessed on 7/27/2009).
8. White Paper. The Clinton Administration's Policy on Critical Infrastructure Protection: Presidential Decision Directive 63, May 22, 1998, http://www.usdoj.gov/criminal/cybercrime/white_pr.htm (last accessed on 7/27/2009).
9. Citation 6 GAO report 03-564T. Progress Made, but Challenges Remain to Protect Federal Systems and the Nation's Critical Infrastructures, April 3, 2003.

10. Executive Order 13130. Federal Register, 64 FR 38535, July 19, 1999.
11. Executive Order 13231. Federal Register, 66 FR 53063, October 18, 2001.
12. White House. The National Strategy for the Physical Protection of Critical Infrastructures and Key Assets, Washington, D.C., February 2003.
13. Homeland Security Presidential Directive 7. http://www.dhs.gov/xabout/laws/gc_1214597989952.shtm (last accessed on 7/27/2009).
14. Clinton, William J. 1998. Critical Infrastructure Protection. *Presidential Decision Directive/NSC-63* (May 22). Washington DC, The White House.

Index

A

Absorption spectroscopy, 428–429
Acoustic-to-optic tunable filters (ATOFs), 430
Adamsite, 335
Aerosols; *see also* Bioaerosols
  Brownian motion, 44
  diffusive and inertial motions, 45
  dispersion, 47–49
  fluctuating force, 44
  generation, 47
  gravity, 46
  human respiratory tract, 43–44
  light transmission, 42
  mobility, 46
  molecular interactions, 44
  properties, 46–47
  residence times, 41–42
  sampling and characterization
    impactor, 49
    liquid impingers, 50
  settling velocity, 46
  typical size ranges, 42–43
Agricultural transmission, biological weapon, 197–198
Agroterrorism; *see also* Biological terrorism
  access and movement, potential targets, 260
  agricultural products, secondary use, 252–253
  agroeconomic protection and response hierarchy
    agroterrorist attack threat, 239
    Geographic Information System (GIS), 240
    Office International des Epizooties (OIE), 239
  agroeconomic systems and vulnerabilities
    distributed attacks, 236
    food supply chain, point attack, 235–236
    plant/animal disease process descriptions, 236–237
  agroeconomic terrorism planning and response
    bioterrorism detection and analysis, 241
    bioterrorism response modeling and bioinformatics, 244–245
    geographic information system (GIS) and remote sensing technology, 241–243
    time series analysis and risk assessments, 243–244
  Animal and Plant Health Inspection Service (APHIS), 234
  anticapitalist and anarchist, 235
  biology, 256
  crops, 262–263
  definition, 252
  economic terrorism, 238–239
  feasibility, 235
  food defense, 252
  genetically modified organisms (GMOs)
    biotech corn, 246
    genetic diversity, 247
    golden rice, 246
    psychological pressure point, 247
    Starlink, 246
  hoof and mouth disease (HMD), 247–248
  lethality, 256
  livestock, 261–262
  money
    financial damage, 257–259
    major international commodity exchanges, 254, 256
    midsize commodities trading client, 254
    profit, 259–260
    profit potential, 254
  risk, 257
  terrorism and terrorist, psychology
    crusader category, 238
    economic hardships, 237
    motivations, 238
    ravaging crops, 237
    vandalism and arson, 238
  turf farm, 252
  U.S. Department of Agriculture (USDA), 252–253
  weapon
    bovine spongiform encephalitis (BSE), 263
    potential agroterrorism weapons, 263–264

Airborne transmission, biological weapon, 194–195
Al-Qaeda organization, 4
Animal and Plant Health Inspection Service (APHIS), 234
Anthrax; *see also* Biological terrorism
  antimicrobial therapy, 59
  copycat terrorists, 54
  mediastinal widening, 59
  Sverdlovsk
    epidemic curve, 60
    geographic epidemiology, 59–60
    postexposure prophylaxis, 60
    weaponization, 61
  swelling and bleeding, 59
  threat
    Capitol Hill, 12
    wounded and medical evacuations, 13
  U.S. Postal Service, Amerithrax, 61–62
  Washington Offices of B'nai B'rith, 53–54
  woolsorter's disease, 58
  Yersinia pestis, 54
Antibody-based biosensors
  analysis, 440
  antibody-coated oscillator, 441
  sensor and reader, 440
APHIS, *see* Animal and Plant Health Inspection Service
ATOFs, *see* Acoustic-to-optic tunable filters

B

Binary chemical weapons, 452–453
Bioaerosols, 47, 50
Biological and Toxin Weapons Convention (BTWC), 458
Biological terrorism
  agents classification, 80
  anthrax
    Anthracis Yersinia, 53
    antimicrobial therapy, 59
    copycat terrorists, 54
    mediastinal widening, 59
    Sverdlovsk, 59–61
    swelling and bleeding, 59
    U.S. Postal Service, Amerithrax, 61–62
    Washington Offices of B'nai B'rith, 53–54
    woolsorter's disease, 58
    Yersinia pestis, 54
  biological attack, nature, 159–160
  biological warfare history, 187–188
  biological weapons
    anthrax, 189
    cidofovir, 190
    smallpox, 189–190
    utility, 158–159
  biowarfare, future, 80–81
  botulism
    antiserum, 72
    Clostridium botulinum, 70
    natural forms, 71
    types, 70
    zinc-dependent metallo-proteinase, 71
  cell- and tissue-based biosensors, 145–147
  Clostridium botulinum, 52
  communications
    public information, 212–213
    responding agencies, 212
  Dark Winter, 154
  electronic resources, 74–75
  epidemiology
    Al Qaeda, 157
    Aum Shinrikyo, 157–158
    Biological and Toxin Weapons Convention, 156
    doomsday scenario, 157
    fervid religious belief, 158
    weapons of mass destruction (WMD), 156
  fermentation
    batch and continuous process, 81
    fermentor, 81, 83
    large-scale, 83
    malt, 81–82
    small-scale, 84
    yeast, 81–82
  history and historical use, biological weapons
    Bacillus globigii, 91
    Biological Weapons Convention, 92
    Biopreparat, 57–58
    black death, 90
    Camp Detrick program, 91
    deployed agents, 56
    Fort Detrick, 57
    plague, 55, 90
    prospective agents, 56
    Salmonella typhimurium, 55
  live animals, 85–86
  live tissue, 84–85
  military grade weapon, 53
  munitions
    alveoli, 94
    chemical and biological agents, dispersion, 94, 96
    cruise missile, sprayer, 94
    Flettner rotor design, 93
    infective dose, 94–95
    lethal dose (LD), 94–95
    primary aerosol, 94
    R-400 bomb, 93
  National Response Plan (NRP), 155
  perspectives, 187
  plague
    oriental rat flea, 66
    rodents, 66–67
    septicemia, 66
    Yersinia pestis, 65–66
  point detection
    aerodynamic particle sizing (APS), 112–113
    air/water systems monitoring, 103

bubblers/impingers, 108–109
charge-based deep level transient spectroscopy (Q-DLTS), 143–144
cyclone sampler, 107–108
flow cytometry, 114–116
fluorescent aerodynamic particle sizer (FLAPS), 113–114
Fourier transform infrared spectroscopy (FTIR), 144–145
high air volume collectors, 109
immunoassay-based identification systems, 127–136
interferometer biosensors, 140–141
mass spectroscopy-based identification, 118–123
Naval Research Laboratory (NRL) array biosensors, 136
nucleic acid-based identification systems, 124–125
piezoelectric crystal balance, 141–142
portable biofluorescence, 116–118
quantitative polymerase chain reaction (Q-PCR), 125–127
quantum dots multicomponent detection, 136, 139
resonant mirror biosensor, 142–143
surface plasmon resonance (SPR), 140
surface sampling, 109, 112
total microbial content assessment, 103
up-converting phosphor technology, 144
viable particle-size impactors, 104–105
virtual impactor, 106–107

prevention
deterrence, 193–194
preemption, 194

release and transmission
agricultural transmission, 197–198
airborne transmission, 194–195
foodborne transmission, 196
secondary transmission, 198–199
waterborne transmission, 195–196
zoonotic transmission, 196–197

research
general research needs, 215–216
genomics, 218
vaccines, 216–218

response
disease surveillance, information source, 203
emergency medications, mass distribution, 209–210
Epidemic Intelligence Service (EIS), 204
illness monitor, 201
immediate detection technology, 200
laboratory, 206
mass medical care, 207–209
mass mortalities, 210
outbreak and criminal investigations, coordination, 205–206
psychological distress, 211–212
syndromic surveillance, 201–202

smallpox
New York city, 63–64
orthopoxvirus family, 62
public health response, 63
skin rash (exanthem), 62
vaccination, 63
virions, 62–63

small-scale deployment, 96

standoff detection system
laser beam and infrared sensor, 101
Light Detection And Ranging (LIDAR) system, 102–103
Micro-Pulse Lidar (MPL) system, 103
standoff monitors, 101
tryptophan, 102
unmanned aerial vehicle (UAV), 103

training
FEMA, 214
general public, 215
Metropolitan Medical Response System (MMRS), 214
Office of Justice Programs (OJP), 213–214

tularemia
aminoglycoside injection, 65
subspecies forms/biovars, 64
Working Group on Civilian Biodefense (WGCB), 65

U.S. defense strengthening, biological weapons
biodefense program, 161
federal government preparedness and operations, 175–179
hospital epidemiologist preparedness, 166
hospital preparedness, 168–170
infection control officer, 166
local civic preparedness, 170–171
medical examiner and coroner preparedness, 166–167
microbiology laboratory preparedness, 163–166
mortuary services preparedness, 167–168
National Electronic Disease Surveillance System (NEDSS), 162
physician preparedness, 162–163
state and public health service preparedness, 171–175
suspected bioterrorism event, 168

U.S. government
federal agencies, 191–192
military, 191
overall authority designation, 192–193
state and local governments, 193

viral hemorrhagic fevers
diagnosis, 69
Ebola virus, 67–68
pathologic process, 68
transmission, 69

viral production, fertile chicken eggs, 84
weaponizing process, 188
Blood agents (cyanides), 367
Boiling point, 350
Boston Tea Party, 18
Botulism
antiserum, 72
Clostridium botulinum, 70
natural forms, 71
types, 70
zinc-dependent metallo-proteinase, 71
Bovine spongiform encephalitis (BSE), 263
Broadcast technology, 26
BTWC, *see* Biological and Toxin Weapons Convention
Bubonic plague, 66

C

Canine explosive detection, 418–419
Charge-deep level transient spectroscopy (Q-DLTS), 434–435
Chemical–biological–radiological (CBR) agents, 24
Chemical terrorism
antibody-based biosensors
analysis, 440
antibody-coated oscillator, 441
sensor and reader, 440
Biological and Toxin Weapons Convention (BTWC), 458
casualties decontamination, 362–363
chemical attack, signs, 359
chemical release, civilians
decontamination, 359–360
evacuation, 360
hyperventilation, 359
scuba gear and eye-sealing goggles, 360
chemicals, properties
advantages and disadvantages, chemical weapons, 352
boiling point and density, 350
enthalpy of vaporization, 352
molecular weight, 342, 347–349
vapor pressure, 350–351
volatility, 352
chemical vapor detection
canine explosive detection, 418–419
detection tickets (colorimetric method), 420–421
gas chromatograph, 419–420
chemical weapon poisoning and management
blood agents (cyanides), 367
choking agents (lung irritants), 367–368
nerve agents, 363–366
psychotomimetic agents, 368
toxin agents, 368–372
vesicating (blistering) agents, 366–367
Chemical Weapons Convention (CWC), 330
chemical weapons, hazards
chlorine and phosgene, 356
dissemination, 356–357
ED_{50} and LD_{50}, 357
inhalational absorption, 356
low level atmospheric turbulence, 357
mustard and nerve gases, 356
riot control toxicity, 357
classification
blister and blood agents, 334
choking agents, 331, 334
defoliants and desiccants, 335
emerging agents, 335–338
explosives and IEDs, 339–340
incapacitating agents, 335
nerve agents, 334
tear and vomiting agents, 335
countermeasures
chemical agent proliferation activities, indicators, 464–465
chemical agent release, remote detection, 465
delivery systems
aerosols, 451–452
binary chemical weapons, 452–453
chemical agent dispersion, factors, 450–451
chemical weapon technologies, 448–449
Honest John missile, 450–451
MC-1 gas bomb, 449–450
methods, 448
munitions, 449
persistence time, 450, 452
shell, simplified diagram, 448–449
small-scale delivery, 453–455
spray tanks, 450
submunitions, 450–451
destruction
advanced oxidation process, 401–402
arsenicals, 393–394
cost, 381–386
electrochemical oxidation, 400
hydrochlorination, 401
hydrogenolysis, 393
incineration, 388–391
molten metal systems, 392–393
neutralization, 394, 399–400
plasma-based destruction, 390, 392–393
pyrolysis, 390
sea dumping, 386
solvent electron technology (SET), 400–401
supercritical water oxidation, 401
timeline, 380–381
wet air oxidation, 401
electromagnetic wavelengths, sensors
millimeter electromagnetic waves (MEWs), 432
nuclear magnetic resonance (NMR), 431
environmental considerations, 358

equipment decontamination
chlorinated lime powder, 406
deep-penetrating solution, 405
foam, 406–407
German Münster emulsion, 405–406
heat treatment, 405
principles, 402
self-decontamination times, 405
tent, 406
toxic gas release, 402
washing and rinsing, 402, 406
exposure, long-term consequences, 369
exposure routes, 357–358
first responders protection
initial objectives, 361
personal protection equipment (PPE), 360–361
self-contained breathing apparatus (SCBA), 360
health services response logistics, 374–376
homespun development, 356
industrial chemicals, terrorist agents, 463–464
ionization-based sensors
electron capture detector, 421–423
field ion spectrometry (FIS), 424–425
ion mobility spectrometry (IMS), 423–424
tandem mass spectrometer (TMS), 425
medical forensic samples, 369, 373–374
neutron-based detection systems
portable isotopic neutron spectroscopy (PINS), 438–439
pulsed fast neutron analysis (PFNA) system, 439
thermal neutron activation (TNA), 437–438
Organization for the Prohibition of Chemical Weapons (OPCW), 458–459
piezoelectric effects
gas chromatograph/surface acoustic wave (SAW), 432
quartz crystal microbalance (QCM), 432–433
plants, 330
point detection methods, 415–417
rescue operations organization, 361–362
risk analysis, U.S. Civilians, 460–463
stages and obstacles, 447–448
standoff detection systems, 412–415
surface effect
charge-deep level transient spectroscopy (Q-DLTS), 434–435
conductivity-based sensors (CBSs), 435
metal-oxide-silicon field-effect transistor (MOSFET), 435–436
surface wipes (SW), 439–440
syndromic medical management, 369, 373
synthesis
agitators and reaction vessels, 340
mustard, 341
phosgene and hydrogen cyanide, 340
sarin, 341–342
thermo-redox (TR) detector, 433–434
toxic chemical, definition, 330, 356
UV-IR-photons spectroscopy
absorption spectroscopy, 428–429
acoustic-to-optic tunable filters (ATOFs), 430
chemiluminescence, 426–427
laser induced breakdown spectroscopy (LIBS), 430
optical fiber sensors (OFS), 429–430
Raman scattering, 427–428
terahertz spectroscopy, 430–431
X-rays, radiation-based sensors, 436–437
Chemical vapor detection
canine explosive detection, 418–419
detection tickets (colorimetric method), 420–421
gas chromatograph, 419–420
Chemical weapon poisoning and management
blood agents (cyanides), 367
choking agents (lung irritants), 367–368
nerve agents, 363–366
atropine, 365
carbamates, 366
oximes, 365
symptoms, 363, 365
toxic exposure limits, 363–364
ventilatory support, 365
psychotomimetic agents, 368
toxin agents, 368–372
vesicating (blistering) agents, 366–367
Chemiluminescence, 426–427
Chimera virus, 81
Choking agents (lung irritants), 367–368
Clostridium botulinum, 70, 81, 84
Communications technology, 25
Conductivity-based sensors (CBSs), 435
Conventional military force, 19
Cyber-terrorism
firewalls, 489–490
individual computer protection
malicious programs, 489
password access, 488–489
nature
Bronze Soldier, 473
definition, 470–471
distinctions, 471
distributed denial-of-service attacks (DDoS), 472
extortion, 473–474
simple attacks, 471–472
terrorists, Internet, 474–475
queuing and network delays, vulnerable network, 483
Little's law, 487
Markov chains, 484
probability flow, 484–485
queuing system, 483–484, 486
transmission delay (t_d) and workstation delay (t_w), 483
security and encryption, 490–491

ubiquitous computing and vulnerability
bacteria, 477
corporate and enterprise intranets, 476
logic bomb, 477
personal computers and personal device assistants, 475
supercomputing clusters, 476
trapdoor, 476–477
trojan horse, 477
viruses, 477–478
worm, 477
vulnerable network
components of computer networks, 479–481
operation of computer network, 481
transmission control protocol/Internet protocol (TCP/IP), 482–483

D

Defense, 21–22, 27–28
Definitions of terrorism, 5, 17–18
Delivery systems, chemical terrorism
aerosols, 451–452
binary chemical weapons, 452–453
chemical agent dispersion, factors, 450–451
chemical weapon technologies, 448–449
Honest John missile, 450–451
MC-1 gas bomb, 449–450
methods, 448
munitions, 449
persistence time, 450, 452
shell, simplified diagram, 448–449
small-scale delivery, 453–455
spray tanks, 450
submunitions, 450–451
Density, 350
Department of Defense (DOD)
Chemical and Biological Incident Response Force, 540
Defense Support of Civil Authorities (DSCA), 539–540
Domestic Preparedness Program, 540
federal military support, 541
federal response, 540
Joint Task Force (JTF), 541
primary mission, 539
Technical Escort Unit, 540
USAMRIID and USAMRICD, 541
Department of Energy (DOE), 542–543
Department of Homeland Security (DHS)
HSPD-5, 512, 518
HSPD-7, 512
National Response Plan (NRP), 512
organizational chart, 510–511
original 22 agencies, 509–510
radiation detection portal monitors, 295
six goals, 510, 512
Department of justice, federal bureau of investigation
command post structure, 536
Domestic Emergency Support Team (DEST), 537–538
investigative and intelligence activities, 536
Joint Operations Center (JOC) structure, 536–538
Special Agent in Charge (SAC), 536
Terrorist Threat Warning System, 537
DEST, *see* Domestic Emergency Support Team
Detector systems, nuclear terrorism
battery-operated survey meter, 275
Geiger–Mueller (GM) counter, 274–275
ionizing radiation, 274
self-alarming personnel dosimeters, 275
Deterrence, 21–22, 28
DHS, *see* Department of Homeland Security
Digital electronic dosimeter, 285–286
Diplomacy, 1
DOD, *see* Department of Defense
DOE, *see* Department of Energy
Domestic Emergency Support Team (DEST), 537–538
Domestic Preparedness Programs, 2

E

EIS, *see* Epidemic Intelligence Service
Electrochemical oxidation, 400
Electron capture detector, 421–423
Enthalpy of vaporization, 352
Environmental Protection Agency (EPA), 543–544
EPA, *see* Environmental Protection Agency
Epidemic Intelligence Service (EIS), 204

F

Federal Emergency Management Agency (FEMA), 191, 539
Fermentation
batch and continuous process, 81
fermentor, 81, 83
large-scale, 83
malt, 81–82
small-scale, 84
yeast, 81–82
Field ion spectrometry (FIS), 424–425
Five-Year Interagency Counterterrorism and Technology Crime Plan, 4
Foodborne transmission, biological weapon, 196
Francisella tularensis, 64

G

Geiger Mueller (GM) counter
alpha particles and beta activity, 287
gamma exposure rates, 286
pancake probes, 286–287
various types, 287

Genetically modified organisms (GMOs), agroterrorism
biotech corn, 246
genetic diversity, 247
golden rice, 246
psychological pressure point, 247
Starlink, 246
German Münster emulsion, 405–406
Global terrorism, 27
Government and voluntary agencies
Concept of Operations, 549–550
continuing actions, 554–555
Department of Defense (DOD)
Chemical and Biological Incident Response Force, 540
Defense Support of Civil Authorities (DSCA), 539–540
Domestic Preparedness Program, 540
federal military support, 541
federal response, 540
Joint Task Force (JTF), 541
primary mission, 539
Technical Escort Unit, 540
USAMRIID and USAMRICD, 541
Department of Energy (DOE), 542–543
Department of Health and Human Services, 544–548
Assistant Secretary for Preparedness and Response (ASPR), 544
CDC, 546–548
Lab Response Network (LRN), 545–546
National Disaster Medical System (NDMS), 545
OPHEP, 546
department of justice, federal bureau of investigation
command post structure, 536
Domestic Emergency Support Team (DEST), 537–538
investigative and intelligence activities, 536
Joint Operations Center structure, 536–538
Special Agent in Charge (SAC), 536
Terrorist Threat Warning System, 537
Environmental Protection Agency (EPA), 543–544
Federal Emergency Management Agency (FEMA), 539
Federal Law Enforcement Assistance, 551–552
initial actions, 552–554
integration of response, recovery, and mitigation actions, 550
lead federal agencies
attorney general, 532
ESFs, 533–536
Joint Field Office (JFO), 532–533
military support, 550–551
National Incident Management System (NIMS), 531
planning assumptions, 548–549
response and recovery actions, 552
GRaDER program, *see* Graduated Rad/Nuc Detector Evaluation and Reporting program
Graduated Rad/Nuc Detector Evaluation and Reporting (GRaDER) program, 280
Green Mountain Boys, 20
Group psychology
face of terrorism
apocalypse, 32
toxic sentiments, 33
large-group identity dynamics
deindividuation, 36
doubling and numbing phenomena, 35
group membership, 36
group vulnerability, 35, 37
Origins of Ethnic Strife, 37
paranoid–schizoid processes, 34
psychological splitting, 35
psychotic processes, 34
Roots of Evil, 35
large groups and totalistic belief systems
authority and leadership, 38
enemies and scapegoats, 37
fostering ethnic cleansing, 39
Group Psychology and the Analysis of the Ego, 38
terrorist acts
Armageddon, 33
projective identification, 34
theatrical nature and suicide terrorism, 33
vulnerability, 34
Guerilla warfare, 17, 19

H

Health and Medical Programs, 2
High-temperature destruction technologies
arsenicals, 393–394
hydrogenolysis, 393
incineration, 388–391
molten metal systems, 392–393
plasma-based destruction, 390, 392–393
pyrolysis, 390
Homeland Security Presidential Directive-5 (HSPD-5), 512, 518
Homeland Security Presidential Directive-7 (HSPD-7), 512
Honest John missile, 450–451
Hospital preparedness
biodefense, 168
epidemiologist, 166
important components, 169–170
MMRS, 170
Hydrochlorination, 401
Hydrogenolysis, 393

I

Immunoassay-based identification systems, biological terrorism
antibody–antigen binding, 127–128

antibody structure, 127
electrochemiluminescence (ECL), 130–131
flow-through assay, 129
fluorescent evanescent wave fiber-optic immunosensor, 134–136
handheld immunochromatographic assay (HHA), 128–129
light-addressable potentiometric sensor (LAPS), 131–133
sensitive membrane antigen rapid test (SMART), 130
Internal terrorism, republic of Texas, 10–11
Ionization-based sensors
electron capture detector, 421–423
field ion spectrometry (FIS), 424–425
ion mobility spectrometry (IMS), 423–424
mass spectroscopy (MS), 425
tandem mass spectrometer (TMS), 425
Ion mobility spectrometry (IMS), 423–424

J

Jacobin movement, 16

L

Lacrimators, 335
Large-group identity dynamics, group psychology
deindividuation, 36
doubling and numbing phenomena, 35
group membership, 36
group vulnerability, 35, 37
Origins of Ethnic Strife, 37
paranoid–schizoid processes, 34
psychological splitting, 35
psychotic processes, 34
Roots of Evil, 35
Laser induced breakdown spectroscopy (LIBS), 430
Lead federal agencies
attorney general, 532
ESFs, 533–536
Joint Field Office (JFO), 532–533
LIBS, *see* Laser induced breakdown spectroscopy
Light Detection and Ranging (LIDAR) system, 102–103
Liquid splash-protective garments, 502
Local civic preparedness, 170–171
Logic of terrorism, 18
Low-temperature destruction technologies
advanced oxidation process, 401–402
electrochemical oxidation, 400
hydrogenation and hydrochlorination, 401
neutralization
amines, 400
hydrolysis, 394, 399
NaOH, 399
solvent electron technology (SET), 400–401
supercritical water and wet air oxidation, 401
Ludlum Model 19 MicroR meter, 288–289

M

Mass medical care, biological terrorism
federal support arrival, 208–209
infection control plans, 207–208
medical field, workforce shortage, 207
regional planning, 208
skeletal staffing, hospitals, 207
Mass spectroscopy-based identification, biological terrorism
electrospray ionization (ESI), 120–122
fast atom bombardment, 119–120
laser pyrolysis, 118–119
matrix-assisted laser desorption and ionization (MALDI), 122–123
MC-1 gas bomb, 449–450
Metal-oxide-silicon field-effect transistor (MOSFET), 435–436
Metropolitan Medical Response System (MMRS), 170, 214
Microbiology laboratory preparedness
contingency plan, 165
Laboratory Response Network (LRN), 163–165
sentinel labs, 163
Millimeter electromagnetic waves (MEWs), 432
MMRS, *see* Metropolitan Medical Response System
Molecular weight, 342, 347–349
Mortuary services preparedness, 167–168
Munitions, biological terrorism
alveoli, 94
chemical and biological agents, dispersion, 94, 96
cruise missile, sprayer, 94
Flettner rotor design, 93
infective dose, 94–95
lethal dose (LD), 94–95
primary aerosol, 94
R-400 bomb, 93
Mustard gas, 341

N

National Electronic Disease Surveillance System (NEDSS), 162
National Infrastructure Protection Plan (NIPP)
critical infrastructure and key resources (CIKR), 558–559, 561
history
Department of Homeland Security (DHS), 561
Executive Order (EO), 560
HSPDs, 561–562
National Infrastructure Assurance Council (NIAC), 561
Presidential Directives, 560
President's Commission on Critical Infrastructure Protection (PCCIP), 560
infrastructure resilience, 558
overarching goal, 558

partnership, 560
risk management framework
assets, systems, networks, and functions, 567
consequences, vulnerabilities, and threats, 567–568
infrastructure prioritization, 568
progress and effectiveness, 568–569
protective programs, 568
Set Security Goals, 567
support, 569
sector partnership model
Critical Infrastructure Partnership Advisory Council (CIPAC), 564–566
cross-sector coordination, 564
Federal Senior Leadership Council (FSLC), 564
Government Coordinating Councils (GCCs), 564
history, 562
Partnership for Critical Infrastructure Security (PCIS), 564
Sector Coordinating Councils (SCC), 564
Sector-Specific Agency (SSA), 563
State, Local, and Tribal Government Coordinating Council (SLTGCC), 564
National planning scenario, 524–526
National preparedness guidelines, 524
National response plan (NRP)
biological terrorism, 155
Department of Homeland Security (DHS), 509–512
first responders–terrorist incident
WMD advanced operations and technician capability level, 523
WMD awareness capability level, 521–522
WMD defensive/operator capability level, 522
WMD performance level B, 522–523
local and state response plan, 513, 515, 518–519
national planning scenario, 524–526
national preparedness guidelines, 524
national response framework (NRF)
emergency support functions, 513, 516–517
four elements, 513–515
NRF definition, 512–513
objective, 512
preparedness cycle, 512–513
terrorist attack, response, 515, 518–521
NEDSS, *see* National Electronic Disease Surveillance System
Nerve agents, chemical terrorism
atropine, 365
carbamates, 366
oximes, 365
symptoms, 363, 365
toxic exposure limits, 363–364
ventilatory support, 365
Neutralization, chemical terrorism
amines, 400
hydrolysis, 394, 399
NaOH, 399
Neutron-based detection systems
portable isotopic neutron spectroscopy (PINS), 438–439
pulsed fast neutron analysis (PFNA) system, 439
thermal neutron activation (TNA), 437–438
NIPP, *see* National Infrastructure Protection Plan
No-tag biosensors
interferometer biosensors, 140–141
piezoelectric crystal balance, 141–142
resonant mirror biosensor, 142–143
surface plasmon resonance (SPR), 140
Nuclear magnetic resonance (NMR), 431
Nuclear terrorism
countermeasures
infrastructure, 326
intelligence programs, 327
nuclear transfers control, 326
nuclear weapons protection, 324–326
detectors classification
digital electronic dosimeter, 285–286
fast neutron recoil nucleus detectors, 292–294
film badges, 284
Graduated Rad/Nuc Detector Evaluation and Reporting (GRaDER) program, 280
liquid scintillation counter (LSC), 290
mobile and transportable systems, 296–301
pocket dosimeter, 281–283
proportional counters, 291–292
radiation detection portal monitors, 295–296
spectroscopic portal monitors, 295–297
survey meters, 286–288
thermoluminescent dosimeter (TLD), 284–285
detector systems
battery-operated survey meter, 275
Geiger–Mueller (GM) counter, 274–275
ionizing radiation, 274
self-alarming personnel dosimeters, 275
nuclear weapons
effects, 314–315
history, 313–314
weapons technology, 315–318
radiation biological effects
delayed carcinogenic effects, 309–310
immediate (or acute) effects, 309
ionization, 309
radiation detection
compounds, 302–303
credible terrorist threats, 311–312
directly ionizing radiation, 279
Geiger–Mueller tube, 311
highly enriched uranium (HEU), 304
indirect ionizing radiation, 279
lethal dose of radiation, 310
scintillation detectors, 311
special nuclear material (SNM), 304

radiation detection history
photographic film, 274
x-rays, 273
radiation dose, 269
radiation dose, natural and manmade, 307–308
radiation shielding, 268–269
radioactive half-life, 270
radioactivity
amount, 268
radiation, 270–271
threats
expertise, 323–324
Khan network, 322
Pu-239, 322–323
Pu-240, 323
revolutions per minute (RPM), 322
targets and delivery means, 324
U-235 and U-238, 322–323
Nuclear weapons
effects, 314–315
history, 313–314
weapons technology
basic principle, 317–318
eta factor, 316
fission process, 315, 317–318
neutron multiplication factor, 315
number density, 316
power density, 318
rate equation, 315
rate of energy, 317
spherical mass of radius, 316

O

Office of Emergency Preparedness (OEP), 214
Oklahoma City Bombing, 9–10
Operation Whitecoat, 57
Optical fiber sensors (OFS), 429–430
Organization for the Prohibition of Chemical Weapons (OPCW), 458–459

P

Personal dosimeters, nuclear terrorism
pocket dosimeter
digital electronic dosimeter, 285–286
film badge, 284
ionization chamber, 281–283
thermoluminescent dosimeter (TLD), 284–285
x-rays and gamma-rays, 281
Personal protective equipment
biological protection, 504
blast protection, 505–506
breathing apparatus, 507
chemical protection
battle dress overgarments (BDOs), 501
chemically protective undergarments (CPUs), 502
National Fire Protection Association (NFPA), 502–503
nonwoven polymer-based clothing, 503
vapor-protective clothing, 502
dermal protection, 501
doctrine, 495–496
equipment selection, 494
Joint Service Defense Technology Objective, 506
radiological protection, 505
respiratory protection
air-purifying respirator (APR), 497–498
atmosphere-supplying respirators, 498–499
respirator designs, 499–501
risk assessment, 494–495
selectively permeable membrane fabrics, 506–507
thermal protection, 505
PFNA system, *see* Pulsed fast neutron analysis system
Physician preparedness, 162–163
Piezoelectric effects
gas chromatograph/surface acoustic wave (SAW), 432
quartz crystal microbalance (QCM), 432–433
Plague
oriental rat flea, 66
rodents, 66–67
septicemia, 66
Yersinia pestis, 65–66
Plasma-based destruction, 390, 392–393
Pneumonic plague, 66–67
Pocket dosimeters, nuclear terrorism
ionization chambers
anode and cathode, 281
ion pair creation, 282–283
sensitivity, 281–282
shapes, 281
working mechanism, 282
x-rays and gamma-rays, 281
Point detection system, biological agents
air/water systems monitoring, 103
charge-based deep level transient spectroscopy (Q-DLTS), 143–144
fluorescent aerodynamic particle sizer (FLAPS), 113–114
Fourier transform infrared spectroscopy (FTIR), 144–145
immunoassay-based identification systems, 127–136
antibody–antigen binding, 127–128
antibody structure, 127
electrochemiluminescence (ECL), 130–131
flow-through assay, 129
fluorescent evanescent wave fiber-optic immunosensor, 134–136
handheld immunochromatographic assay (HHA), 128–129
light-addressable potentiometric sensor (LAPS), 131–133
sensitive membrane antigen rapid test (SMART), 130

mass spectroscopy-based identification
electrospray ionization (ESI), 120–122
fast atom bombardment, 119–120
laser pyrolysis, 118–119
matrix-assisted laser desorption and ionization (MALDI), 122–123
Naval Research Laboratory (NRL) array biosensors, 136
nonspecific detection
aerodynamic particle sizing (APS), 112–113
flow cytometry, 114–116
fluorescent aerodynamic particle sizer (FLAPS), 113–114
portable biofluorescence, 116–118
No-tag biosensors
interferometer biosensors, 140–141
piezoelectric crystal balance, 141–142
resonant mirror biosensor, 142–143
surface plasmon resonance (SPR), 140
nucleic acid-based identification systems
direct target probe, signal amplification, 124
target amplification, 124–125
Q-PCR, 125–127
quantum dots multicomponent detection, 136, 139
sampling devices
bubblers/impingers, 108–109
cyclone sampler, 107–108
high air volume collectors, 109
surface sampling, 109, 112
viable particle-size impactors, 104–105
virtual impactor, 106–107
total microbial content assessment, 103
up-converting phosphor technology, 144
Portable isotopic neutron spectroscopy (PINS), 438–439
Prudent counterterrorist, 23
Psychopath, 17
Psychotomimetic agents, 368
Pulsed fast neutron analysis (PFNA) system, 439

Q

Q-DLTS, *see* Charge-deep level transient spectroscopy
Quantitative polymerase chain reaction (Q-PCR), 125–127

R

Radiation biological effects
acute/immediate effects, 309
delayed carcinogenic effects, 309–310
ionization, 309
Radiation detection, nuclear terrorism
compounds, 302–303
directly ionizing radiation, 279
highly enriched uranium (HEU), 304
history
photographic film, 274
x-rays, 273
indirect ionizing radiation, 279
special nuclear material (SNM), 304
Radiation dose, 269
Radiation shielding, 268–269
Radioactive half-life, 270
Radioactivity
amount, 268
radiation, 270–271
Radionuclide identifiers, nuclear terrorism
fast neutron recoil nucleus detectors
detection efficiency, 294
ionization, 293
maximum energy transfer ratio (METR), 293–294
neutron scattering, 292–293
recoil nucleus energy, 293
liquid scintillation counter (LSC), 290–291
multichannel analyzer (MCA), 288–290
proportional counters
fill gas, 291–292
neutron REM meter, 292
pulse mode, 291
Raman scattering, 427–428
Reign of Terror, 16

S

Salmonella typhimurium, 55
Sampling devices, point detection system
bubblers/impingers, 108–109
cyclone sampler, 107–108
high air volume collectors, 109
surface sampling, 109, 112
viable particle-size impactors, 104–105
virtual impactor, 106–107
Sarin, 341–342
Savvy terrorist, 23
Secondary transmission, biological weapon, 198–199
Second World Trade Center Attack, 11–12
SEMA, *see* State Emergency Management Agency
Septicemic plague, 66
SHIRA, *see* Strategic Homeland Infrastructure Risk Assessment
Smallpox
New York city, 63–64
orthopoxvirus family, 62
public health response, 63
skin rash (exanthem), 62
vaccination, 63
virions, 62–63
Smallpox–ebola weapon, 81
Solvent electron technology (SET), 400–401
Standoff detection system, biological agents
laser beam and infrared sensor, 101
Light Detection And Ranging (LIDAR) system, 102–103

Micro-Pulse Lidar (MPL) system, 103
standoff monitors, 101
tryptophan, 102
unmanned aerial vehicle (UAV), 103
State Emergency Management Agency (SEMA), 170–171
Sternutators, 335
Strategic Arms Limitation Talks (SALT I), 325
Strategic Homeland Infrastructure Risk Assessment (SHIRA), 568
Supercritical water oxidation, 401
Survey meters, nuclear terrorism
GM counter
alpha particles and beta activity, 287
gamma exposure rates, 286
pancake probes, 286–287
various types, 287
sodium iodide detector, microR meter, 287–288

T

Tandem mass spectrometer (TMS), 425
Terrorism and Political Violence, 16
Terrorists
dire expectations, 19
Jewish Zealots, 20
political conditions, 19
tactics, 20, 29
Thermal neutron activation (TNA), 437–438
Thermoluminescent dosimeter (TLD), 284–285
Tokyo subway attack
Aum group, 8
sarin gas, 8–9
Toxin agents, 368–372
Tularemia
aminoglycoside injection, 65
subspecies forms/biovars, 64
Working Group on Civilian Biodefense (WGCB), 65

U

U.S. Army Medical Research Institute for Chemical Defense (USAMRICD), 541
U.S. Army Medical Research Institute for Infectious Disease (USAMRIID), 541
U.S. defense strengthening, biological weapons
biodefense program, 161
federal government preparedness and operations, 175–179
hospital epidemiologist preparedness, 166
hospital preparedness, 168–170
infection control officer, 166
local civic preparedness, 170–171
medical examiner and coroner preparedness, 166–167
microbiology laboratory preparedness, 163–166
mortuary services preparedness, 167–168
National Electronic Disease Surveillance System (NEDSS), 162
physician preparedness, 162–163
state and public health service preparedness, 171–175
suspected bioterrorism event, 168
U.S. government, biological terrorism
federal agencies, 191–192
military, 191
overall authority designation, 192–193
state and local governments, 193
UV-IR-photons spectroscopy
absorption spectroscopy, 428–429
acoustic-to-optic tunable filters (ATOFs), 430
chemiluminescence, 426–427
laser induced breakdown spectroscopy (LIBS), 430
optical fiber sensors (OFS), 429–430
Raman scattering, 427–428
terahertz spectroscopy, 430–431

V

Vapor pressure, 350–351
Vesicating (blistering) agents, 366–367
Viral hemorrhagic fevers
diagnosis, 69
Ebola virus, 67–68
pathologic process, 68
transmission, 69
Volatility, 352
Vomiting agents (sternutators), 335

W

Waterborne transmission, biological weapon, 195–196
Weapons of mass destruction (WMD), 1, 5
Wet air oxidation, 401
Working Group on Civilian Biodefense (WGCB), 65
World Trade Center (WTC) Bombing, 8

Y

Yersinia pestis, 65–66

Z

Zoonotic transmission, biological weapon, 196–197